Social Science, Technical Systems, and Cooperative Work

Beyond the Great Divide

Computers, Cognition, and Work
A series edited by
Gary M. Olson, Judith S. Olson, and Bill Curtis

Social Science, Technical Systems, and Cooperative Work

Beyond the Great Divide

Edited by

Geoffrey C. Bowker
University of Illinois

Susan Leigh Star
University of Illinois

William Turner
CERESI/CNRS, Meudon, France

Les Gasser
National Science Foundation, Arlington, Virginia

Psychology Press
Taylor & Francis Group

New York London

Reprinted 2009 by Psychology Press

Library of Congress Cataloging-in-Publication Data

Social science, technical systems, and cooperative work : beyond the
great divide / edited by Bowker . . . [et al.].
    p.   cm.
Includes bibliographical references and index.
   ISBN 0-8058-2402-2 (alk. paper). — ISBN 0-8058-2403-0 (pbk. :
alk. paper).
   1. Work groups—Data processing. 2. Social sciences. I. Bowker,
Geoffrey C.
HD66.S65 1997
650'.0285'46—dc21   96-40366
                                                    CIP

10 9 8 7 6 5 4 3 2 1

This volume is dedicated to Bruno Latour and Michel Callon,
pioneer navigators of the Northwest Passage—
and to our dedicated and energetic contributors.

—Geof, Leigh, Bill, and Les

Contents

Introduction

Geoffrey C. Bowker
William Turner
Susan Leigh Star
Les Gasser

Things perceived as real are real in their consequences.
—W. I. Thomas and D. Thomas

THE NORTHWEST PASSAGE

Serres (1980) characterized the charting of a passage between the human sciences and the natural sciences as a form of "northwest passage." This image is meant to invoke the sense of uncertainty, the lack of institutional safe havens, the water raging with ever-shifting ice floes that can wreck the ship of the intrepid traveler passing between the old world and the new.

For over two decades, researchers drawn from the shores of both continents have worked to navigate a path, and in so doing have created the conditions of a new partnership. Social scientists (primarily from sociology and anthropology) and computer and information scientists (primarily from software development, requirements engineering, and artificial intelligence) have worked together on a variety of projects, seeking to create information systems more sensitive to human organization and needs. The early story of these attempts pitted the complex, contingent, political, and emotion-laden human landscape against the equally complex, but rational, formal (or formalizable), universal nature of the systems development process. At its extremes, the differences between the two world views took on a caricatured form: the humane, soft-headed social scientists seeing contingency everywhere against the impersonal techno-cratic developers and computer scientists who seek only working systems of information flow. At times, there seemed a great divide between the realms reminiscent of Snow's (1963) famous "two cultures" designation.

Yet, as the scientists came to work together, the divide became much less of a caricature and much more a complex co-education. Rogers' chapter in this volume states that engineers and computer scientists are often sophisticated analysts of usage and human behavior; social scientists are often technically quite able, contributing on the formal side as well as on the translation and management sides of projects. Social scientists are not just adding human factors to system design; computer scientists are not simply providing tools for social scientists to use in their own research.

The mixture of talents across previously distinct disciplines goes be-yond individual versatility or small groups commingling. Rather, this synergy is changing the very nature of social science and of computer science. Indeed, even identities are shifting: As a social scientist, one is just as likely to attend conferences on Computer Supported Cooperator Work (CSCW) or digital libraries as, say, those of the American Socio-logical Association. As a computer scientist, one might read social theo-rists ranging from Georg Simmel or Karl Marx, on one hand, to Gloria Anzaldúa or Patricia Hill Collins, on the other (Star, 1995a). Why? In the first instance, as systems are becoming larger and more networked, they begin to provide cutting-edge examples of phenomena of interest to social scientists. The design and use of large-scale systems sheds new light on old questions of cooperation and conflict, what can be public and what private, and the nature of scalability (level of analysis). These questions are posed and exemplified by an emergent technological infrastructure; for example, as the World Wide Web appears in more and more organi-zations, what will its ubiquity do to already international organizations? How will information be found, certified, curated, and coordinated? In the instance of the computer scientist, equally venerable questions arise in the other direction. What is a community and who is a member of any community (virtual or not)? Social theorists like Collins and Anzaldúa write about the changing meaning of race and nation, how borders and membership are settled between peoples. Thus, they become crucial re-sources for those designing tools for large-scale information spaces, and who seek to understand the nature of community boundaries.

These border crossings have finally reached a frequency, and the con-nections between scholars such a density, that in fact a new discipline and field of research is being born. For some years its name has been debated , it being quite difficult to find one that does not reify one aspect or another of the research. One attempt in the 1980s, indeed, was a white paper with the title "The Unnamable." For instance, "social impacts of computing," which really refers to one important area contributing to the new field, implies that in some sense the computer is an agent external to society that is then introduced. In fact, the design, development, marketing, and use of computers are social and technical, simultaneously and everywhere.

A recent set of conversations between Phil Agre, Brenda Dervin, Steve Griffin, Rob Kling, and Leigh Star turned to the term *informatics* as one possible solution. In Europe, aspects of the early divide were much more attenuated, partly due to the educational structure, particularly in France, Germany, and Scandinavia. Computer research and design that was more philosophically and humanistically informed has been stronger there than in the United States, and *informaticien* does not translate well to "computer scientist" for this reason. However, informatics still lacks the sense of fuller partnership and synergy this volume seeks to understand. *Interpretive* informatics seemed to capture much of what was being said, but proved a bit too unwieldy and unfamiliar for many. Thus, the somewhat broader *social informatics* was agreed on.[1] The goal of this book is to help establish the intellectual foundations on which this community of interests is being built.

The movement toward a highly dense, distributed information technological infrastructure (the Internet and Web, collaboratories, digital libraries, and attendant integrated technologies), places a new urgency on such foundations. Orwell's *1984* seems wholly plausible from a technological standpoint, as do the wilder reaches of pleasurable virtual reality and its manipulation. During this transition time, there is a great deal to learn from the work presented in this volume about how the contingent, messy, and emotional/political aspects of people's work and leisure are linked with new technological developments and visions. The answer rests, in part, on making accessible tools of analysis that will help navigate this northwest passage and so permit the growth of humanly centered technology and technically informed social analysis.

HISTORICAL BACKGROUND

The attempt to understand how human and technical issues come together in computing systems is now widespread, but its inception as an area of academic research goes back to the 1960s. Initially, such research was

---

[1]Thanks to Brenda Dervin, Steve Griffin, Phil Agre, and Rob Kling for lively and thought-provoking discussions of this matter. This volume, of course, does not exhaustively cover the field even in research represented, but we do hope that many of the bases are touched herein.

informed by concerns about automation (e.g., "deskilling," stratification, and job loss), as well as by psychological and management studies of user interface design and efficiency. It also included a healthy dose of social criticism and philosophically informed debate about the nature of thought and decision making. The Scandinavian tradition of participatory design of computing ("co-determination" or "co-design"), began in the late 1960s and was conducted jointly by social scientists, computing scientists, unions, and workers. Researchers from this approach (see Christiansen & Bødker, this volume; Greenbaum & Kyng, 1991) have studied workplaces in an ethnographic style, using the results to fuel the development of easier-to-use systems that seek to enhance the workplace, not impoverish it.

Artificial intelligence—as possibility and as a well-resourced, going concern in computer science research—played a large role in social science/computer science joint research from the 1960s on. Many writers, such as Dreyfus (1972) and Weizenbaum (1976), assembled philosophical arguments about whether human beings could ever be replicated by machines. They claimed a unique cluster of human attributes focused on the drive from artificial intelligence to replicate and model human intelligence. What is human about human beings? Close examinations of machine functioning in real-world settings saw computers as rigid, often agents of power and bureaucracy, but not sentient in their own right.

In the late 1970s and early 1980s, social scientists increasingly found themselves invited to provide researchers in artificial intelligence with metaphors for sophisticated modeling of collective cognitive processes. For example, at the Message Passing Semantics Group at the Massachusetts Institute of Technology in the United States, system designers actively explored the possibility of using the scientific community as a metaphor for large artificial intelligence systems. As robust natural problem-solving entities, it was felt that scientific communities might prove superior to brains or neurons as models for decision making in large distributed systems. They worked with sociologists (Hewitt, 1985; Star, 1989) in a cooperative venture to produce case studies of scientific communities and model the properties into large artificial intelligence systems.

As technological infrastructures improved and personal and networked computing exploded, the nature of relationships between social and computer scientists began to change. The structure of metaphor supplier/model developer began to shift to the richer landscape of partnership and discovery. A few computer scientists in artificial intelligence began to turn to ethnographic studies of practice to understand, not how humans might be replicated, but what humans and computers were really doing together. Such studies continually focused on human creativity and the local nature of contingency in workplaces, making universal, formal, rational systems a seemingly impossible goal (Star, 1989).

Aside from the limits, this work began to point the way to an exciting new landscape of research possibilities. The tendency for people to wrestle with and change the meaning, attributes, and consequences of system design became in a sense a feature, not a bug (a topic, not just a resource). What regularities could be found in these practices? Could a deeper understanding of them inform design itself? Could some of the psychological and cognitive focus of human–computer interaction scale up to the organizational or even cultural level (Bannon, 1990)?

Suchman's (1987) landmark book and Forsythe's (1992) ethnographic work on artificial intelligence research, along with Gasser's (1986) study of people struggling with standardized systems at work, for instance, all emphasized how people always "work around" the rigidities or remoteness of computing from human experience. Each of these studies conveyed a sense of the limits of computers, of formal modeling, and of rationalization.

The idea of computer-supported cooperative work is accepted as a feature of the 1990s work environment, even if results have not always been up to the hopes put into these new technical support systems. Engineers have joined sociologists in wanting to build mechanisms into their systems that will account for the social costs of changing the infrastructural arrangements of working together. Even in the realm of scientific cognition and decision making, the metaphor of scientists as robust problem solvers is now incorporating issues related to such contingent and messy things as disciplinary and professional politics, or the nature, availability, and rights of access to laboratory materials (Berg, 1996; Star & Ruhleder, 1996).

However, the biggest impetus for closer cooperation between system designers and social scientists probably lies outside the realm of artificial intelligence or CSCW and more in the field of information science. Government agencies are actively sponsoring joint research projects and often seek to include social scientists in large computing projects. This has recently been evident, for example, in the new U.S. Digital Library Initiative, which includes social scientists as evaluators of use and impact, and also as theorists of community and work (Bishop et al., 1995). This step is easy to understand in one sense, given levels of public investments in digital highways. As a matter of public concern, will these highways lead to heaven or hell? Will they be a fabulous opportunity for working creatively together or, as many fear, the siren call luring us into the flow of infojunk currently polluting the Web? The dynamic nature of open systems means that the benchmarks needed to fix the cognitive limits of joint action are not easy to determine. Fence building and fence tending in systems like the Internet have become major concerns. What tools can help to build the frames of reference needed to organize and coordinate collective intellectual activity?

Since the 1970s, a shift has occurred in information systems research from individualist, formal cognitive models to models situated in and grappling with complex real-world dynamics (Hutchins, 1995). For example, computer scientists working in such areas as distributed artificial intelligence, or on such questions as modeling artificial life, have developed new approaches to system dynamics based on the hypothesis of unequal individual access to collective information resources. Information is not universally available in central stores (libraries, databases, organizational memories); rather, it is often a private good distributed with parsimony or guarded jealously for a multitude of reasons (Callon, 1994). This shift in perspective has had considerable impact on empirical studies of collective action and on the synergy building up between computer and social science research. It is now common to hear the call for fuller recognition of the following methodological rule: Technology models social structures but is shaped in return by its use in the workplace (see Thomas, 1994, for some rich case studies of technology in organizations; see also Orlikowski & Yates, 1994). As this volume shows, the conceptual and methodological tools needed to understand this adjustment process are still being developed and are the source of ongoing debate. It is this debate that makes work "beyond the great divide" such an intellectual challenge.

Studies of scientific work focused during the 1970s and 1980s on knowledge production practices in a laboratory, producing detailed studies of the production of knowledge. However, it is far from clear that the models, results, and interpretations can be easily transposed to account for these same practices in a distributed, multisite virtual laboratory, or collaboratory, such as those currently being developed in many fields. The collaboratory concept has been defined as a new organizational structure for scientific activity that specifically accounts for computer-mediated collaborations. They are "centers without walls, in which the nation's researchers can perform research without regard to geographical location—interacting with colleagues, accessing instrumentation, sharing data and computational resources, [and] accessing information in digital libraries" (Lederberg & Uncapher, 1989, p. 19). One reason the laboratory studies may not scale has to do with the importance of transorganizational infrastructure.

Bowker (1994a, 1994b) argued that current thinking in sociology has not sufficiently studied the impact of "infrastructural inversion" on knowledge production practices. Simply stated, infrastructural inversion means that in order to understand the dynamics of cognitive change, what has generally been held as a private backdrop to the action played out on the public stage must, in fact, be analyzed as also determining the plot. For example, with the Internet and World Wide Web, a massive densification of networks is underway. More and more people use their personal computers as external memory for their specific knowledge production strategies. These external memories store documents for work underway locally, those that arrive over the net through e-mail, or those again that are downloaded from web sites and other digital repositories. A wide variety of operations—cut, copy, paste, annotate, associate, link, combine—can be applied to these document sets, generating new perspectives suitable for grounding individual plans of action.

Goody (1986) made the point: New cognitive technologies tend to encourage social practices of criticism. These in turn constantly call into question the legitimacy of recognized sources of authority—moral, institutional, organizational, or consensual. On this view, the dense Net–Web infrastructure may be opening Pandora's box. The goal of harnessing technology to the yoke of collective action might destroy the capacity of social groups to work within strategic frames of reference. *It is possible that forms of social solidarity become so transmogrified that they break down.* System designers, notably in France, are working actively to capture the impact of network densification on strategic planning. Using statistical techniques to model information flows, communication patterns, and change in symbolic notation systems, they hope to make visible the background conditions needed to fully understand the limits of collective cognitive actions in a context of rapid network densification. The French group uses the notion of *hybrid intelligence networks* to position its work in the perspective of a new sociology of collaboratories (Turner, de Guchteneire, & van Meter, 1994): Knowledge hybridization makes the development of what is now generally known as knowledge discovery methods in databases (KDD), an integral part of observation practices in the sociology of science field. These techniques are needed to identify the cognitive attractors structuring the information flows that characterize life in collaboratories, and enable the study of how these attractors serve as boundary objects (Star & Griesemer, 1989; Star & King, forthcoming) to articulate a wide variety of individual, and largely independent, knowledge production strategies.

A number of concepts (collaboratories, network densification, infrastructural inversion, KDD, hybrid intelligence networks, strategic planning, and now boundary objects) have been identified in order to show that the sector of research this book deals with is a generative one. The question of how technology models society and society shapes technology, seamlessly, has become central to large-scale networked computing and the "webbed world" that now exists. The great divide that formerly left social scientists stranded on one side of the shore and systems developers on the other is increasingly a thing of the past. Social and computer scientists are actively working together to redefine agendas for action, research, and collaboration.

ISSUES FOR ACTION

Although the chapters in this book display a robust diversity, there are a number of themes common to all workers in social informatics:

Heterogeneity

This is no doubt the subject that has proven to be the most important common meeting ground between social and computer scientists. Borrowing a term from sociology of science, those building and using today's systems become "heterogeneous engineers," that is, engineering both social change and technical development. People and things are mixed up together, and extend each other's capacities, along many dimensions. As well, the objects of social informatics are themselves heterogeneous with respect to medium (both online and offline resources), points of view (multicultural and multilocale), and purposes.

Negotiation and Division of Labor

Large and complex systems are necessarily internally contradictory—multiple viewpoints necessarily arise from different circumstances and different situated actions, and information in the real world is distributed asynchronously. There is no global broadcast system, and the timing and order in which individuals receive information may also change the semantics of that information. The notion of necessary contradiction implies the need to understand better how people manage these contradictions in the workplace and how systems can be designed to provide frameworks for their negotiation. Frames of reference can be devised to run individual strategies along parallel tracks with no overlap—a version of "separate but equal" (or unequal as the case may be). In sociological terms, this is a mechanical division of labor. This solution is unstable, because as soon as cooperation is required, power struggles begin over the nature of shared language. Understanding negotiations at all levels is thus a key theme of social informatics.

Translation

Given different points of view and the need to negotiate and cooperate, problems of translation are crucial in large networked environments. Again, sociology of science has provided some analytic tools. In the classic cases described by Callon and Latour, the symbolic systems of different groups are translated into a coherent and monolithic representational regime (Callon, 1986; Latour, 1987).[2] Graphically, one can see a funnel shape with information channeled into a spokesperson. Members' concerns are re-represented (Star, 1995b) under a single rubric, and people learn to see (or are forced to see) their concerns in a second language. Models are typical translation structures in the sense that they are used by system designers to re-represent the diversity of individual symbolic systems. Translation struggles are often found in attempts to standardize systems components.

The Politics of Formalism

Every design is itself historically and politically situated. Yet, much computing design has relied on formal representations, designed precisely to extend local knowledge past parochial barriers. Although there is no such thing as a neutral vantage point, even for mathematics (or especially for mathematics?), it has been a long conceptual struggle for social informatics to understand how formalisms work pragmatically. Goguen (this volume) poses a continuum of "wetness" and "dryness" of representations, with highly formal representations being quite dry. The empirical investigation of the relation between the two has opened up new ways of thinking about representation itself.

Working Together

What does it mean to cooperate? Who has the power of decision? Shall one be the spokesperson who speaks for others? Or, is power everywhere and nowhere, because it is diffusely distributed over what neural network scientists call the links in the system? Every large system confronts designers and users with this problem. Shall obligatory passage points be set up (rules, standards, centralized control mechanisms) for managing the information flow, or should distributed models be used to diversely activate the information and dynamically connect people, strategies, and

---

[2]In Latour's explication of Pasteur's success, for example, the "germ theory of disease" was represented to different audiences along the lines of their needs: statistics for epidemiologists, demonstrations of sick cows for farmers, fermentation for brewers. Yet all became united under the rubric "germ."

things? There is no one clear answer; rather, the alternative itself becomes a point of research that opens up a wide range of options for creating learning algorithms for working together.

Boundary Objects

A framework for cooperative cognition that preserves the sovereignty of viewpoints is provided by the notion of boundary objects (Star & Griesemer, 1989). How do scientific communities, for example, create lasting arrangements where they address systems of objects that are simultaneously local and global, common and specialized, shared and segregated? The boundary object model assumes the fundamental ambiguity of objects (an idea taken directly from the Pragmatist notion that meaning is given in use, not in antecedent characteristics) and the durability of arrangements to manage that ambiguity in cooperative ventures. The durability implies the need to develop conventional or routine ways of working with the ambiguity; those conventions themselves may be seen as data structures from the design point of view, as material structures from the organizational point of view, or as working treaties from the political point of view.

Conventions and Routines

If everything is open, and all is apt to change, how do durable cooperative arrangements come to exist? Some suggest that a set of organizational, institutional, and symbolic conventions for getting on with routine business despite heterogeneity is required, but if these conventions cannot be assumed a priori, how are they constructed? Others seek to overcome this problem by questioning the need for rule-based behavior for getting most things done. "Good enough" is as good as it ever gets, whether you are speaking formally or informally about any form of social cooperation. But in that case, what about the situation discussed earlier where machines are becoming active members of hybrid intelligence networks: Without rules, how can what is "good enough" for a machine in supporting cooperative work be defined?

Ethics and Global Responsible Thinking

Winner asked the question "Do Artifacts Have Politics?" (1986). His primary example is taken from the construction of infrastructure in the city of New York, where city planner Robert Moses decided to build bridge overpasses between New York City and Long Island that were too low in height to allow buses to pass through. From his racist and classist perspective, people unable to afford cars were not welcome in Long

Island, a rich suburban area, and he built this politics directly into the infrastructure of the roads and transportation systems. What sort of politics will our artifacts have? Will it be possible to include in our systems the possibility for compassion, ethics, and globally responsible thinking?

Technically, many of the problems of social informatics appear as an overwhelming list of differences: heterogeneous representations, incompatible data sources, or the constantly changing contextual meaning of information across dispersed groups are just some examples. Politically, the problem of dealing with differences is one of preserving the primacy and sovereignty of individual experiences without creating regimes of coercion. Be aware that it is impossible to separate the technical from the political, which clearly means recognizing the macroimplications of research as it is taken up and used to build sociotechnical systems for use in the real world.

OUTLINE OF THE BOOK

The book has been divided into three parts, covering in turn social theory, design theory, and the sociotechnical system with respect to CSCW. Clearly, a book about superseding divides does not want to spawn new ones; and, indeed, none of the chapters fit into only one of the categories! However, broadly speaking, the first set of chapters rethinks basic social categories with the development of distributed collaborative computing technology—concepts of the group, technology, information, user, and text. The second set concentrates more on the lessons that can be learned at the design stage: Given that one wants to build a CSCW system incorporating these insights, what kind of work does one need to do and how is an understanding of design affected? The third set looks at the integration of social and technical in the operation of working sociotechnical systems; collectively, they make the argument that the social and the technical are irremediably linked in practice and so the great divide should be a thing of the past, which never should have existed in the first place. An introduction at the beginning of each section points to some of the themes linking the chapters in that section.

ACKNOWLEDGMENTS

This book is the outcome of a conference organized in Paris under the auspices of the Centre National de Recherche Scientifique (CNRS) with a grant from the Department for Specialized Information of the French Research Ministry. The editors wish to thank both for their support and hospitality. It grew out of a series of workshops partly funded by the CNRS and the British Council, the latter of which we should also like to thank.

REFERENCES

Bannon, L. (1990). A pilgrim's progress: From cognitive science to cooperative design. *AI and Society, 4*, 259–275.

Berg, M. (1996). *Rationalizing medical work*. Cambridge, MA: MIT Press.

Bishop, A. P., Star, S. L., Neumann, L., Ignacio, E., Sandusky, R. J., & Schatz, B. (1995, September). Building a university digital library: Understanding implications for academic institutions and their constituencies. In *Higher education and the NII: From vision to reality*. Proceedings of the Monterey Conference. Washington, DC: Coalition for Networked Information.

Bowker, G. (1994a). Information mythology. In L. Bud-Frierman (Ed.), *Information acumen* (pp. 231–247). London: Routledge & Kegan Paul.

Bowker, G. (1994b). *Science on the run: Information management and industrial geophysics at Schlumberger, 1920–1940*. Cambridge, MA: MIT Press.

Callon, M. (1986). Some elements of a sociology of translation: Domestication of the scallops and the fishermen of St. Brieuc Bay. In J. Law (Ed.), *Power, action and belief* (pp. 196–223). London: Routledge & Kegan Paul.

Callon, M. (1994). Is science a public good? *Science, Technology and Human Values, 19*(4), 395–421.

Dreyfus, H. L. (1972). *What computers can't do; a critique of artificial reason*. New York: Harper & Row.

Forsythe, D. (1992). Blaming the user in medical informatics. *Knowledge and Society: The Anthropology of Science and Technology, 9*, 95–111.

Gasser, L. (1986). The integration of computing and routine work. *ACM Transactions on Office Information Systems, 4*, 205–225.

Goody, J. (1986). *The logic of writing and the organization of society*. Cambridge, England: Cambridge University Press.

Greenbaum, J., & Kyng, M. (1991). *Design at work: Cooperative design of computer systems*. Hillsdale, NJ: Lawrence Erlbaum Associates.

Hewitt, C. (1985). The challenge of open systems. *BYTE*, April, 223–242.

Hutchins, E. (1995). *Cognition in the wild*. Cambridge, MA: MIT Press.

Latour, B. (1987). *The pasteurization of French society, with Irréductions*. Cambridge, MA: Harvard University Press.

Lederberg, J., & Uncapher, K. (1989). Towards a national collaboratory. *Report of an invitational workshop at the Rockefeller University*, March 17–18.

Orlikowski, W., & Yates, J. (1994). Genre repertoire: The structuring of communicative practices in organizations. *Administrative Science Quarterly, 39*, 541–574.

Serres, M. (1980). *Le passage du nord-ouest*. Paris: Editions de Minuit.

Snow, C. P. (1963). *The two cultures: And a second look*. New York: New American Library.

Star, S. L. (1989). *Regions of the mind: Brain research and the quest for scientific certainty*. Stanford, CA: Stanford University Press.

Star, S. L. (1992). The Trojan door: Organizations, work and the "Open Black Box." *Systems Practice, 5*, 395–410.

Star, S. L. (Ed.). (1995a). *The cultures of computing*. Oxford, England: Blackwell.

Star, S. L. (1995b). The politics of formal representations: Wizards, gurus and organizational complexity. In S. L. Star (Ed.), *Ecologies of knowledge: Work and politics in science and technology* (pp. 88–118). Albany, NY: SUNY Press.

Star, S. L., & Griesemer, J. (1989). Institutional ecology, "translations," and coherence: Amateurs and professionals in Berkeley's Museum of Vertebrate Zoology. *Social Studies of Science, 19,* 387–420.

Star, S. L., & King, J. L. (in press). Boundaries, scale and aggregation: Problems in design of computerized social process support. *Organization Science.*

Star, S. L., & Ruhleder, K. (1996). Steps toward an Ecology of Infrastructure: Problems of design and access in large information systems. *Information Systems Research, 7,* 111–134.

Suchman, L. (1987). *Plans and situated actions: The problem of human–machine communication.* Cambridge, England: Cambridge University Press.

Thomas, R. J. (1994). *What machines can't do: Politics and technology in the industrial enterprise.* Berkeley: University of California Press.

Turner, W. A., de Guchteneire, P., & van Meter, K. (1996). Merit review, digital library design and cooperative cognition. In G. Chartron (Ed.), *Médiation Scientifique et Réseaux Electronique,* Rennes: Presses Universitaires de Rennes, Solaris No. 3.

Weizenbaum, J. (1976). *Computer power and human reason: From judgment to calculation.* San Francisco: Freeman.

Winner, L. (1980). Do artifacts have politics? *Daedalus, 109,* 121–136.

INTRODUCTION: SOCIAL THEORY AND CSCW

Susan Leigh Star
University of Illinois at Urbana

Theory plays a crucial role in building partnerships between social scientists and computational/informatics workers. Currently, the theoretical mixture is in flux, with people native to both occupational worlds drawing on many different sources. In this section, a lively and impassioned set of chapters makes clear that computational theory sometimes challenges longheld social science beliefs, and sometimes shapes the everyday conception of the designer building artifacts. Social science theory sometimes offers a resource for partnerships and projects, and sometimes constitutes an irritant or barrier to communication. Each author calls for an empirical, often ethical amalgam; each recognizes the intellectual and political challenges involved in so doing.

Giordano and Lea, for example, look to some of the technical features of both structured programming and object-oriented programming as a source for how *group* has been seen in the world of CSCW. There is a bias toward small group computer-mediated communication, they argue, and even in geographically dispersed groups the technology tries to emulate the face-to-face model. Why should this be so? They point out that many human groups before groupware were not necessarily bounded or shaped in this way. The shapes and limitations of the technology have informed imaginations, first because of the limited bandwidth of early computer-mediated communication, and more recently because of the presumptions of object-oriented programming. The object-oriented approach incorporates some conservative assumptions about what is naturally human, including the inheritance of policy over time and a certain fixedness of roles. They note that the object-oriented abstraction process "requires that each object be subject to and conform to the well-defined and explicitly stated rules, or . . . a 'policy' of the problem domain," which may represent only one way of arranging groups with humans, that is perhaps overly dependent on industrial process modeling.

Similarly, Giordano and Lea find that the focus on increased band-widths taps only one sort of human information-processing capacity. For example, the idea of *presence* originally meant one-to-one video linkup communication; it has recently been expanded to include copresence of groups of people. What is gained and what is lost in this shift? Simplistic ideas of the group as voluntaristic and easily scalable will not work for global, complex, and distributed systems; neither will it work when, for example, the Internet becomes a broadcast medium, as it already has both textually and for technology such as virtual classrooms and "Internet radio." Look to the technology, they urge, to learn more about the complexities of human groups. The great divide may have already been closed, not through interdisciplinary work, but by the way in which technology incorporates and reflects group processes, and is often costructured by constraints beyond the control of either computer or social scientists.

In a similar vein, Goguen argues that we still have much to discover about the nature of this coconstruction. What is information? No mere theory of the representation of information will do (a pragmatics of information use is needed, as indeed the authors in this section agree). The pragmatics is both wet (real time, contingent, historically and socially situated) and dry (i.e., constrained by the formal structures of a working information system and especially operating at a metalevel). It is the reconciliation of the two that matters here—an ongoing process, to be sure, and never a complete or absolute one.

How could this reconciliation occur? Rogers and Goguen concur that multiple memberships are key: People juggle identities as members of particular working or playing groups; they are simultaneously analysts and designers. Each group uses a language of information; sometimes one group "desiccates" the findings of another to make them more formal (and also more portable). Each of these activities is laden with values, decisions, and ethics, as the risk of a violating representation is always present. How to get good, respectful knowledge of working processes is not easy. Sometimes people cannot express what they do reflectively; and their very reliance on tacit knowledge limits the use of formal representations. As well, the multiplicity and temporal character of knowledge mean that all representations, in Goguen's words, "leak." As with Sharrock and Button, Goguen turns to ethnomethodology for detailed studies of workplaces to, following the liquid metaphor, at least make the liquids more viscous. He discusses the use of discourse analysis and narrative. In all of these moves, the value-laden quality of the information is central.

Sharrock and Button's chapter "Engineering Investigations" continues a long tradition of ethnomethodological studies of work. Ethnomethodology is a school of social science research that looks at how people accomplish everyday activities, often in great detail and based on empirical cases. It resists reified definitions of "society" or "power" or some of the traditional explanatory categories in favor of investigations that look at the dynamic processes involved in creating such categories. Engineers, they argue, are indeed surrounded by contingency, which is the first thing many social scientists see when entering an engineering workplace for the first time.

Sharrock and Button also look at patterns and consistencies, and at the repertoire of tools any working engineer brings to bear in solving the problems raised by contingency. When trying to understand these commonsense choices, sometimes it is necessary to clear away an underbrush of myth or overly rationalistic descriptions of how work is done. Throughout, Sharrock and Button focus on engineers as intelligent managers of contingencies, rather than victims or heroes. They maintain that "the course of a technology development is thus a contest with contingencies, and the technology outcome is constituted by the wrestling with them on a day-to-day basis." Some of the contingencies take the form of trying to "outthink the users," often involved as imaginary social types, such as the naive user or the key user, that nevertheless serve to organize the work. Work seen from this perspective is never a textbook perfect product; however, understanding the organizational reasons for less-than-perfect products helps us understand how engineering work is really accomplished.

Rogers' chapter provides a historical account of the attempts and problems involved in trying to involve social scientists in the design of technology, beginning in the 1950s with the sociotechnical systems approach. Early attempts to save workers from deskilling and dehumanization did not really approach questions of design or technology, she argues, but primarily rearranged working groups. Somewhat later, when attempts were made to support or inform actual design in the human–computer interaction area, other sorts of problems arose. Often, psychologists and linguists were not focused on particularly design-relevant topics. At times, they took a condescending approach to designers themselves, prescribing at some distance and assuming lack of knowledge of users (or psychology, sociology, anthropology, or politics) on the part of designers and engineers. At the same time, pulling recommendations out of the context of a densely detailed study might overly simplify some of the social science precepts of the researchers trying to cooperate.

What to do? Rogers notes that ethnomethodologists have metaphorically waded into the design room, and produced detailed empirical studies of work such as those of Sharrock and Button. Their efforts improve the situation in that they can provide good, domain-specific information for the general design team. However, she suggests, perhaps they do not go far enough. Social scientists need to work alongside designers, with all the day-to-day articulation work that implies. They can be translators and in-house consultants, as well as bring in interesting theoretical material from social science, such as activity theory (Nardi, 1996) or theories about a specific domain. She warns that such exercises are not easily formalizable, and may become somewhat "schizophrenic" in publication for more specialized audiences. Nevertheless, the participative approach walks away from the reified divides of earlier years, and moves toward a fuller partnership.

Yoneyama discusses the interpretive flexibility of computers. People can be said to "read" information systems and computers in the ways that readers and viewers wrestle the meanings of texts. Using a semiotic approach, he describes how the text moves away from the writer (not totally without structure or constraint, but unpredictably). Texts may generate meanings not anticipated by the writer; similarly, information systems are a generative source of new tricks and workarounds (Gasser, 1986). The interactive nature of the computer, of course, makes "computer systems fall somewhere between the characteristics of interpreting text" and actual discourse. In some ways, the desktop of a computer can be seen as a person in such a discourse frame, although Yoneyama cautions against too simple an interpretation.

Computer semiotics provides a more sophisticated analysis of how such things as icons and cursors might be read as signs in the semiotic sense. They are unique in that they have a kind of transience not found in other kinds of texts, and they are interactive. Using the tools of semiotics and hermeneutics, these features of computer systems may be read as a kind of communication, rather than as a black box or stable text. In this reading, the user is an active coconstructor of the system, but, as all the authors in this section note, he or she is tailoring and designing against a world of both constraints and possibilities. Sometimes parts of a system must be closed or opaque. Part of the art of design beyond the great divide is understanding where the hermeneutic distance is between design and use.

REFERENCES

Nardi, B. (Ed.). (1996). *Context and consciousness: Activity theory and human–computer interaction.* Cambridge, MA: MIT Press.

Gasser, L. (1986). The integration of computing and routine work. *ACM Transactions on Office Information Systems, 4,* 205–225.

Representations of the Group and Group Processes in CSCW Research: A Case of Premature Closure?

Martin Lea
Richard Giordano
University of Manchester, England

This chapter considers the extent to which the representation of the "group" and "group processes" in the design of computer-supported cooperative work (CSCW) and groupware systems reflects some of the wider preoccupations of the computing and telecommunications communities.[1] This is part of a larger concern that activity modelers tend to represent human activities in ways most appropriate to the tools and techniques they have at hand. This implies that their modeling activities go beyond viewing human activities as a set of constrained rational choices or governed by formalizable rules (which is problematic in itself), but that the resulting models of activities have embedded within them elements of the technologies used in creating them. The choice and deployment of technologies in defining and modeling groups and group behavior manifest themselves in the resulting CSCW technologies. Further, rather than there being a great divide between computer scientists and social scientists, the representations of the group in CSCW system designs and evaluations suggest a degree of closure or agreement. This closure, in itself, does not guarantee that resulting systems will be successful, but it may help to explain why certain forms of groupware rather than others tend to dominate the CSCW field.

---

[1]Groupware has been defined as the combination of group processes and computer software designed to support them. CSCW is a field concerned with the research and development of software systems to support "group working." In CSCW, and in related areas of software engineering such as the design of group decision support systems and of "virtual classrooms," the concept of "groupware" has become central.

Certain longstanding technical issues that have confronted the software and telecommunications engineering communities suggest frameworks from which to model the social world, and concern over these issues has restricted the concept of "the group" to a particular type (i.e., small, task-oriented, face-to-face groups), and consequently has shaped analyses of group processes in essentially individualistic (i.e., reductionist) terms. This chapter focuses on two examples of influences that have helped to shape this configuration of the group, and in addition, suggests how the predominant approach to conceptualizing groups in the social sciences (i.e., through small group dynamics) has reinforced this restricted view of the group in CSCW design as both natural and inevitable.

The first illustration considers the object-oriented analysis and design paradigm, and some of the implications of this approach for the representation of the group in system design. Because this work has only just begun, this chapter sketches out one of the areas for consideration, in this case, the concern in object-oriented design over the visibility of objects and their interrelations in the real world and their visual representation on the screen. Other important features of the object-oriented approach to groupware design—such as the classification of objects, the hiding of data, and the reusability of code—will be left for exploration elsewhere. The aim is to demonstrate that certain technical manifestations of the object-oriented paradigm help to define both the group and group interaction within CSCW.

The second illustration focuses on the issue of communication bandwidth. We trace how the problem of bandwidth limitations in communications came to be so powerfully influential in the analysis of mediated human communication. Essentially, the argument is that the consensus between both the telecommunications engineering and social science communities over the utility of the bandwidth concept for modeling communication has been concretized in the design and evaluation of the new telecommunications media. This chapter, then, aims to illuminate some of the ways in which the stabilization of restricted notions about the group and group processes in groupware design has been achieved through consensus between the various relevant parties. It begins, however, by first identifying the predominant view of the group in groupware design, and highlighting some of its restrictions.

THE CONCEPT OF THE GROUP IN CSCW

Despite the centrality of the group as a concept in CSCW design, it remains a largely unelaborated construct. Indeed, the concept appears to have changed little since research into groupware based on computer conferencing systems began in the 1970s (e.g., Hiltz & Turoff, 1978). A brief survey of the literature on CSCW revealed an abundance of systems designed to support small groups under conditions where the co-presence of group members is actual or simulated. Thus, some systems support collections of individuals working together in "electronic meeting rooms," whereas a second, larger category of systems is concerned with supporting groups working at a distance over computer networks. A frequently observed feature of this latter type of system is onscreen representation of the participants' faces through static photos and increasingly as real-time video pictures of the communicators. This potent if rather literal symbol of CSCW developers' concern to simulate face-to-face communication at a distance reflects some important assumptions about groups and the processes by which they operate.[2]

Working from the CSCW literature, the following general characteristics of groups are identified, which are either specified as guidelines for system design (e.g., Cole & Nast-Cole, 1992) or appear to be assumed by systems design (e.g., Madsen, 1989; Mantei et al., 1991; Nunamaker, Dennis, Valacich, Vogel, & George, 1991):

1. A group is a small number of individuals who normally interact face to face in order to carry out a task or to work toward some common goal.

2. The members have a generally positive, cooperative orientation toward each other and toward the fulfillment of the group task.

3. The members have roles in relation to one another. These emerge from structural divisions developed within the group to fulfill the group's goals. Members of the group have responsibility for specific role-related work outcomes.

4. Continued communication is necessary for individuals to influence one another and for individuals to maintain a sense of belonging to the group.

5. The group progresses through a series of fixed, predictable stages during its life span, analogous to the stages of individual development.

---

[2]Examples of electronic meeting rooms include the Capture Lab at the Centre for Machine Intelligence, Ann Arbor, Michigan (Losada, Sanchez, & Noble, 1990), and the Collaborative Management Room at the University of Arizona (Nunamaker, Dennis, Valachic, Vogel, & George, 1991). Systems that number among their concerns the simulation of face-to-face communication include the Computer Audio Video Enhanced Collaboration and Telepresence (Cavecat) system at the University of Toronto (Mantei et al., 1991); the VideoWindow system at Bellcore (Fish, Kraut & Chalfonte, 1990); and the TeamWorkStation system at NTT in Yokosuka-Shi, Japan (Ishii, 1990). More recent collaborative virtual reality systems continue this concern, for example, the Virtual Space Teleconferencing System (Kishino, Ohya, Takemura, & Terashima, 1993).

6. Groups are short-lived; that is, they have no past and no future beyond that associated with the particular group task.

It should be immediately obvious that as a description of groups, this set of assumptions is overly restrictive, and certain kinds of groups are specifically excluded. Although it clearly describes some aspects of groups working in task-related organizational settings (and is reflected in matrix and other flexible management strategies), it implies group control for larger ends—that is, group behavior that is systematic and operates within perceived constraints that are largely externally defined, together with a set of well-defined measurable goals (Alderfer, 1977; Knight, 1976; Leavitt, 1972; Rojek & Wilson, 1987). The parts played by normative influences and situational factors associated with the group in shaping and defining appropriate group behavior and goals are largely ignored.

A second point is that, although CSCW takes the face-to-face group as its natural form (and therefore seeks to simulate face-to-face interaction as far as possible), other examples can be found of task-oriented groups whose members may never, or only very rarely, meet face to face. Pressure groups, for example, may form to produce coordinated action to achieve specific ends without necessarily ever meeting.[3] Similarly, in the European research context it is quite common for international research teams composed of partners throughout Europe to engage in intense, highly coordinated activity in order to write a research contract proposal without ever meeting or interacting face to face.

A third point (and necessarily given the importance attached to group members' face-to-face interactions) is that a physical limitation is placed on the size of the group, which for all practical purposes must be quite small, even though very large groupings also occur, some of which are task oriented (such as in international collaboration in high-energy physics; Kiesler, Heinmiller, Ostell, Traweek, & Uncapher, 1990).

Fourth, that group members are predisposed to act cooperatively tends to be assumed in groupware design, despite the conflicts readily observed in many groups (French et al., 1982; Robey et al., 1989; see also Poole, Holmes, & DeSanctis, 1988) and the social and cultural norms that may act against such cooperation (e.g., proprietary attitudes toward sharing research data in oceanography; Kiesler et al., 1990).

By setting an agenda primarily to provide computer support for small, short-lived, interactive, task-oriented groups who would normally meet

---

[3]There are some well-documented examples of pressure groups formed from individuals who are geographically widely dispersed using the new communication technologies, such as electronic mail, videotex, and fax to produce coordinated action for political ends (Guardian, 1990; Li, 1990; Marchand, 1984; Perry & Adam, 1992).

face to face, the CSCW field is arguably poorly placed to design systems that would support larger, distributed groups, such as (to take an extreme example) a political party. Such a group is very large, has a common goal or set of objectives that is negotiated, is characterized by intragroup conflicts, and is geographically dispersed. It has members of whom the majority have little knowledge of who the other members are, may interact with only a very few other members, or none at all, and who may never meet face to face.

Additionally, CSCW does not appear to consider examples of highly cohesive groups, such as swimming or track and field teams, which do not necessarily interact in the pursuance of group goals. Finally, by constraining both the definition of the group and the interactions among members of groups (and among groups themselves) the field limits itself to a mechanistic and brittle representation of human activity. By doing so, there is no room in CSCW to view group interaction as complex, or groups themselves as adaptive, self-learning, or nondeterministic systems.

Let us consider two ways in which this narrow focus may have arisen.

OBJECT-ORIENTED DESIGN

One possibility is that there is something about the general approach to software system design that favors this constrained conception of the group. This section argues that system designers coconstruct society and technology and thereby model the real world in an image that fits their modeling tools. The "real" world that object-oriented designers model is only as real as the design assumptions built into their modeling tools will allow.

At the root of all system design methodologies is the underlying proposition that real-world activities must be constrained or limited in order to be modeled into systematic processes. The systematic or formalizable activities in the real world are those that are most susceptible to modeling (Shlaer & Mellor, 1988). This has been a long-standing assumption in both system design and software engineering, and became something of an article of faith in the 1970s with the emergence of structured systems analysis and design methodologies. Block-structured languages, such as ALGOL and PL/I, were designed before structured systems analysis methodologies, and were meant to improve the speed by which systems could be coded and, most important, the ease by which systems could be maintained by teams of programmers. Structured systems analysis techniques followed to take advantage of this advance in language design. The primary motivation behind these new languages and the methodologies to build applications from them was rooted in engineering concepts such as the maintenance, documentation, and enhancement of complex computer systems (Coad & Yourdon, 1991; Gane & Sarson, 1979).

In a structured systems paradigm, sources of data and their ultimate repositories (*external entities*) are identified by analysts along with the processes that are dependent or act on that data. The procedural paradigm takes a task-oriented point of view, which begins the support for the design of the solution (systems design) once the solution to the problem has been found (systems analysis). The proposed solution is decomposed by breaking it into a sequence of tasks that act on data. These tasks form the building blocks for a procedural application (Avison & Fitzgerald, 1988). Such block-structured programming languages as ALGOL and PL/I embody the idea that large, complex tasks are decomposed into subtasks (or modules) that are responsible for one, and only one, task. These tasks are arranged in a hierarchy not unlike the kind found in reporting charts in a highly structured or bureaucratic organization, such as the military (Gane & Sarson, 1979). Although such a design paradigm is far too rigid when dealing with concurrent interactive systems (such as a typical desktop environment), the structured systems analysis and design paradigm has nevertheless dominated systems development since the late 1970s, and is still the most widely used formal methodology in large organizations today.

The object-oriented design paradigm takes the modeling point of view. With structured systems analysis and design, the analysis and design phases are clearly separated; a solution is proposed, and a design is constructed to make that solution real, both in hardware and software terms. With object-oriented design, the analysis and design phases work closely together to define a model of the problem domain. The model is constructed by viewing the problem as a set of interacting entities. The software-based models of entities and the relations between them are assembled to form the basic architecture of the application. Although the pieces of the procedural paradigm performed specific tasks, the pieces produced by the object-oriented paradigm are entity descriptions, classes. The model focuses on the real world under study and identifies, classifies, and abstracts what is in the problem. It organizes this information into a formal structure. Similar "things" in the problem are abstracted as "objects," characteristics of these objects are abstracted as "attributes," and reliable associations between objects are abstracted as "relationships."

It should be apparent that the problem domain, objects, and interactions among them become relatively fixed or static once they are modeled. One result of this is that whereas classes do not necessarily represent physical objects in the real world, objects are often stated in the terminology of the problem domain and often represented as physical or real objects. Further, this abstraction process requires that each object be subject to and conform to the well-defined and explicitly stated rules, or in other words, a "policy" of the problem domain (Korson & McGregor, 1990).

Although object-oriented techniques are often used to model and simulate processes in the real world, including social interaction in the case of "process modeling," they are based on languages that are rooted in software engineering. The problems that object-oriented languages, such as Smalltalk, address are related to the capturing of the problem domain, ease of programming and development, inexpensive extensibility of systems, and system maintenance. In this respect, they share a strong lineage with block-structured techniques. By designing systems as a set of virtually autonomous objects, one may reuse or extend objects and thereby facilitate both rapid system development and relatively easy maintenance, which, in turn, saves both money and time.[4] As with block-structured methodologies, object-oriented design principles assume that it is only useful to model information or tasks to be performed when there is something *systematic* going on that needs to be elucidated (Coad & Yourdon, 1991; Shlaer & Mellor, 1988). Of course, this is grossly simplified, and the differences between the approaches and their implications are much wider than this simple comparison implies. It is sufficient, however, to point out that object-oriented analysis, design, and programming is displacing structured techniques in business and industrial settings, and is the preferred approach among practicing computer scientists and engineers designing CSCW systems software.

Despite the important developments in process and information modeling that object-oriented design brings, it is the development of the "advanced personal computing environment" with its distinctive graphical user interface that has arguably been most important for the promotion of the object-oriented approach. Although structured systems are useful for designing large-scale, sequential batch-oriented systems, they are not

---

[4]Simula, which is the earliest object-oriented programming language, was designed in 1967 at the University of Oslo and the Norwegian Computing Center by Dahl and Nygaard. Simula 67 is a general purpose programming language developed as an object-oriented extension of Algol 60. The name reflects its relation to Simula 1, an earlier language, but is rather misleading as simulation is only one possible application. Nevertheless, object-oriented programming has had a dramatic effect on the approach taken to operational modeling. More recent object-oriented programming languages include C++, and Apple's Object Pascal (based on C and Pascal, respectively), which was used to develop some of the software for the Apple Macintosh. However, the most widely used object-oriented programming language today is Smalltalk. According to Meyer (1988), the ideas for Smalltalk were formulated in the early 1970s at the University of Utah by Alan Kay who was attempting to apply the concepts in Simula to his graphics work. Later, when Kay joined Xerox the same principles formed the basis for an advanced personal computing environment. Other important contributions were made by Adele Goldberg and Daniel Ingalls. Parcplace systems, a Xerox subsidiary, was created in 1986 to develop and market Smalltalk as a mainstream software product.

helpful for designing concurrent systems (as one would typically find on a Macintosh or a UNIX platform that can run more than one process simultaneously) nor are they helpful in analyzing and designing graphical icon-based user interfaces.[5] The Smalltalk programming language introduced or popularized many of the familiar advances in this area: windows, icons, menus, and the use of the mouse as a pointing technique. Smalltalk embeds within it so many of the principles of object orientation that many computer science departments, and some books, teach object-oriented design principles by teaching pure Smalltalk.

Indeed, these two strands to the development of object-oriented programming are combined in the Smalltalk environment to the extent that the promulgation of the process modeling application of object-oriented programming is intimately bound to the success of the graphical user interface. Justifications for the adoption of the object-oriented approach to support process and information modeling rely heavily on the idea that it is a *natural* approach that is being exploited. According to Meyer (1988), "when software design is understood as operational modelling, object-oriented design is the natural approach because the world being modelled is made of objects and it is appropriate to organize the model around computer representations of these objects" (p. 51). At the same time, this view of the world is reinforced within object-oriented programming by the provision of libraries of graphical user interface tools that are the means by which these same "objects" and the relations among them can be made visible, tangible, and fixed for a wider audience.

It is obvious, however, that modeling the world around real-world objects stems largely from the earlier concerns of procedural programmers to overcome difficulties related to representing complex physical systems, such as assembly lines, chemical reactions, payroll routines, or computer operating systems. The kinds of objects that populated these worlds were employees, paychecks, and tax returns, as well as well-defined functions or tasks. The problems could be solved pragmatically by representing the physical objects as systems composed of interlocking serial processes depending on a flow of information. (In this regard, such systems have been likened to electronic versions of assembly lines; Gane & Sarson, 1979.) There was no need to consider what symbolic meanings the objects may carry, nor the implications of explaining the system in any way other

---

[5]IBM spent huge resources and failed trying to build applications using structured methods in the OS/2-EE Presentation Manager environment, which uses pull-down menus, multiple windows and processes, icons rather than text commands, and mouse-driven commands. Their only successes were achieved when they abandoned structured techniques and adopted an objected-oriented approach. It can be argued that the paradigm in system development changed at IBM only after the existing structured paradigm failed (Coad & Yourdon, 1991, p. 191).

than by reducing it to its constituent elements, as one would when thinking about the structure of a program. In the object-oriented paradigm, the world is modeled by representing the objects of the real-world problem (tangible things, activities, roles, incidents, interactions, specifications) in the computer system. This approach is reinforced by the availability of graphical user interfaces that enable the representations of objects of the model to be rerepresented visually on the screen, and, thus, those objects and their relations are given solid form.

Both methods of representing the world are, at root, deterministic, mechanistic, rational, and each in its own way reflects industrial processing. As has been observed, the structured paradigm reflects the assembly line. The object-oriented paradigm still reflects a classical vision of organizations where goal-directed, rational routines and their interactions are fundamental building blocks (Finholt & Sproull, 1990). Moreover, these routines can be represented relatively statically, and they can be improved or changed by some external agent. As Hutchins (1991) has observed, such a classical representation looks at the behavior of a system, represents it explicitly, and searches for a better solution. (This, for instance, lies behind much of the work in process modeling and process re-engineering or work on the implications of group work on organizations). The process of change lies *outside* the group through the action of some external agent. The outside observer observes a system's performance and represents it. Thus, once the system is symbolically represented, it can then be altered from the outside much as an engineer would tinker with any machine.

There are at least two problems with this view: First, the intangible world, the complex, the chaotic, the atemporal, the arational is either ignored or given constrained tangible form graphically. It represents on the screen, not negotiated or changing realities, but, in the process of transforming complex interaction into computer code, there emerges a constrained physical system of interacting entities and fixed relations between them guided by explicit rules.[6] The interaction of groups in this mechanical way cannot be scaled-up to model—for instance, the interactions among groups in even a small organization if the organization is viewed (as Hutchins does) as being composed of many parts where each part may simultaneously provide constraints on the behavior of other

---

[6]The transformation of rules from the intangible to the tangible appears to parallel Forsythe's (1993) observations of scientific habits or styles of thought among knowledge engineers. In her study, knowledge engineers represented knowledge or thought as solid when they were transformed into computer code. The fact that engineers thought that thought can be transformed in this way affected how they captured and characterized knowledge. Knowledge engineer's, in Forsythe's view, characterize knowledge as something concrete, a thing can be extracted "like a mineral or a diseased tooth" (p. 459).

parts or be constrained by them, and where agreement on rules and roles emerge as a dynamic equilibrium satisfying the demands of many parties (Hutchins, 1991). This leads to the second problem, which is that such a representation depicts a deterministic mechanical world, not an emerging system that has the ability to adapt to changing internal and external environments on its own. Objects are subjected to rules, but the rules are laid down once by the engineer after observing the system. The rules do not emerge as the system operates, as they would in the real world. Such a system may better reflect the design considerations and software engineering concerns of programming languages such as Smalltalk, and the cognitive or work styles of system engineers, than groupings or phenomena in the real world that CSCW aims to model.[7]

BANDWIDTH

The second factor limiting the conceptualizations of groups and group processes in CSCW system design is the engineering concept of communication bandwidth and its putative social and psychological effects. Within telecommunications engineering, bandwidth is defined as the range of frequencies available for signaling, that is, the difference between the highest and lowest frequencies of a band. However, the important point to note is that the quantity of information that can be transmitted along a given channel, such as a cable, is proportional to the bandwidth multiplied by the transmission time.

The problem of how to increase bandwidth and thus maximize the efficiency and decrease the costs of telecommunications has been a longstanding concern ever since the first experiments with telegraphy in the 1840s. The development of multiplexing systems, new materials for cabling, and satellite technology has ensured that the capacity of major telecommunication highways has been increasing exponentially since then by a factor of 10 every 17 years (Martin, 1971). The origins of the bandwidth approach lie in information theory, and its attempts to construct mathematical formulations of communication that would apply to any situation of information transfer, whether by humans or machines. Central to the information theory approach is the idea that communication can

---

[7]Two examples of systems where rules are not fixed and change over time are *adaptive systems* where the way a system interacts with its parts change with time based on its performance, and *nondeterministic systems,* such as massively parallel systems where individual processors may not be synchronized. Rather than waiting for synchronizations (which may waste time) processors may make decisions based on partial or available information. Thus, when a system is run twice with the same input, the answers may be different.

be quantified in terms of so many bits of information. Problems of uncertainty are reduced to a series of binary questions and the number of such questions required to solve a problem provides the necessary quantitative measures for the application of this essentially mathematical theory to communication analysis (Frick, 1959).

This approach, with its emphasis on the transmission of information rather than the communication of meaning, then paves the way for social evaluations of the relative efficiency and capacity of different communication channels based on a mechanistic analysis of message content. Bandwidth is considered to have important social and political implications. For example, it forms a cornerstone of the vision of a postindustrial or information society (e.g., Nora & Minc, 1978). This vision is predicated in part on the desirability of maximizing the information flow into peoples homes and offices, and the central role of bandwidth in its elaboration is no more clearly seen than in the current debate in the United States over the pros and cons of developing a national information infrastructure—the so-called information superhighway. The need for a broadband network is likened to the development of the interstate highway system and the need for wider roads that not only permit more traffic to flow, but also enable larger loads to be carried. Here then is a vision of a society whose organization would be made more "socially efficient" by virtue of the increased technical efficiency of the major communication networks.

The equation of technical efficiency of a communication medium with its social efficiency also underpins various social psychological analyses of mediated communication that have been collectively termed the "reduced social cues" approach (Spears & Lea, 1992). Here theoretical constructs such as "cuelessness," and "information richness" have been employed to quantify the amount of *social* information carried by different media, whereas the related concepts of "social presence" and "psychological distance" attempt to define the relative information-carrying properties of different media in phenomenological terms. These concepts first gained ground in social science research in the 1970s following a series of social psychological experiments investigating communication by telephone, audio, and video links by the Communication Studies Group, at University College, London, funded by the British Post Office (Short, Williams, & Christie, 1976).

In fact, anxieties and concerns about the social consequences of reduced communication bandwidth had been voiced much earlier in the popular science journals of the 1890s following the widespread diffusion of the telegraph and telephone. These concerns tended to be expressed in the form of anecdotal accounts of dire consequences (such as betrayal, fraud, and abuse), which befell those who naively treated full and attenuated bandwidth as if they were socially equivalent. These reports fueled debates among professional engineers as to what constituted sufficient presence for a medium to be judged as equivalent to face-to-face communication (Marvin, 1988, pp. 86–96). Strikingly similar processes have been traced in the discourses on new computer-based communication media, nearly 100 years later (Lea, O'Shea, Fung, & Spears, 1992; Lea & Spears, 1995). Reports in the popular press about the personal and organizational implications of anonymity in computer-mediated communication have fed directly into social science models of the medium, which in turn have helped shape popular ideas about the kind of medium provided by computers.[8]

Of particular interest here is the extent to which, and the way in which, these concerns have helped to shape the design of CSCW systems along certain lines. The important points to note about the work of Short et al. and subsequent followers of the reduced social cues approach are, first, the scientific, and in some cases, objective status that was given to the notion of presence; and, second, the way in which the concept of presence changed from being one that was appropriate to apply not only to inter-personal communication between two people, but also to groups of people communicating together.

This latter point is discussed further later, however, it is worth noting that Short et al's. experiments failed to find any convincing empirical support for the social presence idea. Further problems lie in the definition and operationalization of the construct (e.g., social presence is defined circularly and post hoc; Spears & Lea, 1992). A subsequent research program that was in part funded by British Telecom attempted to elaborate on the social presence concept in various ways in order to accommodate awkward and contradictory results (Rutter, 1987). Despite the lack of empirical evidence for social presence and its generally loose conceptual status, the concept was nevertheless seized on in the early writings on the new computer-based communication media (e.g., Hiltz & Turoff, 1978) and have remained remarkably influential ever since (e.g., DeSanctis & Gallupe, 1987; Rice, 1984).

The essential proposition in social analyses of communication bandwidth is that different communication media can be ranked according to

---

[8]Numerous examples include the now infamous account of the impersonation of a disabled woman by an able-bodied male psychiatrist (Van Gelder, 1985); the impersonation of presidential candidates on CompuServe in the last U.S. elections (Perry & Adam, 1992); and the use of e-mail networks for griping, flaming, and abuse of management by subordinates (e.g., Emmett, 1985; Zuboff, 1987). Further, related parallels can be seen between the liberatory rhetoric expressed in the last century about electricity as a truly democratic communication medium and similar views expressed about computer-mediated communication today. In both cases, entirely opposite views of the media have also been expressed that focus on their capacity to increase social control and reinforce existing power relations. Protagonists of either optimistic or pessimistic viewpoints, both then and now, have relied at least in part on the anonymity provided by reduced bandwidth to argue their respective corner (Marvin, 1988, chap. 3; Spears & Lea, 1994).

their capacity to transmit *social* information. Media that have a high capacity in this regard are considered to be high in social presence, low in cuelessness and psychological distance, and rich in social information. Video conferencing is regarded as most efficient in this regard, as it communicates both visual and auditory information, similar to face-to-face interaction. Audio-only conferencing and the telephone come next, followed by text-based media (such as electronic mail and computer conferencing), and finally, print-based media (such as letters and memos) are lowest in the hierarchy (Rutter, 1987; Short et al., 1976; Sproull & Kiesler, 1986).

One prediction of these conceptually similar models has some direct implications for groupware use in organizations. If media differ in their capacity to convey social information, their speed of transmission, and the delay in feedback, then it is argued that they consequently differ in their appropriateness for different sorts of communication tasks. For example, media furthest away from face-to-face interaction in terms of the number and type of cues they can transmit (the "information lean" media) are considered to be inappropriate for communicating messages high in ambiguity or uncertainty, in contrast to the "information rich" media (Trevino, Daft, & Lengel, 1990).

Not surprisingly, then, information theory and its derivatives have been enthusiastically applied to the comparative analysis of a wide range of interpersonal communication media including the telephone, audio conferencing, and video conferencing, and more recently computer-based message systems, such as electronic mail and computer conferencing systems, though the relative positions that different media occupy appear to be easily overturned or give way to more important factors (for reviews, see Lea, 1991; Spears & Lea, 1992; Walther, 1992).

Despite some considerable problems with the application of communication bandwidth to social and psychological analyses of interpersonal communication, the consensus between telecommunications engineering and social science over its utility has ensured its influence on CSCW and groupware design. Yet, its appropriateness for shaping analyses of group interaction is particularly questionable and rests on various assumptions about what constitutes the social and social behavior. To be specific, the social is defined in individualistic, physicalist, and "interdependence" terms. Social information, therefore, constitutes the verbal and nonverbal information conveyed in situ and most powerfully in face-to-face interaction. Given these assumptions, it then follows that the goal of CSCW design in supporting the group is to both model and simulate as nearly as possible the face-to-face situation. Furthermore, the means to achieving this goal is through the promotion of interaction and maximizing the exchange of interpersonal information in situ.

REPRESENTING THE GROUP
AND GROUP PROCESSES

Readers familiar with the field of small group dynamics will recognize that many of the assumptions about the group in CSCW match those in the field of group dynamics (for reviews, see e.g., Hogg, 1992, 1993; Hogg & Abrams, 1988). Interestingly, small group research developed in the 1940s and 1950s and flourished on the pragmatic considerations of solving specific problems for the army and industry (e.g., Cartwright & Zander, 1960). Theoretical considerations largely took second place to small-scale hypothesis testing. This pragmatic orientation in which the object of study is the dynamics of relations established at a given moment by given individuals in a given situation would seem to fit quite well with the pragmatic orientation of process and information modeling and its concern with modeling the here and now of physical systems—that is, modeling the real world. The connection of object-oriented design and the modeling of physical or systematic real-world systems as constrained interacting entities and their relations, as well as the wide diffusion of graphical user interface design to represent those entities, would seem to have created favorable preconditions for construing groups as small systems that are composed of interacting entities, operating in the here and now, and in terms of their structural elements.

However, by extending this formal representation of the world to the representation of the structural elements of a group, an important point is overlooked. That is, that "people in groups, unlike atoms in molecules, can contain psychologically the whole within themselves; that is, they can cognitively represent the group for themselves and act in terms of these cognitive representations" (Hogg & Abrams, 1988, p. 101). This contrasts with the structural view also favored by group dynamics, which is of the group as existing outside of the individual and operating on the individual.

One might therefore ask what it is that CSCW considers to determine that a collection of individuals requires support for group processes; that is, what is it that defines them as a group? In CSCW, just as in traditional perspectives on the social group, the fundamental assumption would appear to be that people who are interdependent on one another in order to perform some activity, and who achieve or expect to achieve some satisfaction from completing their tasks, need to develop feelings of mutual attraction in order to become psychologically a group (Turner, Hogg, Oakes, Reicher, & Wetherell, 1987). Given this assumption, then the need to support the group in terms of promoting positive regard and cohesion among group members becomes all important. And, because the cement that binds the group together is construed in terms of positive interpersonal ties, it becomes necessary to support interaction and the exchange of personal information between group members (Hogg, 1992).

So, when the CSCW field asserts the need to support group processes, it focuses not on the group level, but on the interpersonal level, that is, on supporting interpersonal communication between more than two people. As mentioned earlier, one approach is to transmit video pictures of the communicators' faces to each other, another depends on the system collecting data from individuals and then aggregating these in some way so as to draw conclusions about phenomena occurring at the group level. The design of the Group Analyzer system associated with the Capture Lab exemplifies this approach. Systematic observation of interpersonal interaction is coded according to Bales (1950) interaction process analysis and fed back to the group in the form of graphs that indicate the average group functioning.[9] The problem that seemingly confronts the system designers then is how to design an agent that can accurately capture this data and how best to aggregate it and display it to the group (Losada, Sanchez, & Noble, 1990). However, a more fundamental problem lies in the reductionism entailed in this approach. Rather than focusing on a group level of analysis, group processes are construed and measured at an interpersonal level. The approach relies on some kind of arithmetical procedure supposedly to transform this interpersonal information into a measure of group functioning.[10]

The emphasis on the need to support interpersonal ties in order to sustain the functioning group may go some way to explain why the CSCW field has focused its attention on modeling small groups in face-to-face situations, and is therefore poorly placed to design systems capable of supporting larger groups, or communities interacting irregularly over protracted periods where the rules of behavior are not clearly established. This concentration on providing support for small groups is a little curious given that computer networks, if anything, explode the physical limitation on the size of groups and afford opportunities for the formation of very large rather than small groups. For example, they facilitate the connection of individuals with similar interests rather than individuals that are grouped together by structural variables such as membership of the same organization, division, or work team. Examples of discussion groups on

---

[9]The Capture Lab is a computer-supported collaborative environment where participants can gain access to a publically shared screen by the press of one key on their workstations. Behavior in meetings is observed via video cameras and coded by behavioral scientists in an adjoining room. The GroupAnalyzer software is used to support the coders in capturing as much of the ongoing group dynamics as possible. In order to provide the group with feedback, a diagram summarizing the groups current behavior along the Bales dimensions is presented on the public screen.

[10]An additional problem lies in the strong distinction drawn between task-oriented and social or socioemotional dimensions of group activity by this approach. The implication is that task-oriented activity is not itself social activity or socially regulated (Spears & Lea, 1992).

Usenet, for example, already number thousands of members and in some cases, such as when the network is used to support people from the same cultural background who are removed from their country of origin, members clearly have strong identifications with and perceive themselves to be a group (e.g., Li, 1990). Given the present rate of growth of the internet, such groups will soon be able to number millions of members, yet the prospects of designing successful systems to support such mega-groups on the basis of promoting interpersonal ties would seem rather poor. One implicit assumption behind this focus of attention on small groups that would seem unwarranted is the idea of scaling up; that is, what can be designed to support a group of 4 can also work for a group of 400, rather than that there may be something qualitatively different about small face-to-face groups that does not extend to all situations and all groups.

One reason for these problems may be because the CSCW field has not yet considered very fully the implications of the computer as a broadcast medium rather than as a medium of interpersonal communication. Elsewhere, it has been argued that the development of the computer medium is itself contributing to the breakdown in the utility of this traditional distinction between interpersonal and mass communication (Lea & Spears, 1995), as part of a general process that is also reflected in the growing personalization of mass media and the consequent development of pseudo-communities (Beniger, 1987). After all, one of the sociotechnical features of the computer medium is that the difference between communicating interpersonally to another individual, and broadcasting a message for mass consumption by a worldwide audience, is only a matter of a few keystrokes. However, CSCW has generally yet to consider the kinds of support the computer could provide for groups when viewed in this way.[11]

The bandwidth concept also feeds the notion that supporting interpersonal ties is essential for successful group functioning in the computer environment. Yet, although the usefulness of bandwidth as a technical characteristic of media is not disputed, there are various objections that can be leveled against it as a foundation for analyzing media in social terms. To begin with, the assumption of a direct relation between the amount of information transmitted in a technical sense and the amount of social information conveyed seems to ignore the fact that some very influential kinds of social information require minimal bandwidth to be

---

[11]One promising foundation here is in the Advisor system developed for the Andrew Messaging System at Carnegie Mellon University. Designed to support computer users, the user sends a message asking for advice or help to "the advisor," but this is merely the front-end hiding a vast network of bulletin boards that enlist the cooperative efforts of groups of programmers, network administrators, and other university support staff to provide the solutions that appear in the Advisor's response (e.g., Borenstein & Thyberg, 1988).

communicated. This is particularly the case with information at the social (group) level. One obvious example here is gender, which is communicated as a single binary piece of information, but that despite its trivial status in purely informational terms, can have enormous consequences in the construction of social meaning from the communication.

Second, a clear distinction should be made between social cues qua interpersonal cues conveyed in situ (e.g., nonverbal signals, verbal intonation, etc.) and cues to the social (viz. information about the participants), the context, and particularly social category information. Whereas the communication of cues at an interpersonal level would arguably be sensitive to restrictions in communication bandwidth, it is not clear that conveying categorical information depends at all on wide bandwidth. To indicate membership of social categories, such as *female*, or membership of an organizational division or project team, is a matter of conveying binary information that requires minimal bandwidth and can therefore be communicated by the leanest, or most narrow, of media. Nevertheless, this kind of information exerts a powerful social influence and arguably has a greater effect on the kind of communication and its content, than any interpersonal cues conveyed in situ. It can be argued that a medium that is informationally rich in terms of interpersonal and personalized cues might undermine or counteract the group and social categorical bases of interaction, such that a rich medium may paradoxically appear less social than a lean one. Physical isolation and a lean communication medium can therefore have the effect of increasing a person's sense of being part of the group relative to face-to-face conditions (Spears & Lea, 1992, 1994).

The concern with bandwidth and with the transmission of information in situ tends to preclude such ideas about normative, historical, or situational influences on communication and behavior. Social influence as a fundamental group process becomes dependent solely on the amount and quality of information transmitted so that the social has been reduced merely to standing in for the interpersonal. As a consequence, the agenda for supporting group processes in CSCW system design becomes a case of maximizing the flow of interpersonal information.

CONCLUSIONS

A recent paper by Hollan and Stornetta (1992) called for CSCW to relinquish its preoccupation with emulating face-to-face group interaction. However, whereas Hollan and Stornetta still maintain the importance of maximizing the exchange of information in situ (specifically, they try to envisage what kind of system might provide more social presence, or sense of being there, than face-to-face interaction), designers must respond to this call in a different manner and imagine how alternative means of supporting group processes might be found that do not depend on maximizing information exchange or simulating the face-to-face situation or enhancing metaphysical notions such as presence.

If CSCW is to provide support for groups, that is, if it is to provide support for groups rather than aggregates of individuals, and for social and not just interpersonal processes, then it needs to identify processes that are unique to groups and common to all groups, irrespective of physical constraints such as size and geographical dispersion. It also needs to develop greater sensitivity to the contexts in which groups function— that is, the important preexisting social categories, norms, and identifications that position communicators and define their relations to each other—and then to find ways of supporting this context (e.g., by maintaining historical records of the group and by communicating more of the situational influences that affect the extent to which individuals have the sense of being part of a group). In this respect, maximizing the flow of interpersonal information may have a detrimental effect. Furthermore, it should develop interfaces that are sensitive to communicating social meaning rather than displaying information, so that for example social information that is trivial in quantitative terms to transmit could nevertheless be signified by the medium in accordance with its social import. Finally, it needs to recognize the position of groups vis-à-vis other groups, and the positions of group members with respect to these other groups. That is, there is a need to develop an intergroup perspective that acknowledges the multiple, and possibly conflicting, social identities held by interactants and their effects on group functioning.

If the preliminary investigation into computer-supported cooperative work is correct, its dimensions and limitations are not the result of a great divide between computer scientists and social scientists, but instead may be the outcome of the opposite: premature closure or agreement between the two. This suggests that the mixture of different disciplinary or cognitive orientations in designing systems will not in itself engender successful systems. It also suggests that tools designers use in understanding processes and modeling them, are embedded in resulting technologies. By understanding the limits of the tools used to create a technology, students of technology may themselves understand the limits of systems constructed from them.

ACKNOWLEDGMENTS

This work was supported by a fellowship to the first author from the U.K. Joint Research Council Initiative in Cognitive Science/Human–Computer Interaction, and by a grant to the second author from the University of Manchester, Faculty of Science, Simon Fund.

REFERENCES

Alderfer, C. P. (1977). Groups and intergroup relations. In J. R. Hackman & J. L. Suttle (Eds.), *Improving life at work.* Santa Monica, CA: Goodyear.

Avison, D. E., & Fitzgerald, G. (1988). *Information systems development: Methodologies, techniques and tools.* Oxford, England: Blackwell.

Bales, R. F. (1950). *Interaction process analysis: A method for the study of small groups.* Reading, MA: Addison-Wesley.

Beniger, J. R. (1987). Personalization of mass media and the growth of pseudo-community. *Communication Research, 14*(3), 352–371.

Borenstein, N. S., & Thyberg, C. A. (1988). Cooperative work in the Andrew message system. In *CSCW '88: Proceedings of the Conference on Computer-Supported Cooperative Work, September 26–29, 1988, Portland, OR* (pp. 306–323). New York: Association for Computing Machinery.

Cartwright, D., & Zander, A. (Eds.). (1960). *Group dynamics: Research and theory* (2nd. ed.). Evanston, IL: Row, Peterson.

Coad, P., & Yourdon, E. (1991). *Object-oriented analysis.* Englewood Cliffs, NJ: Yourdon Press.

Cole, P., & Nast-Cole, J., (1992). A primer on group dynamics for groupware developers. In D. Marca & G. Bock (Eds.), *Groupware: Software for computer-supported cooperative work* (pp. 44–57). Los Alamitos, CA: IEEE Computer Society Press.

DeSanctis, G., & Gallupe, R. B. (1987). A foundation for the study of group decision support systems. *Management Science, 33,* 589–609.

Emmett, R. (1981, November). Vnet or gripenet? *Datamation,* 48.

Finholt, T., & Sproull, L. (1990). Electronic groups at work. *Organization Science, 1*(1), 41–64.

Fish, R. S., Kraut, R. E., & Chalfonte, B. L. (1990). The VideoWindowSystem in informal communication. In *CSCW '90: Proceedings of the Conference on Computer-Supported Cooperative Work, October 7–10, 1990, Los Angeles, CA* (pp. 1–12). New York: Association for Computing Machinery.

Forsythe, D. E. (1993). Engineering knowledge: The construction of knowledge in artificial intelligence. *Social Studies of Science, 23,* 445–477.

French, J. R. P., Caplan, R. D., & Van Harrison, R. (1982) *The mechanisms of job stress and strain.* London: Wiley.

Frick, F. C. (1959). Information theory. In S. Koch (Ed.), *Psychology: A study of science* (pp. 611–636). New York: McGraw-Hill.

Gane, C., & Sarson, T. (1979). *Structured systems analysis: Tools and techniques.* Englewood Cliffs, NJ: Prentice-Hall.

Get faxed in Dutch. (1990, September, 7). *The Guardian.*

Hiltz, S. R., & Turoff, M. (1978). *The network nation: Human communication via computer.* Reading, MA: Addison-Wesley.

Hogg, M. A. (1992). *The social psychology of group cohesiveness: From attraction to social identity.* London: Harvester-Wheatsheaf.

Hogg, M. A. (1993). Group cohesiveness: A critical review and some new directions. *European Review of Social Psychology, 4,* 85–111.

Hogg, M. A., & Abrams, D. (1988). *Social identifications.* London: Routledge & Kegan Paul.

Hollan, J., & Stornetta, S. (1992). Beyond being there. In P. Bauersfield, J. Bennett, & G. Lynch (Eds.), *CHI '92: Proceedings of the Conference on Human Factors in Computing Systems, May 3–7, Monterey, CA* (pp. 119–125). New York: Association for Computing Machinery.

Hutchins, E. (1991). Organizing work by adaptation. *Organization Science, 2*(1), 14–39.

Ishii, H. (1990). TeamWorkStation: Towards a seamless shared workspace. In *CSCW '90: Proceedings of the Conference on Computer-Supported Cooperative Work, October 7–10, 1990, Los Angeles, CA* (pp. 13–26). New York: Association for Computing Machinery.

Kiesler, S., Heinmiller, R., Ostell, J., Traweek, S., & Uncapher, K. (1990). Computer-supported cooperative work in science. In *CSCW '90: Proceedings of the Conference on Computer-Supported Cooperative Work, October 7–10, Los Angeles, CA* (pp. 239–240). New York: Association for Computing Machinery.

Kishino, F., Ohya, J., Takemura, H., & Terashima, N. (1993). Virtual space teleconferencing system: Real time detection and reproduction of 3-D human images. In G. Salvendy & M. J. Smith (Eds.), *Human-computer interaction: Software and hardware interfaces* (pp. 669–674). Amsterdam: Elsevier.

Knight, K. (1976). Matrix organizations: A review. *Journal of Management Studies, 13,* 111–130.

Korson, T., & McGregor, J. D. (1990). Understanding object-oriented: A unifying paradigm. *Communications of the ACM, 33*(9), 40–60.

Lea, M. (1991). Rationalist assumptions in cross-media comparisons of computer-mediated communication. *Behaviour and Information Technology, 10,* 153–172.

Lea, M., O'Shea, T., Fung, P., & Spears, R. (1992). "Flaming" in computer-mediated communication: Observations, explanations, implications. In M. Lea (Ed.), *Contexts of computer-mediated communication* (pp. 89–112). London: Harvester-Wheatsheaf.

Lea, M., & Spears, R. (1995). Love at first byte? Building personal relationships over computer networks. In J. T. Wood & S. Duck (Eds.), *Understudied relationships: Off the beaten track* (pp. 197–233). Thousand Oaks, CA: Sage.

Leavitt, H. (1972). *Managerial psychology: An introduction to individuals, pairs and groups in organizations.* Chicago: University of Chicago.

Li, T. (1990). Computer-mediated communications and the Chinese students in the U.S. *The Information Society, 7,* 125–137.

Losada, M., Sanchez, P., & Noble, E. E. (1990). Collaborative technology and group process feedback: The impact on interactive sequences in meetings. In *CSCW '90: Proceedings of the Conference on Computer-Supported Cooperative Work, October 7–10, Los Angeles, CA* (pp. 53–64). New York: Association for Computing Machinery.

Madsen, C. M. (1989, September). Approaching group communication by means of an office building metaphor. In J. Bowers & S. Benford (Eds.), *Proceedings of the First European Conference on Computer-Supported Cooperative Work, September 1989* (pp. 449–460). London, England.

Mantei, M. M., Baeker, R. B., Sellen, A. J., Buxton, W. A. S., Milligan, T., & Wellman, B. (1991). Experiences in the use of a media space. In *Proceedings of the Conference on Human Factors in Computing, March 1991* (pp. 203–208). New York: Association for Computing Machinery.

Marchand, M. (1984). Conclusion: Vivre avec le Videotex. In M. Marchand & C. Ancelin (Eds.), *Télématique: Promenades dans les usages.* Paris: La Documentation Francaise.

Martin, J. (1971). *Future developments in telecommunications.* Englewood Cliffs, NJ: Prentice-Hall.

Marvin, C. (1988). *When old technologies were new: Thinking about electric communication in the late nineteenth century.* Oxford, England: Oxford University Press.

Meyer, B. (1988). *Object-oriented software construction.* Englewood Cliffs, NJ: Prentice-Hall.

Nora, S., & Minc, A. (1978). The computerization of society [*L'informatisation de la société*]. Paris: Editions du Seuil.

Nunamaker, J. F., Dennis, A. R., Valacich, J. S., Vogel, D. R. & George, J. F. (1991). Electronic meeting systems to support group work. *Communications of the ACM, 34*(7), 40–61.

Perry, T. S., & Adam, J. A. (1992). Forces for social change. *IEEE Spectrum* (Special Rep./Electronic Mail), October, 22–33.

Poole, M. S., Holmes, M., & DeSanctis, G. (1988). Conflict management and group decision support systems. In *CSCW '88: Proceedings of the Conference of Computer-Supported Cooperative Work, September 26–28, 1988, Portland, OR* (pp. 227–243). New York: Association for Computing Machinery.

Rice, R. E. (1984). Mediated group communication. In R. E. Rice (Ed.), *The new media: Communication, research and technology* (pp. 129–154). Beverly Hills, CA: Sage.

Robey, D., Farrow, D. L., & Franz, C. R. (1989). Group processes and conflict in system development. *Management Science, 35*(10), 1172–1191.

Rojek, C., & Wilson, D. C. (1987). Workers' self-management in a world system. *Organizational Studies, 8*(4), 297–308.

Rutter, D. R. (1987). *Communicating by telephone.* Oxford, England: Pergamon.

Saudis wage fax war from Wembley. (1995). *The Guardian.*

Shlaer, S., & Mellor, S. (1988). *Object-oriented systems analysis: Modeling the world in data.* Englewood Cliffs, NJ: Yourdon Press.

Short, J., Williams, E., & Christie, B. (1976). *The social psychology of telecommunications.* Chichester, England: Wiley.

Spears, R., & Lea, M. (1992). Social influence and the influence of the "social" in computer-mediated communication. In M. Lea (Ed.), *Contexts of computer-mediated communication* (pp. 30–65). London: Harvester-Wheatsheaf.

Spears, R., & Lea, M. (1994). Panacea or panopticon? The hidden power in computer-mediated communication. *Communication Research, 21,* 427–459.

Sproull, L., & Kiesler, S. (1986). Reducing social context cues: Electronic mail in organizational communication. *Management Science, 32,* 1492–1512.

Trevino, L. K., Daft, R. L., & Lengel, R. H. (1990). Understanding managers' media choices: A symbolic interactionist perspective. In J. Fulk & C. Steinfield (Eds.), *Organizations and communication technology* (pp. 71–94). Newbury Park, CA: Sage.

Turner, J. C., Hogg, M. A., Oakes, P. J., Reicher, S. D., & Wetherell, M. S. (1987). *Rediscovering the social group: A self-categorization theory.* Oxford, England: Basil Blackwell.

Van Gelder, L. (1985). The strange case of the electronic lover. *Ms.,* October, pp. 94, 99, 101–104, 117, 123–124.

Walther, J. B. (1992). Interpersonal effects in computer-mediated interaction: A relational perspective. *Communication Research, 19,* 52–90.

Zuboff, S. (1988). *In the age of the smart machine: The future of work and power.* New York: Basic Books.

Toward a Social, Ethical Theory of Information

Joseph A. Goguen
University of California at San Diego

This chapter seeks to take some initial steps toward a theory of information that is adequate for understanding and designing systems that process information, (i.e., information systems in a broad sense). Formal representations of information are needed in designing, using, and maintaining such systems, especially when they are computer based. However, it is also necessary to take account of social context, including how information is produced and used, not merely how it is represented; that is, we need a *social* theory of information. This chapter uses some ideas from ethnomethodology and semiotics, as well as logic and the sociology of science, to explore the nature of information. Ethnomethodology also provides guidelines for collecting high quality information on which to base design, especially in situations where interaction is important. In addition, some case studies and some ideas on how to combine methods are presented. We argue that, as a result of its social situatedness, information has an intrinsic ethical dimension, and that this may have some wider implications.

It is said that we live in an "Age of Information," but it is an open scandal that there is no theory, nor even definition, of *information* that is both broad and precise enough to make such an assertion meaningful.[1]

---

[1] Perhaps none is possible. Bowker (1994) discussed mythologies that support the notion of information. Schiller (1994) discussed the importance of information as "commodity" in postindustrial society, and Haraway (1991) gave a daring modern cyborg myth; Bowkers' discussion of Babbage's mythology (1837) is especially interesting. Agre (1995) argued that the notion of information is itself a myth, mobilized to support certain institutions, such as libraries.

In particular, such a theory should help us understand and design *information systems*—in a wide sense that includes computer-based systems, as well as systems that are paper-based, conversation-based, graphics-based, and so on, and combinations of these. Any system that interacts meaningfully with humans can be seen as an information system in this sense; in particular, business corporations and government agencies may be included. However, a major motivating example is Information Systems in the narrow sense (i.e., computer-based systems for storing and retrieving information, e.g., database systems); capitalization is used to distinguish Information Systems in this narrow sense from the general concept.

The need for such a theory is pressing. Society demands ever larger and more complex systems. For example, billions are spent each year on software, but many systems that are built are never used, and at least one third of systems begun are abandoned before completion. Moreover, many systems once thought to be adequate no longer are. Some sobering examples are given in Gibbs (1994), including the disastrous baggage handling system at the new Denver International Airport; Gibbs concluded that "despite 50 years of progress, the software industry remains years—perhaps decades—short of the mature engineering discipline needed to meet the demands of an information-age society." Since that paper was written, a major computer company has defaulted on an $8 billion contract to build the next generation U. S. air traffic control system. In many such cases, problems with requirements, that is, customer needs, have been implicated as a major source of difficulty. For discussions of the importance of requirements in developing systems, and of social factors in requirements, see Goguen (1994), Goguen (1996), and Goguen and Luqi (1995).

An adequate theory of information would have to take account of social context, including how information is produced and used, rather than merely how it is represented; that is, it must be a *social* theory of information, not merely a theory of representation. On the other hand, the formal aspects of information are inherent to technical systems; computers *are* engines for storing, processing, and retrieving formal representations. Thus, the essence of designing such systems is the *reconciliation* of their social and technical aspects (Goguen, 1994), respectively called the *dry* and the *wet* (Goguen, 1992). Indeed, this chapter argues that all information is grounded in these dual aspects, and later argues that information has an ethical dimension that cannot be separated from these aspects.

This chapter draws on several different approaches to sociology, as well as on ideas from logic and semiotics; in this sense, it is postmodern. Nevertheless, it has a goal: to help make the analysis, design, and construction of information systems more responsive to users and to social context. If it does not serve this purpose, then perhaps it will at least raise doubts and questions about how system development is usually organized at present.

Requirements for a Theory of Information

Before suggesting an approach to information, it may help to present our criteria for success:

1. A theory of information should be useful for understanding and designing information systems, and in particular, Information Systems in the narrow sense.

2. It should address the *meanings* that users give to events, in a broad sense that includes social and political nuances. This is needed because design decisions about information systems have profound implications for how work is done in organizations, and this is something that users of such systems care about very deeply.

3. It must address *ethical* issues, including but not limited to the privacy of information. These too are important to the members of organizations, as well as to society as a whole, and can strongly impact the success of information systems.

4. It must take account of the fact that different individuals and groups can construe meanings in very different ways. For this purpose, and in order to achieve accuracy, it seems important to have a theory that is strongly empirically based, in two different senses:

   (a) the analyst does not enter into a social context with pre-given categories, which are assumed to be relevant to the analysis (such as rank or status);
   (b) the analyst leaves a social context with "hard data," such as videotapes, that document social interaction and can later be used as a basis for design through discussions with other analysts.

It follows that a suitable theory of information must be a *social theory of information*, rather than a *statistical theory of information*, like Shannon's theory (Shannon & Weaver, 1964), or a *representational theory of information*, like the situation theory of Barwise and Perry (1983). In fact, a theory of the kind we need cannot be "objectivist" or "realist," in the sense of assuming a pre-given distinction between subject and object, and an objectively given real world. Thus, traditional semiotics is not adequate as a foundation, because it assumes that signs represent things in a real, objective world; we need a *social semiotics*, rather than a logical semiotics. Although the notion of a sign system is used in our formulation of information, it is in the sense of a (members') category system (see the following section on ethnomethodology), rather than a pre-given system of distinctions. Finally, knowledge representation, in the sense of artificial intelligence, is another objectivist, realist, reductionist theory that cannot meet our needs.

FORMALIZATION AND INFORMATION

After some preliminary concepts, this section suggests a definition of information, and then explores some of its consequences. Ideas from the sociology of science are also used.

Member, Analyst, Designer

Our discussion will proceed more clearly if we first distinguish certain roles. The basic concept for this purpose is that of a *member* of a social group[2]; in particular, we will need to distinguish the members of group(s) of (potential) users of some information system. The words designer and analyst will refer to an individual or group engaged in understanding and designing information systems; the term requirements engineer is also used in computer science.

Distinguishing the activities of members from those of analysts can be very helpful in clarifying the status of various objects and events that arise during design. Analysts form groups that have their own distinct cultures, and it is necessary to evaluate their actions from this perspective. Nevertheless, analysts can benefit from knowing the methods and categories of members, particularly when they want to understand things that members regularly and ordinarily do themselves. Note that analysts can use categories and methods that members of the group they are studying do not use. For example, analysts of an Information System may consider statistical measures of response time that would be incomprehensible to most users of the system. An approach to information should not be so dogmatic as to exclude such technical methods.

Formalization and Metalanguage

Every formalization requires a distinction between an *object* level, for that which is formalized, and a *meta* level, which provides a language for expressing the formalization. The object level models the world of members, while the meta level provides the language of the analysts who do the modeling. The metalanguage may contain technical terms and rules that members would not understand. The distinction between the object

---

[2]We return to the issues of member and group in a later discussion of ethnomethodology.

and meta levels of description is parallel to the distinction between the member and analyst cultures. Note that the interpretation of analysts' technical terms into the social world is an essential part of a formalization; in general, this cannot itself be formalized, and instead is a tacit part of the analysts' culture. It is also worth emphasizing the obvious point that a model of the object level is necessarily situated at the meta level, rather than the object level; it is an analysts' construction.

Perhaps researchers in the social and literary sciences have been more reluctant to use formalization than they should be, because of their deep understanding of the limits of formalization (as discussed later). I hope that this chapter might encourage a wider appreciation of the fact that using a formal language loosely can still be very successful. Indeed, because any use of a formalization must always be somewhat loose, the essential problem is to avoid claiming more (or less) than is justified by the match between the formalization and the domain of interest.

Information

I suggest the following as a working definition:

> An item of information is an interpretation of a configuration of signs for which members of some social group are accountable.

Signs, in the sense of semiotics, do not necessarily have significance, and "mere signs" (i.e., "marks") have no significance. However, this is only a theoretical possibility, because the very notion of sign presupposes a category system (e.g., a certain character set, such as ascii) within which it is a sign. Thus, any sign has at least the significance of being a sign in a certain system (e.g., the letter "t"). Note that the same mark can appear in more than one category system (e.g., "E" in the Greek and Roman alphabets), and as such has different interpretations. A "configuration" of signs is a "text," existing as one choice among many in a system of such configurations; such a system should not be considered closed (the qualities of such systems are discussed later). "Texts" in this sense, like signs, are already the result of interpretation, and of course are not limited to writing, but also include spoken discourse, movies, mime, comics, and so on. The senses of sign and of accountability intended here are based on ethnomethodology.

The foregoing definition ties an item of information to a particular social group through a particular relationship of accountability for a particular interpretation. However, the same configuration of signs could very well be interpreted by different groups in different ways, giving rise to different items of information in our sense. In this approach, it takes *work* to interpret signs as information, and this work is necessarily done in some particular context, making use of the resources available and within the constraints imposed in that context.

De Saussure (1976) is a founder of what is now called *structuralism*, with his conception of signs as arbitrary, attaining identity only through differences, that is, through participation in a system of distinctions. For De Saussure, these systems of distinctions exist as ideal entities, rather than being emergent through social interaction, as with our notion of category system. So-called *poststructuralism* has attacked structuralism on this ground and others, such as its presupposition of a subject–object distinction, saying instead that such distinctions arise out of discourse.

Information that can be understood in a wide variety of contexts can be distinguished from information that is so thoroughly situated that it cannot be understood except in relation to certain very particular contexts. We call these types of information *dry* and *wet*, respectively (Goguen, 1992). Note that there is really a continuum of "humidity" for information (e.g., there is "damp" information, of which cooking recipes are a typical example). In general, information cannot be fully context sensitive (for then it could only be understood when and where it is produced) nor fully context insensitive (for then it could be understood by anyone in any time and place).

In the driest formalizations, the metalanguage is also formalized, so that an object-level model is a formal theory in the metalanguage. In less fully formalized models, the metalanguage may simply be a natural language, such as English, or a somewhat stylized dialect of it. Note that rules about objects are part of the model, whereas rules at the meta level define the language used in the formalization, or else give methodological rules. (Justification for the distinction between object and metalanguage on social rather than logical grounds is considered later)

A fairly extreme case is the "raw data" collected in a scientific experiment; although it may be just a collection of numbers, it is very highly situated, because those numbers only make sense to a very small group who share a very particular context. On the other hand, an equation that summarizes those particular numbers is relatively more dry, and a general physical law is even drier. These considerations suggest the following, which we call the *formalization hypothesis*:

> Formalization is the process of making information drier (i.e., less situated) by using a more explicit and precise metalanguage for expressing information.

Some criteria for measuring the degree of formalization (i.e., the "humidity" of information) are discussed later.

Dry information is usually intended to be interpreted in what counts as the same way for practical purposes in a variety of contexts. However dry it may be, information is always situated in some particular social context: from this point of view, there is no such thing as abstract, ideal information, which is independent of context. In particular, the same configuration of signs can mean different things in different contexts.

The *structure* of information is *how* it is configured; formalization makes that structure more precise and explicit, through use of a metalanguage. The notion of abstract data type (Goguen, Thatcher, & Wagner, 1978) uses the very dry metalanguage of abstract algebra for formalizing structure. This approach also formalizes the notion "representation independence," that the same structure can be represented in different ways. An abstract data type defines the space of all admissible configurations for a class of signs, along with methods for creating, modifying and retrieving configurations. The notion of *situated abstract data type* was introduced (Goguen, 1994) to explicate how information can be both situated and structured.

Tacit Knowledge

It can be difficult to find good data on which to base the design of information systems. Experience shows that simply asking managers what they want often works poorly. They do not (usually) know what is technically feasible, and they cannot accurately describe what their workers really do, what their clients really do, or even what they themselves really do. This is not because managers are incompetent; on the contrary, they are (usually) genuine experts at their own job. Rather, it is due to what philosophers (Polanyi, 1967) call the problem of *tacit knowledge* (i.e., the phenomenon that people may know how to do something, without being able to articulate how they do it). In the social sciences, this is called the *say-do problem*. Some examples are riding bicycles, tying shoe laces, speaking languages, negotiating contracts, reconciling personal differences, evaluating employees, and using a word processor.[3] An important reason for this difficulty is the situatedness of the information involved.

But to build a system that effectively meets a real business need, it is usually necessary to find out what workers, clients, and managers really do. Note that simply asking workers what they do is subject to the same problems as asking their managers. Instead, if we really need this information, it is usually best to go where the work is actually done, and carefully observe what actually happens. Various methods from sociology seem promising for this purpose, and are discussed below. Of course, it may be necessary to abstract away many details of what workers do, so

---

[3]Some groups may have specialized concepts and methods for dealing with certain situations. For example, sailors have a specialized vocabulary for knots that would allow them to describe how to tie shoelaces.

that a new information system supports what is essential rather than what is accidental.

An important way to take advantage of tacit knowledge is to evolve the design of a new system through a series of prototypes, which small groups of workers are invited to use, and while doing so, discuss what they are doing. These interactions can be videotaped and then analyzed. A first prototype could be as crude as some cardboard boxes with drawings of buttons, and with changeable pieces of paper to simulate screen configurations.

Qualities of Information

It seems worth contrasting the view of information and meaning suggested earlier with the *representational theory of meaning* that is standard in computer science and in the Anglo-American analytic tradition of philosophy with which it is closely allied. According to our social theory of information, meaning is an ongoing achievement of some social group; it takes *work* to interpret configurations of signs, and this work necessarily occurs in some particular context, including a particular time, place, and group. The meaning of an item of information consists of the relations of accountability that are attached to it in that context and, as we will see later, the narratives in which it is embedded.

By contrast, a representational theory of meaning claims that a meaningful configuration of signs *represents* something in the real world. In sophisticated representational theories, such as situation semantics (Barwise & Perry, 1983), what is represented by (say) a given phrase in English can vary with the context where it is interpreted, and need not be a simple object, but can be a complex of interconnected relationships, that is, what they call a "situation." This is adequate for some purposes, but even the most sophisticated representational theory leaves out the work of interpretation and the social accountability that is required for interpretation.

That information is tied to a particular, concrete situation and a particular social group has some important consequences, as summarized in the following list of *qualities of information*:

1. *Situated.* Information can only be fully understood in relation to the particular, concrete situation in which it actually occurs.
2. *Local.* Interpretations are constructed in some particular context, including a particular time, place, and group.
3. *Emergent.* Information cannot be understood at the level of the individual, that is, at the cognitive level of individual psychology, because it arises through ongoing interactions among members of a group.

4. *Contingent.* The interpretation of information depends on the current situation, which may include the current interpretation of prior events.[4] In particular, interpretations are subject to negotiation, and relevant rules are interpreted locally, and can even be modified locally.

5. *Embodied.* Information is tied to bodies in particular physical situations, so that the particular way that bodies are embedded in a situation may be essential to some interpretations.

6. *Vague.* In practice, information is only elaborated to the degree that it is useful to do so; the rest is left grounded in tacit knowledge.

7. *Open.* Information (for both participants and analysts) cannot in general be given a final and complete form, but must remain open to revision in the light of further analyses and further events. (At the analyst level, one may say "all theories leak.")

I do not claim this list is complete, let alone superior to other such lists. On the contrary, this list derives its plausibility from its similarity to many other such lists. For example, qualities like these are familiar to anthropologists (e.g., see various comments by Lévi-Strauss, 1996), although anthropologists have not been very precise in distinguishing among different qualities. Also, Suchman (1987) gave a similar list of qualities for plans, which was a major inspiration for the above list. On the other hand, the categories in the list are themselves vague and partially overlapping, and the list itself should be considered open; that is, this list of qualities applies to itself.

These qualities can be applied in many ways. For example, they lead to some basic limitations of formalization. Because any formalization is information, it must be emergent, contingent, local, open, and vague (see Goguen, 1994; Goguen & Luqi, 1995). We can also apply the list to obtain qualities of category systems, signs, interpretations, texts, and so on.

The qualities of information can also be used to understand why it is not possible to completely formalize requirements: They cannot be fully separated from their social context. More specifically, the qualities explain why so-called lifecycle phases cannot be fully formalized. Indeed, the activities necessary for a successful system development project cannot always be expected to fit in a natural way into any system of pre-given categories, and practicing software engineers often report (informally) that they have to spend much of their time circumventing "the system." Robinson and Bannon (1991) show that representations pass through multiple "semantic communities" during the construction of large systems, and suggest this implies that such "work-arounds" should not be surprising in practice.

---

[4]Of course, an "event" is what some group counts as an event.

Sociology of Science

There have been important new developments in the sociology of science. One exciting voice in this field is Latour (1987), who has suggested certain properties that distinguish scientific work from other kinds of work. Latour introduced the phrase *immutable mobile* for a representation that can be interpreted in essentially the same way in a variety of contexts[5]; thus, immutable mobiles are information structures that have been dried out. To illustrate this concept, Latour discussed the use of cartographic maps for navigation: Given the proper instruments and proper conditions (e.g., good weather), such maps can be used anywhere in the world; but each such use is still a local interpretation.

Representations are often what Latour called *re-representations*,[6] which are representations that concentrate previously available information; this is a form of abstraction. For example, a large set of observations of planetary motion might be summarized by a single equation. Latour claimed that the qualities of immutable mobility and concentration are characteristic of the information that occurs in the discourse of science. Formalization tends to increase these qualities, and, indeed, it is natural to suggest the following *success criteria*:

> A formalization is successful to the extent that it exhibits immutable mobility and concentration.

Note that formalized information is not necessarily more immutably mobile or more concentrated.

As Latour (1987) pointed out, the construction of immutable mobiles can be a way to mobilize power. For example, if an analyst compresses large amounts of information into simple graphical representations, then anyone who wishes to disagree must mobilize the resources to acquire and compress comparable amounts of information. This can be seen in the presentation of dataflow diagrams in requirements meetings; in general, such diagrams are beyond the capabilities of users and managers, due in part to the huge volume of information involved in large projects, as well as its formal character. Requirements engineering has developed special tools, such as gIBIS (Conklin & Bergman, 1988), to help collect and organize arguments for various positions on selected requirements issues. However, these tools are based on normatively given presuppositions about the way that projects should be organized, and serve mainly to increase the power of analysts. A tool that tries to make requirements

---

[5]It is not so clear what Latour meant by a "representation," but for the purposes of this chapter, it should simply be considered a configuration of signs, without any necessary representational connection to "real" objects.

[6]These can be considered "semiotic morphisms" in the sense of Goguen (1996).

information more relevant to users and their needs is described in Pinheiro and Goguen (1996), with further motivation given in Goguen (1996).

Star (1988) introduced the term *boundary object* to describe information that is used in different ways by different social groups. For an information system to be successful, it must often serve multiple groups, and so it seems natural to suggest that boundary objects can be usefully applied (e.g., to Information Systems). Indeed, the notion of a database *view* already reflects the idea that it may be useful to present different information in different ways to different users. Similarly, requirements documents must serve a number of different stakeholders, and thus must be boundary objects. This seems a fruitful area for further research.

The Retrospective Character of Explanation

The following, called the *retrospective hypothesis*, seems a basic result in our social theory of information:

> Only post hoc explanations for situated events can attain relative stability and independence from context.

While events are unfolding (and before they happen), they cannot achieve a final social accountability, because members can always revise their assessment of the significance of past events in the light of new events, or of new interpretations for prior events; even what counts as an event is negotiable, as are the criteria for what counts as significant. Thus, information is always subject to revision, and is often revised as events unfold. Empirical support for this view can be found in work on plans and explanations reported in and Linde and Goguen (1978) and Goguen, Weiner, and Linde (1983), and in the important work of Suchman (1987) on situated planing.

This explains why it can be so difficult to determine the requirements for a large system: it only becomes clear what the requirements are when the system is successfully operating in its social and organizational context; requirements evolve as system development proceeds, and a reasonably complete and consistent set of requirements for a large, complex system can only emerge from a retrospective reconstruction. It takes work by members to achieve a retrospective reconstruction, and for large systems, it is unusual to do all this work. Determining whether some system meets its requirements is the outcome of a complex social process that typically involves negotiation, and may involve legal action. Thus, it is usually entirely misleading to think of requirements as pre-given.

Going further, it could be argued that time, in the sense of a linear ordering imposed on events, is itself the result of the retrospective reconstruction of causal chains to explain events (i.e., to give them significance in relation to shared values). The use of causal explanations in this way is characteristic of Western culture, and is a basic constitutive shared value of that culture (see a later section for some discussion of causality in narrative).

HOW TO GET INFORMATION

This section describes and evaluates a number of methods that can be used to get the information needed to support the design of information systems. More details, including more comparison and examples, are given in Goguen and Linde (1993), from which parts of the next two subsections are drawn.

Some Methods and Their Limitations

Perhaps the most common method for designers to get information about users' needs and habits is *introspection*, which amounts to imagining what kind of system the designer would want. Although this can be useful, the introspection of an expert in a different field, such as computer science, is unlikely to reflect the experience of the intended users. Experts tend to use what they remember or imagine of themselves; for user interface design, this experience can be very far from the questions, assumptions, and fears of actual users. For example, an expert might be surprised when a user does not attempt to understand why a word processor unexpectedly centers some material; in fact, users often seem to believe that computers just are sometimes puzzling or irritating, and that it is neither necessary nor valuable to explain their more bizarre behavior. Cognitive scientists may be surprised by this, because their theories suggest that a user who finds that a model is incorrect should correct the model. Designers may be upset because they feel their designs are not being used correctly.

Moreover, designers cannot reliably introspect what work settings are like, or the conditions under which a new technology will be learned or used. For example, many users must learn and use technology in conditions that require multiple and ongoing splitting of attention; this may be due to complex collaborative relationships.

Questionnaires and interviews are also frequently used. Questionnaires are limited by their stimulus–response model of interaction, which assumes that a given question (as stimulus) always has the same meaning to subjects. (Note that questionnaires can be administered either in writing or else in an interview situation.) This model excludes interactions that could be used to establish shared meaning between the subject and the interviewer. Open-ended interviews allow less constrained interaction between the interviewer and the interviewee, who is no longer considered the subject of an experiment. However, this method is still limited by the need for the participants to share basic concepts and methods, without which they will be unable to negotiate shared meanings for the questions asked. Open-ended interviews are also more vulnerable to distortion by interviewer bias. (See Suchman & Jordan, 1990, for a more detailed discussion of this topic, including some examples.)

These limitations also apply to focus groups, and to their cousins in requirements engineering, called JAD (or RAD) groups. In addition, these methods are vulnerable to political manipulations by participants, as many experienced requirements know from bitter experience.

Protocol analysis asks subjects to engage in some task and concurrently talk aloud, explaining their thought processes. Proponents claim that this kind of language can be considered a "direct verbalization of specific cognitive processes" (Ericsson & Simon, 1984, p. 16). Protocol analysis is also used to reflect on problem solving, or some other task, retrospectively (i.e., after it has been accomplished). It assumes that people can produce language that gives a trace of "autonomous cognitive activity." The problem with this assumption is that language is intrinsically social, created for a partner in conversation. (This property is called *recipient design* in conversation analysis.) When an experimenter asks a person to solve a problem and talk aloud, then that person has to imagine a partner with certain desires and try to provide what that partner wants. (Or the subject may be rebellious and try to frustrate the imagined partner.) Thus, protocols are an unnatural discourse form, and moreover, are unnatural in ways that are difficult to specify, as well as being based on an incorrect cognitivist model of human thought that ignores social context; Goguen and Linde (1993) gave a detailed analysis of a protocol demonstrating its unnaturalness on linguistic grounds.

None of these methods can elicit tacit knowledge. The principles of ethnomethodology discussed in the next subsection, such as members' concepts and members' methods, provide a powerful framework for a deeper consideration of the limitations of the traditional methods, as well as a basis for methods that do not have the same limitations.

Ethnomethodology

Traditional sociology has been greatly influenced by what it considers to be orthodox science, where scientists first formulate a theory, on the basis of which they make predictions, which they then test empirically. The aim is to achieve *objectivity*, in the sense that the scientists' desires and biases cannot affect the conclusions. Hence, there is a rigid separation between subject and object, between observer and observed. Physics has already moved rather far from this kind of objectivity,[7] and so it should not be

---

[7]Penrose (1990) gives an elegant and readable exposition that illustrates just how strange the theories of contemporary physics can be.

surprising if sociology, and the social aspects of computing, had to go even further. In particular, if objective information is replaced by situated information, then the orthodox approach of formulating and then testing hypotheses objectively, for example through statistical sampling, will not be valid because the random events observed can no longer be assumed to be statistically independent. However, statistical methods are the foundation for much of traditional sociology, for example, the design and evaluation of questionnaires. This does not mean that statistics and questionnaires are never useful, only that they are *not always valid*, and in particular, that they should not be used in situations where context plays a significant role.

Ethnomethodology began as a reaction against the objective "scientific" and normative approach of traditional sociology (Garfinkel, 1967). Unfortunately, ethnomethodology can be difficult to understand; however, Levinson (1983), Suchman (1987), and Goguen and Linde (1993) gave relatively comprehensible expositions of certain points. Ethnomethodology tries to reconcile a radical empiricism with the situatedness of social data by looking closely at how competent members of a group actually organize their interactions. One basic principle of ethnomethodology is the following *principle of accountability*:

> Members are held accountable for certain actions by their social groups; exactly those actions are the ones constructed as socially significant by those groups.

A member performing such an action is always liable to be asked for an account, that is, a justification.[8] Accountability is the basis of all social interaction, and thus of society. It means that members are held *responsible* for their behavior.

From the principle of accountability, the following *principle of orderliness* can be derived:

> Social interaction is orderly, in the sense that it can be understood by analysts.

This follows from the fact that the participants themselves understand it, because of accountability; therefore, analysts should also be able to understand it, if they can discover how members themselves make sense of their interactions.

In particular, ethnomethodology looks at the *categories* and *methods* members use to render their actions intelligible to one another; this contrasts with presupposing that the categories and methods of the analyst

---

[8]Of course, this does not imply that such accounts are always requested, or even usually requested.

are necessarily superior to those of members. The methods and categories of members are identifiable through the procedures by which members are held socially accountable by other members of their group. We may also say that the analyst is used as a measuring instrument. Through training, such an analyst gradually learns to pay attention to doubts and hints, and to follow them up with further observations and questions. Through immersion in data from some particular social group, the particular competencies are gradually acquired that enable the analyst to be a sensitive and effective instrument in that domain. In this way, subjectivity is harnessed, rather than rejected.

Sacks (1972) demonstrated that members' categories often come as part of *category systems*,[9] which are collections of category distinctions that members treat as naturally co-occurring. Sacks also gave some rules that govern the use of such systems, and showed how these provide a rich resource for interpreting ordinary conversation. Category systems in this sense are the basis for our notion of information; thus, our theory of information is founded on an ethnomethodological semiotics.

Conversation analysis grew out of ethnomethodology through work of Sacks on how speakers organize such details as timing, overlap, response, interruption, and repair in ordinary conversation (Sacks, 1992; Sacks, Schegloff, & Jefferson, 1974). Interaction analysis extends conversation analysis from audio to video data, particularly in institutional settings. See Goodwin and Heritage (1990) for an overview of conversation analysis and Kendon (1990) for a collection of essays on interaction analysis. Both these fields are strongly empirically based, in the sense that any phenomenon asserted by analysts must be "warranted" (i.e., supported) by evidence that members in some way *orient to* that phenomenon (i.e., noticeably use it to organize interaction).

Although the distinction between object and meta levels comes from logic, it can be warranted in concrete situations by observing how analysts orient to different items of information used in their work (e.g., during meetings in which they discuss data such as transcripts of interviews). These categories may not be recognized by users, but they are an important part of the apparatus of analysis.

Members concepts and methods can be formalized using abstract data types (Goguen, 1994). This motivates a reexamination of Sacks' categorization devices as *situated abstract data types*, where the relationships between the formal and informal social aspects are taken into account; Goguen showed that a great many such relationships are possible; this can be seen as an attempt for further develop and formalize Sacks' work.

It seems promising to apply methods from ethnomethodology to the sociology of science. Work that helps point the way has been done by

---

[9]Actually, Sacks (1972) called these "categorization devices."

Livingston (1987) on mathematics, and there are also ethnomethodological studies of several other fields of science (e.g., see Garfinkel, Lynch, & Livingston, 1981, on the discovery of pulsars). Such an approach could help correct the lack of explicit empirical research in much current sociology of science. Another promising direction is to apply category systems to information systems. However, Sacks only analyzed very simple examples, and a good deal more development would be needed for a large Information System project.

Ethnomethodology can also be understood as providing useful general guidelines for how to collect high quality data about social interaction, and conversation and interaction analyses can be seen as embodying these guidelines in ways that are directly applicable to many practical problems in understanding and designing technology (some further discussion and examples are given in Goguen & Linde, 1993). Also, they can be used to obtain tacit knowledge, because they bypass the unreliable explanations of users and managers, and instead examine what actually happens. However, these are far from the only way to elicit requirements and may not be the best methods for some circumstances.

Some Limitations of Ethnomethodology

For the purposes of this chapter (which are understanding and designing information systems), ethnomethodology and the methods based on it have some significant limitations, including the following:

1. Ethnomethodology requires the use of naturally occurring data, which is nonintrusively collected in a situation having significant social interaction, where members are engaged in activities that they regularly and ordinarily do.
2. Ethnomethodology requires the analyst to understand members' concepts and methods. Although it is only necessary for an analyst to understand *certain* members' concepts and methods, to a *certain* degree, to achieve a certain pragmatic goal, it can be difficult to determine what must be understood, and to what degree.
3. Ethnomethodology requires grounding observations in the concrete circumstances of their social production. However, the design of technical artifacts requires the use of abstractions and formalizations that are not so grounded. In particular, methods based on ethnomethodology cannot be applied directly to systems that have not yet been built.
4. From a practical point of view, the most important limitation of methods based on ethnomethodology is that they are labor intensive. In particular, it can take a skilled person a long time to produce a transcript

from a videotape of live interaction. Typical projects can involve hundreds of hours of work in recording, transcribing, and analyzing data.

Regarding the first point, if data is not collected in a natural social situation, then the principle of accountability will not apply, and we cannot be sure that events in the data have any natural social significance. This precludes a number of convenient "quick and dirty" ways of collecting information, such as questionnaires. Controlled experiments are also unsuitable sources of data, as are solitary operators of equipment.

For the second point, there seems to be fairly general agreement that prior to using a method based on ethnomethodology, it is necessary to do some ethnography, that is, to achieve some prior orientation to the social milieu to be studied. Thus, we might look to ethnography for guidelines, as well as to ethnomethodology, because the latter presupposes some appropriate level of understanding. Unfortunately, the ethnographic literature does not provide much help, because ethnographers have not had definite pragmatic goals; perhaps those working on the interface between technology and sociology will have to develop suitable guidelines themselves.

For the third point, note that the design of a technical artifact is typically a formal object. For example, a design may be expressed in a blueprint for a building, or a computer program to control a machine tool or even an entire automated factory. Similarly, the design of an Information System is typically expressed using formal notations; furthermore, the Information System itself can be seen as a formal object in a nontrivial way, because it is (in part) a program written in a formal programming language, running on a formally describable computer.

The fourth point has considerable practical significance, because those who want information systems are often unwilling to wait the long periods of time that ethnomethodological studies may involve; their business environment may be very competitive and fast changing, and they want an effective but not necessarily optimal system in place as quickly as possible. Therefore, it is important to develop practical criteria for determining when we have a sufficient understanding of some situation for practical purposes.

Discourse Analysis

In linguistics, the phrase *discourse analysis* refers most broadly to the study of structures larger than sentences. Both interactional and linguistic approaches have been taken to such structures. The interactional approaches arise from ethnomethodology, and consider how social order arises in conversation. The linguistic approaches arise from sociolinguistics, and consider the internal structure of certain discourse forms; this subsection concentrates on the linguistic approach.

A *discourse unit* is a structural, linguistic unit directly above the sentence. Some common examples that have been studied extensively are the oral narrative of personal experience (Labov, 1972; Linde, 1986; Polanyi, 1989), the joke (Sacks, 1974), the explanation (Goguen et al., 1983), the spatial description (Linde, 1974; Linde & Labov, 1975), and the plan (Linde & Goguen, 1978). A discourse unit has two criterial properties: defined boundaries and a describable internal structure.

The property of *definable boundaries* means that the discourse unit is *bounded*; for example, (with some interesting exceptions) we know when a speaker is or is not engaged in a narrative. Of course, there may be boundary disputes, either at the beginning, during which a speaker negotiates with hearers whether the narrative will be told, or at the end, where the speaker may negotiate the proper response to the unit with hearers (Polanyi, 1978, 1989; Sacks, 1974). However, such negotiations do not mean that the unit is not structurally bounded. Rather, they imply that its boundaries are negotiated, that is, they are social.

One important effect of establishing of the boundaries of a discourse unit concerns turntaking. Other things being equal, the sentence is the potential unit of turn exchange, for example, a second speaker may begin to speak when the first speaker has reached a permissible end of sentence. However, if the first speaker has negotiated permission to produce a recognized discourse unit, such as a joke or a story, then that speaker has the floor until the unit is completed. A second speaker may contribute questions, appreciations, side sequences, and so on, but the discourse unit and topic in progress will not change until the unit is recognized as completed.

The second important property of the discourse unit is that it has a *precise internal structure*. The description of this internal structure is necessary for understanding the interactional process of discourse construction, because the task of hearers is quite different, for example, in different sections of a narrative. Moreover, discourse structure can be described with just as much mathematical precision as sentential syntax (Goguen et al., 1983, and Linde & Goguen, 1978, present an appropriate mathematical apparatus).

The principle of accountability suggests that a member of some group telling a story should establish its relevance to the audience. Labov (1972) showed that narratives of personal experience, in which the narrator is an agent, are discourse units. For the purposes of this chapter, it suffices to consider just two aspects of narrative structure. The first, called the *narrative presupposition*, is that (unless explicitly stated otherwise) the temporal order of events is the order in which they occur in the text, in "narrative clauses." The second, called *evaluation*, refers to the justification or explanation of actions, events, and so on, through reference to shared values. It may seem surprising that values are an integral part of the internal structure of stories, rather than being confined to an optional "moral" given at the end. Evaluative material sometimes appears in explicit "evaluative clauses," but usually appears in more implicit forms (Linde, 1993), and, indeed, its syntactic expression is a significant clue to its importance in a given story.

Narratives seem particularly important for understanding information involved in system development, because much of what is communicated between parties appears as stories (e.g., about what a group does, what it hopes to accomplish with the new system, etc.). For example, a study of experienced photocopy repair personnel (Orr, 1986) shows that they often use narratives for informal training of novices in problems not covered in official manuals and training courses. These "war stories" are an important part of the work life of photocopy repair mechanics, although management may see this activity as "goofing off" rather than a legitimate part of the job.

Let us illustrate these ideas with a nursery rhyme. This is not a naturally occurring spontaneous story, let alone a narrative of personal experience, as studied by Labov (1972). However, it is often read, or repeated from memory, to children in natural social settings, and thus an analysis of its values should reveal something about our society. This analysis omits many details of argument; otherwise, it could be too tedious to read. Here is our text:

> Jack and Jill went up the hill
> to fetch a pail of water;
> Jack fell down and broke his crown,
> and Jill came tumbling after.
>
> Up Jack got, and home did trot,
> as fast as he could caper,
> Jill put him to bed and plastered his head
> with vinegar and brown paper.

(The second verse is one among several variations; see Opie & Opie, 1951, for this and other background information.) The first line is a straightforward narrative clause, recounting an action in the narrative past tense, while the second line is an evaluative clause, giving a reason for the action of the first clause. The third and fourth lines give further narrative clauses (there are two in the third line).

A very basic feature of narrative is that the order of narrative clauses is taken as the order of the events that they report, unless some trouble is taken to indicate otherwise. Thus, in the first verse, they first went up, then Jack fell down, then he broke his crown, and then Jill came tumbling

after. This basic principle is called the *narrative presupposition*. Note that
it is a convention, and *not* a necessary feature of narratives; for example,
Becker (1979) showed that in Balinese narratives, if no special care is
taken, then the events reported in a sequence of narrative clauses are
taken as occurring *simultaneously* rather than sequentially.[10]

Because ordering is significant in English narratives, it is interesting to
notice that Jack always comes before Jill. As far as the semantics is
concerned, this ordering would not matter in the first line, but because
it is part of a general pattern, we can consider it an evaluative feature of
the narrative. (Note the delicacy, and not quite watertight quality of this
argument; rigorous proofs are impossible in this area.)

I think we may conclude that water is important to this (somewhat
mythical) culture, that males are more important than females in it, and
that females may take care of males.

This need not be the end of the analysis (although further elaboration
might push the limits of patience): Further results could be obtained from
the so-called *causal presupposition*, which says that, other things being
equal, given clauses in the order A, B, we may assume that A causes B.
(For example, "You touch that, you gonna die.") As an exercise, the reader
may wish to apply this to the previous text.

Such analyses do not *prove* some assertions, or extract the *truth* from
a text; rather, they uncover a resonance of a text with some context; this
is more like literary criticism. Each such analysis is contingent, local and
open; it is best done in a group, so that the analyst is accountable to other
analysts, in which case the analysis itself becomes emergent and embodied
at that level. Any such interpretation can be considered to be some part
of the meaning of the text; of course, each interpretation will seem more
compelling to some analysts and groups than to others, and some may
seem dubious to most.

This discussion can be related to the work of Lyotard (1984) on
information in the postmodernism age. For Lyotard, *modern* societies rely
on the values in *metanarratives*, or "grand unifying stories," to legitimate
their institutions. The grand narratives of Western civilization support
the domination and exploitation of nature. On the other hand, *postmodern*
societies have many "local language games" that cannot necessarily be
unified, or even neatly classified. Lyotard believed the grand narratives of
Western civilization were being replaced by a multitude of local
narratives, that is, that we are in a postmodern[11] era. Babbage's dream of

---

[10]A computer scientist might say that the default connective for a narrative sequence in
English is sequential composition(";"), whereas in Balinese it is parallel composition (" | | ").

[11]Many other notions of postmodernism appear in the literature, some of which are very
superficial; in general, the word "postmodern" has been overworked. Lyotard's definition
appeared relatively early, and has some substantial content, using ideas from Wittgenstein's
late period.

emancipation through increased order and everlasting information (1837) seems a good example of a grand narrative that is no longer sustainable (Bowker, 1994), while Haraway's (1991) cyborg manifesto seems a good example of a contemporary local narrative.

A school of "narratology" developed in France, especially following Roland Barthes, claiming among other things that our sense of subject and object is created by our participation in narratives. In any case, it seems clear that narratives play a strong role in the production and use of information and even in the belief that there is such a "thing" as information. Such a more human orientation is characteristic of continental philosophy, in contrast to the Anglo-American analytic tradition.

Ethnomethodology and Ethics

Ethnomethodology does not assume any pre-given value systems for members. Nevertheless, values are important to ethnomethodology: The group being studied has values; analysts have values; and the ambient society has values. In each case, the values are produced, sustained, and modified by members of the relevant group, and are important to its identity and its functioning. In general, the values at each level are different, and may interact in complex ways. One might go so far as to say that groups, values, and information are "coemergent," in the sense that each produces and sustains the others; that is, groups exist because members share values and interactions with each other; values exist because they are shared and communicated by groups; and information exists because groups share values in a dynamic world. No one of these three can be considered more basic than the other two; it is creative acts of interpretation that unify social groups, values, and signs, and in that way create information. Thus, values are a necessary presupposition of ethnomethodological analysis: Members' accountability to shared values renders their concepts and methods visible to analysts. Jayyusi (1991) put it as follows:

> What emerges from both Garfinkel's and Sacks' work is the understanding that all communicative praxis presupposes, and is founded in, a "natural" ethic—an ethic, that is, which is constitutive of, and reflexively constituted by, the *natural attitude of everyday life*.

The reflexivity mentioned here is the same as the coemergence already discussed.

The situatedness of information arises from the particular relations of accountability that tie it to a particular social group and the work done in the particular context to produce that particular text and its particular interpretations. Values do not exist as abstract ideal entities, but rather emerge interactively in actual instances of accountability. It follows that *everything* that arises in social life has an inherent ethical component, and attains its *meaning* through the relations of accountability in which it participates. Thus, information has an inalienable ethical dimension.

Values are also critical at the analyst level. Analysts are accountable to other analysts for the accuracy of their analyses, and for how their questions, methods, and conclusions fit in with those of other analysts. There is also the important issue of accountability of analysts to members. Because ethnomethodological analysts try to understand members' own methods and concepts, they often communicate with members in order to test their own understanding. Members are naturally concerned to know the motivations of these strangers among them. A common issue is the confidentiality of certain information. In this respect, it is natural for analysts to offer members a power of veto over publication of data in which they are involved.

Trust between members and analysts is often essential to the success of the analysis. Even in cases where such trust is neither sought nor secured, such as Garfinkel's "breaching experiments" (Garfinkel, 1967), a sense of compassion, that is, of being able to sympathize with members, seems essential to the analysis. This is a fundamentally ethical point.

Case Studies

Case studies have been done to test the practical application of interaction analysis to requirements engineering. One project involved the analysis of videotapes of stock dealers at work, supplemented by ethnographic interviews, including feedback from the dealers on the interpretations of selected video clips. Some results from this study are described in Heath, Jirotka, Luff, and Hindmarsh, 1993. Another case study concerned requirements for an integrated database system for the fault restoration office of a major telecommunications control center; here we discovered that system development work was being greatly impeded by an ideologically motivated "internal market" that kept system developers from direct communication with users. It is estimated that several million dollars were saved as a result of these two exercises, possibly much more if the internal market is abolished.

Goguen and Linde (1978, 1981) developed a method for using discourse analysis to determine a value system for an organization (or part thereof) from a collection of stories and jokes told by members of the organization among themselves on informal occasions, such as coffee and lunch breaks. A related method determines work structure from task-oriented discourse. These methods primarily use narratives of personal experience, in which an individual relates events that were personally experienced (Labov,

1972). The first method classifies the evaluative material (in the sense discussed earlier) of the stories collected, using a formal structure called a *value system tree*, in which higher level nodes correspond to higher level values, and lower level nodes correspond to refinements, applications, or corrections of superordinate nodes. Because members of an organization who tell a story are socially accountable for doing so, the evaluative material they use to justify their telling that story reveals their shared values.

Figure 2.1 shows part of a value system tree obtained by Goguen and Linde (1978) for a small corporate recruitment (i.e., "head hunting") firm.[12] The tip nodes in this tree are *situated* in the sense that they are taken directly from actual narratives by members and may thus require more background information in order to be understood. Many interior nodes, which express superordinate values, are also situated in this sense, but others were created by the analysts, by clustering nodes into larger and larger related groups, in the general style of the KJ method (Kawakita, 1975).[13]

The edges in Fig. 2.1 express relationships of subordination; these are situated to the extent that there is evidence for them in the structure of the discourse; moreover, members could have been asked about them. The nodes at the three topmost levels are analysts' constructions, with support from the data. The phrases at the fourth level are taken from the evaluative clauses of actual stories and jokes. (Some nodes at the fourth level of Fig. 2.1 have two more levels below them that are not shown here.)

Note the contradiction between the first two nodes on the fourth level. This illustrates the fact that real value systems are not necessarily consistent. This seems to be one reason why it is difficult (or even impossible) to elicit values from members just by asking for them. Indeed, value systems, like many other aspects of social life, are tacit knowledge.

Such a structure can help system designers make appropriate trade-offs between conflicting requirements of the client and/or end user. The hierarchical structure of the tree suggests which requirements should be given precedence over others. Also, the nature of any conflicts that appear may be clarified, because the higher level values are more significant. For an even more detailed analysis, weights could be assigned to values based on their frequency in the data that support them.

---

[12]Note that this representation differs from trees on earth, which have their roots at the bottom.

[13]This method was introduced by the Japanese anthropologist Jiro Kawakita for classifying artifacts, and it is now rather widely used by Japanese businessmen and computer scientists. It provides heuristic guidelines for combining clusters, separating clusters, and so on.

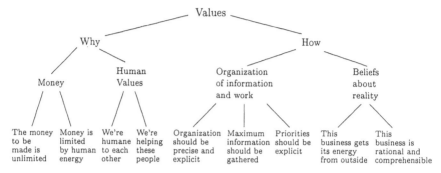

FIG. 2.1. A value system tree.

Combining Methods and Zooming

Despite the limitations of various methods, they can be useful (with the possible exception of protocol analysis). In fact, their strengths seem complementary, so that it could be useful to apply various combinations to particular problems. In particular, it is usually a good idea to start with an ethnographic study to uncover basic aspects of social order, such as basic concept systems used by members, the division into social groups, some typical patterns of work of various social groups, and so on (see Sommerville, Rodden, Sawyer, Bentley, & Twidale, 1993, for a review of ethnography in relation to requirements engineering). After this, one might use questionnaires or interviews to explore what problems members see as most important, how members place themselves in various classification schemes, and so forth. Then one might apply conversation, discourse, or interaction analyses to get a deeper understanding of selected problematic aspects.

Discourse analysis can be useful when verbal communication is important to the system being developed, as illustrated in the case study on values mentioned in the previous section. Conversation and interaction analyses can help to uncover limitations of other methods. Interaction analysis can be used to discover details of nonverbal interaction in real work environments (Kendon, 1990); but the effort required to produce video transcripts suggests that this method should be used very selectively. Ethnography should be used continually to provide context for results obtained by other methods.

To sum up, a "zooming" method of requirements elicitation is recommended, whereby the more expensive but detailed methods are only employed selectively for problems that have been determined by other methods to be especially important (Goguen, 1994). From this point of view, the various methods based on ethnomethodology can be seen as analoguous to an electron microscope: They provide an instrument that is very accurate and powerful, but is also expensive, and requires careful preparation to ensure that the right thing is examined. One should not use an electron microscope without first determining where to focus it as exactly as possible, using either an ordinary microscope or, depending on the nature of the sample, a magnifying glass, the naked eye, or a hierarchical combination of these methods. Similarly, in studying information systems, one should first use ethnography, and perhaps interviews or questionnaires. Discourse analysis can also be useful. Ethnomethodology may be necessary when interaction is important.

CONCLUSIONS

We have used ideas from ethnomethodology and semiotics to define information as an interpretation of a configuration of signs for which members of some social group are accountable. We have argued that methods based on ethnomethodology overcome many limitations of traditional methods for acquiring information on which to base design; in particular, information acquired in this way can be more accurate in complex situations of collaborative work, because it is more fully situated. However, we also noted that ethnomethodology and methods based upon it have some limitations of their own, and we argued that these can be overcome, at least in part, by combining methods; the metaphor of "zooming" helps to explain this. It is not just a complaint about the dangers of methodological dogmatism, but rather a pragmatic suggestion for combining the particular strengths of certain methods.

Ideas from the sociology of science (especially the work of Latour) and logic helped explicate the nature of dry information. Dry information often loses the property of embodiedness, and is also less emergent, contingent, and local. However, even the driest information is still situated, and in particular, is open, emergent, contingent, and even embodied at the meta level, where analysts are accountable for its formalization. Similarly, even the wettest information about social interaction is necessarily partially abstracted from its social context, in order to be presented to an audience of analysts. In particular, analysts necessarily speak (in part) in a metalanguage.

Operations of abstraction, to a varying extent, sever the resulting information from the social contexts in which it was originally situated. This is not the result of an inadequate method, but rather it is necessarily the case that operations of re-representation (such as classifying, summarizing, abstracting, theorizing, and concluding) have such an effect. The construction of immutable mobiles necessarily reduces the situatedness of data and makes it drier, and assertions by analysts necessarily fall into this area. Moreover, dryness comes not merely in different degrees, but also in a wide variety of kinds, resulting from the complex relationships of accountability between different communities, including that of analysts (e.g., see the examples in Goguen, 1994). This applies to the observations of conversation analysis just as much as anything else.

Information Systems are a particularly interesting site for research. By definition, such systems are repositories for immutable mobiles, and also provide the means for producing new immutable mobiles, for transporting them into new contexts, and for further concentrating and summarizing information. This means they can be sources of power. Consequently, the design of an Information System is a natural occasion for power struggles, and it is important that the human interests of all stakeholders be recognized and protected. A *power struggle* can be defined as a difference among two or more groups in how to interpret some signs, or alternatively, as the failure of an information system to effectively function as a boundary object.[14] Boland (1991) provided an interesting case study that illustrates the importance of power struggles in understanding organizations. The failure to take account of such factors explains why many large information systems have failed in practice.

The relation between the formal and the social aspects of information is not one of antagonism, where one must be rejected and the other accepted; rather, these two aspects of information are both essential for the very existence of information, and are also crucial to successful design. The formal context insensitive and the social context sensitive aspects of information are complementary, and can be very complex in that many different facets can arise in different social contexts, with different levels of abstraction, interconnected in complex ways, as shown by examples in Goguen (1994).

It is the nature of technical design to construct dry structures, and design necessarily occurs at a meta level, involving a group that to some degree has separated itself from users. However, a slavish adherence to narrowly prescriptive plans and categories is certainly not necessary, and users can be involved in a variety of ways. In general, abstractions (immutable mobiles) have only a practical utility, and must be interpreted concretely in order for that utility to become manifest. Therefore, effective design can never be fully separated from the community of users, and indeed, I would say that effective design necessarily involves moments of transcending the distinction between the social groups of users and analysts.

---

[14]Thus, there is no such *thing* as "power"; it is merely a reified way of talking about the social distribution of interpretations.

It seems hard to escape the conclusion that the progressive erosion of meaning in modern life arises in large part from the growing formalization of information through mass media, computers, the internet, and the general progress of science and technology.[15] The result has been not only a loss of values in human interaction, but also a devaluation of nature. If nature is seen as fundamentally determined by the laws of physical science, which are mathematical and impersonal, then trees, beaches, mountains—and by extension, buildings, cities, animals, and even people—have no inherent value. This seems to be one source of current environmental and social crises.

Recent trends is philosophy exacerbate these problems. The Anglo-American tradition of analytic philosophy, with its rigorous and even mathematical analyses, has alienated much of its audience, and earned it a reputation for irrelevance. Postmodernism, despite many valuable insights, encourages fragmentation through its attacks on the grand narratives that lend coherence to Western culture; this makes it difficult to respond to, or even conceptualize, contemporary environmental and social crises (Gare, 1995). Ethnomethodology can be seen as taking a relativistic view that would prohibit discussions like that in this and the previous paragraph.

It is my hope that recognizing the intrinsic ethical dimension of information, and more generally of social interaction, will help us find a path toward greater realization of value and meaning in social life and in nature, without rejecting science and technology.

ACKNOWLEDGMENTS

The research reported in the chapter has been supported in part by contracts with British Telecom, Fujitsu Laboratories Limited, and the Information Technology Promotion Agency, Japan, as part of the R & D of Basic Technology for Future Industries "New Models for Software Architecture" project sponsored by NEDO (New Energy and Industrial Technology Development Organization).

This chapter was largely written while the author was with the Programming Research Group of the Oxford University Computing Lab.

I thank André Stern for his interesting remarks about time and requirements, and Susan Leigh Star for several very interesting and helpful

---

[15]Very many writers have explored this theme, but in particular Heidegger (1977) was one of the first as well as one of the most profound critics of the social effects of science and technology.

conversations. Thanks to Frances Page for typing many draft versions quickly and cheerfully. Special thanks to Charlotte Linde for our long collaboration, during which I learned much of what I know about language. Parts of this chapter are drawn from Goguen (1994) and Goguen and Linde (1993). The subject is difficult, and despite all the help that many people have tried to give me, there is no doubt a great deal about which I remain ignorant.

REFERENCES

Agre, P. (1995). Institutional circuitry: Thinking about the forms and uses of information. *Information Technologies and Libraries*, December, 225–230.

Babbage, C. (1837). *The Ninth Bridgewater Treatise: A fragment*. London: C. Knight.

Barwise, J., & Perry, J. (1983). *Situations and attitudes*. Cambridge, MA: MIT Press.

Becker, A. L. (1979). Text-building, epistemology, and aesthetics in Javanese shadow theatre. In A. L. Becker & A. Yengoyan (Eds.), *The imagination of reality: Essays on Southeast Asian symbolic systems* (pp. 211–243). Norwood, NJ: Ablex.

Boland, R. (1991). In search of management accounting: Exploration of self and organization. (Tech. Rep.). Case Western University.

Bowker, G. (1994). Information mythology. In L. Bud-Fierman (Ed.), *Information acumen: The understanding and use of knowledge in modern business*. London: Routledge.

Conklin, J., & Bergman, M. (1988). gIBIS: A hypertext tool for exploratory policy discussion. *ACM Transactions on Office Information Systems*, 6, 303–331.

De Saussure, F. (1976). *Course in general linguistics* (P. Owen, Trans.). London: Fontana.

Ericsson, E. K., & Simon, H. A. (1984). *Protocol analysis: Verbal reports as data*. Cambridge, MA: MIT Press.

Gare, A. E. (1995). *Postmodernism and the environmental crisis*. London: Routledge & Kegan Paul.

Garfinkel, H. (1967). *Studies in ethnomethodology*. Englewood Cliffs, NJ: Prentice-Hall.

Garfinkel, H., Lynch, M., & Livingston, E. (1981). The work of a discovering science construed with materials from the optically discovered pulsar. *Philosophy of the Social Sciences*, 11, 131–158.

Gibbs, W. W. (1994). Software's chronic crisis. *Scientific American*, September, pp. 72–81.

Goguen, J. (1992). The dry and the wet. In E. Falkenberg, C. Rolland, & El-Sayed Nasr-El-Dein El-Sayed (Eds.), *Information systems concepts* (pp. 1–17). Amsterdam: North-Holland, Elsevier.

Goguen, J. (1994). Requirements engineering as the reconciliation of social and technical issues. In M. Jirotka & J. Goguen (Eds.), *Requirements engineering: Social and technical issues* (pp. 165–200). New York: Academic Press.

Goguen, J. (1996). Abstract of "Semiotic morphisms." In J. Albus, A. Meystel, & R. Quintero (Eds.), *Intelligent systems: A semiotic perspective*. Gaithersburg, MD: National Institute of Science and Technology.

Goguen, J. (1996, April). Formality and informality in requirements engineering. *Proceedings, International Conference on Requirements Engineering*.

Goguen, J., & Linde, C. (1978). Cost-benefit analysis of a proposed computer system (Tech. Rep.). Structural Semantics.

Goguen, J., & Linde, C. (1981). Structural semantic analysis of the information structure of organizations (Tech. Rep.). Structural Semantics.

Goguen, J., & Linde, C. (1993). Techniques for requirements elicitation. In S. Fickas & A. Finkelstein (Eds.), *Requirements engineering '93* (pp. 152–164). New York: IEEE.

Goguen, J., & Luqi (1995). Formal methods and social context in software development. In P. Mosses, M. Nielsen, & M. Schwartzbach (Eds.), *Proceedings of the Sixth International Joint Conference on Theory and Practice of Software Development (TAPSOFT 95)* (pp. 62–81). New York: Springer.

Goguen, J., Thatcher, J., & Wagner, E. (1978). An initial algebra approach to the specification, correctness and implementation of abstract data types. In R. Yeh (Ed.), *Current trends in programming methodology* (Vol. 4, pp. 80–149). Englewood Cliffs, NJ: Prentice-Hall.

Goguen, J., Weiner, J., & Linde, C. (1983). Reasoning and natural explanation. *International Journal of Man–Machine Studies, 19*, 521–559.

Goodwin, C., & Heritage, J. (1990). Conversation analysis. *Annual Review of Anthropology, 19*, 283–307.

Haraway, D. (1991). A cyborg manifesto: Science, technology, and socialist-feminism in the late twentieth century. In *Simians, cyborgs, and women: The reinvention of nature.* London: Free Association.

Heath, C., Jirotka, M., Luff, P., & Hindmarsh, J. (1993). Unpacking collaboration: The interactional organization of trading in a city dealing room. In *European Conference on computer-supported cooperative work '93.* IEEE.

Heidegger, M. (1977). *The question concerning technology and other essays.* (W. Lovitt, Trans.). New York: Harper & Row.

Jayyusi, L. (1991). Values and moral judgement: Communicative praxis as a moral order. In G. Button (Ed.), *Ethnomethodology and the human sciences* (pp. 227–251). Cambridge, England: Cambridge University Press.

Kawakita, J. (1975). *KJ method: A scientific approach to problem solving.* Tokyo: Kawakita Research Institute.

Kendon, A. (1990). *Conducting interaction: Patterns of behavior in focused encounters.* Cambridge, England: Cambridge University Press.

Labov, W. (1972). The transformation of experience in narrative syntax. In *Language in the inner city* (pp. 354–396). Philadelphia: University of Pennsylvania.

Latour, B. (1987). *Science in action.* Manchester, England: Open University.

Lévi-Strauss, C. (1986). *The raw and the cooked* (J. and D. Weightman, Trans.). New York: Penguin.

Levinson, S. (1983). *Pragmatics.* Cambridge, England: Cambridge University Press.

Linde, C. (1974). *The linguistic encoding of spatial information.* Unpublished doctoral thesis, Columbia University, Department of Linguistics.

Linde, C. (1986). Private stories in public discourse. *Poetics, 15*, 183–202.

Linde, C. (1993). *Life stories: The creation of coherence.* New York: Oxford University Press.

Linde, C., & Goguen, J. (1978). Structure of planning discourse. *Journal of Social and Biological Structures, 1*, 219–251.

Linde, C., & Labov, W. (1975). Spatial networks as a site for the study of language and thought. *Language, 51*(4), 924–939.

Livingston, E. (1987). *The ethnomethodology of mathematics.* London: Routledge & Kegan Paul.

Lyotard, J.-F. (1984). *The postmodern condition: A report on knowledge: Vol. 1. Theory and history of literature.* Manchester, England: Manchester University Press.

Opie, I., & Opie, P. (1951). *The Oxford dictionary of nursery rhymes.* New York: Oxford University Press.

Orr, J. (1986). Narratives at work: Story telling as cooperative diagnostic activity. In *Proceedings, Conference on Computer-Supported Cooperative Work (SIGCHI).* New York: Association for Computing Machinery.

Penrose, R. (1989). *The emperor's new mind.* New York: Oxford University Press.

Pinheiro, F., & Goguen, J. (1996). An object-oriented tool for tracing requirements. *IEEE Software*, 52–64.

Polanyi, L. (1978). So what's the point? *Semiotica*, 25(3–4), 208–224.

Polanyi, L. (1989). *Telling the American story*. Cambridge, MA: MIT Press.

Polanyi, M. (1967). *The tacit dimension*. London: Routledge & Kegan Paul.

Robinson, M., & Bannon, L. (1991). Questioning representations. In M. Robinson, L. Bannon, & K. Schmidt (Eds.), *Proceedings, Second European Conference on Computer-Supported Cooperative Work*. Dordrecht, The Netherlands: Kluwer.

Sacks, H. (1972). On the analyzability of stories by children. In J. Gumpertz & D. Hymes (Eds.), *Directions in sociolinguistics* (pp. 325–345). New York: Holt, Rinehart & Winston.

Sacks, H. (1974). An analysis of the course of a joke's telling in conversation. In R. Baumann & J. Scherzer (Eds.), *Explorations in the ethnography of speaking* (pp. 337–353). Cambridge, England: Cambridge University Press.

Sacks, H. (1992). *Lectures on conversation* (G. Jefferson, Ed.). Oxford: Basil Blackwell.

Sacks, H., Schegloff, E., & Jefferson, G. (1974). A simplest systematics of the organization of turn-taking in conversation. *Language*, 504, 696–735.

Schiller, D. (1994). From culture to information and back again: Commoditization as a route to knowledge. *Critical Studies in Mass Communication, 11*, 92–115.

Shannon, C., & Weaver, W. (1964). *The mathematical theory of communication*. Urbana, IL: University of Illinois.

Sommerville, I., Rodden, T., Sawyer, P., Bentley, R., & Twidale, M. (1993). Integrating ethnography into the requirements engineering process. In S. Fickas & A. Finkelstein (Eds.), *Requirements engineering '93* (pp. 165–173). New York: IEEE.

Star, S. L. (1988). The structure of ill-structured solutions: Heterogeneous problem-solving, boundary objects and distributed artificial intelligence. In M. Huhns & L. Gasser (Eds.), *Distributed artificial intelligence* (Vol. 3, pp. 37–54). San Mateo, CA: Kauffmann.

Suchman, L. (1987). *Plans and situated actions: The problem of human–machine communication*. New York: Cambridge University Press.

Suchman, L., & Jordan, B. (1990). Interactional troubles in face-to-face survey interviews. *Journal of the American Statistical Association, 85*(409), 232–241.

3

Reconfiguring the Social Scientist: Shifting From Telling Designers What to Do to Getting More Involved

Yvonne Rogers
University of Sussex, England

The development of computer systems may be viewed as a struggle to configure the user. For example, Woolgar (1993) described an ethnographic study of a computer company, where the architects of a new computer system (i.e., the hardware and product engineers, project managers, salespersons, technical support, and others) spent considerable time discussing and arguing over who the new user of the system would be and what kinds of functionality would be appropriate for them. Moreover, Woolgar pointed out that it was the decisions made about the hypothetical user that subsequently became embodied in the new system. In this sense, the user has a *configured* relationship with the system, whereby only certain types of interaction are possible.

This chapter aims to extend the notion of the struggle to configure the user by presenting a critique of the struggle by the social scientist to contribute to the process of system design and use. In contrast to the various company architects, who are directly involved in developing computer systems that configure the user, social scientists (and others[1]) have largely channeled their efforts through more indirect means. In particular, a vast body of prescriptive knowledge has been constructed that is intended to equip designers more appropriately so they can better configure the user than through their existing repertoire of means. The main kinds of knowledge that have been offered include a melee of

---

[1]The term *social scientist* is used loosely here, and refers to academic researchers, ranging from cognitive psychologists to ethnomethodologists, who are involved in applying theories and methods, from their respective fields, to system design.

evaluation and design methods, user models, conceptual frameworks, design toolkits, design principles, and guidelines. The source of such knowledge has largely been drawn from the theoretical and methodological bases of the contributing disciplines, including cognitive psychology, management science, and sociology.

Implicit in the translation of such academic knowledge is an altruistic conviction that current system development is inadequate and can be helped out through input from the social sciences. An underlying assumption is that system designers have all too often overlooked the needs and capabilities of "the user"; the social scientist, on the other hand, having a background in psychology or sociology, is in a much better position of understanding and articulating the user's concerns.

Endemic to the social scientist's approach of indirectly seeking to improve the design of technical systems by focusing more on the user is a further assumption that this can be achieved through informing designers of what needs to be done. For example, in any guidebook on interface design, designers are told at the onset that they must develop systems that are easy to learn and use. Whereas the intentions of those advocating what, when, and how they should design is often fueled by a genuine faith in their ability to provide insightful knowledge for others, it may seem rather presumptuous to the others. Such an authoritative position is particularly problematic in situations in which those in the targeted group have developed their own craft knowledge, skills, and domain expertise to inform their work practice. For example, programmers, graphic designers, and software engineers have all evolved their own set of methods, tools, and skills. Why should they, therefore, take up alternative methods and tools that another set of researchers have developed for them, which may not, in themselves, map onto the problems of the specific domain being designed for? Besides undermining their own expertise and practice, there is often a lack of appreciation of what their work entails; for example, the many constraints and complexities they have to juggle and manage in their day-to-day work activities. Alternatively, a rather stereotyped view of software designers has percolated; namely, they are too narrow and technically minded and hence need to be educated about social or psychological concerns.

The prescriptive approach to bridging the gap between academic research and "better" system design is clearly problematic. The next section explores why this is so in the context of developments in the sociotechnical movement, human–computer interaction (HCI) and more recently computer-supported cooperative work (CSCW). Following this, an alternative approach is proposed that promotes more proactive involvement of the social scientist in the processes of design, deployment, and use of technical systems. One such role is as an intermediary; negotiating, providing feedback, and coordinating between the different parties involved (Rogers, 1994). The emphasis here is more on getting involved rather than prescribing, by helping the users and designers of new technology *reconfigure* their working practices.

THE SOCIOTECHNICAL MOVEMENT

The sociotechnical movement came about largely through a concern by social scientists with the effects that automation was having on the well being of the work force. Most notable was the mechanization of the U.K. coal mining industry. Trist and Bamforth (1951) showed that the new technology installed for cutting and removing coal did not lead to the expected increased productivity gains. Instead, it brought many social problems, such as absenteeism and stress-related illnesses, among the workers. A main problem identified was that the resultant organizational changes considerably upset the existing practices. Prior to mechanization, the miners had worked in small independent units (typically pairs) deciding for themselves whom they worked with and setting their own goals and pace of working. Postmechanization replaced these working practices with the longwall method, whereby the small groups were reorganized into much larger groups, resulting in the miners' having less autonomy to organize their work. Furthermore, the tasks were fractionated (i.e., broken down into simplified and segregated tasks), making it much more difficult for the miners to maintain good working relationships.

Based on the findings of this and other studies, in which automation was introduced into the workplace, the sociotechnical movement proposed that changes in both technical and social systems were needed. Focusing only on the technical system, as happened in the coal mining industry, would lead to suboptimization of the whole system. Accordingly, the goal of the sociotechnical approach was to obtain the right balance between the social and technical aspects of the total system. To achieve this harmony, various sets of principles, tools, and techniques were proposed. These included a set of design principles (Cherns, 1976) and a nine-step program for determining the organizational requirements (Mumford, 1987). Examples of the former include "the process of design must be compatible with its objectives," "people should not be given fractionated tasks," and "variances must be controlled as close to their point of origin as possible." Examples of the latter include assessing whether the "workers believe that their roles meet (their) psychological needs" and "all the hypotheses and proposals considered during the process of analysis must be gathered together, considered, and turned into an action program."

Although Mumford (1993) claimed to have had positive effects in changing various organizations through using her particular program (known as ETHICS), the sociotechnical approach—as it stands—has proved to be difficult for others to put into practice. In particular, Blacker and Brown (1986) discussed the problems of attempting to operationalize such general principles, as those already illustrated, in any applicable way. Even though it may be relatively easy for workers to identify their putative psychological needs (e.g., the need to talk with each other), the difficult problem is turning this knowledge into a course of action. Thus, one of the main weaknesses of the sociotechnical approach is the paucity of advice it provides on how to turn requirements into design specification.

Mumford (1993) attempted to bridge this gap by providing more specific recommendations for job and organizational design. Examples include "each job should not be so routine as to cause boredom nor so demanding as to cause stress." However, whereas the content of such commonsensical guidelines may have escaped the attention of some system designers, they are still not particularly helpful in specifying how to design actual jobs or, indeed, how to prevent boredom and stress in a particular work context.

Furthermore, the sociotechnical movement has never really given much advice on how to design new technology. This is somewhat surprising given that the main thrust of the movement was to optimize both the technical and social systems. Instead, the focus has been, ironically, on privileging the social; taking the technology as a given from which to reorganize work around (Clegg & Symon, 1989). For example, an extensive review by Pasmore, Francis, Haldman, and Shani (1982) found that the most typical solution initiated in over 100 sociotechnical studies was the introduction of autonomous working groups. Only 16% of the studies claimed to have accomplished any technological changes.

One of the main problems with the sociotechnical movement, therefore, is its limited characterization of the process of organizational change as, primarily, a set of generalized job design prescriptions. Besides those who conceived of the prescriptions, others have found them very difficult to use and, in particular, to know how to translate them into concrete specifications that optimize both the social and the technical.

THE RISE AND FALL OF HCI PRESCRIPTION

A major concern of researchers who moved into the field of HCI in the early 1980s was that most computer systems being designed were difficult to learn, difficult to use, and did not enable the users to carry out their tasks in the way they wanted. Such was the extent of "bad" interface design, that the formation of what amounted to the user's charter emerged, in which *user-centered design* became the central philosophy (Norman & Draper, 1986). Aptly described as the rhetoric of compassion (Cooper, 1991), the user-centered approach came up with a range of prescriptive goals for designers, some of which have now become classic slogans (e.g., "know your user!").

The first wave of HCI researchers, mainly cognitive psychologists, attempted to help designers achieve the objectives of user-centered design, by translating their theoretically based knowledge of human capabilities and performance into a bricolage of design support tools. The development of user models, interface design guidelines, design principles, and analytic and empirical methods proliferated. Some researchers aspired to rigorous engineering standards and benchmark tests (e.g., usability engineering; Tyldesley, 1988), whereas others devised more user-friendly techniques that could be performed rapidly (e.g., cognitive jogthrough; Rowley & Rhoades, 1992) with minimum costs and minimal training (e.g., cooperative evaluation; Monk, Wright, Haber, & Davenport, 1993).

Task Analysis

The most pervasive technique to evolve from the translation of psychological knowledge was task analysis. An underlying assumption was that knowing how users cognitively perform their tasks was essential to good system design and so a suitable means of gathering and representing this knowledge was needed. The basic approach was to describe the way users carry out their tasks by breaking them down into smaller and smaller components. Having reduced human–computer interactions into simple unit or atomic tasks, it was assumed that designers would then be able to analyze, predict, and explain the performance of users with different interface and system designs (Brooks, 1991). To distinguish these analyses from the less theoretical approaches that had been established in human factors research, and to show they were based on a cognitive analysis of the user, the methods were typically described as *cognitive task analyses*, each adopting their own reductionist acronym (e.g., CLG, GOMS, CCT, ETIT, TAG, ETAG, DTAG, TAKD; see Diaper, 1989, for an overview).

Although there have been claims for the success of such cognitive task analytic methods in informing design, they have, like Mumford's ETHICS, tended to be for studies carried out by those who have been involved in the development of the methods or trained in the same school (e.g., Gray, John, & Atwood, 1992). In contrast, there have been few, if any, reported studies in which designers or software engineers have taken on board the task analytic methods provided by their HCI colleagues and found them to be truly useful. Besides being intimidating, difficult to learn, and very time-consuming to put into practice, they lack scalability to real-world problems (e.g., see Bellotti, 1988). Above all, they have never really helped the designer design interfaces. Landauer (1991) argued that "the amount of insight into process offered by the keystroke model could be easily exceeded in any real design problem by the empirical evidence of a crude prototype test with a handful of users."

Implications: Design Principles, Rules, and Guidelines

Another approach to helping designers develop more user-centered systems was to transform established knowledge from cognitive psychology, in the form of theories, models, and laws, into "implications" for design. A rationale was to make such knowledge more accessible and usable by designers, by re-presenting it as explicit prescriptions that could be used as a set of criteria from which to evaluate design decisions. Three main forms of implications were developed: principles, rules, and guidelines. The main difference between them is their degree of generalization; the former being the most general and the latter being the most specific. An example of the former is "design for consistency" and an example of the latter is "always place the exit button in the bottom right-hand corner of the screen."

There are two related problems with this re-representation of knowledge: first, finding ways of generating design principles, rules, or guidelines from psychological theory and second, knowing whether and how they can be interpreted in a way that can inform system design. Most attempts have sought to translate empirical findings derived from a theoretically driven context. One of the main problems of taking this approach is that the knowledge base is largely inappropriate. For example, there does not appear to be much in common between the questions addressed by psychologists on how memory is structured and the questions that need to be answered in relation to user interface design. Moreover, many basic theories are too low level, unable to be specified beyond the laboratory settings in which they were determined (Barnard, 1991).

In spite of this dilemma, several researchers have managed to develop extensive sets of interface design guidelines (e.g., Gardiner & Christie, 1987; Smith & Mosier, 1986). Typically, included alongside a guideline, is a brief discussion referring to the psychological theory from which it was derived. An example is the implications of findings from long-term and working memory for interface design. The various limitations and characteristics of human memory are discussed in conjunction with the implications, for example: "As working memory is the bottleneck through which all information has to pass, . . . it implies that complex computer messages may be digested only if they relate to prior knowledge" (Waern, 1989, p. 43).

One of the major problems with this approach is that the meaning of a piece of empirical research can get distorted in the process of translating it into design guidance. A classic example is the misrepresentation of the well-known psychological finding that the capacity of short-term memory (STM) is limited to 7 ± 2 items (Miller, 1956). In some sets of guidelines this has been translated into a design principle prescribing the maximum number of items that should be displayed at any one time. For example, in a set of recommendations for using color displays, Durrett and Trezona (1982, p. 83) suggested: "The average user should not be expected to remember (the meaning of) more than 5 to 7 colours. This is the 'magic number' usually associated with STM. . . . Novel displays should have no more than 4 colours since this is well below the average limit of STM."

Although it is true that overuse of colors at the interface is undesirable, the reason for this is not because individuals can remember the meaning of only a few colors at any time (this of course will depend on the nature of the information being represented by the colors), but because having a multitude of colors on any screen causes problems of distraction and confusion. Individuals may well recognize 250 different animal names (or remember the meaning of 250 different animal names), but the extent to which they can recall a set of unfamiliar animal names that are briefly presented is limited to roughly 7 ± 2 of those (although this can vary depending on various factors such as individual differences, context, and content). The guideline, therefore, is misleading and has led some system designers to think in terms of categorizing and displaying items on the screen in terms of no more than 7, irrespective of the context of use.

Empirical studies of the use of sets of guidelines have also shown them to be difficult to follow. The main problems encountered have to do with interpretation (de Souza & Bevan, 1990; Tetzlaff & Schwartz, 1991). Mosier and Smith (1986) also reported how designers found it difficult to translate "generally worded guidelines into specific design rules" (p. 39). Löwgren and Laurén (1993) also found that in a study of designers who were required to develop a prototype user interface, half did not use the guidelines with which they had been provided. Simply stated, "you never have time to do it under normal circumstances, so why do it now?"

Current Developments in HCI

The previous discussion has shown how both the cognitive task analytic and implications approaches within HCI, for prescribing better system design, have suffered from trying to translate one discipline's knowledge into practical tools for another. Such difficulties, however, have not gone unnoticed within the HCI community. For example, Long and Dowell (1996) commented on how such "one stream" attempts to pull pure science into an applied one, have shown little evidence of significantly contributing to the design of more effective technological systems. Bannon (1991) and Landauer (1987, 1991) also published influential critiques of these kinds of cognitive approach to interface design.

More recently, several HCI researchers have begun rethinking how to best inform system design using alternative theoretical perspectives (see Rogers, Bannon, & Button, 1993). These include adapting concepts from Activity Theory (Bødker, 1991; Nardi, 1996) and using the framework of Distributed Cognition (Flor & Hutchins, 1992; Halverson, 1992; Hutchins, 1995; Hutchins & Klausen, 1992; Rogers, 1993a) to analyze *computer-mediated activities*. Long and Dowell (1996) also argued for a more design-oriented approach to HCI, which is based on more domain-specific theories. They proposed that a new discipline of cognitive engineering needs to evolve that is separate from that of cognitive psychology, that has its own theories that specifically address the concerns of "users interacting with computers to perform work effectively."

Other researchers within HCI have also sought to develop alternative methods that explicitly support the design process more. These include:

1. *Design rationale.* This aims to document and make explicit the implicit aspects of the design process. The idea is that through explicating implicit knowledge more design alternatives can be explored while also providing a set of reusable designs to be readily available (e.g., see Carroll, 1995; MacLean, Young, & Moran, 1989).
2. *Participatory design.* Designers and users both play an active role in redesigning technology and its use in the workplace (e.g., see Greenbaum & Kyng, 1991; Schuler & Namioka, 1993).

It is too early to say whether or not the new methods will prove to be more effective, useful, and usable by designers, than the user-centered ones derived from cognitive theory. It is interesting to note how the rhetoric of compassion has shifted its focus from being about *empowering* the (single) user, to *supporting* groups of users (or actors) through a "turn to design" (Bowers & Pycock, 1994) and a "turn to the social" (Button, 1993). In so doing, a new set of social and organizational phenomena are being brought to the attention of designers. "Interaction," "the organization of work," "context," and the like are now being offered to designers as the important social science concepts that need to inform design (just as the likes of "mental models," "user modeling," and "information processing" were by psychologists in the 1980s).

DESCRIBING AND INFORMING THE DESIGN OF COMPUTER-SUPPORTED COOPERATIVE WORK (CSCW)

A new research area was established, calling itself Computer-Supported Cooperative Work (CSCW), which set itself apart from HCI and other fields concerned with computer design (e.g., management information systems). Instead of just focusing on the needs of one user sitting at one terminal (as has been the traditional framework within HCI), system designers and social scientists alike became concerned with how to support groups of people in their work settings through and with computers. Advances in enabling technologies, in particular distributed computing and networking, made system developers aware of new opportunities for developing groupware and other technological systems that could support groups working and communicating together. Social scientists, especially sociologists and social psychologists, saw their potential for making a contribution to the new field, by providing accounts of the nature of cooperative work and the way technology is used in work settings.

It is interesting to note that the same dilemma facing psychologists, who moved into the HCI field with the objective of applying their knowledge, is now confronting sociologists and other social scientists in the field of CSCW, namely, how to inform the design of technical systems that can more effectively support groups working together. The problem is further exacerbated, however, by virtue of the fact that designing distributed systems for multiple interacting users is much more complex than designing interfaces for single users (Grudin, 1994). Besides having to translate the social needs of individual users as system requirements, there is also the problem of how to re-represent social and organizational knowledge about the interactions between groups of people and their use of technical systems.

In the early days of CSCW, several social scientists followed the same user modeling approach, as the applied psychologists had done in HCI, but extending the modeling activity to group processes. Whereas individual user models were intended to form the basis of individual interfaces, group models were built for systems that would support group activities (i.e., groupware). However, as pointed out by Bannon (1993), many of the early models of group communication and group coordination had little evidence of any practical relevance to the design task at hand. Just as user models had been abstracted in HCI with little regard of the context of use for the systems they were intended to configure, so too were group user models beginning to appear that were unrealistic and divorced from any context of use. For example, many of the first generation of collaborative drawing and writing tools were based on implicit assumptions about the coordinating mechanisms needed, without taking into account the respective user's awareness and informational needs in a given context (see Dourish & Bellotti, 1992, for a review).

Other social scientists, notably ethnomethodologists,[2] took a very different approach and sought to understand existing work practices by carrying out a number of illuminating ethnographic studies of the organization of work and the interactions and actions that are accomplished in different work settings. For example, ethnographic studies of control centers in the London Underground (Heath & Luff, 1991), American airports (C. Goodwin & M. J. Goodwin, 1996; Suchman & Trigg, 1991), and air traffic control (Bentley et al., 1992) have revealed how informal working practices, like inadvertent overhearing and flexible division of labor, are instrumental to the coordination of work and the co-management of unexpected events. Ethnomethodologists have also turned to the design process itself as a social phenomenon in need of ethnographic study. For example, Anderson et al. (1993) focused on the problem of organizational priorities that designers have to contend with when making design decisions, noting how often such organizational concerns tend to override more technical concerns.

Building a body of knowledge about the use of technologies in work settings, where clearly there is a need for a better understanding, is considered in itself a significant contribution to the field of CSCW (see Plowman, Ramage, & Rogers, 1995). Bentley et al. (1992) suggested that the "information provided by ethnography is essentially background information which has provided a deeper understanding of the application domain," whereas Sommerville, Rodden, Sawyer, Bentley, and Twidale (1993) stressed that "ethnographic studies generate nuggets of useful information at unpredictable intervals." Others, too, have emphasized the valuable insight gained from such studies (e.g., Bowers & Pycock, 1994; Cooper, Hine, Low, & Woolgar, 1993; Rogers & Ellis, 1994).

The reported accounts provided from these studies may also play an indirect role in shaping system design. In particular, they can provide researchers and designers with a means of conceptualizing and framing

---

[2]Ethnomethodologists are referred to here as a group of sociologists who reject many of the fundamental tenets of traditional sociology, especially the theorizing and structures of the discipline, and who instead insist on a rigorously descriptive program, through doing ethnographic studies, that accounts for members' (sic) working practices (Button & Dourish, 1996; Shapiro, 1994). Researchers who do field studies and call themselves ethnographers, on the otherhand, can come from a variety of social science backgrounds, including anthropology and cognitive science. They do not adhere to the same agenda as ethnomethodologists (although sometimes the social phenomena they observe, interpret, and describe can overlap).

the concerns, issues, and key questions of CSCW. One example of such a work is by Suchman (1987), who provided both a critique of cognitive approaches to system design and an ethnomethodologically informed study of pairs of people using a photocopier machine. Although it is difficult to demonstrate explicitly how this book and her other writings have influenced the design of actual systems, it seems certain that some designers have become enlightened after reading them, and in so doing, much more attuned to the significance of "everyday working practices" through being exposed to her work (Button & Dourish, 1996; Grudin, personal communication).

On the other hand, many designers and software engineers do not have the background, time, or proclivity to digest the typically rich, poetic, and somewhat rambling accounts delivered by ethnomethodologists. Ethnomethodologists are only too aware of this, having encountered software engineers and system designers who find their descriptions of sociality alien and difficult to comprehend (Hughes, Randall, & Shapiro, 1992). At the same time, there is considerable pressure from the CSCW community, at large, for ethnomethodologists to demonstrate more directly how their ethnographic studies can inform design. This creates a dilemma for ethnomethodologists (Grudin & Grinter, 1995), whose research involves analyzing practice rather than "inventing the future" (Button & Dourish, 1996). Moreover, the conventional route of generalizing and theorizing adopted in the social sciences for applying research findings to design is counter to the atheoretical stance taken by ethnomethodologists, which instead tries to remain faithful to the descriptions of members' accomplishments in their work practices. Hence, unlike cognitive psychologists and other social scientists, who have been able to offer designers all sorts of prescriptive advice and design support tools (leaving aside the usefulness of them at the moment), ethnomethodologists have had a real struggle finding ways of translating their accounts that can be accessible to designers.

Some *applied* ethnomethodologists have tried to circumvent the "purist" requirement of rigorously adhering to the data in their accounts by resorting to a form of "covert theorizing" (Shapiro, 1994). This usually takes the form of adding a short implications for design section at the end of a publication that is often in sharp contrast to the discursive style of the account preceding it. Whereas the implications approach is common practice for other social scientists, when discussing their findings in relation to system design, it seems somewhat ill-suited for ethnomethodological accounts. For example, Anderson, Button, and Sharrock (1993) outlined four "bullet point" implications, from their study of an organization's practice, which seem so commonsensical that it leaves the reader wondering why such a detailed study needed to be carried out in the first place. Arguably, anyone could have come up with such advice. An example of their bullets is that designers need support tools that take up a minimal amount of their time and such tools should be adaptive to the exigencies of changing priorities.[3] Most designers know the former only too well and desire the latter only too much.[4]

A problem with this kind of summarizing, therefore, is that it both belittles the ethnomethodologists' rich descriptive accounts while appearing very tokenistic to designers and the rest of the CSCW community. Another approach to getting round the ethnomethodologist's dilemma has been to follow in the footsteps of applied psychologists by offering designers detailed prescriptive advice with respect to the design of a specific system. For example, Heath and Luff (1991) suggested various detailed recommendations for screen design on the basis of their ethnographic study of how an interface was used. Following the prescriptive route, however, makes them prone to the same set of problems applied psychologists encountered when trying to construct guidelines for interface design (see previous section). Moreover, replacing cognitively oriented sets of design guidelines with sociologically oriented ones may prove to be even more problematic, given that there appears to be little relevance between the descriptive language and sociologically generated analytic categories constructed in ethnographic studies and the practical problems of actually designing computer systems (Button, 1993). Hence, there may be even more susceptibility for misinterpretation of meaning. Furthermore, although the conceptual frameworks and analytic tools used in cognitive psychology and cognitive science have something in common with those used by software engineers and system developers (e.g., formal and semiformal notations for describing system requirements and user–system behavior) the terms used in "ethno-talk" and "techno-talk" would appear to be very different. Button and Dourish (1996), however, argued otherwise; they suggested that much of ethnomethodology is in fact concerned with explicating "generally operative social processes," which can, if operationalized appropriately, provide abstractions for design.[5] How such abstractions can be operationalized (or, indeed, have been by the authors) in system design, however, is not made clear.

Another approach to overcoming the ethnomethodologist's dilemma has been to move more toward a designers' perspective and consider alternative solutions for the redesign of a specific system. For example, Heath, Jirotka, Luff, and Hindmarsh (1993) speculated how to preserve

---

[3]Interestingly, Bellotti (1988) raised the same issue 5 years earlier, with respect to the nonuse of HCI methods for single-user systems.

[4]My apologies to Wes Sharrock for using this study again to make the point.

[5]The example they used to illustrate what they mean by this expression is turn-taking in conversations.

existing work practices in dealing rooms by envisioning how novel technological input devices could be used. Hughes et al. (1992) also constructed interface metaphors as a vehicle for exploring the implications
of their fieldwork for the redesign of a flight strip for air traffic control.
Taking it even one step further, some researchers have proposed new
agendas for integrating ethnographic methods with system design. These
range from a prerequisite that informal ethnographic records must be
written in a way that they can be translated into more formal system
requirements (Sommerville et al., 1993) to practical how-to-do-it guides
intended for designers (or in conjunction with ethnographers) to carry
out field studies (e.g., Blomberg, Giacomi, Mosher, & Swenton-Wall, 1993).

THE WAY FORWARD: PROACTIVE RESEARCH

The value of "packaged prescriptive" advice provided by social scientists—be they cognitive psychologists, ethnomethodologists, or otherwise—for the purpose of improving system design through applying their
theories and methodologies has been questioned. It is argued that approaches putting the onus on designers to translate their advice will
remain largely unused and, hence, have little impact.

It is time for a change. Rather than always take a backseat role, researchers need to become more proactive in their involvement with the
people and objects of their study. This means engaging more in an ongoing
dialogue with the various groups of people working or designing together
(i.e., the users, the managers, and the designers). Researchers should stop
shying away from being involved. On the contrary, they should be seeking
ways of taking a more active role in the design and implementation
process, even becoming "change agents" (cf. Blomberg et al., 1993) where
appropriate. In so doing, ideas can be fed back, discussed, and negotiated
as part of the ongoing practice of research (Cooper et al., 1993). Through
adopting a more reflexive orientation to design the articulation of system
requirements also can be improved (Bowers & Pycock, 1994). It could
also act as a learning experience, enabling researchers and designers to
develop an understanding of what, when, and why methods work in
practice. In turn, this could lead to some truly useful generalizations.

Emergent Involvement in the Implementation
and Use of Technology

It is encouraging to see that a number of researchers are becoming more
involved in the design and implementation processes. One trend has been
to explore and explicate the design requirements and development of

computer products with designers through the use of various prototypes and scenarios (cf. Blomberg et al., this volume; Bowers & Pycock, 1994; Carroll, 1995). Another approach has been to play more of a role in facilitating the implementation of new computer systems in organizations in conjunction with coadapting their work practices.

One experience while carrying out some research at a travel company, illustrates how the latter can be achieved (Rogers, 1993b, 1994). A study was begun under the pretext of trying to understand the problems surrounding the introduction of a new distributed computer system into an established workplace, which provided an opportunity to play an active role in implementing change. Specifically, the potential was there to help the company overcome some of the problems that had arisen through the introduction of the new system.

The company had decided to change from its existing multi-user booking and ticketing system to another one for various reasons, including the benefits of more functionality, a better maintenance package, and more security. None of the reasons, however, were concerned with the usability of the system. It was not surprising, therefore, that when the new system was first introduced in the company, there was widespread discontent among the consultants on the shopfloor. Their main complaint was that the system was cumbersome and unwieldy to use in contrast with the existing system. Moreover, they felt the new system was far more constraining, preventing them from carrying out their work in the flexible manner they had become accustomed to with the old system. On discovering these usability problems, the directors assumed they were simply teething problems that would dissipate once the consultants had become more familiar with the system.

Following discussions with the various consultants using the new system and listening to their conversations, a very different picture emerged from the shopfloor. In particular, their dislike of the system continued to grow. Several consultants complained bitterly that the new system was seriously disrupting their ability to carry out their work.

Gradually, management became more aware that all was not well. Informal feedback from myself and the consultants made them change their minds about attributing the discontent to teething problems and, alternatively, decide to do something. Initially, they felt that priority should be given to getting the software improved. Accordingly, they agreed on an arrangement with the system suppliers, whereby the suppliers would develop enhancements to the software that the travel company felt would substantially improve the usability of the system. Any agreed changes, however, would have to be negotiated with regard to their cost. It was important for the travel company, therefore, to be able to assess the additional costs (determined by the amount of new lines of code required to be written to make the changes) in terms of perceived benefits. To facilitate this process of negotiating required initially collecting a list of all the problems the consultants were experiencing. This required that someone go round to the various departments, collate the information, classify it, and then write it up as a list of requirements in terms that were understandable to the suppliers.

But no one wanted to do this task because it was considered to be additional work load. Originally, one of the directors was going to do it but became too busy; so one of the consultants was given the responsibility. The consultant, likewise, was unable to carry out the task having become too busy coping with the continuous stream of technical problems from the new system. An opportunity arose to help them overcome this impasse.

During weekly visits to the company, the director would see me, which would remind him of the need to deal with the new system "problem" and consequently talk to the consultant in my presence, asking whether the list had been made. The consultant would explain that he never had enough time now and that when he had asked the other consultants they had not volunteered the information. However, as the weeks of procrastination progressed, the director became increasingly concerned. He specifically requested that I join him and the consultant to visit all the different departments and collect the gripes there and then. We collected written lists from the various departments and got the other consultants to explain in more detail what they meant by what they had written down. There was even a joke at the end of this process, that the company could usefully employ me as a secretary to type up the lists.

It was possible to accomplish the task because there were three individuals working together. Hence, in one sense, I acted as a mediator, helping to instigate participation from the consultants to provide input into the redesign of the system to improve its usability. Of course, the consultant responsible for the information-gathering task would have eventually created the list of requirements, but it could be argued that the process was accelerated and legitimized through me being there. Moreover, the explicit discussions that ensued between myself, the consultants, and the director while doing the rounds enabled both the director and the consultant to gain a better picture of the difficulties the consultants were having. I also contributed my own researcher's views on why I thought some interface changes were necessary, which were based on observations and understanding of the problems the consultants were experiencing. In this sense, I was acting very much as a facilitator, using academic knowledge/expertise in CSCW and HCI in a largely implicit manner.

There were also several other instances during the study, where I became implicated in mediating between the consultants, management, and the suppliers. For example, I was involved in the decision-making activities concerning the possibility of introducing a new software package that would have radical effects on the current ways of working (Rogers, 1993c). Each occasion where I became involved was largely opportunistic. In doing so, I moved with the ebb and flow of the tide of obstacles, problems, and developments as they surfaced in the company, providing feedback and facilitating discussion as and when appropriate.

The advantage of being an outside researcher meant that I could avoid the situation of having to be aligned with either management, the consultants, or the software suppliers. I could move freely between the different parties. Trying to remain neutral, however, was sometimes difficult. For example, there were occasions when management attempted to exploit the situation of me being present on the shopfloor, by asking me sensitive questions about the working practices and activities of certain consultants. In such circumstances I used my discretion. I would either give noncommittal answers (e.g., "they seem to be OK") or point out that they could always ask the consultant in question, themselves.

This form of proactive research does not lend itself to any formalization. As such it cannot be regarded as a particular approach to design, but, alternatively, should be viewed as research that both enables an ethnographic study to be reported in the CSCW community of the changes that occur when a new system is introduced into the workplace (Rogers, 1994), while also enabling me as a researcher to play a more active role in helping the particular company to better configure its technical systems and working practices.

Social Scientists as In-House or Corporate Researchers and Consultants

Getting involved with the people who are being studied is of course nothing new; participatory design methods such as those espoused by Mumford (1993) have always stressed the value of researchers as facilitators in helping users specify their own requirements. Likewise, several in-house/corporate HCI groups (and other socially based research teams) together with independent consultancies have sought in vain to be more directly involved in dialogues with the primary architects of design (e.g., see Blomberg et al., this volume; Rousseau, Candy, & Edmonds, 1993). The difficulty that such groups frequently experience, however, is getting their voices heard and being able to have some influence in the design process. Often, the contributions proposed by such researchers and external consultants are not incorporated, because it is too late for the necessary changes to be made in the design process (see Grudin, 1993, for a historical overview of why such obstacles have evolved). A further problem is the degree of relevance and value attributed to HCI/CSCW specialists and other socially oriented researchers by the architects of design. For example, Blomberg, Suchman, and Trigg (chap. 8, this volume) discuss the pigeonholing of their ethnographic work by others in the organization, who regard their findings as being only relevant to product development for particular markets. In contrast, they believe their research has much more universal application.

A difficult problem facing corporate researchers employed in large organizations, therefore, is how to overcome competing demands. There are many other stakeholders involved in the development of systems, whose vested interests often take precedence over the social scientist. In trying to make a case, the corporate social scientist may be forced to justify their contribution through the provision of concrete and tangible results. The danger here is that such visible outcomes will be equated with the creation of prescriptive sets of guidelines and design tools. In contrast, proactive research entails much "articulation work" (Strauss, Fagerhaugh, Suczek, & Wiener, 1985), where informal talking, negotiating, and reflecting with in-house designers are central. The corporate social scientist, therefore, is in the difficult position of trying to convince the other stakeholders of the importance of this form of reflexive activity.

CONCLUSIONS

Previous attempts in the field of HCI to configure the user indirectly through prescribing ways of designing technical systems to be more user-centered have been largely ineffective. Part of the problem stems from the use of an inappropriate knowledge base from which to derive the prescriptive advice. The production of paper and computer-based tools by one community for another, with little consideration of how that community does its work, was also seen as problematic. Alternative means of informing system design that have since emerged within HCI and CSCW were outlined. These include reconceptualizing the area of study, using alternative theoretical and analytic frameworks, and a shift toward understanding and supporting the design processes and the implementation of technology in organizations.

Ethnomethodological and other kinds of ethnographic studies of the workplace and design were seen as playing an important role in shaping the emerging field of CSCW. It was stressed, however, that such research does not have to follow the same misguided path of informing system design through the provision of prescriptive advice, taken by the applied psychologists in HCI and sociotechnical systems. Instead, social scientists could try considering how to be more proactive in their research by engaging in continuous dialogue with the people being studied. In doing so, they may find they can have a more direct (and potentially more useful) contribution; providing constructive feedback and co-articulating ideas with designers on the fly is more likely to have a direct influence on decisions about the design and use of technical systems than channeling research through the traditional, indirect "single stream" methods. Through this form of dynamic, situation-contingent discourse, it is believed that the processes of design and technology use can be articulated better and, in so doing, enable a more constructive bridging of the Great Divide.

ACKNOWLEDGMENTS

Thanks to Victoria Bellotti for her comments.

REFERENCES

Anderson, B., Button, G., & Sharrock, W. (1993). Supporting the design process within an organizational context. In *Proceedings of the Third European Conference on Computer-Supported Cooperative Work* (pp. 47–60). Dordrecht, The Netherlands: Kluwer.

Bannon, L. (1991). From human factors to human actors: The role of psychology and human–computer interaction studies in system design. In J. Greenbaum & M. Kyng (Eds.), *Design at work: Cooperative design of computer systems* (pp. 25–44). Hillsdale, NJ: Lawrence Erlbaum Associates.

Bannon, L. (1993, April). Use, design and evaluation: Steps towards an integration. In *Proceedings of the International Workshop on CSCW Design and Groupware Systems*, Austrian Computer Society, Shärding, Austria.

Barnard, P. (1991). Bridging between basic theories and the artifacts of human–computer interaction. In J. Carroll (Ed.), *Designing interaction: Psychology at the human–computer interface* (pp. 103–127). New York: Cambridge University Press.

Bellotti, V. (1988). Implications of current design practice for the use of HCI techniques. In D. M. Jones & R. Winder (Eds.), *Peoples and computers* (Vol. 4, pp. 13–34). New York: Cambridge University Press.

Bentley, R., Hughes, J. A., Randall, D., Rodden, T., Sawyer, P., Sommerville, I., & Shapiro, D. (1992). Ethnographically-informed systems design for air traffic control. In *CSCW '92: Proceedings of the Conference on Computer-Supported Cooperative Work* (pp. 123–129). New York: Association for Computing Machinery.

Blacker, F., & Brown, C. (1986). Alternative models to guide the design and introduction of the new information technologies into work organizations. *Journal of Psychology, 59*, 287–313.

Blomberg, J., Giacomi, J., Mosher, A., & Swenton-Wall, P. (1993). Ethnographic field methods and their relation to design. In D. Schuler & A. Namioka (Eds.), *Participatory design: Principles and practices* (pp. 123–155). Hillsdale, NJ: Lawrence Erlbaum Associates.

Bødker, S. (1991). *Through the interface: A human activity approach to user interface design.* Hillsdale, NJ: Lawrence Erlbaum Associates.

Bowers, J., & Pycock, J. (1994). Talking through design: Requirements and resistance in cooperative prototyping. In *CHI '94: Proceedings of Human Factors in Computing Systems Conference* (pp. 299–305). New York: Association for Computing Machinery.

Brooks, R. (1991). Comparative task analysis: An alternative direction for human–computer interaction science. In J. Carroll (Ed.), *Designing interaction* (pp. 50–59). Cambridge, MA: Cambridge University Press.

Button, G. (Ed.). (1993). *Technology in working order.* London: Routledge & Kegan Paul.

Button, G., & Dourish, P. (1996). Technomethodology: Paradoxes and possibilities. *Proceedings of Human Factors in Computing Systems* (pp. 19–26). New York: Association for Computing Machinery.

Carroll, J. (Ed.). (1995). *Scenario-based design: Envisioning work and technology in system development.* New York: Wiley.

Cherns, A. (1976). The principles of socio-technical design. *Human Relations, 29,* 783–792.

Clegg, C., & Symon, G. (1989). A review of human-centred manufacturing technology and a framework for its design and evaluation. *International Review of Ergonomics, 2,* 15–47.

Cooper, G. (1991). *Representing the user.* Unpublished doctoral thesis, Open University, England.

Cooper, G., Hine, C., Low, J., & Woolgar, S. (1993). Ethnography and human–computer interaction. *CRICT discussion paper No. 39,* Brunel University.

de Souza, F., & Bevan, N. (1990). The use of guidelines in menu interface design: Evaluation of a draft standard. In D. Diaper, G. Gilmore, G. Cockton, & B. Shackel (Eds.), *Human–computer interaction—Interact '90* (pp. 395–400). Amsterdam, North Holland: Elsevier.

Diaper, D. (1989). *Task analysis for human–computer interaction.* Chichester, England: Ellis Horward.

Dourish, P., & Bellotti, V. (1992) Awareness and coordination in shared workspaces. In the *Proceedings of the 1992 Meeting for the Society of Computer-Supported Cooperative Work* (pp. 107–114). New York: Association for Computing Machinery.

Durrett, J., & Trezona, J. (1982). How to use colour displays effectively. *Byte, 7*(4), 50–53.

Flor, N. V., & Hutchins, E. (1992). Analyzing distributed cognition in software teams: A case study of collaborative programming during adaptive software maintenance. In J. Koenemann-Belliveau, T. Moher, & T. Robertson (Eds.), *Empirical studies of programmers: Fourth workshop* (pp. 36–64). Norwood, NJ: Ablex.

Gardiner, M., & Christie, B. (Eds.). (1987). *Applying cognitive psychology to user interface design.* Chichester, England: Wiley.

Goodwin, C., & Goodwin, M. J. (1996). Seeing as a situated activity: Formulating planes. In Y. Engeström & D. Middleton (Eds.), *Cognition and communication* (pp. 61–95). Cambridge, England: Cambridge University Press.

Gray, W. D., John, B. E., & Atwood, M. E. (1992). The precis of project Ernestine, or, an overview of a validation of GOMS. In P. Bauersfield, J. Bennett, & G. Lynch (Eds.), *CHI '92: Proceedings of the Human Factors in Computing Systems Conference* (pp. 307–312). New York: Association for Computing Machinery.

Greenbaum, J., & Kyng, M. (Eds.). (1991). *Design at work: Cooperative design of computer systems.* Hillsdale, NJ: Lawrence Erlbaum Associates.

Grudin, J. (1993). Obstacles to participatory design in large product development organizations. In D. Schuler and A. Namioka (Eds.), *Participatory design: Principles and practices* (pp. 99–119). Hillsdale, NJ: Lawrence Erlbaum Associates.

Grudin, J. (1994). Groupware and social dynamics: Eight challenges for developers. *Communications of the ACM, 37*(1), 92–105.

Grudin, J., & Grinter, R. (1995). Ethnography and design. *Computer Supported Cooperative Work, 3*(1), 55–59.

Halverson, C. A. (1992). *Analyzing a cognitively distributed system: A terminal radar approach control.* Unpublished masters thesis, Cognitive Science Department, University California San Diego, CA.

Heath, C., & Luff, P. (1991). Collaborative activity and technological design: Task coordination in London underground control rooms. In *Proceedings of the Second European Conference on Computer-Supported Cooperative Work* (pp. 65–80). Dordrecht, The Netherlands: Kluwer.

Heath, C., Jirotka, M., Luff, P., & Hindmarsh, J. (1993). Unpacking collaboration: The international organisation of trading in a city dealing room. In *Proceedings of the Third European Conference on Computer-Supported Cooperative Work* (pp. 155–170). Dordrecht, The Netherlands: Kluwer.

Hughes, J. A., Randall, D., & Shapiro, D. (1992). Faltering from ethnography to design. In *Proceedings of the 1992 Meeting for the Society of Computer-Supported Cooperative Work* (pp. 115–122). New York: Association for Computing Machinery.

Hutchins, E. (1995). *Cognition in the wild.* Cambridge, MA: MIT Press.

Hutchins, E., & Klausen, T. (1996). Distributed cognition in an airline cockpit. In D. Middleton & Y. Engeström (Eds.), *Communication and cognition at work* (pp. 15–54). Cambridge, England: Cambridge University Press.

Landauer, T. K. (1987). Relations between cognitive psychology and computer system design. In J. Carroll (Ed.), *Interfacing thought* (pp. 1–25). Cambridge, MA: MIT Press.

Landauer, T. K. (1991). Let's get real: A position paper on the role of cognitive psychology in the design of humanly useful and usable systems. In J. Carroll (Ed.), *Designing interaction: Psychology at the human–computer interface* (pp. 60–73). New York: Cambridge University Press.

Long, J., & Dowell, J. (1996). Cognitive engineering or "getting users interacting with computers to perform effective work." *The Psychologist, 9*(6), 313–316.

Löwgren, J., & Laurén, U. (1993). Supporting the use of guidelines and style guides in professional user interface design. *Interacting With Computers, 5*(4), 385–396.

MacLean, A., Young, R., & Moran, T. P. (1989). Design rationale: The argument behind the artifact. In *Proceedings of the 1989 Annual Human–Computer Interaction Meeting* (pp. 247–252). New York: Association for Computing Machinery.

Miller, G. A. (1956). The magic number seven plus or minus two: Some limits of our capacity for information processing. *Psychological Review, 63*(2), 81–87.

Monk, A., Wright, P., Haber, J., & Davenport, L. (1993) *Improving your human–computer interface: A practical technique.* New York: Prentice-Hall.

Mosier, J., & Smith, S. L. (1986). Application of guidelines for designing user interface software. *Behaviour and Information Technology, 5*(1), 39–46.

Mumford, E. (1987). Socio-technical systems design: Evolving theory and practice. In G. Bjerknes, P. Ehn, & M. Kyng (Eds.), *Computers and democracy* (pp. 59–77). Aldershot: Avebury.

Mumford, E. (1993). The participation of users in systems design: An account of the origin, evolution, and use of the ETHICS method. In D. Schuler & A. Namioka (Eds.), *Participatory design: Principles and practices* (pp. 257–270). Hillsdale, NJ: Lawrence Erlbaum Associates.

Nardi, B. (1996). *Context and consciousness: Activity theory and human–computer interaction.* Cambridge, MA: MIT Press.

Norman, D., & Draper, S. (Eds.). (1986). *User-centered system design.* Hillsdale, NJ: Lawrence Erlbaum Associates.

Pasmore, W., Francis, C., Haldman, J., & Shani, A. (1982). Socio-technical systems: A North American reflection on empirical studies of the seventies. *Human Relations, 36,* 1179–1204.

Plowman, L., Ramage, M., & Rogers, Y. (1995). What are workplace studies for? In *Proceedings of the Fourth European Conference on Computer-Supported Cooperative Work* (pp. 309–324). Dordrecht, The Netherlands: Kluwer.

Rogers, Y. (1993a). *Adapting to change: A report on the changes that occurred when "Bridge the World" introduced a new computerized travel system into the workplace.* Unpublished report, University of Sussex.

Rogers, Y. (1993b). Coordinating computer mediated work. *Computer Supported Cooperative Work, 1,* 295–315.

Rogers, Y. (1993c, September). From observation to participation: How far should the ethnographer go in informing design? Paper presented at the *Ethnography in Practice* workshop at ECSCW '93, Milan, Italy.

Rogers, Y. (1994). Exploring obstacles: Integrating CSCW in evolving organisations. *Proceedings of the 1994 Meeting of the Society for Computer-Supported Cooperative Work* (pp. 67–78). New York: Association for Computing Machinery.

Rogers, Y., & Ellis, J. (1994). Distributed cognition: An alternative framework for analysing and explaining collaborative working. *Journal of Information Technology, 9*(2), 119–128.

Rogers, Y., Bannon, L., & Button, G. (1994). Rethinking theoretical frameworks for HCI. *SIGCHI Bulletin, 26*(1), 28–30.

Rousseau, N. P., Candy, L., & Edmonds, E. A. (1993). Influence, direction and time available: A case study of HCI practice in software development. *Interacting With Computers, 5*(4), 397–411.

Rowley, D. E., & Rhoades, D. G. (1992). The cognitive jogthrough: A fast paced user interface evaluation procedure. In *CHI '92 Proceedings* (pp. 389–396). New York: Association for Computing Machinery.

Schuler, D., & Namioka, A. (Eds.). (1993). *Participatory design: Principles and practices.* Hillsdale, NJ: Lawrence Erlbaum Associates.

Shapiro, D. (1994). The limits of ethnography: Combining social sciences for CSCW. In *Proceedings of CSCW '94* (pp. 417–428). New York: Association for Computing Machinery.

Smith, S. L., & Mosier, J. N. (1986). *Guidelines for designing user interface software* (Rep. No. EDS-TR-86-278). Bedford, MA: Mitre Corp.

Sommerville, I., Rodden, T., Sawyer, P., Bentley, R., & Twidale, M. (1993). Integrating ethnography into the requirements engineering process. In *Proceedings of the IEEE Requirements Engineering Conference,* San Diego.

Strauss, A., Fagerhaugh, Suczek, B., & Wiener, C. (1985). *Social organization of medical work.* Chicago: University of Chicago Press.

Suchman, L. A. (1987). *Plans and situated actions.* Cambridge, England: Cambridge University Press.

Suchman, L. A., & Trigg, R. H. (1991). Understanding practice: Video as a medium for reflection and design. In J. Greenbaum & M. Kyng (Eds.), *Design at work* (pp. 65–90). Hillsdale, NJ: Lawrence Erlbaum Associates.

Tetzlaff, L., & Schwartz, D. (1991). The use of guidelines in interface design. In *Proceedings of CHI '91* (pp. 329–333). New York: Association for Computing Machinery.

Trist, E. L., & Bamforth, K. W. (1951). Some social and psychological consequences of the longwall method of coal getting. *Human Relations, 4,* 3–38.

Tyldesley, D. (1988). Employing usability engineering in the development of office products. *Computer Journal, 31*(5), 431–436.

Waern, Y. (1989). *Cognitive aspects of computer supported tasks.* Chichester, England: Wiley.

Woolgar, S. (1993). The user talks back. *CRICT Discussion Paper No. 40,* Brunel University.

4

Engineering Investigations: Practical Sociological Reasoning in the Work of Engineers

Wes Sharrock
University of Manchester, England

Graham Button
Rank Xerox Research Centre, England

The chapter illustrates an ethnomethodological orientation to the theme of social science, technical systems, and cooperative work through the study of engineering work in organizations.[1] As a prelude, consider these four points:

The study draws almost exclusively on our own studies of engineering work in the design and development of photocopier hardware and software; it is not reviewing a range of ethnomethodological concerns with technical systems.[2]

The specific lineage of ethnomethodology within which the investigations are located is "studies of work." This means the primary interest is in the organization of work activities and interactions.[3]

---

[1]It is outside the scope of a short chapter to even provide a sketch of ethnomethodology, and consequently those who seek an introduction should refer to Sharrock and Anderson (1986) and Heritage (1984). For a consideration of the place of ethnomethodology in the human sciences, see Button (1991).

[2]These studies were conducted over a 5-year period and encompassed four projects, all concerning the development of photocopier technology. Detailed reports emanating from this work can be found in Anderson, Button, and Sharrock (1993a, 1993b); Button and Sharrock (1994a, 1994b); Button and Sharrock (1997, in press); and Sharrock, Button, and Anderson (forthcoming).

[3]See Garfinkel (1986). Also see Button (1993) for a collection of ethnomethodologicaly affiliated studies of work and technology.

The fact that this work is organized through the complex articulation of the collaborative structure of the project format is what relates these studies to the theme of this book.

These studies of work instantiate ethnomethodology's root concern with *practical sociological reasoning*.

In order to illustrate practical sociological reasoning, Garfinkel (1967) drew on the case of the workings of the Los Angeles Suicide Prevention Center (SPC). Another municipal organization, the Los Angeles Medical Examiner-Coroner's Office, identified cases of death in which it was unclear whether death was caused by suicide or some other cause and referred them to the SPC, which was charged with the task of determining the cause of death. Garfinkel's interest was in how such determinations are made, and with what, as a matter of practical action, is involved in carrying out inquiries to determine cause of death. However, the conditions under which, and the procedures by means of which, the investigators had to do their work were not necessarily distinctive to their occupation, but represent what Garfinkel called "commonsense situations of choice." Garfinkel outlined a number of prominent features of the practices involved in such situations of choice, that have become touchstones for subsequent studies of work done under ethnomethodology's study program. These prominent features include:

> (1) an abiding concern on the part of all parties for the temporal concerting of activities; (2) a concern for the practical question *par excellence*: "What to do next?"; (3) a concern on the inquirer's part to give evidence of his grasp of "What Anyone Knows" about how the settings work in which he had to accomplish his inquiries, and his concern to do so in the actual occasions in which the decisions were to be made by his exhibitable conduct in choosing; (4) matters which at the level of talk might be spoken of as "production programmes," "laws of conduct," "rules of rational decision making," "causes," "conditions," "hypothesis testing," "models," "rules of inductive and deductive inference" in the actual situations were taken for granted and were depended upon to consist of recipes, proverbs, slogans, and partially formulated plans of action. (Garfinkel, 1967, pp. 12–13)

These points are manifest in the following description of the work at the SPC:

> The work by SPC members of conducting their inquiries was part and parcel of the day's work. Recognised by staff members as constituent features of the day's work, their inquiries were thereby intimately connected to the terms of employment, to various internal and external chains of reportage, supervision, and review, and to similar organizationally supplied

"priorities of relevances" for assessments of what "realistically," "practically," or "reasonably" needed to be done and could be done, how quickly, with what resources, seeing whom, talking about what, for how long, and so on. Such considerations furnished "We did what we could, and for all reasonable interests here is what we came out with" its features of organizationally appropriate sense, fact, impersonality, anonymity, of authorship, purpose, reproducibility—*i.e.*, of a *properly* and *visibly* rational account of the inquiry. (Garfinkel, 1967, p. 13)

The ease with which Garfinkel's case can be analogized to that of design and development engineers producing photocopiers is facilitated by one of the first observations made in the course of our studies: Engineers are, no less than members of the SPC, very much *investigators*. Their day-to-day work is overwhelmingly a matter of problem solving and their work load is substantially comprised of what they themselves identify as investigations into the causes of and the viability of candidate solutions to those problems. The work of the engineers closely paralleled the work of those in the SPC for both groups engaged in practical sociological reasoning.

Treating engineering work as a case of practical sociological reasoning enables a simple and direct link to be made between "the technical" and "the social" because, programmatically, given the starting point, it must be appreciated that the practicality of the reasoning and associated conduct is integrally constituted in relation to the socially organized setting of the investigations themselves. As the SPC case illustrates, the investigations are conducted as "part and parcel of the day's work" and, as such, are conducted under the auspices of the SPC organization. The work activities involve an orientation to the features "that anyone knows" of the organization (and its wider occupational environment), its properties and ways, and their management as the condition of "an adequate inquiry." Thus, the engineering work studied was inseparable from its organizational environment, and it was from within their workplace and on the basis of that workplace's and their profession's organized practices that the engineers determined the conditions for adequate engineering practice in any given instance. Just as with the case of the SPC, the matters reported here are those that were well known to those engineers studied, those they recognized as the familiar, and variably tractable, conditions of their day's work. Thus, the engineering investigations were, through and through, embedded inquiries conducted in and through the organized social setting and its ways.

It is not, however, the intention to offer these observations as a sociological thesis, which makes proposals about the constraints under which the engineers must operate, whether or not they were aware of them. Rather, it is to document the way in which this embedded character was attended to by the engineers; something they took for granted and which they would, as a matter of course, take into account as grounds for inference and further action in doing their engineering. Garfinkel's arguments offer, then, the conception of the members of society, including engineers, as *practical sociologists*, who must analyze the social organization of the settings within which they operate as a condition of further conduct within those settings. Members deploy that sociological reasoning in the service of practical purposes and in response to practical requirements, which means that practical sociological reasoning is part and parcel of the work of the settings in which it is done. It is in terms of this conception that a connection is made between the technical and the social, treating the carrying out of the technical engineering work as something which is done on the basis of and by means of practical sociological reasoning.

In order to explore engineers' practical sociological reasoning, three major contingencies of their work and the ways in which they attended to them as practical sociologists were examined: the contingency of engineering outcomes, the contingency of user understandings, and the contingency of collaborative work in an organizational environment.

ORGANIZING AGAINST CONTINGENCY

One persistent theme of recent social studies of scientific and technological work has been the contingency of scientific and technological outcomes.[4] The prominence of this theme owes much to the desire to argue against determinist and necessitarian conceptions of the development of science and technology. This argument can be made by exhibiting the existence of alternate possible ways in which the technology's initial conception and subsequent maturation might have gone, and the way the selection of one possible route for the technology's development was achieved through "political" struggle rather than "logical" or "formally rational" decision processes. Contingency also looms large in ethnomethodological studies. This is not, however, because of its implications for theoretical conceptions of the nature of science and technology, but simply because of the prominence it has in members' working lives, a prominence also manifest in the working lives of the engineers we studied.

The Contingency of Engineering Outcomes

In doing their work, the engineers oriented to a difference between the *project on paper* and the *project in practice* (Bucciarelli, 1994). The project on paper and the project in practice are potentially two different objects,

---

[4]For example: Mackenzie and Wajcman (1985), Bijker and Law (1992), and MacKenzie (1996).

and the extent to which the project on paper provides a viable schematic for the delivery of a product is something that can only be conclusively gauged in attempting to follow the project plans. The schematic nature of the project plans provided for the details of the project to be worked out during its course. Thus, just how the particulars of the specification were to be realized was something that could only be figured out once the development work on a project had begun, and was something that might prove more or less amenable to being worked out. Engineers entered into their projects with the belief that the development could eventually be worked out, but knowing that this would not be straight-forward. They also believed that preserving the demands of the specification within the limits of the timetable and the budget would keenly tax them. They thus initiated work on their projects with firm expectations that contingencies would attenuate the correspondence between the project on paper in terms of its plans, initial designs, and schedules, and the project in practice in terms of its actual progress. The contingencies afflicting any project are numerous, and this chapter holds to a discussion of two sources of contingency relevant to the outcome of a project.

Sources of Contingency: The Intractability of Engineering Material. One source of difficulty and delay in projects was the intractability of the engineering materials relative to the development of technical practice. For example, to photocopier engineers, paper is often a highly intractable material and is difficult to handle by mechanical means. Developing solutions to the particular problems encountered with the material on a particular development will affect the specifications of the product design on which they are working. For example, among other things, paper is inclined to be "sticky," because sheets of paper are prone to develop charges of electrical static that make them adhere to each other, and thus cause jams because they enter the "paper path" in multiples. On one of the projects, engineers, who were seeking to maintain the very high speed of a machine they were re-engineering, confronted a serious problem because their attempts to meet the high speed requirement was creating a critical stickiness problem. To alleviate this they had to design and develop, from scratch, a mechanical solution involving a novel procedure, the installation of a set of additional "fingers" to fan out sheets of paper entering the path.[5] Thus, time that was not provided for in the project schedule was used up, both in discovering that their attempted solutions to their engineering problems had created another serious problem, and then in working out, designing, and testing a solution.

---

[5]This solution was so successful that it became a standard feature on subsequent copier models.

Sources of Contingency: The Organization of the Work. Problems on projects do not just arise from technical difficulties such as those that accrue from the materials the engineers work with, but also from out of the design of the development team and the organization of its work. Thus, for example, the remote distribution of collaborative work can give rise to serious problems. In one case, a collaboration with the Japanese arm of the company meant that the U.K. engineers required information and support from the Japanese engineers. However, it had not been realized, until the project was underway, and just at the moment the information and support was necessary for the next phase of work, that the documentation the U.K. engineers required was in Japanese. Consequently, they sent e-mail messages to their Japanese counterparts but initially these were not answered, giving rise to suspicions about a lack of cooperativeness. It was then realized, when a frustrated U.K. engineer called someone he supposed had worked on the original Japanese version of the machine, that the Japanese engineers with whom they were dealing could not read English. The delay in answering was the result of having to translate the English messages, and it was going to take the Japanese at least a fortnight to reply to simple queries. However, no provision, organizational or financial, had been made for translation.

In another instance, the distribution of code writing between two very distant sites, one in the southeast of England and the other on the west coast of the United States, proved much more problematic than expected. The e-mail and satellite television links provided to enable distributed working were insufficient to manage the communications problems. These difficulties were compounded by interdepartment conflicts between the management on the two sites leading to significant departures from the project schedule.[6]

The fact that these projects fell victim to these particular organizational exigencies was not, however, regarded as a sign of the engineers', or their managers', fundamental incompetence in handling their affairs. Rather, all concerned looked on these as instances of the type of problems that can afflict any project. Every problem of this sort was understood as a specific instance from among the large and open-ended assortment of organizational contingencies that could arise in the course of any project.[7]

Confronting the Contingencies. Project work is highly organized to prevent the occurrence of numerous known contingencies and enabling organized and adaptive responses to the many inevitable but unforeseen

---

[6]More detail on this case can be found in Sharrock and Anderson (1993b).

[7]Engineers could, and sometimes did, make mistakes that they or their colleagues would judge as incompetent or stupid. For example, we were told that the previous site manager had become carried away with an ingenious but seriously flawed design. This was deemed to have been ruinous to his career and the cause of his removal.

contingencies that were to be expected. The very organization of the work into a *project* is itself a species of planning. Many of the features of the project format and of the "processes" the engineers employed in order to work on a particular task were understood as devices designed to inhibit one contingency or another,[8] thus reducing, desirably minimizing, the extent to which the known vagaries of engineering practice and work organization would recreate past problems.

The project format was not, however, expected to eliminate contingencies altogether, and the engineers attempted to make realistic assessments of the inadequacies of their plans to confront contingencies of the sort described. Consequently, there were mechanisms in the project form designed to identify and contend with contingencies as they arose, and to contain their consequences as far as possible, while recognizing that contingencies were multifarious and more numerous than could be anticipated in the project's design, or practically managed without serious troubles and extensive damage to the project's projected order before the problems these contingencies created could even be identified.

To illustrate, consider the way in which the engineers worked to ensure that problems or mistakes were detected early on. A predominant anxiety shared by engineers and project managers was that problems would not be identified until it was too late. This meant that something that had been done, or had been left undone, and could give rise to severe consequences for the project objectives, might not manifest itself in recognizable form until long after the mistake or oversight had occurred. It might then be necessary to redo work previously considered complete and when the difficulty and cost of correcting the mistake would be substantially greater than it need have been had the error been detected at the time it was made.

If the problem or mistake was not detected, then it would, in all likelihood, be further compounded, as subsequent decisions were built on it, and as it was, perhaps, intricately interwoven into the developing design, ensuring that the steps to correct the matter would ramify through other parts of the design making it much more difficult, time consuming, and costly to fix. In the course of building on the mistake the implications for the development would transform the mistake from one that had been made, for example, on a sheet of paper on a designer's drawing board, or in a line of code on a software engineers' workstation, to something that had been incorporated into the physical design or into a complex

---

[8]For any significant problem-solving task, the engineers were expected to define a process by which it was to be carried out, that is, to work out in advance just what means they were intending to employ to carry out the task and in what order the steps would be carried out. This requirement was intended to encourage clarification of the engineer's reasoning, to ensure that the engineer had clearly defined objectives and an equally clear conception of how the relationship between those and the means deployed to achieve them.

structure of software. In this respect, it was commonplace for engineers to contemplate the possibility that their work practices might be masking their mistakes and problems from them, that even as they were making a given decision they might be committing a major error that they might yet live to regret. There were many junctures within the projects at which the engineers did not feel confident that they knew what they were doing, and at which they did not have sufficient information relative to a decision that they must in any case make.

"Too late" a detection of a problem or a mistake could also refer to scheduling considerations. The discovery that there was a problem might be "too late" within a project's schedule, because the corrective measures necessary would make a project that had appeared to be on schedule now overshoot its deadline or would make the schedule slippage problems of an already-late project even worse. "Too late" a detection of a problem or a mistake thus not only had consequences for the actual design of the technology but also for the schedule to which the technology was produced, and all of the engineers had been on projects that had been troubled by too late a detection of a problem or mistake.

In order to attend to the "too late" problem, the engineers used reactive mechanisms within the project format and in the engineer's working practice to "surface," a problem early on. One mechanism was to extensively and frequently review their work. To this end, a great deal of engineer's actual work consisted of the review of their work. They would make presentations about their work and engage in discussions of each other's work on a day-to-day basis. There were many forums within which they did this ranging from informal groups, to formal meetings of subgroups of the project or of the whole project, or, if the project was sufficiently large, of the project's management committee. In the formal meetings, the plans for, or progress of, particular engineering operations would be discussed, and their relationship not only to engineering problems but to the progress of the schedule and the project's accumulating costs would also be monitored. In addition, there were extensive formal reviews of the project that occurred at specified junctures in the projects' "life cycle," such as the transition from developing the initial concept of the project, to the actual design and development phase in which the prototypes would be produced, or at the transition from design and development to manufacture.

The work of reviewing the work was thus conducted at various levels in the project structure. On a day-to-day basis this consisted of being asked, and asking of others, just when a particular activity would be completed, requiring the engineers to review their progress and give estimates as to its completion date, or at weekly problem review meetings at which a subgroup would examine reports on new problems identified and review the list of outstanding problems. These reviews of work were thus occasioned by the run of work that day or that week. The reason for these reviews resided in the intricacy of the interdependence and sequencing between tasks. That is, tasks on a project were often sequentially related to one another, which meant the timing and pacing of tasks were inexorably mutually dependent. The project organization was constituted in the scheduling of activities relative to one another, and in order to accomplish this ongoing scheduling, it was necessary for the engineers to know where they were and where others were relative to the target dates for the completion of activities and whether there were problems developing that would affect these issues.

Much of the engineer's day-to-day work was, thus, directed toward keeping to or correcting for deviations from the project targets: that is, attempting to achieve a clear comprehension of the relationship between "where we (collectively) are" in relation to the progress of project work relative to "where we ought to be" according to schedule, budget, and specification; arranging things to inhibit deviation from the latter, to minimize the degree of deviation where that was unavoidable; and catching up with or otherwise returning to the prescribed target where that was possible. The work of reviewing the work was a mechanism designed to surface problems early on to enable the coordination of the work in relation to the project schedule.

In addition to day-to-day reviews that were occasioned by the run of work that day or that week, there were also formal reviews built into the project schedule. The formal review recognized that a risk of the day-to-day review procedures was that of *partisanship*. Engineers might overestimate the extent of their success, and underestimate the problems. Such misrepresentations might be due to deliberate attempts to conceal bad work, and to buy time to put it right, or it might be more a matter of the "wish being father to the thought." Engineers routinely became committed to the success of their projects, and, it was conjectured that they might, therefore, simply believe they were making better progress than they really were because that was what they wanted to believe. In other words, it was recognized that the review mechanism could itself compound the "too late" problem.

There was a concern with conducting formal reviews in such a way that they could achieve the correct outcome, the early detection of a problem if there was one. The review was thus constituted as objective and its objectivity was "worked up" in a number of ways. For example, members of review panels were selected who were organizationally distant from the participants on the project. Also, engineers were briefed by their managers on how to conduct themselves during the review. Thus, the managers would exhort the engineers to regard honesty as the best

policy, to be as objective as they could in presenting their work, substituting, where they could, objective measures for anything that could be
considered their opinion, and to avoid doing anything that might be
intended to improve the project's chances in the review but might in any
way misrepresent or minimize its present difficulties.

The course of a technology development is a contest with contingencies,
and the technology outcome is constituted by the engineers wrestling
with them on a day-to-day basis, by, for example, working review procedures to surface mistakes or oversights early on. Technology outcomes
are, thus, contingent productions, dependent on the way in which development contingencies are prepared for, prevented, confronted, defeated,
or accommodated.[9] Engineers contend with development contingencies
as practical sociologists, for, as the examples illustrate, they contend with
them in organizing their collegial relationships with one another; in making their relationships with one another organizationally accountable; in
knowing their way around the bureaucratic structures of the organization;
in their management of the goals of the project; in adjusting ends and
means in practical circumstances, and so on. This practical sociological
reasoning is interwoven into their technical deliberations, and is the vehicle through which their technical deliberations are manifest in the technology outcomes. It is as practical sociologists that the engineers confront
the contingencies of a development, and in practical sociology that technology outcomes are constituted.

Contingency of Meaning

Not only have social studies of science and technology been concerned
to show that the outcomes of technology are contingent, they have also
been a concern to argue that "the meaning" the technology has for users
is also contingent. That is to say, there is openness and ambiguity about
the nature of the finished, usable technological product. The terms in
which the contingency of meaning are commonly discussed relate to
whether or not the meaning of technology is or is not intrinsic to the
technology itself.[10]

We have also been concerned with the contingency of meaning with
respect to technology. However, this issue is pursued through an examination of how technology can be ambiguous to users and how the fact
that its meaning is contingent for users was an oriented to fact of technology use for the engineers, one that entered into the practical conduct
of their design and development work. The form in which the engineers

---

[9]The contingencies may also defeat the engineers working with the constraints of time
and budgets, and the cancellation of projects is not a rare occurrence.

[10]Woolgar's (1991) discussion is important here.

encountered the problem of the contingency of meaning was a workaday engineering matter. This manifests itself in their work as attempts to reason about the meaning that could be attributed to their designs, and the settings in which their products would be used in order to "outthink the user."

Outthinking the User. The engineers were attuned to the contingent character of the meaning of their products. They were aware that users would in all probability find something in their designs that they themselves did not intend, or would fail to percieve things they did intend. It was, thus, one feature of their general concerns with the management of contingency that they sought to control some of the possibilities of meaning that users could impute to their technology. The extent to which the engineers had the technological means to anticipate, prepare, and control user reaction to the machine involved a problematic relationship of ends and means. There were (in their current situations) practically irreducible difficulties in bridging the gap between the engineers' own understanding of the machine and its potential and that of users. Many of the design difficulties they experienced arose in efforts to make, unambiguously manifest, the character and role of features of the machine to potential users. Thus, there were cases in which they could see that a discrepancy of meaning would obtain and could project a scenario of users' actions in response to specific features of the machine, but could not easily, nor necessarily successfully, conceive ways of exhibiting their intended requirements of machine use in readily comprehensible, desirably foolproof, ways.

For example, on one of the projects the interface team attempted to figure out how to convey to the user the numerous services that had been built into the design. The machine was equipped with a visual display unit (VDU) interface that could provide extensive information about its services and instructions on how to exploit them. However, the first problem was to find a way of making the user aware that the machine provided a greater functionality than ordinary photocopiers, and then persuade them to invest time in engaging in a tutorial. The project was eventually scrapped before the team was able to devise an interface design that would effectively draw these possibilities to the user's attention and motivate the user (who might be in a hurry and who just wants to get a photocopying job done) to take an interest in exploring these possibilities.

On another project, the engineers found during a testing phase of the development that the testers were not only using the pause button to suspend machine operations, something it was designed to do, but were also pressing the pause button to restart them. This, however, was causing problems because the machine was designed to restart operations after they had been paused by pressing the start button, not the pause button. The engineers could now see their mistake. They had overlooked the fact that it was reasonable to restart the machine by pushing the pause button as a way of canceling the pause operation, for, after all, that is the way in which many other machines with pause functionality (such as tape and video recorders) operate. This realization, however, came too late for all practical purposes because too much had been designed around this functional deployment of the interface buttons to permit redesign of such extent and complexity at this stage, and so this problem was destined to be one of the design faults with which the model would proceed to market.

The engineers on the various projects did not, however, imagine that the users made up a homogenous group and thus they did not design for only for one kind of user. They recognized that to "outthink the user" it was necessary to conceive of the diversity of users involved. They were often attempting to design for as wide a range of envisaged types as they could accommodate. For example, on one of the projects the engineers were developing an add-on to an existing product that would equip it for the particular requirements of lending libraries. The engineers would invoke the "one-time-perfunctory user" as a pivot around which to organize the interface design while at other times, design decisions would depend on the concept of a "key user" who was someone who would be administratively responsible for the machine and would acquire a deep working familiarity with it.

Also, in test operations the machine operators were required to simulate "naive users,"[11] and refrain from invoking their accumulated familiarity with the specific machine they were operating in order to enhance its performance by solving problems that, were they truly naive users, they would in all likelihood be incapable of fixing without a "call out" of a repair operative. Because one of the leading criteria of machine performance in the testing phase was the number of unscheduled maintenance (UM) calls, the engineers did not want the frequency of such call outs to be an artifact of the testing practices.

Consequently, the designers attempted to outthink the user in the very course of their design activities. They oriented to the fact that their technology had a contingent meaning for those who would use it and attempted to invoke the essential ambiguity of the technology in the practical work of designing the machine, using the fact that the user may find the technology to be ambiguous as a resource for working out their designs. However, whereas the engineers sought to envisage, provide for, and guard against a range of types of users, and a range of problems of use created in the

---

[11]"Naive" only in the sense of being fresh to and unfamiliar with this particular model of copier.

contingent meaning of the technology, they did not suppose that their imaginings and preparations were exhaustive, that they had envisaged all the misconceptions and the perceptions that any user could bring to it. As in everything else in the design, there were trade-offs between, on the one hand, working out all the possible and possibly relevant scenarios of machine use and, on the other, of letting this pass and getting back to the other tasks that would be neglected if this one was pursued.

Further, it was recognized that the provision of measures to minimize the ambiguity of the technology for the user may merely provide the resource for further problems of meaning. The engineers recognized that the diversity, perversity, and ingenuity of users is effectively inexhaustible and that, however the machine is designed, it will then provide only a starting point from which users will find ways of (often legitimately or reasonably) wanting just what the designers had never thought anyone would or could want or of doing what the engineers thought they had rendered impractical. In part, then, it is possible to conceive of designers as seeing themselves in something of a contest with users, trying to outthink them, but being aware that they can only do this on specific points. They know they cannot, overall, achieve a comprehensive anticipation of and provision for users, because they must conduct this contest subject to, and handicapped by, severe restrictions of time and resources, severe restrictions on investigative time and opportunity, and equally severe restrictions on design freedom and flexibility.

The User as a Scenic Feature. In outthinking the user, the user is invoked in Lynch's terms, as a "scenic feature" of the designer's operations.[12] The user is, in these instances, a *social type*, not any actual person. In Schutz's (1972) characterization, the social types that are relevant to the engineer's deliberations are what he called *course-of-action types*. That is, in deliberating what the user will do the engineers imagine the *courses of action* that persons will perform in specific circumstances, not the people who will use the machine. Engineers very often produce these types "around-the-table" and they accordingly take on the character of "on-the-spot" productions. Thus, the issue as to what the user might relevantly do is occasioned by some course of design reasoning, for example, how to partition a design solution between the machine and the user's good sense. With respect to the problem of the "pause button," the designers were faced with deciding to either seek to provide designed-in solutions that at that stage would have been costly and problematic themselves, or relying on the user to find and implement some solution.

---

[12]See Sharrock and Anderson (1993a). Lynch's original coinage is to be found in an unpublished paper, "The Judge as a Scenic Feature of the Courtroom."

It was decided to leave the design unchanged and to leave it to the user to figure out (perhaps with some minimum inconvenience) what the problem was and how to resolve it.

The relevance of the user in such discussions is embedded within design and development work processes. The invocation of the user as a course-of-action type allows the engineers to address their problems with the resources they have to hand, and within the practical constraints they face. Thus, the engineers invoke the user as a course-of-action type in order to determine, without discontinuing their current activity, what to do: to decide here and now, around this table, among us, what to do about this matter; to make a decision without having to leave the table, collect evidence, or consult anyone who is not now present; and thus to envisage, now, the user, the appropriate circumstances, and the likely—even the for-sure—response that such a type will produce in those circumstances.

The construction is, further, constituted as a "reasonable one." The proposed features of the course-of-action type, the way in which it is proposed that this person will organize a particular sequence of action, or will feel about the situation is for practical purposes reasonable. Thus, for example, the user confronted with the pause button problem is constructed as not being very much concerned by the minor inconvenience of sorting out the problem, and it is assumed that they will indeed feel it is a minor problem. Thus, the engineers, in discussion, can recognize the user as reasonable, and against this construction they can gauge that what they proposed is intelligible, and can be assented to without disagreement.

The user is, then, a "scenic feature" in that the envisaged conduct of such types is a frequent and decisive feature of the deliberations of the engineers, that they must frequently address the question of what the user will do, will be like, or will feel, as an element in arriving at their design decisions. It is through such reasonable course-of-action type constructions that engineers seek to outthink users.

The Engineer Knows Best.   In outthinking the user through the construction of a course-of-action type, the engineer is clearly engaged in practical sociological reasoning, working out how people will conduct themselves faced with practical problems. In the same way in which the members of the SPC studied by Garfinkel operated as practical sociologists in their investigations into the cause of death, so too does the engineer work as a practical sociologist as an integral and continuous part of design and development reasoning. Thus, just as the SPC investigator must envisage social settings, their orderly ways, situations that develop within them, and typical or possible activities on the part of persons within those scenes and situations as a means of deciding what was really the cause of death in some case, the engineer, in order to reach a design decision, must envisage numerous aspects of social organization and order. For example, they need to envisage the ways of offices, libraries, and other workplaces; the characteristic routines, needs, populations, and problems of such settings; and of the likely, typical, or possible ways in which persons will behave. In short, the engineer exhibits a grasp of anyone's capacity to engage in sociological analysis in the reaching of design decisions.

It is officially deemed, however, by the organization that many matters pertaining to users are not so much within the purview of engineers but of other departments in the organization and that users are subject to the disciplinary rigors appropriate to those departments. That is, the user is subject to other investigator procedures in addition to those of engineering. For example, if the engineers needed to consider refined knowledge of ergonomic features of design, or of the pattern of user response to a particular model of machine, or to matters of safety, then these are officially deemed the competence of other parts of the organization. Thus, Industrial Design and Human Factors (IDHF) is deemed as being equipped with knowledge of and attentive to problems of an ergonomic or humankind. Marketing is responsible for investigations into customer satisfactions and dissatisfactions. Lastly, Customer Care and Education has responsibility for safety matters.

Although officially required, the engineers' compliance with the demands of IDHF and Customer Care were, however, more often more dutiful than convinced. A view predominated among mechanical and electrical engineers that their work was the paradigm of engineering work, and that other elements, such as human factors were lesser forms of practice. Thus, for example, they were apt to look on IDHF as lacking the kind of attested and well-formulated knowledge that they believed they, as engineers, brought to bear in their work. Though they might be ready enough to take note of what, for instance, IDHF had to say about users, the engineers were not convinced that it carried unambiguous messages about what, in engineering terms, they ought to do.

Their view was organizationally exacerbated, for although the company deemed that user matters should be the purveyance of IDHF it, in fact, during the course of the studies, reduced it, as part of organization-wide layoffs, to a rump, with a small number of rather junior staff (one of whom was an undergraduate student on a coursework placement in the organization). The engineers viewed this as reflecting the actual dispensability of IDHF for many purposes. The idea of attaching importance to user issues was one the engineers were willing enough to accept, but the organizational realities of attempts to do this did not strike them as either as helpful or dependable as they would like it to be.

From the point of view of the engineers, then, the formalized methods of departments that are officially charged with user matters are inferior when compared to their engineering methods and practices. Many of the matters they contend with through on-the-spot, around-the-table constructions are those that the engineers are confident about because through their years of accumulated wisdom in the photocopying business they believe they have a good idea of the range of relevances that exist with respect to photocopier use and users. Consequently, they judged that their on-the-spot, round-the-table deliberations are entirely adequate for many purposes. As a practical sociologist, the engineer knows best—certainly better than IDHF.

The engineers, consequently, orient to the fact that the technology they are developing will have a contingent meaning for its users. This fact enters into their practical work in their attempts to divine the ways in which the user will attribute meaning to the technology. The fact that technology may have a contingent meaning for users consequently shapes the technology outcomes for the engineers attempt to outwit the user through their practical sociological reasoning, which for the purposes of contending with the contingencies of meaning the engineers are dealing with is viewed as more reliable than the range of methodologies available to IDHF. This reasoning enters into the very work of design and is occasioned by aspects of it. The contingency of meaning with respect to technology is something that enters into the practical conduct of engineers design and development work through occasioned courses of practical reasoning done to construct the user as a course-of-action social type.

Contingencies of Collaboration

A last general theme in social studies of science and technology that is relevant for these investigations is that of politics in technology.[13] This theme has arisen from at least two sets of considerations. First, the extent to which there are alternative means to any given technological end suggests that the decisions between these alternatives may not be made on the basis of "strictly rational" procedures. The argument is sometimes put that there are, in any case, no strictly rational procedures, at other times that rational procedures do not provide unequivocal support for one of the options. Either way, the choice between alternatives is seen as rooted in political considerations.[14] The second set of considerations that has given rise to considerations of politics in technology concerns the extent to which technical decisions are subject to the power of formal institutions and the large-scale structures of power in the society. Thus,

---

[13]Latour (1996) provided an example in his consideration of the failure of "Aramis," a guided-transportation system intended for Paris.

[14]"Political" roughly means, here, anything to do with conflictual elements of social relationships.

technology development is subject to influences that originate outside of the day-to-day working world of scientists and technologists, residing in the demands and imperatives of the state, of large corporations, of the development of economic globalism, inter alia.

Again, the interest in politics is in the way in which it is built into the practical work of engineering, in this case the way in which it entered into the organization of collaboration between different groupings on a project as a matter of the practical management of the contingencies of collaboration. A starting point is the engineers' assumption that good engineering and political considerations could be (though not necessarily or invariably) inimical to each other, and the two could certainly be elided—typically to the detriment of a technical decisions. Thus, the next sections discuss the ways in which work was organized to keep considerations of "organizational politics" from intruding into technical decisions.[15] There are three aspects of the attempted practical management of the impact of politics on technical considerations: working across boundaries, relations between different engineering specialities, and the role of total quality.

Working Across Boundaries

The engineers took it for granted that their engineering work was socially organized, in the sense that it was done under the auspices of an organization, in accord with its procedural prescriptions, overlooked and directed by its management, and in conjunction with engineers of various types. The organization of working relationships was an essential precondition of the effective accomplishment both of particular organizational tasks, and of the project's ultimate objective of delivering technology to the marketplace. The organization of working relationships was itself among the means of securing engineering objectives, and like the technical means (such as coding languages) that were administered and implemented through those working relationships, they possessed a more or less problematical relationship to engineering objectives. This means that the ways in which the kinds of work are being done can engender troubles, as, for example, when those engaged in different kinds of work get in each other's way. To examine what is involved here, consider the example of "blaming software," the "political" expedient of loading a project's troubles on another group.

The mechanical and other electrical engineers did not regard software engineering (which was located within the electrical engineering depart-

---

[15]It might seem that this proposal begs the argument that one cannot make a distinction between technical and political considerations. However, it is to be remembered that the distinction is not one being proposed or defended, but one found in the practice of the engineers studied.

ment) as a regular, and entirely bona fide engineering venture comparable with their own. If problems of quality, delivery, and cost were problematic for all engineers on a project, then they were looked on as worse with regard to software, which could add disproportionately to the problems of a project. The engineers were not interested in diagnosing the source of problems for purposes of diagnosing and correcting the technical fault alone, but were almost invariably on the lookout for possibilities of blame, of both handing it out, and, perhaps, having to take it. In this context, mechanical engineers and software engineers were each apt to get in each other's way, to look on each other's ways of working as to blame for some of their respective problems.

From the mechanical engineer's point of view, the simple fact was that their need for software would very frequently be holding up their work. They may, for example, have completed the work they could do with respect to a particular phase in the development of the hardware, and would, perhaps, be ready to introduce new functionality into the design but would be unable to do so because the software was not ready. This problem could develop because the production of a product was often conducted in a stepwise fashion with respect to the addition of functionality. Thus, a particular function would be enabled in the machine, and it would then be tested to the point at which the problems with it had been sorted out, and it was running effectively, and then a related function would be enabled. This stepwise development would often be conducted between groups, with the software engineers first providing software developed to the point at which it would support a particular function at the same time that the hardware engineers were developing the corresponding mechanical features, and then providing a next release of software that would contain the next function to develop. This parallel development would often get out of step, characteristically with the hardware engineers awaiting the software release, and unable to progress with their own work. So the software group was viewed by hardware as not only holding up their own work, but actually adding to it because they were being put in a position where they would have to find ways of reorganizing their work to get around the delays induced by software, and to spend time involved in activities designed to help software sort out its problems.

From the software engineers' point of view, matters were regarded differently. They believed that the mechanical engineers often underestimated the extent to which software engineering is the more difficult task, and were only too ready to place blame on the software team for problems that were just a product of the complexities of a multi-engineering environment. From the software engineer's point of view, the mechanical and other electrical engineers were, after all, themselves entirely capable of creating trouble for the software engineers, by, for example, demanding either the modification of the existing design or the addition of functionality. These requests could often have extensive consequences for software rewriting. By way of another example, on one project there was a demand by hardware for the early release software to enable them to keep their own schedules at the expense of the software engineer's timetable, involving the latter in the work of preparing an interim release, which would leave the software problems unresolved and would slow the software development itself.

Further, the software engineers were satisfied that many of the problems attributed to them under the projects fault scoring system were only *apparently* software problems. Software problems might arise from, and also mask, problems in hardware design, but there was no way of being able in any given case to demonstrate that this was so. This meant that software engineers often felt somewhat hard done by because the scoring system to some extent worked against them. Thus, one project had accumulated a substantial backlog of problems that were prefiguring a major schedule slippage. A significant proportion of the total backlog was allocated to software. The software team felt that they were being blamed for the project's problems, and unjustly so. They were not being explicitly blamed, nothing was being said in so many words, but the software engineers were nonetheless convinced that there was, in what was being said, implications to that effect. They could not deny the reality of the record of numerous outstanding problems, nor, though they felt that many of these problems were wrongly ascribed to them, did they possess tangible bases for contesting those ascriptions. They could only resent the injustice that they were being blamed by those who they were sure were often the real culprits, that their work was complicated and protracted by the need to solve problems that were ostensibly those of software design but arose in reality from deficiencies in the machine's hardware and from the mechanical engineers' failure to work thoroughly through many of their own problems.

Social Solidarity

The engineers were attuned to the extent to which considerations of social solidarity provided contingencies of their collaborative, coordinated work. They attempted to grapple with the contingencies of collaboration by strengthening solidarity in a number of ways.

Solidarity Across the Project. One of the predominate ways in which the engineers worked together was through the organization of a division of labor into specialist groups. A contingency of collaboration that could arise from such an organization was, however, that such groups would be what is termed *parochial* in their outlook, and regard the discharge of their immediate responsibilities within the division of labor as their primary if not sole responsibility. In addition, they might also develop their own internal standards for what counted as adequate fulfilment of their obligations.

These possibilities were regarded, at an organizational level, and among many of the engineers, as undesirable, for such an orientation would lead to failures of integration of the contributory parts of the product or in an obstruction of other people's work. There were, therefore, structural mechanisms in the formal structure of projects, as well as project-initiated practices that were intended to combat such parochialism—to engender a sense of solidarity across the project, and to discourage the attitude that problems that were not part of one's immediate responsibilities in the division of labor were therefore somebody else's responsibility. Thus, there were prescriptions for the way in which design work was conducted. These required that the engineer attend not only to the development of, in engineering terms, a successful design, one that, for example, would provide a compact, efficient, reliable, and cheap design. They also required that the engineers bear in mind, as they originated that design, the ease with which it could be accessed for repair or the ease with which it could be assembled during manufacture.

There were, therefore, requirements on the engineers to attend to others in the division of labor, such as maintenance and manufacture groups. Thus, the engineers responsible for design were encouraged to "design for maintenance" and to "design for manufacture." In one project, it was a mandatory requirement that representatives from each of the project's subsidiary working groupings attend the daily Sunrise meeting,[16] whether or not there was specific business affecting them at the meeting. The project manager insisted on this arrangement as a manifestation of the project's official attitude, which was that the mentality that one was only interested in the work of one's own group within the project was not acceptable, that problems, although they were attributed to specific groupings, were nonetheless the project's problems, and therefore everyone's problems.

Solidarity Between Working Groups. The engineers saw good will between working groups as an important element in their collaboration. Through good will they could call on each other to do more than was strictly required in terms of their participation in the division of labor, according to the official procedures or organizational position. For

---

[16]So called because it occurred at the official commencement of the working day.

example, the engineers often found themselves scavenging around the organization for resources—if the resources allocated to the project could often prove insufficient for certain specific needs. Thus, due to the exigencies of its make up, one project we worked on had an unbalanced skill set, the engineers being barely able to cope with some of the work they had to do. The manager made efforts, therefore, to persuade the manager of another project to allow him the use one of the engineers on his project who was particularly skilled in a certain kind of engineering drawing and to persuade an individual who was highly skilled in designing testing arrangements to undertake the design of a test program. The capacity to make such approaches was dependent on an assumption of good relations.

Good relations were important not only for issues such as "looking out" and "coming through" for each other, but also in terms of the extent to which the engineers would be confident that they could trust and depend on each other. When good will broke down, then the project could become disrupted. A near-fatal problem occurred on one project when a problem in integrating the software developed by one group in the United Kingdom and another in California arose. In part, the problem developed because the two groups did not trust one another and labeled each other according to derogatory stereotypes. For instance, the U.K. engineers would bewail the inappropriately laid-back Californian posture of the U.S. engineers toward problems. The disregard of each for the other led to, on the U.K. side, an unwillingness to do anything other than that which was strictly required to assist with the U.S. group's problems. It was voiced that efforts to do this in the past had not been, and further efforts would not be, reciprocated. On the U.S. side, their was an unwillingness to accept that the U.K. engineers really knew what they were doing, and, therefore, to place credence in the reports they made about the problems they were encountering.

The Perpetuation of Shared Understanding. A common understanding of the purpose and reasoning behind particular design steps was considered to be necessary for the reciprocal integration of parts of the design. This common understanding could not, however, necessarily be derived from whatever formal specifications were provided and whatever design steps were taken. For example, the formal specifications themselves contain no instructions as to how they should be applied. Thus, the project structure processes demanded that the code be documented and software engineers should include explanatory comments in with the code. This instruction was an attempt to address the problem that it is difficult to ensure a common understanding of the intention of computer code merely from an inspection of the lines of code.

In this vein, the engineers on one project, though they were working in a common coding language, found that it did not allow them to write in a way that would specify their design purposes closely enough for others on the project to understand what they were writing. To address this problem they developed an additional set of coding conventions to keep their understandings of the code in close alignment. Even so, the reading of the code according to the conventions was not enough for code writers to be able effectively to complement each other's work on the basis of reading each other's code, and one subgroup in the team became the repository of information about the design and structure of the whole system of code. These were the "fault module" engineers, who were writing software that interfaced with all the other modules of software in the system, and who would circulate among the other subgroups of engineers to discuss their own specific problems of integrating fault diagnosis code with other elements in the system, and would develop detailed familiarity with the specifics of others' code, making them the first port of call for queries about the interdependencies and interactions between code.

There were, thus, risks of slippage in shared understandings, especially where the integration of two elements in the design was complex and intricate. The practice of testing understanding was a common occurrence in engineers' discussions and conversations, where they would take what was an apparently agreed conclusion and then proffer a reformulation of that conclusion as a means of ensuring that they correctly understood what had been agreed to. On one project, the software and process subgroups regarded the risk of slippage of understanding a strong and likely prospect. They recognized that the organization of the two groups was comprised out of two very different kinds of specialists with very different kinds of approaches, which meant that each group would have only a limited understanding of the others' expertise, and the interconnections between their two modules was so extensive and close that even small discrepancies in understanding could have far-reaching consequences. To attend to what they considered to be the almost inevitable likelihood of misunderstanding, they established a regular weekly intergroup meeting just to compare, clarify, and update understandings.

Good Organizational Reasons
for Second Best Engineering Practice

The company's Total Quality policy was designed to encourage the pursuit of highest quality engineering results in all circumstances, and to empower engineers to hold out for quality in the face of practical and organizational expediency. This arrangement recognized that technical and organizational rationales could often be in conflict with one another, and that the best engineering decisions risked being preempted by concerns such as keeping to schedule and within budget. Notionally, the objective was to achieve best engineering results, but it was recognized among the engineers on a project that this objective could be somewhat displaced by the need to keep to schedule and within budget. In practice, the concern with the organizational viability of the project, or of the organizational consequences for the engineers involved, were considerations that could preempt technical standards.

The software engineers on one project were equipped with good practice methodologies, such as Yourdon, to improve the standards of their working practice; these methods were designed to impose on them a stepwise, sequential progression of software development.[17] These methods, then, notionally had the support of their management, and the engineers, themselves, favored conformity with the methods. However, they found themselves unable to adhere to them because of pressures to deliver a software release to the hardware engineers. However meritorious the Yourdon method might be,[18] adherence to it would have meant that the hardware engineers would be unable to do their work, because they required test software that would not be available at the appropriate time if Yourdon was followed. The software team was not prepared to take the risk of being seen to cause a situation in which other engineers were left with nothing to do.

The software engineers on the same project found a way around the problem of working with a chip that was incapable of operating to the standard required if its programming was to be written in the prescribed code, C, by using assembler language instead.[19] The chip's inadequacy was, in the engineers' view, a consequence of a mistaken managerial decision, made on grounds of cost, rather than technical requirements. However, they were not prepared to make this deficiency public out of their concern to protect themselves and their interest in the project, and partly to prevent their already difficult relationships with their software manager deteriorating still further.

---

[17]For a more detailed consideration of the use of Yourdon methodology, see Button and Sharrock (1994a).

[18]In many circles methods such as Yourdon would be regarded as retrograde, but this chapter is not delivering a judgment on them here, only reporting the fact that the method was chosen after a complex organizational process of investigation as the best in relation to what the organization required. This was a judgment endorsed by the engineers who were to work with it. In their world Yourdon is certainly prestigious and looked a likely corrective to what they recognized as defects in their method.

[19]See Button and Sharrock (1994b).

Thus, the quality policy in theory, and the quality policy in practice were potentially two different things. The policy was intended to insulate the engineers' engineering decisions from considerations of organizational expediency and from the pressures of otherwise hierarchical work relationships, and, notionally, the individual engineer could expect support from management for decisions made on quality grounds and invoking the best technical standards. The engineers were, however, aware that whether or not such support would actually be forthcoming would be something that remained to be seen, and it was certainly not something to be counted on. The engineers' own working assumption was that when it came to it, wherever the practical and organizational exigencies were significant, these would overwhelm the strictly quality considerations.[20]

CONCLUSIONS

This chapter has reviewed some of the exigencies that loomed large within the concerns of working engineers as they sought to make, on a day-by-day basis, progression toward outcomes that could be quite long term (i.e., up to 5 years ahead). The exigencies they encountered would change as their work moved through the successive periods of activity and as their project moved on, and as new types of activity, with their associated circumstances, difficulties, and risks, became appropriate. A predominate concern in the organization of their work on this day-by-day basis was to ensure that the work's accomplishments were accumulating in the direction of the desired objective, and they were doing so in ways that kept as close a relationship as possible, to design specifications, timetables, and budgets assigned to the project. This correspondingly meant they were extensively preoccupied with the extent to which the work they were doing was in accord with the project's program of work, the extent to which the work in hand was coherent with the work already done, and that it was, as far as could be seen, effectively preparatory for and timely relative to the next steps to be taken. It was also necessary to establish, sustain, and check out ways of keeping their work activities together with sufficient coherence for the purposes of the project and the requirements of its scheme. Their problem was how to achieve a sufficient standard of engineering design and development in such circumstances; how to balance or, if necessary, prioritize the demands of an adequately

---

[20]On one of the projects the project manager was elevated to heroic status because, uncharacteristically for project managers, he was prepared to risk a major schedule slippage in order to sustain quality, and to give his explicit endorsement to his project team that they should themselves put quality first.

undertaken and properly finished piece of engineering work against the requirements of time; collegial demands; and so forth.

In this context, the engineers' investigations were comprised of their reasoning through a problem to a solution, solving, in other words, engineering conundrums. This involved them reasoning through technological questions such as the most efficient way in which to write a line of code, or how to achieve a particular speed specification. However, their investigations were situated ones, situated in the socially organized setting in which their investigations took place. Thus, their investigations were conducted in their utilization of their knowledge of the ways of the setting within which they worked. Consequently, in their engineering investigations they displayed an orientation to the organization of the setting in: being on the look out for being blamed or for the possibility of blaming others; attending to the opportunities the quality processes presented them; concerting their engineering activities through attending to the cohesiveness of their work groups; making their individual work organizationally accountable; attending to the disjuncture between the project as planned and the project in practice within the constraints of time and budgets; developing processes such as those designed to surface a problem; and so much more. Thus, the engineering investigations were, inexorably, situated ones done in and through the organized social setting within which the engineers worked. They consequently worked as practical sociologists, reasoning through their engineering conundrums and utilizing their knowledge of the ways of their organization.

Their investigations also involved them in attending to the ways of people who would use their technology and the ways of the social settings in which their technology would be located. They did this in the construction of people as social actors, the construction of social action types, attributions of judgment, locating their actors in social settings to determine their conduct, analyzing the working environment, and, again, so much more.

The adequacy of their engineering investigations is thus tied to the adequacy of their practical sociology, and it is in operating as practical sociologists that the engineers interweave the social and the technical. From our ethnomethodological orientation, the character of the relationship between the technical and the social is continually being assembled and reassembled for practical purposes in the work of the engineers as they confront the contingencies of technology production. Also, from an ethnomethodological orientation, to tell the engineers this would not be to tell them anything they did not know. The interest here has not been to reveal the entwined relationship of technological systems and the social but to explicate the ordered properties of that relationship as it is constituted in the collaborative work of engineers.

REFERENCES

Anderson, R. J., Button, G., & Sharrock, W. W. (1993a). Getting the design job done: Notes on the social organization of technical work. *Journal of Intelligent Systems*, 3(2–4), 319–344.

Anderson, R. J., Button, G., & Sharrock, W. W. (1993b). Supporting the design process within an organisational context. In G. de Michelis, C. Simone, & K. Schmidt (Eds.), *ECSCW '93: Third Conference on Computer-Supported Cooperative Work* (pp. 47–59). Milan: Kluwer.

Bijker, W. E., & Law, J. (1992). (Eds.). *Shaping technology/building society: Studies in sociotechnical change*. Cambridge, MA: MIT Press.

Bucciarelli, L. L. (1994). *Designing engineers*. Cambridge, MA: MIT Press.

Button, G. (Ed.). (1991). *Ethnomethodology and the human sciences*. Cambridge, England: Cambridge University Press.

Button, G. (1993). (Ed.). *Technology in working order: Studies of work, interaction, and technology*. London: Routledge & Kegan Paul.

Button, G., & Sharrock, W. W. (1994a). Occasioned practices in the work of software engineers. In M. Jarotka & J. A. Goguen (Eds.), *Requirement engineering* (pp. 215–240). New York: Academic Press.

Button, G., & Sharrock, W. W. (1994b). Practices in the work of ordering software development. In A. Firth (Ed.), *Negotiations in the workplace*. New York: Pergamon.

Button, G., & Sharrock, W. W. (1997). Project work: The organisation of collaborative design and development in software engineering. *Computer-Supported Cooperative Work*, pp. 369–386.

Button, G., & Sharrock, W. W. (in press). The organisational accountability of technological work. *Social Studies of Science*.

Garfinkel, H. (1967). *Studies in ethnomethodology*. Englewood Cliffs, NJ: Prentice-Hall.

Garfinkel, H. (1986). *Ethnomethodological studies of work*. London: Routledge & Kegan Paul.

Heritage, J. (1984). *Garfinkel and ethnomethodology*. Oxford, England: Polity.

Latour, B. (1996). *Aramis, or the love of technology*. Cambridge, MA: Harvard University Press.

MacKenzie, D., & Wajcman, J. (Eds.). (1985). *The social shaping of technology*. Milton Keynes, England: Open University Press.

MacKenzie, D. (1996). *Knowing machines: Essays on technical change*. Cambridge, MA: MIT Press.

Schutz, A. (1972). *The phenomenology of the social world* (G. Walsh & F. Lehnert, Trans.). London: Heinemann.

Sharrock, W. W., & Anderson, R. J. (1986). *The ethnomethodologists*. Chichester, England: Ellis Horwood.

Sharrock, W. W., & Anderson, R. J. (1993a). The user as a scenic feature of design. *Design Studies*, 5–18.

Sharrock, W. W., & Anderson, R. J. (1993b). Working towards agreement. In G. Button (Ed.), *Technology in working order: Studies of work, interaction, and technology* (pp. 149–161). London: Routledge & Kegan Paul.

Sharrock, W. W., Button, G., & Anderson, R. J. (forthcoming). *Inside design: Social and organizational aspects of the design process*. Mahwah, NJ: Lawrence Erlbaum Associates.

Woolgar, S. (1991). The turn to technology in social studies of science. *Science Technology and Human Values*, 16(1), 20–50.

5

Computer Systems as Text and Space: Toward a Phenomenological Hermeneutics of Development and Use

Jun Yoneyama
University of Aarhus, Denmark

What happens between the time when a system is completed and it is naturalized into use? This chapter addresses the Great Divide between systems development science and sociological inquiries into actual computer system use by focusing on the hermeneutical aspects of the design and use of computer systems. System development has focused intently on the methodological and procedural aspects leading to the design and construction of computer systems. By focusing on the process leading up to an implemented system, users have been considered through models or by having user representatives involved in the project. Less consideration has been given to the communicative aspects of moving between design and use, and to computer systems as carrier of communication.

This chapter aims to describe hermeneutical aspects of development and use of computer systems at the level of signs. The underlying metaphor is that the symbolic dimensions of computer systems may be addressed as if they were texts, and thereby enabling an analytical perspective on computer systems as more or less open, while at the same time stressing the dynamics involved in meaning production in the process of taking a system into use. The initial metaphor is the traversal of texts from writers to readers. By the application of Ricœur's phenenological hermeneutics (1979, 1981a, 1981b), the interpretation work inherent in the process of establishing usage habits are regarded as a kind of reading.

RICŒUR'S MODEL OF THE TEXT

This section presents Ricœur's hermeneutical philosophy of texts (Ricœur, 1979, 1981a, 1981b). Contrary to the romantic hermeneutics of the 19th century, the interplay between text and reader is central to Ricœur, so the hermeneutical process is not a quest for the intention of the writer but a process of making the text meaningful in the context of the reader. But this is not an a priori choice. It is a consequence of Ricœur's analysis of the phenomenology of text.

Basically, a text is a sequence of sentences, each sentence consisting of a sequence of words, each level contributing to the interpretation process and the phenomenology of the text in different ways. The level of words is covered by structural linguistics, the level of sentences by semantics. This distinction between structuralism and semantics is a stratification developed by Benveniste (1974). Semantics is here understood as the ability of a sentence to refer to a situation. By means of grammatical markings and other devices, the utterer may make the sentence refer to the situation where language is put to use.

Structuralist Signs

Structuralist linguistics (De Saussure, 1966) operates with a clear distinction between language system (langue) and language use (parole). The language system is the "language itself," the systematization of all distinguishable signs in a language. As a resource used in all instances of language use, the language system is not bound to a particular event and has been researched as a transcendental object with an objective existence.

The language system is a system of elements on two levels: an *expression level* and a *content level*. Signs are then defined as a combination of a *content element* and an *expression element*. The expression is the phonemes of word and the content is the corresponding mental representation. On the expression level, all representations are mutually separated from each other making them distinct units. On the content level, all the contents represented by the representations are likewise distinctively separated from each other. The distinctive differences between the elements on each plane are the main organizational principles of structural linguistics.

In the structuralist methodology, these differences may be uncovered through a commutation test. Taking as a premise the conjecture that distinctive differences on one level will show up as a corresponding difference on the other level, the commutation test is simply a substitution test in which parts of the element are substituted with something else. If the substitution causes a change on the other level, then a significant difference has been found.

The following is an example from Andersen (1990). In English, the *ng* and *n* sounds make a significant difference (commute) on the content level in "sing" versus "sin," but not in the word *in(g)cline.*

The commutation test is a methodical consequence of the view that neither content nor expression elements are regarded to have substantial existence but only exist as differences. Another consequence is that the constituting differences are immanent in the system, isolating the signs from the world.

Ricœur argued that structuralism cannot by itself explain texts and language use, because the situatedness of any language use contributes to the production of meaning.

Semantic References

The limitation of the language system is that signs do not refer by themselves to the world. A sign has a distinctive existence by its part being different from any other corresponding part of other signs. Signs may then be said to have a distinctive meaning, but this meaning is enclosed in the language system. According to Benveniste (1974), what makes meaningful dialogue possible when communication is an exchange of signs, is the ability of sentences to refer to a world.

> With semantics we enter the specific mode of meaning caused by the discourse. The problems raised here are related to the language as producer of messages. A message cannot be reduced to a succession of units, which are identified separately; it is not an accumulation of signs, which create meaning. On the contrary it is the meaning (the "intended"), globally conceived, which realizes and divides itself in distinctive "signs," which are words. Furthermore, semantics govern necessarily the totality of referents, whereas semiotics in principle is precluded from and is independent of all references. The semantic order is identical to the world of enunciation and the world of discourse. (Benveniste, 1974, p. 64)

Sentences are more than a simple aggregation of signs; a semantic structure is added that makes the sentence able to refer to the speaker, the listener, the temporal situation (the "now"), and the situation. Ricœur called these references *ostensive,* as they are references rooted in the situatedness of the discourse. There is no doubt about who the "me" in an utterance in a discourse is, because the utterer is present in the situation.

The ability of sentences to refer to the world is dialectically connected to the meaning of the sentence. By ostensive references the sentence is able to point out objects in the context and thereby say something about them. The sentences are meaningful by being able to say something about something.

At this point, Ricœur substituted the Saussurian *parole* with the term *discourse.* Where *parole* is as a simple instance of diachronic application of the language system, *discourse* is a situated use of language by someone, to say something about something, to some other person. Or, in short, discourse is the process where sentences are understood as referential and meaningful units.

Writing

For Ricœur, discourse is an intermediate concept that he used to emphasize the changes brought about by writing "the fixation of the discourse in external marks" (1981b, p. 199).

The externalization separates the writer's situated writing and intention from the range of possible interpretations of the text. The ostensive references of a discourse common to speaker and listener are absent, and even if writers try to use references to their context, readers have to guess what the writers really referred to, as the writers' context is unavailable to the reader.

But texts can have references. The characteristics of textual references are just different from the ostensive references of the discourse. In the intentional act of writing, the references of the text are connected to the intended meaning of the writer. But as soon as the text is written, they lose the immediate meaning that characterized the ostensive references of the discourse. Ricœur called these textual references *nonostensive references*, because it is the immediacy of the ostensive references that are lost. When the immediateness of the references are lost, the act of reading becomes a process whereby the references are made actual in the new context of the reader. Thus, the interpretation of a text is then a quest for the meaning of the text—not as a meaning immanent in the text by itself, but meaning as created in the meeting between the text and the reader. The act of reading is a discourse in the sense of a reinstallment of the text in the immediate situation. In this way, a text is able to refer to more than its writer's discourse, because the references in the text may come to refer to any reader's discourse through acts of reading.

Ricœur listed four kinds of nonostensive references. They each characterize a difference between discourse and text:

> Where the discourse is an event in time, a written text may be read at any time. The "now" of the text is a past for any reader and is thus no more the event as event but the event as remembered or narrated.

> The writer is also absent at the time of reading—if not absent in person then as the writer at the time of writing.

> Just as the "now" of the discourse is immediate, its context is immediate and implicit. But the context of the writer and the context of the reader are different.

A text may be addressed to somebody, but it is not possible to predict who eventually reads it. So where the discourse has a known dialogue partner, a text may be read by anyone capable of reading the language.

Discourse is restricted to the situation, whereas a text is public in a much broader sense. It is available to interpretation for anybody who understands the language. So any ostensive reference to the "now," the "me," the situation, and the "you" is lost in writing and survives in the text as nonostensive references. These references have to be actualized in the world of the reader in order to regain meaning.

Interpretation

Now that the original single intention of the writer is lost and with that, the immediate situatedness of the discourse, the text moves away from its writer, creating a distance between the writer's intention and the literal meaning of the text. This does not mean the writer can be ignored altogether but that the text acquires an independence that a reader no longer can trace back to the writer's intention.

Obviously, this makes it not only possible, but also legitimate, for a text to generate meanings that were not a part of the writer's intention, because of reading circumstances not anticipated by the writer. This should not be confused with misinterpretation, which is an interpretation of a text without sufficient basis in the text itself. When a text does generate unintended meanings, this is not solely an accomplishment of a creative reader, but a result of the interplay between the reader's world and the text's semantic structure. Because the nonostensive references in the text are inscribed in a semantic structure, the text is said to have attained a semantic independence.

STRUCTURALISTIC AND SEMANTIC UNITS IN COMPUTER SYSTEMS

Computer systems and use of computer systems do not fall readily into just one of Ricœur's descriptions of language, discourse, and text. Just like texts, there are permanent features that do not change during use. They may be interpreted and resituated giving new meanings, but they cannot be changed. These features are mainly the elements provided by the designer. So the computer system may be regarded as a kind of work traversing from designer to user, paralleling the traversal of texts from writer to readers.

But this is just one aspect of computer systems. Many computer systems make communication between users possible, thus making the computer system resemble a language and computer use resemble discourse. This makes the use of computer systems fall somewhere between the characteristics of interpreting text and discourse.

As a discourse, the use is an event in time and may refer to the user and elements of the use situation. But the use of computer systems does not usually involve the copresence of a dialogue partner. In a few situations like computer-mediated video conferences, the use situation is more like a true discourse, but more often the dialogue partner present is the computer system itself. The meaning of a discourse is not intended for the computer system but for a known or unknown future user. The discursive result is then a kind of text that traverses from a user to the same or another user. This said, the actual use of a computer system still resembles a discourse as a situated act.

Even if this picture to some extent deconstructs the concepts formulated by Ricœur, the background of his analysis is still relevant for an understanding of computer systems as hermeneutic objects. Following Ricœur's analysis, the first interesting question is whether it is possible to find levels of analysis similar to the structuralistic and semantic levels of the text. This depends on the question of how users may see elements in the computer systems as references to the world.

References

In graphical user interfaces, as exemplified by Apple Macintosh and Microsoft Windows, it is easy to find obvious candidates of references in computer systems. The cursor represents the user, the hard disk and floppy disk icons refer to the corresponding physical units, a mailbox icon may represent another person on the network that may be e-mailed. These elements seem to fulfill the role of ostensive references in the discourse, representing "me," things in the context, and "you," respectively. However, there are two factors that should be considered in this interpretation.

First, the elements are not created by the user but are provided by the developer. In use the cursor is representing "me," but from the point of view of the developer the cursor is representing the user as an "interactive agent" as inscribed into the system (Latour, 1996; Latour & Akrich, 1992). It is not representing me as an actual user—a person with a history, body, and being present in the situation.

Second, how does anybody know that the elements represent what they do? By experience (and hopefully through manuals too) people know the elements should be used in certain ways that are connected with their reference. Dropping a text document on an icon representing a colleague's mailbox icon may really cause the e-mail to be received, but individuals have to interact with the element to know this and need to know or experience which elements can interact with each other.

The interactivity of computer systems has to be considered as an integral characteristic of computer-based signs. In short, how can icons and cursors be analyzed as interactive signs?

Computer Semiotics

An answer to this question may be found in computer semiotics. Computer semiotics is a new discipline being developed primarily by Andersen (1990, 1992, 1993). He developed a semiotic description of computers linking user interface concerns with work language analysis.

In a description of a user interface as signs, the linguistic sign concept is not adequate. Whereas written signs are permanent and, at least in principle, unchangeable, Andersen found two kinds of features unique to computer-based signs: *transience* and *interactivity* (Andersen, 1990, p. 178). *Transient features* are features that may change during use of the system. In Windows, the cursor may change between an arrow and an hourglass indicating changes of program status. *Interactive features* are features open for interaction by the user. The cursor changes position when the mouse is moved, and buttons change shape when pressed; both are examples of interactive features.

But not all changes are commutational. When one applies the commutation test on computer-based signs, not all graphical changes do create corresponding changes in meaning. On the Macintosh, the cursor changes to a clock face when the user is expected to wait. The change between arrow and clock face indicate changes in the interaction status; not every change on the clock face corresponds to meaningful changes.

Semantics of Computer Systems

In use, the buttons and the cursor form a semantic unit. Both the button and the cursor are provided by the designer, and in the following they are regarded as a kind of sentence.

As a semantic unit a button and a cursor together constitute the prerequisites for action, the cursor referring to the user and the button to a functionality built into the system. As an event, the press on the button through the cursor is an act resembling the dicourse. The cursor refers to the user, the "me," ostensively and the action of the button may be dependent of the actual state of the system, the context of the act. The discursive features are rooted in the user's being-in-the-world even when there is no dialogue partner present.

But the cursor + button sentence may also be seen as elements in a system resembling a language. A computer system usually does have a certain proportion of invariant elements. The permanent features obviously do not change through use. Transient features may also be invariant if they only change between a closed set of fixed values, as buttons that may have two states: pressed and not pressed. Also, functionality is usually invariant or only variant inside a closed set of possibilities. All these invariant elements resemble the structuralist concept of a language system because they are "outside time" being permanent regardless of when and where the system is put to use. Whereas the cursor refers to the user as being present in the situation, the button refers to the presence of an available functionality in the system. One perspective on use of a computer system is that use is the application of functionality to data. More generally, the permanent features of a computer system are resources in the act of using the system. The language systemlike features of the semantic unit are rooted in the computer system being a resource for action. Resources that are applied in situ. (This aspect is elaborated later.)

Computer systems also share characteristics with text: the ability to convey information across time and space, possibly being accessible for a wide variety of users, being written in one context and usually being used in another, and so forth. Just as text is detached from the writer, computer systems are detached from the designer. Where the detachment of text is a separation of the writer's intention and the literal meaning of the text, the detachment of computer system separates the designer's intention and the system as an article for everyday use.

This has consequences for computer systems regarded as media. Contrary to linguistic communication, computer-based communication is characterized by involving a third party besides the sender and the receiver (Andersen, 1990). The third party is the *designer*, who establishes the possibility of communication. Whereas the sender is the direct author of the message, the designer is an indirect author by virtue of providing the framework in which the communication takes place.

A *structuralistic analysis* is an analysis of the invariable elements in a text that are objectively observable. But where texts are regarded as unchangeable, computer systems often are developed in versions; so, in contrast to most literary works, computer systems change over time. This makes computer systems resemble other kinds of texts, like laws, regulations, and price lists. This is a difference in genre and not a fundamental difference between texts and computer systems. The prototypical computer system just happens to be nonfiction system and the prototypical text, for Ricœur, is fiction. An interesting prospect could be to conduct genuine narrative analysis of computer games in the adventure genre, as this may show the possiblities and limitations on interactivity in rich semantic settings.

INTERPRETATION OF COMPUTER SYSTEMS

This section is an example of how hermeneutical theory may be applied on specific kinds of computer systems. It is not a presentation of a methodology but a demonstration of how a hermeneutical perspective may change the understanding of well-known systems.

As already noted, computer systems have languagelike features when regarded as providers of communication. The following example is expanded from an analysis in Yoneyama (1992). Here databases are regarded as communication systems connecting different work practices of an organization. As part of this perspective, the conceptual schema of the database may be regarded as a description of the syntactic and semantic rules governing the communication. Usually, records in a database may only have a fixed number of fields and the content of these may be restricted by rules. Changes to the conceptual schema must be done explicitly and changes concern all records of the same type. All records are assumed to have only a single nonoverlapping type.

At the structural level, the conceptual schema may then be viewed as a kind of language system, being a closed system of nonoverlapping classes. The conceptual schema also describes the kinds of records that can possibly be communicated through the database, indirectly referring to the objects that may be the content of the communication. In this example there is a clear distinction between the "language system" level and the "language use" level. Also, the database schema has primacy to the database use, but unlike language the database schema does only change through deliberate actions by a developer.

On the semantic level, the records may be analyzed as varieties of simple sentences. The key refers to and identifies the object concerned and the other fields describe relevant features of the object. As a kind of constative (Austin, 1962/1975), a record is a sentence following the classical subject + predicate form. Like Ricœur's nonostensive references, the sentence cannot refer to a "now," "me," situation, and "you" directly, but have to rely on nonostensive references in the sentence. These nonostensive references have to be actualized in the world of the reader to regain meaning. Usually, there are very few nonostensive references at all in a database record. It may be possible to see the "now" as a simple time stamp, but a time stamp says nothing about the "now" as an event. Likewise, it is usually impossible to see who created the record, and under which circumstances. The only reference left in the record is the symbolic reference to the object.

COMPUTER SYSTEMS AS SPACES
OF ACTION POSSIBILITIES

Computer systems may be interacted with, so their interpretation has to include the possibilities of acting. An interpretation of computer systems is therefore also an interpretation of action possibilities. The implicit question is not simply "what the meaning of" specified elements in the system are, but also "what is the meaning of the possibility of doing this." The question is not only "why does it says that . . . ," but a "why may I . . ." and "why does it do this, when I . . ." Because of this, a hermeneutical understanding of computer systems cannot be just a metaphorical application of an understanding of texts. It also has to include an understanding of computer systems as spaces of action possibilities.

Word processors are designed as flexible writing tools, but their flexibility is limited by cultural conventions. It is usually not possible to write vertically as in East Asia, or to imagine the paper as vertically finite but horizontally infinite. These conventions are inherited from the typewriter; but, in the computer, there are no technical reasons for limitations on either the direction of writing or size of the virtual paper (ignoring the printer). Looking for limitations may reveal implicit assumptions about the use built into the system (Akrich, 1992; see also Berg, in press; Timmermans & Berg, in press).

This line of argument is not a defense of "infinitely flexible systems"—if anything like that were are all possible. The value of word processors is that they offer solutions to recognized problems, but flexibility is a condition for a system to be used in more than specific known situations. The designer cannot predict all premises, so the system has to be flexible to be useful. Flexibility is therefore a kind of sturdiness in unknown or unpredictable surroundings. In this way, flexibility has a family resemblance with nonostensive references.

Users and Developers

A study of spreadsheet users (Nardi & Miller, 1991) observed that the use of spreadsheets blurs the distinction between users and developers. To use a spreadsheet system is to develop a spreadsheet (see also Mackay, 1990; Nardi, 1993).

If users and developers are considered from the concept of "space of action possibilities," then it seems reasonable to see users as people who actualize and use a system's space of action possibilities, and developers as people who create or change this space. From this point of view, it is not possible to distinguish between developers and users by considering whether their work is done before or after the system is finished. Any change affecting the space of action possibilities is development work—even when the sole user of the change is oneself and even if the roles change back and forth all the time.

In Microsoft Word, text may be formatted with styles selected from a selection list. The list is a closed set of styles that may be selected but it is possible to design new ones besides those delivered with the system. When a user starts designing a new style, the space of action possibilities changes and, from this point of view, the user assumes a developer's role.

BETWEEN EXPERIMENTAL AND EXPERIENTIAL USE

According to Ricœur, the literary work as a whole refers to existential problems and myths in the culture. This may also be true when considering narrative computer systems like games and interactive fiction, but the paradigmatic case of computer systems is systems built as tools to solve or support everyday problems. As such, computer systems do not refer to existential problems but to the problems they are built to solve or support. They do this regardless of whether they were built as bureaucratic devices or as flexible tools for craftspeople.

Ehn (1988) discussed the toolness of computer systems as a design ideal that fits the general program of participatory design. Here workers are understood as craftspeople; computer systems should therefore not merely establish efficient bureaucratic orders but also support craftsmanship and the continuous development of the craft. Referring to Heidegger's phenomenology of tools, Ehn proposed toolness as a mode of design that supports and respects users as craftspeople.

In Heideggerian phenomenology, tools may be *ready at hand*, meaning that consciousness is focused at the object of work, and the tool is regarded as an extension to the body. If the tool somehow draws attention to itself, it is *present at hand*—the focus of the mind. This process of changing attention from work-object to tool is called a *breakdown*. By creating and questioning breakdown situations using participative design methods such as mock-ups and prototypes, the user may actively contribute to the evaluation of design proposals experientially.

Ihde (1979) connected the Heideggerian phenomenological analysis of tools with hermeneutical aspects in a discussion of scientific instruments. Here toolness and hermeneuticness are conceived as different kinds of relations between the user and the world. The toolness relation is called an *embodiment relation*, because the instrument is conceived as an extension to the body, amplifying some aspects and reducing other aspects. A telephone amplifies the user's hearing so communication over long distance is possible, but at the same time sight is reduced, which means gestures are not visible to the dialogue partner.

Hermeneutical relations are those where the instrument is a necessity to access parts of the world unavailable through normal senses. The relation between a user and the world is mediated through the instrument. The world is not available directly to the senses, so the output of the instument can only be conceived as something to be interpreted in order to get information about the world it displays. The world is experienced through the machine. Ihde showed these relations as :

Embodiment relation: (User–Machine)–World

Hermeneutic relation: User–(Machine–World)

Computer systems are hermeneutical machines because they show the world symbolically and in a mediated form. Ehn's design ideal points out the possibility of computer systems simulating tools and thereby be used in a kind of symbolically mediated embodiment relation.

In a computer-based drawing tool, all the elements are symbols: the virtual paper, the pencil, the rubber gum, and so on. In use, the system may still be understood as a framework that allows certain computer-based tools to be available for work on computer-based material. Here devices like mice and drawing tablets are important because they can translate human gestures into the symbolic world of the computer system.

This does not invalidate a hermeneutical phenomenology of computer systems. Computer-based tools like pencil, rubber gum, and so on are simulations created by a combination of gesture devices, discursive features, and clever design. Computer-based tools may rest on preunderstanding and experiences with their real-world cousins, but the relation is a metaphorical relation and only selected features are implemented.

In a broader sense, computer systems may be regarded as a kind of tool, in the sense that they are a means to an end. Here the mediated relation between the user and the world is not regarded on an amplification–reduction scale, but as a resource that may be put to use.

This does not make Ehn's use of Heidegger's concepts irrelevant. The ready-to-hand experience of computer-based tools corresponds to what Ricœur described as the *actualization* of the semantic references in the text. In the act of reading, all the intermediate procedures of interpretation are carried out, but the attention is focused on the story. In this mode of reading, the reader is said to understand the text.

Correspondingly, when the text is present at hand, the structuralistic and semantic structures may be read without paying attention to the story. Ricœur stressed that the structuralistic–semantic analysis of a text depends on an understanding of the text as work. In the following examples (paraphrasing Ihde), the relations between the user and different aspects of meaning in computer systems are shown.

The use of a computer system pays attention to the objects of work and aspects relevant to the working situation. This is where the computer system is used as a means to an end and thus resembles the use of tools as resources. In this mode of use, the experience with the system is important. Only if the user is skilled in using the system can the system gain the transparency characteristic of a toollike use. When the system is used as a tool in the user's work situation, the role of the system may be depicted in this way:

Use of system as resource: (User–System)–Work situation

When attention is focused on the system itself, the relation is different. When the system is read as a text, the nonostensive references and the space of action possibilities are regarded as something created by the developer. The reading of a computer system is a reading of the meaning of the system. In this mode, the use of the computer may be experimentally, the reading being an analysis of what is possible in the system and the intended use in the design.

Reading the system: User–(System–Design/Designer)

The last relation concerns the data put into the system by the same or other users. These data may refer to actual objects of interest for the organization or simply be e-mail messages. Here the references are not created by the developer, but by a user. This relation accounts for the difference between the system itself and the accumulation of references entered through former use.

Reading data: User–(System–World of another user)

Sometimes the last set of parentheses may be absent (e.g., when the provider of the data is known as in e-mail messages), but, as noted, in database systems the world of the sender may very often remain opaque because contextual information regarding the situation where the data was entered usually is not maintained in the system.

Computer-based signs have features in common with language, discourse, and text; and, so as long as the features of a tool can be given a symbolic form, the tool may be replicated on a computer.

A HERMENEUTICAL PERSPECTIVE
ON COMPUTER SYSTEMS

Until now, the hermeneutical philosophy of Ricœur has been applied as if the interpretation of computer systems is a possibility for every computer user, as is interpretation of literature for every reader. This does not have to be so, because it is possible to make significant parts of a computer system opaque to a user. Teller machines may show many useful information about accounts, but they do not show that the bank automatically transfers money in and out of the account. Nor do they show how the system is maintained by personnel. So a possible guess is that teller machines are devices that transfer money from the invisible inside of a plastic card to physical bank notes. For a person totally ignorant of how bank accounts are managed, it is impossible to get enough information to see what really happens behind the scenes solely from the user interface of the machine. So it is fair to assume that it is possible to make computer systems opaque, preventing a user to go beyond pure guessing.

A hermeneutic perspective on computer systems is on the other hand of increasing importance. In internal MIS departments, for example, the main development effort is directed at users in the organization and the distance between developers and users is manageable through direct contact. With the growing importance of mass-produced system, this distance increases and users change from being a community to a public. How do developers maintain contact (or even a dialogue) with hundreds of thousands of users spread all over the world? These considerations are not new to other mass market products but raise new challenges for the art and science of developing computer systems. If the hermeneutical issues raised here are shown to be important in understanding the use of computer systems, then hermeneutics may be a useful foundation to the analysis of this distanciation.

CONCLUSIONS

This chapter has shown that the traversal of computer systems from development to use in not a trivial process. Many layers of description are relevant and must be considered to adequately account for the distanciation of the computer system from the context of development to the actualization into the context of use.

Considering computer systems as texts may account for important aspects on the production of meaning in relation to computer systems. Where the hermeneutical distance between developers and users accounts for the openness of possible uses, the phenomenological description still needs to reach behind the metaphors. A conceptualization of computer systems as spaces of action possibilities is suggested as an initial description of what traverses from development to use.

The view presents two challenges for further research: With systems considered as spaces of action possibilities, the system development process does not end with the project, but continues through users' actualization of the computer system when they establish their usage. A "theory of taking systems into use" corresponding to theories of reading, as the complement to system development theory is the first challenge. The relation between development and use, on the other hand, is as much a social process as a communication of computer-based signs, so a symmetric sociological analysis covering both development and use is just as challenging a possibility.

ACKNOWLEDGMENTS

The work in this chapter has been made possible by a scholarship grant from Aarhus University Research Foundation. Randi Markussen, Peter Bøgh Andersen, Kim Halskov Madsen, and Geoffrey Bowker have been most helpful with critique, suggestions, and all other sorts of help and support.

REFERENCES

Akrich, M. (1992). The de-scription of technical objects. In W. E. Bijker & J. Law (Eds.), *Shaping technology/building society: Studies in technological systems* (pp. 205–225). Cambridge, MA: MIT Press.

Andersen, P. B. (1990). *Computer semiotics*. Cambridge, England: Cambridge University Press.

Andersen, P. B. (1992). Computer semiotics. *Scandinavian Journal of Information Systems, 4,* 3–30.

Andersen, P. B. (1993). A semiotic approach to programming. In P. Andersen, B. Holmqvist, & J. F. Jensen (Eds.), *Computers as media* (pp. 16–68). Cambridge, England: Cambridge University Press.

Austin, J. L. (1975). *How to do things with words.* New York: Oxford University Press. (Original work published 1962)

Benveniste, É. (1974). *Problèmes de linguistique générale, II* [General problems of linguistics]. Paris: Gallimard.

Berg, M. (in press). *Rationalizing medical work. Decision support techniques and medical practices.* Cambridge, MA: MIT Press.

De Saussure, F. (1966). *Course in general linguistics.* New York: McGraw-Hill. (Original work published 1916)

Ehn, P. (1988). *Work-oriented design of computer artifacts.* Stockholm: Arbeitslivscentrum.

Ihde, D. (1979). *Technics and praxis.* Dortrecht, The Netherlands: D. Reidel.

Latour, B. (1990). *Aramis, or the love of technology*. Cambridge, MA: Harvard University Press.

Latour, B., & Akrich, M. (1992). A summary of a convenient vocabulary of the semiotics of human and nonhuman assemblies. In W. E. Bijker & J. Law (Eds.), *Shaping technology/building society: Studies in technological systems* (pp. 259–264). Cambridge, MA: MIT Press.

Mackay, W. (1990). *Users and customizable software: A co-adaptive phenomenon*. Unpublished doctoral dissertation, Sloan School of Management, MIT.

Nardi, B. (1993). *A small matter of programming*. Cambridge, MA: MIT Press.

Nardi, B. A., & Miller, J. R. (1991). Twinkling lights and nested loops: Distributed problem solving and spreadsheet development. *International Journal of Man–Machine Studies, 34*, 161–184.

Ricœur, P. (1979). *Fortolkningsteori* [Interpretation theory]. Copenhagen: Vintens forlag.

Ricœur, P. (1981a). The model of the text: Meaningful action considered as text. In J. B. Thompson (Ed.), *Hermeneutics and the human sciences* (pp. 197–221). New York: Cambridge University Press. (Original work published 1970)

Ricœur, P. (1981b). What is a text? Explanation and understanding. In J. B. Thompson (Ed.), *Hermeneutics and the human sciences* (pp. 145–164). New York: Cambridge University Press. (Original work published 1970)

Timmermans, S., & Berg, M. (in press). Standardization in action: Achieving universalism and localization in medical protocols. *Social Studies of Science*.

Yoneyama, J. (1992). *Perspektiver og informationsmodeller* [Perspectives and information models]. Unpublished thesis, Department of Information and Media Science, Aarhus University.

INTRODUCTION: DESIGN THEORY AND CSCW

Les Gasser
National Science Foundation, Arlington, Virginia

This section deals primarily with issues in the design and development of socially integrated collaborative computing across diverse communities. For the most part, they share several perspectives on the key dimensions of the nature of human activity, the nature and role of representation, and on the nature and processes of design.

Change to systems of human activity is a critical dimension of computerization. Bodker and Christiansen, Robinson, and Axel mention that designing socially embedded computing systems means examining the way work is done and changing organizations themselves. Thus, a natural question is what are basic approaches to action and process that designers can use to conceptualize and analyze human activity and change? Similarly, the design of socially embedded systems involves representations in several ways. Representations serve as parts of systems themselves (e.g., as representation of knowledge or of process), and they also serve as tools and methods in design processes. All of the chapters in this section have something to say about the nature and practice of representation, and its critical role in system content and in design process. Treatment of design itself is a third dimension that unites them. Design is seen as a key stage in the process of integrating technical systems and their social contexts. But, in addition, design processes themselves are organized human activities, part of the contingent and dynamic stream of the social life of all design participants. Integrating and balancing the differing roles, worldviews, and interests of designers and users in the midst of system conception and construction is one of the primary tasks to be faced.

ACTIVITY AND ITS ROLE

For these authors the activity of people is complex and modeling that activity is tricky. Robinson's chapter takes the view that models, procedures, and scenarios are "tin ducks" that keep coming back to haunt analysts of computerization. Many analysts, he notes, treat procedures as actions whose outcomes are specified in advance, analogous to the technical notion of algorithms: procedures that are guaranteed to terminate and return an answer. However, for Robinson, procedures do not necessarily exist independently of inquiries that people make about them. Managing the outcome of a procedure also means managing the procedure through its life, and managing the meaning or interpretation of the outcome. There is in principle no "guaranteed outcome." Useful human action is locally situated, whereas procedures are not—they are decontextualized systems of instructions. Formal procedures can be useful as a "way in" to a situation for beginners, and they cover participants themselves against blame: A participant can say "we followed the procedure." Procedures can serve as the core objects in a "dialogue over a boundary," namely, a dialogue among those inside and those outside a work situation. Procedures are not algorithms for producing work (because they are contingent and out of context) but instead are representations for consumption by outsiders.

In empirical studies of the information-management activities of people in relation to libraries (not reported here), Neumann and Bishop reported that people fall into two classes: Novices in a field often search for and retrieve information (e.g., from libraries), whereas more expert users "have been at their work long enough to have built up the social networks and power to be able to avoid libraries and command personal forces in seeking information" (personal communication, Bishop, July 9, 1996). That is, the formal information search and retrieval tools and procedures of libraries are often bypassed by experts, who replace them with ongoing social arrangements through which information flows naturally and continuously, without explicit "search" or "retrieval" activities. Formal tool-supported search and retrieval processes are, in effect, replaced by ongoing dynamic networked social processes for experts.

This notion of activity as informal and widely integrated social networks has important implications for design of computer support for information-intensive applications (e.g., for distributed "digital libraries"). Social tools for information management may become more effective for professional clients by supporting ways to establish and maintain systems of ongoing social relations, as well as by providing indexing, search, and retrieval procedures. Or, looked at another way, technological and nontechnological means for maintaining social arrangements are necessary adjuncts to formal procedures for information management as communities rely more on virtual and "nonmaterial couplings" among their members.[1]

This view of activity is very close to what several of the authors in this section are saying: In many settings, formal procedures of work are irrelevant to the people doing the work; people rely instead of ongoing, distributed, continuously adaptive social relations and processes to get work done. For Axel, people's activity is multifaceted, with no single goal, no unequivocal intent, and continual balancing. For Robinson, using procedures as foundations for designing collaborative computing is a partial solution, because the procedures are not what makes work happen. They are often the post-hoc rationalized accounts of work. Procedures, in effect, become a sort of language or code for collapsing complex arrangements of social relations into what only appears to be a simple and mechanically repeatable system of activity. The issue of how reflective representations of work interact with the work itself is ripe for investigation.

Another feature of activity is the integration of action, communication (in several modes), and artifacts themselves. For Robinson, activity is always social, and is mediated by tools, communication, and the division of labor. Artifacts pass back and forth among roles in activity. Robinson notes that two modes of communication are needed. He calls these "formal," by which he means formal joint manipulation of an artifact or a world, and "cultural," by which he means wideranging, open, poetical, and discourse-oriented communication.

Poitou notes that action is channeled by its human and material environment as much as by the wills of actors (their goals and visions). A key point made by Poitou is that what he calls "intellectual objects" (objects that inherently embody knowledge in some fashion) are organized via, and are ongoing parts of, a "master discourse" of activity and com-

---

[1]Aramis' engineers in Latour (1995) needed to supply "nonmaterial coupling" among the individual train cars to make their flexible distributed transportation system work. This means new forms of nonmaterial coupling among people who are migrating their communities and working practices from the concretely materialized worlds of physical resources such as manufactured parts, paper forms, and hard copy reports, books or journals, to the dynamic distributed, virtual worlds of electronic communications and computational representations of things physical.

munication. This master discourse is an overarching, governing, extra-individual patterning process that helps to shape individual activity. The master discourse is in part a pattern or system of social relations within which action takes place. In this master discourse, or rather as a part of it, an organization is an ever-evolving, dynamic system of alliances.

TYPES AND ROLES OF REPRESENTATION

Representations are critical as both the outcomes of design processes—formal ways of capturing the results of design—and as dynamic tools in that process. The roles of representation in design are complex; in part they are seen as means, not ends. They are seen as complex and reflexive encodings of human activity; and, as Macias-Chapula points out, there may be as many representations as there are participants in a situation.

Tools—the outcomes of design activity and representation—are themselves representations of that activity and of the underlying individual, organizational, and social processes. Poitou notes that "a tool is product of social activity and thus in general embodies more information and possibilities than the individual who uses it." For him, a tool embodies knowledge (e.g., task knowledge) so is a special kind of "intellectual object," not just a random object. This intellectual content is an attribute of "toolness." The same can be said of human spaces, and other materializations of human activity. For Poitou, then, tools are documents that appear in nonlinguistic form.

Robinson's view of the role of models in design is that they are only useful as an active part of the design process—as agents in a dialogue—rather than as passive and objectified representations of a design result, or of a world into which a designed artifact will fit. (Poitou would call such models intellectual objects.) In the abstract, for Robinson, models are materializations that make dialogues possible. Models are not valuable as representations, but rather as reference points for reflective activity. He draws on Lynch's insight to point out that theoretical diagrams are useful in design dialogues as ways analogous to how armatures are supportive structuring devices in movement or sculpture. For Robinson, models must be understood as pointing to an external world, in order to support such reflective (e.g., design) activity, but are seen as separate from that world. By contrast, in Agre's personal project to reform artificial intelligence (AI; a branch of computing deeply involved with core issues of representation), he notes AI's common "tendency to conflate representations and things-represented."

Blomberg, Suchman, and Trigg employed case-based prototypes as representations of systems and activities in design. These prototypes served as triggers for discussion and for mutual learning, not just as product proxies. These researchers studied the development of a group work support system for a law firm that engaged in two different kinds of legal activity: corporate law (drawing up contracts and other documents) and litigation (taking cases to trial). In corporate law, the dominant activity is the creation of documents, whereas litigation usually requires locating and accessing archived documents. Documents in this law firm were are rarely drafted from scratch; prior documents are used as prototypes and modified to fit new circumstances, making the corporate law document creation process a deeply historical one.

The collection of documents that the firm had produced in the past comprised what Blomberg et al. call the "articulated memory" of the law firm and its lawyers. This articulated memory appears in the form of both the office documents themselves, and in the arrangement of those documents. One attorney kept a collection of prototype documents that he called a "form file," spread through his office, on the floor, in file cabinets, and so on. The form file was used by a number of other attorneys—it was a collective repository. The physical arrangement of this collection was—for Blomberg, Suchman, and Trigg—an articulation and materialization of the personal and corporate memory, and as such it became important in the retrieval process (cf. the discussion of information management applications). The physical organization of this sort of repository has implications for joint work when the organizing schemes are shared among the participants in the firm. Converting such a collection (in which the physical manifestation plays a critical role) to electronic format means reorienting the articulated memory from a physical manifestation to a virtual one (it means dematerializing the articulated memory and changing the foundation of its "geography"). It also means, as part of a design process that integrates these representations, managing the geographic transformation over time via a careful system design and implementation process.

In addition to form and physicality, modality of representation can be critical. For the lawyers studied by Blomberg et al., format and structure cues were important for information retrieval, but they were represented pictorially, in the layout of the legal documents; thus, maintaining a pictorial view of these documents, even at reduced scale and in unreadable form, was a critical strategy beyond textual encoding.

Representations require interpretation (they are constructed out of human and social activity—the intellectual objects of Poitou) and must be translated back into human activity to be useful. For Agre, technical specifications and papers are representational narratives to be interpreted. Robinson uses Lynch's compelling images of Audubon's bird illustrations placed in museums, in history texts, or on postage stamps to show how representations take their meanings from their contexts, and how these meanings are constructed through relations with other context elements and within the transactions in which the representations are used.

DESIGN PROCESS AND CONTENT

A process of design is by nature a process of balancing and adjusting interacting demands and interacting processes. The process of design is as important as the products of design, both in leading to workable products, and as the first stage in the ongoing process of assimilating design results into contexts and settings of their use.

For Robinson, design is the management of mutual understanding—managing the collision of heterogeneous "immutable mobiles." Bodker and Christiansen point out that design means embodying and communicating ideas, dropping old conceptualizations and grasping new ones, and facilitating shared understandings (boundary mediation). Axel notes that "the possibility and ease of computerization is thus dependent on the relation between the interpreting, meaning producing, and gap closing aspect of human action and the produced formalistic tools." Robinson points out that because procedures are incomplete and decontextualized with respect to in-vivo human activity, the activity of design (and the human processes that are its outcome) must focus on managing social relations, not on following procedures. As an alternative, Bodker and Christiansen advocate a "tool-box" approach to joint design that they suggest involves checklists, examples, and outlines—not procedures. For Poitou, the aim of design is to discover how to organize intellectual objects in one's workplace as a "storage" for knowledge and then how to use this organization for just-in-time retrieval of that knowledge (and possibly retrieval into direct action, rather than into planning, thought, or reflection).

For Bodker and Christiansen, design leads to change, which is expansion of work practice. A principal question is how (and to what extent) to integrate the worlds of design situations (the practices of designers) and use situations (the practices of users). Blomberg et al. wonder how it is possible to bridge developers' work with work practice and work experience of users in the sites of use. How can developers gain knowledge of the sites of use? For them, this is possible through direct experience in the site, meetings and communications, and through the use of models and prototypes. But the site of use is often a different place from the site of development spatiotemporally, culturally, and in many other ways. It is not in general possible to bring the site of system development and the site of use together in all ways, so the gap is a fundamental and ongoing one. The issue faced by many of these authors is how can this gap be bridged? Robinson's chapter recapitulates this issue, pointing out that designer and user communities do not necessarily intersect in their social relations. But the dilemma is, if they do not intersect, how are meanings to be managed toward the goal of creating "mutual understandings"? On the other hand, if communities' social relations do intersect, the question is, how are interactions managed?

For Agre, the gap is wide and is made visible in the forms of discourse in design and user worlds. His own experience of the divide addressed in this book is made compelling in his statement that "it is useless to speak nontechnical languages to people who are trying to translate these languages into specifications for technical mechanisms." Here again is the dilemma often faced by users dealing with designers. A designer's "extensive network of linguistic forms, habits of thought, established techniques, ritualized work practices, ways of framing questions and answers, genre conventions, and so forth" cannot simply be jettisoned or ignored. This is a continual dilemma of design. Just as Agre was trying to formulate an alternative worldview from a position within the culture and practice of AI, any designer has to formulate an alternative worldview (that of the situation of use) from within the situation and culture of system design. As Agre points out, it impossible both to cast off this culture and to remove oneself from it. He goes on to articulate the four kinds of difficulty: becoming aware of conventions, reducing alternatives to novel technical methods, governing the interpretation of technical methods or artifacts, and actually applying a new method into an existing network of practices heavily conditioned by (and indeed defining and constituting) the existing situation-of-use world.

Bodker and Christiansen lay out a collection of additional "dilemmas of design," which are features that designers must balance. Other authors here view design of socially embedded computing tools as an activity of continual balancing and trading off. Macias-Chapula notes a distinction between "problems" that are amenable to circumscribed "solutions" and "problem situations," situations that include constellations of ongoing and interacting issues in which it is likely that outcomes and approaches will need to be balanced and traded off repeatedly. There are many dimensions to be balanced; some treated in this section include the following:

Integrating situations of design situations with situations of use.

Concentrating effort on understanding potential and postimplementation (future) scenarios versus comprehending present situations.

Exploiting generalized, theoretical understanding, versus practical situated understanding.

Doing planning versus acting, as both designers and users.

Using frameworks, models, and descriptions of circumstances and requirements, versus "letting situations speak."

Using formal descriptions versus active prototypes as media for interactions among designers and users.

Managing these trade-offs is an integral part of design addressed by a number of these authors.

A number of these authors are fundamentally concerned with questions of what aspects and how much of design can be formalized, and what are the boundaries of formalization, both in the sense of formalizing activity and formalizing representations. For example, Axel has the aim "to determine the conditions for the proper application of formal analysis, [and] to differentiate human activity and its formal aspects." For him, formalism can be applied only after a problem has been posed. Agre sees one aspect of formalization as a project to eliminate vagueness. He notes that vagueness has an immoral connotation in some highly technical worlds. For him, an alternative to formalization as a dominant, controlling interest in a complex technical project is attention to detail and to experience; this is analogous to drawing the figure as a foundation of art.

Individualism and collectivism are both possible as methods of intervention. Agre points out that his project to reform AI failed because he thought he could carry out a "revolution" against an individualist/mental discourse. In a sense, he recapitulates the individualist agent fantasy in his project of reform: "When I first started trying to reform AI, I believed in revolutions. It seemed to me that I could clear the ground completely and start over, working out a whole alternative intellectual system that would replace everything that was there before." He has since moved beyond that to a philosophy of more collective action. However, collective action means diversity. "Technical work is performed in and by communities, and a critically engaged practitioner cannot hope to found an alternative community in which everyone shares the same critical premises and methodologies."

Macias-Chapula raises the question of what is the relation between information and health care, and stresses the need to understand the relations between information and outcomes. He provides a discussion of Checkland's Soft Systems Methodology as a way of approaching health care information systems. This analysis and design methodology stresses the iterative integration of many views of a large-scale information system, including descriptions of the transformation process, ownership of the system, the participants or actors, customers of the system's products, environmental constraints, and the worldview under which the system is organized.

CONCLUSIONS

Taken together, these chapters range from detached and empirical analysis to personal, involved, and communicatively "hot" depictions of experience. Agre's memoir is a personal, autobiographical narrative. Robinson's chapter is itself a unity of style and content. Its style is poetic (in the sense of exploiting layered and overlapping denotations of its words) and highly referential (to both itself and others)—a complex interaction between colliding, episodic observations and points of view that communicates some of the feel and the experience of the cross-boundary design issues he is treating. Axel gives some very rich data on the complexity of organizational processes (e.g., what it means to say that something is going right or is going wrong in a setting). Blomberg, Suchman, and Trigg, too, illustrate the workings of the site they investigated with detailed descriptions of the uses of information. Taken together, these chapters provide a mine full of prospects for rich analysis of design problems in socially embedded collaborative computing systems.

REFERENCE

Latour, B. (1995). *Aramis, or the love of technology.* Cambridge, MA: Harvard University Press.

Toward a Critical Technical Practice: Lessons Learned in Trying to Reform AI

Philip E. Agre
University of California, San Diego

Every technology fits, in its own unique way, into a far-flung network of different sites of social practice. Some technologies are employed in a specific site, and in those cases we often feel that we can warrant clear cause-and-effect stories about the transformations that have accompanied them, either in that site or others. Other technologies, such as electric lighting and the telephone, are so ubiquitous—found contributing to the evolution of the activities and relations of so many distinct sites of practice—that it requires considerable effort to understand their effects on society, assuming that such a global notion of "effects" even makes sense (Hughes, 1983; Latour, 1987).

Computers fall in this latter category of ubiquitous technologies. In fact, from an analytical standpoint, computers are worse than that. Computers are representational artifacts, and the people who design them often start by constructing representations of the activities found in the sites where they will be used. This is the purpose of systems analysis, for example, and of the systematic mapping of conceptual entities and relations in the early stages of database design. A computer, then, does not simply have an instrumental use in a given site of practice; the computer is frequently *about* that site in its very design. In this sense and others, computing has been constituted as a kind of imperialism; it aims to reinvent virtually every other site of practice in its own image.

As a result, the institutional relations between the computer world and the rest of the world can be tremendously complicated—much more complicated than the relations between the telephone world and telephone subscribers, or between the electric lighting world and the people who use electric lights in their workplaces and homes. The residents of these borderlands between worlds are many and varied, and increasingly so. They include the people who work on the border between the computer world and the medical world, whether conducting research in medical informatics or encoding patient interactions for entry into a hospital's automated record keeping system. They likewise include the photographers whose livelihood is moving into digital media, the engineers who must employ computer-based tools for design rationale capture, and the social scientists who study the place of computers in society. Each of the borderlands is a complicated place; everyone who resides in them is, at different times, both an object and an agent of technical representation, both a novice and an expert. Practitioners of participatory design (Greenbaum & Kyng, 1991) and requirements engineering (Jirotka & Goguen, 1994), among other disciplines, have done a great deal to explore and transform them. Above all, every resident of these borderlands is a translator between languages and worldviews: the formalisms of computing and the craft culture of the "application domain."

Every resident of the borderlands has a story, and in this chapter I draw some lessons from my own. In 1988 I received a PhD in computer science at MIT, having conducted my dissertation research at the Artificial Intelligence (AI) Laboratory. I started out in school studying mathematics; I moved into computing because it helped pay my school bills and because AI appealed to my adolescent sensibilities; I moved out of computing because I felt I had said everything I had to say through the medium of computer programs; and now I am a social scientist concerned with the social and political aspects of networking and computing. This path has its geographical aspects, of course, and its institutional aspects; at each transition I was able to construct myself as a certain sort of person, and I was usually able to stay employed. Here, though, I wish to focus primarily on the cognitive aspects of my path. My ability to move intellectually from AI to the social sciences—that is, to stop thinking the way that AI people think, and to start thinking the way that social scientists think—had a remarkably large and diverse set of historical conditions. AI has never had much of a reflexive critical practice, any more than any other technical field. Criticisms of the field, no matter how sophisticated and scholarly they might be, are certain to be met with the assertion that the author simply fails to understand a basic point. And so, even though I was convinced that the field was misguided and stuck, it took tremendous effort and good fortune to understand how and why. Along the way I spent several years attempting to reform the field by providing it with the critical methods it needed—a critical technical practice.

In writing a personal narrative, I assume certain risks. Few narratives of emergence from a technical worldview have been written; perhaps the best is Hales' (1980) remarkable account of his time as a manufacturing engineer using operations research to design work processes for chemical production workers. (Heshusius & Ballard, 1996, collect analogous stories from education and social research.) A sociological inquiry is normally expected to have an explicit methodology. The very notion of methodology, however, supposes that the investigator started out with a clear critical consciousness and purpose, and the whole point of this chapter is that my own consciousness and purpose took form through a slow, painful, institutionally located, and historically specific process.

A personal narrative is also open to misinterpretation. I do not wish to engage in public psychotherapy; my emotional investments in AI and its research community are illuminating in their own way, but here I simply wish to recount an intellectual passage. I am not interested in portraying myself as a victim of wrongdoing or an innocent party in a conflict. Perhaps my tale will contribute to the emergence of a critical technical practice, but only if it is taken as a counsel of humility.

A final risk is that I may seem to condemn AI people as conspirators or fools. AI has a long history of conflict with critics, to whom it has often responded harshly (Bloomfield, 1987). Although these responses may reflect the aggressive styles of particular personalities, they may also result from a lack of access to forms of historical explanation that interpretive social scientists and philosophers take for granted. Without the idea that ideologies and social structures can be reproduced through a myriad of unconscious mechanisms such as linguistic forms and bodily habits, all critical analysis may seem like accusations of conscious malfeasance. Even sociological descriptions that seem perfectly neutral to their authors can seem like personal insults to their subjects if they presuppose forms of social order that exist below the level of conscious strategy and choice.

The first few sections of the chapter are concerned with AI as a field. The first recounts some salient aspects of the field's institutional and intellectual history. The next sketches how the field understands itself; it is crucial to comprehend these self-understandings in order to work critically because they will shape the mainstream practitioners' perceptions of proposed alternatives. The chapter goes on to describe some of the discursive practices that have made AI so successful up to a point, while also making it difficult to conceptualize alternatives.

The last few sections describe my own experience and the lessons I have drawn from it. I recount how I emerged from AI's unfortunately confining worldview and began to incorporate influences from philosophy, literary theory, and anthropology into my technical work. Then I discuss what it means in practice to develop "alternatives" to an existing technical practice; for the most part, this notion is misleading. The final section concludes with my own theory of critical engagement with a technical field.

HISTORICAL CONSTITUTION

The field of artificial intelligence arose in the years after World War II, when psychologists and others who had been pressed into wartime research returned to their labs. During the war, these researchers had been greatly inspired by wartime technologies such as signal detection methods and tracking devices for guns. The attraction of these technologies was that they lent themselves to intentional description: A tracking device, for example, could be said to pursue goals and anticipate the future. As such, they provided the paradigm for a counterrevolution against behaviorism—a way to make talk about mental processes scientific and precise.

Wartime research also created an important set of social networks among the military and civilian research communities. MIT in particular came to prominence as a technical university that had made significant innovations in the war effort, and after the war it found itself closely connected to the suddenly much larger government research establishment. With the transition to the Cold War, this epistemic community united around a scientific and technical vision that Edwards (1996) usefully identified as "cyborg discourse"—the whole world as one large technical system. Human beings, on this view, are themselves technical entities who serve as components of organizational systems: Their bodies are machines and their minds are nodes in a hierarchical command-and-control network based on rational analysis and optimization.

As an institutional matter, then, AI was one part of an overall movement with a coherent worldview. It would be unfair to say that AI's founders were conforming themselves to military funding imperatives, just as it would be false to say that the emerging field of AI was intellectually autonomous. Numerous factors converged to reward the search for technologies and mathematical formalisms whose workings could be described using intentional vocabulary. Several technologies and formalisms received serious attention in this regard, including information theory, simulated neural networks, signal detection methods, cybernetic feedback systems, and computational complexity theory. As the field coalesced, though, only a handful of technologies and formalisms emerged to define the first decades of AI research. Most of these technologies and formalisms—formal language theory, problem solving in search spaces, mathematical logic, and symbolic programming—were qualitative in nature, not quantitative, and most were founded on the power and flexibility of the stored-program digital computer.

As the field of AI took form, it mixed elements of science and technology in complicated ways. Many of the founders of AI were psychologists, and they explained the field in terms of computer modeling of human thought processes. Others had a more abstract, less empirical interest in intelligence, and they explained the field with formulas such as "building systems whose behavior would be considered intelligent if exhibited by a human being." Few regarded themselves as engineers seeking purely instrumental solutions to technical problems. Despite this, and notwithstanding the differences among individual investigators' approaches, the research programs at the new AI labs were deeply congruent with the broader military-scientific "cyborg discourse" consensus. As a result, the research in these labs continued for over 20 years with remarkably little detailed oversight or direction from the Advanced Research Projects Agency (ARPA) and the other basic research funding agencies in the military. Broad research problematics such as problem solving, learning, vision, and planning formed a kind of boundary between the individual researchers (and especially their students), who experienced themselves as having considerable autonomy, and their funding agencies, who had a ready vocabulary for explaining the relevance of this research to the agencies' overall technology strategy.

Critics of AI have often treated these well-funded early AI labs as servants of the military and its goals. But, it should be recognized that these labs' relative prosperity and autonomy within a deeply shared worldview also provided the conditions for dissent. In my own case, the first 5 years of my graduate education were paid by a fellowship from the Fannie and John Hertz Foundation. John Hertz, best known as the founder of the Hertz car rental company, was a conservative patriot who left his fortune to a foundation whose purpose was to support military research. The Hertz Foundation fellowship program was, and is, administered largely by scientists at Lawrence Livermore National Laboratory who are associated with the military's nuclear weapons and ballistic missile defense programs. During the late 1970s, when I received my own Hertz Fellowship, the Hertz Foundation was aligned with the military's support for AI research. Numerous other graduate students in my laboratory were also Hertz Fellows, and the foundation officers would speak explicitly about their hopes that the nation's research base—whose health they understood in a broad sense, not simply in terms of immediate contributions to military research programs—would benefit from the large investment they were making in graduate students who were entering AI. They did not favor students whose ideologies were compatible with their own, although they did require us to listen to some luncheon speeches by Edward Teller, and they knowingly gave fellowships to several students who opposed militarism. The Hertz Foundation, and later ARPA, paid me a decent graduate student salary during many months when I supplemented my technical work by reading a great deal of phenomenology and literary theory. The culture of MIT itself included a cult of "smartness," such that students deemed "smart" (including most everyone accepted to graduate school) were given wide latitude to pursue their own research directions, no matter how odd they might seem to their worried dissertation committees. If the field of AI during those decades was a servant of the military, then it enjoyed a wildly indulgent master.

Within academia, the early AI pioneers were largely engaged in a revolt against behaviorism. Behaviorism, in its day, had organized itself largely in reaction against the vague and unreproducible nature of introspectionist psychology. The metaphors provided by new technologies provided a means of placing mentalist psychology on a scientific basis, and a functionalist epistemology emerged to explain what it meant to offer mental mechanisms as explanations for experimental data. Although the participants in this intellectual movement experienced themselves as revolutionaries, mechanistic explanations of mind already had a long history, going back at least as far as Hobbes. Yet, in a curious twist, these mentalists acknowledged little inspiration from this tradition. Instead, they reached back 300 years to identify themselves with the philosophy of Descartes. Although Descartes' defense of a specifically mental realm in a mechanistic universe was a useful symbol for mentalists engaged in polemics against behaviorism, the principal appeal of Descartes' theory was not its ontological dualism, but rather the explanatory freedom that Descartes' dualism afforded. The theorizing of later mechanists—from Hobbes to Locke to the associationists and reflex-arc theorists—was severely constrained by the limitations of their mechanical models. Descartes, on the other hand, could prescribe elaborate systems for the conduct of the mind without worrying how these systems might be realized as physical mechanisms. He intended his rules as normative prescriptions for rational thought; they were explanatory theories in the sense that they would accurately describe the thinking of anybody who was reasoning rationally. Although nobody has mechanized Descartes' specific theory, the stored-program digital computer, along with the theoretical basis of formal language theory and problem-solving search and the philosophical basis of functionalism (Fodor, 1968), provided the pioneers of AI with a vocabulary through which rule-based accounts of cognitive rationality could be rendered mechanical while also being meaningfully treated as mental, as opposed to physical, phenomena.

SELF-CONCEPTION

These aspects of AI's institutional and intellectual origins help to explain its distinctive conception of itself as a field. The central practice of the field, and its central value, was technical formalization. Inasmuch as they regarded technical formalization as the most scientific and the most productive of all known intellectual methods, the field's most prominent members tended to treat their research as the heir of virtually the whole of intellectual history. I have often heard AI people portray philosophy, for example, as a failed project, and describe the social sciences as intellectually sterile. In each case, their diagnosis is the same: Lacking the precise and expressive methods of AI, these fields are inherently imprecise, woolly, and vague.

Any attempt at a critical engagement with AI should begin with an appreciation of the experiences that have made these extreme views seem so compelling. In its first 15 years, AI developed a series of technical methods that provide interesting, technically precise accounts of a wide range of human phenomena. It is often objected that these machines are not "really" reasoning or planning or learning, but these objections can miss the point. The early demonstrations of AI were incomparably more sophisticated than the mechanistic philosophies of even a short time before. As a result, the people who had stayed up many late nights getting these demonstrations to work felt justified in extrapolating their extraordinary rate of progress for one or two or three more decades at least. Critics of their research have often focused on particular substantive positions that have seemed unreasonable—for example, the frequent use of computer symbols such as REASON and DECIDE and GOAL whose relation to the actual human phenomena that those words ordinarily name is suggestive at best. But AI's fundamental commitment (in practice, if not always in avowed theory) is not to a substantive position but to a method. Any particular set of mechanisms will surely prove inadequate in the long run, but a mechanism serves its purpose if it forces issues to the surface and sharpens the intuitions that will guide the development of the next mechanism along. AI people generally consider that their goals of mechanized intelligence are achievable for the simple reason that human beings are physically realized entities, no matter how complex or variable or sociable they might be, and AI's fundamental commitment (again, in practice, if not always in avowed theory) is simply to the study of physically realized entities, not to production systems or symbolic programming or stored-program computers.

In relation to the rest of the intellectual and technical world, then, AI long regarded itself as simultaneously central and marginal. It understood itself as central to human intellectual endeavor, and its integral connection to the cyborg-discourse agenda ensured that its main research centers (MIT, Carnegie Mellon University, and Stanford) would number among the most prominent scientific laboratories in the world. But it was marginal in other, sometimes peculiar, senses. Not only was it intellectually autonomous to a significant degree, but it was also a small world. Research results were communicated through internal report series, IJCAI (the biannual International Joint Conference on Artificial Intelligence), and the ARPANET. Its principal archival journal, *Artificial Intelligence*, was an important publication venue, but the central laboratories did not emphasize journal publication, and graduate students often were not taught how to write papers for journals.

The sense of marginality extended to the culture of the field. Much has already been written about the peculiarities of the "hacker culture" (Håpnes & Sorensen, 1995; Turkle, 1984; Weizenbaum, 1976), with its extreme informality, emotional simplicity, resentment of externally imposed structures and constraints, and the leeway that the hackers afforded to one another's eccentricities. It was, paradoxically, an intensely social culture of seemingly quite asocial people. Whether explicitly or tacitly, they opposed the falseness of bureaucratic life to the principled meritocracy of their craft. Building things was truly the end purpose of the hacker's work, and everything about the methods and language and value system of the AI world was organized around the design and implementation of working systems. This is sometimes called the "work ethic": It has to work. The "result" of an AI research project is a working system whose methods seem original and broadly applicable; an "idea" is a method of building technical systems or a way of analyzing problems that motivates a promising system design; and a research "approach" is a conceptual and technical framework by which problems can be analyzed and transformed into a particular type of technical system (Chapman, 1991, pp. 213–218). The field, accordingly, reckons its history primarily as a sequence of computer systems and secondarily as a history of debates among different approaches to the construction of systems.

It is commonly supposed that work in technical fields proceeds through sharply defined, rational, logical reasoning. Many technical people actually believe this to be the case, but in AI at least, it is not true. The next section describes some consequential fallacies in the field's ideas about precision and rigor, but it is equally important to understand the role of intuition in the AI's own explicit understandings of itself as a technical practice. Whereas industrial computer programming is organized primarily around specifications that govern the input–output behavior of the various modules of a system, research programming in AI is self-consciously virtuosic and experimental. Much of the field's internal discourse has been concerned with the intuitions that guide the design of its complex, ambitious systems. The principle of modularity, for example, might be treated as an axiom or an instrumental expedient in industrial programming. But AI people understand modularity as a powerful but somewhat elusive principle of the universe, akin to a law of nature but much harder to define (Abelson & Sussman, 1984; Simon, 1970). The point is certainly not that AI people are mystics, or that they consciously wish to make anything obscure, but rather that they take seriously the craft nature of their work. AI people, likewise, are constantly discovering that different considerations trade off against one another. Modularity trades off against efficiency, for example, in the sense that systems can usually be made more efficient by breaking down the modularity boundaries that limit the amount of information that two components of a system can share. The expressive power of representation schemes trades off against efficiency as well, inasmuch as symbolic matching and inference tasks become rapidly less tractable as the representation languages provide a greater variety of ways of expressing equivalent concepts (Brachman & Levesque, 1984). Each of these broad generalizations can be made perfectly formal in the context of particular, concrete design decisions, yet the generalizations themselves seem worthy of articulation and reification as lessons learned from research despite their informality. The enormous obstinacy of technical work (if a method cannot be made to work in a given case, then no amount of sloppiness or vagueness will make it work) seems to back these potentially nebulous intuitions with a "hardness" and irrefutability that philosophical or literary research never seems (to AI people anyway) capable of achieving.

DISCURSIVE PRACTICES

The premise of AI, in rough terms, is the construction of computer systems that exhibit intelligence. One encounters different formulations of this premise at different labs, and from different individuals in the field. In philosophical and popular forums, the field is often discussed in terms of a seemingly fundamental question: Can computers think? But little of the field's day-to-day work really depends on the answer to such questions. As a practical matter, the purpose of AI is to build computer systems whose operation can be narrated using intentional vocabulary. Innovations frequently involve techniques that bring new vocabulary into the field: reasoning, planning, learning, choosing, strategizing, and so on. Whether the resulting systems really are exhibiting these qualities is hard to say, and AI people generally treat the question as an annoying irrelevance. What matters practically is not the vague issue of what the words "really mean," but the seemingly precise issue of how they can be defined in formal terms that permit suitably narratable systems to be designed. If you disapprove of the way that we formalize the concept of reasoning or planning or learning, they are likely to say, then you are welcome to invent another way to formalize it, and once you have gotten your own system working we will listen to you with rapt attention. If you disapprove of the very project of formalization, or if you insist on sensitivity to the ordinary vernacular uses of the words (e.g., Button, Coulter, Lee, & Sharrock, 1995), then, they would argue, you are simply an obscurantist who prefers things to remain vague.

In an important sense, then, AI is a discursive practice. A word such as *planning*, having been made into a technical term of art, has two very different faces. When a running computer program is described as planning to go shopping, for example, the practitioner's sense of technical accomplishment in part depends on the vernacular meaning of the word— wholly arbitrary neologisms would not suffice. On the other hand, it is only possible to describe a program as "planning" when planning is given a formal definition in terms of mathematical entities or computational structures and processes. The subfield of "planning research" consists of an open-ended set of technical proposals, joined by a densely organized family relationship but not by any a priori technical definition, about the implementable senses in which words in the semantic field around "planning" ("plan," "goal," "execution," "actions," "policies," and so forth) might be used. Different schools certainly differ in their standards of formalization, from "neat" (that is, explicitly and systematically mathematical) to "scruffy" (demonstrated simply through a compelling program). But they emphatically agree that the proof is in the programming, and a proper research result consists in a method for casting planninglike tasks as technical problems that running computer systems can solve.

This dual character of AI terminology, the vernacular and formal faces that each technical term presents, has enormous consequences for the borderlands between AI and its application domains. The discourse of "domains" in AI is extraordinarily rich and complicated, and the field's practitioners take for granted a remarkable intellectual generativity. Once a term such as "planning" or "constraints" or "least commitment" has been introduced into the field through a first implemented demonstration in a particular domain, AI people will quite naturally shift that term into other domains, drawing deep analogies between otherwise disparate activities. Once an automated design problem, for example, has been analyzed into a large, discrete set of design choices, it immediately becomes possible to ask whether these choices can be made without backtracking—that is, whether the choices can be made in some sequence in which earlier decisions never have unhappy implications for choices that must be made later on. Techniques that arose to support the patterns of back-tracking that were discovered during research on storytelling may then find application in the automated design domain, or in a medical diagnosis domain, or in the domain of planning shopping trips. Having proven themselves broadly useful, these techniques might be abstracted into general-purpose algorithms whose computational properties can be studied mathematically, or they might be built into a programming language. Each technique is both a method for designing artifacts and a thematics for narrating its operation.

AI researchers can build computer models of reasoning in particular domains because their discourse is, in one sense, precise. But they can only make such a wide range of domains commensurable with one another because their discourse is, in another sense, vague. At any given time, AI's discursive repertoire consists of a set of technical schemata, each consisting of a restricted semantic field and a specific family of technical methods. Among the most prominent technical schemata are *planning* and *knowledge.* Each of these words might be given a wide range of meanings in different cultural or disciplinary contexts. In AI, though, their meanings are closely tied to their associated technical methods, and they are not otherwise constrained. Absolutely any structure or purposivity in anybody's behavior, for example, can be interpreted as the result of planning. This is not a hypothesis—it is simply how the word is used. Miller, Galanter, and Pribram (1960), despite its lack of technical demonstrations, is nonetheless the field's original textbook in the rhetoric of planning. Absolutely any enduring competence, likewise, can be interpreted as a manifestation of knowledge; McCarthy's early papers (e.g., 1958/1968) provided one influential AI rhetoric of knowledge in terms of the predicate calculus.

The construction of an AI model begins with these most basic interpretations and proceeds systematically outward from them. Having detected an element of behavioral regularity in the life of some organism, for example, one can immediately begin enumerating the unitary elements of behavior and identifying those as the "primitive actions" that the putative planner has assembled to produce its plan. Miller et al., motivated by Chomsky's linguistic formalisms and Newell and Simon's early problem-solving programs, helpfully suggested that all plans are hierarchical: A morning's activity might comprise several distinct activities (dressing, eating breakfast, answering correspondence), and each of those activities can be understood as itself comprising distinct subactivities, which are themselves composite activities in turn, until finally one reaches a suitably elementary repertoire of actions from which all others are assembled. Miller et al. never offered a definitive set of these primitive actions, and the field has never felt it necessary to do so. (Schank's, 1982, theory of the mental representation of action for purposes of story understanding, though, includes a fixed repertoire of primitive action types.) The purpose of the theory of planning has not been to provide a single technical specification for all domains, but rather to provide a set of technical schemata that can be expanded into a narrative thematics for any particular domain. Much of the practical work of AI, in other words, consists precisely in the deployment of these technical schemata to translate, or gloss, selected features of a given domain in terms that can also be interpreted as the operation of a computer program. The vagueness of AI vocabulary is instrumental in achieving this effect.

The strategic vagueness of AI vocabulary, and the use of technical schemata to narrate the operation of technical artifacts in intentional terms, is not a matter of conscious deception. It does permit AI's methods to seem broadly applicable, even when particular applications require a designer to make, often without knowing it, some wildly unreasonable assumptions. At the same time, it is also self-defeating. It has the consequence that AI people find it remarkably difficult to conceptualize alternatives to their existing repertoire of technical schemata. The idea that human beings do not conduct their lives by means of planning, for example, is just short of unintelligible. At best it sounds like behaviorism, inasmuch as it seems to reject all possible theories of the mental processing through which anyone might decide what to do. The term *planning*, in other words, exhibits an elastic quality: As a technical proposition it refers to a quite specific and circumscribed set of functionalities and algorithms, but as an empirical proposition it refers to anything at all that can plausibly be glossed with the term. This elasticity of meaning is already found in Miller et al. Their formal definition of a "Plan" (they capitalize the term) is "any hierarchical process in the organism that can control the order in which a sequence of operations is to be performed" (1960, p. 16). A Plan is defined as a "process," and yet process is given no technical definition, either in their book or in subsequent planning research. Despite the broad and inconclusive connotations of "any hierarchical process," in practice they use the word Plan much more specifically. In some places it refers to a "TOTE unit," which is a simple kind of feedback loop, and in other places it refers to a parse tree of the type described by formal language theory. This latter version has been the more influential, and virtually all AI planning theories interpret a plan as a symbolic data-structure that functions essentially as a computer program (another connotation that Miller et al. gestured at without formally embracing). As a result of this equivocation, attempts to deny the narrow technical theory of planning sound to the ears of AI researchers like denials that the sequential ordering of human behavior is determined by any coherent process at all.

Miller et al.'s concept of a Plan also exemplifies another prominent feature of AI discourse: the tendency to conflate representations with the things that they represent. Their substantive theory is that behavior derives its structure from the structure of a Plan, and so they taught a generation of AI practitioners how to shift rapidly back and forth between the structure of outward behavior and the structure of internal mental processes, and between the structure of these time-extended phenomena and the structure of static symbolic structures in the mind. This conflation of representations and worldly things is particularly encouraged by the domains that early AI research chose to illustrate its techniques. Newell and Simon's (1963, 1972) problem-solving research, for example, employed logical theorem-proving and puzzle-solving domains for which the distinction between mental representation and corporeal reality was shady. Proving logical theorems in one's head, after all, is a different activity from proving them with pencil and paper, but the essentially mathematical nature of the domain permits the distinction between logical propositions in working memory and logical propositions written on paper to be blurred. In particular, the mental representations readily capture everything about the real-world entities that can ever have any consequences for the outcome of the task. These domains appealed to early AI researchers in part because computer vision and robotics were very poorly developed, and they permitted research on cognition to begin without waiting on those other, possibly much more difficult, research problems to be solved. But the privileged status of mathematical entities in the study of cognition was already central to Descartes' theory, and for much the same reason: A theory of cognition based on formal reason works best with objects of cognition whose attributes and relations can be completely characterized in formal terms. Just as Descartes felt that he possessed clear and distinct knowledge of geometric shapes, Newell and Simon's programs suffered no epistemological gaps or crises in reasoning about the mathematical entities in their domains.

The conflation between representations and things can be found in numerous other aspects of AI research. It is found, for example, in the notion that knowledge consists in a model of the world, so that the world is effectively mirrored or copied inside each individual's mind. This concept of a "model," like that of a "plan," has no single technical specification. It is, rather, the signifier that indexes a technical schema: It provides a way of talking about a very wide range of phenomena in the world, and it is also associated with a family of technical proposals, each of which realizes the general theme of "modeling the world" through somewhat different formal means. Just as disagreements with the planning theory are unintelligible within AI discourse, it makes virtually no sense to deny or dispute the idea that knowledge consists in a world model. The word *model*, like the word *plan*, is so broad and vague that it can readily be stretched to fit whatever alternative proposal one might offer. AI people do not understand these words as vague when they are applied to empirical phenomena, though, because each of them does have several perfectly precise mathematical specifications when applied to the specification of computer programs.

WAKING UP

The portrait of the AI community in the previous three sections is, of course, a retrospective understanding. Although they seem commonsensical now, and may seem commonsensical to others who have never been practitioners in the field, as an autobiographical matter I only came to these ideas through a long struggle. I had gone to college at an early age, having been constructed as a math prodigy by a psychologist in the region of the country where I grew up. (The arrival of court-ordered school integration in that region coincided with an emphasis on identifying talented students and grouping students into classrooms based on their test scores.) I began my college work as a math major before drifting over to the computer science department. My college did not require me to take many humanities courses or learn to write in a professional register, and so I arrived in graduate school at MIT with little genuine knowledge beyond math and computers. This realization hit me with great force halfway through my first year of graduate school, and I took a year off to travel and read, trying in an indiscriminate way, and on my own resources, to become an educated person.

My lack of a liberal education, it turns out, was only half of my problem. Only much later did I understand the other half, which I attribute to the historical constitution of AI as a field. A graduate student is responsible for finding a thesis topic, and this means doing something new. Yet I spent much of my first year, and indeed the next couple of years after my time away, trying very hard in vain to do anything original. Every topic I investigated seemed driven by its own powerful internal logic into a small number of technical solutions, each of which had already been investigated in the literature. My attempts to investigate the area of concept learning, for example, endlessly converged back to a single idea: that all possible definitions of concepts form a mathematical lattice, and all reasonable inferences from evidence about a concept's correct scope could be analyzed in terms of lattice-theoretic operations of meeting and joining. This idea was already implicit in Winston's (1975) early research on concept induction and had been fully worked through by others subsequently. It seemed inescapable, and overwhelmingly so.

With 15 years' distance, I can now see that the idea of concept induction through lattice-crawling is indeed inescapable if one's ideas about concepts and evidence and learning are constrained by the ensemble of technical schemata that operated in the discourse and practice of AI at that time. But 15 years ago, I had absolutely no critical tools with which to defamiliarize those ideas—to see their contingency or imagine alternatives to them. Even worse, I was unable to turn to other, nontechnical fields for inspiration. As an AI practitioner already well immersed in the literature, I had incorporated the field's taste for technical formalization so thoroughly into my own cognitive style that I could not read the literatures of nontechnical fields at anything beyond a popular level. The problem was not exactly that I could not understand the vocabulary but that I insisted on trying to read everything as a narration of the workings of a mechanism. By that time much philosophy and psychology had adopted intellectual styles similar to that of AI, so it was possible to read much that was congenial—except that it reproduced the same technical schemata as the AI literature. I believe that this problem was not simply my own—that it is characteristic of AI in general (and, no doubt, other technical fields as well). This is not to say that AI has no intellectual resources and no capacity for originality. In recent years particularly, the field has made productive connections with several other technical fields, establishing common cause through the sharing of technical schemata.

My own route was different. I cannot reproduce its whole tortuous detail here, and so it will inevitably sound simpler in the retelling than it was in the living. But the clarity of hindsight makes evident that I drew on the internal resources of the field, even as I struggled to find my way out of it. I began by filling my notebook with exhaustively detailed stories from my own everyday life. By this time I had grown preoccupied with planning research, so I decided to gather some examples of real-life planning. In doing so, I was following an AI tradition of introspection that has been described aptly, if unsympathetically, by Turkle (1984). Many early AI researchers were clearly attempting, at one level or another, to reproduce their own psyches on computers, and many of them drew on introspection to motivate their programs. Introspection as a formal research method in psychology, of course, had been comprehensively discredited decades earlier. But AI people have not regarded introspection as evidence but as inspiration; because the functionality of their computer systems provides a fully adequate criterion of the success of their research, they believe it does not matter what experiences might have motivated the systems' design. And introspection is close at hand.

But my own practice was different from introspection in one important respect: Whereas introspection attempts to observe and describe mental processes under specially controlled conditions, I was trying to remember and recount episodes of concrete activity that took place in my own everyday life. Together with my fellow student, David Chapman, I rapidly developed a method that I called "intermediation." Having noticed some interesting sequence of events in the course of washing the dishes or carrying out the trash, I would write it down in my notebook in as much detail as I could remember. Along the way, I would invent names for aspects of the recounted activity that seemed relevant to some technical concern. The method worked best if these names were intermediate in their degree of abstraction, thus the term "intermediation." For example, I became interested in what I called "hassles," which are small bits of trouble that recur frequently in routine patterns of activity. Having noticed a hassle (e.g., an episode in which silverware tried to jump into the garbage disposal while washing dishes), I would write out in some detail both the episode itself and the larger pattern's attributes as a hassle. Having done so, I found that I would then start spontaneously noticing hassles in other activities, particularly hassles that were analogous in some way to the hassles that I had already noticed and written out in my notebook.

I did this regularly for a couple of years, to such an extent that I was continually noticing various aspects of the mundane mechanics of my daily life. I was also continually noticing the many small transformations that my daily life underwent as a result of noticing these things. As my intuitive understanding of the workings of everyday life evolved, I would formulate new concepts and intermediate on them, whereupon the resulting spontaneous obsevations would push my understanding of everyday life even further away from the concepts that I had been taught. It may be objected that a method driven by a priori concepts can only find whatever it is looking for, but that was not at all my experience. When looking for hassles, of course, I would find hassles. But then writing out the full details of an actual episode of being hassled would raise an endless series of additional questions, often unrelated to what I was looking for. It is hard to convey the powerful effect that this experience had on me; my dissertation (Agre, 1988), once I finally wrote it, was motivated largely by a passion to explain to my fellow AI people how our AI concepts had cut us off from an authentic experience of our own lives. I still believe this.

Perhaps someday I will finally write out my treatise on the true functioning of everyday routine activities, based on the great mass of anecdotes that I accumulated by this procedure. My purpose here, though, is to describe how this experience led me into full-blown dissidence within the field of AI. Given that an AI dissertation is based on a computer program, my investigations of everyday routine activities were always aimed at that goal. I wanted to find an alternative means of conceptualizing human activity, one that did not suffer the absurdities of planning but that could be translated into a working demonstration program. To this end, I spent many months working back and forth between concepts to describe everyday activities and intuitions that seemed capable of guiding technical work. Most of these intuitions would be impossible to explain without developing an elaborate apparatus of concepts, and indeed I found that my thinking about these matters had become impossible to communicate to anybody else. A small number of my friends, most notably David Chapman, sat still for long, complex explanations of the phenomena I was observing and the intuitions they seemed to motivate. But, clearly, I had to bring this project back into dialogue with people who did not already share my vocabulary.

In order to find words for my newfound intuitions, I began studying several nontechnical fields. Most importantly, I sought out those people who claimed to be able to explain what is wrong with AI, including Hubert Dreyfus and Lucy Suchman. They, in turn, got me started reading Heidegger's *Being and Time* (1961) and Garfinkel's *Studies in Ethnomethodology* (1984). At first I found these texts impenetrable, not only because of their irreducible difficulty but also because I was still tacitly attempting to read everything as a specification for a technical mechanism. That was the only protocol of reading that I knew, and it was hard even to conceptualize the possibility of alternatives. (Many technical people have observed that phenomenological texts, when read as specifications for technical mechanisms, sound like mysticism. This is because Western mysticism, since the great spiritual forgetting of the later Renaissance, has often amounted to a variety of mechanism that posits impossible mechanisms.) My first intellectual breakthrough came when, for reasons I do not recall, it finally occurred to me to stop translating these strange disciplinary languages into technical schemata, and instead simply to learn them on their own terms. This was very difficult because my technical training had instilled in me two polar-opposite orientations to language—as precisely formalized and as impossibly vague—and a single clear mission for all discursive work—transforming vagueness into precision through formalization (Agre, 1992). The correct orientation to the language of these texts, as descriptions of the lived experience of ordinary everyday life, or in other words an account of what ordinary activity is *like*, is unfortunately alien to AI or any other technical field.

I still remember the vertigo I felt during this period; I was speaking these strange disciplinary languages, in a wobbly fashion at first, without knowing what they meant (i.e., without knowing what *sort* of meaning they had). Formal reason has an unforgiving binary quality—one gap in the logic and the whole thing collapses—but this phenomenological language was more a matter of degree; I understood intellectually that the language was "precise" in a wholly different sense from the precision of technical language, but for a long time I could not convincingly experience this precision for myself, or identify it when I saw it. Still, in retrospect, this was the period during which I began to "wake up," breaking out of a technical cognitive style that I now regard as extremely constricting. I believe that a technical field such as AI can contribute a great deal to our understanding of human existence, but only once it develops a much more flexible and reflexive relation to its own language, and to the experience of research and life that this language organizes.

My second intellectual breakthrough occurred during my initial attempt to read Foucault's *Archaeology of Knowledge* (1972). Foucault suggested that when two schools of thought are fighting, rather than try to adjudicate the dispute, one should investigate whether the opposed schools are internally related components of a single intellectual formation. Having done so, it becomes possible to ask how that whole formation arose historically. I came across this idea at an opportune moment. Although the structuralism of *The Archaeology of Knowledge* has often been condemned by Foucault's critics, this very structuralism nonetheless ensured that I could grasp Foucault's ideas in my habitual patterns of technical thought, and that I could then employ his ideas to objectify and defamiliarize those very patterns of thought. It became possible, for example, to inquire about the nature and workings of the discursive formation that consisted of behaviorism plus cognitivism. This was an extraordinary revelation.

It may be objected that *The Archaeology of Knowledge* is only one possible theory of the history of ideas, and that dozens of preferable theories are available. My point, however, is that my technical training did not include any of those other theories. I later became a zealous consumer of those theories, but it was Foucault's theory that first pierced the darkness—precisely because of its commensurability with the order of technical thought. Having found a means of objectifying ideas, I could then proceed systematically to extricate myself from the whole tacit system of intellectual procedures in which I had become enmeshed during my years as a student of computer science. For this reason, I have never experienced poststructuralism or literary theory as strange or threatening, nor have I ever perceived them as varieties of relativism or idealism. Quite the contrary, they were the utterly practical instruments by which I first was able to think clearly and to comprehend ideas that had not been hollowed through the false precision of formalism.

THE FALLACY OF ALTERNATIVES

After some months of study, these foreign disciplinary languages began to provide an established vocabulary for expressing the intuitions that I had developed by noticing and writing out episodes of routine activity. In broad outline, my central intuition was that AI's whole mentalist foundation is mistaken, and the organizing metaphors of the field should begin with routine interaction with a familiar world, not problem solving inside one's mind. In taking this approach, everything starts to change, including all of the field's most basic ideas about representation, action, perception, and learning. When I tried to explain these intuitions to other AI people, however, I quickly discovered that it is useless to speak nontechnical languages to people who are trying to translate these languages into specifications for technical mechanisms. This problem puzzled me for years, and I surely caused much bad will as I tried to force Heideggerian philosophy down the throats of people who did not want to hear it. Their stance was: If your alternative is so good, then you will use it to write programs that solve problems better than anybody else's, and then everybody will believe you. Even though I believe that building things is an important way of learning about the world, nonetheless I knew that this stance was wrong, even if I did not understand how.

I now believe that it is wrong for several reasons. One reason is simply that AI, like any other field, ought to have a space for critical reflection on its methods and concepts. Critical analysis of others' work, if done responsibly, provides the field with a way to deepen its means of evaluating its own research. It also legitimizes moral and ethical discussion and encourages connections with methods and concepts from other fields. Even if the value of critical reflection is proven only in its contribution to improved technical systems, many valuable criticisms will go unpublished if all research is required to present a new working system as its final result.

Another, more subtle reason pertains to AI's ambiguous location between science and engineering. A scientific theory makes truth claims about the preexisting universe, so it is generally considered legitimate to criticize someone else's theory on grounds of methodological weakness, fallacious reasoning, lack of fit with the evidence, or compatibility of the evidence with other theories. Engineering design methods, on the other hand, make claims in the context of practical problems, and so the legitimate criticisms relate solely to issues of utility. AI projects are sometimes scientific in intention, sometimes engineering, and sometimes they shift subliminally from one to the other. AI people often make substantive claims about knowledge or learning or language, and yet many of them will respond with indignation to arguments that their projects fundamentally misconstrue the nature of these phenomena; in most cases (the primary exception being Newell and Simon's research group at Carnegie Mellon University), they will argue *not* that the claims against their work are empirically false but that they are non sequiturs. Pressed to explain the seeming contradiction, they will generally state that their systems exhibit knowledge-as-such, say, as opposed to human knowledge in particular. But then, it seems, they will turn around and compare their systems' behavior to human behavior without further comment. The underlying problem is not mendacity but a conflict of languages: Norms and discourses of engineering are applied to terms (knowledge, learning, language, and so on) whose meanings are inextricably rooted in the phenomena of human life. As a consequence, I have often encountered an emphatic, explicitly stated injunction against "criticizing other people's work," the idea being that the only legitimate form of critical argument is that "my system performs better than your system on problem X."

A final reason, already discussed, is that AI discourse makes it exceptionally difficult to conceptualize alternatives to the field's prevailing ideas. Indeed, AI does not have "ideas" in any sense that would be familiar from philosophy or literature or social thought; instead, it has technical practices, loosely articulated intuitions about those practices, and ways of talking about the resulting artifacts that combine precision and vagueness in specific ways. If you write a program whose operation you understand in different terms, then somebody will observe that your program can perfectly well be described as having knowledge, executing plans, and so on. Never mind, then, that you choose to talk about the program differently; in fact, they will say, it is nothing new. The seemingly commonsensical demand to provide alternatives is thus, in practice, actually a demand to express disagreements with the existing language within the existing language itself, and this is nearly impossible.

In these ways, AI's construction of itself as a self-contained technical discipline, though seemingly governed by practical-minded criteria of success and failure, is actually a powerful force for intellectual conservatism. Critics will be asked, "what's your alternative?", within a tacit system of discursive rules that virtually rules out alternatives from the start. All the same, I think that the very concept of alternatives is misleading, and that it is actually impossible to achieve a radical break with the existing methods of the field. This is because AI's existing language and technical practice, like any disciplinary culture, runs deeper than we are aware. Having been socialized into the field, by the time I began conceiving myself as a dissident I had acquired an extensive network of linguistic forms, habits of thought, established techniques, ritualized work practices, ways of framing questions and answers, genre conventions, and so forth. It would have been impossible to simply cast off that whole network of cultural forms, any more than I could simply decide to stop being American and start being Thai, or to become transcendentally stateless and cultureless. As a result, attempts to formulate a wholly distinct alternative worldview for AI, or even to secede from the field altogether, are bound to fail. The point is exceptionally subtle: AI's elastic use of language ensures that nothing will seem genuinely new, even if it actually is, while AI's intricate and largely unconscious cultural system ensures that all innovations, no matter how radical the intentions that motivated them, will turn out to be enmeshed with traditional assumptions and practices. When AI people look at an innovation and pronounce it nothing radically new, they will be wrong in some ways and right in others, and it will require tremendous effort to determine which is which. Critical practice is essential to make sense of such things, but the goal of this practice should be complex engagement, not a clean break.

I began to understand this once I had attained a few years' critical distance on two computer programs that illustrated the intuitions and technical ideas that arose through our experiments with intermediation on the workings of ordinary activities; I have described these programs in my dissertation (Agre, 1988) and more recently in my book (Agre, 1997). I wrote the first of these, a program called RA that operates in a conventional AI "blocks world," as an experiment in computational improvisation; rather than constructing a plan that it then executes wholesale, it conducts a fresh reasoning through of its situation as quickly as it can. David Chapman wrote the second, with some participation from me in the later stages of development, a program called Pengi that played a video game by a similar improvisation but with a much more sophisticated model of visual perception.

Although intended as alternatives to the conventional theories of planning, reasoning, and vision, these programs ultimately turned out to recapitulate some of the subtle confusions of the conventional methods. Specifically, both of these programs relate to their "worlds" from a bird's-eye view, or, more precisely, from an orthographic projection, as if the simulated agent were infinitely far away from the action except for the one instrument through which it moves things around: a cartoon "hand" for RA and a cartoon penguin for Pengi. Orthographic projections are ubiquitous in the diagrams of AI papers; they make it seem reasonable that the simulated agent maintains a panoptic representation of its entire environment. This is one particularly insidious manifestation of AI's tendency to conflate representations and things-represented. In the case of RA, this conflation was already hidden by a convention of blocks world: The blocks have their names ("A," "B," "C," etc.) written on them, as if the agent's mental symbols were part of the material world, automatically connected to the things they name. In the case of Pengi, the problem was much more subtle. Pengi's mechanisms for deciding what to do were modeled on RA's. Pengi, however, employed a somewhat realistic model of vision, and so it did not automatically represent the whole of reality to itself. But the adversarial and partially random nature of the video game meant that Pengi could not rely on stable structures in the world or large-scale patterns in its interactions with the world to help it keep track of things. And because Pengi had a body only in a rudimentary sense, and thus no strong sense of being located anywhere in particular, every part of the visible "world" was potentially relevant all of the time. As a result, Pengi (like any player of a video game) was forever scrambling to allocate its attentional resources to the most important objects in its visual world. It could carry on reasonably well by focusing primarily on the objects closest to it. It could only keep track of individual objects, however, by physically tracking them across the screen, much as RA kept track of blocks by knowing their names. In the end, therefore, Pengi did not provide the clear-cut alternative that we had hoped.

Neither of these programs was a failure. To the contrary, each of them introduced technical methods that may have some lasting value. And each of them does point to the utility of different metaphors for the technical work of the field, even if it proves impossible to make a knock-down argument for one set of metaphors over another. At the same time, each program reflects the inherent difficulty of inventing a thoroughgoing alternative to established technical methods. It is thus not surprising in retrospect that I have found myself exchanging published arguments with another AI dissident, Terry Winograd, that one another's alternative technical ideas (his outside of AI and mine inside) are not actually as technically new as their associated rhetoric makes them out to be (Agre, 1994; Winograd, 1995). We are both right, yet neither project is discredited as a result. On a technical level they are inevitably incremental advances, just as AI people insist they are. But the conceptual analysis and philosophical critique that accompany them must be understood as intellectual contributions in their own right, grounded both in a priori analysis of the phenomena and in detailed, critically informed reflection on the difficulties encountered in getting AI models to work.

It is useful, by way of summary, to distinguish four reasons why it is difficult to create alternatives to the standard methods of AI. First, it is difficult to become aware of the full range of assumptions underneath existing practices, from technical methods to genre conventions to metaphors. Second, having formulated an alternative intuition, it is difficult to reduce that intuition to a novel technical method—a new type of artifact, or a new way of building artifacts. Third, having invented a new technical method, it is difficult to prevent that method from being construed as "nothing new" within the elastic boundaries of existing technical schemata. Fourth, having coupled a new technical method with a new way of talking about the phenomena, it is difficult to apply the method to any real cases without inventing a lot of additional methods as well, because any worthwhile system will require the application of several interlocking methods, and use of the existing methods may distort the novel method back toward the traditional mechanisms and the traditional ways of talking about them. This litany of obstacles does not make critical technical practice impossible; it simply defines the terrain on which such a practice must operate.

CRITICAL ENGAGEMENT

I must leave it to others to determine how effective, if at all, my attempts to reform AI have been. I know that the original Pengi paper (Agre & Chapman, 1987) has been extensively cited, but one reason for this paper's popularity is that our innovations in models of situated activity happened to coincide with a shift in military strategy toward autonomous battlefield robots under the Strategic Computing Initiative. There immediately ensued, with scant and mostly disruptive participation from us, another round of consensus-building between ARPA and the AI community about the necessity of "autonomous agents" and "reactive plannning." The vocabulary of planning research soon filled with the military discourse of "uncertain, unpredictable, or changing environments" (e.g., Hendler, 1990). Was our seemingly lonely work in the mid-1980s subliminally influenced by the ongoing changes in military thinking? Were we working through an immanent trend in the logic of AI work that paralleled an immanent evolution in cyborg discourse? Did our laboratory's attunement to shifts in military thinking create conditions, however unconsciously, for the years of toleration of our strange investigations? I cannot know.

Whatever the case may be, we were not alone in exploring an interactionist style of AI. Authors such as Brooks (1986) and Rosenschein and Kaelbling (1986) were working on broadly similar issues, even though their technical concerns were often different and their philosophical approach was less elaborate. Additional related work has been gathered in Agre and Rosenschein (1996). Research in this style is now reasonably well established as one "approach" within the field.

Beyond these technical concerns, Chapman and I attempted in our papers and talks over several years to provoke critical reflection within the field. We were traveling without a map, so most of our strategies are inevitably embarrassing in retrospect. We managed to make ourselves controversial in any event, and some people seem to believe that we and other dissidents and critics of the field (Randy Beer, Bill Clancey, Hubert Dreyfus, Jim Greeno, Jean Lave, Luch Suchman, Terry Winograd, and others) constitute some kind of new establishment unto ourselves. Although I cannnot evaluate this belief with total precision, I can testify that this utterly disparate group has never tried to constitute itself as a school or movement. AI is still very much its own coherent center of mass, though for many reasons it is less centralized than it had been in the 1970s, and no equally coherent "critical" school has arisen to compete with it. It is a real question whether such a scenario would even make sense.

What, then, can be learned? When I first started trying to reform AI, I believed in revolutions. It seemed to me that I could clear the ground completely and start over, working out a whole alternative intellectual system that would replace everything that was there before. The concept of a generative metaphor seemed to hold out particular promise in this direction, given that so much of the underlying substantive problem with AI really can be understood as expressing a single principle—mentalism as opposed to interactionism. It seemed as though one could throw away the old foundation, and everthing on top of it, and start over.

Now I do not believe that it works that way. Instead, I believe in something more like hermeneutics. The intellectual utility of technical exercises, as distinct from the practical utility that they might actually have in the world, lies precisely in their limitations and failures. Perhaps we can learn to approach technical work in the spirit of reductio ad absurdum: Faced with a technical difficulty, perhaps we can learn to diagnose it as deeply as possible. Some difficulties, of course, will be superficial and transient. But others can serve as symptoms of deep and systematic confusions in the field. We are only aware of this possibility if we develop the critical tools to understand the depths below the ordinary practices of a technical field. Some of these critical tools will draw on the methods of institutional and intellectual analysis that have served generations of philosophers, sociologists, and literary critics (Agre, 1995). Others may be responses, each sui generis, to the specific properties of technical work. Research could proceed in a cycle, with each impasse leading to critical insight, reformulation of underlying ideas and methods, fresh starts, and more instructive impasses.

But the language of hermeneutics is not adequate either, because it suggests a solitary "reader" facing the practical reality of technical work as an individual. Technical work is performed in and by communities, and a critically engaged practitioner cannot hope to found an alternative community in which everyone shares the same critical premises and methodologies. As I worked my way toward a critical technical practice, this was the part that I found hardest: maintaining constructive engagement with researchers whose substantive commitments I found wildly mistaken. It is tempting to start explaining the problems with these commitments in an alien disciplinary voice, invoking phenomenology or dialectics as an exogenous authority, but it is essentially destructive.

The constructive path is much harder to follow but more rewarding. Its essence is to evaluate a research project not by its correspondence to one's own substantive beliefs but by the rigor and insight with which it struggles against the patterns of difficulty that are inherent in its design. Faced with a technical proposal whose substantive claims about human nature seem mistaken, the first step is to figure out what deleterious consequences those mistakes should have in practice. If the predicted impasses have actually been detected in the technical work, then the next step is not to conclude that AI, considered as a static essence, has been debunked in a once-and-for-all fashion. Instead, research can now proceed on the basis of a radical interpretation of their significance, inevitably incremental in its practical effect but more sophisticated than it would have been otherwise, leading toward new and different problems. Or, perhaps the predicted impasses are present but have not been recognized as such, in which case one might ask why they have been overlooked. Technical impasses can be overlooked for many reasons; they can be buried in vague or ambiguous language, in notational conventions, in experimental designs, in seemingly unproblematic assumptions, and in many other places. Critical methods might be helpful in discovering other ways in which technical troubles can be inadvertently hidden from view. But nothing can substitute for the daily work of trying to get things built and working. Technical research can only develop from within the designer's own practical work, and it will only progress when the designer's experience is neither channeled by self-reinforcing conceptual schemata from inside the field nor delegitimated by incommensurable philosophies from outside of it. Cultivating the painstaking middle way between these hazards is probably not my own path any more, but it is very much what Collins (1990) had in mind in his philosophically astute but constructively minded research on expert systems, and perhaps it will be a path for others in the future.

A critical technical practice will, at least for the foreseeable future, require a split identity—one foot planted in the craft work of design and the other foot planted in the reflexive work of critique. Successfully spanning these borderlands, bridging the disparate sites of practice that computer work brings uncomfortably together, will require a historical understanding of the institutions and methods of the field, and it will draw on this understanding as a resource in choosing problems, evaluating solutions, diagnosing difficulties, and motivating alternative proposals. More concretely, it will require a praxis of daily work: forms of language, career strategies, and social networks that support the exploration of alternative work practices that will inevitably seem strange to insiders and outsiders alike. This strangeness will not always be comfortable, but it will be productive nonetheless, both in the esoteric terms of the technical field itself and in the exoteric terms by which we ultimately evaluate a technical field's contribution to society.

ACKNOWLEDGMENTS

This chapter has benefited from comments by David Chapman, Harry Collins, Gloria Gannaway, Joseph Goguen, Timothy Koschmann, Warren Sack, Penni Sibun, and Patrick Sobalvarro.

REFERENCES

Abelson, H., & Sussman, G. J. (1981). *Structure and interpretation of computer programs.* Cambridge, MA: MIT Press.

Agre, P. E. (1988). *The dynamic structure of everyday life.* Unpublished doctoral dissertation, Department of Electrical Engineering and Computer Science, MIT.

Agre, P. E. (1992). Formalization as a social project. *Quarterly Newsletter of the Laboratory of Comparative Human Cognition, 14*(1), 25–27.

Agre, P. E. (1994). Surveillance and capture: Two models of privacy. *The Information Society, 10*(2), 101–127.

Agre, P. E. (1995). The soul gained and lost: Artificial intelligence as a philosophical project. *Stanford Humanities Review, 4*(2), 1–19.

Agre, P. E. (1997). *Computation and human experience.* Cambridge, England: Cambridge University Press.

Agre, P. E., & Chapman, D. (1987). Pengi: An implementation of a theory of activity. In *Proceedings of the Sixth National Conference on Artificial Intelligence.* Seattle, July, pp. 196–201.

Agre, P. E., & Rosenschein, S. J. (1996). *Computational theories of interaction and agency.* Cambridge, MA: MIT Press.

Bloomfield, B. P. (1987). The culture of artificial intelligence. In B. P. Bloomfield, (Ed.), *The question of artificial intelligence: Philosophical and sociological perspectives* (pp. 59–105). London: Groom Helm.

Brachman, R. J., & Levesque, H. J. (1984). The tractability of subsumption in frame-based languages. In Proceedings of the National Conference on Artificial Intelligence (pp. 34–37). Austin, TX.

Brooks, R. A. (1986). A robust layered control system for a mobile robot. *IEEE Journal of Robotics and Automation, 2*(1), 14–23.

Button, G., Coulter, J., Lee, J. R. E., & Sharrock, W. (1995). *Computers, minds, and conduct.* Cambridge, England: Polity Press.

Chapman, D. (1991). *Vision, instruction, and action.* Cambridge, MA: MIT Press.

Collins, H. M. (1990). *Artificial experts: Social knowledge and intelligent machines.* Cambridge, MA: MIT Press.

Edwards, P. N. (1996). *The closed world: Computers and the politics of discourse in cold war America.* Cambridge, MA: MIT Press.

Fodor, J. A. (1968). *Psychological explanation: An introduction to the philosophy of psychology.* New York: Random House.

Foucault, M. (1972). *The archaeology of knowledge* (A. M. Sheridan Smith, Trans.). New York: Pantheon.

Garfinkel, H. (1984). *Studies in ethnomethodology.* Cambridge, England: Polity Press. (Original work published 1967)

Greenbaum, J., & Kyng, M. (Eds.). (1991). *Design at work: Cooperative design of computer systems.* Hillsdale, NJ: Lawrence Erlbaum Associates.

Håpnes, T., & Sorensen, K. H. (1995). Competition and collaboration in male shaping of computing: A study of a Norwegian hacker culture. In K. Grint & R. Gill (Eds.), *The gender-technology relation: Contemporary theory and research*. London: Taylor & Francis.

Hales, M. (1980). *Living thinkwork: Where do labour processes come from?* London: CSE Books.

Heidegger, M. (1961). *Being and time*. (J. Macquarrie & E. Robinson, Trans.). New York: Harper & Row. (Original work published in German 1927)

Hendler, J. (Ed.). (1990). *Planning in uncertain, unpredictable, or changing environments. Proceedings of the AAAI Symposium at Stanford* (University of Maryland Systems Research Center Rep. No. SRC TR 90-45).

Heshusius, L., & Ballard, K. (Eds.). (1996). *From positivism to interpretivism and beyond: Tales of transformation in educational and social research*. New York: Teachers' College Press.

Hughes, T. P. (1983). *Networks of power: Electrification in western society, 1880–1930*. Baltimore: Johns Hopkins University Press.

Jirotka, M., & Goguen, J. A. (Eds.). (1994). *Requirements engineering: Social and technical issues*. San Diego: Academic Press.

Latour, B. (1987). *Science in action: How to follow scientists and engineers through society*. Cambridge, MA: Harvard University Press.

McCarthy, J. (1968). Programs with common sense. In M. Minsky (Ed.), *Semantic information processing* (pp. 403–418). Cambridge, MA: MIT Press. (Original work published 1958)

Miller, G. A., Galanter, E., & Pribram, K. H. (1960). *Plans and the structure of behavior*. New York: Holt.

Newell, A., & Simon, H. A. (1963). GPS: A program that simulates human thought. In E. A. Feigenbaum & J. Feldman (Eds.), *Computers and thought* (pp. 279–293). New York: McGraw-Hill.

Newell, A., & Simon, H. (1972). *Human problem solving*. Englewood Cliffs, NJ: Prentice-Hall.

Rosenschein, S. J., & Kaelbling, L. P. (1986). The synthesis of digital machines with provable epistemic properties. In J. Halpern (Ed.), *Proceedings of the Conference on Theoretical Aspects of Reasoning About Knowledge*. Los Altos, CA: Morgan Kaufmann.

Schank, R. C. (1982). *Dynamic memory: A theory of reminding and learning in computers and people*. Cambridge, England: Cambridge University Press.

Simon, H. A. (1970). *The sciences of the artificial*. Cambridge, MA: MIT Press.

Turkle, S. (1984). *The second self: Computers and the human spirit*. New York: Simon & Schuster.

Weizenbaum, J. (1976). *Computer power and human reason: From judgement to calculation*. San Francisco: Freeman.

Winograd, T. (1995). Heidegger and the design of computer systems. In A. Feenberg & A. Hannay (Eds.), *Technology and the politics of knowledge* (pp. 108–127). Bloomington: Indiana University Press.

Winston, P. H. (1975). *The psychology of computer vision*. New York: McGraw-Hill.

7

According Tools With Meaning Within the Organization of Concrete Work Situations

Erik Axel
Copenhagen University, Denmark

In the 1950s, just after the development of the first computers, the Navy Special Projects Office developed a planning system called Program Evaluation and Review Technique (PERT). It was used to assist the construction of the Polaris nuclear submarines meeting schedules, and it is said to have saved the Navy many dollars. The well-known PERT chart was developed in this setting, and the scheduling facilities were gradually computerized. This is an early example of computer-supported cooperative work, where human activity and electronic computing meshed in interactions never seen before. The last decade or so has seen a spate of such systems, their development enhanced by facilities such as networking and graphics. Examples of this kind of computerization are office automation, CAD/CAM systems for the maintenance of plant components, and computer-supported regulation in control rooms.

However, the employment of this kind of system has produced many surprises and has not always met expectations. For example, one hears about architectural firms having stopped using CAD/CAM programs, which they have implemented at great cost. Contractors of computer systems for the maintenance of plant components admit they are hard to use, but then go on to claim that the proper use is a matter of schooling. From a different angle on a similar problem Henderson (1993) reported on the difficulties of using CAD/CAM. She noted that these systems impose one way of designing as the correct one, and detailed how designers surmount these problems and incorporate the systems in their preferred working methods for the task at hand. Taylor, Gurd, and Bardini (chap. 16, this volume) reported on a police force in which new computer-based communications technology was introduced and the police dispatchers substituted with less qualified personnel at the same time. The authors demonstrated how these changes revealed the more supple judgments the police dispatchers had performed in assigning tasks to the police force before the introduction of computers, judgments that the computer system did not incorporate. The introduction of computer systems thus reorganized the workplace, its work patterns, its personnel, and it is also changed in many other respects. The broad scope of these changes is well known to systems developers. One can hear many interpretations of the changes, differing according to the workplace at issue. For example, engineers setting up computerized control rooms state that the new technique makes boredom a core problem in control room jobs. They say there is nothing to do in the control room for long periods, so the operators may doze off, and when dramatic events happen they wake up to a charged situation and react irrationally.

It becomes evident that the introduction of computers in cooperation is not a straightforward task. There are many problems, and their nature is not always clear. Some contractors defend their products by claiming that the operators must be educated in the use of the equipment or by calling them irrational when they make errors. Researchers with investigating minds talk about the constrictions of the gear on work organization, others uncover supple judgments performed by workforces and not recorded until the introduction of computers. Thus, problems are claimed to stem from the machinery or the workforce, and although these explanations need not be mutually exclusive, they are sometimes used as if they were. Hence, not only is the nature of the problem unclear, but it also contested.

Whatever the nature of the problem, the introduction of computers implies a set of challenges—a reorganization of the workforce, which, as in any other introduction of new technology, involves changes in training, wages, employment, and so on. From previous experience, there are some resources and routines—be they adequate or not—with which to handle these challenges. However, it is clear that a striking and specific feature of the challenges can be found in many investigations of the introduction of computers to workplaces. This is the importance of up-until-now hidden and poorly regarded aspects of work tasks. Until the advent of those investigations, it was much easier for a scientific investigator to adhere to a notion of job performance as following rules. When superordinates in a work organization told subordinates to do something to be finished by tomorrow, the superordinates were intent on results and from contact with the shop floor, or from their previous experience, they would probably know what was going on while the job was being performed; this helped them evaluate how to pull the strings in order to get optimal results. Scientific investigators of work organizations or system developers were not looking to get practical results in the first instance, but to get facts. They did not need the intimate knowledge of the superordinate but were bent on minimal, essential knowledge, which gave them an overview. Therefore, it appeared reasonable to them to stick to the belief that the subordinate accomplished the job by following rules; this allowed the investigator to perform formal scientific analysis. But the problems popping up during the computerization of work tasks have forced scientific investigators into another level of surprising particularity. The interaction between computers and humans forces formal analysis down to a level of detail not necessary earlier. Sometimes this fine-grained analysis makes a computerization possible; at other times it is of no use. At the end of the road, the shortcomings of the fine-grained analysis and its diminishing returns become conspicuous, and other modes of description appear. It becomes clear to some that human beings do not manage a job by blindly following formal rules like a computer. It is the computer that necessitates the detailed analysis; human beings only need a general description of the job to get the general idea, and they will fill in the details while acting. As in the previous examples, when humans act, the workforce makes supple judgments in order to complete the job.

We have here hit upon a phenomenon that is to be understood as a limitation of formal analysis. The limitation parallels the fact that an automated machine is never let alone. A human being is always brought in to monitor an automaton; it is not considered safe to let the automaton loose—be it the autopilot in an airplane or a robot in a factory. Something may come up that only the human being would be able to identify and handle; a situation might occur in which the human being would juggle with goals and means to cope with it. A human being works by making ends meet; goals and means are modified and changed according to the needs of the situation. This also implies that errors are identified and modified according to the shifting interpretations of the ongoing activity. According to such a notion, it proves to be necessary to identify the dynamics specific to human activity so that the technology can be implemented as a proper enhancement of human powers.

THEORETICAL DISCUSSION

A whole group of investigators has recognized the necessity of identifying the dynamics specific to human activity (e.g., Garfinkel, 1992; Lave, 1988; Suchman, 1987). Their way of investigating situated human activity has set off a trend that is more or less opposed to a formal analysis of human activity. This trend is contested by people working within the tradition of cognitive science (e.g., Vera & Simon, 1993). The issue up for discussion between these many groups is the relation of the dynamics of human activity to the formalizations that can be programmed into a computer. The positions in the debate are not clear-cut, but two main viewpoints can be distinguished.

It is a common notion in cognitive science that human thinking works according to principles of formal logic (Newell & Simon, 1972). Formal logic consists of finite elements and logical operations on those elements (e.g., if $a < b$ then c). Computers are machines that process numbers according to the rules of formal logic. To discuss whether computers can simulate human thinking is therefore to discuss whether human thinking and its meaning consist of finite elements and operations on those elements. Within cognitive science it is believed that the automaton simulating human thinking does not work yet, because it is not perfect, and is not yet all encompassing. If only all instances were taken care of, if only the analysis could be sufficiently fine grained in the right places, then it could work on its own.

The other position works with identifying specific aspects of human thinking, which cannot necessarily be formalized, so that they may be modeled in a computer. Embodiment and situatedness are concepts to circumscribe these specific traits. In this chapter, a central aspect of human thinking is determined as its ability to identify what kind of object this particular thing is. This is seen as achieved by human beings according meaning to situations in which they act by making ends meet. Furthermore, formalisms are understood as tools, which do not possess meaning, but are used and accorded meaning by human beings in their activity. This position is an elaboration of Critical Psychology (cf. Tolman & Maiers, 1991; Holzkamp, 1983).

Thus, this chapter confronts these two positions and some arguments are given to the effect that human thinking is determined by content and cannot be formalized. Such arguments are of course not meant to deny formalisms their fertility. The advent of the computer with all the kinds of use (also unexpected) to which it has been applied and the profound change of the organization of social activity it has caused, must all be taken as evidence of the fertility of the application of formal analysis to human activity. However, in the end, the fertility of formal analysis is not a proof of its validity as a model of human activity, nor a proof that it governs human activity itself. The chapter accordingly aims at encircling a domain of analysis of human activity, in which formalisms can be of no avail, in order to help the proper domain of formal analysis to stand out more clearly. It argues that each domain should be given due respect according to its characteristics, and attempts to sketch out good reasons for this position. The present position is then part of the change of importance of formal analysis in human sciences, as heralded by Garfinkel's criticism of the notion of rule-based behavior. In the 1950s and 1960s it was a dominant claim that a theoretical analysis should end up in formal statements, a theory in the humanities could only be considered a proper theory if it was "dressed in a formal tuxedo" (to use Leigh Star's expression). This chapter does not posit a counterclaim that only artistic rags will do; the aim is to determine the conditions for the proper application of formal analysis, to differentiate the process of human activity and its formal aspects, and thereby to identify the proper scientific methods for each domain.

First, the formal approach is determined and some of those characteristics are accentuated that stop it from being a valid instrument with which to grasp the process of human activity. Second, some of those aspects of human activity that place it out of reach of formal analysis are determined. Last, some of the points discussed are demonstrated in the work activity of a group of control room operators in a city district heating system.

Cognitive Science as Abstract and Formal

Newell and Simon (1972) characterized their own conception as emerging from a powerful and growing Zeitgeist, having its origins around the turn of the century and coming together just before and after World War II. The Zeitgeist congealed from the formalization of logic and mathematics of Whitehead and Russell, Shannon's information theory, Wiener's cybernetics based on servomechanism theory, and control theory. Thus, Newell and Simon pointed to these developments in formal sciences and engineering, which made the computers and automatic plants of today possible, and hence they based their understanding of human beings on technological developments. As they saw it, the fundamental contribution of formal logic was that the manipulation of symbols "could be described in terms of specific, concrete processes quite as readily as could the manipulation of pine boards in a carpenter's shop. The formalization of logic showed that symbols can be copied, compared, rearranged, and concatenated with just as much definiteness of process as boards can be sawed, planed, measured and glued" (p. 877).

To base one's understanding of human beings on control processes utilized in technological progress is not necessarily problematic in itself. In the industry, the formalisms were planed, measured, sawed, and glued so that plant productions were regulated and controlled in anticipated ways. This feature made the formalizations advocated in Bruner et al.,

(1956) and in Miller, Galanter, and Pribram (1960) appear workable in the behavioral scientist's shop. A conscious control of behavior could be understood as processes that were open to the same kind of scientific control procedures as behavior and the construction of industrial plants. Consciousness was not anymore a volatile phenomenon studied by vitalists; control structures were a theme that made the study of consciousness possible at the behavioral departments of primarily American universities. All the same, it remains an issue whether such formalisms grasp the central aspects of subjectivity. In order to examine this, a discussion of the formal paradigm is necessary.

It would not be very convincing to claim that people are like computers or like the automatic control functions of an industrial plant. "Then it becomes relevant to discover whether man is all bits on the inside" (Newell & Simon, 1972, p. 5). But it can be stated that there is a theoretical identity between computers and people, because they are both instances of the same abstract information processing system. According to Newell and Simon, to proceed in this way makes it possible to disregard the material side of the computer, its fast arithmetic, and its simply ordered memory, and on the other hand human physiological mechanisms. The abtraction allows the study of the precise symbolic process, the implementation of which will be restricted by material considerations, whether the process is implemented in people or machines.

Thus, on the level of the abstract information processing system, the performance of human problem solving is investigated as symbolic behavior. Some aspects of human behavior are omitted, however. Learning is seen as changes in the performance of the individual, and it is claimed that as long as the theory of performance in human problem solving is not well understood, it is better to abstain from the study of learning (Newell & Simon, 1972). Furthermore, unlike computers, human beings possess a fully developed perceptual system. But in perception one can find gestalt phenomena, whose nature is not sequential and has not yet been determined. Because the theory of symbolic behavior works with sequential processes, perception also has been omitted. The study of human problem solving may thus be characterized as a formal theory of how problems are solved, discounting perception, learning, and behavior.

Consider this abstract theory, which emerged from the construction of control structures in automatic machines and then was applied to human beings. In what way would the formal theory of sequential symbolic behavior determine how an operator reacts to alarms in an automated hydraulic system? The answer has not been worked out in detail, but it is possible to sketch the direction such an investigation would take. According to the delimitation of Newell and Simon, it is necessary to disregard perception, learning, and development, and therefore consider an abstract case of recognition, which is pure routine. If everyday life were different from their conception—that is, if you could learn from even the most drowsy routine—Newell and Simon would not be able to detect it, having eliminated learning from the theory and relegated it to other kinds of investigation.

By excluding anything new or changing in the operators' recognition, or in any other aspects of their activity, we gain an ability to formalize the operators' routine. It becomes possible to identify formal symbols, which can be processed in an information processing system, and that denote alarms, pumps, vents, and so on in the plant. To make this formalization work properly all the symbols relevant to the system of the plant must be identified. The elementary operations in the information processing system—those of copying, comparing, rearranging, and concatenating—must be used to construct the complete set of more specific operations on the symbols relevant to the functioning of the plant: acknowledging alarms, turning pumps on and off, opening and closing vents, and so forth. As the behavior of the operator is conditioned, we must set-up the proper conditions for each operation—for turning pumps on or off, for opening or closing vents. Each condition and operation is called a *production*, and these productions may be put together in production systems. For example, this means small episodes like: Turn on the pump when all valves are open and the pressure is too low and monitor the pump until the pressure is at the standard level of the plant, this being the goal level. All the production systems relevant to the operation of the plant are included in a closed problem space, containing all the possible states of the system, and all the possible productions to be performed on the states and all the possible goals of the plant. The problem solving in the information processing system of the operators is then determined in the following way. The plant is in one state (e.g., an alarm turns on when pressure is too low), they know the relevant goal state for this alarm (e.g., attaining the standard level pressure), and they must now identify the set of productions with which they can proceed from the alarm state to the goal state. A fundamental procedure with which to move from the initial state to the solution is a search hierarchy: Each possible production is tested against the initial state, and the new state is analyzed in terms relevant to obtaining the goal. The best production is chosen, a further state is obtained by applying yet another production, and so on.

The concepts of symbol, operation, production, production system, problem space, and search hierarchy have become the common lore of cognitive scientists. They were originally developed through the analysis of small problems, like how to open a safe with 10 turn knobs, each having 10 possible positions. The problem can also be used to illustrate another key concept in cognitive science, which pointed to its further development. The systematic search dictates setting all knobs at the first position, then turning the first knob through all its positions, then setting the second knob on its second position, again turning the first knob through all its positions, and so on, until the knobs were in the position allowing the safe to be opened. If now the click of each knob was detectable when it entered the correct position, then the search would be greatly reduced. This is an example of a heuristic search, in which knowledge about the particular safe shortens considerably the search for the correct position of the knobs. Everyday experience tells that the heuristic search mostly resembles the way human beings work with problems. This consideration is especially valid for operators; they would not perform a systematic search of all the possible production rules applicable to the present state of the plant; they would do something resembling a mixture of a heuristic and systematic search, based on their acquired knowledge of the workings of the plant. The change from general procedures in problem solving to heuristic searches based on knowledge of the problem space was a key development in cognitive science in the 1970s.

To acknowledge the importance of heuristic searches makes the importance of learning evident. Originally, when Newell and Simon defined their new science of information processing, they were scientifically strict by delimiting their approach from learning and perception. As already demonstrated, the formal theories they applied transformed problem solving to formal operations in an axiomatic system, in which all the elements for the solution of the problem are given before the solution is embarked upon. The formalisms can only be applied after the problem has been posed (cf. Seidel, 1976). By excluding perception, learning, and development, in processes one would expect the problem to be encoded, or, better, to be posed, Newell and Simon were hence acting in accordance with their theoretical approach, not necessarily in accordance with the necessities of reality. To introduce heuristics is to introduce the fruits of learning without attacking the problem of understanding learning. In this way, Newell and Simon could continue their investigations into formal procedures, and leave the study of learning to somebody else. Only in cases where it is required by the theoretical approach is it self-evident that performance must be studied without learning. One might as well on the basis of another conception claim that because everything a human being is able to perform is learned and relearned, learning must be studied as performance.

The pressure for issues of learning, arising from work with heuristics and the therein contained work with expert systems, forced cognitive science to take up issues of learning and perception. The late Newell followed this trend with the AI programming system SOAR, which purports to be a general system to build expert systems able to learn (Waldrop, 1988). Simon claimed that problems in perception have been solved with the techniques of neural networks (Vera & Simon, 1993).

The need for a theory of learning and perception, however, does not change the preconditions of formal theories; it is still true that formal theories can only be applied to closed problem spaces in which all elements and operations are determined in advance. A formal description of how operators respond to alarms must still be based on the closed set of representations for alarms, of acknowledging alarms, and the closure purportedly obtained by limiting the problem space to the present set of alarms in the system. This may be taken to mean that by performing the operations of a formal system in a problem space, it may be possible to combine the present elements in as many ways as allowed by the rules for permutation, but it will never be possible to abstract a new kind of symbol or operation learned from the operations or from a formally operating perceptual system. This conclusion is based on an important discussion in philosophy. This chapter only looks at its outlines:

In an abstract formal system the abstraction process is presupposed. This is Locke's idea of concept formation, which became one of the roots of formal logic. Nelson (1974, p. 270) explained that, to Locke, "it is by a process of abstraction that concepts are formed; we observe a number of particular objects and abstract from them those features that are common to several of them. Concepts are formed when objects are classified. Not only must we notice similarities to form a general idea, but we must also set aside particular differences, which are not relevant to the concept in question." This argument has two steps, first we note common features and set aside particular differences in a set of objects, then we classify the objects according to their common features. The classification is normally said to constitute the concept. Cassirer (1953) argued that "the concept, however, is not deduced thereby, but presupposed; for when we ascribe to a manifold an order and connection of elements, we have already presupposed the concept, if not in its complete form, yet in its fundamental function" (p. 17). Cassirer argued that the classification presupposes the abstracted features, and the concept is inherently constituted by the abstracted features, which the classification simply confirms. The classification is the formal process, the abstraction lies before it and sets up the concept. This circumstance parallels an earlier statement that the posing of a problem comes before its formal statement.

This was the reason that Newell and Simon disregarded perception and learning, which are connected with the abstraction process.

Formal statements are only valid after the concept has been established. But could it then be possible to explain the abstraction process itself whether in perception or in learning through a formal system? This question immediately defeats itself. The reason is that in perception and learning the objects appear as the unity of the particular and universal. Logical statements, however, deal with universals and not with specific objects (cf. Passmore, 1994, on Herbarth, p. 159f.). This must mean that as long as the operators of the example have not found out that the specific object in front of them is an alarm, they cannot use formal statements. To put it bluntly, logic will not help them decide whether the blinking light is an alarm, reflections of a moving object, or whatever. According to the formal description, they may reason about their assumptions, and the reasoning may guide them, but the reasoning presupposes preformed concepts to work with and thus the reasoning helps them choose among preestablished conceptual alternatives. Hence, you cannot use conditional statements to establish or identify the universal aspects of this particular thing! There must be other kinds of necessities involved in perception and learning. These other necessities must be able to work in an open space, meaning that they must allow for the possibility of acknowledging that the object confronting the operator was not an alarm of this kind, but maybe of another kind, or maybe something else whose identity must be ascertained.

According to this line of argument, abstraction, perception, concept formation, learning, and human development cannot be explained by formal systems. Furthermore, mathematics cannot be identified with the formalistic school of Whitehead and Russell. There are other mathematical schools that contest whether formalisms constitute mathematics (cf. Davis & Hersch, 1990). Formal systems are tools with which to systematize elements already formed and belonging to a closed space. Within the terms of the formal paradigm and its application on thinking, there are serious problems. The nature of the problems offers reasons of sufficient strength to transcend the paradigm. It now becomes the task to identify how human beings dig meaning out of a situation. Newell and Simon stated that the formal, mechanical operations of copying, comparing, rearranging, and concatenating are just as definite as the processes of sawing, planing, measuring, and gluing pine boards. This statement demonstrates the tool character of formalisms. If formalisms are tools, then go back one step and study the use of tools. It will be necessary to investigate the carpenter's shop, the computer scientist's shop, and the social activity of the subjects in the shops. The central aspects of human subjectivity must be determined.

Human Activity as Embodied and Situated

The discussion of Newell and Simon noted that symbolic behavior was considered an abstract theory on a level above computers and human beings. To allow the formal approach to be applied, the problem space was closed; all symbols, operations, and states belonging to the specific problem to be solved were enclosed in this space. On the one hand, this procedure would be defended by Newell and Simon on the grounds that the abstract level included the essentials of the problem-solving process. On the other hand, intrinsic aspects of the object of study have been locked out. To isolate a theoretical domain on its own is the characteristic feature of essentialism, where the abstracted form is given precedence over content, where the abstract formalisms are located in a realm of their own parallel to concrete reality, and where it hence becomes impossible to connect the two domains (cf. Axel, 1992). The problems of essentialism remain as long as formal, abstract theories are employed. Perception, learning, and development were separated from performance in order to allow for formalizations. When cognitive science does take on the task of theorizing about learning, it is viewed as acquiring existing knowledge, learning is always understood in the past tense. To cognitive science, existing knowledge can be contained in a closed problem space in which the flow of knowledge from node to node can be studied. This excludes invention and reinvention of knowledge, which are difficult problems to cognitive science (Lave, 1993, p. 12). Thus, in trying to mold content (learning) according to form (formal control theory), central aspects of reality have escaped cognitive science.

To avoid losing central aspects of our subject, we must let our theory of human behavior, of human activity, be molded by its subject matter. This means it cannot be extracted out of its realm; we must immerse ourselves in the material process. To step back to see formalisms used as tools in the computer scientist's shop and thus to study concrete human subjectivity, means to enter material human activity. To step back, moreover, means to include ourselves as participants in the social process investigated. We investigators are human beings ourselves, we must be guided by our own participation in the processes. Our participation is our human method— our ethnomethod—with which we explore human activity. The differentiations we make must be relevant to participants, including ourselves. We must begin with the object we confront when stepping back, with the social activity of human subjects in the shop and its meanings. This approach can be generally characterized as working with concrete, real activity and with embodied and situated meanings.

In our case, to study concrete, real activity means to ask ourselves how an operator comes to identify what is in front of him as an alarm, to ask how he recognizes this particular thing in front of him as an alarm, as having universal aspects. If we now claim that we must study how the operator sees the particular thing in front of him, we defy ourselves: we are able to identify it only through universals (e.g., "particular" and "thing" are universals of language presupposing a very general level of discussion). On the other hand, we have claimed that we cannot presuppose universals—to do so would mean relegating their development out of the field of study. The study of concrete, real activity thus includes studying the object of activity as the dialectical unity of the particular and the universal. It means studying how the particularities of the object are determined through its universalities, how the universalities are determined through the particularities, and how the two opposites develop each other in human social activity. Concrete, real activity unites the human being and the situation, and constitutes an active organism–environment relationship. What gives meaning to the human being, what is relevant to it, makes it act. A first broad identification of meanings is their relevance for acting, and meanings as part of the active organism–environment relationship are embodied as well as situated.

The meanings of social activity are embodied. The embodied aspect is a unity of a species specific and biographical perspective in human activity. Even though the term *embodiedness* is not used in Critical Psychology, the species-specific aspects of human activity may be explicated with categories from Critical Psychology. To Critical Psychology, the social nature of human beings implies that they satisfy their needs through socially produced objects (cf. Tolman & Maiers, 1991, pp. 12–15). Therefore, even though specific societies restrict the development of some individuals more than others, such a differentiation in social opportunities is seen as a historically conditioned aspect of society. The fundamental aspect of society is the fact that it provides human beings with objects to consume for the satisfaction of their needs, and this provision is a result of productive human activity. Now, the embodied aspects manifest themselves in the organization of human activity, its immediate as well as its mediated aspects. Human beings as bodies in social time and space must arrange their activities in more or less regular and interwoven rounds: repeated participations in different social activities and their coordination (cf. Dreier, 1994, pp. 72–74; Holzkamp, 1995). Some of the rounds take care of immediate needs like sleep, food, and social contact; others make arrangements between them, like providing shelter, food, and so forth; yet, other activities enter into more mediated and interwoven connections, participation in societal productive activities, or their arrangements. We may take this to mean that, generally, the embodied aspect of meanings concerns a species-specific arrangement of activity rounds based on an individual history of situated changes and developments. When we turn to concrete human beings, the meanings they act on operate within sets of acts, and their arrangements may therefore also be understood as an expression of the unity of the species-specific and biographical perspectives in their activity.

The meanings of social activity are *situated*. This implies that they change according to the relevancies of the situation. The relevancies of the situation change according to the activity of the subject and to situational aspects both here and now and in other locations and at other times—that is, to general and specific aspects of the situation. To cope with situational changes, the individual must develop. Thus, it can be said that situated activity always involves changes in knowledge and action (Lave, 1993, p. 5). Meaning is part of and a product of social history. Furthermore, the circumstance that meaning is situated implies that participants in activity, with their own perspectives, have their own angle on the meanings of the situation. This also has implications for the meaning of tools, and is related to the concept of boundary objects (Star & Griesemer, 1989). Boundary objects are common objects in an institutional setting, where each group of participants organizes specific routines according to those aspects of the boundary objects that are relevant for activities in its site.

Indeed, to step back from seeing formalisms as tools in the computer scientist's shop and thus to study human activity entails studying human subjectivity, investigating purposeful human activity in the shop. It is important to determine the uses of the tool sets, the purposes they serve and the anticipations and organizations they set up. Within the trend of investigating embodied situated activity, Critical Psychology is conspicuous for having developed a category of the subject (Holzkamp, 1983; Tolman & Maiers, 1991). It has already been stated that studying human activity as embodied and situated is to think developmentally. The inherent intent of such a project is to grasp human beings as active participants in their own development dependent on the social circumstances.

The category of subject is meant to grasp these aspects. It is many-sided and systematically developed in Critical Psychology, but here it only can be sketched. Subjectivity is seen as having developed phylogenetically from the need for exploratory activity in mammals. Animals explore unknown aspects in their biosphere in order to master them. Along with the development of human social nature, the need for exploratory activity evolved into a need to explore and cooperatively master unknown aspects of the social situation of the human being—whether these be objects, meanings, social processes having impact on its life, social processes it partakes in, or whatever. This need is called *productive need*. Exploration unfolds through ordinary activity when conditions render it meaningful to subjects, and as an exploring participant in social processes the subjects change themselves by changing changed circumstances. The productive need is thus the origin of human active development, and because any activity (even the most distracted routine) contains possibilities for development, productive needs must be considered to be involved in any activity to a greater or lesser extent.

To think developmentally is to think in possibilities. Accordingly, Critical Psychology opens the way for actions to be seen as not being totally determined by social conditions, but appearing as possibilities for action under certain conditions. It is stated that when a human being acts, it makes use of the conditions of its social position and their meaning for its action possibilities. The category of action potence is a focal point for the category of subjectivity: The determinations of productive needs, action possibilities, and conditions merge in it. A human being is said to have action potence, if the social conditions open up the possibility for that human being to have the ability to participate in the social regulation and development of its life conditions. Here, *ability* means subjective potentials in relation to those of the situation.

Action potence is seen as a species-specific human need. Its need character becomes evident, for example, in the fear of being exposed to adverse social conditions. It is common in social science to find conceptions wherein social beings are either seen as totally socially determined or as totally freewheeling, as if they were able to change their life at will. The category of subject has been developed in order to deal with the circumstance that human beings are active and socially determined. The fact that they are beings socially evolved means that what happens to them and what they become cannot happen without their being active. Human beings relate to, act in, and thereby change their social conditions. Any act is a reciprocal change of circumstances and subjects, the geographical and organizational extent of development being also dependent on the conditions of the act.

The subject makes use of its action conditions. The conditions are not exploited one at a time; all the conditions and their interwoven relations and contradictions in a situation constitute one complex qualitative evaluation of the situation on which the subject acts.

However, even though all meaningful aspects of the situation form part of the evaluation of relevance, the subject focuses on some, and differentiates, selects, or unfolds some, as the most pertinent on the background of the situation. This implies that meaning is neither additive nor abstractable from the situation; it is a situated totality. That is, meaning cannot be pieced together into a closed problem space as we attempted when discussing in what way the formal theory of Newell and Simon would determine how operators react to alarms. On the contrary, the operators estimate the configuration of alarms according to their knowledge of the plant, its general state of disrepair, of how it was regulated by the operators on duty before them, on how much trouble they can take just now, and so on. They made use of all these conditions in their reaction—if you ask them, they will explain. But they did not reflect on each of them and then act. They acted on their complex qualitative evaluation, and then reflected when asked. They could go on giving aspects and reasons for their action for as long as you cared to ask (cf. Garfinkel, 1967, p. 24ff.). There is no closure, and all the same, they made an evaluation of the total situation and acted on a pattern of considerations in the situation.

Had they reflected, they might have prefigured future events, and their reflection on their acts might have made them learn why things happened, and led to a reorganization of future complex qualitative evaluations. But, reflection presupposes that the individuals have experience from activity to reflect on. Furthermore, they are not only acting on immediate considerations such as the set of alarms, but also on mediated ones, as on what happened to the plant on the previous period of duty, on the general state of disrepair of the plant, where their evaluation of the general state is also determined by what they generally expect about repair states in their society, and so forth. Situated meaning is socially mediated (Dreier, 1993, p. 113).

Now, it has been stated that situated meaning is historical and changes according to the relevancies of the situation, and that meanings are accordingly organized specifically on each location in an institution, in a society. From such a location, situated meaning reaches toward other locations. Also, it has been stated that meanings are the meanings of conditions for action possibilities. All this implies that meanings must be understood from the perspective of the subject, though they are not subjective in the sense of being arbitrary or completely free. Each meaning has its material conditions and material consequences, and has its relations to other times and places. Bound up with the subjective perspective, meanings are based on interests to achieve certain anticipated events. The distribution of conditions and resources opens up for configurations of more or less comprehensive, more or less restrictive interests. The distribution is a central element in the formation of the different perspectives on a situation. Among the different perspectives there may be conflicting interests with respect to participation in the social regulation and development of conditions and resources. This implies conflictual negotiations of the state of the system. Like meanings, the conflicting interests are mediated. A conflict between Ms. White and Mr. Blue in a control room is not only an immediate conflict between people, nor a mediated conflict between only professional groups but also is a conflict between classes. As participants, we have no privileged position from which we can judge who is right. The general ambiguity of conflict processes does not allow for an unequivocal definition of the initial problem. Individual points of view on the problem will not totally coincide, and no single contradiction could be resolved into anything other than a contradiction (Dreier, 1991, p. 203).

According to the relative positions and scope of interests of the participants in conflict, *deadlocks* or *developments* are created. Deadlocks may be tense or relaxed; developments may be step by step or in terms of a fundamental reorganization. Conflicts may come into deadlocks for many reasons: The distribution of resources may make a set of restrictive interests possible so that the actions of some block the interests of others. Reciprocal loss of control in conflicts also narrows the viewpoint of participants. In such cases, the conflicts become easily personalized (Dreier, 1991, p. 203).

When conflicts open the way for development, the scope of relevant interests is more comprehensive. One way such a scope can be patterned can be identified in the following case. Ohm (1989) reported on a participatory planning of a new computer system in a botanical garden. Botanists with university degrees defined the institution as one that should serve the scientific classification of plants, whereas the gardeners without university degrees saw the institution as one that should serve the cultivation of rare and not well-known plants. Ohm maintained that this type of conflict seems to be inherent in the organization of botanical gardens, and mentioned that at a certain point in time it lay behind the suicide of a director of one. The introduction of a computer system for the registration of plants created an opportunity for change. On the basis of discussions with the professional groups, a common project was outlined. The extinction of many plants in nature was made the background for setting up the task of storing seeds from plants for future use and for entering their classification into a database along with information on their growth and cultivation. Thus, a new computer system was an opportunity to expand the two specific interests and thus move toward a more comprehensive one.

On the basis of the categories presented, how meanings are established can be explored further. We briefly consider how the process of identifying meanings works—this process that Cassirer argued was presupposed in formal systems. As meanings are embodied and situated totalities, we cannot say that they are abstracted, or pulled out, from a situation; they are focused figures on a situational background. Thus, all possibly meaningful aspects of the situation may form part of the evaluation of relevancies, on the basis of which the subject focuses on a meaningful formation of the situation. The main sides of activity involved in the discussion are its productive, consumptive, and distributive facets and its aspects of time, space, and matter. As meanings are social, they are used (or consumed), but as they change with the situation, they are simultaneously used and reproduced each time anew. As meanings are situated, they are concrete and particular; as they are recognizable from situation to situation, they are universal, or distributed. Meanings are thus determined as the unity of the universal and the particular, of consumption and production in activity.

When social objects (processes, routines, or tools) are consumed or used in activity, they are seen as the unity of the universal and particular aspects of meaning. Regulating or investigating the plant in which I work, and which was designed by contractors with an anonymous operator in mind, I will create a particular reproduction of its general use on the basis of my previous experience. Dependent on the circumstances and my relations to them, my reproduction will modify the universal theme I find in the plant, the modification ranging from the easily overlooked to conspicuous, easily remembered ways of use.

When I observe your particular way of regulating the plant, I notice the contrast between what you do and what I would have done. When I see how you do it, I may wonder what makes you do it that way. Dependent on the circumstances and my relation to them based on previous experience, I may investigate the reasons more or less thoroughly, and deepen my knowledge of the particular circumstances in this case, thereby grasping the universal aspects of the situation better. In other words, the greater my experience, the better I grasp both the universal and the particular aspects of the situation.

My regulation of the plant, and my investigation of your way of doing it, is part of the general social distribution of that kind of plant. The plant or its components must be incorporated in a widespread social practice so that we can find its meaning by identifying differences and similarities, particularities, and universalities in different uses. There are some plants like this one, and we hear what kinds of problems operators of the other plants run into. Our group works each day with this plant, regulates it routinely under different circumstances. I regulate the pump and other professional groups repair them, construct them, and buy them. Thus, we all routinely work with components in the plant for complementary purposes, in different locations, sometimes for the purpose we believe the component is meant for, other times not, and we may for different reasons contest each other's use of the components. In the midst of the conflicts and reciprocal contestations, each of my regular uses of these components acquires an obviousness to each of us, which makes it look as if the meaning of the plant and its components were carried by them. However, if I discover an artifact, a tool, or a language whose use nobody knows, then I may be able to recover its meaning only if I can relate it more or less directly to artifacts whose use is known. The tool acquires its meaning through the kinds of practice related to the one it was meant for, and the meaning cannot be understood only from the form of the tool. The tool is a condition of life for me, and through comparisons between our practices its form becomes meaningful to me by opening new action possibilities, which I may explore further on my own.

When the contractors produced or designed the plant, they gave it a particular form according to their anticipation of its general use. The meaning they found in that kind of plant made them design it in this way. When the operators began to regulate the plant, they may for good reasons the contractors did not know, and had no need to know, use it in ways not anticipated. The contractors cannot claim that the operators have used it wrongly, even though this use was not included in their general apprehension. Such phenomena demonstrate that tools get their meaning through their social use, and there is no crucial difference between the processes of according the tool with meaning when it is used in the general and common way or in a unique way. The general use the designer anticipated is not immanent in the tool. It is not written on the forehead of a chair that one can sit on it, use it as a ladder, as a weapon, as firewood if it is made of wood, and so forth. But when I use a tool in the general and common way, I can say that I use it as intended and be right.

Meanings have here been determined as the meaning of conditions for action possibilities, and thus as based on interests to achieve ends. To be interested in achieving a specific situation is to value it, which is the result of an emotional evaluation of the present and future state of the situation and the subject. To evaluate a future state of a situation is to anticipate what may happen and to strive for one of the possibilities: We are not able to know exactly what the future holds for us. We may have a general idea, we may have a hunch, or a more or less vague perception of what may come, which makes us explore possibilities. I strive to achieve something which I perceive vaguely. I strive differently according to my anticipation, and my endeavor shapes my anticipation: To have a hunch in explorative activity is a basic phenomenon that forces us to admit the existence of cognitive functions in emotions. We cannot say that emotions determine cognition, nor can we say that cognition determines meaning, but we must acknowledge their interrelatedness. This makes us see that we cannot subtract emotion and be left with objective meaning as the remainder. Emotion and cognition as a unity form situated meaning. This also implies that we cannot talk abstractly about either emotion or cognition; when we discuss cognitive aspects of meanings, we are also implying their emotional aspects and vice versa. The hunch, the open idea, ready to be reorganized according to relevancies in praxis that it guides and is guided by, is that objective phenomenon that we take as a guideline to understand even the most stable perceptions in human consciousness. This must mean that a perception in consciousness may always be developed further, and that it is extremely likely that we may in principle at any time do the right thing for the wrong reasons.

Thus, in the reproduction of meaning, emotions and cognition reciprocally determine each other in a process playing on the dialectical unity of the particular and the universal, of necessity and coincidence, and progressing from the arbitrary beginning to the unfolded general meaning. This is implicated when I act and think, and when I think acts. In principle, it is a process that in relation to the object can take its beginning anywhere and stop anywhere. With good reasons its beginning, end, and direction are determined by conditions in the situation, my previous experience and my evaluation. Beginning anywhere means beginning with some aspect of praxis (e.g., either notions, perceptions, or vague feelings). It cannot mean that abstract universals are presumed at the starting point, but anywhere concrete meaning in concrete activity can unfold. Adopting a term from Lave (1988), we could call the process *gap closing*, a process of changing circumstances according to anticipations and anticipations according to circumstances until what unfolds is acceptable as what is strived for.

Even if it is claimed that meaning resides in consciousness, it must be made absolutely clear that meaning is social and dynamic, meaning is the coordinating rhythm of social dance. Meaning does not come from within, from archetypical symbols in hereditary constitution or other conceptions like that. Nor is it inherent in things. But tools have significance for me, I accord them with meaning in the situations of my social activity, in keeping with my way of using them.

This, then, is a conception of situated meaning. Meaning is as stable as the conditions for activity; it changes according to activity and wanes with the conditions of activity. As stated, this does not imply that meaning is immediate and only concerns the situation here and now, but it implies that the focus of an organized system of meaning is determined by the organization of kinds of situations, their anticipations, and tools. I may still have an idea what this alarm means, even if I have not reacted to it for years, but my concrete reaction to it with all its shortcuts, remedies, and smartness comes to me through repeated reaction in the rounds of everyday work situations.

This conception implies that the establishing of situated meaning can best be investigated in everyday life. Work situations are one part of human activity, where all the many-sided aspects of a situation coalesce to accord it with meaning. This process can be identified in the negotiation of errors in the following exploration of some operators working in a district heating system.

AN EMPIRICAL EXPLORATION OF TOOL USE
WITH LOCALIZED MEANINGS

The Plant

We will look at a district heating system—which I will call the Company—from the point of view of its operators. What is said about the localization and funtioning of the Company in the community is to be understood as a perspective coming into view through a confrontation between a researcher and a group of operators. The task will be to demonstrate that the problem-based and localized understanding of the operators emerges as the result of according the plant with meaning in its social connections. The plant as a tool comprises ways of working, which left to themselves would make them wander beyond social meaningfulness. This ongoing process is a central part of the work conditions of the operators. They must bend the ongoing activities by relating to the social needs, demands, and anticipations they are exposed to in their workplace. It will also be important to understand the broader perspectives they talk about as getting their meaning from the daily operation of the network.

The Company must be considered as a societal response from the 1980s to the oil crisis in the 1970s. The response is multifaceted: There is no single goal, no unequivocal intent—to use Bourdieu's phrase: the response is orchestrated with no conductor. Among the aspects of the response, the ecological and economical ones are in the foreground. Each aspect is complex and laden with potential conflicts.

This goes right into the core of the physical process of the plant. From the perspective of the power plants, the heating system is a coolant agent. Water under high pressure in the pipes carries heat away from the plants. The water runs through a number of heat exchangers, which cools the water of the district heating system, and the cooled water returns to remove yet another round of heat. From the perspective of the consumers, be they municipalities or households, the district heating system through the heat exchangers delivers heat, and relatively cheaply compared to other available resources. As a coolant agent, the system must be available according to the production of electricity. As a heating agent, the system must be available according to weather conditions. Many times the conditions will support each other (e.g., during the winter it is cold and dark), therefore the need for heat and electricity are both enhanced; the 24-hour rhythm of the two needs is also a close match. But even in winter, some days are colder than others, although any one day can be as cloudy as another, and so on. The operators say that in the beginning of the operation of the network, old power plants supplied the heat. Prior to the construction of the network, these plants had the control over the level of production of electricity as well as heat. This made the operators of the power plants reluctant to respond to the needs of the Company, and created a lot of tension. The newer plants started up with the Company already present, therefore the operators of those plants easily accomodated the needs of the Company.

This development story contains aspects of a pattern that appears regularly in the operators' explanations. Initially, they describe a situation, which is unappealing because some need is not met and you get a lot of trouble, discord, and conflict between work groups of the network. Then they tell you about the arrival of a new rule or component, either of which solves some problems. If you specifically ask, you will hear that it also creates others and you are reassured that, as an answer to the present state of discord and conflict, a new set of rules or yet a new component is set up, either of which creates order and a smooth operation. If there are still disagreements, then they go through another more fine-grained round. Thus, the vanishing point of their stories is an end state, which they laughingly talk about as unachievable, and which resembles the night shift: The graph giving the trend is a nice, smooth curve, and the operator can lean back in a big armchair and watch everything without having to do anything. Their stories are thus in compliance with the formal approach: It is possible to implement the automation of the plant so that nothing needs to be done.

But by persisting and asking whether conflicts between the cooling of the plant and the heating of the city are really settled, or are still a source for action, one can get a spectrum of answers. Some will tell you that the contradiction still pops up in the anticipation of rare situations. For example, in an emergency situation, the need for electricity must be met before the need for heating. Also, operators of an electrical power plant are not allowed to strike, but operators of a heating plant are. Others will tell you that the conflict between heating homes and cooling power plants will constantly pop up in the acquisition of different components, and give a recent acquisition as an example. You will also hear about rules, which are constantly contested and are set up so that the priority of power production is ensured. Thus, on the one hand, you are presented with an official story in compliance with the general ideology of an automated workplace: The plant will nearly run by itself, if you can just disregard some small annoyances. But, if you persist and scratch the surface, you can collect a set of examples, illustrating conflicts permeating the process of the plant, and having different appearance in the everyday work functions.

The Company was established to save money, and it is organized according to the way power production has been organized in Denmark for many years—a procedure with peculiar resonances in the basic ideological prescription of the 1980s. Even though the Company cannot go bankrupt or be taken over by a competitor, it is driven as a private enterprise and must show profits. Cost-efficiency is in everyone's mind.

The Company is the result of the cooperation of municipalities at different levels of their organization. It is not unusual among the operators to interpret each action of the authorities according to the question "whom does it benefit?" In the network of a certain part of town, the water runs at lower temperatures than other parts. At the same time, there is a limit to the amount of water that can run through that specific network. This means the Company cannot meet demands with cheap heat from its main network. In that case, the municipality is allowed to start up an expensive power plant at the expense of the Company. Because the Company has the monopoly of selling and buying heat, it must buy the more expensive heat from the power plant and sell it to the municipality that owns the plant and runs the network. This, in the opinion of the operators, can only mean that citizens from other municipalities will have to pay for the heat in this part of town.

In the organization the operators can be identified according to their tasks and the tasks of the work group with whom they have the closest relations—the engineers. The widespread adoption of computers in the 1980s has made it possible to automate the regulation of the district heating system on a level not seen before. The operator on duty sits in a control room at a console with seven computer screens and some key-boards for entering commands. Here he monitors and modifies the regu-lation of the network. As a consequence, their workload has been eased in some aspects, but the designers foresaw a new problem: boredom and emptiness. Therefore, they followed a trend in high-tech workplaces in Scandinavia to combine work functions. In the past few decades, before the advent of the computerized plant, these functions were divided as a matter of fact between specific work groups. Now the operators of the Company also perform the regulation of the plant as the maintenance of some aspects of it. They are also involved in the "ripening" of the plant, and in the planning and evaluation of the regulation.

Calibrating Pumps and Valves
or Reconstructing the Plant?

But these work functions are not easily distinguished. They are constantly changing, and what at one time looks like calibrating will at another time appear as mending a faulty component. The following example of work on the heat exchangers demonstrates the change of meanings according to the perceived goals.

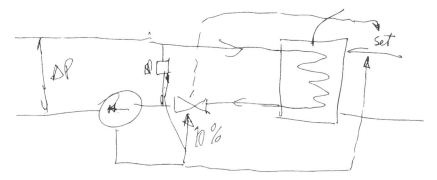

FIG. 7.1. Diagram drawn by operator, showing main components in the control system of the heat exchanger. Pump, valve, heat exchanger, setpoint, pipes, and cables drawn. Delta p, pressure difference between pipes to and from heat exchanger indicated.

The heat exchanger is a complex piece of equipment, which can most easily be identified by four of its main components (see Fig. 7.1). First, there is the heat exchanger itself, where heat is exchanged through metal plates between the water of the Company, the primary side of the heat exchanger as seen from the Company, and the water of the consumer, the secondary side. On the primary side, hot water enters the exchanger, gives off heat to the secondary side, and cooled water then leaves the exchanger on the return side of the primary side. Immediately after the exchanger it passes through a valve and then a pump. These components regulate the amount of water passing through the primary side, determined by the temperature of the water, which leaves the exchanger on the secondary side. Here a regulating device is located, which measures the temperature of the water and compares it to a setpoint. If the temperature is lower than the setpoint, a command is issued to the valve on the primary side to open more up. More water will pour through the exchanger, and the temperature on the secondary side will increase above the setpoint, a command is issued to close down a certain amount, and now less water will pass through on the primary side. This will go on for a while, and the oscillations dampen, and in the end the secondary side will get a stable supply of water at a set temperature. A further refinement is added to this. The regulating valve on the primary side will cause the least disturbance of the pressure in the network, if its opening is within a specific range. If the changes in the amount of water are so large that the opening of the valve is outside this range, then—after some time has passed and the change has thereby proven stable—the state of the pump is changed automatically in such a way that the valve will be within its opening range and the temperature on the secondary side still meets the setpoint.

Now, the interplay of pumps and valves within the network as a whole creates pressure waves, which the designers were not able to calculate before the construction of the system. Therefore, they made it the task of the operators to identify the opening range of the valves, the amount of opening asked for by the regulating device on the secondary side, and the steps in effect the pumps must take when changing the opening of the valves. A part of the construction of the system was thus transferred by the construction engineers to the operators.

This calibration occupied the operators for 4 or 5 months after the initiation of the system. Out of this work emerged two strategies of regulation, each advocated by its originator. One strategy was to let the valves stay as open as possible. This would cause the least loss of pressure, and therefore economize the effect used in the pumps. It also meant that the pumps would accomplish a greater part of the regulation. The other strategy was to let the valve regulate the small changes, and the pump the bigger ones. This would ensure a more stable delivery to the consumer on the secondary side. There would, however, be a slight loss in pump economy, as the pump would have to work for a short time under adverse conditions. But the operator advocating this strategy also had a solution to this slight impediment. He said that the regulating device on the secondary side should also be changed so that it could send a command directly to the pump, if the change in heat was greater than a specified value and lasted for at least a specified time. In this way, one could avoid the two-step regulation of longer lasting large changes in temperature. But the operator could not make the managers pay the expenses for such a change in the working of the regulating device.

Since the inception of the strategies, their originators each worked according to their preferred strategy. When arriving at work, they tuned the system according to their strategy. Being on duty after one of the two advocates, the newcomers did not change the setpoints, but watched their behavior, and tested them. Some apparently did not, however, align in the discussions, whereas others felt the urge to alter the settings, if the system was not stable during their shift. The constant altering of the settings proved to be a source of irritation. The operators had tried to agree on a common policy at some meetings but had not achieved agreement, and the conflict had gone stale. I was told that you could not really discuss the matter anymore. It was common lore in the control room to consider the divergence as a personal difference, maybe even a matter of personal style or taste.

Now, at the time of observation, some problems occurred in a heat exchanger station belonging to a municipality. The engineers working with it contacted the operators in order to get some help. The operator, who advocated the strategy of stable supply, made the contact, and working together they discovered that the regulating device was actually sending the required message to the pump, but somehow the message was getting lost along the way. It would be much too easy to deemphasize this course of events by stating that just after the inauguration of the system the operators simply performed a calibration of the heat exchangers on false premises, and that they might now have to redo it all, if the lost messages can be retrieved.

To understand the use of tools, it is important to stress the following points. As the two operators calibrated the heat exchangers, they did not only follow rules. They related to the working of the stations by investigating the behavior and they evaluated the performance according to the principles that should determine the workings of the system. One operator saw a problem in the uneconomical use of pumps and devised a strategy to optimize the use of effect for the pumps. The other operator—by the way according to rules—gave higher priority to stable delivery of heat and came up with a corresponding strategy. He even outlined a solution, which would reconciliate the differences between the two solutions by minimizing the inefficient use of pumps.

It is evident that the situated activity of manual calibration is not only determined by the immediate circumstances. Many mediated circumstances are involved and contested, each way of calibration is defended with a reinterpretation of general principles for the regulation of the plant. The background of the differences in relation to pump economy was unclear to me, but we note that the deadlock in the conflict narrows its scope down to a matter of personal style. This example also demonstrates the intimate relation between construction, optimizing, and fault finding. The course of the events discussed here can be regarded as a construction anew of smoother regulation principles, a reconstruction, or as the first steps in fault finding; it is determined by the operators according the plant with meaning in its social connections.

Negotiating Errors

To demonstrate that error identification is a functional aspect of a constructive relation to work tasks is to demonstrate the close relation between errors and the ever-changing anticipatory goals of action. Another aspect of this relation can be explored by an example on how different work groups see the same kinds of events.

A meeting was held in the Company in order to discuss a possible renewal of the computer equipment with which the system is regulated. Some representatives of the contractor of computer equipment, two operators, and two operation engineers were present at the meeting. One of the operators wanted to know whether there would be a change in an error, which they had from the beginning and often turned up. If the network on which commands were sent to their relevant locations is loaded, then it could happen that a command was lost, and had to be resent. Would that change with the new system? The contractor knew about this possibility, and related it to the specifications of the network, which would not change with the new equipment. Therefore, this would still be present when the new equipment was delivered. The operation engineers were taken by surprise, and stated that such an error could not be accepted in the system. The contractor argued that this way of functioning was up to specification.

Thus, errors must be understood as being identified according to the actions, interests, and ways of conception of work groups. The system engineers consider the way the communication network handles a command as an inconvenience due to specific features of the system. They may see many reasons for the inconvenience: limitations of present technology, of resources put into the project, and of the quality of the specifications. They are all related to their tasks as designers. Furthermore, the inconvenience is not an error, if the mode of operation is within agreed on specifications. The operation engineers inspect the system and must account for incidences in the system in the organization. Therefore, they consider the mode of operation an error due to its possible consequences, and get annoyed with such an error delivered with a system, for which they payed so much. The operators consider the mode of operation as a silly characteristic of the system not worth mentioning and easily circumvented, but that it would be nice to be without. Furthermore, these are not fixed and determined positions. The operation engineers looked up the specifications and found grounds for action; they made a case for it, and are now negotiating with the contractor how to handle the situation. The outcome of the negotiations will become conditions to which each group must relate, in order to accord them with meaning.

Testing a Pump

Each work group thus accords the process in the system with meaning in keeping with their anticipation of goals, and what counts as errors are part of this production of meaning. The redefinition of what is an error can also be found in the everyday regulation of the plant.

One cool day in winter, an operator got a call from a pump station, which contains pumps able to regulate the pressure in the system. These pumps are called fixed pumps because they cannot regulate but work on a fixed level. One of the fixed pumps had been serviced and the servicepeople wanted to check it. Due to the weather, the pump station assisted the power plant in regulating the pressure so that the regulating pump was on.

As the regulating pump was working, the operator identified his task as changing the workload to the fixed pump, and he thought he would have to do it manually. He would start the fixed pump in its basin, and stepwise he would have to open the valve manually, so that the pump gradually overtook the workload, and the regulating one would automatically recede. Manually opening a valve the right amount is not easy. You are only told how many percent the valve disc has turned, and there is no simple relation between percentage openness and amount of water able to pass through the valve. Furthermore, there is a delay in the feedback, you cannot see in real time the opening of the valve while you issue the command, and as you only know how long it takes to open the valve completely, you must judge how great a percentage openness is required and the time it takes to get there. But the task had to be done; he issued the opening command while counting slowly to 20, which measured the amount of time he thought was needed to open the valve to the required position. But, alas, the pressure went far beyond any anticipated level (see Fig. 7.2). This also meant that the automatic safety measure to protect the system made the pumps at the power plant stop regulating. This was not anticipated; now the two pumps at the pump station were both working, maintaining the pressure of the system. But looking at the situation, the operator discovered he had what he wanted, that is, the fixed pump was working. Thus, there was no need to go for the situation where the fixed pump had overtaken the workload from the

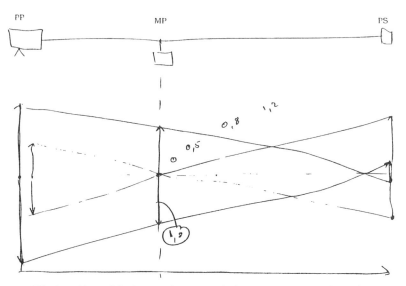

FIG. 7.2. Above: PP—Power Plant; pipes both ways; MP: measuring point; pipes both ways; PS: pump station. Below: Pressure graph; big difference at PP before starting pump at PS; small difference after.

regulating one. He would just have to stabilize the present situation, and then little by little give the work of maintaining the pressure back to the pumps at the power plant. A correction of errors is never pursued relentlessly but is only maintained so far as the functioning is understood as an error. The operator first changed circumstances according to anticipations, then he changed anticipations according to circumstances. What unfolded in front of him was accepted as what they were striving for, he made ends meet. We may also say that gap closing or other consequences of the ambiguity of the tool stopped the error correction in the middle of a jump so to speak, as soon as the context bound meaning of the tool in a concrete work activity has changed.

CONCLUSIONS

The fact that meaning is negotiated does not mean that it is not at times self-evident. And, inversely, the fact that meaning is self-evident under certain circumstances does not mean it cannot change under other circumstances. In everyday life it will not be a contested error if the water slipped out of the tubes into the city streets, but it is possible to imagine situations (for example in wartime) where this was a highly desirable effect for some people. This chapter has examined those processes that establish self-evident true meaning, and would also under other circumstances establish the opposite true meaning as self-evident. This is not relativity. If anything, it is absolute relativity: Meanings have conditions and consequences; meanings mean something.

It is hoped that the cases presented have demonstrated good reasons for exploring concrete everyday practice. Formalism in everyday practice is treated as a tool. It gets its meaning from the anticipations in everyday practice and it is bent and reorganized according to these. This conception has implications for what can and cannot become computerized. They are tentatively sketched out here.

Human beings working in an organization must be viewed as producing formalized procedures and tools. The stability of the formalized procedures, their robustness, will vary according to many aspects of the organizational practice. Formalized procedures set up to regulate physical systems must be modified over time according to changes in the way the system is used as a tool, in the way components are used in the system, and according to the introduction or development of new components. Sometimes the formalized procedures will need only slight modifications even after extensive changes in the physical system. At other times, the formalized procedures must be thoroughly rewritten due to small, but significant changes. The formal procedures produced to regulate the flow of tasks or the decisions in a bureaucratic organization, may, depending on the task at hand, be relatively open to interpretation. Thus, formalisms for date stamping of letters and journals, produced and used for matters of accountability, might relatively easily become computerized. Dependent on the action of the workers they can be set up as a well-defined and finite set of procedures on a specified set of elements. But the formalisms for much casework are harder to objectify in computers. Here the interpretational or gap closing aspect of the use of formalisms has a less controllable function, because it is much more an expression of the dynamic development of social life. The formalisms of casework cannot be determined definitively by being specified in minute detail, they come about as the result of localized conflict resolution in social organizations. You cannot determine the pension of Ms. Smith using formal procedures relying on, among other things, a minutely specified description of her invalidity; what she gets will be the result of social conflict ridden negotiation among the involved parties.

The possibility and ease of computerization is thus dependent on the relation between the interpreting, meaning producing, and gap closing aspect of human action and the produced formalistic tools. The good reasons to study the concrete everyday practice are that you can reach sensible decisions about computerization on the basis of the relation between, on the one hand, work functions producing meanings and, on the other hand, formal procedures. Where the meaning producing aspects can be controlled in such a way that the formal procedures can meaningfully be considered as a closed, well-defined set of procedures stable over time, the procedures can be computerized. In these cases, it is also important to establish a set of work routines that open up the possibility of developing challenging, rich, situated experience, on the basis of which regulation and monitoring can be performed efficiently. Only then can technology be implemented as a proper enhancement of human powers.

REFERENCES

Axel, E. (1992). One developmental line in European activity theories. *Quarterly Newsletter of LCHC, 14*(1), 8–17.

Bruner, J. S., Goodnow, J. J., & Austin, G. A. (1956). A study of thinking. New York: Wiley.

Cassirer, E. (1953). *Substance and function and Einstein's theory of relativity.* New York: Dover.

Davis, P. J., & Hersch, R. (1990). *The mathematical experience.* London: Penguin.

Dreier, O. (1991). Client interests and possibilities in psychotherapy. In C. W. Tolman & W. Maiers (Eds.), *Critical psychology, contributions to an historical science of the subject* (pp. 196–211). Cambridge, England: Cambridge University Press.

Dreier, O. (1993). Re-searching psychotherapeutic practice. In S. Chaiklin & J. Lave (Eds.), *Understanding practice, perspectives on activity and context* (pp. 104–124). Cambridge, England: Cambridge University Press.

Dreier, O. (1994). Personal locations and perspectives: Psychological aspects of social practice. *Psychological Yearbook, 1*, 63–90.

Garfinkel, H. (1992). *Studies in ethnomethodology.* Cambridge, England: Polity Press.

Henderson, K. (1993). *On line and on paper: Mixed practices in the visual culture of design engineering.* Paper presented at an invitational workshop within CSCW, at Centre Nationale de Recherches Scientifique (CNRS), Paris. Printed in Conference report: *Social science research, technical systems and cooperative work* (pp. 131–150).

Holzkamp, K. (1983). Grundlegung der Psychologie (Foundation of Psychology). Frankfurt/Main, New York: Campus Verlag.

Holzkamp, K. (1995). Alltägliche Lebensführung als subjektwissenschaftliches Grundkonzept (Conduct of everyday life as a category of the science of the subject). *Das Argument, 212*, 817–846.

Lave, J. (1988). *Cognition in practice.* Cambridge, England: Cambridge University Press.

Lave, J. (1993). The practice of learning. In S. Chaiklin, & J. Lave (Eds.), *Understanding practice: Perspectives on activity and context* (pp. 3–32). Cambridge, England: Cambridge University Press.

Miller, G. A., Galanter, E., & Pribram, K. H. (1960). *Plans and the structure of behavior.* New York: Holt, Rinehart & Winston.

Nelson, K. (1974). Concept, word, and sentence: Interrelations in aquisition and development. *Psychological Review, 81*(4), 267–285.

Newell, A., & Herbert, S. (1972). *Human problem solving.* Englewood Cliffs, NJ: Prentice-Hall.

Ohm, C. (1989). Verknüpfung von partizipativer Systementwicklung, Qualifizierung und Arbeitsforschung von unten. Bericht aus der Praxis kritischer Arbeitspsychologie (Connecting participatory design, qualification and workplace research from beneath. A report from the praxis of Critical Work Psychology). *Forum Kritische Psychologie* (24), 5–36.

Passmore, J. (1994). *A hundred years of philosophy.* Harmondsworth, Middlesex, England: Penguin.

Seidel, R. (1976). Denken—Psychologische Analyse der Entstehung und Lösung von Problemen (Thinking—A psychological analysis of the emergence and solution of problems). Frankfurt/Main: Campus Verlag.

Star, S. L., & Griesemer, E. M. (1989). Institutional ecology, 'Translations' and boundary objects: Amateurs and professionals in Berkeley's Museum of Vertebrate Zoology, 1907–1939. *Sociological Quarterly, 28*(2), 147–169.

Suchman, L. (1987). *Plans and situated actions: The problem of human–machine communication.* Cambridge, England: Cambridge University Press.

Tolman, C. W., & Maiers, W. (1991). *Critical psychology: Contributions to an historical science of the subject.* Cambridge, England: Cambridge University Press.

Vera, A. H., & Simon, H. A. (1993). Situated action: A symbolic interpretation. *Cognitive Science, 17*, 7–48.

Waldrop, M. M. (1988). Toward a unified theory of cognition. *Science, 241*, 27–29.

8

Reflections on a Work-Oriented Design Project

Jeanette Blomberg
Lucy Suchman
Randall H. Trigg
Xerox Palo Alto Research Center, Palo Alto, California

1. INTRODUCTION

For some years, we have been engaged in research aimed at developing new ways to conceptualize and structure relations between work and technology design. We take our project to be understanding relations of work and technology in ways that draw from and contribute to current theory and practice within anthropology and computer science. To that end, we conduct theoretically informed, empirical investigations of everyday work practices and technologies in use, in relation to work and technology (re)design. Our approach differs from conventional business process and marketing analyses in its focus not only on the detail of how activities are organized and interrelated, but also in its concern with practical problems and solutions as they appear to organization members in the course of doing their work. We are interested in exploring how such analyses can contribute to more effective change initiatives and to better adapted and therefore more useful technologies.

Our goals for the project reported in this article were to deepen our understanding of document work practices, to gain experience in cooperative design, and to explore the opportunities and obstacles for doing cooperative work-oriented design within our company. At the time of this writing, there is little in the way of work-oriented design practice within our company's product divisions.[1] For the most part, intended users of new technologies are involved in design and development only through participation in focus groups, as respondents to questionnaires, and through usability testing. As others have pointed out, concerns with usability, although necessary, are not sufficient to the development of genuinely *useful* systems (Beyer & Holtzblatt, 1995; Nardi, 1993; Wixon & Comstock, 1994). Whereas *usability* refers to the general intelligibility of systems, particularly at the interface, *usefulness* means that a system's functionality actually makes sense and adds value in relation to a particular work setting.[2]

In what follows, we first sketch our approach to work-oriented design, with a focus on cooperative development of prototype applications. We then briefly describe the work site in which our project was located, and the rationale for taking up two design efforts within that site. The remainder of the article discusses those two efforts, highlighting distinctive issues that arose for us in each. In raising these issues we hope to make explicit an experience that we believe is quite common to design efforts based in actual work settings: the simultaneous pursuit of a design agenda and negotiation of complex, often contested organizational ground. The different and sometimes disconnected forms of engagement that are called for in response to these two aspects of cooperative design are reflected in the two cases that we present here. Our hope is that the diverse issues raised by the two cases will be recognizably consistent with the experience of others who have engaged in work-oriented, Participatory Design projects.[3]

2. A COLLABORATIVE RESEARCH APPROACH

Our early research focused on the application of interaction analysis and ethnography to questions of information systems design and use (Blomberg, 1987, 1988; Suchman, 1983, 1987, forthcoming; Suchman & Trigg, 1991). More recently, we have been exploring possibilities for incorporating work-oriented design practices into product development within our organization. The starting premises for our current work are the following:

---

[1]Notable exceptions include, for example, Anderson and Crocca (1992). More recently others in Xerox—for example, Bowers, Button, and Sharrock (1995) and Brun-Cottan and Wall (1995)—have been developing work-oriented design agendas in relation to product divisions.

[2]Both concerns are important, and each is potentially complementary to the other. However, they are not equivalent; making a system usable does not ensure its usefulness, and useful systems (e.g., DOS) may not be particularly usable.

[3]For overviews of PD, see Muller and Kuhn (1993) and Schuler and Namioka (1993).

- Detailed analysis of how people work using existing and prototype technologies provides a basis for innovative design and better-integrated technologies.
- Individual technologies "add value" only to the extent that they work together in effective configurations.
- Delineating the space of effective technology configurations requires applications development within actual use environments and with the active participation of end users.

Based on these premises, our research strategy has been to establish relations with specific work settings and to use those as sites for cooperative applications design. Our approach involves cycling among studies of work, codesign, and user experience with mock-ups and prototypes of new technologies (Kyng, 1995; Tang, 1991). Through this approach, work practice studies are embedded in design activities, whereas design efforts contribute to work analyses.

A challenge for us in attempting to create a work-oriented design practice is to develop innovative ways of making insights that we gain from our research projects available to product development.[4] Because not all developers are able to accompany us to worksites, we use various means of bringing what we learn from the site to relevant development efforts. As part of our own work in the site, we record interviews with members of the organization, instances of their everyday work, and meetings that we convene or to which we are invited. The materials that we accumulate (e.g., documents, field notes, and video records) are a resource in our ongoing communications about the project. For example, customized video collections are sometimes used in short presentations to our research colleagues and as a resource in meetings with developers.

We also use case-based prototypes as a way to support the imagination of future work practices, augmented with new technologies. As with all prototypes, *case-based prototypes* constitute partial implementations of envisioned technologies and their interfaces. Prototypes have long been used as stand-ins for designs in progress, where they are often employed in structured meetings in which users perform tasks designed to test particular parts of the system (Gould, 1988). In our work, prototypes are employed in a way more akin to what Bødker and Grønbæk (1991) call *cooperative prototyping*.[5] As with all rapid prototyping approaches (see,

---

[4]For further discussion of the relations between ethnographic studies of work practice and design see, for example, Blomberg (1995), Blomberg, Giacomi, Mosher, and Swenton-Wall (1993), Forsythe (1992), Hughes, Randall, and Shapiro (1993), Jordan (1996), Shapiro (1994), and Simonsen and Kensing (1994).

[5]See Bødker and Grønbæk (1991) and Grønbæk (1991) for descriptions of the cooperative prototyping approach.

e.g. Miller-Jacobs, 1991), cooperative prototyping includes the notion of iterative development as a means of gaining user input throughout the development cycle. Changes to the prototypes can be made in direct response to feedback that users provide during prototyping sessions. In addition, cooperative prototyping views prototypes not just as proxies for future products or as means to gain user feedback, but as triggers for discussion and mutual learning.[6] In this way, our prototypes are co-constructed artifacts that depend on participation from work practitioners. Finally, our prototypes incorporate a significant body of materials (e.g., documents and categorization schemes) actually in use at the worksite. We use the term *case-based* to underscore the ways in which our prototypes address the work of particular practitioners, reflect our shared understandings of their work, and incorporate their work materials.

In our projects, we attempt to work in close collaboration with individuals from particular worksites. We choose to focus on a single worksite and, within that site, to look closely at specific work activities. These choices are motivated by two considerations: our desire to obtain detailed, in-depth views of specific work practices as opposed to more superficial accounts of a wider range of activities, and our commitment to work closely with worksite participants. Although generalizing beyond our specific cases is constrained by these objectives, we believe that many of our findings do apply to other activities and settings. Where warranted, therefore, we point to the more general implications of our work.

Finally, to enable the investigation of work practices and the development of case-based prototypes in actual work settings, our projects are structured as research collaborations among ourselves as researchers, technology designers, and developers within our own organization, and prospective users of new technology in an interested outside organization. Structuring the relationship as a research collaboration means, on one hand, that our funding comes from our own organization; the prospective user organizations with which we are cooperating do not provide us with any direct payment, but only with their time. On the other hand, this arrangement also means that we do not promise to deliver a working system at the project's end. Instead, what we aim to provide as compensation for the engagement of organization members is (a) a clearer appreciation for their own work practices and associated technology requirements and (b) new insights into the state of the art and foreseeable future directions of emerging technologies. This type of relationship is one way to create the space for exploration and learning that seems to be required for the detailed envisionment of new work and technological possibilities.

---

[6]For accounts of how prototypes can trigger or "provoke" discussions in work settings, see Mogensen (1992), Mogensen and Trigg (1992), and Trigg, Bødker, and Grønbæk (1991).

3. THE WORKSITE: A SILICON VALLEY LAW FIRM

The site selected for this project was a large law firm. The choice was motivated partly by the forms of work that we expected to find there and partly by the apparent likelihood of a fit between the work and the technologies that we were interested in developing.[7] The business division with which we set up our initial collaboration was involved in developing products that bridged paper and electronic documents, incorporating new approaches to search over electronic documents as well as machine analysis of marks on paper. Legal practice involves extremely document-intensive forms of work, in environments in the midst of transition from paper-based to increasingly electronic media. Both of these characteristics seemed relevant to our interests.

Our initial discussions concerning the scope of our project and our early interviews and observations were with members of the firm's technology advisory committee. Through them we learned that the firm provides its clients with two forms of legal services: corporate law and litigation. These two forms comprise distinct organizations within the firm and involve significantly different document-related work practices. Put simply, the work of corporate law centers on the creation of documents, based in large part on the reuse of existing documents, many of which were generated in house. Litigation, in contrast, involves locating and accessing crucial documents from a very large corpus generated outside of the firm, within the client's organization, and available almost entirely in paper form.

Our initial interest in exploring advanced applications for a suite of image processing technologies led us first to focus on the litigation side of the firm's practice, specifically on the work of creating electronic indices to the paper documents used in litigating large cases. Later, we turned our attention to the practices of document reuse on the corporate side of the firm, in response to a decision by the developers within our company to include text database retrieval technologies in their next product. Our aim was to investigate how those technologies might support the identification and retrieval of relevant documents from electronic files. In the end, we focused our work practice studies on both the practice of document retrieval and reuse in corporate law and the database production

---

[7]Note that this differs from some early participatory design projects where the system developers/consultants had fewer a priori commitments to specific technologies, and could be more freely responsive to the needs of workers. A well-known example was the Utopia project (Kyng, 1991), which developed computer systems in cooperation with graphic workers at a Swedish newspaper. For a description of the relations between the project and technology vendors, see Bødker, Ehn, Romberger, and Sjögren (1985).

activity in litigation, exploring the possible applications of text database retrieval and image processing technologies respectively.

4. DEVELOPING A CASE-BASED PROTOTYPE: AN ATTORNEY'S "FORM FILE"

Attorneys at the law firm expressed to us a central tenet of their practice that effectively states, "If at all possible, avoid drafting anything from scratch." That is, if a "model" or boilerplate document (often referred to as a *form document*) can be located—for example, a buy–sell agreement or a venture capital loan agreement—it should be used as a starting point for the creation of the new document. At times the form document requires only minor modification; perhaps only the date or names are changed. In other cases, the form document provides "language" for a new document that is otherwise unlike the form document. A third possibility is that the form document provides information to help guide composition of a new document.

In response to the challenge of locating relevant form or model documents, attorneys at the term employ a variety of strategies. These often include retaining documents from previous transactions that might prove useful in the future and "walking the halls," asking other attorneys if they have ever drafted a particular type of document or one with specific provisions. Attorneys differ in how systematic and diligent they are in keeping and organizing their form documents. Some attorneys are known to others for their dedication to maintaining their form file. They and their form files become resources to others in the firm who do not keep such extensive sets of files themselves. We worked closely with one attorney, M, who keeps a lateral file cabinet containing several thousand documents organized by topic in alphabetically arranged file folders (see Fig. 8.1). Another attorney with whom we worked keeps a more ad hoc, distributed "form file" (throughout his office, on the floor, on the desk, and in file cabinets), that, although useful for his own work, is less of a resource for others.

At the outset of the project, we were interested simply in understanding M's current use of his paper form file. We asked him to describe the organization of the documents in his form file and observed a few occasions on which he referred to the file, either to assist in document composition or in response to requests from colleagues. However, because M's use of the form file was occasional and unpredictable, we asked him to let us leave a video camera in his office so that he could record his use

FIG. 8.1. Attorney M at the form file.

of the file for us. We requested that he record himself when using the file either for his own purposes or in response to colleagues' requests.

The utility of M's file for other attorneys depends on his knowledge of its contents and organization, derived in turn from his creation, maintenance, and regular use of the file. Other attorneys rely on M to help determine whether the form file contains documents relevant to the transaction on which they are working, to point them to likely places in the file where relevant documents might be found, and to justify the choice of particular documents (e.g., "This agreement is good for the protection it affords the lender"). During discussions with M about the document for which they are looking, junior attorneys can also learn about other issues relevant to the transaction. M views the effort he expends in maintaining the form file as worthwhile because it provides him with a suitable collection of model documents to work from (reducing the number of times he needs to compose a new document from scratch), it helps him keep informed about the status of projects around the firm, and his overall value to the firm is enhanced by maintaining the form file for use by other attorneys.

Informed by observations of the use of paper document collections like M's form file, we began to explore with M the potential for technological support, in particular an electronic document collection that could offer advanced search capabilities and (eventually) shared access. In what follows, we discuss our prototyping work in collaboration with M and our subsequent attempts to engage product developers in discussions around these ideas.

4.1. Defining and Developing a Prototype

Our application-development effort on the corporate side of the firm was informed by our general understanding of the centrality of document reuse in the practice of corporate law. We focused specifically on supporting the maintenance and use of M's form file, because of his highly developed organization and use of the file, his willingness to allow us access to a subset of the documents (for scanning), and his interest in working with us. Other attorneys also contributed to our application design effort by reflecting on the overall value of making form documents available electronically and by evaluating the usefulness of particular design features.

We decided to build a prototype that would give M electronic access to a sizable fraction of the documents in his form file. Our prototype was developed in two major iterations. The pilot version was based on 36 documents taken from several of M's most frequently accessed folders that we scanned, using optical character recognition (OCR) whenever possible. Using this version, we conducted a cooperative prototyping session with M and another attorney. Our goal was to obtain feedback on the prototype and assess whether we should proceed to incorporate a larger number of the documents from the form file. The session raised important technological and work practice issues relating to the requirements for image-based browsing and text-based retrieval. Given M's clear interest in continuing to develop the prototype, we borrowed, copied, and quickly returned approximately a quarter of the documents (862) in his file cabinet. By scanning and OCRing these documents ourselves, we allowed our design effort to focus on issues of searching and browsing the corpus rather than the problems of inputting new documents.

In building our prototype, we made use of a platform being developed in our research organization to support "retrieval-centric" applications (Rao, Card, Johnson, Klotz, & Trigg, 1994). Although our original plan was to build the prototype on a product platform (making later integration with the product easier), this was not possible due to organizational and technical problems in the development organization (Blomberg, Suchman, & Trigg, in press). The research platform did provide us, however, with an interface to text database technologies as well as browsing of document

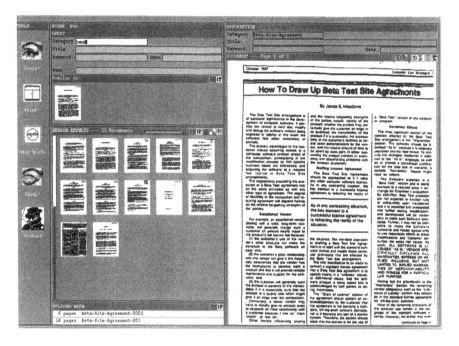

FIG. 8.2. Electronic file cabinet prototype. The left side of the window contains reduced "thumbnail" images of the documents returned from a search. The right side shows a "full size" image of one of a chosen document's pages. Other options include displaying the OCR'd text for a document and laying out intermediate-size images of its pages. See Rao et al. (1994) for a full description of the prototype.

page images. The case-based prototype we created reflected particular aspects of M's work practice, and included the images and text from his document corpus (Fig. 8.2).[8] Viewed as an electronic document collection, our prototype was an exploration of the possibilities for combined use of text and images in the work of searching and browsing. More specifically, our prototype supported search with a full-text information retrieval program (Cutting, Pedersen, & Halvorsen, 1991). Because only minimal labeling information (e.g., folder name) was associated with the docu-

---

[8]The development of the prototype involved a three-way collaboration among M, the authors of this article, and Ramana Rao, a research colleague at Xerox PARC. Although Rao's platform provided the basis for the implementation, he also participated in design discussions at the law firm regarding both the pilot and later versions of the prototype. He played a key support role during the weeks when the prototype was left running in M's office, and was primarily responsible for several rounds of customization of the platform necessary to meet the evolving needs of M's application (cf. Footnote 16).

FIG. 8.3. M using/demoing the prototype with a visitor.

ments,[9] the prototype also provided small scale "thumbnail" reductions of the documents' first pages as a way to present the results of searches. Browsing through a scrollable display of these first page thumbnails, M could select one document, step through individual images, lay out reduced images of all the pages, or scroll through the OCR'd text.[10]

Once the prototype was relatively stable, we left it in M's office for over 2 weeks. Again we requested that he record himself using the prototype or discussing and demonstrating it for visitors (Fig. 8.3). In addition to providing us with a record of his attempts to use the prototype as occasions arose, we found that the camera became a communication channel from M to us during the time that the prototype was in his office. M's comments to the camera included requests for new features, complaints about the speed of the system, general observations as to its utility, and a few humorous asides. For some of M's requests and complaints, we were able to respond with patches to the prototype and new documentation intended to clear up possible confusion.

---

[9]The lawyers reported having no time to assign keywords or titles to documents.

[10]We have recently built a World Wide Web-based version of the prototype, which is shareable and integrates images into search as well as browsing.

4.2. Bringing the Case to Developers

Given the limits on product developers' ability to engage directly with the project, we used a variety of project materials (including video recordings of work at the firm) to engage developers in discussing the implications of our observations and experiences. For example, we met with programmers and quality assurance engineers charged with developing a product aimed at supporting document management. The meeting consisted of a series of topical discussions, each triggered by a short video segment from our collection. Our initial suggestions of technical questions raised by each segment were followed by free-ranging discussions of relevant implementation issues. During the discussions, we answered questions and volunteered information about the setting and our understanding of the attorneys' work practices (see also Blomberg & Trigg, in preparation). As a result of these discussions, several features were added or modified on the developers' "to do" list for the current product plan.

A video clip of an attorney critiquing the words used to classify search clusters, for example, led the developers to rethink their design of the stopword list. *Stopword lists* are used to eliminate certain common words from the text before building indices over which retrieval algorithms search. Normally the stopword list is taken to be standard across applications (assuming only that the text is in English). During a cooperative prototyping session with M and another attorney, however, we found that additional stopwords were required; words like *corporation* and *agreement* are as nondistinguishing at the law firm as *and* and *the*. It was apparent to the developers on seeing this video clip that the attorneys would need the ability to edit their own stopword lists. In discussing the problem of reindexing the corpus when stopwords change, a developer made the proposal that their document management product should allow stopword lists to be assigned on a per-corpus basis. This requirement came from seeing the need for customizability and from recognizing that stopword lists might not be identical for all attorneys in the firm.

Another design topic that came up during this same meeting with developers involved the role of on-screen page images in search and browsing. The software platform on which our prototype was built combines document page images with OCR'd text. Support for corpus-wide searches is based on the text, whereas browsing through smaller collections of documents and document pages is facilitated using reduced page images arrayed on the screen. Our discussions of this topic with the developers revolved around several video clips showing M searching for documents, browsing using the "thumbnail" reductions of the documents' first pages, and browsing within the document using intermediate-sized page images laid out in rows and columns. We noted the attorneys' ability to identify quickly the "genre" or style of a document (e.g., memo, letter, financial statement, etc.) from a vastly reduced image of its first page. We also pointed out that attorneys found intermediate image sizes useful for quickly browsing through the pages of single documents and for jumping to larger images of particular pages.[11] In viewing these video clips, the developers were interested in the degree to which the attorneys relied on cues about the form and structure of the document. These cues could be gleaned from reduced page images, but were lost in ASCII text renderings. Also of particular interest to the developers was the precise point at which M shifted from refining a search by, say, adding new keywords, to using what one of the developers called "pictorial browsing": browsing using scaled page images. This observation underscored the potential value of support for combined image and text-based search strategies.

5. ENCOUNTERING ORGANIZATIONAL POLITICS: THE WORK OF LITIGATION SUPPORT

As we noted earlier, the law firm conducted litigation as well as corporate law. Along with an opportunity for a second prototyping project, our engagement with the litigation side of the firm revealed an ongoing contest within the organization over the status and future of one aspect of the work of litigation. In what follows, we focus less centrally on our cooperative prototyping efforts with workers in litigation and more on our navigation of the political complexities that we met in the course of those activities.

Litigation work within the firm comprises defense of corporate clients against suits brought by other corporations or by shareholders. The material grounds for these disputes take the form of documents, in some cases numbering in the hundreds of thousands, gathered from the client's files. Every case includes a legally binding process known as *document production,* in which documents taken by the firm from the client's files are turned over to the opposing side. This same corpus provides the basis for the firm's preparation of its own case.

No generalized account of the process of document production can adequately represent the overwhelming logistical requirements of actually managing a large document corpus, in relation to the multiplicity of actors

---

[11]In the last version of our prototype, four page image reduction sizes were supported, all of which M used and appreciated. For more on changes made to the prototype based on M's use of an early version, see Rao et al. (1994).

involved and the unfolding interests of the case at hand. How documents are taken from client files, photocopied and returned, searched and indexed, in what order, and by whom is only partly rationalizable, due to these practical exigencies. Ideally, however, document production begins with the assignment of a unique identification number to each page of every document, followed by a rapid sort of the entire document corpus into those documents that are "responsive" to the case—that is, that must he turned over to the opposing side—and those that are not. This sorting is done by junior attorneys, relatively new both to the practice and to the firm. The set of responsive documents is then "computerized." This does not mean that all documents are transformed into electronic media, but rather that an online index is created to the paper documents. Creation of this database, done by workers in "litigation support," involves coding each document by representing its type and aspects of its content in a standardized format. That information is entered into a database, which can then he queried according to various criteria of interest to attorneys. The results of queries, typically submitted by paralegals, are presented in a report that is used as a pointer for retrieval of the paper documents.

Having developed an initial sense for the document-related work practices of paralegals and attorneys, we decided to look directly at the work of coding documents and creating the database index. From what we had heard, we had reason to believe that the relations of paper and electronically based media involved in this practice were particularly well suited to our design agenda. Through inquiries, we located the firm's litigation support operation. There we found a former paralegal, with extensive experience in the maintenance and use of computerized databases, supervising an office of temporary workers, many with bachelor's degrees. These "document analysts," as their supervisor called them, were engaged in carefully examining and representing the thousands of documents for a given case with the goal, vigorously instilled by their supervisor, of creating a valid and useful database.

At the time we began to look at the work of litigation support, coders were recording information about each document on a form, which was then handed to coworkers who entered the information into the database (Fig. 8.4). It became clear to us that representing the documents involved coders in an interweaving of tedious activity and mindful judgment. What interested us was the possibility of embedding bits of automation into the coding practice in a way that would relieve the tedium, while maintaining interactive control required for the exercise of necessary judgments. The image processing technologies that we were interested in exploring supported machine "interpretation" of certain classes of marks on paper (e.g., constrained handprinted characters, checked boxes, and circled text). We decided to work with the supervisor of litigation support

FIG. 8.4.   A document coder at work.

and her staff to mock up a redesigned document-coding practice, incorporating some of our technologies.

Maintaining alignment between our design efforts and the work
practices of litigation support during this time was a significant challenge
for us. The litigation support staff were continuously experimenting with
alternative strategies for coding documents. One lesson we (re)learned
was the degree to which workers themselves are engaged in reflecting
on and redesigning their own practice.[12] Our design proposals had to stay
attuned to these ongoing changes in work practices.

5.1. The Politics of Invisible Work

The place of the "routine/knowledge work" distinction in divisions of
labor and its implications for technology development came to life for us
in our work with the law firm. A powerful construct in the representation
of divisions of labor within organizations is the distinction between
so-called routine and knowledge work. The standard organizational icon
of the pyramid, for example, is stratified according to the attribution of

---

[12]Andrew Clement (1994), among others, has argued eloquently for the place of workers'
active and *independent* involvement in work and technology design.

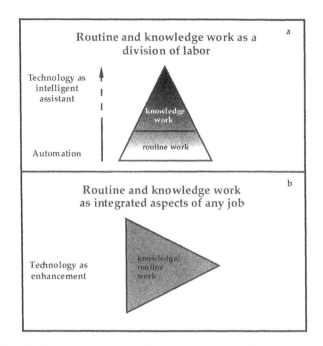

FIG. 8.5. Two views of the distribution of routine and knowledge work.

progressively more knowledge work as one moves from bottom to top (Fig. 8.5). The bottom layers in this view are made up of relatively large numbers of workers with relatively few skills, engaged in appropriately routine tasks. The top layers comprise smaller numbers of workers with greater knowledge and skills, engaged in correspondingly more knowledge-intensive forms of work. With respect to technology development, this image argues that efforts to replace labor by capital investment should begin with displacement of routine work by automation or outsourcing. As this logic is brought to bear on increasingly more powerful organizational actors, technology is reconstructed from a replacement for one's labor to one's "intelligent assistant."

In the case of the work of litigation support, we were presented with two very different views of the work. On one hand, our initial contact with the firm was through a senior attorney who described the process of document coding as made up of two types; what he termed *subjective*, or issues coding done by attorneys, and *objective* coding which he described as follows:

You have, you know, 300 cartons of documents and you tear through them and say, I'm going to put Post-Its on the ones we have to turn over to the other side. And then, ideally, you hire chimpanzees to type in *From, To,*

Date. And then, ideally, you then have lawyers go through it again and read each document, with their brain turned on.

This characterization was repeated on several occasions in which the attorney recapitulated for us how the document production process is organized. At the same time, at no point during the period in which we talked with and recorded the work of attorneys did we encounter the work of objective coding directly. Literally as well as figuratively, that work was invisible from the attorneys' point of view. In contrast, once we began to observe and engage with the work of litigation support, the supervisor of that operation expressed to us her belief that, given the coders' familiarity with the document corpus, they could be responsible for certain other aspects of the document production process now handled by junior attorneys (e.g., the assignment of subjective codes). She also expressed her view that the attorneys underutilized the database, due to their ignorance of its capabilities and how to exploit them.

We found ourselves, in other words, in the midst of a contest over conflicting characterizations of the work of subjective and objective document coding and its requirements. Our observations of the work of the attorneys revealed no small measure of mundane or tedious activities, which when brought into the attorneys' awareness were accepted by them, albeit ruefully, as inevitable accompaniments of their practice. At the same time, the more we looked into the work of document coding and data entry, the more we saw the judgmental and interpretive work that the document coders were required to bring to it. Given our knowledge of previous studies, these observations came as no surprise.[13] Nonetheless, in contrast with the simple characterization provided by the senior attorney, the interpretive demands of something as basic as, for example, finding the "documents" in a box of papers, were remarkable. That is to say, document coders were presented with boxes containing hundreds of pieces of paper and asked to establish document boundaries within them.[14] Although some pages might be attached together with a paper clip, the coders knew that they could not rely on those physical markers alone; they needed to make sufficient sense of each page so as to assess

---

[13]We are thinking here of previous studies that have revealed, on one hand, the mundane activity required for the accomplishment of what has come to be called knowledge work, in particular in recent studies of science and technology (e.g., Bijker, Hughes, & Pinch, 1987; Collins, 1985; Fujimura, 1987; Knorr-Cetina & Mulkay, 1983; Lynch, 1993; Lynch & Woolgar, 1990) and on the other hand, the judgment and reasoning required for the accomplishment of so-called routine work (e.g., Garfinkel, 1967; Goodwin & Goodwin, in press; Orr, 1990; Suchman, 1983; Whalen, 1993; Zimmerman, 1969).

[14]This because "documents," not pages, needed to be entered into the database. A document is entered as a range of page ID numbers; for example, a given memo might be coded as XYZ000134 to XYZ000138.

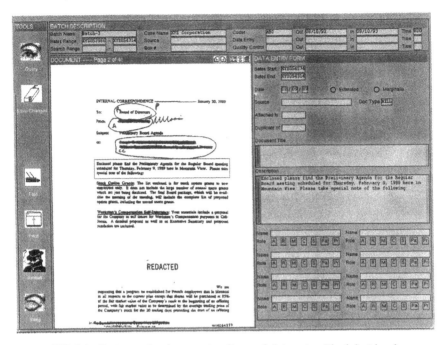

FIG. 8.6. Prototype for document coding and data entry. The left side of the window shows a document page image. The document analyst has circled and labeled various names of interest on the original hardcopy. The right side shows an electronic data entry "form," the fields of which some have automatically been filled in. A region containing text has been specified in the page image, automatically OCR'd, and pasted into the Description field in the data entry form.

its association with or independence from those that came before and after. Similarly, deciding on the date of a particular document—given, for example, an agreement that was written on one day, signed on another, and faxed on a third—might involve choosing which of several dates would be most useful to an attorney engaged in a search for documents relevant to a particular issue in the case. And so forth.

5.2. Supporting Document Coders' Knowledge Work

Our aim of relieving some of the tedium of the document coding process, while at the same time allowing flexible control over the work, led to a prototype design that supported automatic recognition of document codings where possible, while also providing image views of documents and editable text fields (Fig. 8.6).[15] Our design allowed coders to use paper

---

[15]For more on the work of document coding and our design proposal, see Suchman (1996).

coding forms that later could be scanned and automatically recognized, or to code directly on the documents by circling and labeling relevant regions of text. Coding forms, document page images, and previously circled text regions could then be displayed on the screen, giving coders the ability to edit the coding forms, correct OCR'd text, or "lift" text regions directly from the document images for on-the-fly OCR into the database. This design supported the coders' review, correction, and enhancement of entries into the database, allowing them to bring their experience and accumulated knowledge to hear on the task at hand.[16]

After working for some time on this design for litigation support, we learned from the firm's director of technology that, in the interest of cost cutting, the senior management of the firm was seriously considering closing down the in-house coding operation altogether and shipping the documents for coding to the Philippines. Because we had reason to believe that this decision was being made without full knowledge of what was actually involved in the work of document coding, we arranged to provide the director of technology and whomever else he felt was appropriate with an update on our work, including our observations and proposals regarding document coding. We hoped that this presentation would have some influence on the firm's deliberations.

In the meantime, the supervisor of litigation support and her staff had been moving proactively to respond to what they recognized as potential challenges to their continued operation, by increasing their productivity and lowering the cost of their services. This was in part accomplished by coding documents directly into the database rather than in two separate passes for document coding (on forms) and data entry (from forms into the database), as they had been doing. As a result of their efforts, at the time our project ended their place within the firm seemed relatively secure.

Our representations of the work of litigation at the firm and our design of a prototype application involved reconceptualizing the work from activities divided clearly into two types—knowledge and routine—to different orders of practical reasoning and action. The implications of the invisibility of practical reasoning and action are different for differently positioned organization members. For those whose work has been mythologized, making the actual work visible implies a process of demysti-

---

[16]As with our prototype on the corporate side (Footnote 8), the development involved the law firm's litigation support staff, the authors of this article, and Ramana Rao. Again, the prototype was based on Rao's platform, augmented by text editing and image mapping functionality he added per our request. This time, we took responsibility for the user interface customizations necessary for the document coding application and for design discussions with litigation support staff.

fication. For those whose work has been trivialized, in contrast, making the work visible is about recognizing and acknowledging the skills that are actually involved in doing it. Rather than premising our design proposals on a distinction between mindless labor and knowledge work, we attempted to show that routine activities and the exercise of judgment coexist at all levels of the organizational hierarchy (Fig. 8.5). Although the conditions of our own working practice meant that our design efforts ended with a research prototype, we hope to have contributed to the standing of litigation support at least by seeing their work and acknowledging what we saw, both in our representations of it and our designing for it.

6. GENERAL FINDINGS AND RECOMMENDATIONS

The project reported here has contributed to our knowledge, both specific and general, of how documents are actually created and used within working practices, to our understanding of what it means to do work-oriented design, and to our appreciation of the problems and possibilities for more work-oriented design practices within our company. In concluding we offer some general observations and recommendations from our experience.

6.1. Working Document Collections

Our work in the law firm provided us with a rich view of document work practices not only as they occur within the specific practice of law but, we believe, in ways generalizable to other settings as well. In particular, M's form file is an example of what we are calling a working document collection. Such repositories comprise documents that are selectively saved for future reference and reuse by their creators as well as others. Though working document collections are created for long-term and possibly infrequent use, the documents they contain must nonetheless he readily available for the task at hand. In the law firm, their location in attorneys' offices, in file cabinets, on bookshelves, or in stacks on the floor provided this accessibility. Working collections seem to occupy a niche between archives (often stored remotely) and active documents (kept, e.g., in stacks on the desktop). Although documents requested from a remote archive are frequently returned within days or weeks, a document from a working collection needs to be retrievable within the shorter time frames dictated by an immediate task. In the law firm, for example, if a form file document cannot be found quickly, it may not be worth retrieving at all.

To continue working on the task, attorneys might, for example, resort to drafting from scratch the language they had hoped to reuse.[17]

At the same time, the scope of working collections extends beyond just those documents currently in use. Moreover, a collection may become quite large in size, and any specific document in a collection may be used only rarely.

Work with a document collection involves adding new documents to the corpus, transforming them as necessary (e.g., printing or copying the document, or labeling it with filing instructions to an assistant). In addition, ongoing maintenance of the collection includes activities of cleaning up and reorganizing, throwing away outdated and duplicate documents, shuffling documents between folders, and consolidating and removing folders. Finally, the reuse of documents in the collection involves searching and browsing as well as transforming and integrating found documents into current work. Transformations include copying a borrowed document from the collection so that modifications can be indicated by marking up the document, or reading aloud from a document into a dictation machine while making changes to the language for a new version.

Our observations of M's work with his collection indicate several other characteristics of the dynamics of these practices:

1. Activities are ordered and interleaved in complex and opportunistic ways. For example, before adding a document to the form file, M might search to see if something like it is already there. Similarly, maintenance of the collection may happen as part of the activities of storing and searching. For example, M might rearrange folders in the midst of responding to colleagues' query for a document

2. Access to the collection involves tightly linked consideration of both a document's visual characteristics and its content. We saw, time and again, the ease with which attorneys could identify document genre as well as other document characteristics (e.g., the source of the document) simply by leafing through a folder.

---

[17]Reporting on two studies of the practices of organizing online information, Barreau and Nardi (1995) proposed three information types: ephemeral, working, and archived. Their sense of *archived* matches most closely our term *working document collections* in terms of the longer "shelf life" and less frequent access. Barreau and Nardi claimed, moreover, that this category of information has been overemphasized in the literature, perhaps reflecting the "researchers' own needs for archival support" (p. 42). We suspect, however, that their impressions may be a result of studying patterns of information organization by individuals. Though only a minority of the members of an organization may spend the time to manage "archived" information, the entire organization may benefit from their librarian-like work. Indeed, the law firm we studied pronounced the attorneys' working document collection "corporate assets" and began investigating how to centralize them.

3. The collection's creator and primary maintainer plays a crucial role in facilitating shared access to the documents because of their knowledge of the collection's organization and contents. Moreover, a request for a document provides an opportunity for discussion about points of law, the status of projects, and so on. Those posing requests may be querying not only the files but the creator's expertise as well.

Our cooperative prototyping with M centered on the second observation. That is, our prototype did not support either the scanning of new documents into the corpus or the easy rearrangement of documents between folders. Furthermore, the standalone status of the prototype limited our ability to explore issues of shared access. We were, however, able to develop new insights regarding the value of combined image and text-based document search, and to convey those insights and their implications to our collaborators at the worksite, to other researchers, and to product developers.

6.2. Case-Based Prototypes

Although at the time of this writing our work at the law firm has drawn to a close, we continue an extended process of communicating what we have learned in the project to other researchers and to product developers. Rather than "delivering" the results of our studies and prototypes to these relevant others, we are committed to finding ways to engage them directly in exploring with us the implications of our work for their ongoing projects. Given the realities of occupational specialization, we believe there will always be a need for persons and artifacts that mediate between work practice and design. At the same time, we agree that "participatory design is a collaborative approach to design, not a rigid set of design methods" (Good, 1992, p. 441). To us this means that mediating artifacts and activities must be flexibly adapted to the demands of the situation. We recognize that to be accessible to the work of design, the details of working practices need to be explicated, interpreted, and contextualized. But this is a different and, we believe, more challenging process than developing abstract representations of those practices. A basic tenet of our approach is that the details of practice are an essential part of what must be addressed in system design.

Perhaps the single most important lesson that we take from this project with respect to these issues is the power of case-based prototypes. Such prototypes are working artifacts that demonstrate the potential of one or more technological innovations. They incorporate a significant body of material from an actual worksite, and are informed by the practices and needs of those who work with the material. Such prototypes thus embody real-world cases as well as new technological possibilities.

Case-based prototypes and their contents can be made available in an ongoing and iterative way to the work of research and development. They offer design input that is different from and complementary to other techniques for bringing experience of work practice to bear on product design.[18] Moreover, we believe, perhaps paradoxically, that prototypes that are "specific" in the sense described here are more likely to be generally useful. This is because the richness of their contents and the observable details of their use connect in varied and evocative ways to a wide range of other settings and practices.

At the same time, the work of case-based prototyping does require investments of time and resources. Building a case-based prototype requires not just a knowledge of the relevant technology, but also understanding and incorporation of materials and practices from a particular work site. Case-based prototyping also requires maintaining an ongoing relationship with workers with whom the prototype is iteratively defined. Moreover, the prototype does not simply speak for itself, but must continually be "read" for its significance and lessons in ways that connect with the particular concerns of researchers, developers, and intended users. Communication through and around a case-based prototype in this respect remains a labor-intensive undertaking.

7. CONCLUSION: TOWARD MORE WORK-ORIENTED PRODUCT DEVELOPMENT

The project we report here was organized at the outset as a collaboration between researchers, product developers, and work practitioners. We set out to work with particular partners in the product divisions of our company to incorporate more work-oriented design practices into the product development process. However, conditions within the product development organizations made it difficult to sustain the kind of collaboration that we had hoped for. Briefly, shifting technology directions and inadequate allocations of resources for use-oriented design activities made it difficult for developers to maintain real engagement with our project. Given these conditions and the constraints they placed on the direct involvement of developers in any form of work-oriented design, we found ourselves as researchers in the position of trying to maintain some kind of alignment between the work site and product development activities.[19]

Nonetheless, our continued belief is that ongoing relations between technology developers and strategically selected worksites can deepen

---

[18]For example, Carroll and Rosson (1992), Karat and Bennett (1991), and Nardi (1992) suggest that scenarios can be productively employed in connecting design to work activities.

[19]For a more extended discussion of these difficulties, see Blomberg et al. (in press).

developers' understanding of the problems that workers face and expand workers' understanding of the technological possibilities. At the same time, we recognize that system development is a highly specialized, somewhat fragmented enterprise, with tremendous differentiation among the participants even within a given job category. Individuals have different objectives tied to their particular backgrounds and interests, and even in the best of circumstances there are different levels of involvement with prospective technology users on the part of developers. Moreover, the increase in outsourcing, third-party development, partnerships among companies, and the like means that there is greater ambiguity as to who actually makes up the product development team. As a consequence there will always be a need for people who can bridge between groups variously positioned with respect to a product development effort (Fromherz, 1996).

Our goal in this project was not to define a new bridging role in system development, but rather to propose new kinds of activities that might occur in a variety of places internal and external to system development organizations. From our efforts to develop our own practice of work analysis and case-based prototyping, we can offer some recommendations that might productively inform any project that combines work practice studies and design interventions. These recommendations are based in the approaches of anthropology and action research, two of the traditions underlying Participatory Design. One tells us how to study people and their practices respectfully, and the other how to turn our interventions into cooperative, mutually enriching and reflective engagements.

Look for "invisible" work. In the case of the law firm, this led us to see not only the taken-for-granted aspects of an attorney's work with his form file, but ways in which the work of litigation support was obscured systematically from the view of firm management in their plans for change. Our view onto the work's actual requirements suggested new directions for both work and technology redesign.

Find the knowledge work in what is characterized as routine, and the routines in what is characterized as knowledge work. Again, this orientation led us to see knowledgeable aspects of the work of litigation support that were missing in its being stereotyped as routine, and to articulate routine aspects of attorneys' work with documents. Both are relevant to the design of new supporting technologies, within a design ethic of relieving tedium while enhancing judgment-based activities.

Expect and encourage joint project design and definition with worksite participants. Our strategy of collaborative research begins with an interest in finding productive relations between a particular form of work and a range of emerging technologies. From there, our projects are shaped in interaction with organization members.

Assume that change is already and always in progress. Understand the politics of change and where you stand within them. In our experience, all organizations are engaged in some ongoing forms of self-assessment and redesign. These initiatives often reproduce or make more visible existing contests over divisions of labor and associated distributions of material and symbolic reward as well as implying changes to them. Navigating responsibly within such settings requires an awareness of one's own values and commitments with respect to those contests.

Understand how extended contexts (e.g., institutional and global) constrain the scope of what can be accomplished in a given setting, and attempt to question or take advantage of those contexts as appropriate. In this project, the constrained conditions of product development, and the movement toward increased outsourcing of litigation support in the law firm, brought us into contact with intensification and shifting configurations of work within and among organizations locally, regionally, and worldwide (Greenbaum, 1994). To some extent we were required to incorporate these conditions, as given but also problematic, in the direction of our own research.

It is our hope that the project reported here and others like it will help bring traditions of anthropology and action research a step closer to the world of product design. In the end, however, developing a work-oriented design practice requires time and space for exploration and learning. As researchers we may be in a better position at present to develop cooperative, work-oriented design practices than our coworkers in product development or, for that matter, than prospective technology users. Making work-oriented design an integral part of system development and use ultimately will require resources to be committed to alternative forms of design practice, within both product development organizations and the sites in which technologies are intended to become useful.

ACKNOWLEDGMENTS

An earlier version of this article was presented at the 1994 Participatory Design Conference in Chapel Hill, North Carolina. It was subsequently published in *Human–Computer Interaction, 11*, 237–265. Copyright © 1996 by Lawrence Erlbaum Associates, Inc. Reprinted with permission.

We are grateful to our collaborators at the law firm and to Herb Jellinek, Walt Johnson, Susan Newman, Mike Powers and Ramana Rao for their participation in this project. Liam Bannon, Finn Kensing, Susan Newman, William Turner and several anonymous reviewers provided useful comments on prior drafts of this paper.

REFERENCES

Anderson, W. L., & Crocca, W. T. (1992). Experiences in reflective engineering practice: Co-development of product prototypes. In M. J. Muller, S. Kuhn, & J. A. Meskill (Eds.), *Proceedings of the PDC'92 Participatory Design Conference*, 13–22. Palo Alto, CA: Computer Professionals for Social Responsibility.

Barreau, D., & Nardi, B. A. (1995). Finding and reminding: File organization from the desktop. *SIGCHI Bulletin, 27*(3), 39–43.

Beyer, H. R., & Holtzblatt, K. (1995). Apprenticing with the customer. *Communications of the ACM, 38*(5), 45–52.

Bijker, W., Hughes, T., & Pinch, T. (Eds.). (1987). *The social construction of technological systems*. Cambridge, MA: MIT Press.

Blomberg, J. (1987). Social interaction and office communication: Effects on user's evaluation of new technologies. In R. Kraut (Ed.), *Technology and the transformation of white collar work* (pp. 195–210). Hillsdale, NJ: Lawrence Erlbaum Associates, Inc.

Blomberg, J. (1988). The variable impact of computer technologies on the organization of work activities. In I. Greif (Ed.), *Computer-supported cooperative work: A book of readings* (pp. 771–782). San Mateo, CA: Kaufmann.

Blomberg, J. (1995). Ethnography: Aligning field studies of work and system design. In A. F. Monk & G. N. Gilberg (Eds.), *Perspectives on HCI: Diverse approaches* (pp. 175–197). London: Academic.

Blomberg, J., Giacomi, J., Mosher, A., & Swenton-Wall, P. (1993). Ethnographic field methods and their relation to design. In D. Schuler & A. Namioka (Eds.), *Participatory design: Perspectives on systems design* (pp. 123–154). Hillsdale, NJ: Lawrence Erlbaum Associates, Inc.

Blomberg, J., Suchman, L., & Trigg, R. (in press). Back to work: Renewing old agendas for cooperative design. In M. Kyng & L. Matthiassen (Eds.), *Computers in context*. Cambridge, MA: MIT Press.

Bowers, J., Button, G., & Sharrock, W. (1995). Workflow from within and without: Technology and cooperative work on the print industry shopfloor. In H. Marmolin & Y. Sundblad (Eds.), *Proceedings of the ECSCW'95 Fourth European Conference on Computer-Supported Cooperative Work*. Stockholm: Kluwer.

Brun-Cottan, F., & Wall, P. (1995). Using video to re-present the user. *Communications of the ACM, 38*(5), 61–71.

Bødker, S., Ehn, P., Romberger, S., & Sjögren, D. (Eds.). (1985). *Graffiti 7—The UTOPIA project: An alternative in text and images*. Stockholm: Swedish Center for Working Life, Stockholm: Royal Institute of Technology, and Aarhus, Denmark: University of Aarhus.

Bødker, S., & Grønbæk, K. (1991). Design in action: From prototyping by demonstration to cooperative prototyping. In J. Greenbaum & M. Kyng (Eds.), *Design at work: Cooperative design of computer systems* (pp. 197–218). Hillsdale, NJ: Lawrence Erlbaum Associates, Inc.

Carroll, J. M., & Rosson, M. B. (1992). Getting around the task–artifact cycle: How to make claims and design by scenario. *ACM Transactions on Information Systems, 10*(2), 181–212.

Clement, A. (1994). Computing at work: Empowering action by "low-level" users. *Communications of the ACM, 37*(1), 52–63.

Collins, H. M. (1985). *Changing order: Replication and induction in scientific practice.* Chicago: University of Chicago Press.

Cutting, D., Pedersen, J., & Halvorsen, P.-K. (1991). An object-oriented architecture for text retrieval. *Proceedings of the RIAO'91 Conference on Intelligent Text and Image Handling,* 285–298. Amsterdam: Elsevier.

Forsythe, D. (1992). Using ethnography to build a working system. In M. Frisse (Ed.), *Proceedings of the 16th Symposium on Computer Applications to Medical Care* (pp. 505–509). New York: McGraw-Hill.

Fromherz, M. P. J. (1996). Collaborative, mediated technology design and development (Technical Report SPH–96–027). Palo Alto, CA: Xerox Palo Alto Research Center.

Fujimura, J. (1987). Constructing "do-able" problems in cancer research: Articulating alignment. *Social studies of science, 17,* 257–293.

Garfinkel, H. (1967). *Studies in ethnomethodology.* Englewood Cliffs, NJ: Prentice-Hall.

Good, M. (1992). Participatory design of a portable torque-feedback device. *Proceedings of the CHI'92 ACM Conference on Human Factors in Computing Systems,* 439–446. Monterey, CA: ACM.

Goodwin, C., & Goodwin, M. H. (1996). Formulating planes: Seeing as a situated activity. In Y. Engeström & D. Middleton (Eds.), *Communication and cognition at work* (pp. 61–95). New York: Cambridge University Press.

Gould, J. D. (1988). How to design usable systems. In M. Helander (Ed.), *Handbook of human–computer interaction* (pp. 757–789). Amsterdam: Elsevier/North-Holland.

Greenbaum, J. (1994). Windows on the workplace: The temporization of work. In A. Adam, J. Emms, E. Green, & J. Owen (Eds.), *Women, work and computerization: Breaking old boundaries—building new forms* (pp. 295–309). Amsterdam: Elsevier.

Grønbæk, K. (1991). *Prototyping and active user involvement in system development: Towards a cooperative prototyping approach.* Unpublished doctoral dissertation, Computer Science Department, Aarhus University, Denmark.

Hughes, J. A., Randall, D., & Shapiro, D. (1993). From ethnographic record to system design: Some experiences from the field. *Computer Supported Cooperative Work, 1*(3), 123–147.

Jordan, B. (1996). Ethnographic workplace studies and computer supported cooperative work. In D. Shapiro, M. Tauber, & R. Traunmueller (Eds.), *The design of computer-supported cooperative work and groupware systems* (pp. 17–42). Amsterdam: North Holland/Elsevier.

Karat, J., & Bennett, J. L. (1991). Using scenarios in design meetings—A case study example. In J. Karat (Ed.), *Taking software design seriously: Practical techniques for human–computer interaction design* (pp. 63–94). San Diego: Academic.

Knorr-Cetina, K., & Mulkay, M. (Eds.). (1983). *Science observed: Perspectives on the social study of science.* London: Sage.

Kyng, M. (1991). Designing for cooperation: Cooperating in design. *Communications of the ACM, 34*(12), 64–73.

Kyng, M. (1995). Making representations work. *Communications of the ACM, 38*(9), 46–55.

Lynch, M. (1993). *Scientific practice and ordinary action: Ethnomethodology and social studies of science.* New York: Cambridge University Press.

Lynch, M., & Woolgar, S. (Eds). (1990). *Representation in scientific practice.* Cambridge, MA: MIT Press.

Miller-Jacobs, H. H. (1991). Rapid prototyping: An effective technique for system development. In J. Karat (Ed.), *Taking software design seriously: Practical techniques for human–computer interaction design* (pp. 273–286). San Diego: Academic.

Mogensen, P. (1992, August). Towards a prototyping approach in systems development. *Scandinavian Journal of Information Systems, 4,* 31–53.

Mogensen, P., & Trigg, R. H. (1992). Artifacts as triggers for participatory analysis. In M. J. Muller, S. Kuhn, & J. A. Meskill (Eds.), *Proceedings of the PDC'92 Participatory Design Conference* (pp. 55–62). Palo Alto, CA: Computer Professionals for Social Responsibility.

Muller, M., & Kuhn, S. (Eds.). (1993). Special issue on participatory design. *Communications of the ACM, 36*(4).

Nardi, B. A. (1992). The use of scenarios in design. *SIGCHI Bulletin, 24*(4) 13–14.

Nardi, B. A. (1993). *A small matter of programming: Perspectives on end user computing.* Cambridge, MA: MIT Press.

Orr, J. (1990). Talking about machines: An ethnography of a modern job. Unpublished doctoral dissertation, Cornell University (*PARC Technical Report* SSL–91–07 [P91–00132]). Palo Alto, CA: Xerox Palo Alto Research Center.

Rao, R., Card, S. K., Johnson, W., Klotz, L., & Trigg, R. (1994). Protofoil: Storing and finding the information worker's paper documents in an electronic file cabinet. In B. Adelson, S. Dumais, & J. Olson (Eds.), *Proceedings of the CHI'94 Conference on Human Factors in Computing Systems* (pp. 180–185). Boston: ACM.

Schuler, D., & Namioka, A. (Eds.). (1993). *Participatory design: Principles and practices.* Hillsdale, NJ: Lawrence Erlbaum Associates, Inc.

Shapiro, D. (1994). The limits of ethnography: Combining social sciences for CSCW. *Proceedings of the CSCW'94 Conference on Computer-Supported Cooperative Work, 417–428.* New York: ACM.

Simonsen, J., & Kensing, F. (1994). Take users seriously, but take a deeper look: Organizational and technical effects from designing with an intervention and ethnographically inspired approach. In R. Trigg, S. I. Anderson, & E. Dykstra-Erickson (Eds.), *Proceedings of the PDC'94 Participatory Design Conference* (pp. 47–58). Palo Alto, CA: Computer Professionals for Social Responsibility.

Suchman, L. (1983). Office procedures as practical action: models of work and system design. *ACM Transactions on Information Systems, 1*(4), 320–328.

Suchman, L. A. (1987). *Plans and situated actions.* Cambridge, England: Cambridge University Press.

Suchman, L. (1996). Supporting articulation work. In R. Kling (Ed.), *Computerization and controversy: Value conflicts and social choices* (2nd ed., pp. 407–423). San Diego: Academic Press.

Suchman, L. (forthcoming). Centers of coordination: A case and some themes. In L. B. Resnick, R. Saljo, C. Pontecorvo, & B. Burge (Eds.), *Discourse, tools and reasoning: Situated cognition and technologically supported environments.* Heidelberg, Germany: Spriner-Verlag.

Suchman, L., & Trigg, R. H. (1991). Understanding practice: Video as a medium for reflection and design. In J. Greenbaum & M. Kyng (Eds.), *Design at work: Cooperative design of computer systems* (pp. 65–89). Hillsdale, NJ: Lawrence Erlbaum Associates, Inc.

Tang, J. C. (1991). Involving social scientists in the design of new technology. In J. Karat (Ed.), *Taking software design seriously: Practical techniques for human–computer interaction design* (pp. 115–126). San Diego: Academic.

Trigg, R., Bødker, S., & Grønbæk, K. (1991). Open-ended interaction in cooperative prototyping: A video-based analysis. *Scandinavian Journal of Information Systems, 3* 63–86.

Whalen, J. (1993, August). *Accounting for "standard" task performance in the execution of 9-1-1 operations.* Paper presented at the annual meeting of the American Sociological Association, Miami.

Wixon, D. R., & Comstock, E. M. (1994). Evolution of usability at Digital Equipment Corporation. In M. E. Wiklund (Ed.), *Usability in practice: How companies develop user-friendly products* (pp. 147–193). Cambridge, MA: Academic.

Zimmerman, D. (1969). Tasks and troubles: The practical bases of work activities in a public assistance agency. In D. Hansen (Ed.), *Explorations in sociology and counseling* (pp. 237–266). Boston: Houghton Mifflin.

9

Scenarios as Springboards in CSCW Design

Susanne Bødker
Aarhus University, Denmark

Ellen Christiansen
Aalborg University, Denmark

The design of computer applications is not solely a matter of constructing something technical. The constitution of the design situation as well as the situations of use have many social aspects. In particular, the interplay between design and use is an important yet often neglected topic. And, despite the fact that the design of computer artifacts inevitably implies social change, designers are given little help to consider and reconsider the outcome of creating something new, as far as the social setting of use is concerned. Furthermore, designers live on the borders between several communities of practice, surrounded by conflicting interests and requirements. They are easily caught in a dilemma between awareness of tradition and orientation toward transcendence: on the one hand starting out from current practice and history, on the other hand making sure that something qualitatively new gets shaped in the process. The designers may face this dilemma in various ways: as reflected in what may seem a contradiction between abstract theoretical and situated practical understanding; as a dilemma between planning and responsiveness; or between using a framework or a description method to structure the analysis of the situation, and an open-minded "letting the situation speak to you." These dilemmas point to a methodological question. But, before turning to the issue of methodology, consider some overall concerns.

This research has a multidisciplinary background. For many years, the goal has been to understand systems design processes in general, and user participation in particular. Research in systems design and user participation has been concerned with the dilemma between tradition and transcendence from the perspective of social change within the workplace. There have been various action-oriented research projects, which have been set up to inquire into the social aspects of design. Attempts to interpret the findings have brought about the realization that designing tools also means designing work, because new tools mean new work environments and new work practices and thereby, to some extent, a whole new social situation at work. This insight points to the question of how to conduct design so that the inevitable social change is not inevitably secondary and derivative to the technical, but a matter of the expansion of work. Attempts to answer this question have drawn mainly on activity theory.

Methodologically, experience has led to the rejection of formal descriptions as the central design tool, and to replace it with more experience-oriented devices such as prototypes. An understanding of such experience-oriented devices was developed through the UTOPIA project (Bødker, Ehn, Kammersgaard, Kyng, & Sundblad, 1987; Ehn & Kyng, 1984), as well as the later AT project (Bødker et al., 1993), and described in detail in Greenbaum and Kyng (1991).

In these endeavors there has been a constant challenge to deal with both social and technical perspectives in the same process. As yet there have been no satisfying suggestions for merging these different perspectives into a single unified one. The idea presented here instead aims to let the different perspectives talk to each other, providing opportunities for the participants to switch between multiple views through joint activities and emphasizing conflicting concerns.

The result of this effort has become a prototypical device, a thinking tool for designers engaged in developing computer-supported cooperative work. The tool *box*, as it has come to be called, consists of *checklists* addressing social as well as technical issues, *examples*, and an *outline* of how to work with scenario-making throughout the design process. Some ideas about thinking tools, each of which illuminates an important aspect of the benefits of using the tool box, are presented next.

TECHNICAL AND SOCIAL CHANGE IN THE LIGHT OF ACTIVITY THEORY

As for establishing an understanding of technical and social change, activity theory is interesting in that it proposes to understand communities of practice (Lave, 1988) as human activity systems, upheld by mechanisms of the (inter)action of the actors, their practice by which they produce an outcome and reproduce themselves as competent actors.

Leontjev (1978, 1981), one of the founders of activity theory, distinguishes between three levels in human activity: activity—the overarching, collectively constituted integration of actions oriented toward and defined by a shared objectified motive, of which the individuals may or may not be consciously aware; goal-oriented individual actions of which the individual is consciously aware, can plan, discuss, and modify; and automatic operations depending on the specific conditions in the actual setting. For example, when starting to learn to ride a bike, maintaining balance is the activity. Once having learned that, maintaining balance turns into an operation, something individuals accomplish unconsciously adjusting to the conditions (the weather, the road, etc.); or biking becomes an action they can discuss as an option in line with other means of transportation, and they are free to think about where to ride the bike.

Through attempts to perform actions in relation to an object, sets of unconscious actions and overviews allowing for further expansion are produced. By the transformation of actions into operations and the expansion of actions into overview, complexity is reduced and the activity as a whole is expanded. Leontjev (1978, 1981) suggested taking these levels as a hierarchy, subordinating operations to actions, and actions to activity.

This should not be taken as if the actors act directly on the object. On the contrary, according to activity theory, all activity is inherently social, and all action is mediated by communication, tools, and working divisions of labor, all inherent in the culture that meets the actor on a first encounter. Because activity theory aims to understand an activity in its historical, developmental context, the theory pays much attention to the role of mediation. Mediation is taken as crystallized action, and thereby as a source from which to dig out developmental structures and transformations. The focus on mediation is, more than anything else, what makes activity theory so stimulating for reflections about design. In this conception, an artifact is seen as constituted through its different roles, depending on the relations to the object and among the actors. A *role* is a label for a position under constant and mutual definition depending on these relations. Furthermore, the artifact is the outcome of other activities, and may pass back and forth between these roles.

The following sections stress three specific "role models" of the mediating artifacts, or *affordances* (to use a well-known term used by Gibson, 1979, and later by Norman, 1991, in describing usefulness).

Mediators of Production and Communication

Wartofsky (1979) suggested a hierarchy of roles of artifacts analogous to Leontjev's hierarchy of activity: At the operation level, he talked about "primary artifacts." Here, the role is said to be transparent. If the artifact really serves as a tool, individuals are not consciously aware of it. At the level of action, individuals are consciously aware. The role of "secondary artifacts" is to preserve and transmit skills in the production and use of the primary artifacts. In this way, secondary artifacts become representations of the primary level. Wartofsky also suggested a tertiary role for artifacts corresponding to the activity level. Engeström (1990) built his understanding of "tool-ness" on the work of Wartofsky; he talked about the artifact's playing a certain role in contextualization of actions (i.e., in answering questions of "for what," "how," and "why" artifacts are used). Accordingly, he referred to the Wartofskian hierarchy in terms of "upward" and "downward" contextualization. The "what role," or the role as primary artifact, corresponds to the level of operations, whereas the "how roles" and "why roles," or roles as secondary artifacts, serve the purpose of preserving and transmitting skills in the production and use of primary artifacts. A tool playing this role represents the level of operations in the sense of being a symbolic externalization or objectification. At the tertiary level, as "imaginative" artifact, no "what," "how," and "why" question is answered because the reference point is no longer the immediately known presence but the activity under expansion.

Bødker (1991) dealt with how to create artifacts that do not cause breakdowns in the fluid conduct of work. This is what Engeström (1990, p. 194) called *downward contextualization*. However, as Engeström pointed out, if the intention is to expand and transcend already-known possibilities within a given work context, an *upward contextualization* is needed as well: It has to be anticipated how the artifact-to-be will support overall conceptualization and point to new possibilities.

Springboards: Triggers of Social Change

Engeström, from a basis in activity theory, developed a theory of social and psychological expansion. In it he tried to identify the mechanisms through which change is brought about.

Engeström labeled such expansive tools as *springboards*. He outlined their meaning in the following way: "A springboard is a facilitative image, technique or socio-conversational constellation . . . misplaced or transplanted from some previous context into a new" (p. 287). Springboards do not come about smoothly or automatically, and they are not as such solutions to the problem that one is facing. They are starters that may lead to an expansive solution. Engeström (1990) observed an important interdependency between the roles/levels: His results seem to point out that unless a tool that is meant as an imaginative artifact and instrument for expansion is anchored also in the primary level, people tend not to use it.

Boundary Objects: Facilitators of Communications Across Different Communities of Practice

In order for an artifact to serve as a springboard and address the future, it also has to address the present. Star and Griesemer (1989) introduced the notion of boundary objects characterizing common intellectual tools. Boundary objects fulfill the role of containers and carriers: Boundary objects are "both plastic enough to adapt to local needs and constraints of the several parties employing them, yet robust enough to maintain a common identity across sites. They are weakly structured in common use and become strongly structured in individual site-use. Like a blackboard, a boundary object 'sits in the middle' of a group of actors with divergent viewpoints" (Star & Griesemer, 1989, p. 46).

If a tool serves as a boundary object in a design situation, it represents and refers to a known use situation at the same time as it embodies the meaning assigned and taken for granted within the community of users. Following Engeström's observation, an artifact intended to serve as a springboard must also, in collaborative settings such as design, serve as a boundary object.

DESIGNING TOOLS

Design is a particular kind of activity that crosses, or lives on, the boundaries of several communities of practice relating the future to the past. Design processes have a double orientation: toward the product and toward the process. Because what is going to be created is by definition new and unknown, at least to some extent, neither product nor process can be fully known or planned in advance.

Systems development methods in general are rather detached from practice, and they often present themselves as cookbook recipes, without concern for the specifics of the design setting or the qualifications of the designers. Furthermore, such methods often prescribe a stepwise process, from an analysis of the present work situation to the programming of the system, as if the "new" either comes out of the blue, or is ensured by the stepwise construction process.

Designers need guidelines and plans, not for total prediction, but to guide the process and to come to grips with the shaping of the artifact. Thus, they need help to assess current use, as well as to anticipate and transcend current use in a planned way and in a specific direction. The designers need to represent and hypothesize about the computer artifact and its use, and in this endeavor they need to be supported by thinking tools. This view on design is in line with the findings of the Amodeus project, which showed how design consists of iterative processes of idea generation and evaluation (Nielsen, 1991).

Reflecting on some experiences with the design of computer-supported collaborative work (CSCW), three major sets of requirements have been elicited, which the support of thinking in design has to meet: First, there is a constant need to embody ideas and communicate them. Second, there is a need to find ways to let go of old conceptualizations and give rise to new. And third, there is a need to facilitate a shared understanding between participants coming from different professions, workplaces, and bringing different sets of constraints to the process.

This generally stated, multifunctionality of artifacts is definitely a challenge to design products and intermediaries: Not only is the artifact to "do something for you and remind you of something you can do" (Ehn, 1988), which in activity terms means that an artifact is mediating as well the productive as the reproductive aspects of the action, it is to do so for different people involved in the activity from different angles and with different capacities. And, it has to do so in a way oriented toward the unknown, that is, the future work situation.

If a tool serves as a springboard, then it represents meaning for the designers and embodies design ideas. Such embodiments do not refer to some kind of present or future use reality, for which reason they will not be of much use in stepwise refinement and modification of what is already there. Instead, they may, while being created within a community of designers holding mutual perspectives and experiences, facilitate the creation of something new.

The idea of springboards has been brought together with that of artifacts serving as boundary objects in design. A brief sketch is given of the present situation in systems development as far as design tools are concerned. Because what is going to be created is, according to Engeström (1987), "a living movement leading away from the old," neither product nor process can be fully known or planned in advance (p. 287). This fundamental condition traditionally has been dealt with in systems development by enforcing abstract systemic thinking on the situation where designers use their technical expertise as a shield and as a power instrument.

Design implies a focus on the process as well as the product: Focusing on the process means focusing on cooperation in the process, on working division of labor, resources, and so on. Focusing on the product means focusing on properties of the product (to be) and the activities that are part of this. The artifacts used in design carry a double determination: engendering the decisions made in design and being a vehicle of communication among participants. Most techniques describing the product do (e.g., enforce a certain way of proceeding with the process). In systems development this has provoked an ongoing discussion of what comes first, formalisms or exploration, where one side holds theory as the prime source of knowledge and the other practice. Floyd (1987) argued that both the theory-driven and the situated way of dealing with the design is necessary. Where Floyd put the main emphasis on the theory-driven side in most cases, this research has been more exploratory and empirical (Bødker & Grønbæk, 1991a, 1991b; Bødker et al., 1991, 1993).

Boundary objects facilitate communication and cooperation between different but cooperating communities of practice. There are at least two reasons why systems development tools deserve the label "boundary": the "container function" and the semantics that gradually emerge while a group of designers (and users) are working together to embody a design idea. As far as the container function is concerned, tools play a role in supporting and keeping track of the systematic reflection about the content of design ideas. Representing the mutual experience of constructing and exploring the design ideas, they make the ideas sharable and assessable for modification and critique. Emerging semantics arise during the conduct of the design activity, in the subgroups where subtasks are done. When participants in a large project want to work along common lines according to a shared overall understanding, representations that can serve as boundary objects are necessary in order to establish a shared "task semantics."

Bødker and Hammerskov (1984) showed how traditional descriptions alone are unsuitable to engender the shaping of the product or to serve as vehicles of communication, because the proposed general semantics for this is insufficient. When it comes to communication, the main problem is that the shared understanding is created in the construction process; it is not inherent in the outcome (i.e., the description; see, e.g., Munk-Madsen, 1978). This is the "representation-embodiment problem" once again: The map is not the territory, and even more important, the territory does not necessarily exist yet.

Even though it is impossible for designers to make representations that stand for "the whole truth," some kinds of representations—of, for example, a computer application being designed—are necessary in order to hold on to the construction. The question is how to make such representations. To support idea generation as well as systematic reflection, *scenarios* are the candidates: They may embody the negotiation process as well as hypotheses that, to some extent, embody the product to be.

The thinking tool box needs to guide the users in reducing the empirical situations to manageable dimensions as well as in clarifying and completing the description.

Lynch (1990) dealt with the process of visualizing and mathematizing scientific phenomena. He pointed out that the stepwise process from an empirical mess to a scientific drawing is not only a matter of reducing information to manageable dimensions. Instead, representations are added features to clarify, complete, extend, and so on, the incomplete state of the specific, unique phenomenon represented. In this process scientists apply generic pedagogy as well as abstract theorizing. Thus, they move the representation toward the essential and typical, away from the specific and unique. Scenarios may be able to represent the essential and typical in situations. In analogy to this, asking appropriate theory-driven questions about the computer application in use is useful. A potentially useful representation of such questions may be in the form of *checklists*.

As already stated, the social issue of how to convey and develop ideas across different communities of practice present a major communicative problem. Engeström's (1987) cycle of expansion has already been pointed to as a way to work with expansion across boundaries between communities of practice. He outlined in detail how to work the way from the experience of a need state and a double bind in one community of practice to the consolidation of the new in wider contexts. Taken as a prototypical way of conceptualizing technological change, his model applies to the experiences gained through research projects such as the UTOPIA project (Bødker et al., 1987; Ehn & Kyng, 1984), and the AT project (Bødker et al., 1993).

To sum up, the actors in a "design-as-change-and-expansion process" need boundary objects as springboards that capture the ideas and present them in an open-ended way, as well as checklists for systematic reflection. These are the kind of tools researchers have been trying to bring about, taking a point of departure in an understanding of tools from within activity theory.

THE TOOL BOX

The aims of the tool box have been to support shared understanding of the product and of the semantics for bringing it about, combined with generation, development, and evaluation of hypotheses. A major part of the tool box represents knowledge from practical design, from theoretical foundation, and from inquiries and investigations, put together in forms of questions and caselike descriptions to support thinking in the space between theory and reality.

Work with the practical formulation of the elements of the tool box was carried out in Esprit project 6155, called EuroCODE, the aim of which was to develop a design environment for CSCW applications. The idea of the tool box has been to facilitate communication about the platform and exemplary products of EuroCODE, emphasizing the social, educational, and organizational aspects of process and product. The tool box was developed in close interplay with the development of the platform and exemplary products in collaboration with different contractors. In the later part of the development of the tool box, various kinds of empirical experiences with the use of parts of the tool box have been collected, and attempts have been made to extend the tool box in various ways (see Bødker et al., 1993; Bødker, 1995; and Bødker, Christiansen, & Thüring, 1995).

All the tools in the tool box are meant to both speak to and contradict each other to stimulate discussion and dialogue. That is, for example, the main reason why there are two separate checklists (and the possibility of adding more)—one for *work* and one for *technical matters*—and why redundancy is intended.

Checklists and Paradigm Cases

The technical and work-oriented checklists each are formulated under 12 headings, formulating various thought-provoking questions. These questions were compiled from activity theory, from existing CSCW frameworks and from the technical concerns of the EuroCODE shell and demonstrators. They are meant as heuristics to support examination of hypotheses and to help clarify and complete the scenarios, in the fashion described by Lynch (1990). Furthermore, to support the understanding of possible answers, and to give an outline of the current state of the art, a set of key points in CSCW and CSCW applications ("Technical solutions looking for a problem") are offered to users. These paradigm cases constitute points of departure for idea generation. These examples are ways of helping the designer understand the consequences of design choices by making analogies to well-understood and clear-cut examples.

Creating Scenarios

Scenarios exist in the borderland between experience and expectation, the borderland characterized by Ricoeur (1988, chap. 10) as being between space of experience and horizon of expectation, and they have the power to provoke idea generation. This approach seeks to establish this relation by offering examples of crucial and critical aspects of work that might be affected by design, and examples of possible technological solutions. Dressed up with examples and theory, it is assumed that designers will be ready to think (i.e., to create scenarios themselves).

Scenarios are representations of the meaning that designers assign to embodiments of ideas of the future artifact and its use (see, e.g., Campbell, 1992; Carroll & Kellogg, 1989; Carroll & Rosson, 1992; Kyng, 1992, 1995). To understand more precisely what this means, analogies to the role of representations in scientific practice are made. Indeed, Latour (1990) pointed out, using the example of Galileo, that the development of tools for representation has been of major importance for scientific break-throughs, which underscores the importance for the creative processes of a good tool box.

Viewing scenarios in the role of tertiary artifacts, the role of which is "to give identity and overarching perspective to collective activity forma-tions" (Engeström, 1990, pp. 173–174), is a way to help groups of designers ask questions like "Who has access to these files, at what level?" and "Who shares this material, in relation to which processes?" Because sce-narios are not empirical situations, they should be "stories" located in time and space, "traces" featuring details, not "novels," and they should be designed based on knowledge about typical ways of doing things, but addressing specific, critical instances of the typical.

In the creation process, the scenariomakers may get support from the following narrative scheme, considering *what is done* (product of activity from the point of view of the organization and from the point of view of the different groups of involved actors), *where* (situating the activity sys-tem, including artifacts), *by whom and when* (working division of labor and the order according to which the activity is carried out), *by what means* (the role of the artifacts: position in division of labor, tool functionality, and communications-functionality), and *in what way* (the underlying cul-ture, norms, and values).

The following summarizes the qualities of the use of scenarios in design:

They support the build up and use of a shared understanding among the design group.

They exist in the borderland between experience and expectation.

They are meant to provoke new ideas.

They constitute a theoretical anchoring of an empirical "chaos."

The scenarios as such are not physical entities. They need to be em-bodied to provide hands-on experiences with problems and situations. This means that the tool box is primarily a professional designer's tool. The scenarios need to be explored in various games and workshops (future workshops, simulations, organizational games, dilemma games) or in prototyping, where users can get their hands on the situation.

Using Scenarios in the Design Process

So far, specifying procedures of how to use the tool box have been avoided. EuroCODE designers have freely chosen any tool they felt help-ful for the task at hand. Moreover, the tool box does not propose or constrain how to combine its components with other techniques. One way of using it in interplay with other tools and methods, however, may be the following:

1. A series of scenarios runs through the design project.

2. These scenarios help span out a theory-oriented exploration of design situations, while grounded in the specific empirical setting.

3. Numerous design activities take place within the overall design activity, ranging from initial interviewing and observation to programming and testing.

4. Some of these activities, as well as the actual shaping of the scenarios, are cooperative activities among users and designers; others are primarily done by professional designers.

5. The scenarios as such do not embody the technology, so they are not available for hands-on experiences by the users. Scenarios will primarily form the basis for other activities in which they are embodied and explored. Such activities include setting the stage for and pointing at problems and solutions to be dealt with in cooperative prototyping (Bødker & Grønbæk, 1991a, 1991b), when using mock-ups (Ehn & Kyng, 1991), simulations, or in more systematic explorations of a running computer application for evaluation or education.

6. Furthermore, the scenarios can be designed and explored in other types of design-by-doing situations such as future workshops (Kensing & Madsen, 1991), organizational games (Ehn & Sjögren, 1991), dilemma games (Mogensen, 1993). The scenarios may be used, as well, with other design approaches (e.g., data flow analysis, object-oriented analysis and design, or transaction cost analysis).

To summarize and hypothesize a little more about the use of scenarios in design, consider an example (Fig. 9.1). Scenario 1, the present work situation, is a scenario based on interviews and observations of work, studies of present technology, and so forth. The scenario may be the outcome of a future workshop, or it may be developed in an iteration with the future workshop (e.g., an early draft may set the stage for the workshop, whereas a more finished version may be produced after the workshop). The work checklist will serve to raise questions to be dealt with in the scenario. The scenario will span typical as well as critical situations of the present (potentials, problems, and bottlenecks). It represents hypotheses about the problems of the current situation, thus pointing in directions for the change to be initiated. The scenario is a boundary object serving to point to a mutual understanding of problems of the current work. It will delineate and represent an area of interest for the design/change process.

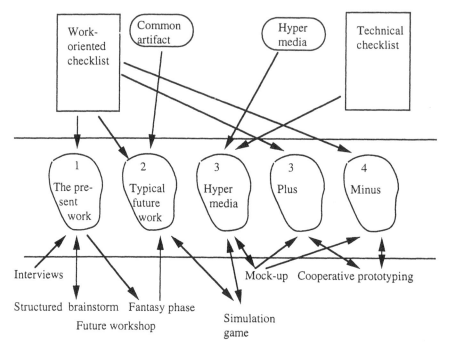

FIG. 9.1. Scenario-centered design.

Scenario 2 may be based on the fantasy phase of the future workshop. It explores primarily typical situations in the future changed work. The common artifact example is used to help generate the fantasy as qualified guess, and the work checklist to help consider the consequences of the choices made. This scenario represents a thinking from a third point, and may serve as a springboard. It may be explored in a simulation game, resulting in some modifications.

Scenario 3, a hypermedia solution, may be explored in close interplay with mock-ups and early prototypes based on the EuroCODE shell and hypermedia. Initially, this scenario will deal with typical situations of technical nature, perhaps moving more and more into critical situations as the prototypes evolve. Alternative prototypes may be applied to explore these critical situations. The hypermedia example is used to enhance the technical imaginations, and the technical checklist to consider the potentials, problems, and bottlenecks of the situations, in examining the scenarios.

Scenarios 4 and 5 are plus and minus scenarios for the use of the prototypical technical solution. These scenarios represent qualified guesses about "a good" and "a bad" use situation around the activity. These solutions "talk to" the experience of users as well as designers, making it possible to discuss what is and is not wanted. They may be explored also in other design activities such as dilemma games, and they may be used in setting the stage for cooperative prototyping activities. Work-oriented and technical checklists are used to examine the consequences, as well as to clarify and extend the representation by asking critical questions about well-known consequences.

Scenarios for evaluating prototypes usually move from typical to critical as the prototypes develop vertically and horizontally (and what is typical and critical may change). As the prototyping proceeds, the process changes character from a focus on the typical work centered on the prototype to one where it is important to explore and get hands-on experiences with a more and more complete prototype, covering increasingly specific and peripheral work activities. This is both because it is hard to evaluate critical situations if the typical situations are not yet in place, and because the breakdowns in use spread more and more into extreme, critical situations.

PARAPHRASING *LIFE OF BRIAN*:
WHAT HAVE WE GAINED?

We come from nothing and we go to nothing, so what have we lost?—nothing.
—Monty Python (1979)

In evaluating current attempts to create a thinking tool box for the design of CSCW, Monty Python's sentence might be paraphrased by saying: "We come from a scenario and we go to a scenario, so what have we gained— another scenario?"

In HCI, the topic of theory-driven versus ad-hoc design has been discussed vividly for many of the same reasons. The group around Jack Carroll has developed the use of scenarios to account for usability of the computer artifacts, and the analysis of the psychological theory "embedded" in the artifact (see, e.g., Campbell, 1992; Carroll, 1995; Carroll & Kellogg, 1989; Carroll & Rosson, 1992). As Bannon and Bødker (1991) pointed out, this is extremely problematic; without analyzing it in its setting, it is easy to overemphasize aspects of the artifact that may not be crucial in the use setting (see also Wixon, Holtzblatt, & Knox, 1990). When it comes to CSCW applications, the ability to conceptualize the social setting of design and use is crucial because these applications are dealing with social situations that are far more complicated than the one user–one computer situations, which have been the human–computer interaction (HCI) foci for many years (see, e.g., discussions in Carroll, 1991).

Campbell (1992) tried to categorize scenarios, based on the assumption that a scenario refers to "representative instances of interaction between user and system." As Kyng (1992) pointed out, these categories are presented as a goal per se in much of the literature, rather as an instrument to be used in cooperation between users and designers (e.g., in relation to evaluation of prototypes, future workshops, etc.). They are all dealing with almost fully specified systems, whereas the notion here is one where an early idea about a system may be explored as well. Scenarios are a way of referring back to user practice, again without making them ends in their own right.

Making scenarios is a creative process: They are hypotheses or qualified guesses about the future computer application, as embodiments of it. Thus, the tool box cannot be used in a stepwise derivation of scenarios. Checklists may be used for producing documentation, and for systematic evaluation of the design ideas, and they may be used to clarify and extend the scenarios by pointing to directions to be covered.

Checklists or individual items on the lists may introduce conflicts around the computer application and its use. This discussion has deliberately tried not to resolve such conflicts theoretically a priori, because it is in this creative space of conflicts and contradictions that something new is created (Engeström, 1987). Conflicting points of view can only be dealt with in terms of specific empirical situations. Here they may result in solutions that transcend the dilemma, or where deliberate choices are made in favor of one side of the dilemma. Furthermore, it is important to work with alternative scenarios illustrating alternative paths.

Looking at the theoretical side of design of CSCW applications, most frameworks give rather idealistic descriptions of group work (what it is supposed to be). One exception from this is the work by Schmidt and others (Bannon & Schmidt, 1992; Schmidt, 1993). The use of this framework in design has been dealt with in detail in Bødker and Mogensen (1993). Such a frame creates problems because it pigeonholes work as cooperative or not, instead of asking questions about how a certain technology makes work more, or less, cooperative. Though it claims to view cooperation as an emerging phenomenon, it describes cooperative work as something static. This design is a process of cooperative thinking in which scenarios crystallize a shared understanding of the product (to be), thus populating the space between theory-driven and situated design. In this way, this study tried to avoid the ontological "trap" of discussing what CSCW is or is not. Instead, a tool box has been provided, allowing for an exploration of better computer support for cooperative work in the specific work settings. This exploration is inspired and directed by theoretical concerns, as well as "ideal cases" (good or bad) that constitute state of the art in investigations of CSCW applications.

This effort is not just another scenario or guidelines for making better scenarios. It is support for embodiments of the future product—embodiments that are open enough to allow for dialogue and sufficiently precise to provoke breakdowns in assumptions, or in Engeström's words "living movements away from the old."

ACKNOWLEDGMENTS

The work has been funded in part by Esprit project 6155—EuroCODE. The scenario idea owes much to discussions with Lucy Suchman and Wendy Mackay. The idea of a thinking tool box has been developed in discussions with Morten Kyng, Kaj Grønbæk, Preben Mogensen, Kim Halskov Madsen, Peter Axel Nielsen, and Mike Robinson. The EuroCODE T1.1 group has played a major role in shaping up the idea. In particular, Manfred Thüring, who has been our writing partner, has taken on the much appreciated, though little popular, role of the devil's advocate. We owe much to Morten Kyng, Leigh Star, and Chris Darrouzet for critical comments on drafts of this chapter.

REFERENCES

Bannon, L., & Bødker, S. (1991). Beyond the interface: Encountering artifacts in use. In J. M. Carroll (Ed.), *Designing interaction: Psychology at the human–computer interface* (pp. 227–253). New York: Cambridge University Press.

Bannon, L., & Schmidt, K. (1992). Taking CSCW seriously. Supporting articulation work. *CSCW Journal*, 1(1–2), 7–40.

Bødker, S. (1991). *Through the interface—a human activity approach to user interface design.* Hillsdale, NJ: Lawrence Erlbaum Associates.

Bødker, S. (Ed.). (1995). *Deliverable 1.4.2: The EuroCODE conceptual framework: Finalization, the process.* Aarhus, Denmark: Department of Computer Science, Aarhus University.

Bødker, S., et al. (1993). *Deliverable D 1.1: The EuroCODE conceptual framework: Preliminary.* Bonn: Empirica.

Bødker, S., Christiansen, E., Ehn, P., Markussen, R., Mogensen, P., & Trigg, R. (1991). Computers in context. Report from the AT project in progress. *Report of the 1991 NES-SAM conference, Ebeltoft, Denmark* (pp. 153–158). Copenhagen: NES/SAM.

Bødker, S., Christiansen, E., Ehn, P., Markussen, R., Mogensen, P., & Trigg, R. (1993). *The AT-Project: Practical research in cooperative design* (DAIMI No. PB-454). Aarhus, Denmark: Computer Science Department, Aarhus University.

Bødker, S., Christiansen, E., & Thüring, M. (1995, January). A conceptual toolbox for designing CSCW applications. In *COOP '95, International Workshop on the Design of Cooperative Systems* (pp. 266–284). Juan-les-Pins.

Bødker, S., Ehn, P., Kammersgaard, J., Kyng, M., & Sundblad, Y. (1987). A utopian experience. In G. Bjerknes, P. Ehn, & M. Kyng (Eds.), *Computers and democracy: A Scandinavian challenge* (pp. 251–278). Aldershot, UK: Avebury.

Bødker, S., & Grønbæk, K. (1991a). Cooperative prototyping: Users and designers in mutual activity. *International Journal of Man–Machine Studies, Special Issue on CSCW, 34,* 453–478.

Bødker, S., & Grønbæk, K. (1991b). Design in action: From prototyping by demonstration to cooperative prototyping. In J. Greenbaum & M. Kyng (Eds.), *Design at work: Cooperative design of computer systems* (pp. 197–218). Hillsdale, NJ: Lawrence Erlbaum Associates.

Bødker, S., & Hammerskov, J. (1984). ISAC—A case study of systems description tools. In M. Sääksjärvi (Ed.), *Report of the Seventh Scandinavian Research Seminar on Systemeering* (pp. 201–210). Helsinki: Helsinki School of Economics.

Bødker, S., & Mogensen, P. (1993). One woman's job is another man's articulation work—an essay about the design of computer support for cooperative work. In M. Robinson & K. Schmidt (Eds.), *Developing CSCW systems: Design concepts.* Report of the CoTECH WG4 (pp. 149–166). Roskilde, Denmark: Risø National Laboratory.

Campbell, R. L. (1992). Will the real scenario please stand up? *SIGCHI Bulletin, 24*(2), 6–8.

Carroll, J. M. (Ed.). (1991). *Designing interaction: Psychology at the human–computer interface.* New York: Cambridge University Press.

Carroll, J. M. (Ed.). (1995). *Scenario-based design. Envisioning work and technology in system development.* New York: Wiley.

Carroll, J. M., & Kellogg, W. (1989). Artifact as theory-nexus: Hermeneutics meets theory-based design. In K. Bice & C. Lewis (Eds.), *Proceedings of CHI '89 Conference on Human Factors in Computing Systems* (pp. 7–14). New York: ACM Press.

Carroll, J. M., & Rosson, M. B. (1992). Getting around the task-artifact cycle: How to make claims and design by scenario. *CACM, 10*(2), 181–210.

Ehn, P. (1988). *Work-oriented design of computer artifacts.* Hillsdale, NJ: Lawrence Erlbaum Associates.

Ehn, P., & Kyng, M. (1984). A tool perspective on design of interactive computer support for skilled workers. In M. Sääksjärvi (Ed.), *Proceedings from the Seventh Scandinavian Research Seminar on Systemeering* (pp. 211–242). Helsinki: Helsinki School of Economics.

Ehn, P., & Kyng, M. (1991). Cardboard computers: Mocking-it-up or hands-on the future. In J. Greenbaum & M. Kyng (Eds.), *Design at work: Cooperative design of computer systems* (pp. 169–195). Hillsdale, NJ: Lawrence Erlbaum Associates.

Ehn, P., & Sjögren, D. (1991). From system description to scripts for action. In J. Greenbaum & M. Kyng (Eds.), *Design at work: Cooperative design of computer systems* (pp. 241–268). Hillsdale, NJ: Lawrence Erlbaum Associates.

Engeström, Y. (1987). *Learning by expanding.* Helsinki: Orienta-Konsultit.

Engeström, Y. (1990). *Learning, working and imagining. Twelve studies in activity theory.* Helsinki: Orienta-Konsultit.

Floyd, C. (1987). Outline of a paradigm change in software engineering. In G. Bjerknes, P. Ehn, & M. Kyng (Eds.), *Computers and democracy—a Scandinavian challenge* (pp. 191–212). Aldershot, UK: Avebury.

Gibson, J. S. (1979). *The ecological approach to visual perception.* Boston: Houghton Mifflin.

Greenbaum, J., & Kyng, M. (Eds.). (1991). *Design at work: Cooperative design of computer systems.* Hillsdale, NJ: Lawrence Erlbaum Associates.

Kensing, F., & Madsen, K. H. (1991). Generating visions: Future workshops and metaphorical design. In J. Greenbaum & M. Kyng (Eds.), *Design at work: Cooperative design of computer systems* (pp. 155–168). Hillsdale, NJ: Lawrence Erlbaum Associates.

Kyng, M. (1992). Scenario? Guilty! *SIGCHI Bulletin, 24*(4), 8–9.

Kyng, M. (1995). Creating contexts for design. In J. M. Carroll (Ed.), *Scenario-based design. Envisioning work and technology in system development* (pp. 85–108). New York: Wiley.

Latour, B. (1990). Drawing things together. In M. Lynch & S. Woolgar (Eds.), *Representations in scientific practice* (pp. 19–68). Cambridge, MA: MIT Press.

Lave, J. (1988). *Cognition in practice.* Cambridge, England: Cambridge University Press.

Leontjev, A. N. (1978). *Activity, consciousness, and personality.* Englewood Cliffs, NJ: Prentice-Hall.

Leontjev, A. N. (1981). *Problems of the development of the mind.* Moscow: Progress Publishers.

Lynch, M. (1990). The externalized retina: Selection and mathematization in the visual documentation of objects in the life sciences. In M. Lynch & S. Woolgar (Eds.), *Representations in scientific practice* (pp. 153–186). Cambridge, MA: MIT Press.

Mogensen, P. (1993). *Cooperative analysis.* Unpublished doctoral thesis, Aarhus University, Denmark.

Munk-Madsen, A. (1978). *Systembeskrivelse med brugere* [Systems description with users]. (DUE-notat no. 9). Aarhus, Denmark: Aarhus University.

Nielsen, J. (1991). *Designers decision making. Design of a user interface for a picture search database. Description and analysis of an experimental workshop.* Amodeus Project document RP7/WP, The Amodeus Project, ESPRIT Basic Research Action 3066.

Norman, D. (1991). Cognitive artifacts. In J. M. Carroll (Ed.), *Designing interaction: Psychology at the human–computer interface* (pp. 17–38). New York: Cambridge University Press.

Python, M. (1979). *Life of Brian* [93m WB-Orion C].

Ricoeur, P. (1988). *Time and Narrative* (Vol. 3). Chicago: University of Chicago Press.

Schmidt, K. (1993). The articulation of cooperative work—Requirements for computer support. In M. Robinson & K. Schmidt (Eds.), *CoTech WG4 report. Developing CSCW Systems: Design Concepts* (pp. 37–104). Roskilde, Denmark: Risø National Laboratory.

Star, S. L., & Griesemer, J. R. (1989). Institutional ecology, "translations" and boundary objects: Amateurs and professionals in Berkeley's museum of vertebrate zoology, 1907–39. *Social Studies of Science, 19,* 387–420.

Wartofsky, M. (1979). Perception, representation and the forms of action: Towards a historical epistemology. In *Models, Representations and Scientific Understanding* (pp. 188–210). Dordrecht: Reidel.

Wixon, D., Holtzblatt, K., & Knox, S. (1990). Contextual design: An emergent view on systems design. In J. Chew & J. Whiteside (Eds.), *Empowering people CHI'90 Conference Proceedings* (pp. 329–336). New York: Association for Computing Machinery.

10

Building a Collective Knowledge Management System: Knowledge-Editing Versus Knowledge-Eliciting Techniques

Jean-Pierre Poitou
Université de Provence, France

Technical cognitive processes occur in a technical and a social division of labor. The technical division of labor—both vertical (the segmentation of the operating cycle) and horizontal (multiple workstations for the same operation in the cycle)—entails a distribution of knowledge. The situation created by the social division of labor (Poitou & Chabot, 1991) is illustrated by this statement from Bonnet, Haton, and Truong-Ngoc (1986): "The expert withholds some capital. The knowledge engineer is paid to take it away from him" (p. 165). Such is the context in which cognitive processes in the firm are to be analyzed.

This context is first described under the present economic circumstances. Then some considerations are presented as to the importance of documents in the cognitive functioning. The term *document* is given an extended meaning, and understood as an "intellectual object" (Janet, 1935). In the case of industrial business, the meaning of documents is extended to include as intellectual objects almost every component of the shop or of the office.

One consequence of the social division of labor is that knowledge is traded off neither between individuals nor between workposts but rather between "places." This concept is presented in detail later, and its relations with the management of collective knowledge are discussed further.

Finally, drawing on the foregoing considerations, two systems for computer assistance to the management of corporate knowledge (CKMS) are presented.

THE COLLECTIVE MANAGEMENT OF KNOWLEDGE AND THE DIVISION OF LABOR

The technical and the social divisions of labor are conditioned by the changes in the economic circumstances. Accordingly, the distribution of knowledge in the firm is itself ever-changing, because the structures over which it is spread change continuously under the effects of financial, administrative, and technical reorganization in the firm and its branches.

The development of knowledge and diffusion of expertise are partitioned and segmented in nature. They are segmented in time, according to the ups and downs of competition between firms, between branches within firms, between departments within the branches, and as a function of individual social conflicts and rivalries resulting from competition between members of the workforce. They are segmented in space, by the division into departments, each subjected to different, sometimes contradictory, industrial policies. And, finally, they are hierarchically segmented.

These divisions are sources of conflict due to power relations between the economic agents, buyers, and sellers of labor. In such a context, pieces of knowledge are elements of professional qualification, and consequently, become goods bitterly fought over. The outcomes of these conflicts determine the distribution of knowledge in the firms, and, as becomes evident, the absolute nonequivalence of places in the firm.

The current economic conjuncture causes further instability and discontinuity in the generation and use of knowledge in industry. Under these circumstances, the evolution of knowledge and skills is neither linear nor consistent but dictated by the particular, rarely synchronized, patterns of economic expansion, technical change, and product innovation.

During the 1960s, a large supply of essentially unskilled workers carried off mass production. Then, during the next decade, the resulting polarization of the workforce followed by the massive layoff of the least skilled workers, the disappearance of numerous large-scale production units and their corresponding collective skills, and the lower level of investment in general and vocational training all contributed to making the professionally qualified a rare commodity. At the same time, solvent demand became increasingly rare. Manufacturing became more capitalistic. Financial capitalization of the economy required faster and greater returns on investments. Competition increased on the few solvent markets for high value-added products. The healthiest businesses in the industrialized countries tended to concentrate on the production of complex products, which demand rigorous management of resources and knowledge. Indeed, they relied on the proliferating computer tools to supplement knowledge-processing capabilities. Yet, with the emergence of new technologies in sectors of strong capitalistic concentration, professional skills and competence became the productive qualities that could be wisely used to a larger and more profitable extent. Management has become aware of the need to capitalize the knowledge assets of the firm, especially in the face of rapid renewal of product and tool complexity (Poitou, 1983, 1987).

Those industrialists wealthy and wise enough to invest in both human resources and technical solutions have attempted to resolve the difficulties of the current conjuncture by attacking them from both ends: from the bottom up, with psychosociological and ideological solutions such as progress groups, quality clubs, and so on; and from the top down, with costly investments in the automation and rationalization of human intellectual activity. But many industrialists have looked for exclusively technical solutions, which did not quite fulfill the hopes they had raised—expert systems being one case in point.

The current conjuncture is a highly contradictory one. The immense potential of science and technologies is being checked by the production crisis. In previous periods of technical and organizational changes, every new managerial technique was supported by a legitimacy founding discourse, which Hatchuel and Weil (1992) called a *rationality myth.* They concluded four case studies of expert systems by pointing out that the rationalization process now in progress does not involve an overall unifying notion of productive rationality, which might appeal to every member of the firm. A better understanding of the collective management of knowledge is needed in order to improve the cooperation of the members of the firm toward the implementation and use of computer-assisted production techniques.

THE MAN–TOOL RELATION: INTELLECTUAL OBJECTS AND OBJECTAL KNOWLEDGE

To say that the tool comes before the intelligence (Leroi-Gourhan, 1962) is to say that, being the product of some social activity, it embodies more varied pieces of knowledge and in greater number than the individual's own perception of how to use it.

Intellectual Objects and Objectal Knowledge

The tool is adapted not only to its use, but also to its user. The tool teaches individuals how to work efficiently. It also teaches them how to cooperate with their fellow workers. This is particularly the case with tools of artificial intelligence, but it holds true for any tool, however unsophisticated: Every tool is an "artificial thought device" (Poitou, 1991b).

More precisely, every tool embodies what the ergonomists call a *user's model*. Whether empirical or scientific, whether implicit or explicit, the user's model is the result of accumulated technological knowledge about the role and efficiency of both the tool and the worker in the production process. In order to be efficient, workers have to conform to the user's model, inasmuch as they perceive and understand it (of course, the actual user's model does not necessarily coincide with the model the designer of the tool had in mind). Because it embodies knowledge, which it conveys to its user, the tool can be called an "intellectual object" (Janet, 1935). With regard to its capacity to incorporate and transmit knowledge, every tool is a document in an extended meaning of the term.

The knowledge embodied in an intellectual object can be termed *objectal*. Objectal knowledge can also be found in the organization of the workplace, of the shop, of the plant. More generally, the organized space (Bolt, 1984) can be considered as the objectal form of *situated* knowledge.

Once having resolutely admitted the objectal character of knowledge, it is possible to consider a special class of tools, mostly verbal (and/or graphic) in kind: instructions for use, recipes, and norms that constitute the technical literature. This verbal form of knowledge is an elicitation, only partial, of the knowledge embodied in the objectal forms. Such elicitation of situated knowledge takes place in training situations of various kinds, for instance, when experts teach an apprentice their trade, or instruct a newcomer to a new job. It is meant to help the unskilled operator to "read" objectal knowledge.

In order to improve the management of knowledge, Engelbart (1963) suggested considering not the individual agent, but a larger system he called "H-LAM/T: Human using Language, Artefacts and Methodology in which he is Trained" (p. 40). By proper assistance to the objectal part of this system, intelligence could be amplified:

> *Intelligence amplification* seems applicable to our goal (of augmenting the human intellect) in that the entity to be produced will exhibit more of what can be called intelligence than an unaided human could demonstrate. That which possesses the amplified intelligence is the resulting H-LAM/T system, in which the LAM/T augmentation means represent the amplifier of the individual's intelligence. (Engelbart, 1963, p. 45)

Language–Artefact–Methodology is the part of the system where the best can be made of computer assistance. Basically, it means designing *methodologies* and tools for giving fast, exhaustive, and reliable access to accurate and pertinent knowledge, in both its objectal (*artefacts*) and its verbal (*language*) forms. Or, put otherwise, it means improving the management of documents (in the extended meaning of the term).

But in order to do this, it is necessary to first understand how the knowledge embodied in the machine and the intelligence of the human performer combine into technical intelligence, forming a *man–machine dialog formation* (Poitou, 1991c, 1991d; Poitou, Caquant, & Peri, 1993).

Knowledge Processing: A Three-Stage Process

First consider music as an example. Strictly speaking, music only exists in practice. It is only present, real, and alive for music lovers during its execution, in action. The performance makes use of tools (the musical instruments), written documents (the score), motor programs (the way the musicians play), an organization (the orchestra), a division of labor (the hierarchy of music stands), an organized process (the conductor's control of the execution), and so on. None of these elements are the music, but the music does not exist without the presence and cooperation of each of them.

Music can be recorded "live"; the recording, however, will not contain live music, but its trace. One can describe and thus transmit the conditions under which it is reproducible—that is, its execution components, ranging from the score to the comments jotted down by the conductor (the tempi, for instance), including the composition of the orchestra and the types of instruments (contemporary or baroque for example). However, each execution is unique.

So music exists under either of two conditions: either as a sound, when performed, or otherwise, as a collection of artefacts of various kinds; either as a performance, or as a set of material conditions under which music can be produced. Music as sound, living music, being transient and unique, can be experienced, though not described or transmitted; the conditions of music, sleeping music so to speak, can be described and transmitted.

This metaphor helps to distinguish between two notions whose terms are relatively arbitrary but whose distinction is well grounded: *expertise*, which refers to a potential, directly observable only when actually performed, and *knowledge*, which refers to a result. Knowledge, as the outcome of the prior development of expertise and as the condition for the developments currently in progress, is embodied in artefacts. It can be located, described, transmitted, and acquired. Expertise is the *performance* of knowledge. The output of this performance consists of intellectual objects, documents for more knowledge, and possibly new knowledge, which will be put into use in another performance. As already illustrated, with the example of music performance, expertise cannot be "encapsulated" or "boxed." Only its output can. Knowledge can be viewed as raw material for expertise or dead expertise. Reciprocally, expertise is living knowledge.

Between the passive state of knowledge, and the active state of exper-tise, a transition stage has to take place, which consists of *knowledge management*. Knowledge management implies a set of practices supported by particular skills, enabling the agent to exploit intellectually the envi-ronment, and the intellectual objects it contains, in order to have passive knowledge realized into productive efficient actions (i.e., into expertise).

Expertise Reconstructed

Bourdieu (1972) recommended concentrating efforts on observing those unique, concrete sequences, in which the knowledge of an expert is put into action, in the form of an improvisation adapted to the circumstances of the current interaction with the surroundings, one's addressee, or one's opponent. The action is adjusted step by step, both in the course of the sequence, and sequence by sequence, over time. The meaning of a se-quence emerges move after move, and becomes completely understood by the actors themselves only when the sequence is completed. The action is thus controlled at least as much by the human and material environment as by the actors' will. Regularities in the sequences of actions stem from the constants introduced into the environment by the effects of the culture: the organization of space and time, the tools, and so on.

Ethnomethodology has developed its dialog-based view of the con-struction of meaning to study human activity. This idea again uses the idea that actions, like statements, are not completely programmed, even if they are part of a plan. Nor are they completely willful, even if they are guided by intent. They are not completely explicit either, nor fully stated, because they are meaningless unless they are considered in refer-ence to the circumstances under which they were produced (indexicality). These conditions, which may seem to lead to inefficiency, are on the contrary a guarantee of adaptation, and therefore, of efficiency.

Finally, research in ergonomics (Lacoste, 1990; Pinsky & Theureau, 1987) and studies on the microsociology of everyday life (Bratman, 1987; Conein, 1990, 1991; Zimmerman, 1973) have shown knowledge to be distributed over the places and objects the agent uses. Tools and materials are arranged in space following configurations that correspond to rough plans and not to detailed programs. When getting to action, the operators retrieve—via contact with the various materials and tools and according to paths governed by the arrangement of the places—the relevant knowl-edge about the implementation of their action scheme. Then the action sequences occur, periodically interspersed with the recurrent display of the technical device. This uncovering of meaning through the use of a significant set of tools is what Pinsky and Theureau (1987) termed the *course of action*. Far from corresponding to the execution of predefined algorithms or to the processing of stored information, the course of action implies the activation and organization of knowledge, an integral part of the preparation for action.

These various theoretical approaches of what might be called a dialog-based understanding of practice provides the necessary background for discussing the main constituents of corporate knowledge.

TECHNOLOGICAL BASE, COGNITIVE FORMATIONS, AND MENTAL OPERATORS

The Technological Base

The notion of technological base (Poitou, 1987) simultaneously refers to the lore of technical knowledge from which agents draw in order to carry out their production practices, and to the heterogeneous collection of pieces of equipment, in which it is embodied: shops, offices, workplaces and workstations, tools and equipment, organizations as well as flow charts, documents, and technical instructions.

For all of the reasons stated in the first part of this chapter, this body of knowledge is neither complete nor permanent, nor is it universally accessible or equally distributed. On the contrary, it is always contingent on conjuncture-oriented transformations and is often what is at stake in conflicts between opposed parties. However, due to the cooperative nature of production, in general, and of knowledge production, in particular, there is some degree of solidarity among the constituents of the technological base. To characterize the mode of organization and operation of this base, the term *formation* is more appropriate than *system* because it allows for a kind of solidarity that is compatible with or even founded on antagonism, and therefore allows for weak points and inconsistencies.

Skills—whether social or technical, collective or individual—are the basic components of the knowledge management process (Poitou, 1983, 1992). They correspond to the agents' ability to actualize, in practice, the knowledge stored in objectal form, by adjusting ever more precisely to the actual user's model of the tools and other artefacts they are in charge of.

Individual Management of Knowledge

Representation-Free Cognitive Functioning

When considered quite in the abstract, and at the individual level, the management of knowledge, however skillful, seems to be a rather simple matter.

According to Kirsh (1990), a system capable of reacting to local conditions in an automatic and expert fashion possesses a kind of flexibility that allows it to adapt a previous plan to the current situation. Such a plan does not necessarily have to consist of much more than the following elements: a roughly ordered set of intelligent perception–action modules, a set of landmarks and possible signs, a few heuristics and tricks, some reminders, a set of means that proved to be effective in the past, and some pointers indicating specific examples (or fragments of examples) that might be useful. The prerequisite reasoning for such a system involves retrieving, sorting, and using potentially useful cases. This type of method can reduce complexity if the user is willing to pay the initial price of setting up the pointers and reminders for subsequent use. In this way, Kirsh defined the minimal conditions allowing an automaton to organize its activity in a natural environment. This calls for a theory of activity that accounts for behavior as determined by the situation rather than based on an internal model (Agre & Chapman, 1987). Such a theory of intelligent thought is founded as little as possible on representations (Brooks, 1991).

At first sight, Kirsh's model seems quite adequate for describing individual knowledge management in industrial settings. The technical organization of production is aimed at such a situation-regulated and representation-free cognitive functioning of the workers. The ongoing effort to organize production involves ordering and arranging the agent's environment so that it will be as controlled as possible while still being loaded with knowledge. This environment is deliberately pigeonholed with pointers, reminders, landmarks, and signs, which can later be used at low cost. These multiple and redundant cues mark the path for navigation in a controlled and meaningful environment. This environment might be called a knowledgeable workplace, insofar as it enables mental functioning without an excessive load of representations, because knowledge is already written in the environment.

In such an environment, the individual knowledge management consists of organizing the intellectual objects at one's workplace as a convenient storage for knowledge, and exploiting the knowledge stored in the workplace according to the most efficient rules of stock management, including: alleviating the mental load by locating knowledge as much as possible in external storage, elaborating and implementing "just in time" procedures for retrieving adequately needed knowledge, and supplying knowledge in order to carry on mental activity with "zero stock" and "minimal outstanding."

However, workers are not an automaton in a natural or technical environment, but agents working at their own specific place in a network of social relationships. This situation has, according to Pêcheux (Pêcheux,

1969; Pêcheux & Fuchs, 1975) several implications with respect to the operator's understanding of spoken or written statements. When considering tools, and more generally the whole work environment as documents, accordingly it becomes necessary to consider the implications of the concept of place in the understanding of the knowledge embodied in work artefacts, and of the cooperation processes between workers. Before considering the collective managment at the level of the technological base, this chapter first examines the concept of *place*, and its implications for the meaning of documents and the mutual understanding among co-workers.

The Concept of Place

The term *place* is used in its topographical sense, of course, as the physical workpost, and in its cognitive sense, as a place for the storage of knowledge. This place belongs to someone, because there can be no practice without a subject, no place without an agent. Thus, a place should also be understood in its social sense, as a situation in the social relations of production, indicated by wages, job assignment, qualification, and skill requirements. The fundamental relations between the instrument and the performer (Poitou, 1978) and between the instrument and the knowledge (Pêcheux & Fuchs, 1975) are nested in the network of place relations. Thus, the relations between places determine the possibility for the performer of a task to capture the knowledge embodied in the environment, in order to actualize it as expertise (i.e., to perform the task).

Place and the Construction of Meaning. In developing his automatic discourse analysis program (AAD), Pêcheux (1969) made a strong claim: Analyzing the social conditions of discourse production is absolutely required for any semantic analysis, because every text produced is a selection of elements among the constituents of a higher level *master discourse*, which is dependent on the specific production conditions. For all speakers bound by them, these social conditions govern which elements are selected from the master discourse and how they are linked together in the thread of each individual discourse.

The master discourse can be viewed as a virtual hypertext, where parts of the discourse are linked to other discourses or texts, which serve as references or rather as paraphrase. Understanding means thus navigating through this hypertext and using the associated discourses, or cotext, in order to enlighten the text actually read. Navigation through the hypertext is determined by the linguistic cues that serve as shifters from node to node, the organizational cues that help to identify places, and the social relation between the speakers' places and the listeners' or readers' places.

Morphosyntactic Markers. *What* is said in a document is understood through the *way* it is told or written. Not only the vocabulary, but the argumentative style, the grammar, the enunciation marks also serve to build meaning by indicating how to navigate within the text, and between the text and its cotexts. Linguistic characterization of the text, using lexical and morphosyntactical markers, are currently developed in the line of the paraphrase-based tools for textual description derived from the work of Harris (1952) and Pêcheux (1969). They can be used to establish relations between different parts of the same text, and among texts between documents (Stiegler, 1993).

Organizational Markers. Knowing *where from* (i.e., from which place) a speech or text comes also matters in understanding (Pêcheux & Fuchs, 1975). Organizations are usually careful in making clear who addresses whom, and what the respective *positions* in the corporate structure are. Organizational indices concern the authorities (in terms of department, offices, positions) and agencies that issued the document, the people to whom it was directly or indirectly addressed, and the specific functions the document fulfills in the organization (whether it is a memo, an agreement, a bill, etc.). Industrial writings contain a great many markers of this sort, which are evidence of the fact that the construction of meaning by both the writer and the readers is heavily dependent on these organizational cues. Accordingly, organizational references should be taken into consideration in order to index documents in a knowledge management system.

Relations Between Places. Although different places in a firm determine a different understanding of knowledge, identical places in the same circumstances determine the production of meanings that are "paraphrases" of each other. Readers try their best to take advantage of the various linguistic and organizational cues in order to identify the functional and *social* relations between places, and to select accordingly in the cotext the paraphrases relevant to the text. Comparing the text to its paraphrase allows readers to dispose of ambiguity.

This analysis is based on the idea that the antagonistic nature of the social relations of production determine the social conditions of discourse production, from which meaning results. Knowledge in a cognitive formation is neither freely accessible nor freely activated by the agents, but instead, is distributed according to the places they hold in the social relations of production, and consequently, in the work process. These very determinants regulate the forms of knowledge actualization.

In matters of trade and job, understanding is total between two agents whose places are identical. It is restricted to common sense (i.e., to almost nothing) when the places are completely disconnected, as is the case for instance between any expert and a knowledge engineer. Knowledge engineers are wrong in interpreting the knowledge eliciting problems they encounter as being due to enunciative, mnemonic, or logical imperfections of the communication process. These difficulties reside in the impossibility of "swapping places" with the people they interview. Knowledge engineers are not "in the work processes" they analyze. Their "place" in the social relations is not that of the expert with the knowledge and skills needed to perform in a local context. Accordingly, between a trainer and a trainee for instance, an optimal distance (not too great, and not too small) has to be found between their respective places, such that trainers have something to teach, and a capability to make themselves understood, and the trainees have a desire to ask questions, and a capability to understand what they are taught. This is the basis for the Method 3A.

More generally, the way in which a given technographical item (be it verbal or artefactual) is put into practice will depend on the place of the performer who makes use of it. The reconstruction of expertise from available knowledge is circumstantial; it occurs at the performer's place and is the performer's job. Also, the performer's place is necessarily the place where knowledge is integrated in view of its subsequent actualization in productive practice. And, finally, the integration functions are necessarily the responsibility of the performers and not of systems of any kind, because knowledge implementation is circumstantial, conjunctural, and contentious.

This idea is clearly in opposition to current knowledge representation theories, which generally consider that knowledge can be represented and representations supplied irrespective of the place where knowledge is to be used. It does not coincide perfectly either with a representation-free conception of performance, as illustrated by Kirsh's model. It assumes short-term transient representations of the situated knowledge to be converted into expertise. Such representations are reconstructed on the spot, in a rather broad fashion, and are continuously restructured in order to be adapted to the situation.

In opposition with the representationalist view, this chapter proposes that any computer aid to knowledge management should not attempt to assign any meaning to a document nor to *re-present* the meaning of a document. A more modest, but also more efficient and practicable, goal is helping the users to reconstruct meaning by and for themselves.

Collective Management of Knowledge

An automaton according to Kirsh, or an animal according to Gibson (1979), are able to "read" their environment directly. As Gibson noted, the information embodied in the human environment is accessible to individuals not directly as an "affordance," but through "displays." As a matter of fact, it has always been necessary in cooperative production to describe knowledge, and to engage in the endless process of enumerating, locating, situating, diffusing, and processing knowledge descriptions of all types. This process has produced in each and every organization a body of empirical practices and methods for "displaying" elements of the technological base.

The aim of these practices is to establish, maintain, and restore mutual understanding between members of the firm with respect to the technological base. They are the methods naturally developed in order to capitalize knowledge and to circumvent (as much as possible) the obstacles to communication of knowledge, through the elaboration of accessible documents (either oral or written), which, because of the division of labor, do not flow through a network of open channels connecting equivalent positions but between sets of places in the firm. These practices of technological base management result in verbal elicitation (either oral or written) of objectal knowledge. That is, they transform documents (in the extended meaning of the term) into documents in the ordinary sense. This process is endless because the firm is an ever-evolving, antagonistic/cooperative body.

Cognitive Formations and Mental Operators. As noted earlier, the individual cognitive functioning can be viewed as an interaction between individuals and their tools, or more generally between individuals and their tool-fitted workplace. In industrial settings, cognitive functioning occurs within the cooperation of people interacting with their own tools and interacting with their fellow workers in a network of workplaces. Or, to use Engelbart's terminology, cooperation occurs within a network of H-LAM/T. Such a network might be called a man–machine dialog formation (Poitou et al., 1993). Performing an industrial task implies processing knowledge into expertise within a man–machine dialog formation. *Cognitive formations* are the knowledge thus processed, by one or more agents, distributed among various hierarchical levels and places throughout the company. Such formations are the basic cognitive components of a technological base. They are the conjuncture-dependent outcome of the interplay between knowledge-as-speech (the technology or "instructions for use") and objectal knowledge in the form of work devices (Poitou, 1978, p. 61).

Even simple and representation free as Kirsh's automaton is, it has to have a few things "in mind," such as perception–action modules, pointers, and so on. It is difficult (at least up to the present stage of theorizing) to give these elements a definite status. On the one hand, they belong to the environment, as cues, signals indicating what kind of knowledge is to be found where they lie. They are either natural stimuli, or more often displays indicating what is there to be known. On the other hand, they belong to expertise, they are the releasers (*Auslöser*) of action subprograms. These *mental operators* are the gears of the utilization of cognitive formations in the practices of agents. Through this utilization, technical knowledge is converted into efficient behaviors.

Mental operators are to be considered as constituents of professional qualification. Skilled workers organize mental operators in well-ordered sets in order to set up the most convenient storage of knowledge at their workplace, and exploit the knowledge stored in the workplace according to the most efficient rules of stock management, that is:

To alleviate the mental load by indexing knowledge in external storage under mental operators as easy to discriminate as possible.

To order mental operators in accurate series, so as to retrieve adequate knowledge "just in time."

To re-externalize knowledge, when no more needed, under well-ordered mental operators in order to carry on mental activity with "zero-stock" and "minimal outstanding."

Training and professional achievement consist in improving the set of mental operators by increasing their accuracy and the adequacy of their ordering. This is precisely what individual knowledge management is about, and what cognitive psychologists should concern themselves with. But, it results from a social process.

The functioning of a company is not a technical process but a social practice, such that a given workplace is ruled by speeches and texts that contradict each other because at that place they represent inconsistent, divergent, or antagonistic interests. More generally, the way in which a given technographical item is put into practice will depend on the place of the performer who calls on it. Thus, one cannot arbitrarily assign any inherent, specific, and stable meaning to a document or artefact.

As a consequence, it is impossible to represent the knowledge inherent to a document or to an artefact independently of the place where they are in use. Furthermore, knowledge is already present in its objectal or verbal form. The management problem is to provide easy retrieval and access just in time. The computer, then, will be more helpful as assistance to documentation, rather than to knowledge representation.

However, within the network of places where it is used, the knowledge embodied in artefacts and workplaces can be described. The sharing of a common technical culture—or, more precisely, the fact of belonging to a common man–machine dialog formation—makes the description of activities and the elicitation of knowledge possible, or at least easier. In many situations such as training, objectal knowledge is converted into verbal knowledge. The usual in-house methods of training can suggest a methodology for the survey of the existing technical practices, their description, and their regular updating by the performers themselves.

Thus, if computers are to be used in making mental operators more efficient in the processing of knowledge, then the integration of their output must remain the responsibility of the performers. What is really needed in order to make the knowledge capitalized in the corporate technical heritage more readily available to its members, is assistance in preparing, storing, retrieving, and processing documents (i.e., *editing* knowledge, instead of *eliciting* knowledge). Such was the basic idea underlying the proposition for computer aid in the collective management of corporate knowledge (Poitou, 1983, 1987, 1991a, 1991b, 1991c, 1991d).

COLLECTIVE KNOWLEDGE MANAGEMENT SYSTEMS

Such systems are exemplified by two applications in development at present: SG2C[1] (Poitou et al., 1993) and DIADEME (Ballay & Nuwendam, 1994), which is being developed at Electricité de France (EDF), a French electric power production and supply corporation.

The specifications of both systems were stated at about the same time, SG2C being more of a conceptual model, and DIADEME being intented for actual implementation in the research department of EDF. The two systems are conceived along pretty much the same lines, and since 1995, the designers of SG2C and of DIADEME are cooperating in assessing the users' expectations about, and satisfaction with the later system (Ballay & Poitou, 1996; Poitou, 1996).

SG2C

The objectives of a CKMS are not different from the goals of the usual management of knowledge in the firm. However, a CKMS present user with computer assistance in order to get the easiest access to documents, and with new, fast, accurate, and exhaustive means for reworking the meaning of information when conditions and needs change.

This requires being able to explicitly delineate the heterogeneous conditions under which knowledge is used in the company (i.e., to locate

---

[1]"Système de gestion collective des connaissances" is French for "collective knowledge management system."

knowledge in the technological base and to describe accurately how it is "started-up"); to thoroughly collect the knowledge in that base without making assumptions about its meaning (i.e., draw up a descriptive catalog, *"catalogue raisonné,"* of knowledge existing in the base, by formally describing the documents that record it); and to present the users of knowledge, who are the actual performers of expertise, with an instrument for retrieving knowledge in order to use it as *they* see fit.

Describing the Technological Base

In order to display a complete description of the technological base, the extant verbal documentation has to be supplemented by further descriptions of the objectal knowledge and of its location in the organizational structure. A description of the technological base will record the men–machines dialog formations, together with the corresponding cognitive formations and the main mental operators. This cannot be sized "from the outside." It has to be done within the "place" relations, by the performers themselves. As already noticed, members of the firm know how to explain a job, what has to be known in order to perform it, where lies the information, and what are the decisive cues for appropriate action. This is rather common practice. The methods thus used should be observed and recorded in order to improve them, and to provide better check of their effectiveness.

To that end, a method is being developed for the autonomous analysis of activities (Method 3A; Poitou, 1991a), which offers practitioners a procedure for describing their own activities, in line with the self-confrontation methods. The method is based on a trainer–trainee relation; it requires the participation of three persons: an expert, whose activity is to be described, an "observer–trainee," and a naive trainee.

In order to analyze the knowledge underlying or inherent to the activity of a given expert at his workplace, the first step is to select an "observer-trainee." Performing a different task in the same office or shop would qualify a person for that role. It will permit enough familiarity with the job situation for basic understanding, while carrying enough uncertainty for accurate and relevant questioning about the particulars of the task to be described. The selected observer is then introduced to the observation and interviewing techniques of the Method 3A.

Observers must first observe and record the behavior of their "instructor," their fellow worker in charge of the job to be analyzed. They will observe and question their trainer up to the point where they will be able to actually perform the task. The correct performance of the job by the trainees evidences that knowledge has been efficiently elicited in terms and statements clear enough for any member of the firm. Thus, the performance validates the complete elicitation of the cognitive formation.

Observer–trainees must also write down a notice of instruction about the job, technique, or device they had to master. This verbal record of knowledge is then read by the second trainee, completely new to the job. When the second individual can perform the job to the satisfaction of the expert, then the recording of knowledge is considered to be valid. Not only the device is correctly described, but the modus operandi is accurately recorded, in terms of adequate mental operators. Otherwise, the instruction notice is improved, and the validation procedure iterated until a correct performance is obtained from the naive trainees.

On the basis of these purely empirical tests, it can be assumed that knowledge has been converted from its objectal into its verbal form within the limits of the same cognitive formation. Such *technographical* record increments the corpus of descriptions of the technological base.

Now attention is turned to the task of editing knowledge, whether elicited in documents or through descriptions by Method 3A.

The Descriptive Catalog

Documents only become completely comprehensible if they are related to the work situations and operations to which they refer. The link has to be created between the organization and technical operation of the company, on the one hand, and the descriptions of the in-house technical practices, on the other hand.

A three-file descriptive catalog (*catalogue raisonné*) of the activities carried out in the firm, and of the knowledge associated with these activities, will be established and kept up to date. It will serve to locate and record knowledge in the technical base.

The first stage in editing knowledge from the technological base consists in creating linkages between documents or parts (excerpts) of documents. Links are established according to organizational and linguistic considerations.

An indexing system based on organizational references and linguistic cues will allow the extraction of a set of relevant quotations from all the texts dealing with the object of the request. In other words, users are not presented with rewritten knowledge, nor with a representation of knowledge, but with items already available in the technological base, edited according to the organizational and linguistic mores of the firm, in order to help them construct or improve their representation of the item of interest.

The descriptive catalog—a simplified version of which is presently being planned and designed in order to test its capabilities—rests basically on three files: a document inventory, a data file, a lexical file.

The Document Inventory. Existing documents (most of them on paper) are registered according to the usual rules of the documentation service and indexed with respect to their organizational markers. The writing of new documents is computerized and structured according to norms aimed at making their electronic edition and circulation as easy as possible.

The record of each document in the inventory file includes, in addition to the usual archive indexes, complete references about: its origin, authors, addressees direct or lateral; its history (i.e., which documents have preceded, which it modifies); the data it refers to; and the concepts it refers to.

Documents are processed in order to select data and concepts they contain. It should be noted that the whole document is processed, including not only the text itself, but also the identification marks it bears (such as name of the authors and addressees, departments that released it, and so on). Excerpts are fed into the records of the relevant entries in the data file and in the lexical file. Excerpts relevant to these data and concepts are made with the help of a parser computer program. To this end, NOMINO, a program developed by Pierre Plante at the ATO Center, at the University of Quebec at Montreal, Canada (Dumas, A. Plante, & P. Plante, 1995; P. Plante, 1995; P. Plante & Dumas, 1995) is being tested.

The Data File. Items in the data file are the names of "individuals" (person, part or subpart of the organization, object or collection of identical objects) that are recognized entities in the firm. Every data has its own record. An item record consists of the name of the data (e.g., a registration number in a stocklist), the category to which the data belongs (i.e., the relevant noun word from the lexical file), the excerpts where this very item is mentioned, the references to the documents where the excerpts come from, and key words (i.e., relevant concepts from the lexical file).

Thus, a data item is described in a file entry that presents the entity under consideration in precisely the terms used by the agents or in company documents, and only in those terms. The key words used to index the documents consist solely of the items in the lexical file entries.

The Lexical File. The lexical file is an in-house dictionary of corporate knowledge. Entries in this file are noun phrases parsed out from the firm documents. Under the heading of a noun phrase, there are:

A definition made of the relevant excerpts, which allow for the construction of a concept of the heading.

A list of related notions (i.e., other noun phrases co-occurring in some excerpt with the entry of the record).

A list of "see also" or associated notions. Associated notions are the results of "navigation" in the file. A record is kept of the consultations made in the file. When, even through sheer "mental association," several lexical entries are "browsed through," they are said to be associated.

Of course, every excerpt quoted in a lexical record is given with the references to the document it comes from. Updating the files is exclusively additive: Deleting a previously recorded excerpt is strictly forbidden. The purpose of this rule is to make sure that every change in thinking, doctrine, or usage affecting in-house knowledge is recorded.

The descriptions that occur in the files are not the outcome of the file-entry writer's analysis or representation of what is written in the main documents. The descriptions are collections of excerpts taken from the main documents processed. This procedure makes it possible to avoid introducing into the texts any special vocabulary other than that found in the technological base under study (i.e., the lexicon of the parlance common to the members of the company), guarantee the local and historical validity of the definitions, and preserve the significant idiosyncrasies of the company members' own syntax.

An item's description thus provides a means for linking together the various pieces of information about that item, while preserving the particularities or even contradictions in the various usages made of it by the practitioners who employ it and were consulted on the matter.

DIADEME

A complete description of DIADEME could be found in Ballay and Nuwendam (1994), and Nuwendam and Ballay (1994). The basic idea of the system is that the main resource for knowledge managing is documentation. Knowledge management can thus be bettered by improving documentation at two levels: production and exploitation. At both levels, various types of computer assistance are available that can be interfaced and coordinated.

At the production level:

Documents should be standardized as much as possible, through norms both external (such as SGML) and internal (standardized text processing and edition format, assistance to structured writing).

Documents should be computerized in order to make them more easily accessible, and more durable.

Documents should be contextualized through automatic hypertext interconnection.

At the exploitation level:

Documents should be made more accessible and open by the organization of databases, with coherent and automatic indexation.

Documents should be made more informative through multimedia edition.

Databases should be made more cohesive and navigable thanks to hypertext connections.

Automatic recording in archives should improve knowledge capitalization.

A document never expresses its meaning; it only presents the reader with words or symbols. If this were not true, then all knowledge would be immediately accessible to all those who speak and read the language of the document. Unfortunately, this is far from the case! The same goes for artefacts. Intellectual objects do embody objectal knowledge. However, the knowledge embodied in even the simplest artefact can never be immediatly sized. It has to be displayed.

Such is the purpose of systems like SG2C or DIADEME: to take advantage of computerized text description and document linkage techniques in order to display the technical knowledge of a company to its agents, in the form of a *supertext* of sorts, that is, a text that is larger, more comprehensive, and extendable (if not already extended) to all documents used in the company; more ordered by thorough and multiple-level references; more effectively broken down, on the basis of surface marks; more carefully tied together by the links defined by the morphosyntactic themes in the texts; and, finally, dynamic, because it is equipped with instruments for online exploration and processing.

It is easy to imagine that such tools might lead to new functions in the organization of cooperative work, and will contribute to the emergence of new social modes of organization and cognitive functioning in industry. The thorough achievement of this purpose requires not only significant technical developments, but also changes in the organization, administration, and criteria applied to business management. These requirements are largely outside the scope of the cognitive sciences, but their underlying objective may constitute one of the "rationality myths" that Hatchuel and Weil (1992) considered to be an essential component for industrial rationalization.

ACKNOWLEDGMENT

I wish to thank W. Turner for his helpful comments in the preparation of this chapter.

REFERENCES

Agre, P., & Chapman, D. (1987). PENGI: An implementation of a theory of activity. In *Proceedings of the National Conference on Artificial Intelligence* (pp. 268–272). Menlo Park, CA: American Association for Artificial Intelligence.

Ballay, J. F., & Nuwendam, F. (1994). *Outils et méthodes informatiques pour les cas-tests de DIADEME* [Computer tools and methods for DIADEME tests]. (Research Rep. No. HM-75/94/016). Clamart: EDF.

Ballay, J. F., & Poitou, J. P. (1996). DIADEME: a collective knowledge management system (CKMS). In J. F. Schreinemakers (Ed.), *Knowledge Management. Organization, competence and methodology* (pp. 265–285). Würzburg: Ergon Verlag.

Bolt, R. (1984). *The human interface: Where people and computers meet.* Belmont, CA: Lifetime Learning Publications.

Bonnet, A., Haton, J. P., & Truong-Ngoc, J. M. (1986). *Systèmes experts, vers la maîtrise technique* [Expert systems: Toward technical control]. Paris: Inter Editions.

Bourdieu, P. (1972). *Esquisse d'une théorie de la pratique, précédée de trois études d'ethnologie kabyle* [Outline of a theory of social practice, with three studies in Kabyle anthropology]. Genève: Droz.

Bratman, M. (1987). *Intentions, plans and practical reason.* Cambridge, MA: Harvard University Press.

Brooks, R. (1991). Intelligence without representation. In D. Kirsh (Ed.), Foundations of artificial intelligence [Special issue]. *Artificial Intelligence, 47,* 139–160.

Conein, B. (1990). Cognition située et coordination de l'action. La cuisine dans tous ses états [Situated cognition and coordinated action. About cooking]. In M. de Fornel (Ed.), Opinion, savoir, communication [Special issue]. *Réseaux, Communication, Technologie, Société, 43,* 99–109.

Conein, B. (1991). L'action située est-elle sans plan?: Sur les rapports entre recette et action culinaire [Is situated action without a plan? About the relations between recipes and cooking actions]. *Technologies, Idéologies, Pratiques, 10*(2–4), 353–367.

Dumas, L., Plante, A., & Plante, P. (1995) *Nomino; Version 1.0b.* (Tech. Rep.). Montreal: Centre d'Analyse de Texte par Ordinateur ATO, University of Quebec at Montreal.

Engelbart, D. (1963). A conceptual framework for the augmentation of man's intellect. In P. Howerton (Ed.), *Vistas in information handling* (Vol. 1, pp. 1–29). Washington, DC: Spartan.

Gibson, J. J. (1979). *The ecological approach to visual perception.* Hillsdale, NJ: Lawrence Erlbaum Associates.

Harris, S. Z. (1952). Discourse analysis. *Language, 28,* 1–30.

Hatchuel, A., & Weil, B. (1992). *L'expert et le système. Suivi de quatre histoires de systèmes-experts* [The expert and the system. With four case studies of expert systems]. Paris: Economica.

Janet, P. (1935). *Les débuts de l'intelligence* [The beginnings of intelligence]. Paris: Flammarion.

Kirsh, D. (1990). Préparation et improvisation [Preparation and improvisation]. In M. de Fornel (Ed.), Opinion, savoir, communication [Special issue]. *Réseaux, Communication, Technologie, Société, 43,* 111–120.

Lacoste, M. (1990). Interaction et compétences différenciées [Interaction and differentiated skills]. In M. de Fornel (Ed.), Opinion, savoir, communication [Special issue]. *Réseaux, Communication, Technologie, Société, 43,* 81–97.

Leroi-Gourhan, A. (1962). Apparition et premier développement des techniques [Beginnings and early developments of techniques]. In M. Daumas (Ed.), *Histoire générale des techniques: Vol. 1. Les origines de la civilisation technique.* Paris: Presses Universitaires de France.

Nuwendam, F., & Ballay, J. F. (1994). *DIADEME, état de l'art et analyse des technologies informatiques pour la gestion des connaissances* [DIADEME, state of the art and analysis of computer technologies for knowledge management]. (Research Rep. No. 94NO00019). Clamart: EDF.

Pêcheux, M. (1969). *Analyse automatique du discours* [Automatic discourse analysis]. Paris: Dunod.

Pêcheux, M., & Fuchs, C. (1975). Mises au point et perspectives à propos de l'analyse automatique du discours [Automatic discourse analysis revisited: State of the art and prospects]. In M. Pêcheux (Ed.), Analyse du discours, langue et idéologie [Special issue]. *Langages, 37,* 7–81.

Pinsky, L., & Theureau, J. (1987). *L'étude du cours d'action, analyse du travail et conception ergonomique* [The course of action: Job analysis and ergonomics]. Paris: Conservatoire National des Arts et Metiers.

Plante, P. (1995). NOMINO [Computer program]. Montreal: Centre d'Analyse de Texte par Ordinateur ATO, University of Quebec at Montreal.

Plante, P., & Dumas, L. (1995). *Nomino-signet—un assistant à la construction de bases de connaissances sur les textes* [NOMINO-SIGNET, an assistance to knowledge base building based upon texts]. Montreal: Centre d'Analyse de Texte par Ordinateur ATO, University of Quebec at Montreal.

Poitou, J. P. (1978). *La dynamique des groupes, une idéologie au travail* [Group dynamics: An ideology at work]. Paris: Centre national de la Recherche Scientifique.

Poitou, J. P. (1983). *Savoir vif, savoir mort* [To know life, to know death]. Paper presented at the Symposium "Les cultures populaires" of the Société Française de Sociologie and the Société d'Ethnologie Française, Nantes.

Poitou, J. P. (1987, June). The expert and the system. *ORIA 87. Artificial Intelligence and Sea* (pp. E1–E12). Marseille: Institut International de Recherche en Informatique et Automatique de Marseille.

Poitou, J. P. (1991a). *Définition d'une méthodologie de recueil et d'extraction des connaissances au service des systèmes experts en amont de la formalisation des connaissances* [Defining a methodology for extracting and collecting knowledge before formalization in expert systems]. (Research Rep. No. 89 D0041). Paris: Ministère de la Recherche et de la Technologie.

Poitou, J. P. (1991b). Le mythe, la cathédrale, l'atelier: Trois dispositifs artificiels de pensée. Essai d'anthropologie cognitive [Myths, cathedrals, and shops: Three artificial thought devices]. *Technologies, Idéologies, Pratiques, 10*(2–4), 67–85.

Poitou, J. P. (1991c). Sciences cognitives et forces productives [Cognitive sciences and productive forces]. *La Pensée,* no. 282, 55–67.

Poitou, J. P. (1991d, September). *Technologie et psychisme* [Technology and psychism]. Paper presented at the Symposium MASTECH "Problématique, Instrumentation, Maîtrise sociale de la technologie" Lyon.

Poitou, J. P. (1992). Nouvelles technologies et élévation des qualifications: À propos du rôle de la visuo-motricité et de la motricité graphique dans l'activité cognitive globale du technicien de bureau d'étude [Improving skills through new technologies: The role of visual and graphical motor behavior in the global cognitive activity of draughtsmen]. *Intellectica, 1/2*(13–14), 185–217.

Poitou, J. P. (1996). *Etude des pratiques actuelles de gestion des connaissances au service ERMEL* [Managing knowledge today at the ERMEL Department]. (Research Rep. No. HN-51/96/201). Clamart: Électricité de France.

Poitou, J. P., & Chabot, R. (1991). Vers un outil de gestion des connaissances [Toward a knowledge management tool]. In D. Hering-Aimé, R. Dieng, J. P. Regourd, & J. P. Angoujard (Eds.), *Knowledge modeling and expertise transfer* (pp. 459–470). Amsterdam: IOS Press.

Poitou, J. P., Caquant, D., & Peri, L. (1993). *Intégration des connaissances, systèmes de gestion collective des connaissances et systèmes experts dans la construction: Application aux risques des eaux et aux nuisances acoustiques* [Integrating knowledge. Collective knowledge management systems and expert systems in building industry: The cases of flood risk and of acoustic nuisance]. (Research Rep. No. 91N86/0063). Paris: Plan "Construction et Architecture" et du PIRTTEM/CNRS.

Stiegler, B. (1993). Projet OPEN. In J.-P Barthès (Ed.), *Proceedings of the Symposium COMETT 93 Gestion du savoir-faire et des connaissances de l'entreprise. Problématique, modélisation ; intérêt et limites de l'approche "objet."* Compiègne, Institut International pour l'Intelligence Artificielle.

Zimmerman, D. (1973) The practicalities of rule use. In J. Douglas (Ed.), *Understanding everyday life* (pp. 221–223). London: Routledge & Kegan Paul.

"As real as it gets. . . ." Taming Models and Reconstructing Procedures

Mike Robinson
Department of Computer Science & Information Systems
University of Jyvaskyla, Finland

Abstract: very

INTRODUCTION

(with thanks and apologies to John Bowers)

MULTIPLICITY OF COMMUNITIES OF PRACTICE

This chapter is a speculative essay on dialogues between different communities of practice. It is concerned with the twin "dead ducks," *procedure* and *model*, which periodically pop up at the computer-supported collaborative work (CSCW) feast. What roles do these spectres have in the alignment and misalignments between different communities of practice? What roles might they have if they were invited to sit down and take a little ethnomethodological wine with us?

Bowers (1992) repeated his historical claim that Copernicus should not be seen primarily as the person who "decentred Man from the Universe." Instead, he should be seen

> at the *centre* of a tangled web of *representation paths* connecting him with the previously scattered and unconnected monasteries, courts, libraries and mosques of Europe, Africa, and the Middle East. Copernicus discharges intermediaries who bring back inscriptions of astronomical observations from the periphery to the centre. It is at the centre that Copernicus can *manipulate* inscriptions and *see* discrepancies, much as any contemporary business analyst might *manipulate* columns of figures, graphs, pie-charts and see the state of the market. On this view, it is the humble tasks and the mundane technologies of representation which raise the world. A supreme irony indeed!

With reference to the concept of "immutable mobiles"[1] (Latour, 1987) such as those Copernicus worked on and produced, Bowers raised the problem of just how it is that multiplicity and heterogeneity of "ascription practices" (assigning properties and meanings to artifacts and representations) is managed and with what consequences. This chapter aims to look at how different communities of practice do or might manage the heterogeneity, multiplicity, and the *manipulability* of the colliding, mutating, immutable mobiles that pass between and amongst them; a situation where we have indeterminately many interacting "centres" of the "tangled web of representation paths."

Partly because this is an indefinitely large subject, two notions that seem deeply implicated in the mess—procedure and model—have been picked out for special scrutiny. Procedure is something to do with "alignment of practice," and model (the recurring ghost of representations past) is as good a name as any for the otherwise unpronounceable "manipulable, mutating, immutable mobiles."

---

[1]"Representations which can convey information over a distance (displacement) without themselves changing (immutability). It is in terms of the manipulation of such objects that many historical developments can be accounted for, and *not* in terms of notions such as *zeitgeist* or through psychologistic or mystical celebrations of the genius of individuals" (Latour, 1987).

PROCEDURES AND MODELS

These related notions, as the basis for computer applications, have been in the firing line for almost a decade now. The critiques are established and definitive (some are mentioned later). Yet, like a row of tin ducks in a fairground, every time a new punter[2] comes along, the ducks are back—just waiting to be shot down again.

Procedures may not have any weight as computer representations of what people do. But they do have some sort of existence in organizations. People talk about themselves as following them, and expect others to. They are a reference point for action and accountability, and a pretty good cover if things go wrong. They are a way of understanding what others do. So it is fairly natural for people, most people, to believe they are "implement-able," and for managers to believe they "should be implemented." And until someone comes up with a convincing story that accounts for what procedures do "do" (and how what procedures do "do" relates to what computers do "do"!), the tin ducks are going to keep coming back.

Models are even worse. At least procedures have a limited range of false moustaches and beards.[3] Roles and workflows is about the best they can do. As for models, Well! We have pictures, representations, images, icons, scenarios, what-ifs, projections, prototypes, abstractions, generali-zations, assumptions . . . . whole rows of tin ducks. And, even within the CSCW community, there is a noticeable ambiguity (down with mod-els, long live scenarios!), sometimes even an ambivalence about the same label ("representation") that has been described as a love–hate relation-ship.

The problem with models is that they can be (or attempt to be) ex-tremely coercive when "implemented," but it is also difficult to see how to get a computer system of any sort that does not build on, and embed a model of some sort.

PROCEDURES

Procedures Are Not Algorithms

The three most organized and most quoted[4] attacks on "procedure" have come from Sheil (1983):

---

[2] A new term for "user" . . . . . .
[3] . . . albeit ghostly ones, with a slightly duckish shape.
[4] subjective impression . . . . .

I had approached those offices convinced . . . that office procedures were, at least in principle, clearly defined methods of processing information. Programs, in other words. Things that could be transcribed, analysed, maybe even reprogrammed for a different "machine." But, above all, I assumed that they existed, independently of my enquiries. And that is fantasy.

from Gerson and Star (1986):

without an understanding of articulation, the gap between requirements and the actual work process in the office will remain inaccessible to analysis. . . . When the articulation of the work is deleted in representations of that work, the resulting task descriptions can only be uneasily superimposed on the flow of work.

and from Suchman (1987)[5] a reference to the observation that even a mundane activity like "turning on a light" can be achieved in many recognizable ways, "even if we had never seen or thought about that pattern previously" (Allen, 1984). On which Suchman comments:

Allen's point is two-fold. First, the "same" action as a matter of intended effect can be achieved in any number of ways, where the ways are contingent on circumstance rather than on definitional properties of the action. And secondly, while an action can be accounted for post hoc with reference to its intended effect, an action's course cannot be predicted from knowledge of the actor's intent, nor can the course be inferred from the observation of the outcome.

The notion of procedures understood as sequences of action specified in advance or in abstract has turned out to be defeasible in principle and defeated in practice.[6] Procedures, says the chorus repeatedly, are not algorithms. Keil-Slawik (1991) has even elucidated a design principle of *avoiding enforced sequentiality*.

Procedures as Secondary to What People Do

Numerous sociological studies pertinent to, or directed at CSCW, have shown that the order reflected in "procedure" originates in, and is maintained by, artful practice that takes into account relevant, specific, concrete circumstance and contingency—in other words, shows that meaningful coherent action is "situated." Good practice that involves social and or-

---

[5]Because "procedure" does not even get a mention in the index of "Plans and Situated Actions," this chapter takes the liberty of assuming that all the points made about plans also apply to procedures understood as sequences of action specified in advance or in abstract.

[6]Take that, Duck!

ganizational competences over, beyond, and sometimes straightforwardly outside "procedure" is described, for example and inter alia, by Button (1993), Darnton, Hughes, and Randall (1993), Schmidt (1991), Wilkinson (1986), and Wynn (1991).

Procedures as a *Useful* Gloss. . . .

There is an implicit, general agreement, at least within the CSCW community, that "procedure" is a "gloss" on work that is done. There is, however, no study that looks at the work done by this "gloss." Because procedures are ubiquitous, can be found in all but the rockiest microcompanies, can be found in many embodiments, and usually many instances of them can be found, it seems relevant to ask what is it exactly that they are used for?

H. Dreyfus and S. E. Dreyfus (1986) gave an indication of one role for procedure ("context-free rules") in learning skills, which was later applied by Ehn (1988) to the skill of design. Context-free rules are a way into skills for novices, and become increasingly less relevant as contextual knowledge and situational "feel" develop.

So procedures are a "way in" for beginners. Extrapolating from this, it seems that procedures are also a way around an organization for outsiders (people who are not about to join the organization or learn its skills). If something has gone wrong, or appears to have gone wrong, then some knowledge of procedure is helpful in knowing where to start enquiring, who to ask. In this case, the procedure can be helpful even if it is a very superficial gloss. Procedures also cover the workers themselves against blame, because it is hard to blame someone if they have been following a "correct procedure." One can reflect that on many occasions the person (boss, manager) doing the blaming will not have, and maybe not even care about, the situated skills necessary to do the work. In all three cases (novice outside the skill, person outside the organization, outside judgment), a procedure provides a ground for dialogue over a boundary. In general, it seems that procedures are for consumption not production. They are for consumption by outsiders, so, in many ways, the glossier the better. They are not algorithms for producing work by insiders.

Procedures are also a ground on which dialogue can be organized, so they seem to be "boundary objects" (Star, 1989, 1992; Star & Griesemer, 1989) in the full sense described here:

> Boundary objects are objects which are both plastic enough to adapt to local needs and constraints of the several parties employing them, yet robust enough to maintain a common identity across sites. They are weakly structured in common use, and become strongly structured in individual-site

use. . . . A boundary object "sits in the middle" of a group of actors with divergent viewpoints. (Star, 1992)

MODELS

The Models We Love to Hate. . . .

The main objection to "pictures" of organizations has been that they are "objectivist." They can reify a simplified, abstracted version of the work, which is then "implemented" in some sort of system and reimposed on the work—a process lovingly described in Robinson and Bannon (1991) where the guilty parties are named as COSMOS, AMIGO MHS+, AMIGO Advanced, and MacAll II (Henessey, Benford, & Bowers, 1989),[7] and where the intent of these European projects was to create "abstract models of groups communication" as "critical limitations" in existing services. But, of course, the criticism is about the (mis)use of models. It does not address the nature of models themselves. In fact, criticisms of use assume it is in the nature of models to (purport to) represent, where "represent" in turn is taken to mean implying a "correspondence theory of truth," "verifiability" in a positivist sense, and so on. But is this the case? If not, what is the nature of models? And what are the implications for and of the use of models in CSCW design?

Taming Models (by making them very wild indeed!)

A Thought From Sartre. In one of the first substantial attacks on mental images as "little pictures in the head," Sartre (1965) used the well-known image of the Parthenon. His challenge, for those that have visited or otherwise know the Parthenon, is to conjure a mental image and then count the number of pillars.

Of course, this cannot be done unless one knows the number in the first place. Images are not like photographs. One only *puts* into them what one knows. Images are produced in active consciousness; they are not things. This chapter suggests that the same holds true of models, that is, that the main utility lies not in what *is there*, but in the activity of *putting there*.

Some thoughts from Lynch (1991b). . . . "Biologists' representations are not transparent windows on an independent reality, since in many fields of biology, visual and other forms of representation are the only way phenomena can become materially witnessable." The paragraph continues with some brief examples and a restatement of this initial point, this time

---

[7]It should be stressed that these examples are not, by a long way, the *only* guilty parties.

couched in terms that oppose a correspondence theory of truth, and the basic positivist "verification" position:

> Researchers cannot directly observe living brain cells, ribosomes, strands of DNA, or bird migration routes without making use of complex procedures for technically visualising these phenomena as picturable, graphable, mappable, or measurable configurations. Even the low-tech observations made by the early ornithologists were mediated by methods of drawing and engraving. In many cases there is no way to compare a representation of a biological phenomenon to the "real" thing, since the thing becomes coherently visible only as a function of the representation work. (Lynch, 1991b)

Lynch also commented on "social theoretical" pictures used by philosophers and sociologists:

> . . . their communicative functions can be very challenging to decipher. They are not "transparent" in the sense of providing an illusory "window" from which to view an independent object or scene. In a way, theory pictures answer to semioticians' dreams by approximating a "pure" semiotic system whose intelligibility is unencumbered by any resemblance to things external to the text. (Lynch, 1991a)

These studies concentrate on the creation and refinement of diagrams, photographs, and visual constructs. This chapter focuses on use. While it is true that a visual construct adds not a potato to the text, they (at least in some cases) can add quite a lot to discussion around the text. They can add manipulability. When this angle is taken into account, the social theory pictures (see Fig. 11.1) whose decomposition Lynch is concerned to hasten, take on some of the nature of "illusory windows." The elements can be moved about, added, modified, deleted, and so on. Even the scrawniest of tin ducks such as Lynch's "sensible picture" can provide an indexical focus for a debatative feast. . . .

Some Thoughts on Manipulable Artifacts. Many artifacts can be thought of as a linguistic substrate. The notion of "common artifact" has its origin in an attempt to understand the specialized uses of "language through an artifact" (or "formal language") in CSCW applications (Robinson, 1991a).[8] Here, building on Sørgaard's (1988) exposition of

---

[8]The term *common* was chosen because of an overlap of three (English) meanings, all of which are relevant to the notion of "common artifact": belonging equally to more than one person ("to hold in common"); frequent, vulgar, mundane, ordinary, commonplace; (as a noun) "a tract of open land, used in common by the inhabitants of a town, parish, etc.," where use is *"by right,"* the "community" is *indeterminate*, and there is *no common objective.*

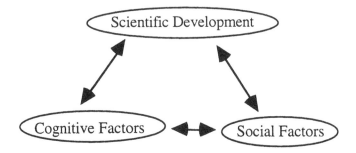

FIG. 11.1. A "sensible picture" reproduced by Lynch.

"implicit communication," it was noted that "successful" CSCW applications seemed to allow two modalities of communication. Natural, fairly unrestricted conversation, with explicit dialogue and high ambiguity tolerance was termed the *cultural* level. Communication via action on an artifact, where the actions are constrained by its material and structure (effectively formation and transformation rules) was termed the "formal" level. Participants in cooperative work need to create and change a structure using rules—*what* they are talking about needs some degree of fixity and predictability—and they also need to *discuss* their work. Both modalities of communication are necessary, and together are termed "double level language."

Common artifacts can be "read" like texts. States can be taken as signs, symbols, or intentional actions by others. It is often impossible to know which parts of the grammar reside in social convention and which in the structure of the artifact. But, it is possible to see that some artifacts resist "grammatical usage": They impede communication. Robinson (1993) argued that common artifacts have the following characteristics, or affordances. They should

- be an effective *tool* for getting a job done,
- help people see at a glance what others are doing (*peripheral awareness*),
- support *implicit communications* through the material being worked on,
- provide a focus for discussion of difficulties and negotiation of compromises (*double level language*),
- afford an *overview* of the work process that would not otherwise be available,
- embed a *partial model* of the situation to be managed,
- perform other functions (e.g., template, enduring record),

- and be *multifunctional*—in the sense that it should perform all (and at least most) of these functions.

Exhibits of common artifacts with embedded models that support "overview" (perspectives over space and/or time that could not be immediately available), "implicit communication" (sensing rather than having explicit statements of what others are doing), and "peripheral awareness" (seeing "at a glance" what others are doing) were:

A hotel keyrack—embedding a formalized model of hotel rooms; supporting implicit and explicit communication between guests and staff.

A London Underground timetable[9]—embedding a schematized model of stations and train movement in time; in a control room, annotations allow staff updated overviews, implicit communication, and focus for questioning.

A "flight strip" in air traffic control[10]—embedding a combined model of ground control and certain properties of a specific aircraft in flight; annotations on and placing of strips alerts other controllers to changes and problematic flights.

The "wage bargainer"[11]—spreadsheet embedding a model of wage scales and work groups; supported expression of claims by groups of workers, and overviews of consequences for other groups; provided negotiating tool and focus.

A hospital worksheet system[12]—embedding a model of the layout of beds in a ward; supported overview, work projections, and coordination.

A "complex sheet" in Airport ground control[13]—embedding a model of planes against passenger and baggage movement; facilitated overview, identification of problematic situations, and coordination.

The focal point in Robinson (1991a) was that all these artifacts, as embedding models, were manipulable. In that lay their utility, and their "ability" to reduce dramatically their potential discursive overhead of cooperative working. All the examples focused on the use of the model bearing

---

[9]Drawing on Heath and Luff (1991).
[10]Drawing on R. R. Harper et al. (1989).
[11]Drawing on Robinson (1991b).
[12]Drawing on Bjerknes and Bratteteig (1988).
[13]Drawing on Suchman and Trigg (1991).

common artifacts within a single community of practice (receptionists, aircraft or plane or ground movement controllers, nurses, etc.). The movement of manipulable (and hence mutating) "immutable mobiles" between communities of practice was not considered. Such considerations take us into considerably deeper water.[14]

Suchman and Trigg note that the "complex sheet" in the ground control "Ops Room" is an "enduring physical record." With the exception of the keyrack (which generates no history of its own states), the use of all the artifacts mentioned earlier generate such an "enduring physical record." Potentially, in unfortunate circumstances, this could be used in a very different community of practice: a law court!

The difficulty of such transitions, the problematic, the origin of hard debates and lengthy proceedings can be seen by applying the thoughts of Sartre and Lynch on images and representations. It can be speculated that the embedded model in a common artifact—the characteristic of the artifact that constrains both the actions that can be taken and the types of meaningfulness that can be attributed to them—is not valuable because it "represents." It is valuable because it is a ground, reference point for and reflection of activity—a way of constituting the "reality," of making it "materially witnessable." Paradoxically, this is only possible if the model is believed to represent, even if it does not or cannot do any such thing. The model is "as real as it gets," but it needs to be *understood* as pointing, as going beyond itself.

This paradox only raises difficulties when a mutating immutable is mobile between communities, and meets itself on the way back . . . .[15]

SOME ILLUSTRATIONS OF TAMED MODELS
AND RECONSTITUTED PROCEDURES

> *Warning:* this section contains dangerous explicit pictures and should not be read by those of a nervous or sensitive disposition.

So far it has been, somewhat aphoristically, argued that procedures can be reconstituted as "boundary objects," and models can be tamed by regarding them as constituting "reality" ("as real as it gets") while being understood as "pointing beyond themselves"—paradoxically, since this is something they are generally not able to do.

---

[14]with no water-wings, concrete boots (and laughter from the ducks!)

[15]when the soft underbelly of the tin duck is revealed in the need to reconcile and align orthogonal practices.

One way of understanding this seemingly impossible state of affairs is to regard the models (pictures, representations, images, prototypes, etc.) as the substrate around and through which dialogue happens.

The Easy Cases

Pictures, images, and models can go to different contexts, different communities of practice, mean different things, and be judged by different criteria. Because the product is formatted, it can be reformatted, or transformed, either within its original "practices" or by applying a different "practice set." Another example from Lynch:

> Audubon's bird illustrations become different objects when hung on the wall in a museum, reproduced in a folio edition of Audubon's work, copied for a text on the history of ornithology, printed on a postcard or stamp, printed on an announcement for a local meeting of the Audubon Society, or placed in a popular guide for identifying North American birds. Audubon's original artwork becomes aestheticized, commodified, fetishized, bowdlerized, and naturalized depending on the textual sites, institutional settings, and pragmatic contexts into which it is inserted. Each copy of the picture contributes to these social contexts while simultaneously deriving its particular illustrative and aesthetic functions from them. (Lynch, 1991b)

This is an easy example because the artwork goes from Audubon *out* to different communities of practice. It does not "meet itself coming back." The communities need not, and probably do not interact. They have no need to reconcile the multiplicity of ascriptions. Such a process of diffusion (from the perspective of a tin duck) looks like Fig. 11.2.

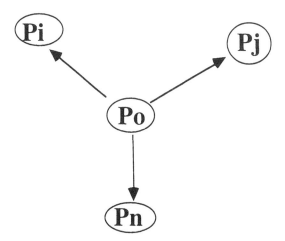

FIG. 11.2. An easy case.

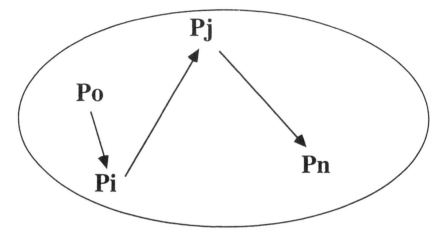

FIG. 11.3. Another easy case.

Another easy case is when an artifact or model is successively transformed within a "discipline," or community of practice (Fig. 11.3). For
instance, consider the different modifications that can happen to a set of
accounts (sorting receipts and invoice copies into date order, checking
entries, summing entries, making a balance sheet). Given all this happens
in the same offices, though by different people, questions can be asked,
clarification sought, mistakes repaired, and so on.

The Harder Cases

A harder case (Fig. 11.4) is where artifacts with embedded, manipulable,
and mutating models can pass between "disciplines," with various trans-

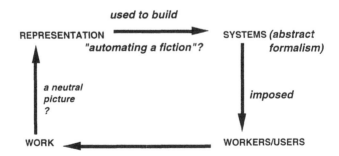

FIG. 11.4. A harder case. A sketch of some steps in the design-use cycle.
From *Proceedings of the Second European Conference on Computer-Supported
Cooperative Work*, edited by L. Bannon, M. Robinson, and K. Schmidt, 1991,
Amsterdam: Kluwer. Copyright © 1991 by Kluwer. Reprinted with
permission.

formations being made as they go, before *arriving back* at the point of origin. The orthogonality of different practices suddenly needs to be reconciled. The site of the problem is the model now under multiple transformations that are incomprehensible to the recipients. Any computer application, initially designed with the users' needs in mind, can undergo this process.

A second, harder case is where multiple communities of practice meet head-on to try and explicate the incomprehensible mess left by some variant of the previous example (see Fig. 11.5). An excellent example is provided by Sharrock and Anderson (1993). Software for different functions of a laser printer designed to support networked workstations had been written on different sites with different technical and organizational practices. One site in the United Kingdom dealt with the software to transfer image onto paper, whereas the U.S. site dealt with image generation and print job organization functions. When the mutated models met themselves on the way back they did not mesh as planned. Identified problems stacked up faster than they could be cleared. Sharrock and Anderson exhibited a transcript of part of a conversation where the key mismesh (an "out of paper" signal) was identified. The remarks happened 90 minutes into a discussion lasted some 6 hours, and involved five software developers. In this case,

> participants in the project typically manifest an intensely detailed knowledge of the features, operations, and ways of "the machine" as it figures in designs and specifications and that they are equivalently aware of the characteristics and performances of the prototypes in operation, down to the history of individual machines. This knowledge is one which they typically carry around "in their heads," and against this background it is not, therefore,

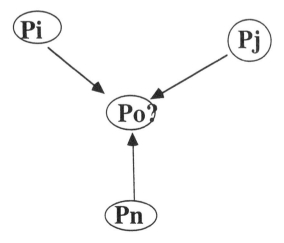

FIG. 11.5. Another harder case.

surprising that the parties set out to reconstruct the organisation of the software by talking it through rather than consulting records of its design.

Stepping through the interleaving processes, with commentary, debate, questions, confirmations, and social management of all of this leads inexorably to the conclusion that the "management of mutual understanding" is complex, time consuming, and skilled. Both "technical work" and the "production of technology" are naturally and uncontentiously "socially organized." Communities of practice, even closely related ones— even given common artifacts, immutable[16] mobiles, and procedures—do not mesh easily.

A REALLY HARD CASE,
OR THE DISASTER AFTER NEXT....

Taking the worst cases of the aforementioned examples, and combining them into one beautiful whole, the potential for the next generation of organizational and interorganizational, fully interactive CSCW systems. . . . . . . (Fig. 11.6).

So far, CSCW has mainly been restricted to interactions between individuals and within small(ish) groups. Approaching the organizational frontier will provide many interesting opportunities to link and interconnect different communities of practice. For instance, to use an example not a million miles from home, consider a hospital. In terms of computerization, constructing a "dossier representatif" (Schneider & Wagner, 1993) has been found to be practically extremely difficult and probably politically impossible. Yet coordination-cooperation remains a significant goal.[17] So why not a "dossier unrepresentatif"? Why not an X[18] that would link the different working applications, the common artifacts and their embedded models; that would support "multiple users in modifying the mechanisms of interaction while being immersed in the very flow of distributed activities"[19]; that would allow interchanges from different perspectives operated from different practices in different locations. Why not indeed?

Would it not be useful (and buildable) for a hospital to have such a "dossier unrepresentatif"? The receptionists could fill in and change patient information, addresses, allergies, dates, from their viewpoint—*forms*.

---

[16]sort of?

[17]ignoring the question of whose goal. . . . . .

[18]where X could be a set of (hyper)linked documents, a set of sets of "objects," even a database modified to lift the veil of "transparency."

[19]Remark overheard in a bar.

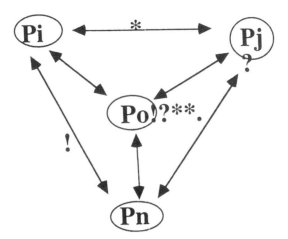

FIG. 11.6. A really hard case.

The nurses could add, modify, and track medicines and symptoms from their symbiotically linked perspective—*worksheets*. Surgeons' diagnoses and scheduling, for their own and public purposes are *freeform* addenda to the growing dossier. Administrators can view and change and suggest modifications to the "patient flow" from their *graphical overviews* and *critical paths*. The bookkeepers and accountants see the whole panoply laid out as a *spreadsheet*. And these diverse activities could impact each other directly. Like cyberspace, such "viewpoint" systems already exist!

It can be remarked that, historically, welding together these and much larger heterogeneous communities of practice is a major societal accomplishment, usually achieved by much breaking of eggs.[20] The most noteworthy element is opaqueness of process and of result. We are beyond the bounds of rationality and of any specifiable competences. Planning future fusions involves much quacking about procedures and models. Managing the collisions, bridging the "pragmatic divide" will not be done by a technical fix, or a "dossier unrepresentatif." But the attempt to provide computer support for the incomprehensible may (just possibly, with luck) result in reconceptualizations that inform both large social interactions and system design.[21]

CONCLUSIONS

none . . . . . .

---

[20]Leninist duck metaphor for violence and violation.

[21]As happened on the small scale with cooperation and CSCW.

DREAMS . . . . . .

The story from Sharrock and Anderson cited earlier shows that it is not easy[22] to reconcile the interacting mutated mobiles that embed different practices and perspectives in the divergent transformation histories of what may have started out as one design. A *skilled* understanding of the transformations embodied in and witnessed by the *presence* of the artifact is needed, together with an ability to reach out and into the practices of other communities. Entrance into these necessarily alien practices happens within the space provided by the "boundary objects" of procedures.

Technically and socially, it may not be too difficult to arrange for manipulable and manipulated models (mutated mobiles) to meet themselves on the way back. Making sense of the collisions will involve taking procedures and models, albeit reconceptualized, more seriously. The first attempts are not likely to be spectacularly successful. But even the limited support for conversation and working across the divides of multiple communities of practice provided by elementary articulations of models (as manipulable and mutating mobiles) and procedures (as "boundary objects") gives cause for optimistic dreams as well as pessimistic projections. As Lynch (1991a) so eloquently put it:

> Perhaps there is a more sociable alternative. As I have noted above, theory pictures create a space for a hermeneutic passage, a dialogic movement between writing and figure. This movement offers the potential for interrupting theoretical monologues with dialogical operations—operations that are not simply exchanges between different "voices," but are passages back and forth across pragmatic divides. Once we are used to thinking of theoretical diagrams as armatures in a movement rather than as pictures of something (or of nothing), we can articulate the beginnings of a theoretical language that has yet to be spoken.

[exit stage left to cheers from the ducks . . . . . .]

ACKNOWLEDGMENTS

The author would like to thank the COST 11 COTECH Working Group IV (CSCW Design) for stimulating many of these worries, and the Euro-Code and COMIC ESPRIT Research Projects for a little time to write them down.

---

[22]. . . to understate by about two orders of magnitude.

REFERENCES

Allen, T. J. (1984). *Managing the flow of technology*. Cambridge, MA: MIT Press.

Bjerknes, G., & Bratteteig, T. (1988). The memoirs of two survivors: Or the evaluation of a computer system for co-operative work. In D. Tatar (Ed.), *Conference on Computer-Supported Co-operative Work, September 26–28, Portland, OR* (pp. 167–177). New York: ACM.

Bowers, J. (1992). The politics of formalism. In M. Lea (Ed.), *Contexts of computer mediated communications*. Hassocks: Harvester/Wheatsheaf.

Button, G. (Ed.). (1993). *Technology in working order: Studies of work, interaction, and technology*. London: Routledge & Kegan Paul.

Darnton, G., Hughes, J., Randall, D. (1993). Customers on Cooperation. In G. de Michelis, C. Simone, & K. Schmidt (Eds.), *Proceedings of the Third European Conference on Computer Supported Cooperative Work—ECSCW '93*. 13–17, September, Milan, Italy. Dordrecht, The Netherlands: Kluwer.

Dreyfus, H. L., & Dreyfus, S. E. (1986). *Mind over machine*. Oxford, England: Basil Blackwell.

Ehn, P. (1988). *Work-oriented design of computer artifacts*. Stockholm: Arbetslivscentrum.

Gerson, E. M., & Star, S. L. (1986). Analyzing due process in the workplace. *ACM Transactions on Office Information Systems, 4*(3), 257–270.

Heath, C., & Luff, P. (1991). Collaborative activity and technological design: Task coordination in London underground control rooms. In L. Bannon, M. Robinson, & K. Schmidt (Eds.), *ECSCW '91: Proceedings of the Second European Conference on Computer-Supported Cooperative Work* (pp. 65–80). Amsterdam: Kluwer Academic.

Henessey, P., Benford, S., & Bowers, J. (1989). Modelling group communication structures: Analysing four European projects. In *Proceedings of the First European CSCW '89 Conference*, Gatwick, London.

Keil-Slawik, R. (1991). Artifacts as external memory: An ecological perspective. In *Position paper for the symposium "Knowing and knowledge: Re-specifying the role of formalization in computer and social sciences," Oksnoen, Norway, June 19–20.*

Latour, B. (1987). *Science in action*. Milton Keynes: Open University Press.

Lynch, M. (1991a). Pictures of nothing? Visual construals in social theory. *Sociological Theory, 9*(1, Spring), 1–21.

Lynch, M. (1991b). Science in the age of mechanical reproduction: Moral and epistemic relations between diagrams and photographs. *Biology and Philosophy, 6*, 205–226.

Harper, R. R., Hughes, J. A., & Shapiro, D. Z. (1989). Working in harmony: An examination of computer technology in air traffic control. In *EC-CSCW '89: Proceedings of the First European Conference on Computer Supported Cooperative Work, Gatwick, London, September, 13–15* (pp. 73–86).

Robinson, M. (1991a). Double-level languages and co-operative working. *AI & Society, 5*, 34–60.

Robinson, M. (1991b). Pay bargaining in a shared information space. In J. Bowers & S. Benford (Eds.), *Studies in computer supported cooperative work: Theory, practice, and design*. Amsterdam: North-Holland.

Robinson, M. (1993). Design for unanticipated use. In *ECSCW '93: Third European Conference on Computer Supported Cooperative Work, Milan, Italy*. Amsterdam: Kluwer.

Robinson, M., & Bannon, L. (1991). Questioning representations. In L. Bannon, M. Robinson, & K. Schmidt (Eds.), *ECSCW '91: Proceedings of the Second European Conference on Computer-Supported Cooperative Work* (pp. 219–233). Amsterdam: Kluwer.

Sartre, J. P. (1965). *The psychology of imagination*. New York: Citadel Press.

Schmidt, K. (1991). Computer support for cooperative work in advanced manufacturing. *International Journal of Human Factors in Manufacturing, 1*(4), 303–320.

Schneider, K., & Wagner, I. (1993). Constructing the "dossier representatif": Computer-based information sharing in French hospitals. *Computer Supported Cooperative Work, 1*(4), 229–254.

Sharrock, W., & Anderson, B. (1993). Working towards agreement. In G. Button (Ed.), *Technology in working order: Studies of work, interaction, and technology* (pp. 149–161). London: Routledge & Kegan Paul.

Sheil, B. (1983). Coping with complexity. *Office: Technology and People, 1*.

Sørgaard, P. (1988). Object oriented programming and computerised shared material. In S. Nygaard & K. Gjessing (Eds.), *Second European Conference on Object Oriented Programming (ECOOP '88)* (pp. 319–334). Heidelberg: Springer Verlag.

Star, S. L. (1989). *Regions of the mind: Brain research and the quest for scientific certainty.* Stanford, CA: Stanford University Press.

Star, S. L. (1992). The Trojan door: Organisations, work, and the "Open Black Box." *Systems Practice.*

Star, S. L., & Griesemer, J. R. (1989). Institutional ecology, "translations" and boundary objects: Amateurs and professionals in Berkeley's museum of vertebrate zoology, 1907–39. *Social Studies of Science, 19,* 387–420.

Suchman, L. (1987). *Plans and situated actions: The problem of human–machine communication.* Cambridge, England: Cambridge University Press.

Suchman, L. A., & Trigg, R. H. (1991). Understanding practice: Video as a medium for reflection and design. In J. Kyng & M. Greenbaum (Eds.), *Design at Work* (pp. 65–89). Hillsdale, NJ: Lawrence Erlbaum Associates.

Wilkinson, B. (1986). *The shopfloor politics of new technology.* Aldershot, England: Gower.

Wynn, E. (1991). Taking practice seriously. In J. Kyng & M. Greenbaum (Eds.), *Design at Work.* Hillsdale, NJ: Lawrence Erlbaum Associates.

12

An Approach to Identifying the Role of "Information" in a Health Care System: Implications for the Quality of Health

Cesar A. Macias-Chapula
Universidad Autónoma de Mexico

Curative and preventive developments in acute and chronic diseases have been obtained in the last two decades. Through research and development activities, physicians have risen to the challenge of resolving difficult problems. Medicine has indeed reached new pinnacles in providing benefits to patients, but the care provided today is also highly complex. Concerns now being raised about patient care have been buttressed in part by well-performed studies that suggest that physicians do not consistently apply available knowledge in the care of patients and that uncertainty about the most effective diagnostic and therapeutic approaches is pervasive (Brahams, 1988; Brittain, 1985; O'Leary, 1988; Silverman, 1994).

These observations—as well as the financial incentives to conserve resources, the growth of for-profit hospitals and demands from purchasers—are among the forces today increasing the need for improved methods that measure quality in health care (Berwick, 1988; Hopkins, 1987; Jencks, 1994). This has become a public policy issue.

Quality assessment is a vehicle for reaching the elimination or reduction in aberrancies of care, and the improved provision of care as it is performed today. These objectives, as end products, can be attained through the appropriate gathering and use of scientific and technical information.

The increasingly sophisticated databases and managed care procedures for the delivery of care present new opportunities to observe and correct quality problems. However, according to Berwick (1988), research targets of measure and methods of measurement have not yet produced managerial useful applications for quality measurements in real-world settings. For example, in order to measure specific outcomes, much confusion still exists as to what information is needed for specific activities (Balla, Elstein, & Christensen, 1989; Black, 1989; Shortliffe, 1989; Smith, Grabham, & Chantler, 1989).

Clearly, the health care "need-provision" process is not given in isolation but within a "conceptual system" that operates in an environment that imposes boundaries and constraints on its activities. The boundaries and constraints include relations with patients, with the community or society, with the level of professional knowledge and technology, and with other subsystems within the system, as well as with certain conventions and rules for procedures.

In this context, information plays an important role, not only as an element in a transformation process within the system, but also in decision making and in quality of health care. According to Donabedian (1988), in order to measure quality of health, information needs to be available at all levels of health care. To assess the impact of information on quality of health care, however, information needs not only to be available, but also "used" as a resource. With this rationale, improvements in the use of information at the structure level of health care would lead to improvements at the structure-process, and outcome levels, thus increasing the quality of health.

The purpose of this chapter is to emphasize the importance of the role of information in a health care system, detect problems in information access and use, describe the use of a soft systems approach to these problems, and explore the implications of this analysis to quality of health care.

The chapter provides a brief description of the health care system in which quality of health and information are considered relevant factors for the functioning of the system. It describes what is perceived as the "problem situation." Then, it summarizes the methodology used to structure and approach the problem. Next it describes other applications in which soft systems have been useful. Finally, the chapter concludes on the importance of further interdisciplinary research needed to bridge the gap between the actors involved in the information production/information systems design side, and those in the information use/applications.

THE HEALTH CARE SYSTEM

Conceptually, medical intervention is considered to be a dual function, consisting of the direct provision of personal health care services and the indirect provision of information and management support services (Tenney, 1976).

The first, or clinical, task is patient care or problem processing. Its elemental unit is the doctor–patient relationship. Basically, this consists of a two-way transaction of personal expectations, with psychosocial determinants including both parties' personalities, roles reference groups, and subcultures in a sociocultural environment matrix. For the patient, antecedents are the multiple factors related to perception of a need for medical intervention, translating it into demand and assuming the patient role; for the physician, they are the acquisition and maintenance of knowledge and skills to analyze and manage patient problems effectively (Donabedian, 1973; Merill & Vallbona, 1984; Tenney, 1976).

The second, or support task, is management or information processing. According to Tenney (1976), it is an essential part of medical intervention directed toward patient care and also toward total community health maintenance, health professional education, biomedical and health services research, and social policy direction. Moore (1970) particularly emphasized information support and described the entire "medical care system" as a predominantly informational one, depending largely on the acquisition, storage, and interpretation of information by both the patient and the doctor.

Quality of Health Care

According to Donabedian (1988), the goodness of technical performance is judged in comparison with the best in practice. In this context, the interpersonal process is the vehicle by which technical care is implemented and on which its success depends. The behavior of the "client" and that of the "provider," however, is not only limited to a "person-to-person" basis; it can also be extended to groups of actors, or else, to the community as a whole. Indeed, it should also be judged according to the social distribution of levels of quality in the community. This depends, in turn, on who has greater or lesser access to care and who, after gaining access, receives greater or lesser qualities of care.

To increase quality, the concepts of what quality consists of must be translated to more concrete representations that are capable of some degree of quantification. These representations are the criteria and standards of structure, process, and outcome (Donabedian, 1982, 1986, 1988). When outcomes are used to assess the quality of antecedent care, there is the corresponding problem of specifying the several states of dysfunction and of weighting them in importance relative to each other, using some method of preferences. The greatest difficulty arises when one attempts to represent as a single quantity various aspects of functional capacity over a life span (Donabedian, 1988). Though several methods of valuation and aggregation are available, there is still much controversy about their validity.

Information and Health Care

In the medical field, the state of the art suggests that evaluation of the impact of scientific and technical information on the quality and cost of health care is reduced to the feedback from users' comments on questions that current literature "directly influenced" the management of specific patients (Greenberg, Battison, Kolisch, & Leredu, 1978; Scura & Davidoff, 1981); or that having the "key article" is as important as having the laboratory investigation reports (King, 1987; Marshall & Newfeld, 1981).

Ideally, health professionals should be aware of or have ready access to the best published evidence to consider in clinical decision making. Unfortunately, studies have demonstrated that a lack of awareness of published findings is critical to patient care, indicating the problems health professionals have in remaining abreast of the literature (Brittain, 1985; Covell, Uman, & Manning, 1985; Stross & Harlan, 1979).

Obstacles to case-related use of the literature by physicians are well documented (Brittain, 1985; C. L. Bowden & V. M. Bowden, 1971; Covell et al., 1985; Haddock, 1985; Siegel, 1982; Tabor, 1985). The "information explosion" and varying qualities of information complicates the task of remaining aware of and locating useful literature (Bernier, 1985).

If the existing health information systems are related to the quality of care assessment model, as proposed by Donabedian (1988) (viz. structure, process, and outcome), then most of the work is found to be related to the process–outcome elements. For example, the medical records information systems in hospitals are the key sources of information about the process of care and its immediate outcome.

A major field of research in the "process" element is medical decision making; the work of McNeil et al. (1971) is the most highly cited in the literature (Pyle et al., 1988). The point of departure for quantitative research in medical decision making is the process of patient care (Cebul, 1988).

Decision-making research has divided into *descriptive work*, which analyzes the process by which decisions are actually made, and *prescriptive work*, which attempts to define how decisions should be made in an environment of uncertainty and real-world constraints. Other applications of information at the same level of "process" are those of computer-assisted instruction (Evans, Brown, & Heestand, 1994; Weed, 1986); computer simulation (Kelly et al., 1988); artificial intelligence (Banks, 1986; Kahn, 1994); and computer-assisted diagnosis (Carson, 1989; de Dombal, 1994). Literature on these topics abounds.

Donabedian (1988) stated that all the activities of assessment, as related to quality of health care, depend on the availability of suitable, accurate information. He failed to mention, however, the risk that although "available," information (or data) does not necessarily lead to its "use." This is an angular point for research because several factors may affect such information use. In other words, information use and outcome, rather than availability, needs to be guaranteed.

THE PROBLEM SITUATION

In selecting a methodology for problem solving, a distinction between "hard" and "soft" problems is necessary. A "hard," or structured, problem is one that is exclusively concerned with a "how" type of question. This kind of problem is the domain of the design engineer, for example, who seeks effective and economic answers on "how" to transport "x" from "y" to "z," at minimum cost. Structured problems are what hard systems thinking and most operational research are concerned with. A "soft," or unstructured, problem, on the other hand, is one that is typified by being mixtures of "what" and "how" questions (Checkland, 1981).

According to Checkland (1981), the concept of "problem" is also one that has been found to be inappropriate. The notion that a problem can be defined suggests that a solution can be found that removes the problem. This is not unreasonable at the hard end of the problem spectrum, but at the soft end, problems do not occur in a way that enables them to be readily isolated. It is more usual to find sets of problems that are highly interactive and it has been found to be more useful to examine, not a problem, but a "problem situation" (i.e., a situation in which there are perceived to be problems; Wilson, 1984). Checkland (1981) defined a *problem situation* as "a nexus of real-world events and ideas which at least one person perceives as problematic: for him other possibilities concerning the situation are worth investigating" (p. 316).

For the purpose of this work, the following problem situation was explored: Scientific and technical information is widely available through different means. The new information technology has facilitated both the storage and prompt retrieval of information in all fields of knowledge. Online and CD-ROM databases, library networks, health information systems, and the automation of technical processes in the production, storage, retrieval, and dissemination of information are becoming cost-effective means of "handling" information in the health sector. Yet, it remains unknown how all this information and the new technologies are providing benefits to patients and to the health care system. The following questions are raised:

Is health care delivery or quality of health improved?

Is productivity increased?

What is the role of technology in the access/use of information?

What are the patterns of communication among the actors (providers/users) involved in the health care process?

What/which are their information flows?

What is the role of the patient, the medic/paramedic and the health manager in the design of information systems?

The answers to these questions are of particular relevance to health and information science researchers in order to understand the impact of information on quality of health care. Here, the interaction of hard and soft elements gives rise to a nonstructured situation. Hard elements are, for example, those related to the design and implementation of the information system; some soft elements are those related to the satisfaction of the end-users in using the system.

In this context, there seems to be a gap between the designers of scientific and technical information systems, and the end-users of information. On the one hand, information systems seem to be designed with a top–down, prescriptive approach, so as to sell a "product" in a market. On the other, end-users, although free to choose the information source that best meets their needs, have to decide not only in terms of how well the information system performs, but also on other values such as "how well the information obtained is going to benefit his patient or the community." This gap has serious implications for the quality of health care.

The problem now is not "how" to obtain/access information regarding a particular need, but how to link the fact that such information (as an element in a system) is going to "transform" certain processes (e.g., the application of knowledge in the doctor–patient relationship), so as to "impact/improve" an outcome (e.g., results of the health program on the prevention and control of chagas disease in Chiapas, Mexico) in terms of "quality." Can information systems be designed with this "quality-goal" orientation? They are certainly desirable, but are they viable?

To date, the end-user is unable to "modify" the information system to impact quality of health. The information systems designers, on the other hand, construct systems mostly to satisfy short-term needs and are usually problem oriented, without perceiving midterm goals of quality procurement. Bibliographic retrieval systems, for example, are limited to satisfy immediate information needs. Their design may be oriented to increase either "recall" or "precision" in a given information search strategy. Such systems, although able to perform their tasks, are by no means concerned with the "outcome" of the information use, as assessed by the end-user.

Clearly, in order to bridge the gap, an interdisciplinary approach needs to be used.

Modeling languages need to be constructed in order to explore how the element "information" is being accessed and used, and how it interrelates to other elements at the structure, process, and outcome levels of the health care system. The development of such models can provide some insight so as to understand about the linkages among the different information sources, the information technologies, the users, and the overall impact to the health system, as they affect quality of health.

In a recent study (Macias-Chapula, 1992b, 1996), some of the factors identified to affect the access and use of information at the structure level of health care, were classified according to the user of the information sources, the information sources themselves, and environmental factors. The following scheme was obtained:

User/personal factors: education/training on how to use information sources; awareness of the existence of the sources; personal experience/familiarity with the information sources; lack of a value, as assigned to information; lack of time to be spent on searching for information.

Information source factors: existence of the source; accessibility; ease of use; cost; technical quality/credibility; organization; language.

Environmental factors: existence of a communication channel between the information source and the user; work role; interpersonal relations; existing policies/politics; external influences; bureaucracy.

The challenge now is to relate these factors to quality of health care, and then to develop further models, linking processes and outcomes, to obtain a wholistic picture of the situation.

APPROACHES

Substantial efforts have been dedicated to the analysis, development, and refinement of methodologies for problematic situations (Flood & Carson, 1988). "Reductionist" efforts have investigated specific methodologies (Rhodes, 1985; Woodburn, 1985). Of equal importance is the consideration of a wholistic approach to methodology, whereby various methodological approaches are linked or integrated into a system that reflects the wide variety of situational classes that may exist.

The benefit of such an approach is to marry appropriate methodological approaches to types of problematic situations. If feasible, ideally this would give some real directions as to which methodology should be used (Flood & Carson, 1988). Efforts in this area include Jackson and Keys (1984), and Klir (1985). According to Flood and Carson (1988), the former work is conceptually based in social systems theory, whereas the latter has a strong relation to general systems theory and its associated mathematical foundations.

Other attempts at wholistic classification are found in Boulding (1956), Checkland (1981), and Jordan (1981). Wilson (1984) purported that the motivation to undertake the development of systems design methodologies arose because of the following four characteristics that affected the postwar industry: technical systems were becoming more complex; market environments were becoming highly competitive; new projects were increasingly more expensive; and computer developments made complex calculations more feasible.

These features gave rise to the need for integrated design methodologies capable of producing "optimized" designs and the need to see design as part of business development planning. Thus, it was realized that technical system design was part of a wider environment that had to be accommodated in the design process (Wilson, 1984). Plant design methodologies were thus developed (Williams, 1961).

As well as being concerned with design, systems engineering as a discipline was directed toward the development of methodologies for problem solving in general. Examples of these are the methodology described by Hall (1962), developed as a result of the experience with Bell Telephone Laboratories, and that of the RAND Systems Analysis (Quade & Boucher, 1968).

Both of these methodologies emphasize a "systemic" approach to problem investigation, though neither takes the basic definition of a system to be more than the general definition (i.e., an interconnected set of entities). They both place considerable emphasis on the definition of the problem and on the need for consensus over objectives. The methodologies detail the stages involved in a complex analysis but give no guide as to how each stage should be taken (Wilson, 1984).

Another systems approach to complexity is Beer (1985). For Beer, a system is viable if it is capable of responding to environmental changes, even if those changes could not have been foreseen at the time the system was designed.

Jenkin's (1981) methodology of systems analysis, design, implementation, and operation attempts to be both systemic and systematic. However, it still made the assumption that systems exist in the real world—that is, the distinction had not been made between designed physical systems and human activity systems, the latter being defined by Checkland (1981) as notional purposive systems which express some purposeful human activity, activity which could in principle be found in the real world. Such systems are notional in the sense that they are not descriptions of actual real-world activity (which is an exceptionally complex phenomenon) but are intellectual constructs; they are ideal types for use in a debate about possible changes which might be introduced into a real-world problem situation. (p. 314)

The measure of performance of Jenkin's methodology is expressed solely in economic terms. This stems from the concern that the systems should function efficiently. Furthermore, this methodology was based on the idea that engineering the system within which the problem lies would solve the problem (Wilson, 1984).

As the kind of problems encountered became softer, modifications to the Jenkin's methodology were found to be necessary. For example, it was found to be useful to derive measures of performance that were not economic and to consider system boundaries that were not coincidental with organizational boundaries (Wilson, 1984). However, real difficulties were found when it was realized that, in general, objectives could not be taken as given.

Indeed, there is usually no basis for assuming at any level of an organization that published objectives really represent what is being aimed for, or that there is anything like a consensus about them. What was needed, therefore, was a methodology that explicitly faced this problem and attempted to expose and counterpose the various "worldviews" in order to reach some valid consensus concerning possible changes based on an appreciation, by the actors involved, of their own and others' values and beliefs (Mingers, 1980). Based on a program of action research within real-world situations, Checkland (1981) developed such methodology, now known as Checkland methodology or soft systems methodology (SSM).

Given a set of methodologies, the question "which methodology should be used?" arises. Flood and Carson (1988), in dealing with complexity, were not able to find universal acceptance with either of the approaches reviewed. On the other hand, Wilson (1984) argued that the assembly of systems concepts (i.e., methodology) needs to be appropriate to the situation and to the particular personality of analysts themselves. In this context, analysts should choose the methodology that "works" for them and that, of course, produces results that the organization will agree are useful.

In order to approach the problem situation exposed in this work, SSM can be used to understand and learn about the role of information on quality of health. The next section briefly describes the methodology.

SSM

SSM can be described as a process of analysis that uses the concept of a human activity system as a means of getting from "finding out" about a situation, to "taking action" to improve the situation. The systems thinker works simultaneously at different levels of detail, on several stages. This has to be so because the methodology is itself a system and a change in one stage affects all the others.

The methodology contains two kinds of activities: *real-world activities* necessarily involving people in the problem situation, and *systems thinking activities* that may or may not involve those in the problem situation, depending on the individual circumstances of the study. The language of the former is the normal language of the problem situation. That of the latter is the language of systems, for it is in these stages that the real-world complexity is unraveled and understood as a result of translation into the higher level language of systems (Checkland, 1981).

Models are thus developed that are relevant to the problem situation. To develop such models, *root definitions* need to be identified; these are defined by Checkland (1981) as "concise, tightly constructed descriptions of human activity systems which state what the system is; what it does is then elaborated in a conceptual model which is built on the basis of the definition. Every element in the definition must be reflected in the model derived from it" (p. 317). Smyth and Checkland (1976) concluded that adequate root definitions should contain five elements explicitly. These elements include a "transformation process"; "ownership" of the system; "actors"; "customers"; "environmental constraints"; and "world-view" of the system.

After a process of iteration, the activities selected in the root definitions are analyzed so as to integrate a "conceptual model"; that is, a systemic account of a human activity system, built on the basis of that system's root definition. Such models should contain the minimum necessary activities for the system to be the one named in the root definition. Only activities that could be directly carried out should be included. This model should be tested and brought to the "real world," where debate and consensus is created about the feasible and desirable changes that are needed to improve the existing situation. This is manifested in a *plan of action*.

The methodology can thus be seen as a general problem-solving approach, appropriate to human activity systems. In contrast to other types of system, human activity systems can never be described (or modeled) in a single account that will be either generally acceptable or sufficient. For a system of this kind there may well be as many descriptions of it as there are "actors" who are not completely indifferent to it (Checkland,

1981). This is the characteristic of the real world that forces the methodology to become a means of organizing discussion, debate, and argument rather than a means of engineering efficient solutions.

APPLICATIONS

SSM has proved invaluable for revealing structural problems in a given organization; for example, parts of the organization that have simply absorbed new requirements without explicitly adapting to meet them, and where the expectations of clients have not been recognized and allowed for. In organizational reviews, SSM can be applied by designing a notional system model that reflects the primary task of the organization in question, then comparing the model with what is happening in the real world, indicating where to improve actions/situations. Systems thinking can identify values that can be shared at all levels by the different actors involved. Through debate, a consensus can be obtained about feasible changes in a given situation (Smallwood, 1990; Youssef & Jackson, 1989).

Organizational analysis, on the other hand, is at the root of using SSM to advise on the requirements for new technology, because it encourages the analyst to consider the purpose of the organization, develop root definitions and conceptual models to illustrate this purpose in systems terms. Ideally, the technology chosen supports the organization's purpose, rather than simply mechanizing particular procedures, as would be the case in a top–down, prescriptive approach.

Similarly, where a significant change of role is anticipated, a model can be developed that reflects the new requirement, which is then compared through debate, with a model that reflects the existing role. This approach was used with positive results when examining the future requirements of Colleges of Further Education in light of new legislation, in the United Kingdom (Patching, 1990).

In the medical field, Eggington (1988) used SSM to examine the information requirements of health care systems throughout Europe. After a process of iteration, she obtained a conceptual model that can be used to design an integrated health information system for the European Community.

Checkland and Scholes (1990) applied the methodology at the community level, within the National Health Service in the U.K. They obtained models of both a system that decides what health care to provide through which agents and a system to provide health care. The models were tested and shown to be appropriate using three projects in East Berkshire as examples, and were incorporated into a model of a system to evaluate any health care project. This latter model was based on the idea of health as a changing "norm" rather than an attainable goal. In this context, the norm will be threatened by influences in the environment, and management skills will be required by the owners of the system to maintain the health of the population within the range of the norm, which will itself be determined by societal, cultural, political attitudes, the state of health technologies, and the resources available. SSM allows to consider these elements in interaction when developing the conceptual models.

In a recent study (Macias-Chapula, 1992b, 1996), SSM was used to approach the information problems that existed at the structure level of a health care system. In this research, a conceptual model was obtained to identify the information-processing procedures of Regional Coordinators for Biomedical Education and Research within Mexico's Social Security Institute (Instituto Mexicano del Seguro Social). Using a model, the barriers to information access and use were identified and their impact to quality of health was explored. Results indicated that the main barrier was the lack of a communication channel between the information source and the user. This was corroborated through debate. Feasible and desirable changes could be proposed through a plan of action.

Regarding current criteria available by which to judge research on SSM, Checkland (1989) reported its use, transferability, and teachability. From using SSM in this research it was learned that the methodology can be used both to approach information problems at the structure level of health care, and to enrich the different concepts of human activity systems that participate in the delivery of health care.

A model was constructed to base this approach (Macias-Chapula, 1992a, 1995). Based on this model, information sources can be investigated at the structure, process, and outcome levels of health care; as well as at primary, secondary, or tertiary levels of care. This model becomes a circular task that, through assessment, becomes a continuous monitor of changes.

The "new process" of SSM, as described by Checkland and Scholes (1990), is particularly relevant to this analysis at lower levels of resolution, where roles, norms, values, and power need to be analyzed as part of the cultural stream of the process, along with relevant systems.

In measuring the impact of information on quality of health care, the criteria for efficacy, efficiency, and effectiveness in model building plays a vital role in the later comparison between the model and the perceptions of the real world.

CONCLUSIONS

Elements of structure, process, and outcome need to be identified, defined, and monitored in order to assess quality of health care. In this effort, a mixture of technical and social elements are interconnected. Technical elements are, for example, the application of knowledge by the health care providers and the available infrastructure to provide health care such as equipment or supplies. Social elements on the other hand are, for example, the interpersonal relations between the physician and the patient, and the degree of organization by a given community to demand and receive health care services. In order to analyze and understand the interaction of these elements, much effort is required by researchers from varying disciplines. Up to date, most of the research on the assessment of quality of health care has been conducted by physicians alone. This is explained by the fact that much of the analytical work has taken place at the operational (process) level of health care. This is not a surprising finding because most of the data and information is collected directly from the medical record.

Sociologists, anthropologists, psychologists, and information scientists need to collaborate through interdisciplinary teams in order to contribute to a better understanding of the aforementioned elements. Sociologists, for example, may want to understand the elements affecting the organization of social groups and communities to respond to health care processes. Anthropologists may want to analyze the cultural elements where health care is provided and accepted. Psychologists may, on the other hand, conduct research on the different behaviors and attitudes to health both by the health care providers and users. It is hoped that the use of different methodologies, as used to approach from different worldviews, will contribute to a better understanding of the interaction of the elements that lead to assess quality of health.

Similarly, information scientists can contribute through the analysis of the element "information" within the system. Such analysis requires a wholistic approach to integrate the different "views" of the actors involved in the life cycle of information. These include, for example, the information system designers, health managers, end-users, programmers, and intermediaries, to mention but a few. Here, prescriptive, top–down approaches need to look at situational diagnoses, systemic analyses, and bottom–up approaches, in an effort to bridge the existing gap between real-world information needs and the efficient application of information technologies.

The methodology that draws on the systems approach to this situation is SSM. It stresses the human and organizational components of human activity systems. There is a recognition in this approach that organizations are complex and unclear. Its philosophy lies in its attempt to understand a given organization wholistically, analyzing the structure of organizations as a whole and from many viewpoints.

In this context, using SSM, information can be analyzed as a contributing element to quality of health care from top managerial levels, down to the outcome level. For example, given a health care problem in a community, information can be analyzed at different levels so as to understand its role and promote its use in order to improve quality of health care. Thus, a situational diagnosis needs to be performed on the information-processing procedures performed by the actors involved in the problem. This includes, for example, the head of the community health district, the providers of health care (including physicians, nurses, para-medics), and the community itself, including patients. SSM can help construct conceptual models to take action to improve the existing prob-lem through the appropriate use of information and linked to improve quality of health care, as a viable and desirable outcome. The same approach can be followed to transfer information technologies, promote the prevention and control of communicable diseases, or conduct research for development activities where information access and use plays a vital role.

REFERENCES

Balla, I. J., Elstein, A. J., & Christensen, C. (1989). Obstacles to acceptance of clinical decision analysis. *British Medical Journal (Clinical Research), 298*(6673), 579–582.

Banks, G. (1986). Artificial intelligence in medical diagnosis: The internist/caduceus approach. *Critical Reviews in Medical Informatics, 1*(1), 23–54.

Beer, S. (1985). *Diagnosing the system for organizations.* Maidenhead: Wiley.

Bernier, C. L. (1985). The ethics of knowing. *Journal of the American Society for Information Science, 36*(3), 211–212.

Berwick, D. M. (1988). Toward an applied technology for quality measurement in health care. *Medical Decision Making, 8*(4), 253–258.

Black, N. (1989). Information, please—and quick. *British Medical Journal (Clinical Research), 298*(6673), 586–587.

Boulding, K. (1956). General systems theory: The skeleton of science. *Management Science, 2*(3), 197–208.

Bowden, C. L., & Bowden, V. M. (1971). A survey of information sources used by psychiatrists. *Bulletin of the Medical Library Association, 50*(4), 603–608.

Brahams, D. (1988). Bad professional relations and risks to patients. *The Lancet, 2*(8609), 519–520.

Brittain, J. M. (1985). *Consensus and penalties for ignorance in the medical sciences: Implications for information transfer.* London: Taylor Graham.

Carson, E. R. (1989). Systems thinking and knowledge technology in medicine. In R. L. Flood, M. C. Jackson, & P. Keys (Eds.), *Systems prospects: The next ten years of systems research.* New York: Plenum.

Cebul, R. D. (1988). Decision making research at the interface between descriptive and prescriptive studies. *Medical Decision Making, 8*(4), 231–232.

Checkland, P. B. (1981). *Systems thinking, systems practice.* Chichester, England: Wiley.

Checkland, P. B. (1989). Researching systems methodology: Some future prospects. In R. L. Flood, M. C. Jackson, & P. Keys (Eds.), *Systems prospects: The next ten years of systems research*. New York: Plenum.

Checkland, P. B., & Scholes, J. (1990). *Soft systems methodology in action*. Chichester, England: Wiley.

Covell, D. G., Uman, G. C., & Manning, P. R. (1985). Information needs of office practice: Are they being met? *Annals of Internal Medicine, 103*, 596–599.

De Dombal, F. T. (1994). Computer-assisted diagnosis in Europe [letter]. *New England Journal of Medicine, 331*(18), 1238.

Donabedian, A. (1973). *Aspects of medical care administration*. Cambridge, MA: Harvard University Press.

Donabedian, A. (1982). *Explorations in quality assessment and monitoring: Vol. 2. The criteria and standards of quality*. Ann Arbor, MI: Health Administration Press.

Donabedian, A. (1986). Criteria and standards for quality assessment and monitoring. *Quality Review Bulletin, 12*, 99–108.

Donabedian, A. (1988). The quality of care. How can it be assessed? *Journal of the American Medical Association, 260*(12), 1743–1748.

Eggington, E. (1988). Health care information in Europe. A soft systems approach. Unpublished master's thesis, Department of Information Science, City University, London.

Evans, L. A., Brown, J. F., & Heestand, D. E. (1994). Incorporating computer-based learning in a medical school environment. *Journal of Biocommunication, 21*(1), 10–17.

Flood, R. L., & Carson, E. R. (1988). *Dealing with complexity*. New York: Plenum.

Greenberg, B., Battison, S., Kolisch, M., & Leredu, M. (1978). Evaluation of a clinical medical librarian program at the Yale Medical Library. *Bulletin of the Medical Library Association, 66*(3), 319–326.

Haddock, D. R. W. (1985). Information problems surrounding the diagnosis and treatment of exotic diseases in the United Kingdom. In J. Brittain (Ed.), *Consensus and penalties for ignorance in the medical sciences*. London: Taylor Graham.

Hall, A. D. (1962). *A methodology for systems engineering*. Princeton, NJ: Van Nostrand.

Hopkins, R. (1987). Doctors as general managers: To be or not to be. *British Medical Journal (Clinical Research), 295*(6609), 1360–1361.

Jackson, M. C., & Keys, P. (1984). Towards a system of systems methodologies. *Journal of the Operations Research Society, 35*(6), 473–486.

Jenkins, G. M. (1981). The systems approach. In The Open Systems Group (Ed.), *Systems behavior* (p. 142). London: Harper & Row.

Jencks, S. F. (1994). HCFA's health care quality improvement program and the cooperative cardiovascular project. *Annals of Thoracic Surgery, 58*(6), 1858–1862.

Jordan, N. (1981). Some thinking about "systems." In F. Emery (Ed.), *Systems thinking*. Harmondsworth: Penguin.

Kahn, C. E., Jr. (1994). Artificial intelligence in radiology: Decision support systems. *Radiographics, 14*(4), 849–861.

Kelly, D. H., Carley, D. W., & Shannon, D. C. (1988). Periodical breathing. *Annals of the New York Academy of Science, 533*, 301–304.

King, D. (1987). The contribution of hospital library information services to clinical care: A study in eight hospitals. *Bulletin of the Medical Library Association, 75*(4), 291–304.

Klir, G. J. (1985). *Architecture of systems problem solving*. New York: Plenum.

Macias-Chapula, C. A. (1992a). Application of soft systems methodology to develop information flow models at the information system design process. A case report. In

New worlds in information and documentation (p. 81). FID 46 Congress and Conference. Madrid: FID.

Macias-Chapula, C. A. (1992b). *Soft systems approach to information problems at the structure level of health care.* Unpublished doctoral thesis, Department of Information Science, City University, London.

Macias-Chapula, C. A. (1995, May). A soft systems approach to understand the impact of health information on patient care. In E. M. Lacroix (Ed.), *Health information for the global village: Proceedings of the Seventh International Congress on Medical Librarianship* (pp. 174–178). Washington, DC.

Macias-Chapula, C. A. (1996). Development of a soft systems model to identify information values, impact and barriers in a health care information system. *Journal of Information Science, 21*(4), 283–288.

McNeil, B. J., et al. (1971). Primer on certain elements of medical decision making. *New England Journal of Medicine, 284,* 416–424.

Marshall, J. G., & Newfeld, U. R. (1981). A randomized trial of librarian educational participation in clinical settings. *Journal of Medical Education, 56,* 409–416.

Merill, J. M., & Vallbona, C. (1984). A theoretical model of sources of physician error. In W. van Eimeren, R. Englelbrecht, & C. D. Flagle (Eds.), *Third International Conference on System Science in Health Care.* Berlin: Springer-Verlag.

Mingers, J. C. (1980). Towards an appropriate social theory for applied systems thinking: Critical theory and soft systems methodology. *Journal of Applied Systems Analysis, 7,* 41–49.

Moore, F. J. (1970). Information technologies and health care: 1. Medical care as a system. *Archives of Internal Medicine, 125,* 157–161.

O'Leary, D. S. (1988). Quality assessment. Moving from theory to practice. *Journal of the American Medical Association, 260*(12), 1760.

Patching, D. (1990). *Practical soft systems analysis.* London: Pitman.

Pyle, K. I., Lobel, R. W., & Beck, J. R. (1988). Citation analysis of the field of medical decision making. *Medical Decision Making, 8*(3), 155–164.

Quade, E., & Boucher, W. I. (1968). *Systems analysis and policy planning: Application and defence.* Amsterdam: Elsevier.

Rhodes, D. J. (1985). Root definitions and reality in manufacturing systems. *Journal of Applied Systems Analysis, 12,* 93–100.

Scura, G., & Davidoff, F. (1981). Case-related use of the medical literature: Clinical librarian services for improving patient care. *Journal of the American Medical Association, 245,* 50–52.

Shortlife, E. H. (1989). Testing reality: The introduction of decision-support technologies for physicians. *Methods of Information in Medicine, 28*(1), 1–5.

Siegel, E. R. (1982). Transfer of information to health practitioners. In B. J. Dervin & M. J. Voight (Eds.), *Progress in communication sciences.* Norwood, NJ: Ablex.

Silverman, W. A. (1994). The Windermere Lecture 1994. The line between "knowing" and "doing": Medicine's dilemma at the end of the twentieth century. *Archives of Diseases of Children, 71*(3), 261–265.

Smallwood, S. (1990). The district nurse and patient assessment. Unpublished master's thesis, Department of Information Science, City University, London.

Smith, R., Grabham, A., & Chantler, C. (1989). Doctors becoming managers. *British Medical Journal (Clinical Research), 298*(6669), 311–314.

Smyth, D. S., & Checkland, P. B. (1976). Using systems approach: The structure of root definitions. *Journal of Applied Systems Analysis, 5*(1).

Stross, J. K., & Harlan, W. R. (1979). The dissemination of new medical information. *Journal of the American Medical Association, 241,* 2622–2624.

Tabor, R. B. (1985). Penalties for ignorance in the medical sciences and health care fields: Implications for library and information services. In J. M. Brittain (Ed.), *Consensus and penalties for ignorance in the medical sciences.* London: Taylor Graham.

Tenney, J. B. (1976). The medical intervention subsystem and health services research. In H. H. Werley, A. Zuzich, M. Zajkowski, & A. D. Zagornik (Eds.), *Health research: The systems approach.* New York: Springer.

Weed, L. L. (1986). Knowledge coupling, medical education and patient care. *Critical Reviews in Medical Informatics, 1*(1), 55–79.

Williams, T. J. (1961). *Systems engineering for the process industries.* New York: McGraw-Hill.

Wilson, B. (1984). *Systems: Concepts, methodologies, and applications.* Chichester, England: Wiley.

Woodburn, I. (1985). Some developments in the building of conceptual models. *Journal of Applied Systems Analysis, 12,* 101–106.

Youssef, E. A., & Jackson, M. C. (1989). Using systems ideas to explore the problems of the textile public sector in Egypt. In R. L. Flood, M. C. Jackson, & P. Keys (Eds.), *Systems prospects: The next ten years of systems research.* New York: Plenum.

III

INTRODUCTION: THE SOCIOTECHNICAL SYSTEM AND CSCW

William Turner
CERESI/CNRS, Meudon, France

An appropriate closing to this book is a set of chapters by people who have elected to take up residence in the great divide. This notion has been used throughout as a means of distinguishing between the social and the technical, between the human, emotion-laden, contingent context of cooperative work (CW) and the formal, rational, and potentially universal character of computer support (CS). The chapters in this section set out from a different perspective. The message is simple and clear: Little headway, if any, will be made if the collective aim is to build bridges between the two terms of the previous equation. Bridgebuilding exercises are not necessary; what is needed is a better empirical understanding of how sociotechnical systems work in practice as well as appropriate cooperative work theories in order to guide their construction. In more concrete terms, the perspective on CSCW research provided here leads to the following question: What precisely is the nature of the relation between sociotechnical systems and CSCW research? As the authors show, at least three different answers can be given.

SOCIOTECHNICAL SYSTEMS LIMIT THE SCOPE
OF CSCW RESEARCH

The sociotechnical system is an observable object for empirical research that is concretely embedded in a work environment. It gives substance to the CSCW concept and limits its scope to the heterogenous set of social and technical elements brought together and combined in a variety of ways when systems are built. The reasoning presented here has been developed and defended for a good number of years by actor–network theorists (Callon, 1980; Latour, 1987). Basically, the argument says that cooperation takes shape and becomes meaningful because of the work done to build locally coherent sociotechnical systems. People might have different ideas about the ethical, moral, political, economic, or social basis on which coherence should be based, but normative questions of this kind cannot be successfully addressed by an outside observer. The mystery of cooperative work—the fact that despite their differences, people actually are able to build things together (programs, machines, strategies, society, etc.)—has to be formulated in another way. The focus is on the procedures through which groups achieve a relative autonomy with respect to their environment and, at the same time, develop the necessary economic, social, and political skills needed to defend this autonomy. How are stable systems achieved? Cooperative work is looked on as being more of an engineering problem than one that raises the theoretical issues of normative social science. The final structure of an engineered system is determined much less by the intentions, worldviews, and fundamental motivations of its designers than by their concrete decisions to incorporate specific elements into the system, to link them together in a specific way, and to codify interactions by a given set of rules and procedures.

Engineers do not seriously expect to be able to take an initial design and use it as a blueprint for building a workable system in the real world. They expect to have to adjust their plan to local conditions and, according to actor–network theorists, it is precisely this adjustment process that has to be described, analyzed, and explained. In the chapters that follow, Berg applies this approach to show that computer-based decision support tools do not just slip into a niche within medical practice, but concretely transform practice while the routines and design decisions embodied in the tools are transformed at the same time. His chapter illustrates the point already made: A computer-supported cooperative work application is a sociotechnical system that is fine-tuned to operate in a given context; consequently, it will be possible to pierce the mystery of cooperative work and understand the techniques, routines, and strategies of doing things together if appropriate observational skills are developed to document the ongoing negotiations about making systems work.

Ira Monarch et al.'s chapter takes a similar point of view but raises the methodological problem about how descriptions of cooperative work practices can be obtained in distributed environments. Their chapter starts off by showing the extent to which design is a geographically decentralized activity, distributed over an open conception space populated by a great many actors who might or might not know one another and who, in any case, work in a great many different contexts. The problem of describing how a multitude of distributed stakeholders actually build their design and implementation strategies requires providing them with what the authors call an "inscription space." Participants in a cooperative engineering activity are invited to create their documents, sketches, and more formal models using tools that not only facilitate the creation of these products but at the same time maintain their accessibility to multiple stakeholders over the lifetime of a project and beyond. Moreover, the authors discuss how this suite of tools will not just passively record and store this information for later recall, but will actively support design participants in organizing both the information itself and the processes for producing it. The aim is to provide engineering communities, including so-called end-users, with reflexive tools for both constructing and monitoring collective agreements and work processes. And why is this goal appropriate? The answer given by the authors to this question clearly illustrates the particular flavor of work being carried out by those at home in the great divide. Engineers might answer that machine augmented intelligence applied to information flows in distributed work environments will prove useful in organizing the ongoing negotiations and adjustments inherent in cooperative cognition. Sociologists might reply with skepticism pointing to such normative questions as: Who benefits and what kinds of social arrangements will flourish when machines are used in the prescribed way? The fact is, however, that without the developmental work and empirical research undertaken by the authors, the gulf of incomprehension between the two communities is only likely to grow. A new kind of hybrid is taking roots in the great divide (aptly called by the authors), an engineer/sociologist, who is both builder and skeptic in turn.

CSCW RESEARCH INCREASES THE OPTIONS
AVAILABLE FOR DESIGNING SOCIOTECHNICAL
SYSTEMS

Design requires answering a normative question: What are the requirements of users if they are going to work with a system? Accepting from the outset that any answer to this question is very strongly theory ladened, the idea defended earlier becomes suspect: It is not at all clear that an understanding of cooperative work solely depends on observing how system skills are deployed. An engineering approach to CSCW research can be criticized because it pays little attention to how blueprints for action are defined in the first place (Goguen, chapter 2, this volume; Jirotka & Goguen, 1994). It is comparatively less important in this approach to understand where ideas come from than to explain the adjustment dynamics associated with their implementation. The point is, however, that the range of negotiations open to stakeholders during implementation is limited in a very real way by the initial assumptions made about user needs. Two chapters in this section address this question and, in doing so, look critically at the conditions that have to be met in order to carry out empirical research into cooperative work processes. They use a reflexive mode of argument in order to show how concrete experience in the CSCW field can be used to define options for the design of new sociotechnical systems. Both are written by people who have actively carried out empirical research and who raise the very fundamental question of how to capitalize on past experience: What methodology should be applied to integrate the results of case studies into an appropriate frame of reference for constantly improving sociotechnical design?

Wagner's experience as a member of a multidisciplinary design team led her to analyze the "norms" of participating disciplines in order to explain how an appropriate statement of system and user requirements might be systematically achieved. After showing that conflicting norm structures constitute a source of misunderstanding that undermines a team's capacity of working together, she makes a series of concrete proposals for building a shared working culture for multidisciplinary design. These proposals define what might be called a "negotiation space" by using four general categories to offer an initial framework for structuring sociotechnical options. According to Wagner, design options become reality by adjusting conflicting points of view about subject-oriented as opposed to process-oriented design; "workable" as opposed to "true" representations of requirements; conditions for confidence building over disciplinary boundaries; and, finally, borderline questions concerning the respective limits of human and machine autonomy in their ongoing interactions.

In his chapter, Bannon sets out from another perspective but arrives at the same conclusion as Wagner, namely, that appropriate frameworks for action can be developed and filled out by ongoing research. Bannon is much more critical than Wagner of the idea that multidisciplinary projects require building a shared working culture. He provides a historical account of research in both human–computer interaction (HCI) and CSCW to show that both fields have developed boundary objects that focus common interests and allow for cross-disciplinary interaction and mutual learning. His chapter indicates a series of arenas that provide settings for boundary object generation. These arenas are articulated around the "interface debate" in HCI and around the "cooperative work debate" in CSCW. He comes out very strongly against the idea of transcending these debates by efforts aimed at developing a sort of interdisciplinary Holy Grail. Conflicts stimulate ongoing research practices: It is important that different disciplinary points of view and interpretations be brought to bear on such things as moving research out from the laboratory into the workplace, defining user needs and requirements, and conceptualizing the design process itself. Theory is much less important in his eyes than appropriate list management techniques for providing a constantly updated overview of the boundary objects emerging in these different arenas. Although Bannon's argument in favor of a bottom–up approach to multidisciplinary dynamics differs from Wagner's, intuitively speaking, one would expect that elements on Bannon's boundary object list could be distributed over the categories derived from Wagner's analysis of disciplinary norms.

WORLDVIEWS FOR UNDERSTANDING WORK
AND EXPLAINING SYSTEMS

Improving sociotechnical design implies efforts aimed at building an appropriate framework for integrating the results of case studies into an ongoing, collective CSCW research program. But, another way to consider the framework problem is to assume that yet another level of generalization is needed. Global semiotic systems structure understanding of the experienced world (Yoneyama, this volume). They define the cultural values and outlooks that individuals generally admit without question, given the processes of socialization at work in a vast range of institutions from the family, to school, and the workplace. Local frames of reference for CSCW research are necessarily embedded in these global worldviews. So it is not enough to simply work up from experience to theory; it must be understood how the constitutive order of semiotic systems impinge on people's actions and understanding. The final two chapters in this section work down from worldviews to theory. The first derives specifically from work in engineering, the second from work in the social sciences, but both examine the same question: How do people position themselves in order to observe what goes on around them? This, of course, is a crucial question for understanding how global systems impinge on individual freedom of action.

Design of computer-supported applications depend on the way in which individuals represent a cooperative work problem in organizations and as Taylor et al. argue in their chapter, this representation will be different if the individuals are located in a system or outside it. People experience things differently: "It is experientially not the same thing to understand an airline from the perspective of its passengers, for whom it is a sequence of distinct activities, one after the other, as it is from that of the airline employees, for whom it is a single configuration of activities, repetitively generated for each new batch of passengers: take off, serve a meal, run the movie, land, disembark." Passengers are objectively in the system as entities connected to their food, their seats, and their film through the actions of the airline employees. They make up the material world in exactly the same way as particles of any physical system constitute the objects on which a process of work is concentrated when they are combined in some way or another. Airline employees, on the other hand, objectively manage the system from the outside, organizing the events proposed to the passengers, making the links between them and controlling for their efficiency. In the real world, people are constantly stepping into and out of systems: subjects in one, objects in another. As they move from one worldview to the other, the material objects that surround them are perceived differently. The computer, for example, will be considered as just another information-processing node of a network on an equal footing to men and women in the material, particle-oriented worldview. But, when it is seen as an entity capable of managing events, of linking them together and of building autonomous interpretations, the design question is no longer that of optimizing network configurations for information processing; it becomes one of augmenting human intellect by using an external memory to extend the mind.

Keller takes the argument one step further by insisting on the fact that it is not enough to link worldviews to everyday experience of organizing and being organized in order to fully understand different conceptions of computer design. The link is certainly useful in explaining different design premises, but explaining does not mean understanding. Explaining is a conventional scientific issue: It often means in the social sciences making explicit and communicable actions that individuals perform, perceive, and understand in everyday praxis without any need to codify, formalize, or objectify. If explaining means knowing, understanding means doing, and the point that Keller makes is that individuals only "know" about social life in very restricted, instrumental ways. Researchers know how to build sociotechnical systems—that is, manage events, link them together, and evaluate results—but much more needs to be done in order to understand cooperative work (i.e., the collective construction of a social identity). Keller argues that global semiotic systems result from the interplay of social processes and concepts of social identity and presents a methodology for analyzing this interplay. His point is that merely explaining sociocultural issues has become inadequate for CSCW projects;

whereas functions and systems can be explained, people and social processes have to be understood. Sociotechnical design has yet to show that it can effectively and efficiently contribute to the collective construction of a social identity.

These chapters have been classed in terms of their focus on empirical, theoretical, or worldview features of sociotechnical design for CSCW. However, they are presented in two groups in order to show first an engineering and then a social science perspective: The first group is composed of the chapters by Monarch et al., Bannon, and Taylor et al.; the second by those of Berg, Wagner, and Keller. This ordering should help readers see the relation between sociotechnical systems and CSCW research as depending on both the level of analysis and the type of perspective used to examine the subject.

REFERENCES

Jirotka, M., & Goguen, J. (Eds.). (1994). *Requirements engineering: Social and ethical issues.* London: Academic Press.

Callon, M. (1980). Struggles and negotiations to define what is problematic and what is not. The socio-logic of translation. In K. Knorr-Cetina, R. Krohn, & R. Whitely (Eds.), *The social process of scientific investigation: Sociology of the sciences* (Vol. 4, pp. 187–219). Dordrecht: Reidel.

Latour, B. (1987). *Science in action.* London: Open University Press.

13

Formal Tools and Medical Practices: Getting Computer-Based Decision Techniques to Work

Marc Berg
University of Maastricht, The Netherlands

Medical practice, in the eyes of many, is in bad shape. Physicians from different regions or different hospitals treat similar complaints in astonishingly varying ways, and many argue that this variability goes far beyond any rational basis (Eddy, 1990; Wennberg, 1984). Underlying these problems, it is argued, are some recurring obstacles. Physicians are drowning in an ever-increasing flow of information and are working in environments that are getting more and more complex. These high demands, so the reasoning often goes, are just too much for their limited cognitive abilities.[1]

To counter these variations, to ameliorate the quality of care and to prevent unnecessary waste of resources, many in and around the medical profession have argued for the implementation of decision support techniques. These tools would rationalize the practice of medicine without subordinating it to direct bureaucratic control. Protocols, computer-based decision tools, and decision analysis, these authors suggest, are the means by which medical practice can become fully scientific, so that the "encroaching control" from outside the medical profession (the government, insurance companies) will not be tempted to intrude further (Hornbein, 1986; Komaroff, 1982).

---

[1]On how this is a *specific* discourse see Berg (1995), which describes medicine's encounter with cognitive science: its new notions of and tools for problem solving and decision making.

This chapter looks at the development and implementation of one type of these tools: computer-based decision techniques.[2] These are tools that, given an array of medical data, attempt to make a diagnosis or decide on a therapy. Implicitly or explicitly, these tools want to supplant the physician's decision making with more thorough, more systematic, and less easily biased reasoning. They seek to do the work that allegedly goes on in physicians' minds when they make a decision and do it better (Berg, 1995; Lipscombe, 1989; Shortliffe et al., 1973). In focusing on the moment of decision, in merely taking control out of the physicians' hands at a single moment in time, these tools attempt to leave the whole wider context of the medical practice intact so as to constrain their freedom and room for flexibility as little as possible.

This chapter concentrates on two examples of such systems: ACORN, an expert system built in a London hospital, and the Leeds' acute abdominal pain system (de Dombal et al., 1972, 1990). The former system, in its present form, builds on logical, symbolic rules to decide whether emergency patients with chest pain need urgent admittance to the coronary care unit. The latter tool utilizes a statistical formula known as Bayes' Theorem to calculate the most probable diagnosis for acute abdominal pain, given a set of symptoms and signs.[3] The central questions posed here are: What happens when these tools are implemented in medical practices? How are these practices restructured? How is the tool itself reconstructed in these attempts at implementation? The materials consist mainly of interviews with the builders, hands-on experience with the systems, and literature dealing with these tools.[4]

First, the chapter provides a brief description of the construction of ACORN, the problems the designers encountered, and the solutions produced with which to deal with them. Subsequently, this case, interwoven with fragments of the Leeds' story, is used to discuss the questions already

---

[2]For a study also looking at decision analysis and protocols, see Berg (1997). "Computer-based decision tools" is just one of the many denotations these types of tools (or subcategories hereof) have been given over the years, and different authors will often use the same words in a different manner. Other terms include "expert systems," "intelligent systems," "knowledge-based systems," or "computer-supported decision-making tools." The tools focused on are tools that want to intervene in the medical decision process; not tools that, e.g., function as electronic medical textbooks.

[3]Bayes' Theorem is a way to calculate the (conditional) probability of a patient having a disease D given the presence of certain symptoms S: $P(D \mid S)$. Among others, one needs for this formula: the probability of the patient having the disease (disregarding symptoms), $P(D)$, and the (conditional) probability of having the symptoms given the disease $(P(S \mid D))$.

[4]The reasons for the selection of these two tools are manifold. In order to set up a meaningful argument, it was necessary to focus on tools that had at least partially succeeded to actually *function* in a medical practice—which thoroughly limits the available choice. Also, my interest in ACORN was triggered by a nicely reflexive article by its designers, concerning the practicalities of system design (Wyatt & Emerson, 1990).

raised. More specifically, the argument is made that implementation of computer-based decision tools always results in a transformation of the medical practices involved. Contrary to the ideal-typed views system builders often hold, these tools do not simply slip into a niche within a practice.[5] Rather, getting a computer-based tool to work involves continuous negotiations with all the various elements that constitute this practice—nurses, physicians, patients, but also laboratory tests, blood cells, and auscultatory sounds.[6] In these negotiations, designers try to adjust the practice to the requirements of their formal tool, which implies a disciplining of that particular practice to that formalism. Expert system builders, for instance, often mention that the medical domain for which the tool is built should be "somewhat formalized." A domain like dermatology, they state, is probably not ripe for decision tools because the "subtle differences in abnormalities of the skin [are often] incapable of verbal description." Hence, there is not enough information and there are no well-defined models for the system to deal with.[7] However, the formality of a domain is not an unalterable, given characteristic, but can be actively constructed. Moreover, this formalization is not limited to solely the nature of the medical problem: The process stretches itself out over all disparate elements involved.

Just as this transformation of practices is an inevitable result of the introduction of a decision tool, the tool itself is modified in this process as well. Inescapably, tools that work have had to give up much of the original, ideal typed ideals about the power, range, and universality of the tool. Many tools appear to work only in one specific medical practice instead of in a universal range of practices; other tools end up confining themselves to a very small part of the spectrum of medical problems they may have wanted to address. This is called the *localization* of the tool: the functional "shrinking" of its potential universality—whether in space, scope, and/or rationale. Avoiding localization implies increasing the disciplining to the formalism; but, in an unruly world of medical practices, designers never succeed in exerting enough control. Thus, localization is a widespread and inescapable phenomenon, continually thwarting attempts to spread the usage of these tools over broader terrains.[8]

---

[5]For an excellent discussion of these views, see Forsythe (1993a, 1993b). See also Kaplan (1987).

[6]Sounds heard through a stethoscope.

[7]Consult Szolovits and Long (1982); cf. Schwartz, Patil, and Szolovits (1987); Engle (1992); and de Dombal (1990). For an introductory discussion of the notion of "formal systems" in the context of artificial intelligence, see Haugeland (1985).

[8]In this chapter, the focus is primarily on the process of *getting* a system to work, not so much on the actual work of medical personnel with the tools. For studies on systems-in-use, see, e.g., Gasser (1986), Button (1993), and Berg (1997).

Finally, this chapter touches on two paradoxes that this analysis shows to be an innate part of computer-based decision tools. First, these systems will not do away with the medical practice variations so deplored by many, rather, they will add to this variety. Second, in the need to discipline a broad range of elements to the formal tool, the computer-based techniques fundamentally drift away from the ideal-typed promise they entail: the single-moment intervention.

The heterogeneous nature of the processes depicted here is stressed. So, this chapter speaks of *negotiations* with nurses and laboratory tests, and mentions physicians, electrocardiography (ECG) machines, and auscultatory sounds as being the *spokespersons* for the heart. This terminology, which may be odd to readers unfamiliar with some of the recent studies of science and technology (see, e.g., Bijker & Law, 1992; Clarke & Fujimura, 1992; Latour, 1987, 1988; Law, 1991),[9] is an attempt to keep a *symmetrical* perspective. One of the central tenets of recent science and technology studies is that the development of a technology cannot be properly understood from perspectives that treat nature and society as separate realms, and confine explanatory power to either one of them. Just what the disciplining of a practice, or the localization of a tool, exactly means can never be understood from standpoints centering merely on, for example, the nature of a medical problem or, conversely, the actions of medical personnel. Rather, the physical and social aspects of computerized medical practices are the *outcome* of the historically contingent events that have led to their current configuration. By treating them symmetrically it will be possible to gain an understanding of the success or failure of decision support techniques. Only by focusing on the way these heterogeneous networks take shape and break down will it be possible to come to terms with the fundamental issues at stake in the production and use of technical systems in (medical) practices (Bowker, 1994; Suchman, 1994).

THE STORY OF ACORN

Acute chest pain patients form a well-known problem for U.K. emergency department personnel. Decisions about whether or not such a patient needs urgent admittance to a coronary care unit (CCU) must be made quickly based on limited information. CCU beds are scarce and expensive,

---

[9]On the importance of these perspectives for research on medical practices, see Berg (1992) and Berg and Casper (1995). The main arguments of this chapter are strongly inspired by Star (1989, 1991), Bowker and Star (1994), Bowers (1992), Woolgar (1991), Latour (1987, pp. 177–257), and Callon (1991). Also, the work of Collins (1990) is important here—although, in a fundamental way, his perspective lacks the symmetry argued for here (see, e.g., the discussions in Pickering, 1992). Similarly, in, e.g., Kling and Scacchi (1982), Kling and Iacono (1984), and Kling (1991), many similar points can be found.

so unnecessary admissions should be kept to a minimum. On the other hand, delaying a needed admission can be a matter of life and death. Acute myocardial infarct, dysrhythmias, and unstable angina all have a high early mortality rate. For these patients, the benefit of being treated in a CCU is greatest in the first few hours after an attack.

Delays and erroneous decisions, however, often occur in emergency departments. Emerson et al. (1989) found that in a series of 604 patients attending their emergency department with chest pain, 14 (11.8% of those requiring admission to the CCU) were erroneously discharged. Furthermore, 32 patients were admitted unnecessarily (16% of all patients not requiring admission).[10] Finally, the median time that patients who were admitted to the CCU spent waiting in the emergency department was no less than 78 minutes! There appeared, Wyatt (1989) noted, "to be a role for a decision-aid that could rapidly process relevant information about a chest pain patient, and help casualty staff to solve the urgent problem: Should a patient be Admitted to the CCU OR Not?" (p. 97). Emerson, who worked in this emergency department as a chest physician, started to think of a computerized decision tool to help nurses make these decisions.[11] His previous experience with decision analytic methods led him toward the set-up of a Bayesian tool, similar to the already well-known acute abdominal pain system in Leeds. Fed with clinical data gathered by nurses, it would make a diagnostic decision relevant in selecting further steps of action.

A first problem, however, was immediately encountered. Which data items would be used? They had to be either examinations nurses could perform, or questions the nurse could ask the patient.[12] Emerson set out to ask some of his experienced colleagues (all physicians) which items they would deem relevant. The three lists of items gathered in this way,

---

[10]Judgments about the "real" necessity of admission to the CCU were made retrospectively, by letting two experienced physicians review all relevant information (including information on what happened after the decision to admit had been made).

[11]As Wyatt told me in an interview (February 2, 1994), Emerson had been thinking of building a system like ACORN for some time already. The first few paragraphs of "ACORN's story," as depicted here, constitute an "origin myth" that could easily be told otherwise (it could be argued, as Wyatt did, that the program started out to reduce the number of tests done in the emergency department). The problem, however, is that *each* alternative could be told otherwise—such is the nature of origin myths. Because all the issues mentioned did, at some stage, play an important role, and the arguments of the chapter are not dependent on the specific origin myth chosen, I chose to keep the first paragraphs of the story more or less as Wyatt (1989) recounted it.

[12]"Could," here, implies not just the ability to gather the item, but also the legal and professional issues involved. Nurses, for instance, could not be given the responsibility to judge an ECG report—something that, in practice, experienced nurses often do much better than junior physicians (see, e.g., Hughes, 1988). On the skill of ECG reading, see Hartland (1993b).

however, were often in conflict with each other. There was widespread opinion about how significant different symptoms and signs were. "If an attempt had been made to build a system from the collected personal constructs of this group of experts," Wyatt and Emerson (1990) stated, "the resulting repertory grid would have defied all known methods of analysis" (p. 70). Through a first rough selection as to their expected importance and ease of collection, this list was cut down to 54 items: forty-five questions on the history and the characteristics of the pain and "nine simple nursing observations about pulse rate and rhythm, temperature, blood pressure and the general appearance of the patient" (Emerson et al., 1988, p. 38). In February 1984, a questionnaire containing these items was drawn up to collect data from presenting patients complaining of chest pain.

Using this list, a database of some 400 patients was created. Analysis of this database soon made it clear that many of the physicians' insights were not reliable. Compared with statistically determined powers of discrimination, the physicians often overestimated the relevance of isolated signs and symptoms. They would attach much weight to the type and the duration of pain, while the statistically measured predictive value of these items for a cardiac condition requiring admission to the CCU appeared to be very low. Also, many data items suggested by the physicians could not be used, because the nurses were not able to elicit them consistently. Many questions seen as relevant by the doctors failed this requirement: A question like "is the pain sharp in nature?" was found to have a repeatability of only 66%. (*Repeatability* was measured by the mean percentage agreement between a first and a second elicitation of the data item; in the case of a yes/no question, of course, 50% repeatability is expected by chance.) Finally, the large number of items ran counter to the original goal of the system: Having to ask 45 questions in addition to 9 investigations was not very helpful in reducing delays!

To deal with these problems, the designers set out to curtail the item list. By eliminating those items that either had statistically low predictive values and/or could not reliably be collected, they managed to reduce the number of items to 22. With these 22 items, a Bayesian formula (see note 3) was devised. It then appeared that an additional 10 items could be dropped without any relevant impact on the outcomes of the Bayesian analysis, which left the final number of items at 12. Figure 13.1 schematizes the setup of the system at this point.

Now, however, Emerson and his coworkers ran into another critical difficulty: The tool did not work. Using patient data from the database, it appeared that this "simple Bayesian approach failed to produce a viable decision aid, because over 30% of patients fell into a middle probability band between the 'Send home' and 'Admit to CCU' thresholds" (Hart &

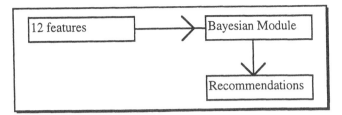

FIG. 13.1. The structure of an early version of ACORN.

Wyatt, 1989, p. 116).[13] Moreover, ACORN would sometimes suggest clearly impermissible actions, such as sending a patient home who, to the nurse, looked very ill and in shock.

It was concluded that "a system based on probabilities alone was not sufficiently accurate and that additional symbolic rules were needed to complement the Bayesian analysis" (Emerson et al., 1988, p. 38). This hybrid system started out like the first version did, that is, by processing the list of 12 indicators with Bayes' Theorem. It decided whether the probability of the current case being a high-risk cardiac was either low, middle, or high. Subsequently, a small expert system, containing some 200 rules, processed up to 12 further clinical features, including the item on the "general appearance of the patient." This analysis would result in one of the following advices:

1. Admit to the CCU immediately as a case of acute ischemic heart disease. No further investigation required.
2. Classification as a noncardiac case not requiring an ECG (with a recommendation about whether or not to order a chest X-ray). (The ECG yields diagnostic information as to the rhythm of the heart, and as to whether, e.g., the heart seems to be ischemic.)
3. Do an ECG (in those patients in whom the computer had insufficient information to decide on either options 1 or 2).

When the last advice was given, the nurse performed an ECG, had the doctor interpret it, and went back to ACORN to put this information in as well. In Fig. 13.2, the structure of ACORN as it looked at this point is outlined.

This system, then, was installed on the department and tested to see whether it would be of help to the nurses. To the disappointment of the system designers, however, three new, serious problems emerged. First, ACORN performed poorly. It had a false-positive rate of 19% and a false-negative rate of 11.8%, which is far too high to be an acceptable decision

---

[13]A test set of 133 patients had been kept apart from the set with which the Bayesian formulae had been devised.

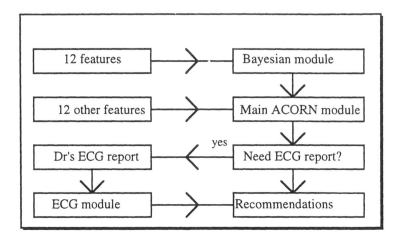

FIG. 13.2. The structure of the hybrid ACORN. Adapted from Wyatt (1989).
Copyright © 1989 by Elsevier. Adapted with permission.

aid.[14] Also, the nurses often did not use the system immediately. When they finally entered the data, they had often already made the important decisions. Third, the nurses complained that the system was too complex and told them to do things they were not allowed to do. For example, to admit a patient to the coronary care unit is formally a doctor's job.

The designers, confronted with these problems, made some fundamental changes to the system. First of all, they decided that a main reason for all the problems mentioned was the fact that the program still tried to accomplish too complex a task. It was trying to do too much with a relatively limited set of data. For example, ACORN tried to figure out whether pneumonia of pulmonary infarct was likely to be the cause of the chest pain—in which case it would ask for an X-ray. As Wyatt and Emerson came to realize, however, they "could not get anywhere near accurate diagnosis of noncardiac pain with the items used" (personal interview with Emerson, July 21, 1993). They decided to limit themselves solely to the question of whether the patient could have a cardiac condition requiring acute admission to the CCU. A more general approach to the problem of acute chest pain, they felt, was not feasible.

Closely linked to this modification was the decision to stop trying to determine whether or not a patient needed an ECG. "It was more and more becoming practice to do an ECG on virtually anybody with chest pain," Emerson noticed (interview). Moreover, incorporating the ECG results from the very beginning would speed up the process that, as

---

[14]A false positive rate of 19% indicates that of all patients who did not have a cardiac condition requiring acute admission, 19% were nevertheless admitted.

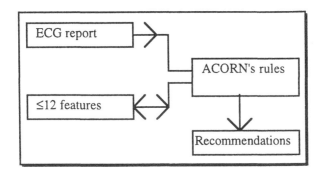

FIG. 13.3. The final structure of ACORN.

already described, sometimes involved two separate sessions with the system.

To make this change feasible, however, another main problem had to be tackled. ACORN's builders found that the delay and inaccuracy of ACORN's advice was primarily due to the fact that the ECG depended on physicians. Because their reading was often both inaccurate and late, the designers decided to eliminate this dependency. Instead, an automated ECG interpreting machine was installed, which provided "more accurate ECG reports within seconds" (Wyatt & Emerson, 1990). The nurse now had to take an ECG, answer ACORN's questions on the ECG, and then subsequently answer up to 12 questions on the history, symptoms, and signs. By now, Wyatt had left the team, and Emerson had completely abandoned the probabilistic part of their system; it now solely consisted of symbolic rules (the schematic outline of the new ACORN is shown in Fig. 13.3).

Other changes were made as well. Because part of the delay was caused by the computer's being too slow and located in a separate room, ACORN's ease of use and mobility was improved by installing the program on a fast laptop PC fixed to a trolley with wheels. Finally, it was decided that the 13 advice options originally provided by ACORN "did not fit in with the nurses' 'triage' system." Suggestions to perform additional tests and conclusions about possible diagnoses appeared to be too elaborate. They were reduced to three: "admit urgently," "see the doctor soon," and "wait in the queue to see the doctor." The designers furthermore arranged that a new policy was formally agreed on: When ACORN advised the nurses to do so, they could admit a patient to the CCU without the intervention of doctors.[15]

---

[15]Since these alterations have been implemented, the system has been on and off the ward continually. Emerson has since then mainly been working on a direct link between the ECG interpreting machine and ACORN: Until recently, nurses had to interpret the ECG machine's statements, and type a summary into ACORN.

DISCIPLINING THE PRACTICE TO THE FORMALISM

The introduction of a technology into an existing practice is a process of continual *negotiations*. ACORN is not a wholly malleable object, accommodating all the idiosyncracies of this emergency department. Rather, ACORN contains specific notions of what nurses, for example, are and are not allowed to do, and which patients' signs are and are not relevant. In other words, ACORN has an inscribed *script* delineating who or what the relevant elements in the involved practice are and what their respective roles consist of (Akrich, 1992; Akrich & Latour, 1992). When a technology such as ACORN is introduced, the originally inscribed script may be challenged by any of the heterogeneous elements it affects. In the negotiations that follow, these elements, including the technology itself, can all be transformed.

So, the *nurses*, at first, did not subscribe to ACORN's script: In the first field test they often did not use the tool. The tool had to be modified so that it was made more mobile and gave less elaborate advice. Moreover, the designers arranged an official redelegation of responsibilities between physicians, ACORN, and nurses: Now, when ACORN told them so, nurses no longer had to call on physicians to admit a patient to the CCU.

The *physician-experts* could also challenge ACORN's script. From the outset, the designers had realized that the functioning of ACORN would be impossible without their backing. These doctors, after all, had to formally endorse the system's decisions. In order to gain and sustain this support, they were among the first consulted in the project, and thus strongly shaped the form ACORN would take. When these experts began expecting routine ECG's from all emergency department patients complaining of chest pain, the designers had little choice but to adapt ACORN to these changed circumstances.

As a last example, it was of course vital to the successful incorporation of ACORN that the *patient's chests* conformed to ACORN's script. If ACORN too frequently sent healthy hearts to the CCU and returned ischemic hearts home, it would be a failure. The chests, however, did not speak for themselves: A host of medical data were the elements that spoke for them.[16] These at first made the creation of ACORN seemingly impossible. They were too numerous, they spoke contradictory voices, and often spoke too indistinctly (or too late, in the case of the ECG) for the nurses to hear them clearly. Again, subtle negotiations took place between the nurses, ACORN, the physicians, and the data. To make ACORN possible in the first place, the list of items had to be cut down. In order not to lose

---

[16]See Latour (1987) for the notion of "spokesperson." See also the last paragraph of the introduction.

the physicians in the process, ACORN kept the list of medical data cited by them as its central core. Subsequently, using statistical techniques, those data items that spoke most clearly and uniformly were selected; and, at one point, all items dealing with noncardiac diagnosis were thrown out. Finally, in order to keep the nurses' role feasible, those data items that spoke too indeterminately were thrown out, and the ECG interpretation was delegated to a machine.

In the implementation of a decision tool, thus, the practice within which the technique becomes embedded is thoroughly transformed. ACORN's designers, in introducing their tool in this emergency department, did not restrict themselves to working solely on their tool. They redesigned the department's practice as well.[17] They tinkered with the department's elements in order to accommodate them to the needs of the tool. They skipped all the data items that were not usable as elementary data items, and introduced an automated ECG interpreting machine to get rid of the noise introduced by the doctor's late and inaccurate ECG readings. They drilled the nurses to use the machine before making the important decisions, and restructured the department's work policy so that nurses, when told to do so by ACORN, could admit patients without first having to consult a physician.

These changes are not arbitrary. Like other decision support techniques, computer-based decision tools are formal tools. They operate using a collection of specific, explicit rules—whether statistical (as in a Bayesian system) or symbolic (as in an expert system). In ACORN's case, feeding in the requested patient features generates a piece of advice; in the Leeds' acute abdominal pain system, the input of some 30 data items results in a diagnosis. Being a formal system has several consequences. First, formal systems require a well-defined set of clear-cut, elementary bits of information as their *input*. Whether the rules are statistical or symbolic, an input data item must at all times match a possible starting point contained in the rules. The current version of ACORN, for example, asks the question, "what is the site of the pain?" It then draws 14 little puppets on the screen, each with a different shaded area over their chests. The nurse should select *one*. Actually, you cannot do otherwise: The program will not proceed until you have done so. There is no room for "it is between this one and this one" because ACORN has no rules to deal with that—it can only deal with these 14 different answers. Moreover, ACORN also imposes a definite set of input items, and a definite sequence in which they are to be obtained. The ECG comes first, for example, and, without an ECG, ACORN does nothing.

---

[17]Hence the term *heterogeneous engineering*, coined by Law (1987).

Second, the *output* of formal systems is predefined within the rules. Generally, a system will contain a circumscribed set of prefixed statements, from which it selects one or several. So, ACORN's final advice always consisted of one of at most 13 possibilities.[18] A seemingly innocent consequence of this feature is that, at all times, all possible outputs must be feasible in the practice in which the tool is positioned. If, for example, one of the output statements requires the performance of an additional test that is not available in that particular setting, the system is useless. Similarly, users have to be drilled to act on the advice, and to do so in the way intended by the designers. The hybrid version of ACORN contained, as one outcome, the advice to obtain an ECG. When the users of the system always already do that, however, the whole purpose of the tool becomes meaningless.

A formal system, thus, requires disciplined users to enter well-defined input, and expects the practice to be able to live up to the predefined output statements. In addition to these demands, the script of a formal tool also requires a certain stability in the relations between the data items used as input and the content of the statements generated as output. A data item like "the location of the pain" is only of use if it can be linked, through one or several rules, to one of the output statements the system contains. If the location of the pain has no relation whatsoever with the cause of abdominal pain, then it is obviously senseless to include it in the Leeds' data item list. Also, a data item is useless if, for example, the existence of a relation is dependent on a host of contingent factors. For example, a data item like "blood pressure" can be linked to the cause of the pain. A large myocardial infarct, for instance, often reduces the blood pressure. On the other hand, stress can increase blood pressure, and so can many other circumstances. In such a situation, an item like "blood pressure" cannot be used by a formal system because it does not behave predictably enough. No unequivocal rule can be designed that links this item in a meaningful way to one of the possible output statements. Similarly, to build a system like ACORN, the question of whether the patients can enter the CCU cannot depend on too many contingent circumstances. Whether the CCU is full or is expected to be full, whether the patients want to be admitted, or whether patients live near another hospital where they would preferably be sent to cannot be too important. If many such contingent considerations could play a role, then there would

---

[18]Not all formal systems contain a prefixed list of statements as their outcome. Decision analysis does not: There, the outcome is a set of numbers, generated through the application of the decision analytic method on the input data (see, e.g., Weinstein et al., 1980). The outcome is just as much predefined within the rules, however: It is *always* a similar set of numbers.

again be no way to link the input data items with the possible advices given as output.[19]

All in all, a formal system carries a script requiring many of the diverse elements constituting the practice to behave in a uniform, stable, and predictable way. It is not only the "nature of the clinical problem" that has to be well-defined, as many system-builders argue.[20] It is not just a matter of finding a group of diseases with clear-cut symptoms and explicit criteria for deciding on diagnosis and therapy. It is a whole, hybrid practice that has to be sufficiently docile—including the nurses, physicians, the data items, and the organizational routines.

Moreover, as ACORN's story makes clear, whether a practice is disciplined enough for the tool to work is not a prefixed, given fact. In the active "redescription" of ACORN's emergency department practice, many heterogeneous elements were transformed to make their behavior definite, uniform, and predictable enough for the formal system ACORN to work. A sufficiently disciplined practice, here, was an *actively achieved accomplishment*. The patients' chests were no longer represented by vague terms as "such and such type of pain," or equivocal ECG interpretations. Rather, the input was "digitized" through obtaining direct input from the ECG interpreting machine and forcing the nurse to select one of a small number of preset answers at each question.[21] The chests now spoke a language a formal system can deal with. Similarly, the nurses had to be disciplined to use the system properly and were taught how to translate patients' complaints into the signs and symptoms required by ACORN. Finally, the department's organization was restructured so that the physicians no longer had a say in the admittance decision—thus circumventing, again, this group of actors who were apparently not easily controlled.

Similarly, to ensure suitable input, the group from Leeds introduced a specific form "in which the patient's case history could be to some extent 'formalized' " (Horrocks et al., 1972, see appendix). Through this form,

---

[19]On similar issues in MYCIN, see, e.g., Lipscombe (1991). And, see Davis et al. (1977), who, in discussing MYCIN's rulebase, states that a domain should have "a limited sort of interaction between conceptual primitives." If more than six clauses start appearing in the premises of a rule, the "premise becomes conceptually unwieldy." In other words, when too many factors can impinge on a relation between a data item and, say, a given outcome, these relations become practically infeasible. Similarly, he argued, it is needed that "the presence or absence of each of those factors can be established without adverse effect on the others," otherwise the results will "depend on the order in which the evidence is collected" (pp. 116–117). MYCIN, the most well-known medical expert system, has never functioned in medical practice (Buchanan & Shortliffe, 1984; Lipscombe, 1991).

[20]See note 7.

[21]Collins (1990) describes the "digitization" of the input and "interpretation" and "repair" of the output of formal tools that is necessary for such tools to actually work in a concrete practice. See also Star (1989, 1991) and Gasser (1986) on the "invisible work" needed to keep such tools going.

they forced the investigating physicians to enter their findings in the required "structured and well-defined" way (de Dombal, 1990). This also implied another requirement secured through the form: All the data items had to be entered at the same time. The physicians could not fool around with this demand, because they had to hand over the form to a research assistant. Only then would the form be encoded and sent to the main computer. Similarly, the cooperating physicians had to be trained so that they would all mean the same thing when stating that, for example, the pain was "severe." Without adequate forms and training, they found the observer variation to be far too large for any computer-based decision tool to work with. In a study where three physician observers witnessed one clinician interviewing a patient, "the three observers were unable to agree in 20.4% of circumstances as to whether or not a particular question was asked. [Moreover, they] were unable to agree in 16.4% of instances as to whether the patients answer was positive or negative" (Gill et al., 1973, p. 110). As de Dombal's team stated, it took new staff "some six to eight weeks during which the personnel familiarised itself with the terminology" and during which "the system performed much poorer" (de Dombal & Gremy, 1976, p. 155; cf. Horrocks et al., 1976; Wilson et al., 1977).[22]

In the implementation of these tools, thus, the involved practices were disciplined to the formalisms in which they were represented. The networks of elements constituting these practices were made sufficiently "tight" for the tools to function (Callon, 1991). Now this argument should not be understood as if the disciplining of practices so as to "fit" with the tool in question is solely the active work of system builders. This is obviously not the case: These local networks are, after all, not independent of other, intermeshed practices. Developments as increasing bureaucracy, standardization efforts, the increasing usage of uniformly packaged technologies, increasing computerization of laboratories, and so on, all also converge in the process of making practices more amenable for tools as described here (cf. Bowker, 1994; Bowker & Star, 1994; Fujimura, 1992; O'Connell, 1993). Also, the term *disciplining* should not be seen as a condemnation of this process. Through this disciplining of nurses, for

---

[22]As with ACORN, it was an interwoven, heterogeneous assembly that needed disciplining. De Dombal's tool, for example, could not work with data items that took time to gather. Like Emerson's ACORN, this tool dealt with emergency situations: Data items could only be used if they could be collected and entered quickly. Unlike Emerson's team, however, de Dombal and his coworkers worked with physicians doing the investigation. So, more physical examination items could be used. Also, it appeared that with these data items, enough stable relations could be drawn to cover the great majority of acute abdominal pain patients coming to the emergency ward. Here again, it was only through training the physicians, introducing specifically developed forms and hiring research assistants that they were able to do so. Here again, thus, the tool could only work due to the disciplining of a very diverse and entangled range of elements.

example, their responsibilities may be enhanced; through the implementation of this tool, physicians may be relieved of some duties they did not really like. Similarly, this disciplining of the nurses relieves them of a prior form of discipline involving, among others, having to find a doctor for each and every admittance decision (cf. Kling, 1991).

Disciplining a practice to a formalism, thus, is neither a purely local affair, nor an easy one to judge. Similarly, not all attempts to adjust the practices to these tools were successful. In many instances, the designers' control over several of the practices' elements did not go far enough. In the case of ACORN, some data items might have been highly relevant to the physicians, but when the nurses cannot be taught to elicit them reliably, such items are not the required stable input items a formal system requires. Also, with this limited set of data items, the designers were not able to let ACORN distinguish among different noncardiac causes of chest pain. The relations between items such as "the location of the pain" or "the nature of the pain" and the noncardiac afflictions were neither strong nor stable enough to make meaningful conclusions feasible.[23] Finally, the designers did not succeed in transforming the local practice so that all 13 advice options of the hybrid ACORN would become meaningful. The physicians were willing to give up their authority when it came to the decision of whether or not to admit patients. They would not, however, allow the system to judge the necessity of an ECG. Neither were the nurses very happy with all these actions that were ordinarily seen as typically medical decisions—and thus not their responsibility. The control of ACORN's designers over these groups was just not strong enough to ensure appropriate niches in the practice for all 13 possible output statements.

LOCALIZATION: "ONE STARTS WITH GREAT EXPECTATIONS"[24]

Implementing formal tools like ACORN or the Leeds tool, thus, implies a disciplining of the medical practices involved. This disciplining of the *practice*, however, is but one side of the coin. The continous negotiations during the process of constructing and implementing the technique result in a *tool* that is thoroughly *localized*. Localization points to the double meanings of that term: The tool's functional universality diminishes, and the tool becomes more and more particular. Localization occurs in one or more of three (often intertwined) ways: in *space*, *scope*, and *rationale*.

---

[23]I am not arguing that no system could do so. Rather, the point is that *in this specific practice*, with this set of data items available, this local population of patients, this group of nurses, etcetera, it was not feasible.

[24]Interview with Emerson 7/21/93.

First, a tool can become *localized in space*. The script of the final ACORN can be read as reflecting the continual need to "give in" to local needs in order to get ACORN incorporated in the emergency department. ACORN uses rules and data items elicited from local experts (and then again only those items elicitable by local nurses, with locally available techniques, and speaking for local hearts[25]), its advice is adjusted to local customs, and so forth. Localization in space is a process that already starts at the first conception of the technique and continues well after its introduction into practice. Even after implementation, local routines may develop that do not necessarily correspond with the intended operation of the tool (Button, 1993; Gasser, 1986; Wynne, 1988).

A system can become so thoroughly imbued with specifically local idiosyncrasies that it can only work at that one site. In fact, this is what has happened to most computer-based decision tools. Only very few have moved beyond the limits of the practice in which they were developed. The large majority of computer-based decision tools are, like ACORN, in operation (if they are at all) in just one location. Now, no attempt had at the time of this writing been made to export ACORN to another hospital, so whether this could be done remains an open question. When asked about this possibility, Emerson sighed and remarked that "the situation would obviously be very different in other hospitals. I do not particularly feel the need to put such a lot of time in that. It wouldn't just 'work'; you would need a lot of effort to reset the whole thing" (personal interview, July 21, 1993). De Dombal's acute abdominal pain tool, on the other hand, is one of the very few tools that has succeeded in doing so. Focusing on this tool sheds light on what this effort amounts to.

A first phenomenon de Dombal and his coworkers continually ran into is that "databases don't travel" (personal interview with de Dombal, July 18, 1993). Their system calculates the probability of a given patient having disease X by drawing on a database listing past patients' symptoms and diagnoses (see note 3). Every time the system is implemented in a different hospital, de Dombal stated, you need to check whether the computer still performs as well as it did in Leeds—and usually it does not. When they tested the system in a Swedish hospital, for example, the computer's

---

[25]This may sound somewhat cryptic, but the statistical method by which the design builders selected the "powerful" from the "weak" data was based on a database containing only a selection of the *local* population of "patients with chest pain coming to this emergency ward." In other words, the same symptoms and signs might have very different statistical weights in different settings. That this is a very concrete problem is clear from the efforts of Bayesian system builders like de Dombal. Time after time again these authors find that a Bayesian system, working with a database generated in, say, Leeds, will function much more poorly when transported to, say, a city in Sweden (Fenyo et al., 1987; Horrocks et al., 1976; see also further).

accuracy dropped from 80% to 50%. The reasons for this phenomenon are manifold. For one, it often happens that a different *type* of patient is encountered. Sometimes, for example, the system is located in an emergency department, whereas elsewhere it is installed on the surgery ward. One difference between these locations is that on the former department, patients can just walk in, whereas on the latter all patients have been referred by a physician. This preselection thoroughly affects the prior probabilities: The referring physician will have stopped many nonserious cases of acute abdominal pain from entering the ward. Therefore, the chances of such a patient having acute appendicitis on a surgery ward are much higher than in an emergency department. Also, de Dombal and his coworkers encountered huge terminological differences between regions. Different areas appeared to use completely different definitions of acute abdominal pain. Some included urological patients, and others did not.[26] Similarly, while introducing the system elsewhere, different forms had to be designed, symptoms had to be carefully defined, and physicians had to be trained anew to ensure that in saying "the pain is colicky" they would mean the same thing as the Leeds' doctors had been taught to do. Finally, in some cases, the presentation of some diseases seemed to vary between places. Pancreatitis, for example, behaved very differently in Copenhagen than in Leeds, which caused the Leeds' program to falter (Bjerregaard et al., 1976; Fenyo et al., 1987; Horrocks et al., 1976; cf. Mol & Law, 1994).

But it is not just a matter of nontransferable databases. Other problems arise due to different organizational configurations. Consider, for example, the following remarks, made by a physician about the difference between the system in a surgical ward (Airedale) and in an emergency department (Leeds, where this physician worked). He pointed at the myriad detailed organizational features that all inhibit smooth transfer from one location to the next:

> The constraints of using the system are, compared to Airedale, not as strict here. [The form] is not part of the patient file, for example. They have to seperately pick up the form here; they can very well do without it. These

---

[26]When asked about the definition of acute abdominal pain, de Dombal replied in 1976: "Of course everybody else has their own definition, and this may differ from place to place. At the moment, we don't even know what these differences are—but we must certainly find out" (de Dombal & Gremy, 1976, p. 174). In building computer-based decision tools, many authors have come up against this issue as a hindrance to their goals (cf. Barnett, 1968; Lusted, 1968). De Dombal (1989) illustrates the persistance of this problem: As the first "obstacle to progress, [standing] in the way of widespread implementation," he mentioned the lack of clear medical terminology (p. 14). "Medical questions and answers have to be simplified, pre-defined, and agreed in advance by wide consensus," he argues (cf. Gill et al., 1973).

are different worlds, the ward at Airedale, and the emergency department here. There is no one standard way of implementing the system. At Airedale, physicians have 10–20 minutes to talk with each patient. Plenty of time. Here, five minutes, and you've got to make a decision. It's a mess here. You can't find the form, what do you do? You've got to deal with the patients; it's so much more hectic in a place like this.

The problems described here recur time and time again. In an introduction to a volume on computer-assisted medical decision making, Reggia and Tuhrim (1985) called this issue "the unresolved question of transferability of a successful system from its initial development site to other geographically distant locations." They continued, "[t]his is more than the usual problem of physical portability of a program: it also involves resolving differences in medical definitions, varying standards of practice, and differences in patient populations" (p. 35). Shortliffe, Buchanan, and Feigenbaum (1979) referred to the differences in standards of practice when they criticized a system built by Bleich (1972): Its " 'Bleich-in-the-Box' feature," they argued, hindered widespread acceptance.

Constructing a feasible, workable decision support tool always implies that *the local context is built into the technique.* Inevitably, idiosyncratic, unique features of the specific site involved become embedded in the tool's script. As the example of de Dombal's tool shows, however, combating localization in space is possible—but it requires much additional work. Swedish physicians had to be trained to adapt the same terminology and investigational techniques as their Leeds colleagues, organizational setups had to be screened or altered, emergency department physicians had to be enticed to use the system as their surgery ward colleagues. Also, much larger, international databases have been gathered to ensure their validity across regions—albeit with varying success.[27]

This latter issue points at the intricate relation between the processes of disciplining the medical practice to the formalism representing it and the localization of the tool. To overcome this type of localization, additional disciplining is needed.[28] Stable relations between data items and outcomes, now, have to stretch out over regions. Physicians in different

---

[27]Interview de Dombal, and see Ikonen et al. (1983), de Dombal (1988), Chatbanchai et al. (1989), and de Dombal et al. (1991).

[28]Bowker and Star (1994) argued a similar point brilliantly in their discussion of the International Classification of Diseases. Compare also Fujimura (1987, 1992), Star (1989, 1991), Star and Griesemer (1989), Kling and Scacchi (1982), and Webster (1991). Three studies of information technologies in medical domains that show (among others) the same phenomenon are Dent (1990), Saetnan (1991), and Bloomfield (1991). Finally, Lipscombe (1991) and Hartland (1993a) cover a whole range of different medical expert systems in which the phenomena of localization discussed in this section can be seen time and time again.

locales have to be trained to use the system and the involved terminology uniformly; organizational differences have to be flattened out. Similarly, when this disciplining fails, localization in space is one way to cope with this failure. As has already been pointed at, there were many instances in which de Dombal's team did not succeed in adjusting the practices to the requirements of widespread usage of their tool. In messy and complex practices such as hospital wards, control is never complete. Nurses, physicians, patients, and hospital administrators all have divergent viewpoints. All are unruly and undisciplined—just like the data items and the patients' afflictions. In those cases where this unruliness could not be overcome, de Dombal and his coworkers went back to their system and tinkered with its setup so that these problems would not result in the total breakdown of the project. Whenever they did not manage to flatten out the organizational differences between different locations, for example, they just created different tools for each different site.

In addition to this localization in space, tools can also become *localized in scope*. This occurs when a system limits its field of application to an increasingly small subset of tasks. This can mean, for example, that the range of disorders the system can handle is reduced, or that the scope of actions it can undertake is limited. In ACORN's practice, the designers did not succeed in incorporating noncardiac causes of chest pain. Also, the tool had to be made "less intelligent": The 13 detailed advice options were cut down to three. Here again, ACORN is quite typical of the overall category of computer-based decision tools. Within limited domains, it is frequently argued, such tools can work. "Skilled behavior" is seen in "many relatively well-constrained domains." However, "most serious clinical problems are . . . broad and complex," which causes the "plateau and cliff effect": "The program is outstanding on the core set of anticipated applications, but degrades rather ungracefully for problems just outside its domain of coverage" (Szolovits, 1982; Szolovits, Patil, & Schwartz, 1988, p. 15).[29] Increasing the scope, however, leads to problems: Unforeseen interactions among the rules appear, the system loses precision, or fails to function altogether. De Dombal's team repeatedly tried to enlarge the scope of their system beyond the small domain of acute abdominal pain to include, for instance, gynecological disorders, dyspepsia, or Crohn's disease. None of these attempts was very successful: The system would always perform much better with the added categories left out.[30]

---

[29]See for similar self-diagnoses of the "current state of the art" in computer-aided decision tools, for example, Miller and Masarie (1990) and Schwartz et al. (1987).

[30]See Wilson et al. (1977), and de Dombal interview. See for similar experiences, for example, Davis et al. (1977) and Engle (1992).

Like localization in space, localization in scope is a result of failing control. It is a matter of unruly, heterogeneous elements that cannot be brought in line with the system. It is never just a technical matter of the nature of clinical problems, as many decision support tool builders often state (cf. Forsythe, 1993b; see also Szolovits' remark quoted in the previous paragraph). It is not that ACORN failed in the realm of noncardiac causes of chest pain because of the inherent difficulty of that problem. The situation is both more complex and more mundane. If ACORN's designers had succeeded in arranging nurses to elicit additional data items (as, e.g., an X-ray, blood tests, or auscultatory sounds), it might have been possible to create a set of data items that could be used to distinguish between several pulmonary afflictions. This, however, was not feasible: The physicians would not let the nurses do these tasks, and the nurses themselves did not want them much either. Also, it would have taken additional time to gather these items, and it would have generated new problems like, for instance, how to turn X-ray interpretations (which are notoriously vague) into clear-cut, unequivocal pieces of input. All in all, the failure to increase the scope of a tool is thus as much a failure of *political*, or *social* control as it is a problem of the intractability of the relations between data items and disease categories. Including pulmonary diseases in ACORN would have required a stronger grip on nurses, physicians, on the interpretation of X-rays and on the links between test data and their implications, than was feasible in this place, at this time. In this sense, it was not so much a mysterious inherent difficulty in the nature of chest pain, as a *practical* failure to adequately constrain the closely intertwined, heterogeneous elements of this emergency department.[31]

The third and last type is *localization in rationale*. This occurs when the designers must agree to a setup in which the potential, ideal-typed precision, accuracy, or scientificity of the system is not realized. As in the previous types, localization in rationale inevitably occurs as a result of the ongoing negotiations during the development and implementation of a tool. Also, faltering attempts to formalize parts of the practice can be managed in this way. Again, ACORN provides examples of this phenomenon. When Emerson started out building his tool he was "a devoted Bayesian." He was interested in "rationalizing medicine"; in the "mathematical approach to decision making" (personal interview, July 21, 1993). Already when selecting the items, however, they had to give up some of this ideal. Potentially powerful data items had to be left out because the nurses either could not or would not elicit them. This "corruption" of the Bayesian ideal grew worse when they had to incorporate all kinds of

---

[31]See Evans (1990), who made an instructive comparison between the overall failure of AI in medicine and the troubles of "implementing" the new function of nurse-practitioner.

symbolic, ad hoc rules to prevent impermissible actions like sending patients home who looked gravely ill. Finally, Emerson and his coworkers abandoned the statistical ideal and embraced a clinical logic: ACORN's final version is a rule-based expert system in the classical sense.[32]

Likewise, in the case of de Dombal's tool, the limited scope led to the requirement that the physician should make the first selection: Is this patient suitable for the tool at all? This necessity for the subjective judgment of the physician is, of course, a pollution of the purity of the ideal of statistical inference. Also, over the years, de Dombal's tool has evolved toward a rather different philosophy. Some continually stress that the tool is not a decision maker. It is "just a test," or even only an educational tool; it yields nothing more than an indication as to what might be the case for a given patient. The decision itself is returned completely to the hands of the physician. From the perspective of the original Bayesian ideal, this is a complete capitulation: an invitation to let the painfully fought arbitrariness back in (de Dombal, 1991; de Dombal, Dallos, & McAdam, 1991).

Similar steps are being taken within the domain of rule-based expert systems. Many authors are abandoning the traditional artificial intelligence approach in favor of building tools that function more like electronic textbooks. The time of the 'Greek Oracle model' (Miller & Masarie, 1990) is over. No longer should individuals work on computers employing "seemingly superhuman reasoning capabilities to solve the physician's diagnostic problem" (p. 2), whereas the latter would be merely a "passive observer."[33] Here as well, the tool has stepped back from the claim that it outperforms the physician at the moment of decision. Here as well, the original ideal of mimicking and even ameliorating expert reasoning has been thoroughly watered down.

PARADOXES AND CHANGING PRACTICES

The previous two sections have described the intertwined processes of disciplining and localization. In the process of getting a decision support tool to work, both phenomena inevitably occur. The medical practice rewrites the tool's script and vice versa; the end result is a configuration in which both are mirrored within the other. The different types of localization (in space, scope, and rationale) can be fought through trying to strengthen control; through tightening the network of nurses, patients'

---

[32]On how this is a very *different* type of rationality, see Berg (1997).

[33]See also Miller et al. (1986), Barnett et al. (1987), and Lipscombe (1991). On this phenomenon as a broader trend, see, e.g., Perrolle (1991).

bodies, physicians, ECG machines, and so forth. The limits of the "formalizability" of a medical domain, thus, is not a preset given: It is a *moving frontier*, a place of struggle for control. On the other hand, it was shown that difficulties to adequately constrain the heterogeneous constituents of medical practices can be coped with by localizing the tool. In a formalized practice, what is legal and what is illegal behavior is clearly distinguished. Only some movements are allowed by the script; as Bowers (1992) phrased it, only "some orders or compositions can be realised or recognised in a particular formalism" (p. 242). When resistances occur, when illegal conduct (by either people or, e.g., laboratory tests) is too frequent and unamenable to correction, the tool can be tinkered with to save it from complete failure. By reducing the scope or the rationale of the tool, or by accomodating local idiosyncrasies in the tool's design, a project can survive.

The different types of localizations, of course, are not meant as an exhaustive set of mutually exclusive categories. Nevertheless, they allow the evolution of both individual and classes of decision support techniques to be viewed as attempts to avoid some type of localization—with the frequently occurring consequence that some other type of localization seeps in through the back door. ACORN's designers, for example, in statistically pruning the list of items generated by the physicians, can be said to have traded localization of its rationale with localization in space. In order to increase the predictive power of the data items used, the designers utilized a statistical technique that took into account only a very specific population: patients with chest pain coming to this specific emergency department. So, although they increased the accuracy of their tool, they simultaneously linked it more tightly to the local context of the specific emergency department with which they were dealing.

The remainder of the chapter draws attention to two final points, which directly touch the ideals of the decision support tool builders mentioned in the first section. First, computer-based decision tools do not do away with medical practice variations but, rather, tend to increase them. Second, the ideal-typed notion of a *single-moment intervention* is an illusion: Only through disciplining a broad array of elements can this pointlike mode of operation be achieved.

The First Paradox: Increasing Diversity

Implementing a computer-based decision tool, it was shown, involves the mutual transformation of the decision support technique and the practice in which it is incorporated. In this process, knowledges and decision-making strategies, embedded in the changing practice, also change—and in an idiosyncratic and intriguing way. Returning to the early, Bayesian version of ACORN, for example, shows how the creation of the data item list began as a list generated by physicians, which was subsequently cut down by checking the individual items' reliability in the hands of the nurses involved and by statistically determining their discrimination power. Through a subtle negotiating process between nurses, physicians, the physical capabilities of ACORN, the possibilities of the statistical techniques and the patients' hearts, a list of 24 items, with their mutual relations, was obtained. The knowledge incorporated in the department, including this new tool, was a compromise between the needs of the heterogeneous elements involved. The end result would have been a practice that comprised fundamentally incomprehensible decision strategies—from both a purely statistical or a purely clinical point of view. The computer, for instance, omitted questions deemed fundamental by clinicians (as to the nature of the pain). On the other hand, the statistical techniques were not invoked until the list of data items, which was created by questioning the clinicians, appeared too large. Moreover, the list of data items was cut down further by a very pragmatic requirement: the repeatability of the data item in the hands of nurses.

The ensuing logic of this practice is of a new, irreducible kind; an intricate mix of, among others, clinical and statistical logics. Similar mixes can be found in every situation in which a decision support tool has become part of a medical practice. The construction of ACORN's later, expert system version, for example, started out with a reduced version of the data item list already described, and worked from there. So, it began with building blocks that already formed an impure mixture. Moreover, the endless ad hoc cycles of refining the rules, debugging unwanted interrelations between them, altering the advice options, and so on, created a system that further distances the system from a simple "simulation" of physician's reasoning.[34] On the contrary, as the end result of the complex negotiations in the implementation of computer-based decision tools, there are practices that embed decision strategies unknown and unfathomable for any physician. Questions are omitted that would be deemed essential, and other data items take on relevancies unintelligible to doctors.

Tools championing a statistical logic, like Bayesian systems, as indicated, cannot escape this destiny either. Ongoing negotiations during construction and implementation strip all purity away. Statistical relations are neglected to ensure, for example, physician's cooperation; important predictive items cannot be used because the nurses cannot elicit them.

---

[34]Again, this is a phenomenon that can be seen time after time. For, e.g., MYCIN, see the wonderfully detailed book by Buchanan and Shortliffe (1984). On INTERNIST, another one of the Great Old Systems, see, e.g., Miller, Pople, and Myers (1982); Pople (1982); and Miller et al. (1986).

As a first conclusion, thus, it appears that in the practice of getting a computer-based decision tool to work, knowledges and decision strategies change beyond recognition. Different logics are mingled with each other and infused with a host of ad hoc alterations resulting from resistances encountered in the medical practices involved. This generation of idiosyncratic, impure logics, aside from being an intriguing phenomenon in itself, runs counter to the hopes and goals of those who want to "cleanse" medical practice of its problem of medical practice variations. Rather than cleansing medical practice of diversity, ACORN introduces a new, additional variety—an approach to patients with chest pain that is equivalent to no physician or practice anywhere else. Stated somewhat more generally, computer-based decision techniques do not do away with the heterogeneity of logics in medicine.[35] They do not bring the sound, unitary logic of science hoped for. Medical practice variations will not be abated through these tools. On the contrary, they introduce new logics, new rationalities, and thus continue, or even intensify, the multiplicity they started out to erase.

The Second Paradox: Disciplining a Practice to Produce a Single-Moment Intervention

As stated, computer-based decision tools contain an ideal of a single, discrete intervention. At the moment of decision, some type of mechanical inference (whether statistical or symbolic) should take over from the physician and replace the latter's imperfect decision-making capacities. The practice of medicine, in this perspective, is defined as essentially an individual, *cognitive* activity; decision making consists of the combination of bits of information and rules. Whatever happens outside of this realm, like the actual gathering of data or the administration of a selected therapy, is of secondary importance and need not be tampered with. In fact, it is an important claim that these issues should not be tampered with. As mentioned earlier, the computer-based decision tools scorn rigidity, and critique striving for standardization for its own sake. Rather than strangling the physician in bureaucratic webs, these tools want to intervene only and superbly at that single moment where they are most needed: the moment of decision.

It should be clear by now, however, that the introduction of computer-based decision tools inescapably entails that the heterogeneous elements of the involved medical practice be kept in check. In order to function, it was argued that these tools require that physicians, nurses, data items, and organizational routines all behave in definite, uniform, and predictable ways. This not only requires that "suitable clinical problems" be

---

[35]On this notion of logics, see Mol (1993) and Mol and Berg (1994).

selected. It is not enough that the "domain has attained a certain level of formalization so that judgmental rules can be written" (Davis, Buchanan, & Shortliffe, 1977, p. 116; cf. Szolovits, 1982, pp. 9–10; Shortliffe & Clancey, 1984). Rather, the latter requirement is inseparably interwoven with increasing restraints on the actions of nurses, physicians, and patients. Now, of course, it was the ambition of the computer-based decision tool builders to create formal systems that would not require such a disciplining of medical practices to these formalisms. Ideally, these authors hoped, the rules within the tools would become so fine grained and so all-encompassing that no disciplining would be necessary. The tool would smoothly slide into the practice, its input and output features articulating effortlessly and powerfully with the ongoing activity. This hope, however, has remained just that: an aspiration that, in the meantime, has lost most of its luster.[36] Meanwhile, all tools that have been constructed, whether or not they were ever implemented, have required their share of disciplining.

The computer-based tools discussed here take the reasoning process out of the hands of the physician and into their own realm. As Lipscombe described it, the practical control of the process of decision making is transferred to the machine (Lipscombe, 1989, 1991). As discussed earlier, this realm remains fundamentally unintelligible to the physician dealing with the tool. The doctor, thus, really has no choice but to either accept the tight lead offered by the tool, or to abandon the tool altogether. In addition, the tool often simply does not allow for shortcuts and unforeseen situations. Physicians are presented with a prefixed series of questions to which they must enter predefined input. And if, for example, they can get away with not or partly answering a question, they have no way of estimating the consequences. The tool's rationale is hidden within a literally opaque, black box. Moreover, the whole process of interaction with the tool is unidirectionally geared toward the single-moment intervention; due to the "plateau and cliff effect," any deviation in the route toward this moment might push the system inadvertently off course.

Paradoxically, thus, these tools, in order to generate a one-moment intervention, require the disciplining of a much broader realm of activities. It could be said that their failure to live up to their ideal projects outward into the surrounding practices. To compensate for the inner limitations

---

[36]For a harsh insiders' critique, see Sutherland (1986). For convincing and far-reaching arguments why this ideal is misguided at heart, see Dreyfus' classical work (1992), and Collins (1990); both (in interestingly different ways) taking issue with the fundamental question of what computers can and cannot do. Lipscombe (1991) argued a similar point as Collins for the field of medical expert systems. In a somewhat different vein, the excellent work of Suchman (1987) and Lave (1988) shows how human action and even "cognition" cannot be "captured" by the formal rules and symbolic logic so fundamental to both cognitive psychology and its computer-based siblings: the decision tools described here.

of these tools, a tight hold on their environment becomes necessary to maintain their functioning. The computer-based tool becomes somewhat like a Trojan Horse: While pledging to turn medical practice into a science, while hoping to free medical practices from the "encroaching control" from outside the medical profession, the tight network it necessitates will rather merge with this encroaching control than detain it.

ACKNOWLEDGMENTS

This chapter is part of a broader research project of the construction of decision support techniques and the roles they play in the ongoing work within medical practices (discussed in Berg, 1997). I would like to thank Geof Bowker, Monica Casper, Harry Collins, Diana Forsythe, Annemarie Mol, Leigh Star, Lucy Suchman, and Gerard de Vries for their comments and support. I am also grateful to the late F. T. de Dombal, his group, P. Emerson, and Jeremy Wyatt for their kind help.

REFERENCES

Akrich, M. (1992). The de-scription of technical objects. In W. E. Bijker & J. Law (Eds.), *Shaping society—building technology: Studies in sociotechnical change* (pp. 205–224). Cambridge, MA: MIT Press.

Akrich, M., & B. Latour (1992). A summary of a convenient vocabulary for the semiotics of human and non-human assemblies. In W. Bijker & J. Law (Eds.), *Shaping technology, building society: Studies in sociotechnical change* (pp. 259–264). Cambridge, MA: MIT Press.

Barnett, G. (1968). Computers in patient care. *New England Journal of Medicine, 279,* 1321–1327.

Barnett, G. O., Cimono, J. J., Hupp, J. A., & Hoffer, E. P. (1987). DXplain. An evolving diagnostic decision support system. *Journal of the American Medical Association, 258,* 67–74.

Berg, M. (1992). The construction of medical disposals: Medical sociology and medical problem solving in clinical practice. *Sociology of Health and Illness, 14,* 151–180.

Berg, M. (1995). Turning a practice into a science: Redrawing the nature and flaws of postwar medical practice. *Social Studies of Science, 25,* 437–476.

Berg, M. (1997). *Rationalizing medical work. Decision support techniques and medical practices.* Cambridge, MA: MIT Press.

Berg, M., & Casper, M. (Eds.). (1995). *Constructivist perspectives and medical work: Medical practices and science and technology studies.* Special issue of *Science, Technology and Human Values, 20*(3).

Bijker, W. E., & Law, J. (Ed.). (1992). *Shaping technology—building society: Studies in sociotechnical change.* Cambridge, MA: MIT Press.

Bjerregaard, B., Brynitz, S., Holst-Christensen, J., Kalaja, E., Lund-Kristensen, J., Hilden, J., de Dombal, F. T., & Horrocks, J. C. (1976). Computer-aided diagnosis of the acute abdomen: A system from Leeds used on Copenhagen patients. In F. T. de Dombal & F. Gremy (Eds.), *Decision making and medical care* (pp. 165–171). Amsterdam: North-Holland.

Bleich, H. (1972). Computer-based consultation. Electrolyte and acid–base disorders. *American Journal of Medicine, 53,* 285–291.

Bloomfield, B. P. (1991). The role of information systems in the UK National Health Service: Action at a distance and the fetish of calculation. *Social Studies of Science, 21*, 701–734.

Bowers, J. (1992). The politics of formalism. In M. Lea (Ed.), *Contexts of computer mediated communication* (pp. 232–262). Hassocks: Harvester.

Bowker, G. (1994). *Science on the run. Information management and industrial geophysics at Schlumberger, 1920–1940.* Cambridge, MA: MIT Press.

Bowker, G., & Star, S. L. (1994). Knowledge and infrastructure in international information management: Problems of classification and coding. In L. Bud (Ed.), *Information acumen: The understanding and use of knowledge in modern business* (pp. 187–213). London: Routledge & Kegan Paul.

Buchanan, B. G., & Shortliffe, E. H. (Eds.). (1984). *Rule-based expert systems. The MYCIN experiments of the Stanford heuristic programming project.* Reading, MA: Addison-Wesley.

Button, G. (Ed.). (1993). *Technology in working order. Studies of work, interaction, and technology.* London: Routledge & Kegan Paul.

Callon, M. (1991). Techno-economic networks and irreversibility. In J. Law (Ed.), *A sociology of monsters: Essays on power, technology and domination* (pp. 132–161). London: Routledge & Kegan Paul.

Chatbanchai, W., Hedley, A. J., Ebrahim, S. B. J., Areemit, S., Hoskyns, E. W., & de Dombal, F. T. (1989). Acute abdominal pain and appendicitis in north east Thailand. *Paediatric and Perinatal Epidemiology, 3*, 448–459.

Clarke, A. E., & Fujimura, J. H. (Eds.). (1992). *The right tools for the job. At work in 20th-century life sciences.* Princeton, NJ: Princeton University Press.

Collins, H. M. (1990). *Artificial experts. Social knowledge and intelligent machines.* Cambridge, MA: MIT Press.

Davis, R., Buchanan, B. G., & Shortliffe, E. H. (1977). Production Rules as a Representation for a Knowledge-Based Consultation Program. *Artificial Intelligence, 8*, 15–45.

de Dombal, F. T. (1988). The OMGE acute abdominal pain survey. Progress report, 1986. *Scandinavian Journal of Gastroenterology, 23* (Suppl. 144), 35–42.

de Dombal, F. T. (1989). Computer-aided decision support in clincial medicine. *International Journal of Biomedicine and Computing, 24*, 9–16.

de Dombal, F. T. (1990). Computer-aided decision support—glittering prospects, practical problems, and Pandora's box. *Baillière's Clinical Obstetrics and Gynaecology, 4*, 841–849.

de Dombal, F. T. (1991). The diagnosis of acute abdominal pain with computer assistance: Worldwide perspective. *Annales de Chirurgie, 45*, 273–277.

de Dombal, F. T., Dallos, V., & McAdam, W. A. (1991). Can computer aided teaching packages improve clinical care in patients with acute abdominal pain? *British Medical Journal, 302*, 1495–1497.

de Dombal, F. T., & Gremy, F. (Ed.). (1976). *Decision making and medical care.* Amsterdam: North-Holland.

de Dombal, F. T., Leaper, D. J., Staniland, J. R., McCann, A. P., & Horrocks, J. C. (1972). Computer-aided diagnosis of acute abdominal pain. *British Medical Journal, 2*, 9–13.

Dent, M. (1990). Organisation and change in renal work: A study of the impact of a computer system within two hospitals. *Sociology of Health and Illness, 12*, 413–431.

Dreyfus, H. (1992). *What computers still can't do: The limits of artificial intelligence.* Cambridge, MA: MIT Press. (Original work published 1972)

Eddy, D. M. (1990). The challenge. *Journal of the American Medical Association, 263*, 287–290.

Emerson, P. A., Wyatt, J., Dillistone, L., Crichton, N., & Russell, N. J. (1988). The development of ACORN, an expert system enabling nurses to make admission decisions about patients with chest pain in an accident and emergency department. In *Proceedings of Medical Informatics: Computers in Clinical Medicine* (pp. 37–40). London: British Medical Informatics Society.

Emerson, P. A., Russell, N. J., Wyatt, J., Chrichton, N., Pantin, C. F. A., Morgan, A. D., & Fleming, P. R. (1989). An audit of doctor's management of patients with chest pain in the accident and emergency department. *Quarterly Journal of Medicine, New Series, 70*, 213–220.

Engle, R. L. (1992). Attempts to use computers as diagnostic aids in medical decision making: A 30-year experience. *Perspectives in Biology and Medicine, 35*, 207–219.

Evans, R. G. (1990). The dog in the night-time: Medical practice variations and health policy. In T. F. Anderson & G. Mooney (Ed.), *The challenges of medical practice variations* (pp. 402–411). London: Macmillan.

Fenyo, G., Clamp, S. E., de Dombal, F. T., Engstrom, L., Hedland, M., Leijonmarch, C., & Wilczek, H. (1987). Computer-aided diagnosis of 233 acute abdominal cases at Nacka Hospital Sweden. *Scandinavian Journal of Gastroenterology-Supplement, 128*, 178.

Forsythe, D. E. (1993a). The construction of work in artificial intelligence. *Science, Technology and Human Values, 18*, 460–479.

Forsythe, D. E. (1993b). Engineering knowledge: The construction of knowledge in artificial intelligence. *Social Studies of Science, 23*, 445–477.

Fujimura, J. H. (1987). Constructing "do-able" problems in cancer-research: Articulating alignment. *Social Studies of Science, 17*, 257–293.

Fujimura, J. H. (1992). Crafting science: Standardized packages, boundary objects, and "translation." In A. Pickering (Ed.), *Science as practice and culture* (pp. 168–211). Chicago: University of Chicago Press.

Gasser, L. (1986). The integration of computing and routine work. *ACM Transactions on Office Information Systems, 4*, 205–225.

Gill, P. W., Leaper, D. J., Guillou, P. J., Staniland, J. R., Horrocks, J. C., & de Dombal, F. T. (1973). Observer variation in clinical diagnosis—A computer-aided assessment of its magnitude and importance in 552 patients with abdominal pain. *Methods of Information in Medicine, 12*, 108–113.

Hart, A., & Wyatt, J. (1989). Connectionist models in medicine: An investigation of their potential. In J. Hunter, J. Cookson, & J. Wyatt (Eds.), *Proceedings AIME 89: Second European Conference on Artificial Intelligence in Medicine* (pp. 115–124). Berlin: Springer-Verlag.

Hartland, J. (1993a). *The machinery of medicine. An analysis of algorithmic approaches to medical knowledge and practice* Unpublished doctoral thesis, University of Bath, UK.

Hartland, J. (1993b). The use of "intelligent" machines for electrocardiograph interpretation. In G. Button (Ed.), *Technology in working order. Studies of work, interaction, and technology* (pp. 55–80). London: Routledge & Kegan Paul.

Haugeland, J. (1985). *Artificial intelligence: The very idea.* Cambridge, MA: MIT Press.

Hornbein, T. (1986). The setting of standards of care [editorial]. *Journal of the American Medical Association, 256*, 1040–1041.

Horrocks, J. C., McAdam, W. A. F., Deuroede, G., Gunn, A. A., & Zolkie, N. (1976). Some practical problems in transferring computer-aided diagnostic systems from one geographical area to another. In F. T. de Dombal & F. Gremy (Eds.), *Decision making and medical care* (pp. 159–163). Amsterdam: North-Holland.

Horrocks, J. C., McCann, A. P., Staniland, J. R., Leaper, D. J., & de Dombal, F. T. (1972). Computer-aided diagnosis: Description of an adaptable system, and operational experience with 2,034 cases. *British Medical Journal, 2*, 5–9.

Hughes, D. (1988). When nurse knows best: Some aspects of nurse/doctor interaction in a casualty department. *Sociology of Health and Illness, 10*, 1–22.

Ikonen, J. K., Rokkanen, P. U., Grönroos, P., Kataja, J. M., Nyliamen, P., de Dombal, F. T., & Softley, A. (1983). Presentation and diagnosis of acute abdominal pain in Finland: A computer aided study. *Annales Chirurgiae et Gynaecologiae, 72*, 332–336.

Kaplan, B. (1987). The medical computing "lag": Perceptions of barriers to the application of computers to medicine. *International Journal of Technology Assessment in Health Care, 3*, 123.

Kling, R. (1991). Computerization and social transformations. *Science, Technology, and Human Values, 16*, 342–367.

Kling, R., & Iacono, S. (1984). The control of information systems developments after implementation. *Communications of the ACM, 27*, 1218–1226.

Kling, R., & Scacchi, W. (1982). The web of computing: Computer technology as social organization. *Advances in Computers, 21*, 1–90.

Komaroff, A. L. (1982). Algorithms and the "art" of medicine. *American Journal of Public Health, 72*, 10–12.

Latour, B. (1987). *Science in action*. Milton Keynes: Open University Press.

Latour, B. (1988). *The pasteurization of France*. Cambridge, MA: Harvard University Press.

Lave, J. (1988). *Cognition in practice*. Cambridge, England: Cambridge University Press.

Law, J. (1987). Technology and heterogeneous engineering: The case of Portuguese expansion. In W. E. Bijker, T. P. Hughes, & T. J. Pinch (Eds.), *The social construction of technological systems. New directions in the sociology and history of technology* (pp. 111–134). Cambridge, MA: MIT Press.

Law, J. (Ed.). (1991). *A sociology of monsters: Essays on power, technology and domination*. London: Routledge & Kegan Paul.

Lipscombe, B. (1989). Expert systems and computer-controlled decision making in medicine. *AI and Society, 3*, 184–197.

Lipscombe, B. (1991). *Minds, machines & medicine: An epistemological study of computer diagnosis*. University of Bath, UK: Ph.D. thesis.

Lusted, L. B. (1968). *Introduction to medical decision making*. Springfield, IL: Thomas.

Miller, R. A., & Masarie, Jr., F. E. (1990). The demise of the "Greek Oracle" model for medical diagnostic systems. *Methods of Information in Medicine, 29*, 1–2.

Miller, R. A., McNeil, M. A., Challinor, S. M., Masarie, F. E., & Myers, J. D. (1986). The INTERNIST-1/QUICK MEDICAL REFERENCE project - status report. *Western Journal of Medicine, 145*, 816–822.

Miller, R. A., Pople, H. E., & Myers, J. D. (1982). INTERNIST-1: An experimental computer-based diagnostic consultant for general internal medicine. *New England Journal of Medicine, 307*, 468–476.

Mol, A. (1993). What is new? Doppler and its others. An empirical philosophy of investigations. In I. Löwy (Ed.), *Medicine and change: Studies of medical innovation* (pp. 107–125). Paris: Les Editions INSERM.

Mol, A., & Berg, M. (1994). The principles and practices of medicine: The co-existence of various anemias. *Culture, Medicine and Psychiatry, 18*, 247–265.

Mol, A., & Law, J. (1994). Regions, networks and fluids: Anaemia and social topology. *Social Studies of Science, 24*, 641–671.

O'Connell, J. (1993). Metrology: The creation of universality by the circulation of particulars. *Social Studies of Science, 23*, 129–173.

Perrolle, J. A. (1991). Expert enhancement and replacement in computerized mental labor. *Science, Technology and Human Values, 16*, 195–207.

Pickering, A. (Ed.). (1992). *Science as practice and culture*. Chicago: University of Chicago Press.

Pople, H. E. (1982). Heuristic methods for imposing structure on ill-structured problems: The structuring of medical diagnostics. In P. Szolovits (Ed.), *Artificial intelligence in medicine* (pp. 1357–1360). Boulder, CO: Westview Press.

Reggia, J. A., & Tuhrim, S. (Eds.). (1985). *Computer-assisted medical decision making*. New York: Springer-Verlag.

Saetnan, A. R. (1991). Rigid politics and technological flexibility: The anatomy of a failed hospital innovation. *Science, Technology and Human Values, 16*, 419–447.

Schwartz, W. B., Patil, R. S., & Szolovits, P. (1987). Artificial intelligence in medicine. Where do we stand? *New England Journal of Medicine, 316*, 685–688.

Shortliffe, E. H., Axline, S. G., Buchanan, B. G., Merigan, T. C., & Cohen, S. N. (1973). An artificial intelligence program to advise physicians regarding antimicrobial therapy. *Computers and Biomedical Research, 6,* 544–560.

Shortliffe, E. H., Buchanan, B. G., & Feigenbaum, E. A. (1979). Knowledge engineering for medical decision making: A review of computer-based clinical decision aids. *Proceedings of the IEEE, 67,* 1207–1224.

Shortliffe, E. H., & Clancey, W. J. (1984). Anticipating the second decade. In W. J. Clancey & E. H. Shortliffe (Eds.), *Readings in medical artificial intelligence. The first decade* (pp. 199–208). Reading, MA: Addison-Wesley.

Star, S. L. (1989). Layered space, formal representations and long-distance control: The politics of information. *Fundamenta Scientiae, 10,* 125–154.

Star, S. L. (1991). Power, technologies and the phenomenology of conventions: On being allergic to onions. In J. Law (Ed.), *A sociology of monsters: Essays on power, technology and domination* (pp. 26–56). London: Routledge & Kegan Paul.

Star, S. L., & Griesemer, J. R. (1989). Institutional ecology, "translations," and boundary objects: Amateurs and professionals in Berkely's museum of vertebrate zoology, 1907–39. *Social Studies of Science, 19,* 387–420.

Suchman, L. (1987). *Plans and situated actions. The problem of human-machine communication.* Cambridge, England: Cambridge University Press.

Suchman, L. (1994). Working relations of technology production and use. *Computer Supported Cooperative Work, 2,* 21–39.

Sutherland, J. W. (1986). Assessing the artificial intelligence contribution to decision technology. *IEEE Transactions on Systems, Man and Cybernetics* SMC-16, 3–20.

Szolovits, P. (Ed.). (1982). *Artificial intelligence and medicine.* Boulder, CO: Westview Press.

Szolovits, P., & Long, W. J. (1982). The development of clinical expertise in the computer. In P. Szolovits (Ed.), *Artificial intelligence and medicine* (pp. 79–117). Boulder, CO: Westview Press.

Szolovits, P., Patil, R. S., & Schwartz, W. B. (1988). Artificial intelligence in medical diagnosis. *Annals of Internal Medicine, 108,* 80–87.

Webster, J. (1991). Advanced manufacturing technologies: Work organisation and social relations crystallised. In J. Law (Ed.), *A sociology of monsters. Essays on power, technology and domination* (pp. 192–222). London: Routledge & Kegan Paul.

Weinstein, M., Fineberg, M. U., Elstein, A. S., Frazier, H. S., Neuhause, D., Neufra, R. R., & McNeil, B. J. (1980). *Clinical decision analysis.* Philadelphia: Saunders.

Wennberg, J. (1984). Dealing with medical practice variations: A proposal for action. *Health Affairs, 3,* 6–32.

Wilson, D. H., Wilson, P. D., Walmsley, R. G., Horrocks, J. C., & de Dombal, F. T. (1977). Diagnosis of acute abdominal pain in the accident and emergency department. *British Journal of Surgery, 64,* 250–254.

Woolgar, S. (1991). Configuring the user: The case of usability trials. In J. Law (Ed.), *A sociology of monsters: Essays on power, technology and domination* (pp. 57–99). London: Routledge & Kegan Paul.

Wyatt, J. (1989). Lessons learned from the field trial of ACORN, an expert system to advise on chest pain. In P. Manning, O. Zhineng, & B. Barber (Eds.), *Proceedings Medical Informatics 1989, Singapore* (pp. 97–101). North Holland: Elsevier.

Wyatt, J., & Emerson, P. (1990). A pragmatic approach to knowledge engineering with examples of use in a difficult domain. In D. Berry & A. Hart (Eds.), *Expert systems: Human issues* (pp. 65–78). Cambridge, MA: MIT Press.

Wynne, B. (1988). Unruly technology: Practical rules, impractical discourses and public understanding. *Social Studies of Science, 18,* 147–167.

14

Mapping Sociotechnical Networks in the Making

Ira A. Monarch
Suresh L. Konda
Sean N. Levy
Carnegie Mellon University

Yoram Reich
Tel Aviv University

Eswaran Subrahmanian
Carol Ulrich
Carnegie Mellon University

CROSSING THE SOCIOTECHNICAL DIVIDE

Engineers and sociologists, when questioned or when given to think about it, would acknowledge that engineering design is both social and technical. However, disciplinary allegiances underplay the extent to which the social and the technical are interrelated or overplay the extent to which one or the other is important. These tendencies have been challenged by some sociologists and historians of technology who have been building a case for interweaving social, technoscientific, and economic analyses in a seamless web (Bijker, Hughes, & Pinch, 1987; Callon & Law, 1989; Hughes, 1987). Callon (1987) took these analyses one step further arguing that engineers who participate in the design, development, or diffusion of technology constantly construct hypotheses and forms of argument that pull them into the field of sociological analysis, transforming them into engineering sociologists—that is, hybrids, who may nevertheless be sociologists par excellence. For Callon, the realm of the engineering sociologist is the practice of engineering at the local level where particular design and development work is taking place and where the social technical divide is routinely crossed, blurring the distinction between what is social and what is technical.

Callon envisioned a reciprocal relation: The engineer being pulled into sociology, but sociology being transformed as a result. Engineers become engineering-sociologists because their designs are inextricably bound up with social analysis and society building, and these designs are socially evaluated, according to Callon, in terms of market share, rate of expansion, or profit rate. For Callon, sociology can be transformed if sociologists are willing and able to trace the engineer's practice of society building and to emulate the sociological analysis and evaluation embedded in the engineer's practice. Sociology is asked to borrow the design engineer's practice, not the engineer's machine, as model.

THE INSCRIPTION SPACE OF THE
ENGINEERING-SOCIOLOGIST HYBRID

Even if it makes sense and is clarifying to view engineers as building and maintaining sociological structures in the fabrication of technologies, and even if their designs can be sociotechnically evaluated, they do not appear to engage in, even from the point of view of a rational reconstruction of their work, any systematic recording of the empirical or conceptual analyses of the sociotechnical aspects of design. The inscription space necessary for articulating a sociotechnical theory or empirically analyzing it seems to be missing from engineering practice.

Any sociotechnical information recorded by design teams is often unorganized and scattered across several online databases, and in paper folders. The latter may come under the purview of an accidental, but fairly familiar, company librarian—much of whose work is invisible, idiosyncratic, not budgeted, and not institutionalized. Such a librarian usually has only very incomplete and skewed knowledge of and access to the virtual organizational archive, which includes memos, meeting notes, notebooks, guidebooks, internal reports about product and process, and the scientific factors bearing on either, external reports (e.g., audits or assessments), newsletters, collections of annotated relevant standards, regulatory requirements (safety and environmental), patents, journal articles and conference proceedings, excerpts from handbooks, and domain specific encyclopedia. These virtual archives are distributed across personal, group, organizational, and sundry public repositories. Moreover, people in organizations are unfamiliar with the multiple kinds of information distributed in "available" repositories and often do not know where to look and how to find the information they need.

Although design engineers perform some, even extensive, sociotechnical analyses, these analyses are not usually detached from practice, or they are buried in the mass of textual and other data produced during design. They are not recorded in a durable inscription space that can be returned to and reflected on (Schon, 1983), even during the lifetime of a project, let alone after a project is over or the design team breaks up.

This is not to say there are no inscription spaces currently in effect for design practice. Some inscriptions are detached and maintained so that necessary information structures can be synoptically held together, at least enough for coherent design to take place. Some empirical and theoretical information is shared by practitioners in the form of shared under-standings of the design enmeshed in its sociotechnical web and commu-nicated in conversations, sketches, models, designs, documents, and other objects that circulate around a design network. However, it is a premise of the work that this communication can be improved to the extent that such representations can be efficiently and effectively returned to and reflected on. This requires extending and making more durable these tenuous inscription spaces for recording information generated in design work (see also Gronbaek, Kyng, & Mogensen, 1992). Later sections explore the organizational settings and information infrastructures needed to create, extend, and maintain these inscription spaces. The more extended and receptive the inscription space, the greater the potential for empirical feedback, theory articulation, shared understanding, and improved prac-tice. The chances for establishing such inscription spaces are increasing as the Internet World Wide Web (WWW) provides more collaborative tools and infrastructure to create intranets.

THEORY BUILDING IN ENGINEERING PRACTICE: A PROGRAMMING EXEMPLAR

It might be argued that creating inscription spaces for theory articulation is not really necessary because practicing engineers do not build theories anyway, or, at the very least, it is unclear what is meant by "theory" in this context. To clarify what is meant, and thereby address both objections, Naur's (1985) approach to theory building in engineering practice is discussed. One of his primary aims was to raise the status of programmers as seen in the typical industrial management view of them as workers of fairly low responsibility and only brief education. To realize this aim, Naur argued that programming is primarily a building up of knowledge of a certain kind; any documentation, at least in the current sense, being an auxiliary, secondary product. For Naur, programming knowledge is generated, in part, through "matching some significant part and aspect of an activity in the real world to the formal symbol manipulation that can be done by a program running on a computer" (pp. 37–38). In addi-tion, such knowledge is generated "in time corresponding to the changes taking place in the real world activity being matched by the program execution, in other words program modifications" (p. 38). On Naur's view, the continued adaptation, modification, and correction of errors in certain kinds of large programs is essentially dependent on a certain kind of knowledge possessed by a group of programmers who are closely and continuously connected with these programs. For Naur, programmers' knowledge is encapsulated in a theory that enables programmers to explain, justify, and answer queries about their program, and explain what aspect or activity of the world is matched by the program text and why each part of the program is what it is. As a result, a programmer is able to respond constructively to any demand for a modification of the program so as "to support the affairs of the world in a new manner" (p. 41).

On the face of it, Naur presented a naive realist view of theory (for an alternative, see Feyerabend, 1975), though what he said about programs matching the real world to symbols does begin to translate an intuitive view of theory into an unfamiliar context. Moreover, it is understandable that Naur wanted to differentiate the current notion of documentation from that which would capture the knowledge he believed is produced via programming as theory building. Nevertheless expanding documentation to include requirements, specifications, problem reports, and change reports, increases the likelihood of it containing important conceptual elements that can be made explicit through effective analysis. Coword analysis or the extraction and interpretation of networks of co-occurring terms may indicate key factors or concepts as well as underlying themes characteristic of the knowledge generated in theory building. In any case, it is Naur's insistence that the knowledge generated in theory building is somehow not detachable from the programmers who are closely and continuously tied with the programs being built that is most in need of being challenged.

He made this claim quite explicit when he asserted that the theory associated with a program "is something that could not conceivably be expressed, but is inextricably bound to human beings" (p. 44). Unfortunately, in his aim to raise the status of programmers, he too restrictively circumscribed the knowledge generated in theory building. Surely, knowledge of the "significant part and aspect of an activity in the real world" and of the "changes taking place in the real world activity" is knowledge woven into the theory of the program. It is knowledge gained through negotiations and reconciliations with many nonprogrammers involved in the real-world context of a software design, including those involved in, for example, the production and marketing of the software and those who will be its end-users. This is part of the *social construction of sociotechnical knowledge and artifacts* (Bijker et al., 1987). Such negotiation and reconciliation already involves significant conceptual and empirical contributions by all participants—programmers and nonprogrammers alike. These contributions are, in effect, part of the theory built in the creation of the software.

Although there is a certain tacit element in the knowledge of a program that ties it to human beings working in a specific context, this knowledge can be captured, expressed, and communicated beyond this context. It may seem otherwise because of the tenuousness or inadequacy of current inscription spaces, but, as discussed later, it may be possible to overcome these factors by creating a new kind of engineering design environment combining organizational and computational elements. Even in present environments, a combination of organizational and inscriptional means enables programmers on a team to express the theory of the program to each other. That is, they must detach the theory in some sense, because if they cannot maintain the theory outside of themselves, it is not clear how they could communicate it, even to themselves at a later time. But if these theories are detachable and maintainable outside of immediate practice, then more effective environments for inscription and interpretation should make it easier for programmers and nonprogrammers to share, to an even greater extent, in theory building. There is no doubt a cost for making the effort to share social technical knowledge, but there is also a cost of not sharing it. This chapter contends that the theories produced in engineering practice, as those produced in science, are not the sole possession of any one individual or group.

CIRCULATING AMONG AND BEYOND
THE DISCIPLINES

Research and experience show that practicing design engineers typically communicate across disciplinary boundaries and are quite responsive to economic, social, political, or cultural considerations, even if they do not always acknowledge this as a significant part of their work. Design and development practice involve negotiation and reconciliation of heterogeneous knowledge and experiential sources in a specific but changing and elusive social context. For example, in the design of information systems, designers must be prepared to delve into disciplines such as telecommunications computer science, software engineering, knowledge engineering, information science, and human–computer interaction—each a discipline in its own right. They also need to know the capability of the development team and development environment, get familiar with the domain application, and competing software applications, determine which software modules need to be developed or acquired, institute policies and procedures for documenting code and creating user documentation, and translate potential customer or marketing visions into something that the development team can deliver. The diversity of equipment, machines, institutions, knowledge, skill, and judgment needed in engineering design practice always involves a collective that accumulates information from multiple disciplines and even information not part of any discipline. Such information and the networks that produce and circulate it are called *cross-disciplinary* and *beyond disciplinary*, respectively.[1]

Science and engineering disciplines, although embedded in many intersecting collectives, achieve a relative autonomy and insulation from each other and from social and economic factors through their rites of passage and gate-keeping procedures. These rites and procedures are manifest in examinations, granting of degrees, refereed journal articles, acceptance of papers to conferences, and in the publication of standards documents, handbooks, and various other kinds of reference documents. Such practices and resources contribute to the maintenance of meaning that determine the boundaries of disciplinary understanding. Disciplines have already forged inscription spaces in which theories are built and evaluated. These inscription spaces take the form of, for example, professional journals and professional meetings where theoretical analyses and the empirical analyses relevant to them are presented, discussed, and published. In the case of disciplinary communication, developing information technology tools can leverage the regularities and constraints of disciplinary configurations like sublanguages (Harris, 1989) into features of an information management and theory-building support system.

Engineering practice, on the other hand, spills across boundaries of many disciplines and needs to be responsive to economic, social, political, and cultural considerations. Designers and developers must translate this multiple and heterogeneous knowledge to enable a design to work in the contexts in which it will be manufactured, marketed, transferred, sold, and used. In doing this, designers and developers cannot appeal to well-established disciplinary constraints on language and interpretation to bring about and maintain understanding, closure of discussion, and decisive action among design participants. Design practice is typically initiated in the construction of local heterogeneous networks consisting of actors, natural objects, and artifacts that enable the creation and maintenance of pockets of agreement and shared meaning that support decisive action in the face of many different disciplinary, economic, political, and cultural interests (Callon, 1987; Law & Callon, 1992). It is based on these shared understandings that theory building and evaluation in local engineering networks takes place. Design practice starting in local heterogeneous networks does not have established inscription spaces at its dis-

---

[1]In cases later in the text, "transdisciplinary" will be used for both "cross-disciplinary" and "beyond disciplinary."

posal. Local networks may expand into more global networks and in the process, develop or adopt discipline like inscription spaces, but the fate of many local networks of design practice is not to get this far (Callon, 1991, 1994). Local engineering networks may have a better chance to expand or maintain themselves if new inscription spaces were established for recording and reflecting on their theoretical and empirical analyses that currently are often lost or inaccessible. Establishing these inscription spaces will also enable local networks to make better use of disciplinary structure and knowledge. Much of the information that will be captured in the new inscription spaces will be information gathered from a variety of disciplines. Regularities and constraints of disciplinary configurations like sublanguages might be useful for structuring both cross-disciplinary and beyond disciplinary information. Cross-disciplinary and beyond disciplinary networks are discussed more fully in the next sections.

Cross-Disciplinary Networks
of Engineering Design Practice

The design of any artifact that draws on multiple disciplines requires the reconciliation of differences in terminology, visualization, and modeling that are the result of different perspectives, interests, and aims indigenous to the disciplines involved. This follows from the general observation that design is, among other things, the collaboration of individuals from different disciplines (Bucciarelli, 1988). Because members of heterogeneous design groups working on the same artifact do not share the same experiences, concepts, perspectives, exemplars, methods, or techniques, they partition the artifact very differently. Engineering design requires the creation of cross-disciplinary information and knowledge through careful mutual linking and translation of terms, visualizations, and models across groups.

When it comes to engineering practice, there is no single set of disciplinary mechanisms to ensure a bounded set of concepts, visualizations, techniques, or methods. Nor is there a single set of skills for using them that pertains to design participants. Moreover, changes in design practice are not governed by the kind of bounded set of rules and norms as are changes in disciplinary practices. Design situations and processes, especially as they are performed in local networks lacking intermediaries or with only weak links to intermediaries, are much more a result of what has been called *methodological* and *theoretical anarchism* (Feyerabend, 1975), and are one source of technological innovation (Callon, 1994). Not all are innovative. Many local networks just act, or are economically pressured to act, in accord with more global networks where design practice is more bounded and less innovative (Callon, 1994). Global networks are subject to certain systemic (Hughes, 1987) and potentially irreversible (Callon, 1991) factors that are very difficult to avoid. The more local and innovative the network, the more contingent it is and the more subject to negotiation and translation in a situation of contested power and authority. Establishing cross-disciplinary and even beyond disciplinary inscription spaces and associated tools supporting theory building and evaluation in local heterogeneous networks should increase the chances of disseminating innovation. Both local and global socioeconomic factors are crucially implicated in sociotechnical innovation (Blomberg, Suchman, & Trigg, 1995; Callon, 1994).

The distinction between disciplinary and cross-disciplinary networks is not hard and fast. For example, a discipline may divide along different subgroups due to differences in working contexts (as, e.g., among chemical engineers in academe, in manufacturing plants, in design shops, in pharmaceuticals, in petrochemicals, etc.) readily demonstrated in a host of case studies (e.g., Bucciarelli, 1988; Sargent, Subrahmanian, Downs, Greene, & Rishel, 1992). All technical disciplines are composed of subdisciplines with communication between them being cross-subdisciplinary. In addition, members of disciplines do pay attention to other disciplines and there is always a potential for interdisciplinary work to lead to the establishment of new disciplines (biophysics, bioengineering, biochemistry, biopsychology, social-biology, engineering-sociology). Because of this, it is not very clear where disciplines begin and end. Disciplines always include cross-fertilization with other disciplines, as well as many other forms of information transfer relevant to the cascades of representation in any technical work (Latour, 1988; Star, 1989).

Extended Participatory Design:
Beyond Disciplinary Networks

Design and development practice not only extends across disciplines, it can extend beyond disciplines to include all who affect or are affected by a design outcome, including potential users, customers, manufacturers, and marketers. This potentiality follows from the irreducibility of design to a single kind of expertise that typically can be imparted to and exercised by a single individual. Being a design participant is not just a matter of a certain kind of training or affiliation in one professional group or another (Reich, Konda, Monarch, & Subrahmanian, 1992), but also a matter of who is affected by a design and who can contribute to its being more effective. It is the irreducible heterogeneity of design and associated development that are resistant to being bounded.

Who is implicated in a design or artifact, and, more importantly, who is considered a design participant, is negotiable as part of the engineering design process. Determining who is a design participant is part of the process of determining what the design is or should be, just as determining who is the subject of knowledge is mutually dependent on determining the object of knowledge (Latour, 1990). Determining who is a design participant sometimes becomes a process of enrollment and reduction of participation and sometimes a process of extending participation in a process of mutual translation where more than one network is enhanced and more than one analysis/practice is elaborated. Any attempt to draw boundaries and exclude participation is always subject to a factionalization of the power and authority to do so. For this reason, end users of an artifact can be in a position of power with respect to a design by being experienced in the context of its use. However, this also means that to the extent that these end-users are in power as design participants, they are also responsible for the success or failure of the design (Bjerknes, Ehn, & Kyng, 1987; Floyd, Mehl, Reisin, Schmidt, & Wolf, 1989)

It is worth inquiring whether emphasis on extensive participatory design can be a fruitful alternative to views that underemphasize the active role of the user in the design process (Whyte, Greenwood, & Lazes, 1991). For example, in the case of sophisticated (i.e., complex) products and processes, user needs are either not known or are, at best, inchoate. In these cases, not only does user participation seem to be called for, but also sophisticated means may be needed to support this participation. In general, articulating user needs by including users early and, when feasible, throughout design life cycle(s) may be of benefit and should be explored. It is not necessary that design extend participation or be committed to extensive participation. However, a more open, experimental attitude is important in this regard. This is, perhaps, of most importance to the engineering sociologist who might appreciate the provision of an inscription space enabling the recording and structuring of negotiations and reconciliations in extended design participation. Although it might be utopian or in the realm of the literary fantastic to imagine an inscription space in which designers and end-users build and evaluate theories together in conjunction with the development of an artifact or end product, the engineering sociologist might find useful a recording device that catches nascent extended participation in the act and that provides tools for structuring the information captured as well.

Empirical Findings on Extended Participatory Design

Whereas there are enormous difficulties in institutionalizing such extensive participation in existing organizations, some initial steps have been taken and their results observed. It has been found that participation resulting in the cross-fertilization of ideas from very different perspectives may promote innovation (Kodama, 1991). Gardiner and Rothwell (1985) contended that good and innovative designs often emerge in situations where customers closely participate in the early design stage. Moreover, highly sophisticated innovations can come from users themselves, though usually in subsequent versions of the product. There are other considerations as well. For example, the perception that extending design participation reduces design efficiency is not borne out by experienced outcome (Hirschheim, 1985). The issue of the efficiency of participatory design cannot be addressed without clarifying what is meant by efficiency. If by efficiency is meant the rate at which the design phase is completed as opposed to the rate at which successful products reach the market, then the case for the usefulness (as opposed to the correctness) of participation may be weak. However, if by efficiency is meant the rate of successful products to market, then an argument for participation can be made, because in the long run significant inefficiencies might result from the failure to address mutually agreed on needs despite the short run potential for inefficiency of extensive participation.

A similar problem arises concerning the question of whether participation will necessarily lead to better designs. There are many studies. A large number of these report positive (Adams, 1988; Baronas & Louis, 1988; Blomberg et al., 1995; Chen & Sanoff, 1988; Corbin, 1988; Gardiner & Rothwell, 1985; Oberdorfer, 1988; Sanoff, 1988; von Hippel, 1988, Whyte et al., 1991) and some report negligble or no significant (Olson & Ives, 1981; Tait & Vessey, 1988) results of user participation on the quality of designs. By and large, the cases in which user involvement had no significant influence on the outcome are characterized by differential power between management and users, planners and citizens, or lack of legitimacy of participation groups (Mohrman & Ledford, 1985), that is, by the exercise of a distorted type of extended participation. As long as the focus is not on the long-term viability of the product, the issues of efficiency and efficacy of participation in design are biased toward the negative.

Taking Extended Participation Seriously

Taking seriously the notion of extending design practice and memory beyond disciplines has had important implications in ways of thinking about design environments and tools. The creation of suitable communication channels between design participants—the actual "bandwidth" varying dynamically depending on the context and the participants—is critical. Design communication needs to be seen as a continuous process of perspectival, conceptual, and information exchange, always requiring interpretation and translation of all design participants who are learning, building, and evolving shared meanings of the current design (Reich et al., 1992; Schrage, 1991). Each group of design participants needs to learn about the needs of those who will use the designed artifact, about the context in which the problem is posed, and about how alternative solutions will suit the needs and culture of users. Moreover, each group needs to learn about alternative possible designs and how these might change perceived needs. In this ideal, each participant traces, follows, influences, and is influenced by the evolution of views of the other. In these respects, the views expressed here differ from some proposals for computer-supported participatory design (Duursma, 1990; Quayle, 1987), or GDSS.

Even with the infusion of computational aids, taking extended participation seriously will still increase the cognitive and other demands made on participants. This may mean that many people will be even less inclined then ever to participate. The contention is that the appropriate way to resolve the issue of whether those who ought to participate will, is by collecting empirical data on people's choices when they are allowed to participate in a variety of forms and contexts. Note that it is particularly critical to investigate those who did not participate in order to discover the underlying reasons for their decision, so that new forms and support of participation can be developed. This again is another case for the engineering sociologist, though one that may require attention to more indigenous sociological techniques. The infusion of computational systems should give rise to accumulation of data and information not otherwise possible.

There is, however, a downside to the infusion of computational tools. Users may be more attracted to programs that deemphasize their active involvement by relying on a tool rather than exercising their own judgment (Chu & Elam, 1990). Moreover, data containing participation records can be used to monitor and control users/designers (a panoptical effect; see Foucault, 1979; Zuboff, 1988). This chapter argues that such factors can be minimized by involving users as much as possible in the development of computational tools for participation and by providing tools with the flexibility to be evolved as participants see fit.

IMPROVING TRANSDISCIPLINARY COMMUNICATION IN ORGANIZATIONS

Clark and Fujimoto (1991) noted that Japanese industries have directed their attention toward organizational integration of human specialists. Enhancing communication between design participants with different perspectives is possible using organizational methods that assign team member responsibilities by placing the designers in close proximity and using techniques such as Quality Function Deployment (QFD) for matching quality control and customer preferences (Hauser & Clausing, 1988).

Such organizational approaches do not provide the basis for maintaining disciplinary and transdisciplinary knowledge in an organization, at least in the sense of representing, organizing, and accessing sociotechnical information distributed in an organization's repositories. Even when an informal project, department, or organization librarian exists, much information is still lost, remains relatively unorganized, and inaccessible. Moreover, organizational memory residing only in individuals makes the organization vulnerable to loss of memory, given the mobility of people and their well-known cognitive limitations. Aside from memory limitations, the previous organizational approaches are less helpful or unhelpful in realizing integration objectives of more timely and more extensive information sharing among those separated by perspective, space, and time. A much more explicit and formal process is needed that identifies important sources of information; specifies procedures for jointly collecting, indexing, organizing the information and making it accessible for mutual participation and joint learning; and creates multiple and varied opportunities for joint learning and mutual construction of organizational memory. Such organizational processes enable and are enabled by information technology, but special attention must be devoted to avoiding the potential centralized and hierarchical (or asymmetric) panoptic power of this technology (Foucault, 1979; Zuboff, 1988), which can lead to excessive control and domination. (For a relatively optimistic view on these matters see Castells, 1996.)

Specifying such a formal process and creating a material infrastructure for building and maintaining knowledge is not just a matter of creating accessible databases and interfaces. It involves an analysis of how individuals create and negotiate shared understandings, reach agreements, and generate decisive actions. It also involves an analysis of what special languages, visualizations, models, and so on are used in order that different individuals are able to share knowledge and experience. In addition, common procedures, substrates, and mechanisms must be a seamless part of the way people go about their work. They must provide effective support for the modeling activities and decision making necessary in the design of artifacts. Only by persistent and thoroughgoing sociotechnical analysis, strategic experiments, and the evolution of information technology prototypes will viable and respectful procedures and infrastructure be achieved—those that build and maintain both disciplinary and transdisciplinary knowledge satisfactorily capturing experience, good or bad, for reuse or avoidance in future design situations.

Reconfiguring organizations and integrating computational tools into new organizational processes is not easy and is both initially expensive and a long-term project. Even in the limited case of Toshiba's "software factory" (Brackett, 1991), a system to maximize software reuse took nearly a decade to create positive payoffs, and was very expensive. Hence, a short-term perspective will render the creation and organization of new inscription space prototypes and experiments infeasible.

Organizational support of new (with respect to the organization) information and knowledge management systems is absolutely crucial. More negatively, certain kinds of organizational structures, established solution strategies, and reward systems act against the use of such systems or, worse, act for the creation of panoptical surveillance of work. Creating new organizational and information infrastructures may require a transformation of work and power. In short, there is no avoiding the need for viable and respectful organizational structures, which may then be enhanced using technology (Clark & Fujimoto, 1991).

CURRENT ISSUES IN THE DESIGN
OF INFORMATION INFRASTRUCTURE

Design participants create and accumulate texts, representations, models, boundary objects (Star, 1988; Star & Greisemer, 1989), and immutable mobiles (Latour, 1988) as they go about the work of design, theory building, and evaluation. This work could be facilitated if these information objects could be coordinated and managed for use in a timely fashion by all participants. Making information objects and structures accessible is supported by providing an evolving map of the sociotechnical network. This evolving map is created through coordination and management activities that include, for example, collecting, analyzing, indexing, annotating, linking, organizing, and presenting the resulting information structures as models and maps of the information. Organizational and infrastructural facilities are needed for creating this shared map or networked memory. Infusion of computer-based information technology currently available, and on the horizon, has the potential for improving, perhaps immeasurably, the mapping and memory creation facilities that are currently tenuous and sporadic (Chen, Schuffels, & Orwig, 1996). Next is a discussion of these techniques and systems for both information and knowledge management.

Issues in Providing Disciplinary
Information Infrastructure

Organizational and technological infrastructure supports disciplinary knowledge creation and maintenance work reasonably well. Scientific and engineering disciplines are maintained, in large part, through institutional practices for circumscribing discussions that are publicly recorded and archived. These constitute important conditions and norms for the creation and maintenance of disciplinary knowledge. The information structures embedded in these discourses are, to a certain extent, made explicit through databases, keywords, indices, nomenclatures, classifications, handbooks, reference manuals, and the like. However, what is currently made explicit is done so from viewpoints of technical practitioners, who are limited in time and biased in perspective, and indexers, who are limited in the depth of their knowledge. Subject categories and nomenclatures for various fields can take months or years to update. To the extent that disciplines contain subdisciplines, groups, or individuals who scout other disciplines, information maps can become very helpful. Members of disciplines and design practitioners who may be scouting a field are always at risk for missing relevant information structures, exacerbated by the fact that current maps of the information terrain are rather one dimensional. Techniques in information visualization and retrieval are currently being developed that will improve this situation (Hemmje, Kunkel, & Willett, 1994; Olsen, Korfhage, Sochats, Spring, & Williams, 1993).

Use of automated techniques that have access to the textual data being generated in a discipline will enable the processing of more data than anyone in the field or any indexer or knowledge engineer will ever have time to read. These automated techniques should be seen as support tools interacting with the members of a discipline, knowledge engineers, and others engaged in managing and producing, for example, indices, subject headings, and thesauruses. Such support tools make extraction, representation, and organization of information more effective in terms of timeliness, coverage, and maps of greater dimensionality. An important set of these tools is based on the principle that constraints on the co-occurrence of words and phrases contribute to a pragmatically useful stabilization of meaning of the sentences in a given sublanguage, reflecting the structures of information in that sublanguage. These constraints can be discovered through computational analysis of the co-occurrence of words and phrases in a corpus of texts (Callon, Law, & Rip, 1986; Harris, 1989). Insofar as these structures of information can be made explicit, they can be used to index, classify, map, and retrieve information important in the discipline (Callon et al., 1986; Chen, Schatz, et al., 1996; Coulter, Monarch, Konda, & Carr, 1996; Monarch, 1994, 1996).

Issues in Providing Transdisciplinary Information Infrastructure

Although there are important differences in information management between disciplinary and transdisciplinary networks, mappings of disciplinary networks can be a useful first step in mapping transdisciplinary ones. Multidimensional mappings of disciplinary knowledge are useful to designers and developers as guides for finding relevant information from various research fronts. They are also useful as a basis for negotiating how disciplinary information is going to be linked into the inscription spaces and information structures generated in design practice. In addition, these mapping techniques will be useful for bringing to light and maintaining the structures and links in cross-disciplinary aspects of organizational information.

A major difference between designing information infrastructures for global disciplinary networks as against local, innovative transdisciplinary networks is the latter have typically inadequate inscription spaces. Information technology must be carefully developed and adapted to facilitate design practice while also, unobtrusively, capturing, structuring, and making accessible local design knowledge.

Currently, popular research and development efforts, such as integration frameworks, though seemingly addressing some knowledge linking and integration issues, are partially misleading. They still, by and large, refer to creating consistent interfaces to and between the specialized tools of a particular profession and not to creating channels of communications supporting the collaborative use of tools among professionals. Modern research projects developing multiple-expert "AI" design systems are concerned with the problem of combining several diverse single-purpose tools to address a common problem. They avoid the problems of reconciliation and integration because they assume they can communicate through the medium of the software representation of the artifact itself (e.g., Bowen & Bahler, 1991; Cutkosky et al., 1993). However, Cutkosky et al. (1993; based on their PACT investigation of tool integration through encapsulation and communication in a common language—predicate calculus) acknowledged that reconciliation of assumptions about time, term definitions, geometry, and units among tools have to be achieved before linking and integrating different understandings of the artifact. Experience in integrating materials databases also reveal the importance of negotiating links between representations of the domain (Sargent et al., 1992). Major problems involved the negotiation of names, objects, constraints, and trade-offs that characterize a particular product and the organizing and distilling of design history (methods, failures, etc.) for subsequent use. To reiterate, the knowledge crucial for design practice is difficult to collect, represent, model, and map because it is the product of multiple perspectives and sublanguages.

These are difficult problems that have led some to argue that knowledge generated in engineering practice is irretrievably embedded in it. In contrast, the contention of this chapter is that such practical knowledge is manifest in practices and is retrievable. The problem is to capture it, to the extent possible, in all its multiple dimensions and make its structure explicit and hence useful within a given project and for future projects. To some extent, projects and organizations do capture information and knowledge generated during design privately in the form of, for example, design manuals, technical letters, and glossaries. Such private repositories are a sedimentation of past negotiations and reconciliations constrained by a single organization's interactions with the marketplace, and the information structures disclosed may reflect a very skewed perspective. How can such practical experience achieve theoretical insight into the design? The answer, already hinted at, is to mobilize organizational support and infrastructure for infusion of information technology that creates and installs inscription spaces for capturing practical information otherwise lost or inaccessible. The infrastructure provides analysis and structuring tools for the creation of linked information structures that underlie local transdisciplinary theory building and evaluation.

A MODELING SYSTEM TO CAPTURE
AND STRUCTURE PRACTICAL DESIGN
INFORMATION

One aim of discussing the development of new inscription spaces and their supporting analysis and structuring tools has been to make some common borders of cognitive science, information technology, and social studies of science and technology stand out. Using this map of common borders, one might search for metaphors extendible and combinable into designs of information systems. In many ways, the aim has been to offer an alternative to the AI goal of building machine simulacra of individual intelligence or memory. The alternative is to build machine infrastructures that graft onto and extend artifactual and organizational supports already in place to supplement individual memory. The result is shared memory (Konda, Monarch, Sargent, & Subrahmanian, 1992) or the ability of heterogeneous communities to link and share information in computationally supported inscription spaces using analysis and structuring tools to build and evaluate theories as designs are constructed.

Individual memory and shared memory are mutually dependent. Individual memory is clueless without inscription surfaces, information objects, and memory technologies (e.g., writing, print, various electronic devices). However, the shared memory made available by sociotechnical supports is viewed and put into effect through the interpretive capacity of individual memory. This approach suggests a new kind of augmented intelligence (AI), emphasizing intelligence distributed in a networked collective of inscription spaces supported by analysis and structuring tools.

The alternative goal of augmenting the memory of groups instead of simulating individual human memory and intelligence has been pursued through the development of an information modeling system for engineering design called *n*-dim, short for *n*-dimensional (Levy et al., 1993; The *n*-dim Group, in press; Reich, Konda, Levy, Monarch, & Subrahmanian, 1993; Subrahmanian et al., 1993). The aim has been to build a system that would support information recording, management, and modeling activities in the very process of doing design, thus facilitating building design theories as well as capturing and retrieving relevant information to evaluate them. This infrastructure would enable designers to store, select, multiply view, and modify shared structures of information (text, geometry, layout, sketches, pictures). The environment would permit asynchronous (different time, different place) group activity and support the retention of time sequence and threads of exchange. Facilities would be provided to enable the management, annotation, analysis, retrieval, and presentation of heterogeneous design information. Most importantly, perhaps, is the focus on modeling in design practice—not just of the design artifact but of the processes and organizational structures necessary to develop designs.

The support of *n*-dim for the creation and linking of models across sociotechnical lines not only provides facilities for designers to do their work but also, in conjunction with other facilities for tracking this work, is capable of providing an informative design history. Part of the social technical analysis work that needs to be done is determining which combinations of information and modeling structures are most effective in supporting engineering practice and informing theory building and experimentation in practice. They go hand in hand. Several avenues are being explored (see Monarch, 1996; Monarch & Gluch, 1995; Reich et al., 1993; Subrahmanian et al., 1993, for some alternatives). For example, it might be useful to produce, through various computational means such as coword analysis, maps of the sociotechnical networks implicated in carrying out design work. These can be elaborated and formalized into several interlinked models representing the varied perspectives or the evolving design, reducing the amount and duration of misunderstanding among design participants. The following describes some typical models and how they might be multiply linked.

There might be models representing and structuring information from public documents including relevant standards documents, regulatory requirements (safety and environmental), patents, journal articles and conference proceedings, excerpts from handbooks, domain specific encyclopedia; information from internal organization documents including reports, memos, guidebooks, meeting notes; the design artifact—its parts, their function, and performance; the design process—procedures, methods, policies, and schedule; project personnel—what they are responsible for and how they are linked to each other; design issues, including issue statements linked to comment, elaboration, and resolution statements; the chain or web of formal engineering analyses along with suitable annotations, emendations, and translations (Subrahmanian et al., 1993). Most importantly, all of these models can be interlinked in a shared modeling space (e.g., nodes in the design issue model can be linked to nodes in any of the other models). Representing an issue in the design issue model may involve cross-links to several parts of the design artifact model, to information structures in the public and internal documents models (as discovered, for example, by sublanguage co-occurrence analysis), to potentially conflicting roles in the personnel model, and to possible schedule overruns with respect to nodes in the process model.

Certain kinds of models (like gIBIS; see Conklin & Begeman, 1988) and modeling support techniques like sublanguage or coword analysis have been found to be useful. They can be used to enable different perspectives to be represented via term network maps elaborated into multiple taxonomies and models derived from and structuring a corpus of information. Users need to view information from various abstraction levels as they see fit. This is why a shared modeling facility has been provided in *n*-dim. Studies have shown that engineers use a wide variety of modeling techniques (see summary in Subrahmanian, 1993). Therefore, it is important to support the creation of new modeling techniques as well as maintain those that have proven useful.

SHARED MODELING IN *N*-DIM

Shared modeling forms a sort of critical mass with three other main features of *n*-dim: *flat space, generalized modeling*, and *publishing*. Together they provide an overview of *n*-dim's main features.

Flat space enables individual information objects, such as chunks of text, to be situated in multiple contexts where they are placed in relation to other things. One can search not only over the contents of information objects but also the structures (models) in which they appear. Furthermore, a given object can appear in an arbitrary number of places (models) where each appearance is not a copy of the original but the original itself. Hence, there is no problem of maintaining the integrity of multiple copies with an original. Finally, not only different designers but the same designer can have multiple arrangements (models) of information objects—thus providing a way of representing the same object in different contexts.

This means that different collaborators can reference and talk about the same object even though they see it from very different perspectives (models). Flat space is one important factor supporting an inscription space enabling information to be recorded as originally presented but then multiply structured in models according to various points of view and updated information. Flat space always preserves an information item's initial entry into the inscription space of the collective.

Generalized modeling allows models to serve as prototypes, that is, models can serve as the starting point for other models, in the sense that they can be copied and the copy modified in ways only selectively constrained by the original (unlike class–instance relations). Exploration of ideas can be structured without having to commit to a taxonomic structure that could inhibit exploration of important ramifications. This allows local (e.g., at the project level) heterogeneous communities of practice to draw on information and conceptual models from many disciplines and non-disciplines without being bound by any particular disciplinary matrix (Kuhn, 1970) in proceeding with empirical and conceptual analyses, theory building, and evaluation.

Models can also serve as modeling languages: paradigms for structuring information. Modeling languages are represented as models themselves (i.e., as things to be designed, negotiated, etc.). In this sense, models can act as types for the creation of other models. Modeling languages are distillations of interrelations between information objects and can be useful beyond the current design situation by codifying formal and informal knowledge (Subrahmanian et al., 1993). Languages for structuring formal knowledge can be used to code expressions, constraints, and production rules that can be manipulated by inference mechanisms. Informal languages can be used to annotate documents, drawings, and formal structures of knowledge. These languages provide the necessary facility for coding design knowledge, organizational procedures, task allocation, and so on. Modeling languages enable the specification of a design to be increasingly standardized and automated thereby serving as a tool to help manage the growth and reconfiguration of a sociotechnical network by formalizing shared arrangements.

Using *n*-dim would thereby establish an inscription space in which doing design work would involve inscribing information objects in models whose evolving history could be maintained and available for reflection and further development.

Publishing is a mechanism for making models formally exchangeable and persistent. Hence, traces of the evolution of information and its structure over time can be found in the growing repository of published objects. Information can be captured in potentially branching paths of models created by designers. Backtracking is possible. Information sequence is maintained by the publishing mechanism. Once a user publishes a model, it is immediately available to anybody in the group or organization subject to access control at the individual, group, or division levels. A published model is inalterable (persistent) but is copyable by any person in the group. In an inscription space, publishing enables a temporal record to be kept of the sequence of potentially important events in design work establishing the basis for design history.

The n-dim system maintains pedigree information in the form of revision models. Their primitives are such that most mechanisms proposed for maintaining different versions based on user, time-stamp, and so on, are directly derivable from the revision model of any model in the n-dim system. Evolution of ideas and negotiations on the development of the artifact can be captured as a sequence of transformations to the models (including the creation of modeling languages and their instances) across time, product versions, and customers.

Thus, n-dim not only supports collaborative modeling but also captures design history as a by-product. Most importantly, design history can be created and maintained without additional burden on the designers.

CONCLUSIONS

This chapter has discussed some aspects of theory and practice in design, focusing on the problem of crossing the social–technical divide, especially at the borders of inscription spaces, mapping, modeling, and information technology. It has set forth the belief that research into engineering design practice (seen here as inherently a group activity) and systems that support it need to be evaluated and modified by an active engagement in design practice. An extension of design participation demands a new kind of design practice and reflection. There is continuing debate over whether such a practice/reflection is viable given current economic constraints, how to modify practice/reflection so it is viable, whether the practical limitations are too difficult to overcome, and how to overcome them as much as possible in the context of the work that comes along. As groupware becomes available on the Internet, WWW and (intra- or inter-)organizational intranets become established, there may be increased opportunities for creating new spaces of design practice/reflection. These are dependent on an ensemble of relays and negotiation.

Design practice and the theory of design practice involves information in multiple forms and in multiple perspectives. Their improvement may depend on identifying patterns and trends extracted from designs in the making. A computational environment can be evolved to record designs in the making if the working space of design practice is also an inscription space in which information is captured as it is created. Such an environment could help address the specification of designs, especially with respect to acquiring, reconciling, translating, and structuring cross-disciplinary and beyond disciplinary, that is, context-specific or local knowledge. Moreover, it could aid in keeping track of how decisions are reached and how information structures are built in an ongoing design project. In other words, such a computational environment could support the creation and maintenance of shared memory that can be used to inform future negotiations within and across design projects. It would be an environment for creation and reflection where the process of artifact construction could be at the same time a process for theory construction both in design and of design and where theory and practice could be integrated both in design and in research about design.

REFERENCES

Adams, W. G. (1988). Participatory programming for Digital Equipment Corporation, Inc. *Design Studies, 9*(1), 14–24.

Baronas, A. M. K., & Louis, M. R. (1988). Restoring a sense of control during implementation: How user involvement leads to system acceptance. *MIS Quarterly, 12*(1), 111–123.

Bijker, W. E., Hughes, T. P., & Pinch, T. K., (Eds.). (1987). *Social construction of technological systems*. Cambridge, MA: MIT Press.

Bjerknes, G., Ehn, P., & Kyng, M. (Eds.). (1987). *Computers and democracy—a Scandinavian challenge*. Aldershot, England: Avebury.

Blomberg, J., Suchman, L., & Trigg, R. (1995). Back to work: Renewing old agendas for cooperative design. In *Proceedings: Computers in Context: Joining Forces in Design, Third Decennial Conference* (pp. 1–9). Aarhus, Denmark: Aarhus University, Department of Computer Science.

Bowen, J., & Bahler, D. (1991). Supporting cooperation between multiple perspectives in a constraint-based approach to concurrent engineering. *Journal of Design for Manufacturing, 1*, 89–105.

Brackett, J. (1991). *Software reuse in Japan: A close look at Toshiba experience*. Slides from a lecture at Software Engineering Institute. Pittsburgh, PA: Carnegie Mellon University.

Bucciarelli, L. L. (1988). An ethnographic perspective on engineering design. *Design Studies, 9*(3), 159–168.

Callon, M., Law, J., & Rip, A. (Eds.). (1986). *Mapping the dynamics of science and technology: Sociology of science in the real world*. London: Macmillan.

Callon, M. (1987). Society in the making: The study of technology as a tool for sociological analysis. In W. E. Bijker, T. P. Hughes, & T. K. Pinch (Eds.), *Social construction of technological systems* (pp. 83–103). Cambridge, MA: MIT Press.

Callon, M., & Law, J. (1989). On the construction of sociotechnical networks: Content and context revisited. *Knowledge and Society: Studies in the Sociology of Science Past and Present, 8*, 57–83.

Callon, M. (1991). Techno-economic networks and Irreversibility. In J. Law (Ed.), *A sociology of monsters: Essays on power, technology and domination* (pp. 132–161). London: Routledge & Kegan Paul.

Callon, M. (1994). Is science a public good? Fifth Mullins Lecture, Virginia Polytechnic Institute, 23 March 1993. *Science, Technology, & Human Values, 19*(4), 395–424.

Castells, M. (1996). *The rise of the network society.* Cambridge, MA: Basil Blackwell.

Chen, T. S., & Sanoff, H. (1988). The patients' view of their domain. *Design Studies, 9*(1), 40–55.

Chen, H., Schatz, B., Ng, T., Martinez, J., Kirchoff, A., & Lin, C. (1996, August). A parallel computing approach to creating engineering concept spaces for semantic retrieval: The Illinois Digital Library Initiative Project. *IEEE Transactions on Pattern Analysis and Machine Intelligence, 18*(8), 771–782.

Chen, H., Schuffels, C., & Orwig, R. (1996, March). Internet categorization and search: A self-organizing approach. *Journal of Visual Communication and Image Representation, 7*(1), 88–102.

Chu, P. C., & Elam, J. J. (1990). Induced system restrictiveness: An experimental demonstration. *IEEE Transaction on Systems, Man, and Cybernetics, 20*(1), 195–201.

Clark, K., & Fujimoto, T. (1991). *Product development performance.* Cambridge, MA: Harvard Business Press.

Conklin, J., & Begeman, M. (1988). gIBIS: A hypertext tool for exploratory policy discussion. *ACM Transactions on Office Information Systems, 6*(4), 303–331.

Corbin, D. S. (1988). Strategic IRM plan: User involvement spells success. *Journal of Systems Management, 39*(5), 12–16.

Coulter, N., Monarch, I., Konda, S., & Carr, M., (1996). An evolutionary perspective of software engineering research through co-word analysis. *Software Engineering Institute Technical Report*, Software Engineering Institute of Carnegie Mellon University, Pittsburgh, PA.

Cutkosky, M. R., Engelmore, R. S., Fikes, R. E., Genesereth, M. R., Gruber, T. R., Mark, W. S., Tenenbaum, J. M., & Weber, J. C. (1993). PACT: An experiment in integrating concurrent engineering systems. *IEEE Computer, 26*(1), 28–37.

Duursma, C. M. (1990). Support for understanding and participation in a distributed problem solving system. In D. Diaper, D. Gilmore, G. Cockton, & B. Shackel (Eds.), *Human-Computer Interaction. INTERACT '90, Proceedings of the IFIP TC 13 Third International Conference* (pp. 1009–1010). The Netherlands: North-Holland, Amsterdam.

Feyerabend, P. K. (1975). *Against method.* London: New Left Books.

Floyd, C., Mehl, W., Reisin, F., Schmidt, G., & Wolf, G. (1989). Out of Scandinavia: Alternative approaches to software design and system development. *Human–Computer Interaction, 4*(4), 253–350.

Foucault, M. (1979). *Discipline and punish: The birth of the prison* (A. Sheridan, Trans.). New York: Vintage.

Gardiner, P., & Rothwell, R. (1985). Tough customers: Good designs. *Design Studies, 6*(1), 7–17.

Gronbaek, K., Kyng, M., & Mogensen, P. (1992). CSCW challenges in large-scale technical projects—a case study. *CSCW 92 Proceedings.* Toronto, Canada: ACM.

Harris, Z. (1989). *The form of information in science: Analysis of an immunology sublanguage.* Boston: Kluwer.

Hauser, J. R., & Clausing, D. (1988). The house of quality. *Harvard Business Review,* May–June, 63–73.

Hemmje, M., Kunkel, C., & Willett, A. (1994). Lyberworld—a visualization user interface supporting full-text retrieval. *SIGIR 94: Proceedings of the 17th International Conference on Research and Development in Information Retrieval.* Berlin, Germany: Springer-Verlag.

Hirschheim, R. A. (1985). User experience with and assessment of participative systems design. *MIS Quarterly, 9*(4), 295–304.

Hughes, T. (1987). The evolution of large technological systems. In W. E. Bijker, T. P. Hughes, & T. K. Pinch (Eds.), *Social construction of technological systems* (pp. 51–82). Cambridge, MA: MIT Press.

Kodama, F. (1991). *Analyzing Japanese high technology: The techno-paradigm shift.* London: Pinter.

Konda, S., Monarch, I., Sargent, P., & Subrahmanian, E. (1992). Shared memory in design: A unifying theme for research and practice. *Research in Engineering Design, 4*(1), 23–42.

Kuhn, T. (1970). *Structure of scientific revolutions* (2nd ed.). Chicago: University of Chicago Press.

Latour, B. (1988). Drawing things together. In M. Lynch & S. Woolgar (Eds.), *Representation in scientific practice* (pp. 19–69). Cambridge, MA: MIT Press.

Latour, B. (1990). Postmodern? no, simply amodern! steps towards an anthropology of science. *Studies of History and Philosophy of Science, 21*(1), 145–171.

Law, J., & Callon, M. (1992). The life and death of an aircraft: A network analysis of technical change. In W. E. Bijker & J. Law (Eds.), *Shaping technology/building society: Studies in sociotechnical change* (pp. 21–53). Cambridge, MA: MIT Press.

Levy, S., Subrahmanian, E., Konda, S., Coyne, R., Westerberg, A., & Reich, Y. (1993). An overview of the *n*-dim environment (Tech. Rep. No. EDRC-05-65-93). Pittsburgh, PA: Engineering Design Research Center, Carnegie Mellon University.

Mohrman, S. A., & Ledford, G. E., Jr. (1985). The design and use of effective employee participation groups: Implications for human resource management. *Human Resource Management, 24*(4), 413–428.

Monarch, I. (1994). An interactive computational approach for building a software risk taxonomy. In *The Third SEI Conference on Software Risk*, Pittsburgh, PA, April 5–7, 1994.

Monarch, I., & Gluch, D. (1995). *An experiment in software development risk analysis* (Tech. Rep. No. CMU/SEI-95-TR-014). Pittsburgh, PA: Software Engineering Institute of Carnegie Mellon University.

Monarch, I. (1996). Software engineering risk repository. *1996 SEPG Conference*, Atlantic City, NJ, May 20–23, 1996.

Naur, P. (1985). Programming as theory building. *Microprocessing and Microprogramming, 15*, 253–261.

The *n*-dim Group (in press). Networked information systems for collaborative product development: The *n*-dim approach. Manuscript submitted for publication.

Oberdorfer, J. (1988). Community participation in the design of the Boulder Creek branch library. *Design Studies, 9*(1), 4–13.

Olsen, K., Korfhage, R., Sochats, K., Spring, M., & Williams, J. (1993). Visualization of a document collection: The vibe system. *Information Processing & Management, 29*(1), 69–81.

Olson, M. H., & Ives, B. (1981). User involvement in system design: an empirical test of alternative approaches. *Information & Management, 4*, 183–195.

Quayle, M. (1987). Computer-aided participatory design: SITESEE. *Journal of Architecture and Planning Research, 4*(4), 335–342.

Reich, Y., Konda, S., Monarch, I., & Subrahmanian, E. (1992). Participation and design: An extended view. In M. J. Muller, S. Kuhn, & J. A. Meskill (Eds.), *PDC'92: Proceedings of the Participatory Design Conference* (pp. 63–71). Cambridge, MA: Computer Professionals for Social Responsibility.

Reich, Y., Konda, S., Levy, S., Monarch, I., & Subrahmanian, E. (1993). New roles for machine learning in design. *Artificial Intelligence in Engineering, 8*, 165–181.

Sanoff, H. (1988). Participatory design in focus. *Architecture and Behavior, 4*(1), 27–42.

Sargent, P., Subrahmanian, E., Downs, M., Greene, R., & Rishel, D. (1992). Materials' information and conceptual data modeling. In T. I. Barry & K. W. Reynard (Eds.), *Computerization and networking of materials databases: Vol. 3. ASTM STP 1140.* Philadelphia, PA: American Society for Testing and Materials.

Schon, D. (1983). *The reflective practitioner: How professionals think in action.* New York: Basic Books.

Schrage, M. (1991). *Shared minds: The new technologies of collaboration.* New York: Random House.

Star, S. L. (1988). The structure of ill-structured solutions: Boundary objects and heterogeneous distributed problem solving. In M. Huhns & L. Gasser (Eds.), *Readings in distributed artificial intelligence 2.* Menlo Park, CA: Kaufman.

Star, S. L. (1989). Layered space, formal representations and long-distance control: The politics of information. *Fundamenta Scientiae, 10*(2), 125–154.

Star, S. L., & Greisemer, J. R. (1989). Institutional ecology, "translations" and boundary objects: Amateurs and professionals in Berkeley's museum of vertebrate zoology, 1907–39. *Social Studies of Science, 19*, 387–420.

Subrahmanian, E., Konda, S. L., Levy, S. N., Reich, Y., Westerberg, A. W., & Monarch, I. (1993). Equations aren't enough: Informal modeling in design. *AI EDAM, 7*(4), 257–274.

Tait, P., & Vessey, I. (1988). The effect of user involvement on system success: A contingency approach. *MIS Quarterly, 12*(1), 91–108.

von Hippel, E. (1988). *The sources of innovation.* New York: Oxford University Press.

Whyte, W. F., Greenwood, D. J., & Lazes, P. (1991). Participatory action research: Through practice to science in social research. In W. F. Whyte (Ed.), *Participatory action research* (pp. 19–56). Newbury Park, CA: Sage.

Zuboff, S. (1988). *In the age of the smart machine: The future of work and power.* New York: Basic Books.

15

Dwelling in the "Great Divide": The Case of HCI and CSCW

Liam J. Bannon
University of Limerick, Ireland

A major theme of this volume is the development of frameworks for the analysis and understanding of the world, which reconceptualizes the set of overly simplistic distinctions that have hitherto held sway in the social and technical sciences. Master narratives in the field of science, technology, and society, such as social relativism and technological determinism, are being discarded as too crude and superficial. Instead, a wide variety of approaches are appearing that reinvent concepts of both the social and the technical, and attempt to deal with their inevitable and inextricable interweaving. For example, some studies extend the concepts of agency, actors, and networks (Callon's "actor–network" model, 1991). On the other hand, there are ethnomethodological studies on how technology is literally constructed, by and through the actions of people in specific organizational settings (cf. contributions in Button, 1993). In some of these approaches, new vocabularies are being constructed to describe objects and relations in these newly discovered or more correctly, newly named, universes of discourse.

This chapter, although not engaging in these larger issues concerning the construction of new discourses, has a more modest goal, that is, to describe the state of affairs in two scientific fields that are undeniably interdisciplinary, and to see what lessons can be learned from the successes and failures of these interdisciplinary enterprises. In other words, this chapter attempts to provide some answers to the questions posed by Leigh Star in her introductory remarks to the original workshop on which these chapters are based, namely, how it is possible to overcome the "great divide" between the social and technical sciences and learn to live, in a sense, "in between" them. The chapter investigates this question by discussing two areas of interdisciplinary activity—namely, human–computer interaction (HCI) and computer-supported cooperative work (CSCW). In each case, a variety of viewpoints on the nature of the field is presented, followed by dissection of a key concept utilized within these areas. It appears unquestionably the case that there are serious difficulties with certain central concepts in both these fields, certainly as regards their widespread acceptance and utilization within each area.

Yet, it is also the case that somehow, despite the lack of agreement about concepts, progress is being made in each field. It is argued that one of the reasons why there is some movement in each field is due to the pressures and concerns of practitioners (designers and users) who have real problems that they seek answers to, rather than to the development of any more inclusive or grounded conceptual apparatus. This is not to argue for the elimination of theory, but to realize that in the areas studied, the gap between theory and application is vast, and much more work is required in developing better understandings of the nature of the phenomena under discussion (classifications, taxonomies, etc.) as a prelude to further theorizing. In a sense, both areas require an engineering rather than a scientific approach, especially given the constructive nature of the two fields discussed here. Some implications of such a position, regarding the nature of interdisciplinarity, and the role of disciplines in defining the boundaries of a field are discussed later.

CASE 1: UNDERSTANDING THE HUMAN–COMPUTER INTERACTION (HCI) FIELD

Over the last decade, the area of human–computer interaction has grown enormously, both within academic research environments and corporate research laboratories. The field attracts interest from very disparate concerns—a variety of academic disciplines, principally cognitive psychology, but also educational psychology, organizational studies, graphic design, media studies, software engineering, artificial intelligence, sociology, and differing groups involved in the production and consumption of computer-based goods (i.e., manufacturers, marketing people, labor unions, consumer groups).

This section intends to show how a community of people, both practitioners and academic researchers, developed the field of HCI over a number of years and gave the field some identity and shape, without, surprisingly, having any apparent shared understanding of the exact focus of the new field. This is examined specifically with respect to a central concept in the HCI area, namely, the very concept of the *interface*. Although undoubtedly this lack of an agreed meaning has caused some problems, and led to various kinds of boundary disputes in the field, the point here is to note how at the same time this underdefined concept gave shape to a community, and thus in some sense served as a "boundary object," in Star's sense of the term (Star & Griesemer, 1989). The *interface*, and the HCI area more generally, thus served as a frame within which a variety of groups could work, despite their differing perspectives. At the same time, the problems associated with the differing interpretations of the term have over time also lead to some of the problems inherent in the enterprise and these confusions and disagreements can also be seen in the field. However, attention to the needs of practitioners has helped the field to focus on relevant issues, and kept it from becoming bogged down in what could have become just sterile academic debates about "proper" definitions.

Next, several competing viewpoints on the nature of the HCI field are presented. This is followed by a documentation of the confusion existing in the HCI literature concerning the fundamental idea of interface. A later section notes how, despite the lack of an agreed terminology or conceptual frame, the field can be described as having made progress over the past decade, and to have shifted in its concerns, due principally to their listening to the voices of people engaged in practical activities at the coal face, rather than confining themselves to arcane disputes about concepts, fueled by disciplinary biases. It is in such a manner that, perhaps, real interdisciplinarity can occur—when it is driven by content questions, not disciplinary concerns.

Perspectives on HCI

HCI as Simply an "Umbrella" Term. For many people, the label HCI simply denotes a very ill-defined category of issues and studies concerned in some way with the relation between individuals and computers. According to this perspective, the field is not characterized by any particular conceptual framework or methodological approach. The HCI "community" comprises people from many diverse disciplinary backgrounds, with a range of interests stemming from theoretical to pragmatic concerns. On this viewpoint, there is no such thing as a set of shared definitions of basic concepts for the field, nor are they required. Simply helping to bring together these different interest groups, for example, at the annual ACM SIGCHI conference where literally thousands of people (researchers, consumers, vendors, developers) put out their stalls and mix and match is useful in and of itself, so nothing further is needed or required. The community thus formed can be characterized simply by the fact that they attend such gatherings, rather than sharing any conceptual framework.

HCI as a New Research Field. For others, the emergence of HCI as a separate entity from the human factors (HF) field (one of its progenitors) in the early 1980s, signaled that there was something distinct about the new field. It was setting out a stall that focused on computers in particular, rather than machines in general, and also explicitly addressed (albeit in a rudimentary way) the need to understand how people could, or should, interact with computers. For many people who accepted this perspective, a key element was the move toward a more cognitive approach to ergonomics, as distinct from the earlier "knobs and dials" behavioral approach of much human factors work. A number of academic groups adopted HCI as a legitimate focus for education and research activity, based primarily in psychology and computer science departments. The older field was seen as lacking in theoretical motivation by cognitive scientists. What was required, it was claimed, was a better *cognitive coupling* between the human and the new universal machine, the computer, and not simply improved surface characteristics of displays. This approach argued for a principled position on the nature of "users," who were to be viewed as information-processing devices that could be studied in ways akin to the study of other information-processing devices (viz. computers). Thus, the field could be built on the bedrock of cognitive psychology and computing concepts, and appropriate methods of investigation of HCI phenomena should consist of experimental investigations and simulation studies.

HCI as the User Interface. The simplest and strictest definition of what HCI is about has been adopted by those who accept that the term is synonymous with the study of the design and use of interfaces to computer systems. This particular approach is prevalent among many computer scientists, especially in the software engineering area. There is a clear distinction made between the interface and the application, with work on the functionality being the province of the engineer, whereas some outside advice on the interface (e.g., from psychologists) might be permissible. For example, Robinson (1990) noted that "the interface stands as a defining and sustaining boundary for the business of HCI, both conceptually and literally" (p. 43). The issue of how the interface is actually constituted is discussed later. In this approach, there is an interest in developing guidelines for engineering the interface, developing dialogue frameworks, and so on.

HCI as a Paradigm Shift. Yet another viewpoint found in the community is one that explicitly recognizes the importance of the human element in computing and explores alternative forms of interaction that might be possible between people and machines. This view is more encompassing than the previous perspective focusing on the interface. It does not attempt to regulate or sharply delineate the area, but is content to advocate the importance of taking a "user-centered" approach toward the design of computer systems.

Given such a variety of orienting perspectives evident among the loosely constituted HCI community, it is perhaps not too surprising to discover, when examining some of the basic concepts utilized within the HCI field, ambiguities and uncertainties about the supposed core concern of HCI—namely, the interface.

Uncovering the "Interface"[1]

[The interface is] "that part of the program that determines how the user and the computer communicate." (Newman & Sproull, 1979)

"Instead of seeing it (the interface) as a part of the program I propose that we view it as a relation between program and use context. . . . It does not make sense to say that a system in isolation has an interface; interfaces 'emerge' when the system is used." (Andersen, 1990)

As indicated in these quotes, the interface concept is open to a number of interpretations. It is often not even clear if people are referring to the *computer interface* or the *user interface* when they talk of the interface as if it is a well-defined entity. Whereas the latter term is most often used, this distinction is not merely academic: ". . . Our equation of 'the user interface' to software and I/O devices means, ironically, that 'user interface' denotes the computer's interface to the user, not the user's interface to the computer" (Grudin, 1993, p. 115). What Grudin called the "computer's interface to the user" can be viewed as the (traditional) software engineering view of the interface, to emphasize that this view of the interface is shared among a professional community. This community has an overlapping set of interests with that of the heterogeneous HCI community, although it has a specific disciplinary orientation. Viewing the interface in this way is problematic in terms of understanding how the overall human–computer interface is perceived by members of the user community, as the users' view of the interface to the system has this larger compass that goes outside of the computer hardware and software itself. Thus, one source of misunderstanding of the term *interface* has been uncovered, one based on different understandings of the inclusiveness of the term and of the perspective from which the interface is viewed (be it from that of the software engineer or that of users).

---

[1] This section is adapted from Kuutti and Bannon (1991).

Although the HCI area is acknowledged to be an interdisciplinary one, the loudest voice has usually belonged to psychologists. A line of demarcation between programmers and psychologists in software design is sometimes drawn by focusing on the separation of the interface from the underlying "functionality" of the system. Robinson (1990) noted that

> The interface stands as the boundary between what is the work of HCI and what is the work of the software engineer. The "true" nature of the system—what it does—is defined by the state of the software "behind" the interface . . . the neutral and objective functionality of the "internal" state (of the machine) may be realized by alternative interface designs. (p. 43)

Such an approach has had the unfortunate effect of reifying the interface concept for much of the HCI community as the prime object of study. This reification has also tended to result in an undue emphasis on rather "surface" aspects of interface design, within many of the different interpretations of the interface that are commonly used. Yet, paradoxically, this reification of the interface as the domain of HCI has actually marginalized its impact. For example, Papert (1990) commented: "I think the interface is part of a larger thing. I think that putting the emphasis on the interface somewhat confuses the issues. . . . If only the interface (is changed), and what lies behind it and what you can do with the system isn't changed, you're only scratching the surface. The interface is only the surface" (p. 230).

More recently, this particular view of "what the interface is" has become the subject of debate within the HCI community. Specifically, the interface–functionality separation is seen as misleading. As Laurel (1990) noted, "The noun, interface, is taken to be a discrete and tangible thing that we can map, draw, design, implement, and attach to an existing bundle of functionality. One of the goals of this book is to explode that notion" (p. xi). It can be seen as a possible territorial division of responsibility between software engineers and HCI people. In designing a program or system, obviously attention must be given to the needs of the user and the use situation, and to how the design will meet these needs. The idea that in such situations a neat separation between interface and functionality can be accomplished is open to question. The connotation of the interface as a "surface" issue is seen as marginalizing the concerns of the intended users of computer systems. For example, Norman (1990), one of the doyens of the HCI community, commented:

> What's wrong with interfaces? The question for one. The interface is the wrong place to begin. It implies you already have done all the rest and want to patch it up to make it pretty for the user. That attitude is what is

wrong with the interface. . . . In the future I want less emphasis on "interfaces" and more on appropriate tools for the task. (p. 6)

Similar concerns can be found elsewhere, for example, in Gorasson, Lindt,
Pettersson, Sandblad, and Schwalbe (1987) and in Bannon and Bødker
(1991).

Faced with this seeming confusion about a central HCI concept, there
have been a number of calls for clarifying this and other terms in HCI,
through the development of a *common dictionary* of concepts, to which all
communities must adhere in their discussion of computer systems. Such
a grand unifying vision is fraught with many kinds of problems. The
problems cannot be resolved simply by making more exact definitions.
This is because the use of the terms is spread across a variety of disciplines,
and it is impossible to enforce a single meaning of a term already in use
across these quite distinct, even if overlapping communities. The least
that could be done would be try to make the contexts of use of the term
clearer for all the parties involved, so that all can recognize that use of
the same term does not imply similar meanings. On the other hand, in
practical development work these distinct communities should be able to
cooperate, and in order to do so the plain recognition of differences is
not enough, but the different contexts of use should be related and
different meanings bridged, at least locally and temporally. Note that this
does not imply that people thus "share" concepts, but that they can get
by in specific situations. It is thus possible for different groups to be aware
of different uses of concepts and take these into account. This is quite
different from engaging in terminological wrangles based on arguments
from first principles. Many disputes about the field have more to do with
disciplinary turf battles than with any serious issue of concern to practitioners. Nevertheless, a number of changes in the field of HCI are not
brought about through the academic refinement of ideas and concepts
but rather driven by the concerns of designers and users of computer-
based systems.

The Changing Nature of HCI

Despite the advances that have been made in various arenas of human–
computer interaction, there has been serious criticism of the field for its
lack of relevance to practitioners in systems design. There is no clear set
of principles that has emerged from this work. The experience of certain
designers has been loosely codified, various design guidelines are available, and a large number of evaluations of existing systems have been
produced, but the attempt to place this applied science on a more rigorous
footing has been difficult. The general lack of contact of the work with

real-world design situations has been noted. From the perspective of the designer, the work to date can highlight some pertinent issues, but new ways of thinking about and developing systems are necessary. It is precisely because of these problems that there is a current interest in "alternative" approaches to the study of HCI—both in conceptual frameworks (from psychological to sociological), research methodologies (from lab experiments to field studies), and design practice (from sequential to iterative design models). The net has been cast wide, and the relevance of a variety of different approaches to the study of work, technology, and organization have been explored. Such approaches as sociocultural activity theory, the ethnomethodological approach, work analysis, and participative design methods have been the subject of debate and discussion. What holds the assorted collection of topics together is that they all are pertinent to understanding how to contribute to a better understanding of technology in use, as they give insight and suggestions for changes in the actual nature of the HCI design process itself, incorporating the voices of actors that have been voiceless previously.

Searching for Alternative Conceptual Frameworks. Much work on the relation between people and computers, concerning design, use, and evaluation of systems, has assumed a cognitive science perspective. Despite the often exaggerated claims made by proponents of this perspective as to its achievements, a number of people have admitted there are problems in this approach. Norman (1980) pointed to the gaps existing in the then-fledgling new science. He was particularly concerned about the basic building block in this approach, which he referred to as the *model human–information processor*: "The problem seemed to be in the lack of consideration of other aspects of human behavior, of interaction with other people and with the environment, of the influence of the history of the person, or even the culture, and of the lack of consideration of the special problems and issues confronting an animate organism that must survive as both an individual and as a species" (p. 2). Much of this critique remains unanswered today. What has been changing, at least in some circles, is the uncritical acceptance of this paradigm as the only, or even a sufficient one to handle the queries he raised. Some critics focus on the *individualistic* nature of much cognitivist theorizing, arguing for greater attention to the setting in which cognition takes place and how it is shaped by this setting: "Cognition observed in everyday practice is distributed—stretched over, not divided among— mind, body, activity and culturally organized settings (which include other actors)" (Lave, 1988, p. 1). Some have argued for a radically different epistemology for the discipline, eschewing the "Cartesian model" for a hermeneutical interpretation. Such a radical critique has been popularized within the computing fraternity by the work of Winograd and Flores starting out from the work of Heidegger, Maturana, and others. The cognitive paradigm has also been attacked at a foundational level by certain sociologists, particularly those who favor an ethnomethodological approach (see, e.g., Coulter, 1983). Yet another long-standing critique of Cartesianism comes from the dialectical materialist tradition within Soviet thought, developed from ideas about activity present in the work of Hegel, then elaborated by Marx and applied within a psychological framework by psychologists such as Vygotsky (1978) and Leontiev. Backhurst (1988) referred to this alternative tradition as "communitarian" in distinction to the "individualistic" Cartesian tradition. Such an approach requires an understanding of the social as a prerequisite to understanding the individual, the opposite of what many theorists and researchers, in the human and even branches of the social sciences, have argued previously. The use of this approach in HCI is currently being developed (Bannon & Bødker, 1991; Bødker, 1989; Kuutti & Bannon, 1993).

Recognizing That "Users" and Settings Are Heterogeneous. The concept of computer "users" has tended to mask a large variety of different kinds of work activities with computers under a generic label that ignores the different aptitudes, interests, and even more importantly, skills possessed by people, as well as the differences in their context of use. The majority of experimental studies in HCI focus on first-time learners of computer systems or applications. Typically, performance is monitored for the first hour or two on the system. Exceptionally, perhaps use of an application is observed over a few days, but rarely for longer periods. Granting that there is some need for studying such users, the paucity of studies that are concerned with the process of development of expertise with a computer application is remarkable. The issue is not simply that expert performance needs further examination, but that greater attention should be paid as to how users become skilled in the use of the computer application. What obstacles or incentives are there within the system to encourage the growth of competence? Additional issues relate to the difference in system learning and use between freshman university students and particular work groups with their own already established set of work practices, which may hinder or support learning and development of competence on the computer system. The issue here is not one of "typing" users into psychological categories, but rather of understanding the different contexts in which people utilize computers in order to accomplish their work, in terms of the tasks involved, the work setting, and the length of time people have been doing this work.

The majority of HCI research studies to date also take as their focus the individual user working on a computer system. This research focus totally neglects the way work actually gets done in most work situations, and the importance of coordination and cooperation between people in accomplishing their work. The applied field has been more astute than the theoretical here, for system designers have been more aware of this coordinated aspect of work activity and have tried to support it at some level, albeit rather crudely. With a better understanding of how work gets accomplished coming from social science researchers such as Suchman, Wynn, and Blomberg, designers have been developing a better "model" or understanding of the work from which to build. The word "model" is in quotes here because, of course, what such research shows is that a strict model of human action in most work situations is not possible or appropriate, rather, human action is driven by the concrete situation that exists at any moment and is constantly changing. This implies that office workers should be supported in their activities rather than building office automation systems. Extending the focus of concern from the human–computer dyad to larger groups of people and machines engaged in collaborative tasks has become an important area for research in the new field of computer support for cooperative work (CSCW), discussed further later.

Moving From the Laboratory to the Workplace. Much of the early research done in the HCI field was confined to rather small controlled experiments, with the presumption that the findings could be generalized to other settings. It has become increasingly apparent that such studies suffer from a variety of problems that limit their usefulness in any practical setting. First, by the time these studies are done, advances in technology often make the original concerns outdated. Also, important contextual cues for the accomplishment of tasks were often omitted in this transfer from the real world to the laboratory, and so the results of the lab studies became difficult to apply elsewhere. Increasingly, attention is shifting to in situ studies, in an effort to "hold in" the complexity of the real-world situations, and a variety of observational techniques are being employed to capture activities, especially video. This concern with understanding the context in which work gets done, and the role of technology in supporting or disrupting these activities, has lead to the need for researchers skilled in observational techniques (such as ethnographers, coming from sociological and anthropological backgrounds) in the HCI/CSCW field.

Reconceptualizing the Design Process: Scandinavian Initiatives. The field of HCI encompasses aspects of the design process, and is specifically concerned with the relation between user requirements and systems design. This is an area where it has been acknowledged that existing methods of requirements analysis, and the tools available to support analysts and users are inadequate. Likewise, their is growing concern about the methodologies for assuring what is termed *user input* to design specifications. Many of the criticisms of such approaches have been orchestrated by Scandinavian researchers, who have argued for an alternative model over a number of years (see Bjerknes, Ehn, & Kyng, 1987; Ehn, 1988b; Greenbaum & Kyng, 1991). These critiques cover a wide range of issues, only some of which are mentioned here, as fuller accounts of this approach are presented in this volume (Bødker & Markussen).

Currently, workers are often asked to evaluate the descriptions made of their work processes by analysts, yet this is often unproductive, as the representational formalisms adopted are often obscure to the workers. In many cases, rather than clarifying things, they simply obscure actual work processes in a cloud of abstractions that make little sense to the people whose work is supposedly being modeled. Worse, these abstractions are then utilized as the basis for building the information system, with the result that the inadequacy of these descriptions becomes clear to all in the failure of the resulting system.

An alternative approach pioneered by different groups in Scandinavia, and sometimes referred to as *Cooperative Design* is to work with users in the whole design process, accepting that needs analysis documents will inevitably be incomplete, and that even with the best of intentions, users find it difficult to articulate how they work, especially if asked to use some form of modeling notation with which to describe or interpret it. Alternative ways of allowing users to map their work processes and the contradictions they currently experience are required. Such methods as Future Workshops, role playing exercises, and games can assist this process (see chapters in Greenbaum & Kyng, 1991, for examples). Such an approach presents a radical critique to much current systems development methodologies, yet due to the concern over acknowledged problems in traditional methods, there has been increased interest in these alternative ideas in recent years. However, it would be a good idea to review more carefully the successes and failures of these experiments, in order to see what aspects of these experiences can be usefully taken up in settings quite different to those of the original studies (see Grudin, 1991b). Paradoxically, some of this work is now itself being taken out of context and being promulgated by some as a panacea for almost any systems development problems one might encounter. Nevertheless, the growth of interest in the Participatory Design conferences of recent years (see Schuler & Namioka, 1993) attests to the concerns on the part of the design community for more effective ways of developing requirements and designing information systems.

So a number of shifts in the field of HCI can be discerned over the years, brought about more by attention to the concerns of people "on the ground" than to any developments in the conceptual aramentarium deployed. Before any further discussion on the implications of such findings, a second case is outlined from the emerging interdisciplinary field of CSCW, closely related on some dimensions to HCI; once again, the discussion notes the pattern of a variety of perspectives on the field being evident, and similar uncertainty about its basic concepts. However, it too is an example of an interdisciplinary area attracting a very heterogeneous mixture of interest groups that somehow manages to evolve and develop despite such shortcomings.

CASE 2: COOPERATIVE WORK AND ITS COMPUTER SUPPORT

The birth of the term *computer-supported cooperative work* (now commonly abbreviated to CSCW) can be definitively traced to the computer scientists Greif and Cashman back in 1984, when they coined this term as a suitable theme for a small invited workshop focusing on the development of computer systems that would support people in their work activities. At that time, they did not actually have any specific view on what exactly was meant by the term *cooperative work*. Since that time, much effort has been spent attempting to define the bounds of the research area (Bannon, 1993; Bannon & Schmidt, 1991; Grudin, 1991a; Hughes, Randall, & Shapiro, 1991). The area has attracted a growing community of researchers, practitioners, and pundits, coming from a motley collection of disciplines including computing, software engineering, cognitive and social psychology, work sociology, anthropology, and organizational theory, to name but a few. The purpose here is to show how the area is characterized by a variety of perspectives and note the amount of dissension and debate around a key concept underlying the field, namely, cooperative work.

Perspectives on CSCW

Despite interest in the new field, there is still no universally accepted definition of CSCW. Indeed, whether CSCW can be viewed as a new field of research in its own right has been questioned by some. As a way into some of the confusion and controversy, at least four distinct ways of viewing CSCW can be distinguished (Bannon, 1993). Readers should note how these different perspectives are related to those viewpoints described for the HCI field earlier.

CSCW as an Umbrella Term. At the simplest level, it can be argued that *CSCW* is simply an umbrella term with little content other than the idea that it is concerned with people, computers, and cooperation in some form. The utility of such a seemingly vacuous definition is that it allows people from a variety of different disciplines, with partially overlapping concerns as to the current state of technology development and the understanding of use contexts, to come together and discuss issues of mutual interest. CSCW in this view is an "arena" where different groups vie for the attention of participants, rather than a coherent focused field. In his remarks at a panel at CSCW'88, Howard described two distinct though very varied communities within CSCW. He coined the term *strict constructionists* to describe those in the field focused on the development of computer systems to support group work, who tend to use themselves as objects of analysis in the provision of support tools. These people, mainly implementers, are interested in building tools (widgets), and they see the area of CSCW as a possible leverage point for creating novel applications. Most of these people equate the CSCW field with Groupware, as they focus on new software applications. Howard called those who make up the remainder of the CSCW field *loose constructionists*, a heterogeneous collection of people, some of whom are drawn to the area by their dissatisfaction with current uses of technology to support work processes, others because they see in this area a chance for communities who traditionally have not had a voice in the design of computer systems to have one. Kling (1991) articulated a somewhat different view of the CSCW community. He saw CSCW as a conjunction of "certain kinds of *technologies*, certain kinds of *users* (usually small self-directed professional teams), and a *worldview* that emphasizes convivial work relations" (p. 83). This issue, of whether or not CSCW implies anything about shared goals of group members, or convivial work relations, has been the subject of some dispute (Bannon & Schmidt, 1991).

CSCW as a Paradigm Shift. Hughes et al. (1991) argued that CSCW should be conceived of as a paradigm shift in the way of thinking about designing computer support systems of all kinds, rather than as a distinct research field. This position has similarities to the views of Suchman (1989), who described CSCW as "the design of computer-based technologies with explicit concern for the socially organized practices of their intended users" (p. 1). Both these views deny any special prerogative to particular user groups, technologies, or forms of work in what constitutes CSCW. Rather, the emphasis is on "the turn to the social," realizing that much work on people–technology systems has systematically avoided issues of the social organization of work and their implications for the design of appropriate support technology.

CSCW as Software for Groups. A quite different conception of what the field is about can be discerned among those who focus on the computer support of "groups" or teams as the hallmark of the field. This has given rise to the term *groupware* to distinguish the computer products marketed in this area (Johansen, 1988). Although this view is most commonly found among information technology and business consultants, it can also be found among software developers and researchers. For example, Greif (1988), one of the originators of the term *CSCW*, defined it as "an identifiable research field focused on the role of the computer in group work" (p. 5). As noted by Kling (1991), many adherents of this view tend to focus on small teams or homogeneous groups with convivial work relations, and thus ignore settings in everyday organizational life where issues such as power and politics play a large role. The "group" focus has also been criticized, based on difficulties of enumerating properties of "groups" as found in the workplace. The relevance of many group studies undertaken in lab situations to workplace situations have also come under criticism.

CSCW as Technological Support of Cooperative Work Forms. Bannon and Schmidt (1991) defined CSCW as "an endeavor to understand the nature and characteristics of cooperative work with the objective of designing adequate computer-based technologies" (p. 5). Here the emphasis is on understanding cooperative work as a distinctive form of work (Schmidt, 1992), and on supporting these cooperative work forms with appropriate technology. This broadens the scope of the field considerably beyond that of computer support for groups. In this framework, cooperative work does not imply any notion of shared goals or conviviality, but rather people engaged in work processes related as to content. Critics of this approach argue that the distinction between cooperative work and individual work is problematic in everyday work situations, and that this approach has too functionalist a perspective, neglecting subjective factors of participation and cooperation.

CSCW as Participative Design. As noted in the comments of Howard (1988), the CSCW community contains within its ranks a number of people who are proponents or practitioners of participative, or participatory, design (see the review by Clement & Van den Besselaar, 1993). Their focus is on developing alternatives to traditional systems design, alternative ways of doing design, of involving users, and so on (see, e.g., Greenbaum & Kyng, 1991). It is the involvement of what has come to be called the Scandinavian school of systems developers in the CSCW community that has led some people to equate the CSCW area with participative design (PD) practices. This is a clear mistake that can only add to confusion surrounding both fields. Certainly various forms of user involvement are important to the development of successful CSCW systems, so use of such techniques or ideas does not automatically signify any focus on cooperative work as variously discussed earlier. Nor, in many cases, are PD researchers interested directly in computer support for the design practices they are proposing. Indeed, many successful participative design practices (e.g., future workshops, wall charting, etc.) are noticeable by the complete absence of computers in supporting the ongoing work of the group. At the same time, the interests of PD and CSCW can overlap. For example, the software development process itself can be seen as a form of cooperative work that is supported by computers, and thus is an interesting and quite legitimate domain for CSCW studies. However, equating CSCW and PD entails unnecessary restrictions for each field of endeavor, and serves to confuse their different research goals and agendas. Part of the confusion has been caused by the fact that a number of members of the CSCW community are also members of the PD community. This should not obscure the differences between the nature of the two fields.

Having described some of the different perspectives evident in the CSCW field, the next section looks briefly at the confusion surrounding a central concept within this field, *cooperative work*, akin to the confusion found in the HCI field around the interface.

Understanding Cooperative Work

Just as the interface was a defining feature of the HCI field, so the concept of cooperative work plays a central role in the CSCW field. Yet, once again, on deeper investigation, there is no shared understanding of what is meant by "cooperative work" among the CSCW community.[2] Analyzing the meaning of cooperative work is necessary due to the wildly disparate uses of the term in the field at present.

All Work Is Cooperative Work. Ehn (1988a) and Bowers (1991) argued that all work is essentially cooperative, in that it depends on others for its successful performance. Taking this stance would seem to imply that there is no additional clarification achieved by adding the term *cooperative* to that of *work*.

Cooperative Work Is Autonomous Group Work. Sørgaard (1987) had a very specific set of criteria for what would count as cooperative work,

---

[2]The following material is adapted from Bannon and Schmidt (1991) and Schmidt and Bannon (1992).

for instance, that it is nonhierarchical, nonspecialist, relatively autonomous, and so on. This is seriously problematic, as there are many forms
of work that are cooperative in the sense of there being the need for some
form of coordination to handle the division of labor, but it has no
necessary relation to group work as commonly discussed.

Cooperative Work Implies Shared Goals and Motives. From yet
another perspective, that of Howard (1987), the term *cooperative work* is
inappropriate because of the ideology inherent in the term, a "too sweet"
label for the realities of everyday work situations. He preferred an
allegedly more open term, *collective work.* Kling (1991) also referred to
similar possible connotations of the term *cooperative work.*

Cooperative Work Is a Distinct Form of Work. Yet another perspective relies on the traditional usage of the term in work sociology.
According to Bannon and Schmidt (1991):

> "Cooperative work," the term picked by Greif and Cashman to designate
> the application area to be addressed by the new field, happens to be a term
> with a long history in the social sciences. It was used as early as the first
> half of the 19th century by economists as the general and neutral designation
> of work involving multiple actors and was picked up and defined formally
> by Marx (1867) as "multiple individuals working together in a planned way
> in the same production process or in different but connected production
> processes." (p. 5)

In this perspective, the concept of cooperative work does not imply any
particular degree of participation or self-determination on the part of the
workers, nor a particularly democratic management style.

So once again, there is an interdisciplinary area that by all accounts is
growing in importance and numbers, yet apparently is able to exist
without having any shared set of concepts accepted by members of this
interdisciplinary community. The parallels between the HCI and CSCW
areas in this regard are striking, but what are the implications concerning
the viability and coherence of interdisciplinary fields of study?

LEARNING FROM EXPERIENCE
WITH INTERDISCIPLINARY STUDIES

This chapter has discussed two interdisciplinary fields, HCI and CSCW.
It has noted the wide variety of perspectives on the nature of the field
held by sectors of these communities, and also the fundamental uncertainties about key concepts in each field. Despite such apparent chaos,

both fields seem to have prospered and have been able to handle this extreme heterogeneity of disciplines, methods, and orientations. That the nature of these fields has been, and continues to be, the subject of debate is not necessarily problematic. In any area of science, the definition of the field—its core concerns and its boundaries—is best viewed as "contested terrain," even more so as the field struggles to find a unique identity, so it can set itself apart from its progenitors. The simple fact that there is dispute could be viewed as being symptomatic of a healthy debate about the underlying issues of interactivity, interface design, computer support, the nature of work, the role of groups in organizations, and so on, which should be clarified over time.

But perhaps such statements are painting too "rosy" a picture. A more jaundiced observer might respond that, really, little in the sense of real interdisciplinarity has occurred in these fields, as different groups carry on using their traditional methods, and produce results that are inter-preted within traditional disciplinary frameworks, with perhaps some lip service to interdisciplinary aspects. Thus, for example, psychologists within HCI perform experimental studies on limited corpora of material in the lab and then proffer implications of this work for the general workforce in a multitude of settings, or computer scientists in CSCW continue to analyze work activities utilizing paper descriptions of job tasks and then build models that are interpreted as being pertinent to real-world work activities. In both cases, it appears that the essence of the interdisciplinary field is being violated, as there is no attempt to take seriously the viewpoints of other groups, based either on differing disci-plinary bases or theoretical or practical concerns.

So, back to the issue of what really has been achieved by these inter-disciplinary fields. Is there a prospect of developing some form of inter-disciplinary theory for particular research fields, to which all members of the community could subscribe to, or is such an idea just a chimera? If such an overarching conceptual framework is not possible, what is left? It has been noted how the supposed new research fields of HCI and CSCW are characterized by a wide range of perspectives. Which of these perspectives is correct? Perhaps this is the wrong question to ask, as perspectives can be more or less illuminating, in certain contexts, rather than being clearly right or wrong in any absolute sense. However, it is important to be aware of the different frames of reference that people apply to an area, in order to better interpret their position. Thus, there are some implications of the different perspectives, in terms of an agenda for research and development, which should be noted. For example, for those who view either HCI or CSCW as simply umbrella terms, HCI and/or CSCW is simply a convenient rack or stall on which to hang a variety of topics, around which communities gather, and may be replaced rather easily by another name, or fad, so long as it brings along some of the communities currently gathered around the HCI/CSCW showcases. In other words, whereas the HCI/CSCW phenomena may have been useful in community building, they are a hollow shell. This may be regarded as an overly cynical position, but it might also be labeled extremely pragmatic, and is the view held by many outside observers of the HCI or CSCW field, who see little in the way of distinct conceptual frameworks, methodologies, or research agendas in either of these fields.

The Possibilities for Interdisciplinarity

Although debate continues about the core issues in HCI and CSCW, few would disagree with the observation that their *interdisciplinary* nature is a key feature. This attempt to meld viewpoints from such diverse fields as anthropology, drama studies (Laurel, 1993), and software engineering has, not surprisingly, created some difficulties and confusions. What the product of such melding could or should look like, and indeed, whether the very idea of "melding" different frameworks makes sense, are open to question. Certainly, a variety of different disciplines can contribute to these areas, utilizing different conceptual frameworks, methods, and so on, but the sense in which this *multidisciplinary* research can be said to be truly *interdisciplinary* is open to question.

This brings up the question of exactly what people mean when they discuss interdisciplinary studies. One view holds that HCI is interdisciplinary simply because a variety of different disciplinary backgrounds may be applied to study aspects of human–computer interaction (psychology, linguistics, software engineering, etc.). This might be termed the *weak* view, as it supports the notion of HCI as simply an additive combination of relevant disciplines, without much relation or interpenetration. According to this weak view, CSCW may be viewed as "HCI-plus" (i.e., HCI with the addition of social science disciplines, such as social and organizational psychology, sociology, and anthropology). But, it is not clear that such a simple additive model can be defended. The domains of interest of the different disciplines cannot be so neatly delineated, and findings subsequently combined, as this model assumes (cf. Bannon & Hughes, 1993).

An opposing perspective, which might be termed the *strong* view, argues that what is needed for truly interdisciplinary work is a radical attempt to develop either a completely new set of concepts and terminology for the new field, or to "wed" concepts from existing disciplinary fields together in order to create a new interdisciplinary theoretical framework. This could be accomplished, for instance, by constructing common dictionaries of terms and concepts that the different disciplines are supposed to utilize, or making mappings across conceptual frameworks, thus attempting to ensure some "shared understanding" among researchers. The ambitions of creating genuinely new interdisciplinary theoretical frameworks for any domain have not been very successful to date.[3] There have not been any exemplary projects that have both argued for this approach and, more importantly, produced interesting results, when viewed from any of the participating disciplines. Likewise, the attempts to create a shared perspective through simple legislation of core definitions of terms across fields seems to have limited utility.

Part of the problem here is that what is involved in assuming a particular theoretical stance toward a subject is often not sufficiently appreciated. At times, it appears that discussions of the need for interdisciplinarity revolves around the utility of a variety of different instruments or methods for gathering data, but it is important to note that a disciplinary perspective is not defined simply by the methods used. The recent interest in ethnographic field studies in CSCW is a case in point. Whereas anyone can rather quickly become proficient at interviewing or taking notes, the essence of this approach lies in the perspective adopted in framing the research, the way the individual chooses to interpret the findings, the authorities that person invokes to support a particular interpretation, and so forth—in sum, the whole conceptual framework within which an individual's approach to the world is framed. Note that the argument here is not that different disciplines are unable to contribute to a joint project, but that the aim of building some form of theoretical base to subsume a variety of conceptual frameworks from different disciplines implies a fundamental misunderstanding of different disciplinary perspectives. These different positions emerge out of different backgrounds, research traditions, perspectives, and so on, which are not commensurable (certainly not in any simplistic fashion). For example, attempting to build some form of hybrid unified framework to encompass an empirical functionalist systems approach with an interpretative constructivist approach seems doomed to failure, as the issue is not simply over different meanings to terms, but relates to fundamentally different *worldviews*. Certainly, theories can be broadened to include factors or circumstances previously omitted—it can be seen how CSCW concerns have prompted cognitive scientists to pay more attention to how artifacts change tasks (Norman,

---

[3]Some have attempted to construct a *hierarchical*, or *levels*, framework that allows for a family of theories—with different concepts—to deal with different aspects of a common object of research. Indeed, Kuutti and Bannon (1993) attempted to use such frameworks in order to structure some of the discussion within the HCI field. Although such frameworks can allow an individual to work with different conceptual frameworks on the same object, it still requires adherence to some minimal shared perspective on how the individual perceives or constructs the world.

1991) and to the distributed nature of cognition, across people and tasks (Hutchins, 1995)—but such extensions do not thereby subsume other theoretical frameworks.

The main point is that *interdisciplinarity* should not be conflated with *interdisciplinary theory qua theory*. The latter concept is fundamentally flawed and posits a Holy Grail that is inherently unattainable. But this does not at all imply that therefore interdisciplinary studies are impossible. Rather, it simply rejects one particular view of what could constitute the way forward in interdisciplinary studies. Part of the argument here is that both HCI and CSCW have indeed developed over time without any single defining disciplinary perspective, due principally to a focus on practice rather than theory.

CONCLUSIONS

One of the hallmarks of exemplary HCI and CSCW work is how it attempts to bridge the gap between the human and social sciences and computer science issues. The argument is not that one should leave behind one's particular disciplinary concepts and methods—indeed, it is important that work is concretely anchored within a well-defined framework— but that if, for example, ethnographic work is to count as HCI or CSCW it must at least attempt to address software design issues (e.g., to the extent of focusing attention on crucial aspects of human interaction that need to be supported via any technology). Likewise, computer science work should be informed by what is known of how people actually work, and show how the technology in fact supports features of this work. This is the challenge facing people from a variety of different backgrounds who wish to be active in HCI or CSCW, as distinct from experimental psychology or computer science. Of course, such work cannot be accomplished overnight. A certain amount of mutual learning between people working on common projects who bring their different perspectives and skills to the table is required. This process of learning is currently underway. Simplified views of people's abilities and the nature of human work activity and the potential for automating it have been replaced by an understanding on the part of information systems developers of the need to explore the human and social world of work. Within CSCW, for example, one can see how this "turn to the social" has lead to at least the beginning of a process of mutual learning between computer and social scientists (Sommerville, Sawyer, Rodden, & Bentley, 1992). In turn, certain social scientists, for example those involved in detailed ethnographic studies in a particular setting, are having to take seriously issues concerning the generalizability of their findings, and their implications for technology support, rather than simply presenting their interpretations of current work practices.

Finally, returning to the discussion of the great divide posited by Star, and based on the experiences of the HCI and CSCW fields, perhaps no such great divide exists. Rather, there exist a number of differing interpretations of what the object of interest is, and how it should be studied. Part of the success of the CSCW field to date has been in the ability of a number of researchers and practitioners, from a variety of disciplines, to take seriously the question of how to construct the common object for their endeavors (cf. especially Kuutti, 1991). The success of this work can be seen in the nature of the discourse within the field, where arguments over which discipline "owns" a problem have given way to genuine attempts to bring particular disciplinary biases to bear on the common object of research. To the extent that this is successful, a new interdisciplinary field is emerging.

Examining the fields of HCI and CSCW from this perspective, some differences can be discerned. Within HCI, as currently constituted, one witnesses a certain amount of fractionation into subgroups due to the lack of agreement on any set of common objects as a focus for their interdisciplinary efforts. Whether new objects can be found or constructed within the arena of HCI to keep it as a thematic entity is currently an open question. On the other hand, CSCW currently shows more hope in this regard, due to the ongoing and sustained attempts by members of the community to construct and articulate a set of common objects that would serve as foci for the field, as noted earlier. This does not imply that all members of the community share exactly the same concepts, but that although they may focus on different issues, there is a core set of common objects—such as the division of labor and mechanisms of interaction in work settings, which serve as boundary objects for both research and practice.

ACKNOWLEDGMENTS

Thanks to the workshop participants for useful discussions, to Bill Turner for his comments and patience, and to the EU Esprit COMIC Project 6225 for support. My understanding of issues in CSCW owes much to discussions with John Hughes and Kjeld Schmidt.

REFERENCES

Andersen, P. B. (1990, December). A semiotic approach to construction and assessment of computer systems. In H.-E. Nissen, H. K. Klein, & R. Hirschheim (Eds.), *Proceedings of ISRA-90 Conference*, Copenhagen, Denmark.

Backhurst, D. (1988). Activity, consciousness, and communication. *Quarterly Newsletter of the Laboratory of Comparative Human Cognition, 10*(2), 31–39.

Bannon, L. (1993). CSCW: An initial exploration. *Scandinavian Journal of Information Systems,* August, 3–24.

Bannon, L. J., & Bødker, S. (1991). Beyond the interface: Encountering artifacts in use. In J. Carroll (Ed.), *Designing interaction: Psychology at the human–computer interface* (pp. 227–253). New York: Cambridge University Press.

Bannon, L., & J. Hughes (1993). The context of CSCW. In K. Schmidt (Ed.), *Report of COST14 "CoTech" Working Group 4 (1991–1992)* (pp. 9–36). Denmark: Risø National Laboratory.

Bannon, L., & Schmidt, K. (1991). CSCW: Four characters in search of a context. In J. Bowers & S. Benford (Eds.), *Studies in computer supported cooperative work: Theory, practice and design* (pp. 3–16). Amsterdam: North-Holland.

Bjerknes, G., Ehn, P., & Kyng, M. (Eds.). (1987). *Computers and democracy—a Scandinavian challenge.* Aldershot, UK: Avebury.

Bowers, J. (1991). The Janus faces of design: Some critical questions for CSCW. In J. Bowers & S. Benford (Eds.), *Studies in computer supported cooperative work: Theory, practice and design* (pp. 333–350). Amsterdam: Elsevier North-Holland.

Button, G. (Ed.) (1993). *Technology in working order.* London: Routledge & Kegan Paul.

Bødker, S. (1989). A human activity approach to user interfaces. *Human Computer Interaction, 4*(3), 171–195.

Callon, M. (1991). Techno-economic networks and irreversibility. In J. Law (Ed.), *A sociology of monsters: Essays on power, technology and domination.* London: Routledge & Kegan Paul.

Clement, A., & Van den Besselaar, P. (1993). Participatory design projects: A retrospective look. *Communications of the ACM, 36*(6).

Coulter, J. (1983). *Rethinking cognitive theory.* London: Macmillan.

Ehn, P. (1988a). Remarks in panel discussion on "CSCW: What does it mean?" (L. Bannon, moderator). In *CSCW '88: Proceedings of the Conference on Computer-Supported Cooperative Work, September 26–28, 1988, Portland, Oregon.* New York: ACM.

Ehn, P. (1988b). *Work-oriented design of computer artifacts.* Falköping, Sweden: Arbetslivscentrum/Almqvist & Wiksell International, Lawrence Erlbaum Associates.

Goransson, B., Lindt, M., Pettersson, E., Sandblad, B., & Schwalbe, P. (1987). The interface is often not the problem. In J. Carroll & B. Tanner (Eds.), *Human factors in computer systems IV.* New York: North-Holland.

Greenbaum, J., & Kyng, M. (Eds.). (1991). *Design at work: Cooperative design of computer systems.* Hillsdale, NJ: Lawrence Erlbaum Associates.

Greif, I. (Ed.). (1988). *Computer-supported cooperative work: A book of readings.* San Mateo, CA: Kaufmann.

Grudin, J. (1991a, April–May). CSCW: The convergence of two development contexts. In *Proceedings ACM SIGCHI—CHI '91,* New Orleans, LA.

Grudin, J. (1991b). Interactive systems: Bridging the gaps between developers and users. *IEEE Computer,* April, 59–69.

Grudin, J. (1993, April). Interface: An evolving concept. *Communications of the ACM, 36*(4), 110–119.

Howard, R. (1987). Systems design and social responsibility: The political implications of "computer-supported cooperative work": A commentary. *Office: Technology and People, 3*(2), 175–187.

Howard, R. (1988). Remarks in panel discussion on "CSCW: What does it mean?" In *CSCW '88: Proceedings of the Conference on Computer-Supported Cooperative Work, September 26–28, 1988, Portland, Oregon.* New York: ACM.

Hughes, J., Randall, D., & Shapiro, D. (1991). CSCW: Discipline or paradigm? In L. Bannon, M. Robinson, & K. Schmidt (Eds.), *Proceedings of the Second European Conference on CSCW—ECSCW'91* (pp. 309–323). Dordrecht: Kluwer.

Hutchins, E. (1995). *Cognition in the wild.* Cambridge, MA: MIT Press.

Johansen, R. (1988). *Groupware. Computer support for business teams.* New York: The Free Press.

Kling, R. (1991). Cooperation, coordination and control in computer-supported work. *Communications of the ACM, 34*(12), 83–88.

Kuutti, K. (1991). The concept of activity as a basic unit for CSCW research. In L. Bannon, M. Robinson, & K. Schmidt (Eds.), *Proceedings of Second European Conference on CSCW (ECSCW-91)* (pp. 249–264). Amsterdam: Kluwer.

Kuutti, K., & Bannon, L. (1991). Some confusions at the interface: Re-conceptualizing the "interface" problem. In M. Nurminen & G. Weir (Eds.), *Human jobs and computer interfaces* (pp. 3–19). Amsterdam: North-Holland.

Kuutti, K., & Bannon, L. (1993, April). Searching for unity among diversity: Exploring the interface concept. In *Proceedings ACM/IFIP Conference InterCHI'93 (Human Factors in Information Systems),* Amsterdam.

Laurel, B. (Ed.). (1990). *The art of human–computer interaction design.* Reading, MA: Addison-Wesley.

Laurel, B. (1993). *Computers as theatre.* Reading, MA: Addison-Wesley.

Lave, J. (1988). *Cognition in practice.* Cambridge, England: Cambridge University Press.

Newman, W. M., & Sproull, R. F. (1979). *Principles of interactive computer graphics.* New York: McGraw-Hill.

Norman, D. (1980). Twelve issues for cognitive science. *Cognitive Science, 4,* 1–32.

Norman, D. A. (1990). Interview. In B. Laurel (Ed.), *The art of human–computer interaction design.* Reading, MA: Addison-Wesley.

Norman, D. (1991). Cognitive artifacts. In J. M. Carroll (Ed.), *Designing interaction: Psychology at the human–computer interface* (pp. 17–38). New York: Cambridge University Press.

Papert, S. (1990). Interview comment. *BYTE,* September, 230.

Robinson, H. (1990). Towards a Sociology of human–computer interaction. In P. Luff, N. Gilbert, & D. Frohlich (Eds.), *Computers and conversation* (pp. 39–50). London: Academic Press.

Schmidt, K. (1992). Cooperative work: A conceptual framework. In J. Rasmussen, B. Brehmer, & J. Leplat (Eds.), *Distributed decision making: Cognitive models for cooperative work* (pp. 75–109). Chichester, England: Wiley.

Schmidt, K., & Bannon, L. (1992). Taking CSCW seriously: Supporting articulation work. *Computer Supported Cooperative Work (CSCW): An International Journal, 1*(1–2), 7–40.

Schuler, D., & Namioka, A. (Eds.). (1993). *Participatory design: Principles and practices* (pp. 79–97). Hillsdale, NJ: Lawrence Erlbaum Associates.

Sommerville, I., Sawyer, P., Rodden, T., & Bentley, R. (1992, September). Sociologists can be surprisingly useful in interactive system design. In A. Monk, D. Diaper, & M. Harrison (Eds.), *Proceedings of HCI '92.* Cambridge, England: Cambridge University Press.

Star, S. L., & Griesemer, J. R. (1989). Institutional ecology, "translations" and boundary objects: Amateurs and professionals in Berkeley's museum of vertebrate zoology, 1907–39. *Social Studies of Science, 19,* 387–420.

Suchman, L. (1989). *Notes on computer support for cooperative work.* (Working Paper WP-12). Dept. of Computer Science, University of Jyvaskyla, Jyvaskyla, Finland.

Sørgaard, P. (1987, August). A cooperative work perspective on use and development of computer artifacts. In *10th Information Systems Research Seminar in Scandinavia (IRIS),* Vaskivesi, Finland.

Vygotsky, L. (1978). *Mind in society.* Cambridge, MA: Harvard University Press.

16

The Worldviews of Cooperative Work

James R. Taylor
Université de Montréal

Geoffrey Gurd
University of Ottawa

Thierry Bardini
Université de Montréal

It has often been claimed that information technology is the key to increased white-collar productivity. Reliance on technology as a substitute for human effort worked for the resource industries and for manufacturing; it seemed that the same principle should also apply to office work. Their supposed contribution to productivity became, for a time, the main selling point of computer systems.

By the mid-1980s, it was becoming evident that the optimistic claims of enhanced productivity were premature. Although there were success stories, there were equally many instances of subperformance: Computerization was as likely to be associated with declines in productivity as with increases (Baily, 1986; Roach, 1987; Strassman, 1985). Attewell (1992, 1993) reported to a computer-supported cooperative work (CSCW) conference in Toronto the results of his exhaustive examination of the literature: There was no clear correlation between the level of implementation of the technology and organizational productivity. Not long after, at a workshop held at Brunel University's Centre for Research into Innovation, Culture and Technology, Paul (1993, p. 8) remarked that "the most generous observation that one can make about current I.S. developments is that most, if not all, systems disappoint."

The learning curve has proved to be more radical than was predicted—more like what Bateson called "deutero-learning" than the ordinary garden variety kind (Bateson, 1972; Star & Ruhleder, 1994). The transposition of the logic of the factory floor may have been made into that of white-collar work too fast, without stopping to ask what an administratively focused organization is, as a fabric of cooperative work, and what is the place of technology in it.

The most salient feature that strikes one on even the most superficial reading of the literature on computerization is not the presence or absence of effect, but the contradictory nature of the evidence. For almost any conclusion based on one study, it is possible to find a contrary result in another (Attewell, 1993; Dumais, Kraut, & Koch, 1988; Rule & Attewell, 1989). It is this absence of a clear pattern that is intriguing.

This chapter offers an explanation for why technology implementation in white-collar contexts may lead to difficulties. There is an equivalence, in the sociological study of organizations, to the relativity principle in physics. Among physicists, it is understood that whether light is intrinsically wave or particle is a question that has no definite answer: It depends on what the experimenters are looking for and how they set up the apparatus for recording its behavior. What is being said is something similar, that there is no unique standpoint for looking at organization or technology nor any single way to arrive at an objective view of either. Again, as in physics, what is recorded depends on how the observers of organization position themselves. An epistemological principle in organizational research is postulated that is called *worldview*. The term *worldview* means the observational standpoint of the analyst or actor—a set of assumptions about reality so basic that they are no longer present in consciousness, like the default conditions in an operating system of software. The objective of the chapter is to explicate this principle and its application to the computerization phenomenon. This chapter argues in particular that difficulties arise when a technology selected on the basis of one worldview is implemented in a context of work more properly characterized by the other—when, in effect, the images of work and computerization interact with institutional constraints and bureaucratic realities of the distribution of power and resource allocation to produce a mismatch.

WORLDVIEW

The notion of worldview has long been familiar in computer simulation (Gordon, 1969; Krasnow & Merikallio, 1964; Pritsker, 1986; Tocher, 1964, 1966). A simulation of a system of activities is realized in a description of its (most commonly) discrete events. There are, in general, two ways a set of discrete events can be identified. A *particle-oriented*, or *material-*

based, perspective (Gordon, 1969) is part of a worldview that focuses attention on the entities in the system, by following the changes that occur as the entities move from activity to activity.[1] *Particles* are any kinds of object streams on which a process of work is concentrated: products of manufacturing, clients in a clinic, documents to be edited—the material of enterprise, in other words. An *event-oriented*, or *machine-based*, worldview describes the operations or activities, by following their history as they are applied to different entities. The operations, similarly, should be interpreted broadly to include all sorts of productive process.[2]

Practically speaking, the difference for a simulator has to do with how times of events are generated (and hence which simulation language to use), because in the first case the time at which system changes occur is treated as an attribute of the entity, and in the second as an attribute of the operation. The issue is not the time taken by the event itself, but the temporal trajectory within which it is situated. Because the determination of the time of an event is calculated using a statistical function of the time elapsing between events (or waiting time), the event sequence of an object or particle being treated is obviously different from that which characterizes the activity of the operator responsible for the activity. From this distinction, simulation languages are said to incorporate one of the two perspectives and therefore to express contrasting worldviews.

A convenient way to visualize the different worldviews is to think of the set of system events as making up the elements of a matrix whose abscissa lists the activities of the system and whose ordinate specifies the particles they are responsible for treating (Fig. 16.1).

The interpretation of the system depends on the marginal reading that is selected: A horizontal reading (e.g., x - o - x . . . x, x - x - o . . . o, etc.) results in a compilation of particle tracks, a vertical reading (e.g., x - x - o . . . x, o - x - x . . . x, etc.) in a journal of activity reports. Within the framework of simulation, the difference of perspective is not crucial in that whichever method of event generation is chosen, a protocol of system

---

[1]The use of the term *particle* is in no way connected to the physicist's usage with respect to light. The expressions *particle-oriented* and *event-oriented* are not particularly felicitous, but, because they are established, they are used in this article. It becomes evident that the connotations go far beyond the realm of computer simulation.

[2]The difference of perspective—and emphasis—is similar to that made in linguistics to distinguish the parts of the predicate: Particle versus event is equivalent to direct object versus the transitive verb to which it is linked. The simulation logic takes as given, and ignores, the logical subject, equivalent to the agency function in a sentence (Halliday, 1970). Its two worldviews are derived from direct object and verb only. This is, in fact, a very significant omission: It objectifies the world being studied by abstracting from its subjective (agentive) context.

ACTIVITIES

		A₁	A₂	A₃	...	Aₘ
	P₁	x	o	x	...	x
	P₂	x	x	o	...	o
PARTICLES	P₃	o	x	o	...	x
	...	...	...	...	...	...
	Pₙ	x	x	x	...	o

FIG. 16.1. A system as a set of events. From *Rethinking the Theory of Organizational Communication: How to Read and Organization*, by J. R. Taylor, 1993, Norwood, NJ: Ablex. Copyright 1993 by Ablex. Reprinted with permission.

behavior is still successfully produced.[3] In the concrete world of an actual organization, however, the difference, because it is now the basis of an interpretation of a *lived* (not a *simulated*) experience, takes on another level of significance: It is *experientially* not the same thing to understand an airline from the perspective of its passengers, for whom it is a sequence of distinct activities, one after the other, as it is from that of the airline employees, for whom it is a single configuration of activities, repetitively generated for each new batch of passengers: take off, serve a meal, run the movie, land, disembark. Similarly, a hospital does not feel, or look, the same to patients as to doctors and nurses. The same events are involved, but the image of them is reversed in polarity: What is figure in

---

[3]Not, perhaps, totally trivial though, because the following question remains: *Which protocol?* How the system is to be modeled, representationally, is fundamental to the whole unfolding of the total cycle of system design and development. Within the culture of design, the type of representational mode that is adopted (e.g., data-flow versus entity-relation diagrams, object-oriented analyses, etc.) is of course foundational, in the sense of setting the framework for the actual production of code. This issue, although of considerable importance to the pragmatics of system development, is peripheral to the line of argument; it is noted in passing but no more is said about it.

one is ground in the other. It is the difference between being the subject or the object of an operation—an agent versus a patient.[4]

This latter subject–object distinction points to a critical difference in the two worldviews: In one case, for example, the airline passengers or the hospital patients, the operation of the system is seen from the *outside*. The activities to which the customers or patients are exposed have a kind of "black box" feel to them, in that what is occurring within the world of the operators remains, by and large, a mystery to the clients being served. To those responsible for the activities, on the other hand, the organization in question, the airline or hospital, is seen from the *inside*. It is phenomenologically present in a way that is not at all the same as for the clients being served.[5]

To the extent that attention is focused on a particular system of activities (passengers and patients are, of course, caught up in another experiential universe, their own, that is extraneous to the model of the organization), the gulf is between the perspective of the *observer*, and that of the *participant*. Looking at an organization from the outside is not only experientially different from conceptualizing it from the inside; it leads to some quite different conclusions as to what an organization is, and how to study and design it.

It is important, for the argument developed here, to note a worldview fact: It is conceptually impossible to entertain, simultaneously, two worldviews. The technical reason is easy to see (cf. Fig. 16.1): An individual cannot simultaneously read off both of the marginal quantities of a two-dimensional matrix. An individual may, first, record and analyze the rows of the matrix, or, if that person prefers, the columns first, or, in the interests of exhaustivity, first one and then the other; but, both analyses may not be accomplished at the same time, because each reading is in itself a summa-

---

[4]Leigh Star (personal communication, 1994) points out the classic observation of Everett Hughes that "one person's routine is another's emergency." Organizational communication is considered to be a weave of asymmetrical relationships bringing into interaction agents, patients, and beneficiaries (who may be identical with the patient, if the latter is human). The agent acts on the patient for the beneficiary, or, in the negative case, against the victim. The categories of agent, patient, and beneficiary are the fundamental parts of a sentence (subject, direct object, and indirect object—the functional relations linking them being mediated by a transitive verb, which is taken to be equivalent to an operation, or activity). As the term "patient" is used in linguistics it need not be restricted to the usual quasi-medical connotation, but refers to any object being operated on, animate or otherwise (Halliday, 1970). Worldview is thus taken to be a basic principle of semantics, and a foundation for organizational pragmatics (Taylor, 1993). As pointed out elsewhere (Taylor, 1982), there is also a similarity with the well-known distinction in organizational theory between *process* and *function* links.

[5]It is this difference, inside versus outside, that is taken to be the origin of Suchman's (1995) concept of "invisible work" (i.e., work that is complex to those involved in its accomplishment, but simple to those who are not).

tive description of the values of the matrix, neither of the two being, a priori, to be preferred to the other (which one is chosen indexes a preference of the analyst, not an inherent property of the matrix). Although each reading is complete, each is, nevertheless, distinct, and furnishes a different picture, even in trivial cases, of what the matrix means when it is interpreted.

The difference is greatly magnified when the entries in the matrix recording events are colored by subjectivity (i.e., as part of someone's personal experience and involvement). Coolly reading off the values of a matrix, as an abstract exercise in analysis, is one thing; living through the events that it records (before they have been transformed into mere numbers) is quite another: The heat has not gone yet. It is not yet simply a unit of analysis, but is still phenomenologically embedded in the particular space, time, and scale making up the surround of a real person. You cannot both be a heart attack patient in an emergency clinic and, at the same time, manage the clinic's queueing system. When it is reduced to just a matrix, the analysts can retrace the reading path: Having looked at one set of marginal values, they can then start over, this time inspecting the other marginal quantities. In real life, the luxury of starting over is not available; there is no way of turning back the clock and to relive past experiences, this time from a different perspective. We are stuck in the groove of our existential singularity.

Of course, computer programmers, like the people they are modeling, come to have a worldview, whether or not they think of themselves as having one. (The consequences of this are discussed further at the end of this chapter.)

WORLDVIEW IN SOFTWARE DESIGN: IMAGES OF THE COMPUTER[6]

When von Neumann wrote the design for a programmable digital computer in 1945, he did more than solve a technical problem: He fixed an image.[7] A computer, as he conceived it, was an instrument that could read in data, store them, and transfer them when needed to a central processing unit where they could be recombined following the dictates of totally explicit operating routines, following which the results of the computations could be exited as an output. The "event" was the computing itself, the data constituted the "material" called the "particles," and the CPU was the "machine" (the latter being a terminological innovation that dates from Turing,

---

[6]For discussion see Bardini (1994) and Bardini and Horvath (1995). A book (Bardini, forthcoming) is in preparation.

[7]The authorship of this design has remained a bone of contention (Goldstine, 1972). For our purposes, it is convenient to think of it as von Neumann's work, whatever the facts of the case.

1936). Following Shannon's (1948) monograph on communication theory, the particles of data came to be regularly referred to as "information" and computers to be thought of as "information-processing machines."

Obviously, this new device was itself, internally, an organization made up of parts, and thus could be interpreted in either of the worldviews described (Weick, 1990). From a particle orientation, it can be observed that a computer describes a trajectory of data flow, where the data are elementary symbols, inscribed in electronic code: from terminals to registers to processing unit and back. From an event orientation, the CPU is an operator that processes data. It is tempting, therefore, to extrapolate what one knows about a computer to make it into an image of the organization as a whole, human this time, where, although the computing function is embedded, it is taken to be an authentic simulacrum of the larger universe of operations. It is a logic that is not so much metaphoric (Morgan, 1986), as metonymic.

The social significance of the computer revolution in technology only started to become organizationally salient in the 1960s and 1970s, because it was then that computing moved out of batch processing into real-time processing of data and online networks with time sharing. Until then, the interface between computing and organizational practice had been highly constrained—just a few specialized operations, such as the processing of scientific and financial data. When online service became available, the limited input–output and storage facilities of the past began to give way to an expanded network that included workstations manned by "users." Such users, having now become components of the extended machine, however peripheral to its central operating dynamic, would now themselves have to be conceptualized. It is at this point that something like two distinct organization-related worldviews of computing emerged—no longer the computer as an organization (its internal structure) but the computer *in* an organization (as a component of the latter). Technology is a domain of applied, not pure science, so that the true identity of a machine only becomes evident when people put it to work. How they put it to work, in turn, depends on how they conceive it, and that implies the intervention of a worldview, not just of the designers, but also of the buyers.

The Particle Perspective: An Information-Processing View of Computerization

What would turn out to be the mainstream view in computing applications by the early 1970s, was to look at the users as a new source of data. What made this view attractive to designers was that it left the care and tending of the machines where it had always been, in the hands of the experts, while it opened up a new design challenge, because the kinds of data that could potentially be treated were rapidly expanding from numeric to alphabetic, with graphics a distinct possibility looming on the horizon. Even within the seemingly limited sphere of numbers, once the whole community of organizational users had become an eventuality, there was a range of new functions that computing could be used for, when harnessed to the purposes of the enterprise.

Even more important was the image of the computer that informed the advertising directed to potential buyers. The emphasis was on *functions*, that is, the different operations that a computer can be made to accomplish in the processing of a variety of data, at different points in the data stream. At the same time, it was being made clear to customers (management) that computers could be treated as substitutes for people, to take over the functions the latter had previously been responsible for, thus realizing important economies. A subtle transposition of sense was implied: People could now also be thought of as functions, which is to say black boxes (self-contained objects)—this is an idea, it was clear, that had considerable appeal to corporate customers. The sales literature was a potent ideological force in the implementation of a particle-oriented worldview, and the latter soon became the dominant way to think about computerization, among its proponents and its critics alike.

Out of this evolving process of expanding uses of computing there emerged an image of the fully integrated organization, with all of its parts linked into one composite network, supported by central servers, ported to the outside world and linked to every user's own desk or machine. The term *office automation* that became popular in the early 1980s captured the image of one giant information factory. The culmination of the movement was conceived to be, finally, the eventual realization of the long-held dream of management information systems (MIS): The information would all be fed into one great operating system, computed (using sophisticated algorithms derived from statistical decision and game theory), and then massaged for the councils of top management, to instruct its strategic decision making.

The "information workers" in this system were thus not only people; they were also the computers themselves, machine intelligence incarnate—the mythology given concrete manifestation. In its most extreme form, today's version of the particle-oriented model, where every step in every process is controlled by computer, and individual skills count for little, has been described as the "electronic sweatshop" (Garson, 1988) or the "McDonaldization of society" (Ritzer, 1993). It is a model of computing in enterprise that has become widely accepted in our society.[8]

---

[8]According to Garson (1988), some 8 million Americans, or about 7% of the total labor force, will have worked at McDonald's and will have experienced, even if only for a time, what it means to work in a situation where normal processes of organization are blocked at every turn. And McDonald's is only one such situation among many. As part of our ongoing research program, Jourdennais (1992) documented the human effects of a similar managerial philosophy at Canada Post.

The Event Perspective: The Computer
as Augmentation of the Human Intellect

MIS was not the only path the software community pursued as computers began to enter the mainstream of organizational life. From the beginning, there had been more than one view about computing (Bush, 1945). A very different conception from that being described, inspired in part by Bush, is illustrated by Licklider (1960), who proposed a program of action to further what he called "man–computer symbiosis."[9] In his conception, humans would be communicating with each other using computers as their channel of communication. Computers, to him, meant interactivity.[10] In 1962, Licklider had a platform to turn his philosophy into practice when he became head of the information-processing techniques office of Advanced Research Projects Administration (ARPA), a Department of Defense initiative under President Kennedy.[11]

Licklider, and his successor Taylor, funded a number of innovative research projects into the interactive potentials of computing. The most original was directed by Douglas C. Engelbart, then at Stanford Research Institute (SRI). In Engelbart's conception, the computer should be an instrument for the "augmentation of the human intellect." In his imagination, the screen of the computer would be like a mirror in which intellectual workers (such as Engelbart himself) could let their thoughts take form, visually, to provide an immediate, almost sensual, feedback to the thinker. Engelbart reasoned that the human brain has a limited ability to handle data, which the computer can greatly supplement, so that the range of intellectual tasks a skilled person could accomplish would be notably increased, if only the computer could be made sufficiently responsive. The limitations of computing as it was known in the 1960s were far too narrow to accomplish all he imagined—graphic artists, for example, watching a design take shape on the screen as their hands

---

[9]Both points of view, MIS and business applications, and the vision about to be considered had always been present in the computing community, at least in such elite institutions as MIT. The different cultures of computing began to become more salient, however, as computing became increasingly integrated into organizational practice.

[10]"Creative, interactive communication requires a plastic or moldable medium that can be modeled, a dynamic medium in which premises will flow into consequences, and above all a common medium that can be contributed to and experimented with by all. Such a medium is at hand—the programmed digital computer" (Licklider & Taylor, 1968, p. 22). Some of the inspiration for this approach comes from an earlier paper by Bush (1945) on what he called a "memex."

[11]He was subsequently to be succeeded by another young psychologist, Robert W. Taylor, who was later to migrate to Xerox PARC, taking several members of the ARPA network with him. At PARC, the tradition continued and eventually had a powerful influence on the development of Apple's Macintosh computer.

manipulated the equivalent of a drawing pen (or mouse, an invention of the SRI group). Thirty years later, multimedia has become a practical possibility, but the conception was already there in the 1960s.

As Engelbart (1962) saw it, there would have to be a coevolution of the computer and the human being; it would be a kind of mutual learning in a context of iterative adaptation of one to the other as each discovered how to map one's symbolic universe onto the other's, interactively networked with other users to allow for collective intellectual work. He called this process "bootstrapping." To Engelbart, the focus should be neither on product nor on artifact, but on process, to attain a rather abstract goal, namely, the augmentation of the human intellect. No longer tools to extend the capacity of the human *body* to accomplish work, as in the past, this was a tool that would be an extension of the *mind*—a kind of intellectual prosthesis, not just a form of artificial intelligence.

The user, fully as much as the computing tool itself, was for him a virtuality to be discovered—computing not as a link in a data trajectory, but a mixed human–machine act of creation and intellectual discovery, pushing outward the frontiers of human intelligence. And this means not just a user in isolation, but *users*—a community of intellectual workers (a term shortly to be softened, under the influence of Drucker (1966, 1969), to the less elitist expression, "knowledge workers"), projecting onto a common medium of communication their unfolding ideas, in real time, to play with, elaborate on, erase, substitute, or do whatever they pleased in a context of interactivity. For Licklider, Taylor, and Engelbart, the computer would not be a machine to process data, but a tool to enable creative process, both individual and collaborative, based on nonlinear access and display of spatial and conceptual patterns.

Under the influence of these researchers, and others such as Nelson and Kay, an alternative worldview of computing had become evident. For them, the fascination was less with the computer as an instrument to control the flow of data in complex networks of exchange than it was with the event itself, which they conceived as man–machine interaction where the true nature of the resulting event was yet to be discovered, because there would have to be a prolonged interaction in a highly situated context of experimentation and development before the full potential of the technology became evident. To the particle oriented, computing was a means to an end, but to the event oriented, it was the machine and its interaction with its user that was seen as an end in itself (with the result that the language of inventors such as Engelbart, insofar as the eventual utility of his work was concerned, tended to the vague, and verged on the grandiose).

It was this alternative view of computing that would eventually culminate (after 1975) in what has come to be known as the era of "personal computing." Radio Shack sold more than $100 million worth of computing equipment in its first 1.5 years and Commodore half as much again (Osborne, 1979, p. 33), yet not one of the 30 or so established computer manufacturers in the mid-1970s benefited from this new market. "Why," Osborne asked rhetorically, "was this entire industry left to reckless entrepreneurs, lucky amateurs, and newcomers to computer manufacture?" His reply: "The answer is that this new market was too bizarre to fit any predictions made by established means." It was an instance of the constraining influence of worldview on the ability to imagine alternatives.

WORLDVIEW IN ORGANIZATIONAL RESEARCH: IMAGES OF COOPERATIVE WORK

A claim has been advanced, namely, that when people represent the events that go to compose a system of activities, they make, whether or not consciously, a choice. They see the world in one of two ways, and how they then record what they see is set in a pattern called a *worldview.* This section considers what the abstract distinction that has been postulated between "particle-oriented/material-based" and "event-oriented/machine-based" worldviews means when translated into the vision an organizational researcher brings to inquiry. How the world of work becomes turned into a scientific account of it is not simply a matter just of what is there but how the investigator sees what is there; it is an issue of epistemology, before it is one of ontology. Particle versus event worldviews become, in this context, lenses for perceiving and recording the nature of organizational processes (and ultimately, of course, of designing a technology to support them).

The Particle-Oriented/Material-Based Perspective on Cooperative Work

A particle-oriented worldview emphasizes the transformation processes involved in the application of a sequence of different organizational energies to the processing of something—a material. In the context of computerization, that "something"—the material being processed—is information: In this worldview, computers are just machines that do information work. Information is thought of as particles to be exchanged to link one event to another.

   This has led a number of researchers to concentrate on the various aspects of information work in the work milieux they were studying: the work itself, its information environments, its task fields. Information work, according to Paisley, "denotes effort involving the production, distribution, transformation, storage, retrieval, or use of information"

(Paisley, 1980, p. 118). Paisley argued that much can be learned about information work by examining "what sequence of information and non-information tasks the work consists of; how each information task is performed; what the effects of information tasks are on the performance of non-information tasks; and what the overall effects of information tasks are on the productivity of the work overall" (p. 120).

Stinchcombe (1990) conceptualized the information system of the organization as a response to environmental uncertainties. Huber and Daft (1987) similarly used the term *information environments* to frame their discussion of information work. Depending on the task activity that individuals are part of, individuals are assumed to function in multiple and changing information environments and to be responsive to different sources of information that permit them to perform a task. An individual's work consists of a variety of inputs and outputs going to and coming from different sources. The concatenation of these input–output functions makes a picture of the way the organization is structured.

Stoelwinder and Charns (1981) proposed a task field model for explaining multiple goals in complex organizations (such as hospitals). A key component of the patient care task field, in their discussion, is the exchange of information:

> The activity of the secondary component is initiated by information crossing this boundary from the primary component. The output of the secondary component must again cross the boundary and be incorporated within the transformation process, which also requires an exchange of information. A variety of information systems can be developed to handle these exchanges of information. Manual information systems, such as laboratory request forms, and laboratory result forms, drug orders, diet lists, etc. exchange information from physicians and nurses in the primary component to the support departments in the secondary component of the patient care task field. (Stoelwinder & Charns, 1981, p. 757)

Huber and Daft (1987) called this view of information work the *information logistics* perspective. It emphasizes the instrumental collection, transformation, and use of information in organizations. In it, messages connect different social actors and information systems.

The concept of a trajectory perhaps captures better than any other term the essence of the particle-based metaphor.[12] An information trajectory

---

[12]Strauss, Fagerhaugh, Suczek, and Wiener (1985), although coming out of a very different tradition that emphasizes the articulatory complexities and contingencies of professional work and the centrality of interpretive activities, nevertheless also visualize hospital work as trajectories. An illness trajectory, as they see it, is a framework for understanding the activities encompassing the social organization of medical work involving a patient's illness. Obviously, from a particle-oriented perspective, for every illness trajectory there would be an associated information trajectory.

emphasizes the task activities by which information is collected, processed, disseminated, transmitted, and so on, from the first events of a complex process to the last.

Inherent in the particle-oriented worldview is a principle of objectification of events, that is, seeing them from the outside. If it is assumed that the activities occurring within the organization can be viewed objectively, then social actors can also be taken to be rational and their work to be instrumental. Individual tasks come to be thought of as functionally situated within a larger structure of events and people are conceptualized as having roles that are defined by the functions associated with them. Once committed to this idea of a rationally articulated, objectifying structure, it is a simple step, logically, to the building of a model, and a number of researchers have been concerned to develop this kind of description of how people work, when events occur, types of task activities, and technologies (cf. Hirschheim, 1986). Rothemund's model (1986), for example, visualizes the task processes involved in a surgeon operating on a patient (Fig. 16.2). The model represents both passive elements (states of the system, rooms, files, channels, conditions, etc.) and transition elements that represent active system components (processes, activities, functions, events, etc.). (The circles and squares represent, respectively, system states and transitions. The circles with vertical lines on the left are expanded to the right to show more detail.)

The commitment to this, or similar, approaches implies not just a view of technology (the formal models are easily turned into data flow diagrams), but also of organization: Scott (1972), for example, stated that "to focus on the technology of an organization is to view the organization as a mechanism for transforming inputs into outputs" (pp. 145–146).

The Event-Oriented/Machine-Based Perspective on Cooperative Work

The development of an event-oriented perspective has indexed a growing interest in the subjective experience of work, and an increasing emphasis during the 1980s on ethnographically inspired, interpretivist approaches to the study of people at work. Sociologists have, for example, explored facets of medical work from a social constructivist perspective (Atkinson, 1981, 1995; Atkinson & Heath, 1981; Hughes, 1977; Macintyre, 1978; Silverman, 1987; Strong, 1979; Wadsworth & Robinson, 1976). In this tradition, Atkinson (1981, p. 95) documented how medical students learn to weigh their clinical experience against theoretical or scientific knowledge: "In the course of their diagnostic work, students find themselves working in a complex field of semiology—a field of manifestation which must be interpreted in order to produce a competent diagnostic picture, and to

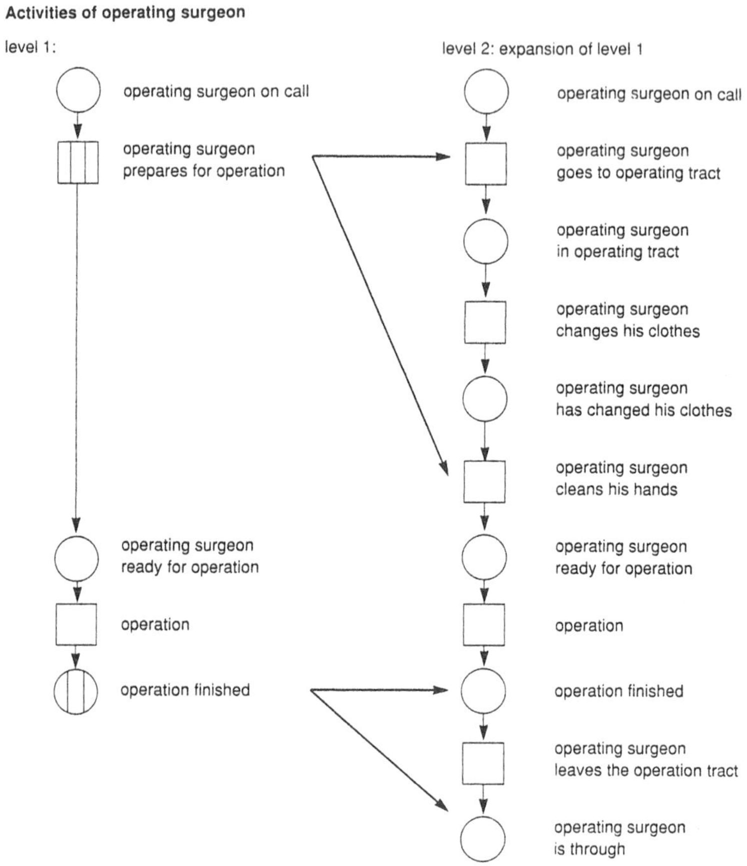

Activities of operating surgeon

FIG. 16.2. A Petri-net representation of a medical operation. From Rothemund M. Modelling Medical Organizational System with Nets. Meth. Inform. Med 1986; 2: 87–89.

allow for the credible and warranted attribution of some label—that of a known disease or abnormality." Students have to deal with two kinds of data: signs (objective data obtained from the physical examination) and symptoms (subjective data obtained from the patient history). The traditional understanding would have been that "talk of 'objective signs' seems to foreclose any discussion of culturally influenced interpretation, of actors' own understandings and so on. Insofar as such phenomena were to be regarded as objective 'facts,' then they would tend to be taken on trust, and implicitly exempted from sociological scrutiny" (p. 96). Instead, Atkinson purported that doctors habitually employ Garfinkel's documentary method:

There are two levels of interpretation involved in the production of diagnoses: they are closely and dialectically related. In the first instance it is the task of medical investigations to treat signs and symptoms as indexing underlying physiological conditions. Though not always successful, they try to relate these indices in order to read off a coherent diagnosis, indicating the presence of an identifiable illness, disorder or syndrome. At the second level, the patient's condition is itself an "index" or a "case" of the disease in question. (p. 102)

The distinction being made is between "hard" and "soft" data. Hard data requires little interpretation; soft data means a resort to judgment, intuition, common sense, experience, and acquired skill—all the facets of knowledge work that are hardest to inscribe in a formal algorithm. Thus, although the word "information" is still central, the idea of what information is has undergone a subtle change, from data based to hypothesis driven. This enters into the realm of professional understandings, which are part of the culture that has to be passed on from generation to generation.

Atkinson (1977, p. 99) focused on bedside teaching as an instance of how medical knowledge is produced and reproduced. "Reproduced" is used in two senses here. The first is in terms of the transmission of medical knowledge from the clinicians to the students. Second, knowledge is reproduced "through the enactment of *versions* of medical work." According to Atkinson,

Although the teaching takes place within the hospital ward, it is to some extent insulated from it, and although there is constant activity in the wards, it does not necessarily impinge on the bedside teaching as such. As it progresses, the teaching round seems almost completely isolated from the other goings-on in the ward. As the clinician and his students stop at each bed they form an "ecological huddle"; as it moves round the ward forming and re-forming round each patient, the group is enclosed by a relatively impermeable "membrane." (p. 92)

Hughes (1977, p. 129) similarly emphasized the importance of everyday medical knowledge in categorizing patients: "The general point is that knowledge conventionally labelled 'medical' is embedded in, and in certain senses dependent for its significance upon, the kind of knowledge usually thought of as 'common-sense.' " This perspective

maintains that the sensible character of ongoing situations is largely dependent on the applicability, on each successive occasion, of typified knowledge of the dimension of the social world. Staff members in the casualty setting experience their tasks as episodes in the mundane working day. Like everyone else they are continuously engaged in a task of making their environment meaningful and intelligible by ordering their experiences in terms of familiar categories. Outside of their working lives they construct definitions of situations and make identifications of objects and events in much the same way as others, and there are very many occasions when this ability is utilised in the practice of medical categorization. (p. 130)

In Cicourel's (1985, p. 162) words, "the hallmark of procedural or commonsense knowledge is that comprehension is contingent on their embeddedness in, and sensitivity to, the setting in which their elements emerge and are used in daily life." The danger of rationalizing work activities in order to computerize them is that it may overemphasize the logical and objective nature of the organization of work and in doing so miss the importance of actors' subjective interpretations of their work.

The vulnerability of system designs grounded in the idea of the organization as an information-processing system is illustrated by a number of fieldwork studies (Fafchamps, 1988; Osheroff et al., 1991; Pettinari, 1988). Fafchamps (1988), for example, documents written and oral information work in a surgical intensive care unit (SICU). The traditional system design focus was on the information itinerary, and specifically its written path. In health care settings, these itineraries are the formal, institutionalized conventions for written communication; the nursing Kardex, the nursing chart, the discharge summary, and so on. Fafchamps' study reveals breakdowns in communication that render the conventional forms of written communication ambiguous. She attributed these problems in the communication network to the "dichotomy between process—decision-making, and products—the record keeping of data" (Fafchamps, 1988, p. 105). For example, doctors use different names for the same drugs, requests by physicians to change drug dosages are often delivered orally (and at other times on scraps of paper inserted into the patient's chart without the knowledge of the nursing staff). As a result, the process of tracing who requested what order and when is time consuming at best and, given the context, dangerous for patients at worst. The implication is that the effective coordination of information between nurses on different shifts, between nurses and the physicians assigned to the SICU, and between nurses, unit physicians, and visiting specialists cannot be regulated just on the basis of written documents. The breakdowns that Fafchamps recorded in the SICU were matched by a number of oral communication repair strategies for sorting out the validity of the information under question. She concluded that a conventional system design would normally lead to the computerization of the institutional, written forms of communications and fail because such systems would not be able to account for the breakdowns and repair strategies.

Osheroff et al. (1991) found that the notion of information need is too narrowly defined in most studies because it only refers to formal kinds of medical information. Such an idea presumes that the solution for doctors' information needs is better access to databases and online textbooks. This formal view of information needs is rejected by the authors. The results from their participant observations indicated that there were many informal types of information needs that could be met by a computer system only with great difficulty. Local knowledge that residents and doctors require in order to make medical decisions is crucial.

Pettinari (1988, p. 129) questioned the link between the operating room report (an institutionally dictated text) and the actual surgical event on which it is based by comparing the talk in the operating room with the dictated content of the report, by an analysis of the internal structure of the text (the relation between prosodic and grammatical features and the episodic structure as perceived by the resident dictating the report), and by recording the change in reporting style over time (the contrast between reports dictated in the first and last years of residency training). Pettinari's claim that written reports are loosely coupled with the events they represent supports Fafchamps' contention that there is an important difference between process and product.

Each of the previous studies rejects a formalistic conception of information work and emphasizes interpretive work. Technology is just one more object in the workers' environments that requires interpreting. In Blomberg's (1988) words, "A new technology does not exert a singular force on the people who adopt it, nor is its meaning shared equally by all. It is important to consider the interplay between the technology and the social organization of use, exploring the ways in which pre-existing social patterns alter responses to the use of such technologies. A technology can only be described and its significance appreciated in the context of its uses and its users" (p. 780). As Barley (1986, 1988) demonstrated, the same technology implemented in two superficially similar work environments is reconstructed in quite different ways and produces very different results. Any approach that abstracts from the influence of the local work culture risks arriving at conclusions that turn out to be merely partially valid (and, all too frequently, are outright *in*valid).

In Summary

The adoption of a worldview is a means to display an aspect of organizational reality, but it remains an aspect and a *display*. This is not a claim about the ontology of organization, but about the epistemological con-

straint that operates on the field of vision of the managers/designers/re-
searchers, to shape the premises on which they build.[13]

A particle-oriented worldview highlights the connections between people and information in the work process, often involving several services
linked in a complex pattern. It does so, however, by ignoring the situational meaning of the information for the people who are doing the
work, locally. Only thus can information be thought of as objective data.
Activities (as events) are treated as if they were black boxes, in that the
fine detail of what goes on inside can be ignored, so that it is possible to
concentrate on the inputs and outputs. The "fine detail," however, as
Fafchamps' study illustrated, is ignored at one's peril, because if, in the
information-recording process, an erroneous image is inscribed, the subsequent "information processing" (of spurious data) becomes a caricature
of what is really happening on the floor.

An event-oriented view of information, on the other hand, treats data
as indices that are not meaningful in and of themselves, because they are
merely clues in a guessing game where ambiguity is an everyday reality.
Social actors are no longer objects that process data from and for other
people. Instead, the data's significance is grounded in the subjective
sense-making strategies that actors use to interpret an information field
in relation to other bits of data, all of them treated as indexical (Weick,
1995). Although there is skill involved in recognizing patterns in the data
of experience, it is mixed with gut feelings and hunches.

The limitation of the event-oriented worldview lies in the loss of an
overall sense of how different processes interconnect. It is, in the purest
sense of the term, an egotistical (or what Hughes, Randall, and Shapiro,
1992, called "egological") perspective; it is potentially so situation specific
as to inhibit generalization. The preoccupation with local events and
subjective understandings potentially blinds agents to the benefits gained
from viewing work processes more globally, making it difficult to gen-
eralize beyond an individual department to a whole organization.

Which worldview is adopted, in practice, normally depends on the
perspective of the person involved. To professionals, for example, caught
up in the immediacy of their own work, the events are present in all their

---

[13]Speaking reflexively, some of these epistemological constraints may be deeply
embedded in the "worldview" concept itself. The worldview vocabulary ("vision,"
"highlight," "black-box," etc.) obviously emphasizes vision over other senses. This
conception itself is in a certain respect a "meta-worldview," very much in tune with the
historical development of scientific thought. Bohm (1980, p. 144), for instance, insisted on
"the very close relationship between instrumentation and theory [that] can be seen by
considering the *lens*, which was indeed one of the key features behind the development of
modern scientific thought." See also Crary (1990) for a historical account of the configuration
of vision in the 19th century.

complexity and uncertainty; to management, typically, the same events are black boxed, rendered "invisible," parts of a rationally conceived trajectory (Suchman, 1995). Because of the worldview gap dividing the people who, typically, purchase the systems, and the people who use them, computerization often turns out to be a singularly complex process (and one deeply imbued with organizational politics).

MISMATCHES OF WORLDVIEW: CASE STUDIES OF THE IMPLEMENTATION OF COMPUTER TECHNOLOGY

Why does the computerization of professional work so often end in disappointment? This is the question asked at the start of the discussion. A hypothesis is that problems arise when there is a worldview mismatch between the technology and the cooperative work to be performed. To illustrate, consider three specific cases of implementation that each led to a disappointing outcome. Be on the lookout for the mismatch and its origin. The point is to find a pattern.

Case Study 1: The 9-1-1 System Study

The first study concerns the implementation of a new dispatching system in a large metropolitan police force.[14] Previously, centrally located 9-1-1 operators had recorded incoming emergency calls on an ordinary file card, which was then passed on physically to a police dispatcher in an adjoining office. The latter was typically a line officer (male) with years of experience. It was his duty based on his judgment, assisted by a more-or-less adequate card filing system, to forward calls on an open channel to officers in the cars. The inefficiencies and lack of security of this system were obvious to everyone and the department decided to install a computerized system. Convinced that the new system, already in use elsewhere, had enough built-in intelligence to substitute for the street savvy of the existing dispatchers, the police department, in the interest of economy, hired civilian dispatchers, although only after a bitter battle with the Police Brotherhood.

This case study was based on observation of behavior and interviews conducted in both selected patrol cars and the dispatching center. It showed that, technically, the system worked quite well and, at this level, was generally appreciated. The substitution of computer programs and

---

[14]Based on research for a master's thesis (Akzam, 1991). See also Taylor and Van Every (1993).

databases for the intuitive knowledge of the older dispatchers had, how-ever, both positive and negative benefits: On the one hand, although there were evident improvements in the quality of information now available to cars on demand (to check license plates, or verify the crime history of a certain location, for example), there were also flagrant breaches of good sense when, for example, the dispatcher, relying on what showed on the computer screen, would call a car from one side of its territory clear over to the other, even though another car was standing by in an adjoining territory just minutes from the scene. The technology had no way of seeing, much less displaying, an overall picture. No gains in efficiency were recorded and, in fact, there were actual losses (measured by an increase in overtime).

Where the new system proved to be dangerously inadequate was in destroying the tissue of trust relations supporting the information system. Police work is dangerous and officers now found themselves heading into risky situations on the basis of intelligence that they had no confidence in because they had no confidence in the people, or the technology, supplying it. The relations between long-serving officers (median length of service, 16 years) and the dispatchers, young, predominantly female civilian employees, were tense and not particularly friendly. One clear dysfunction emerged as a result. The old dispatchers were not only information purveyors, but also acted as disciplinarians. They were the ones with the discretion to tug on the reins when people in the cars were goofing off and, on the other hand, show latitude when a reasonable degree of slack was indicated (at mealtimes, or whether to assign a call to someone just going off shift). They had a sense of the difference between a false alarm and the real thing that no program could capture. The new dispatchers, lacking the same hard-won experience in actual situations of work, were in no position to exercise discipline effectively, other than by rigidly following the book, and the officers routinely began to take ad-vantage of them. This tendency was supposed to be corrected by increas-ing activity from district station commanders, but that turned out to be an unrealistic assumption. The net effect of these trends was a loss of authority overall, and no compensating gains in productivity. In an authoritarian world, a vacuum of authority is an anomaly.

The world of the police is one that, perhaps more than most, is self-con-tained (Van Maanen, 1973, 1978, 1983). To a remarkable degree, it conforms to a self-organizing model: It is self-perpetuating from one generation to another, tends to see itself as isolated in a hostile public environment, is resistant if not impermeable to influences from the outside (including, not infrequently, its own commanders), a potent agency of socialization for those who join it, a complex world of meaning and subtle understandings that supports what is, in the end, a very dangerous lifestyle.

One expression kept cropping up over and over in interviews: The new computer-based system, people complained, was not "police minded"—that is, neither it nor the people who mediated for it as dispatchers had a grasp of the many, many unarticulated understandings that make police work effective—the "inside" conversation. The complex understandings that had grown up in the police culture as to who was responsible for what were an intrinsic component in the information-flow network, not an add-on, as the designers of the new system supposed. The attempted substitution of what Suchman (1983) called procedural (and Cicourel, 1985, declarative) knowledge for the commonsense (the "situated") created confusion, and, in the end, reduced productivity, even though everyone knew that a better information system was needed, and appreciated it when it came.

Case Study 2: The CareFile Study[15]

The CareFile Medical System was developed in a major metropolitan hospital by a practicing doctor with skills in software design. It is a set of interconnected modules for the storage and transmission of information. There are five modules: *CareFiler*, a database for the entry of patient demographic and clinical data, generator of referral/report letters; *Care-Analyzer*, a program for the performance of retrospective analyses of patient data; *CareEditor*, a program for the customization of clinical data storage templates and reports; *Care Book*, an appointment scheduling system; and *CareBiller*, a module to permit billing. In addition, a function was foreseen to allow the downloading of data from the hospital mainframe. Perhaps because the system had been developed by a doctor in the same hospital, the system was widely, if somewhat haphazardly, implemented. Our research was initiated as an evaluation study of its eventual use, supported by the hospital administration, some time following the initial implementation.

The core of the system is the database, made up of CareFiles. A CareFile is used to store information about patients and their medical conditions. The conception behind it is that diagnostic procedures in medical practice are sufficiently repetitive that they lend themselves to structured and standardized data entry and recording. In essence, when doctors perform an examination, the idea is that they follow a checklist of conditions and symptoms. A database should incorporate this judgmental information, as well as demographics, and the results of objective tests. The checklist would, of course, vary depending on specialization, and it was for this reason that a CareEditor was included in the original design, so that a

---

[15]Based on research for a doctoral dissertation (Gurd, 1994).

sector of practice could tailor its database to its own liking. If doctors could be persuaded to use the system, there would, it was felt, be important supplementary benefits: easier communication between doctor and secretary, a bridging to the mainframe system of the hospital, efficient writing of reports and consults, easier billing, and a new facility, analysis of cumulative diagnostic data, for the production of scientific reports.

As it turned out, the CareFile system was used fully by only one doctor in the whole hospital—the designer himself! Many doctors used it in part, but mostly to handle billing (as well as some booking), so that in fact it was not the doctor who handled the input of data but a secretary. Appointments, for the most part, continued to be made using conventional journals (although sometimes both means were employed). Use of Care-Filer tended to be limited to demographic data (again a secretarial responsibility). There were some technical glitches, in that the bridge to the mainframe was not fully possible, but the real difficulties had an origin that was not technical: The system turned out not to match up well with the way medical practice works. For one thing, whereas most medical cases can be described as routine after the fact, this is not necessarily how things appear at the start of the treatment of a patient. Doctors make value judgments (on the worth of a given test, on the reliability of the advice coming from another specialist, on the patients themselves) and this transcends simple checklisting. They dislike writing standardized consults. They spend a good deal of time out of their office, in informal situations of talk, where critical decisions get made. Their relationship with secretaries goes well beyond the strictly procedural, because the secretary mediates between the doctor working in a frequently disorderly work environment and the patient to whom an image of order has to be communicated. Overall, the results confirm those of Fafchamps, cited earlier: Work is not just procedural, at least in the doctors' view of things.

It was not that no advantages were found. The system, for example, permitted a single secretary to make bookings for several doctors (thus alleviating the problem of occasional absences). Even here there was a down side, because it turned out that the making of bookings works best when the secretary understands the idiosyncracies of particular doctors, including such things as how they deal with new patients. One doctor went to the length of constructing CareFile templates for his speciality, only to discover he had ended up with 15 screens, each with upward of 50 fields for entering data. Having gone this far, he concluded the system was too unwieldy, and dropped it. Most doctors continued to prefer recording their notes on a piece of paper, where they could draw simple pictures, if they wished. Also, diagnostics, when they are exchanged between doctors, are evaluated in function of the confidence the receiving doctor has in the source's competence and credibility. There is seemingly an irreducible element of subjectivity in medical practice that the software had failed to capture. The system was by and large unused to anything like its supposed potential.

Case Study 3: The Network Facility Study

The third case study tracked the development of a new administrative software.[16] It followed the steps from the signing of a contract with a large client to the initial phase of actual implementation. The germ of the idea had already been worked out by software designers in the company: a generic tool for the construction of an administrative form that could be configured by users. The initial step, once the proposal had been accepted by the client company, was to collect data on the basis of which the system could be modeled. The data came from methods and analysis officers (in other words, the people who wrote procedures for employees to follow, not the people who had to carry them out). On the basis of this information, using what is called "structured analysis" (De Marco, 1978; Gane & Sarson, 1977; Yourdon, 1989), data flow diagrams were prepared to map the trajectories of information linking the diverse services of the company. The fields making up the administrative form that would support the new system were intended to reflect the functions that had been identified as being associated with each node in the network (assign lines, update inventory, open accounts, forward to traffic, inform marketing, complete forms, etc.). In the imagination of the designers, the transparency of the work organization they were studying was such that they conceived of the entire process as controlled from a single workstation.

When this analysis had been completed, it was time to hand the technology over to another group who would be interacting with the actual client population (or their representatives) in order to incorporate more situation-specific information on priorities, authorizations, and so on. User manuals would have to be composed and again some knowledge of actual work conditions would be useful. Liaison committees were set up with the user groups and responsibilities assigned for filling in the missing information. This is where the project came close to foundering. Communication breakdowns and misunderstandings dogged the process to the point where progress ceased. Even when the two sides were seemingly using the same language, they were not talking about the same things. The intuitive knowledge of how the company actually worked, in the heads of the users, seemed to be quite different from the rational flow diagrams of the developers. One simply did not map onto the other. Meeting followed meeting, and tempers grew frayed.

---

[16]Based on research for a master's thesis (Hovey, 1992). See also Taylor and Van Every (1993).

Gradually, however, the mist began to lift. As it did, the inadequacies in the initial representation of the company and its operations became progressively clearer, including all that had been left out, and the design team set about to make a radical reinterpretation of its original plan, beginning with a redefinition of what users are and how to identify them. What the designers had not understood was that identity is an emergent property of organization, and context dependent, and far from standardized, even where the job titles and descriptions suggest otherwise. The extraordinary differences in corporate culture that emerge over time in a large firm, from one service to another, and one region to another, could be seen. In the end, an acceptable compromise was reached, the designers in effect went back to the drawing board and eventually field trials began.

Because the initial design, in this instance, was predicated on a trajectory logic (the whole system potentially run from one workstation), it conformed to what has been described as a particle-oriented approach (the flow diagram was all about inputs and outputs). The designers, in the interests of keeping their client, were forced, during the implementation phase, to rewrite their software to take account of the perspectives of a user community that was predominantly event oriented. This rewriting took the form of what was called, possibly somewhat prematurely (because it is not sure what long-term effect it had),[17] "conversation in the software development process" (Hovey, 1992; Taylor & Van Every, 1993). The incorporation of an event-oriented perspective into what started out as particle oriented involved more, however, than just an intellectual shift in a software writer's point of view; instead, it embroiled the designers in a new kind of social dynamic—one for which, it seemed, nothing in their formation in a school of computer science had in any way prepared them.[18]

Discussion

If there is a common pattern here, it is this:

1. *The people who bought and designed the systems were not the people who used them.* This was clear in the case of the police. No consultation with the eventual users took place. In the network facility it was the senior management of the company, without consultation, who bought the system. In the hospital case, the decision was taken by the computer com-

---

[17]At this point, our link with the project was also, unfortunately, terminated.

[18]Most of the designers were recent graduates of computer science programs, and their approach followed conventional lines of analysis and design.

mittee, which although it did include doctor representatives nevertheless made a centralized budgetary plan.

2. *The technology incorporated an image of the work environment that was based on a representation of individual task functions.* In the case of the police, the functions centered on tasks carried out by the cruisers; in the hospital case, by the physicians; in the network facility case, such things as assigning lines, billing, recording, and so on.

3. *Once implemented (or, as in Case 3, nearing implementation), it was evident that the representation inscribed in the technology was in fact a misrepresentation: The work was more situated, more contingent, more locally variable, and more dependent on sociality than the design had allowed for.* Although the circumstances varied, this conclusion held for all three cases. The representation was inadequate in two ways: It failed to represent the data field in which professionals work adequately, and it failed to capture the social embedding of workers engaged in cooperative work.

4. *The result was unexpected inefficiencies, confusion of authority, rejection, or an inability to produce viable software.* These were the observed effects; they varied from outright neglect of the technology in the hospital case, to adoption but reduced efficiency in the police case, to major design difficulties in the network facility case.

5. *There was no way to adapt the technology once it had been implemented, and there was in any case, not much systematic feedback on performance either to the buyer (management) or the developers.* This latter conclusion is somewhat less firm. There are no follow-up data on all the cases reported, but the finding is in conformity with other fieldwork completed where the period of observation extended past the implementation period.

All of these observations are hypothetical, and meant to be tentative, but they seem to be supported by some other work reported recently.[19] Sachs (1995) developed a line of explanation that has clear parallels with that being described. She too argued (Sachs, 1995, p. 36) for the coexistence of "different conceptions of work" that "represent different lenses through which people in the organization peer." One of these conceptions she characterized as "organizational, explicit" and the other as "activity-oriented, tacit." The "organizational, explicit" view is represented by "sets of defined tasks and operations such as those described in methods and procedures"; the "activity-oriented, tacit" view "suggests that the range of activities, communication practices, relationships, and coordination it

---

[19]In recently completed work (Khalil, 1996) a case has been documented where the pattern is again to be found: centralized planning and implementation, followed by difficulties in implementation. The context is that of a large government department, staffed by members of the legal profession.

takes to accomplish business functions is complex and continually mediated by workers and managers alike." "When companies seek to transform the workplace," she continued (Sachs, 1995, p. 38), "they do so by employing a perspective that represents the point of view of only one part of this social complex of work: the organizational view"—a view exemplified by business process engineering. The problem is that "the efficiency of work is in fact determined not so much by the logic and sequencing of task flow as by the capabilities of people for troubleshooting vexing problems in complicated situations, which inevitably arise in all workplaces." To illustrate her thesis, she then reported on the implementation of a scheduling, work routing, and record-keeping system in a large telephone company. As in the examples, the result was not greater efficiency, but confusion of responsibilities, breakdown of essential channels of communication, and loss of morale.

Star and Ruhleder (1994, pp. 253–254) distinguished between "a set of rationalistic or 'mechanistic' ideas about artifacts and infrastructure" and "careful empirical analyses, which repeatedly demonstrated that even 'simple' and 'well-defined' tasks could only be understood as part of complex organizational contexts" where "the complex, embedded and historical nature of usage and adoption" is crucial to understanding the work world. The rationalistic view assumes that "tasks to be automated are well-structured, the domain well-understood, and that system requirements can be determined by formal, *a priori* needs assessment." The models taught in software engineering courses assume that "all work can be observed and routinized, all information codified. Users are sources of requirements, and eventually become systems recipients." The methodologies, in their words, "form complex *myth*ologies of systems development and use in 'real-world' domains." Their research, conducted in what might seem an ideal site for the implementation of a computerized communication infrastructure, a distributed group of biological researchers, nevertheless also found limited utilization of the facility that turned out to have grounds that could not just be explained by "user resistance."

The design group at Lancaster University in Great Britain (Hughes et al., 1992; Rouncefield, Hughes, Rodden, & Viller, 1994; Randall, Bentley, & Twidale, 1994) noted the gulf separating contrasting views of work; Rouncefield et al. (1994, p. 275) observed the "importance of understanding the 'real world' conditions of work rather than having design rely on idealizations which tend to ignore the circumstances, the contingencies, the mix of skills, the local knowledge, and more, which are ineradicable ingredients of 'real world' work." "By and large," they conceded, "designers lack the appropriate intuitions about the nature of work." Their experience (Hughes et al., 1992, p. 117) in the development of a technology for the United Kingdom Air Traffic Control Center emphasizes such features of work as sociality, context, contingencies, situatedness, discretion, judgment, tacit knowledge, accountability within a working division of labor and an orientation to one's own activities. These are not properties associated with organization/explicit or rationalistic/mechanical conception of work.

Groleau (1995) reported on three field studies in diverse areas of procurement, accounting, and design in an advertising firm. She found that the implementation of computerization produces unexpected difficulties in reading information display. Although the software simplifies certain information-related functions, it renders others opaque, and obliges users to develop what Sachs (1995) called "work-arounds." With the reduction of sociality that implementation brings, backups that previously could be counted on in dealing with contingencies are lost, and the result is greater vulnerability for both individuals and the organization. Finally, she observed in her study of the ad agency design group that what looks like an enhancement of designers' capabilities on a superficial reading of the process turns out to have negative consequences when the larger situation of the office is taken into account: Economies effected at one stage of work produce losses of efficiency at another, and creative autonomy is adversely affected.

A Computerization Syndrome?

The accumulation of these and other results of empirical research, when taking into account institutional realities that underpin the design, procurement, and implementation of technology in large organizations, adds up to what might well be thought of as a computerization syndrome. There are four organizational actors involved in a computerization scenario (Taylor, 1994): senior management (who control the budget and authorize the purchase), the systems department (who either develop themselves or take responsibility for the purchase of a new system), the implementers (those who install the machines and do the training), and the actual users.

First, management takes a panoptic view: For them, the organization is a global structure of functions and processes. As Suchman (1995) observed, the work ordinary people do in their organization tends to become invisible to management, as far as its situatedness is concerned. Managers' image of the organization, encouraged even further by the predominant tendency of the formal literature on organizations, is overwhelmingly particle oriented. As Weick (1985) pointed out, "Top management in complex organizations does not design operating structures, it designs decision structures. . . . Management does not actually manage the organization. Instead, it manages the process that manages the organization" (p. 114). Similarly (Star & Ruhleder, 1994; Sachs, 1995), the image of work held by software designers tends to be, by and large, particle oriented: The users, through the intermediary of a model, have been transmuted from subjects into objects. The implementers are on a schedule, with typically stringent mileposts, so that they are in no position to question the dominant image of the developers and buyers. The actual user community's *image* is not the critical issue; the *reality* of their day-to-day work is event oriented. Rather than contest the technology, given the facts of organizational power, they mostly grouse among themselves, and develop "work-arounds" (Sachs, 1995).

There is normally no formal means of feedback by which the mismatch between the prescriptive worldview of the technology is seen to be in contradiction with the descriptive worldview of actual work, and even if there were there is typically no way such negative testimony can be conveyed to either management, or the developers.[20] Management is screened by the hierarchy: No one wants to be the bearer of bad tidings where their boss is concerned. The developers have gone on to another project. So both management and the developers remain confined to their initial worldview, even where, to their occasional surprise, the results turn out to be not what they had expected. It is a case of what Boudon (1977) called an *effet pervers*, a "perverse effect" or dysfunction. What seemed a rational decision (economize on human resources by substituting a machine) is—once the whole context is taken into account—in fact irrational (make it harder for people to deal with the contingencies of daily work).

According to Weick (1985, p. 119),

> Most computer sales are vendor-driven. The customer seldom asks, "Do I really need that capability?" Instead, in order to keep up with the competition, hardware is purchased and then employees are urged to use the hardware in order to justify the purchase. Thus, the machine now becomes a required step in every process. Existing controls are disrupted and parts of the system that previously had been self-regulating are disconnected. No one knows what is occurring and everyone knows less about the organization than they did before, because interdependencies have been made more variable.

Consider adding one nuance: In large organizations it is not the vendor but the systems division that commonly is the promoter of the project,

---

[20]This depends somewhat on the users. Khalil (1996) finds lawyers in a large bureaucracy taking political action; Gurd (1994) found similar political clout among doctors in a large hospital. In both cases, issues remained open, and there was more or less open warfare among users and administrators.

which it sells to senior management on the basis that computerization is the key to reduced costs, personnel reduction, and productivity. That commitment—to productivity—locks in a worldview, both for management and the systems department. Of course, there is always "user resistance to change" to serve as a scapegoat. Multiplied thousands of times over, the cumulative result of repeated worldview mismatches ends up as an economic statistic of the kind Attewell (1992, 1993) reported.

What Is Cooperative Work?

How the user community's communication patterns are conceived of is the critical factor in how technology is designed, bought, and implemented. A set of program statements that claim to be, in their totality, a representation of the work world would be tenable if, and only if, communication were just moving information; it is not tenable if it is assumed that communication is a manifestation of what Weick (1979) called "organizing." When a new computer system is introduced, it brings with it its own worldview, partly because of the way the software was written, partly in the approach to implementation that management adopts when it arrives. The case studies reported are about what happens when a settled system of accommodations is asked to alter its basic transactional arrangements to fit the worldview of a new presence in its midst.

If the organization of work is treated as strictly particle oriented and material based, the effect is to program out of existence the self-organizing properties of the group that is engaged in cooperative work. To treat a system of work as nothing but a sequence of discrete operations is a useful approach only to the extent that no local initiative is expected, nor required, unlike the instances of the police (Case 1), or the doctors (Case 2), or the members of a complex administration (Case 3). But then it would no longer be very meaningful to use the term *cooperative work* because the "cooperation" is not generated from within the group itself, but enforced from the outside: coercion, not cooperation.

The problem in the case studies was that local initiative could not be wished out of existence, nor inscribed completely into the software. Because the designers and implementers of the system concentrated on information flow, they ignored the interpretive processes and relational structures that make work go—the conversational dynamics of everyday existence. By imposing a text-inspired system on an interactive system, they implemented a procrustean solution: Do not build a system to match the variety of the natural conversation, but compel the conversation to fit itself into the constraints of the technology. Ironically, it is the technical innovations of Engelbart's group at SRI (mouse, split screen, cut-and-paste, hypertext thinking, etc.) that have become part of every computer programmer's bag of tricks; the philosophy (prolonged user–computer mutual adaptation in a context designed to favor learning) has all too often, unfortunately, been subverted, buried under the institutional rubble of organizational politics.

The result will invariably be dysfunctional: confusion as to the locus of responsibility and authority (Case 1), subutilization (Case 2), and the risk of aborting the entire project after a huge initial investment in time and money (Case 3). No wonder the link from computerization to productivity has been so shaky! What started as a laudable goal to make the information system linking local communities of work into a structured network went adrift because the internal logic of cooperative work—not text driven, but conversational—was ignored.

CONCLUSIONS

The expression "computer-supported cooperative work" combines two terms, *computer-supported* and *cooperative work*. If there is indeed a "great divide"[21] separating, on the one hand, the people who design and develop software-based communication systems for organized contexts of work (the system designers) from, on the other, the people who try to comprehend the human and social dynamics of work into which the new systems are introduced (the social scientists), it is well expressed by the double-barreled character of CS/CW, associating as it does people with ideas about computers with others more accustomed to dealing with human societies, in the process generating a new kind of potentially explosive sociotechnical mixture, part engineer, part sociologist. Whereas both of the participating communities appear to be focusing on the same object of concern—computer-mediated communication—the presuppositions they bring to the meeting of minds are drawn from different disciplinary wells and may express rather different philosophical points of view, particularly as to the nature of work and human organization.

---

[21]The expression "great divide" is taken from a call for papers for an invitational workshop on social science research, technical systems, and cooperative work, held in Paris at the CNRS (Conseil National de la Recherche Scientifique), March 1993. The "great divide" was described in these terms: "Engineers are working on the technical side of the frontier, social scientists on the organizational side and, between the two, there has been a sort of no-man's land. The paradox of this situation is that in many cases engineers are building theories of social intelligence into their machines while social scientists are busy accumulating empirical observations and data on cooperative work processes, often without realizing how valuable each might be to the other." An earlier version of this chapter was presented as a paper at that workshop.

The crux of the matter lies not so much in the acceptability of information-processing technologies, nor whether they can assist people at work (because that is a common preoccupation of both communities). It is rather in the conceptualization of *cooperation* and *work* (and hence of *organization*), and what kind of technology *computers* are, that people bring to the discussion—especially because these are all notions that are so much part of daily discourse that they may seem on this account transparent.

The difficulty in finding a common ground of productive interaction between the disciplines arises less from what is said explicitly, however, than from the *implicit* buried presuppositional semantic structures that underlie, and frame, their respective discourses: their worldviews. These different presuppositional frameworks are not just a matter of abstruse academic concern—an interesting but purely theoretical debate among people of a philosophical bent; on the contrary, what people believe cooperative work *is*, what organization *is*, and what computerization *is*, translates into a set of practical design premises about the organizing of cooperative work itself, and may be, as our field research shows, *the* key to predicting whether the systems will finally succeed or fail.

Fundamental questions of both an ontological and epistemological nature are thus being posed by the computerization of work, and they are made even more salient by the fact that computer-based groupware has become a widely used support for collective enterprises, extending cooperative work beyond unmediated, face-to-face copresence. The implementation of computer-supported interaction forces a reexamination of assumptions previously taken for granted, but that may no longer be, if a constructive dialog that crosses disciplinary boundaries is to be advanced: What is cooperative work? How is it organized? What, indeed, is organization? What is the appropriate way to study, and design, technology, for people at work? Are the ideological premises underlying the design of computer systems compatible with those of the communities they are meant to support? What kind of two-way dialog, if any, is possible, that would link the makers of the systems, the users, and the people who study their implementation, social scientists?

And, it is a dialog that has to include management. The developer–user dialog, mediated or not by an explicit ethnography, is one that occurs within the framework of organizational realities, where there is a third actor, the ownership and management of the enterprise where computerization occurs. As things stand, this institutional frame has a built-in bias that tends to frustrate the opening up of user–developer dialog and perpetuates the worldview mismatch documented.

The purpose in this chapter has been to propose a conceptual framework, against which to situate the different positions in the CSCW dialog.

The claim is that, underlying them all, there is a root opposition that separates conceptual perspectives on organization, and knowledge work, and the use of computers, into two basic orientations called *worldviews*. This opposition is at the heart of the great divide: It marks how people both conceptualize the technology, and the contexts of its use. It explains some of the confusing results of computerization.

CSCW is not just about how to develop better support for cooperative work. It is itself cooperative work. If it is to take shape as a field it will be as a conversation, because no text not realized in a conversation can succeed organizationally. The issue is what will be the premisses of that conversation. It has not been the objective to show that there is a single *right* worldview. However, a recognition of the relativistic basis of organizational studies and of the computerization phenomenon as such will make a better starting point for future dialog in CSCW than more reductionist, single-minded points of view.

REFERENCES

Akzam, H. (1991). *Implantation technologique et adaptation organisationnelle: Période d'expérimentation* [Technological implementation and organizational adaptation: The experimentation period]. Unpublished master's thesis, Département de Communication, Université de Montréal.

Atkinson, P. (1977). The reproduction of medical knowledge. In R. Dingwall, C. Heath, M. Reid, & M. Stacey (Eds.), *Health care and health knowledge* (pp. 85–106). London: Croom Helm.

Atkinson, P. (1981) *The clinical experience: The construction and reconstruction of medical reality*. Farnsborough, UK: Gower.

Atkinson, P. (1995). *Medical talk and medical work: The liturgy of the clinic*. London: Sage.

Atkinson, P., & Heath, C. (Eds.). (1981). *Medical work: Realities and routines*. Farnsborough, UK: Gower.

Attewell, P. (1992, October–November). *The productivity paradox*. Paper presented at the ACM Conference on Computer-Supported Cooperative Work, Toronto.

Attewell, P. (1993). *Information technology and the productivity paradox*. Working Paper, Department of Sociology, Graduate Center of the City University of New York.

Baily, N. (1986). What has happened to productivity growth? *Science, 24*(October), 443–451.

Bardini, T. (1994, April). *The principles of the augmentation of human intellect: The genesis of Douglas Engelbart's framework*. Talk delivered at Stanford University.

Bardini, T., & Horvath, A. T. (1995). The social construction of the microcomputer user: The rise and fall of the reflexive user. *Journal of Communication, 45*(3), 40–65.

Bardini, T. (Forthcoming). *The lab that (almost) augmented us: Douglas Engelbart, the framework for the augmentation of human intellect, and the genesis of personal computing*. Stanford: Stanford University Press.

Barley, S. (1986). Technology as an occasion for structuring: Evidence from observations of CT scanners and the social order of radiology departments. *Administrative Science Quarterly, 31*(March), 78–108.

Barley, S. R. (1988). The social construction of a machine: Ritual, superstition, magical thinking and other pragmatic responses to running a CT scanner. In M. Lock & D. R. Gordon (Eds.), *Biomedicine examined* (pp. 497–539). Dordrecht: Kluwer.

Bateson, G. (1972). *Steps to an ecology of mind.* New York: Ballantine.

Blomberg, J. (1988). The variable impact of computer technologies on the organization work activities. In I. Greif (Ed.), *Computer-supported cooperative work: A book of readings* (pp. 771–781). San Mateo, CA: Kaufman.

Bohm, D. (1980). *Wholeness and the implicate order.* London: Ark.

Boudon, R. (1977). *Effets pervers et ordre social* [Perverse effects and social order]. Paris: Presses Universitaires de France.

Bush, V. (1945). As we may think. *Atlantic Monthly, 176*(1), 101–108.

Cicourel, A. (1985). Text and discourse. *Annual Review of Anthropology, 14,* 159–185.

Crary, J. (1990). *Techniques of the observer: On vision and modernity in the nineteenth century.* Cambridge, MA: MIT Press.

De Marco, T. (1978). *Structured analysis and system specification.* New York: Yourdon.

Drucker, P. (1966). *The effective executive.* New York: Harper & Row.

Drucker, P. (1969). *Ages of discontinuity: Guidelines to our changing society.* New York: Harper & Row.

Dumais, S., Kraut, R., & Koch, S. (1988). Computers' impact on productivity and work life. In *Proceedings of the ACM/IEEE Conference on Office Information Systems, Palo Alto, CA* (pp. 88–95).

Engelbart, D. C. (1962). *Augmenting human intellect: A conceptual framework.* Menlo Park, CA: SRI International, Report to the Director of Information Sciences, Air Force Office of Scientific Research.

Fafchamps, D. L. (1988). *Conventions and strategies: A framework for understanding communication in a surgical intensive care unit.* Unpublished doctoral dissertation, Stanford University.

Gane, C., & Sarson, T. (1977). *Structured systems analysis: Tools and techniques.* Englewood Cliffs, NJ: Prentice-Hall.

Garson, B. (1988). *The electronic sweatshop: How computers are transforming the office of the future into the factory of the past.* New York: Penguin.

Goldstine, H. H. (1972). *The computer from Pascal to von Neumann.* Princeton, NJ: Princeton University Press.

Gordon, G. (1969). *System simulation.* Englewood Cliffs, NJ: Prentice-Hall.

Groleau, C. (1995). *An examination of the computerized information flow contributing to the mobility of tasks in three newly computerized firms.* Unpublished doctoral dissertation, Department of Communication, Concordia University.

Gurd, G. (1994). *Computerization as the intersection of two logics: A hospital case study.* Unpublished doctoral dissertation, Département de Communication, Université de Montréal.

Halliday, M. A. K. (1970). Language structure and language function. In J. Lyons (Ed.), *New horizons in linguistics.* Harmondsworth, Middlesex, UK: Penguin.

Hirschheim, R. A. (1986). *Office automation: A social and organizational perspective.* Toronto, Ontario: John Wiley.

Hovey, M. (1992). *Conversation in the software development process.* Unpublished master's thesis, Department of Communication, Concordia University,

Huber, G., & Daft, R. L. (1987). The information environments of organizations. In F.M. Jablin, L. L. Putnam, K. H. Roberts, & L. W. Porter (Eds.), *Handbook of organizational communication: An interdisciplinary approach* (pp. 130–164). Newbury Park, CA: Sage.

Hughes, D. (1977). Everyday and medical knowledge in categorizing patients. In R. Dingwall, C. Heath, M. Reid, & M. Stacey (Eds.), *Health care and health knowledge* (pp. 128–140). London: Croom Helm.

Hughes, J. A., Randall, D., & Shapiro, D. (1992). Faltering from ethnography to design. *CSCW 92 Proceedings,* 115–122.

Jourdennais, M. (1992). *Changement organisationnel et reconstruction de marges de manoeuvre à la Société Canadienne de Postes* [Organizational change and reconstruction of the "Marge de manoeuvre" at Canada Post]. Unpublished master's thesis, Département de Communication, Université de Montréal.

Khalil, Marie-Josée. (1996). *Étude qualitative d'une implantation informatique dans un ministère de la fonction publique, le cas de Justice Canada* [Qualitative study of a computer system implementation in a federal government department, Justice Canada]. Unpublished master's thesis, Department of Communication, Université de Montréal.

Krasnow, H. S., & Merikallio, R. (1964). The past, present and future of general simulation languages. *Management Science, XI*(Nov.), 236–267.

Licklider, J. C. R. (1960). Man–computer symbiosis. *IRE Transcations on Human factors in Electronics, March*, 4–11.

Licklider, J. C. R., & Taylor, R. (1968). The computer as a communication device. *Science and Technology, April*, 21–31.

Macintyre, S. (1978). Some notes on record taking and making in an antenatal clinic. *Sociological Review, 26*(3), 595–611.

Morgan, G. (1986). *Images of organization*. Newbury Park, CA: Sage.

Osborne, A. (1979). *Running wild: The next industrial revolution*. Berkeley, CA: Osborne/McGraw-Hill.

Osheroff, J. A., Forsythe, D., Buchanan, B. G., Bankowitz, R. A., Blumfield, B. H., & Miller, R. A. (1991). Physicians' information needs: Analysis of questions posed during clinical trials. *Annals of Internal Medicine, 114*(7), 576–581.

Paisley, W. (1980). Information and work. In B. Dervin & M. Voigt (Eds.), *Progress in Communication Science* (Vol. 2, pp. 113–165). Norwood, NJ: Ablex.

Paul, R. J. (1993). Why users cannot "get what they want." *ACM SIGOIS Bulletin, 14*(2, December), 8–12.

Pettinari, C. (1988). *Task, talk and text in the operating room: A study in medical discourse*. Norwood, NJ: Ablex.

Pritsker, A. A. E. (1986). *Introduction to simulation and SLAM II*. New York: Wiley.

Randall, D., Bentley, R., & Twidale, M. (1994, October). Ethnography and collaborative systems development. *Tutorial notes, ACM 1994 Conference on Computer Supported Cooperative Work (CSCW)*, Chapel Hill, NC.

Ritzer, G. (1993). *The McDonaldization of society: An investigation into the changing character of contemporary social life*. Thousand Oaks/London/New Delhi: Pine Forge Press.

Roach, S. S. (1987). *America's technology dilemma: A profile of the information economy* (Rep. No. 6652). New York: Morgan Stanley.

Rothemund, M. (1986). Modelling medical organizational systems with nets. *Methods of Information in Medicine, 25*, 87–100.

Rouncefield, M., Hughes, J. A., Rodden, T., & Viller, S. (1994). Working with "Constant Interruption": CSCW and the small office. In *CSCW '94 Proceedings* (pp. 275–286).

Rule, J., & Attewell, P. (1989). What do computers do? *Social Problems, 36*(3), 225–241.

Sachs, P. (1995). Transforming work: Collaboration, learning, and design. *Communications of the ACM, 38*(9), 36–44.

Scott, W. R. (1972). Professionals in hospitals: Technology and the organization of work. In B. Georgopoulos (Eds.), *Organization research on health organizations* (pp. 139–158). Ann Arbor, MI: Institute for Social Research, University of Michigan.

Shannon, C. (1948). The mathematical theory of communication. *Bell System Technical Journal, 27*(10), 379–423, 623–656.

Silverman, D. (1987). *Communication and medical practice: Social relations in the clinic*. Newbury Park, CA: Sage.

Star, S. L., & Ruhleder, K. (1994). Steps to an ecology of infrastructure: Complex problems in design and access for large-scale collaborative systems. In *CSCW '94 Proceedings* (pp. 253–264).

Stinchcombe, A. L. (1990). *Information and organizations*. Berkeley, CA: University of California Press.

Stoelwinder, J. U., & Charns, M. P. (1981). The task field model of organization analysis and design. *Human Relations, 34*(9), 743–762.

Strassman, P. A. (1985). *Information payoff: The transformation of work in the electronic age*. New York: The Free Press.

Strauss, A., Fagerhaugh, S., Suczek, B., & Wiener, C. (1985). *The social organization of medical work*. Chicago: University of Chicago Press.

Strong, P. M. (1979). *The ceremonial order of the clinic: Patients, doctors and medical bureaucracies*. London: Routledge & Kegan Paul.

Suchman, L. (1983). Office procedure as practical action: Models of work and system design. *ACM Transactions on Office Information Systems, 1*(4), 320–328.

Suchman, L. (1995). Making work visible. *Communications of the ACM, 38*(9), 56–64.

Taylor, J. R. (1982). Computer aided message systems: An organizational perspective. In N. Naffah (Ed.), *Office information systems* (pp. 631–651). New York: INRIA/North-Holland.

Taylor, J. R. (1993). *Rethinking the theory of organizational communication: How to read an organization*. Norwood, NJ: Ablex.

Taylor, J. R. (1994). Les défis du management public à l'ère de l'information [The challenges facing public management in the Information Age]. *Transactions of the Royal Society of Canada*, sixth series, *5*, 31–57.

Taylor, J. R., & Van Every, E. (1993). *The vulnerable fortress: Bureaucratic organization and management in the information age*. Toronto, Ontario: University of Toronto Press.

Tocher, K. D. (1964). Review of simulation languages. *Operations Research Quarterly, 16*(2, June), 189–217.

Tocher, K. D. (1966). *Some techniques of model building*. White Plains, NY: IBM Corporation, Data Processing Division.

Turing, A. M. (1937). On computable numbers, with an application to the Entscheidungs problem. *Proceedings of the London Mathematical Society, 42*, 230–265; *43*, 544.

Van Maanen, J. (1973). Observations on the making of policemen. *Human Organization, 32*, 407–418.

Van Maanen, J. (1978). On watching the watchers. In P. K. Manning & J. Van Maanen (Eds.), *Policing*. New York: Random House.

Van Maanen, J. (1983). The boss. In M. Punch (Ed.), *Control in the police organization*. Cambridge, MA: MIT Press.

Von Neumann, J. (1945). *First draft report on the Electronic Discrete Variable Computer (EDVAC)*. Working Paper, Moore School of Engineering, University of Pennsylvania.

Wadsworth, M., & Robinson, D. (Ed.). (1976). *Understanding everyday medical life*. London: Martin Robertson.

Weick, K. E. (1979). *The social psychology of organizing* (rev. ed.). New York: Random House.

Weick, K. E. (1985). Sources of order in underorganized systems: Themes in recent organizational theory. In Y. S. Lincoln (Ed.), *Organization theory and inquiry: The paradigm revolution* (pp. 106–136). Beverly Hills, CA: Sage.

Weick, K. E. (1990). Technology as equivoque: Sensemaking in new technologies. In P. S. Goodman & L. S. Sproull (Eds.), *Technology and organization* (pp. 1–44). San Francisco, CA: Jossey-Bass.

Weick, K. E. (1995). *Sensemaking in organizations*. Thousand Oaks, CA: Sage.

Yourdon, E. (1989). *Modern structured analysis*. Englewood Cliffs, NJ: Yourdon Press/Prentice-Hall.

17

On Multidisciplinary Grounds: Interpretation Versus Design Work

Ina Wagner
Technische Universität Wien, Vienna, Austria

In fields such as computer-supported cooperative work (CSCW), participants typically come from a variety of disciplines. Producing systems that are informed by both social science and technical knowledge requires building a common working culture. The aim of this chapter is to reflect on the "disagreements" that frequently develop in such multidisciplinary projects. It simultaneously asks how participants cope with the practical problems of finding a shared language and developing common grounds and analyzes the epistemological roots of their points of dissent.

Its empirical basis are firsthand experiences with a project on computer-supported time management in a surgery clinic (Egger & Wagner, 1992, 1993; Wagner, 1993). They are used to highlight some general antinomies inherent in multidisciplinary design. These experiences are read as illustrations of conflicting research paradigms: a subject-centered versus a process-oriented perspective, a truth-oriented versus a success-oriented approach, different modes of trust building, and "opaqueness" versus control.

COTERM: A CASE AT HAND

Four researchers with different academic backgrounds in computer science and sociology collaborated in this 2-year research project. It was their first joint project. A strong interest in multidisciplinary design and in developing a CSCW application provided some shared ground. The team hoped to be able to pool their varied experiences and backgrounds in work ethnography, sociology of work and organizations, feminist theory, software engineering with a strong focus on user–interface design, and methods of user participation. The decision to build computer support for time management tasks was based on a shared interest in time—on the sociologist's side, issues of time and power and on the computer scientists' side, previous research on graph-theoretic specifications as an approach to representing time. Although the members of the group had jointly defined the multidisciplinary framing of their work, they were unable to clarify some major ambiguities and disagreements. This, however, did not impede academic activity—the team produced a series of research papers and a "product" (a prototype).[1]

When looking for a case that would allow to study time management practices in-depth, a surgery clinic offered the opportunity for field work and a rich and highly turbulent environment promising some challenge. Work ethnography as an approach meant to develop a dense description of organizational practices of scheduling surgical operations as seen by the different occupational groups involved. The team assumed the understanding of these practices gained through field work would form the basis for building a supporting system (or at least some prototype version of such a system). *Users* were defined as actors in and interpreters of their social world. They were seen as offering accounts of time management practices, as spelling out problems and as helping to develop directions for solving these problems. Access to these accounts was sought through observation and inquiry.

Although the relevance of such an approach was not disputed, its consequences were not clear and acceptable to all involved. Practicing an integrative approach to design was one of the leading ideas of the computer-supported time management (COTERM) project. This would have called for a more fluent division of tasks and activities, based on a certain redundancy of functions. Still, the stage model of design implicitly persisted for several reasons. Those primarily responsible for system design did not participate in what they considered the case study "phase" of the project. Repeated conflict in the clinic and the unwillingness of the leading surgeons to get involved in organizational change made more extensive forms of user participation, apart from repeated discussion with single interested staff, seem impossible. Consequently, an important source for engaging in an iterative design process with multiple contact with the world of users (as distinct from a more structured approach, based on a requirement analysis, control flow diagrams, etc.) was lacking.

---

[1]Use of the terms *systems designers* and *social scientists* is done to denote disciplines rather than persons (e.g., one team member, a computer scientist by training, carried out large parts of the ethnographic study of time management practices).

A considerable amount of integration work was needed to bridge the resulting gaps, with the project's ethnographers acting as surrogate users (Bentley et al., 1992). This seems to a certain extent unavoidable, in particular, in organizations in which people act under time pressure. Still, it turned out to be extremely difficult to create a site-specific ethnographic understanding of relevant practices and problems that could be shared by all team members in ways that would genuinely inform design.

There was also ambiguity about the role of users' needs in the project. According to a classical hermeneutic approach, field work as well as frequent and regular exchange between the different sources of expertise—work, design, and ethnography related—offers the opportunity for an iterative alignment of researchers' implicit models of the organization's reality and users' practices and interpretations. The idea was to reach some shared reality that includes users' interpretations and visions as well as the team members' own ideas on how to support more cooperative practices of distributing temporal resources. This approach, however, seemed too fuzzy to those responsible for systems design. They hesitated to accept and trust a mix of perspectives and methods that combines descriptive and normative elements from a variety of sources.

Equally iterative, from the sociologists' perspective, was the relation between the detailed narrative of this specific case and a theory of time management. The case, when placed into a carefully constructed web of arguments derived from a variety of theoretical and empirical sources, would reveal structures and patterns of meaning that may be considered typical of many different cases. The team's systems designers felt uncomfortable with this type of reasoning. What might have helped to convince them was a classical test of the "findings" in a wide range of user organizations.

There was a second contested aspect of the "generalizability" question. Designing for many different situations of use was considered much more challenging and rewarding than building a tailored system. However, it was not clear whether the design would be applicable to a variety of domains and support different practices of scheduling surgical operations or, even more generally, cooperative decision making over the distribution of scarce resources. The team's systems designers were interested in developing a "universal method" that would support the modeling and design process for this variety of domains. When it became clear that the case was far too complex to apply scheduling algorithms or a formal specification language, this was felt as severely limiting the project's scientific value.

Similarly controversial was the question about what kind of knowledge would be useful for building a system. Discussion of sociologists' sitespecific ethnographic understanding of time management soon made clear that a series of steps beyond a theory-oriented and narrative description of practices were needed. In several consecutive meetings, a sociological model of computer-supported surgery planning was discussed and further detailed. This model offered a vision of the system within the organization, defining its basic functions as well as clarifying normative foundations and critical points of human intervention. The team's systems developers found it difficult to take this model as a basis for the design work. They felt that in order to be able to start their own proper task, they needed a *specifically abstracted* version of this narrative (e.g., a detailed procedural model that can be the source for control flow diagrams or other detailed descriptions of activities and roles). Repeatedly, incongruencies between the two types of scenarios—the ethnographic descriptions and the view derived from designers' specifications—became visible. Reaching a shared view was further complicated by the expectation that the description resulting from the field work be complete. This was in conflict with the work ethnography revealing a high level of contingency and ambiguity in time management practices. Translation work between the two sets of understandings required considerable effort on both sides.

SUBJECT VERSUS PROCESS

One of the central questions is how to better inform the decisions arising in design work. Work ethnographies do not automatically produce the kind of knowledge on which to base design decisions. They always require an analysis, and which aspects of the richness of work are essential and what are the appropriate concepts for coming to grips with them are continuously debated. Shapiro (1994) pointed at the interpretive character of ethnographic accounts, noting that "there is a 'residual move' of explication and interpretation which goes beyond what is directly to be found in the materials and effects some kind of transition to concepts, categories and arguments which relate to sociology's concerns more conventionally conceived" (p. 419). These concerns are grounded in an interest in the socially constructed subjectivity of individuals as producing meaningful, interpretable action and in the social structures that are enacted through and give shape to this action. Communication in this perspective is seen as allowing actors to create, contest, and modify shared (intersubjective) understandings while reassuring their own subjectivity. Human actors are the "reference systems" for understanding the process of producing and reproducing knowledge. In contrast to this subject-centered (largely hermeneutic) tradition, Luhmann (1992) proposed a systems theory perspective that looks at the communication process itself as producing what is perceived of as meaningful action.

The relation between communication and communicating actors is indirect, Luhmann argued. Communication needs participants who "irritate" and thereby locomote the process by commenting, proposing, interrupting, pointing to some shared material, and so on. They make sense of the difference between what has been articulated and what they understand, thereby stimulating consecutive communicative acts. Given the self-referential complexity and intransparency of psychic systems, it would be impossible for the communication system "to check all the time" whether the participating individual "consciousnesses" follow closely, understand fully, do not deliberately produce misunderstandings. Communication is restricted to themed events that in themselves offer an immense abundance of semantic choices. It evolves, continues, is interrupted, and driven by "irritations"—an unexpected piece of information, a gesture, a technological intervention, a new participant entering the scene. Winding itself through these themed differences, incongruities, and disruptions, it enhances and modifies its sensitivity and the complexity of its operations. Both systems, the flowing communication process and the individual "consciousnesses" that keep it going, while happening parallel and simultaneously, are structurally coupled. This means the systems share events, but each system processes these events independently (Luhmann, 1992).

Luhmann suggested distinguishing between the problems of ensuring that ongoing communication be continued, reinitiated, and held alive on one hand, and the problems of understanding, interpreting, and responding that preoccupy the individual "consciousnesses" on the other hand. It is this distinction that may also help to reflect on some of the basic communication problems between social scientists and systems designers in the COTERM project. A process perspective looks at structural attributes of a temporal order and how these influence the flow of activities in time, whereas a subject view focuses on interpretive aspects and on how these shape temporal practices of individuals and organizations. Barley (1988) drew on this distinction when arguing that "the temporal order of a workplace (therefore) serves simultaneously as a template for organising behaviour as well as an interpretive framework for rendering action in the setting meaningful" (p. 125). Table 17.1 contrasts both perspectives.

The work ethnography produced in the COTERM project to a large extent focused on actors' "subjectively meaningful action." Cultural differences in perceiving, evaluating, and scheduling time were explored in-depth and there was a strong interest in corroborating that time is an intensely social and subjective phenomenon. Great care was applied to

TABLE 17.1
Contrasting Process Perspective and Subject Perspective

Process Perspective	Subject Perspective
Structured maps or timetables specifying: • duration • rate • temporal location • sequence/simultaneity • synchrony • (dis)continuity • temporal links/dependencies	Temporal symmetry or asymmetry with respect to: • evaluation of temporal requirements • value of time of person/activity • priorities (allocation) • coping with time constraints • making temporal commitments • time-autonomy • poly/monochrony
Times as a resource/constraint	Time as a medium of self-regulation, control, resistance, etc.
Representations • time quanta • mathematical (graphs, etc.)	Representations • interpreted time • temporal practices

making clear that those occupational groups that have to coordinate their activities as part of a surgery team use different time reckoning systems. Illustrating examples of different ways of evaluating the temporal requirements of different activities, of coping with time constraints, of making temporal commitments, and of time autonomy were searched for and related to the diversity of occupational milieus to be found in a hospital. What was left from this elaborate analysis from the point of view of systems designers was "just the conclusion": Given the subjective nature of time and the high level of temporal ambiguity, time management cannot be reduced to a scheduling problem. Process-oriented descriptions that helped to understand the "mechanisms" of time management and of making time-related decisions were considered as more useful then an in-depth study of time-reckoning systems.

This "disagreement" reflects an ongoing debate within the CSCW research community. Ethnographic techniques help make more visible a dimension of people's work, in which they actively, flexibly, and reflexively reform, reorient, and recombine their actions to fit the exigencies of the work as it unfolds. Although the focus on context, situatedness, and contingency is seen as indispensable for an understanding of work practice, there is less agreement on the appropriateness of a process perspective that can be translated into (basically procedural) protocols for action (Simone & Schmidt, 1993). The process perspective focuses on cooperation and communication as an unfolding flow of activities. It registers the use of language, manipulations of shared objects, the use of plans, rules, and procedures, and so on, as "enablers" or "preventers" of this flow. It helps to view and design a system as supporting actors to get in touch, to clarify misunderstandings, to work on a shared artefact, and to interrupt an activity. Most systems today build on a process perspective (which is not necessarily procedural in the sense of prescribing prefixed sequences of action). The Coordinator is an interesting example of this way of thinking, stressing "conversation for action" and a commitment to complete language-initiated action. It uses a strongly structured and discipline-oriented approach that identifies ambiguity and gliding transitions between commitments as obstacles to effective completion rather than as potentially productive sources of ongoing action (Flores et al., 1988).

These two perspectives and their relations should not only be explicitly identified in a multidisciplinary design project. They should be used in developing grounded scenarios—"rich descriptions of particular relevant practices" (Blomberg, Suchman, & Trigg, 1993). Ideally, a scenario should be a dynamic resource. It should be co-constructed, respondent both to the needs of developers for "representations of work which can be a source for models, while at the same time not losing their grounded nature in the work at a particular setting." In the COTERM project, a useful layered scenario would embrace both the subject and the process perspective; it would also perhaps:

> Provide a rich description of temporal conflicts in the surgery clinic that helps both the developing team and the hospital staff understand the individual and collective meanings behind these conflicts (differing priorities, power issues, professional orientations).

> Make the interaction mechanisms on which time management practices rest more transparent (what is negotiated, shared, protected, hidden, imposed, voted for, documented, modified in which way?).

> Make the functionalities of objects for time management transparent (what types of common artefacts are used in the process and in which ways do they serve as "irritators" of communication?).

> Provide some detailed procedural knowledge that is translatable into protocols, where this is possible and meaningful.

TRUTHFUL VERSUS SUCCESSFUL

In many phases of their work, systems designers "are less interested in theoretical reasoning than in immediate effects within their structural concepts" (Ropohl, 1979, p. 292). Their thinking focuses on what can be successfully applied to make an artefact, such as an information technology system, work. Sociologists, on the other hand, are interested in generating an interpretative framework. A theory (and for some a good case in addition) is what makes an argument shine. Only those statements are considered "precise," which are based on a carefully structured chain of arguments and backed up by multiple references. In a research-oriented environment like the COTERM project, these differences in team members' orientations are important for an understanding of the problems that arise in multidisciplinary projects. There may be a profound misunderstanding of the "rules" that determine the production and use of knowledge in a field of inquiry, scientific or practical, making it different.

Design work is dominated by a success-oriented, constructive methodology (Knorr, 1985). In many phases of a design, the theoretical substantiation and elaboration of a design decision is less relevant than the applicability of some "heuristics"—"explicable rules of thumb, standard practices etc." (Collins, 1987, p. 336). The lesser the degree of abstraction and idealization of the objects and systems, the more likely systems designers will have to resort on these standard practices (also referred to as methods) that are only partially explicable. This is typical of many engineering professions in which "extensive use of informal, theoretically arbitrary conventions and judgements is still necessary in applying theoretical models to practical design problems" (Whitley, 1988, p. 392). Moreover, a method, rule, or procedure is not simply followed, but made to work in the context of a specific design situation.

This focus of design activities on the "workable" is in itself controversial. Success of a design in an engineering approach is not defined in purely practical terms, but measured against a whole catalogue of norms and standards, such as design simplicity, consistency with a real-world analogue, or anticipation of low frequency events (Grudin, 1991). Computer scientists' understanding of what makes a program valid very much depends on their conceptions of what a program is and there are a variety of legitimate standpoints. Fetzer (1988) discussed the tensions that arise between thinking of programs as algorithms and logical structures or as causal models of those structures that will be executed by a machine. Design does not only consist in making a function (which may be explicated in a formal theoretical framework) applicable, it identifies it at the same time with the action system of a potential user (Ropohl, 1979). Whereas formal methodologists put emphasis on program verification as a formally valid way of assessing the correctness of a program, participatory approaches stress the accountability of a design to the work on site. This also involves a notion of "truthfulness" in the sense of reflecting aspects of the use situation (in a necessarily incomplete way).

Although design work is in many phases oriented along a "successful–unsuccessful" axis (with partial theoretical grounding), the acceptability of ethnographic descriptions very much depends on their "truthfulness." Again, there are conflicting views of what makes an ethnographic finding truthful. Geertz's (1987) idea of dense descriptions emphasizes the need to "keep adding the 'telling' details in any given setting until you have a veridical narrative, one that is close to being there in some sense" (Leigh Star, personal communication, 1994). This is close to the notion of grounded scenarios as being recognizable by the inhabitants of a world as a true description of their practices and beliefs. "Progress" is accomplished by reaching deeper into a phenomenon, it is nonlinear and nonhierarchical (Geertz, 1987). Geertz used the image of studies proceeding "shoulder to shoulder" (rather than on the shoulders of previous research). Grounded theory, on the other hand, simultaneously seeks authentic descriptions and generalizations. Truth is approached through an iterative process in which theory and "data" interact to create more valid interpretations.

In the COTERM project, the truth versus workable distinction in its controversial and varied versions became acute when the design work started and efforts were made to narrow down a rich description to a specific version and vision of reality. Several problems were encountered.

Standing Back Versus Taking Decisions

When capturing social practices and their meaning, a "good" sociological analysis reaches beyond a neutral description ("first-order observations"; Shapiro, 1994, p. 419). It presents a critical approach to those practices by grounding them in ethical, political, or personal concerns. In the COTERM project, this meant explaining the web of connections that influence time management practices and the power structures on which they are based. Descriptions pointed to priorities that lacked transparency, no participation in decision making, authority relationships and unresolved conflicts. Surgeons, nurses, anaesthesiologists, and interns were expected to recognize the situation as described and be open to the conclusions drawn with respect to ways of enlarging the space for cooperative planning.

Although providing interpreted accounts from multiple perspectives (some of them of a partisan character), the sociologists in the team hesitated to get more directly involved in setting a stage for action. Systems designers, on the other hand, make design decisions that may support certain actions while excluding others. CSCW research seeks to provide flexible and malleable tools for use in specific computational environment, but there are still numerous technical limitations to be accounted for. Design choices are partly influenced by the available tools and by theoretical considerations only loosely connected to the case at hand. The design of the COTERM prototype reflects these dilemmas of making the transition from a descriptive, critical, but open mode, to one that fixes a framework for action. Instead of modeling a group decision process on scheduling surgical operations, the design ideas focused on improving actors' basis for ongoing negotiation, arguing that "one central problem such a 'project' faces is the (in)compatibility of automatic scheduling with co-operative decision-making. . . . A 'right mix' between temporal complexity and plurality on one hand and stable rules and procedures on the other hand can only be negotiated, not imposed" (Egger & Wagner, 1993, p. 273).

Preserving Professional Identities

At this point it also became clear that the transition from ethnographic representations of work to design implies a "stripping" down of research findings and interpretations that weaken their disciplinary identity. This conflict more generally applies to the relations between "Wissenschaft" and "Praxis." Making knowledge workable in a practical context—be it politics, counseling, teaching, or designing a system—requires integrating this knowledge into the relevance structures that reflect the particularities and practicalities of a specific context. This is what Beck and Bonß (1989) observed in an essay on the tensions between the "enlightenment" and the "engineering" approach in the social sciences: " 'Shaping' a practical context—and this is what 'using' means—necessarily disconnects the identity thread. To become practically successful, sociological interpretations need to 'disappear,' without leaving a trace, within everyday or practical political knowledge so that they can only be deciphered within the practical context (they 'have been applied to')" (p. 2). Accepting such transitions and transformations may be extremely difficult for sociologists, even if they directly participate in this transition work. Much of what makes a description truthful and sensitive to the complexity of a case disappears as useless or residuary in design work.

The "workable versus true" distinction is tightly connected to questions of accountability. Reflecting on their work on litigation practices in a law firm, Blomberg et al. (1993) identified conflicting structures of accountability: to the variety of people whose organization and practices they describe and interpret, to the developers who will base their design decisions on the provided ethnographic understanding, to the technology development corporation for which they work. Working for a company that seeks to develop marketable technologies creates expectations, opportunities, and constraints that fundamentally differ from those present in a research environment. Accountability not only depends on the roles and responsibilities a person assumes, but also on what is considered the most relevant outcome of a project: Academic publications that will be reviewed by a highly specialized community of researchers; a prototype that acts as an approximation of a future product or rather helps users and developers to explore opportunities.

In multidisciplinary design projects, participants may find themselves immersed in conflicting roles, structures of accountability, and conceptions of what is relevant. Their discussion is made difficult by the ambiguous character of definitions of what "true" or "workable" means. Some of this ambiguity results from the uncertainties involved in translating an ethnographic description into design decisions. Additional inconclusiveness arises from the fact that particular design decisions are only loosely coupled to how a fully developed and implemented system will affect work at a particular site. On one hand, it is clear that through the technical features of the system—the language in which it has been developed and the social conventions that have been frozen in it—potential uses are prescribed (and others excluded). On the other hand, a system is only partly formed and its uses and implications will vary according to the particular ways it is implemented and how the work practices surrounding it will develop (Clement, 1994).

Layered scenarios draw simultaneously on the subject and the process-perspectives of work, with each layer being a possible source of conflict amongst the members of the project team, as we have just seen. In order to cope with conflicting points of view, a definition of project outcomes to be sought at each level might be useful. A list might include: the basic sociological insights into the nature of time management; the scenarios that have been created and serve as boundary objects, accountable to design work and work at site; the model or "universal method" for supporting time management systems designers develop; and a prototype that may ultimately result in a usable system.

An additional possibility would be to create rich descriptions of the accountability structures the various actors find themselves embedded in, including the conflicting commitments that this web of connections creates for them. This involves a form of stakeholder analysis that seeks to identify who has interests (de facto and legitimate) in the process, how these interests are pursued, and where they coincide and diverge, it being understood that team members are themselves stakeholders and accountable for their actions. (As we have already said, their commitments and obligations influence the ethnographic and design work they produce). A stakeholder analysis would focus design on questions of commitment fulfillment, coalition formation and supportive networks for trust-building.

TRUST BUILDING

Creating a shared understanding of work at site and a vision on how to improve and support it through designing a computer system is intimately connected to how actors arrive at knowing something is true, works, is a failure, and leads into a wrong direction. This in turn depends on the ways trust is established. Disciplines differ in the ways trust—confidence in the reliability of an observation or an interpretation, or in the correctness of abstract principles in the face of contingent outcomes—is built.

Trust in the social sciences to a large extent depends on sense making. Implied in this understanding is a peculiar relation between "the general" and "the particular," or unique. Sense making requires establishing and activating relations of what is familiar and what is strange, of a diversity of events, situations, and contexts that may have some characteristics in common while differing with respect to others. Natural languages reflect this relation. They provide general categories that allow the expression of the "uniqueness" of experiences and thoughts in ways that can be communicated to others, without, however, capturing fully what makes them particular and different (Habermas, 1968). This is at the roots of what is often described as the metaphorical, loose, and indexical character of concepts used in sociology. As Habermas pointed out, social scientists' access to social reality is not radically different from the layperson's: "They have to be part of the 'Lebenswelt' whose elements they seek to describe. In order to be able to describe them, they have to form an understanding; and, in order to understand, they have to be able to participate on principle in their production; and participation presupposes belonging to" (Habermas, 1987, p. 160). Confidence in a piece of sociological analysis has to be worked out on the basis of self-reflection and communication. Hands-on experience and contextual knowledge—walking through the hospital, getting a feeling for the place and the people involved, seeing an emergency come in and be scheduled—support the building of trust. Dupuy (1980) viewed "becoming acquainted with the things of life inside a meaningful environment" as a precondition for what he (quoting Hannah Arendt) called "autonomous action of radical novelty"—the capacity of perceiving previously hidden aspects, being surprised, developing a new perspective.

Some of these conditions for trust building apply to systems designers as well. Many argue that seeing a system work in a meaningful environment be indispensable for developing confidence in the design. For Flores et al. (1988) the "effectiveness of a work of design, and of a theory as a basis for design, must be assessed in the context of the consequences of the intervention." This implies that designers need to see their system effectively perform the interventions for which it has been developed. Trust in design work is not solely established through the successful functioning of a prototype or system in a particular environment. It also depends to some degree on the embeddedness of the design in abstract systems. Other types of "proofs" are necessary, such as the internal consistency of a design, its simplicity, having used a formal specification language, and so on. Formal methodologists would require a formal verification as proof of a program's correctness.

The tensions between communicative methods of trust building, which come close to "being there," and more formal approaches point to a more general phenomenon. In his discussion of modernity, Giddens (1990) sketched four dialectically related frameworks of experience: "Displacement" requires "reembedding: the intersection of estrangement and familiarity. Intimacy and impersonality: the intersection of personal trust and impersonal ties. Expertise and reappropriation: the intersection of abstract systems and day-to-day knowledgeability. Privatism and engagement: the intersection of pragmatic acceptance and activism" (p. 140). These observations also apply to the different modes of trust building sociologists and systems designers use. Obviously, bridges need to be built that help both to confide in the observations, interpretations, and devices the other develops. Some of the trust needed for working together builds over time, as the team learns to appreciate the contributions of others without necessarily knowing why. As Star noted (see part I, this volume), this is a process in which the initial disciplinary norms and conceptions are significantly modified and a team develops its own "local rubrics." However, conflicts over what is meaningful and useful cannot always be solved in a spontaneous way. The contextual, embedded nature of ethnographic findings does not lend itself readily to the kind of disembedding that happens when a feature is taken out of its context and reembedded in some abstract system. Trust building under such conditions becomes a project in itself. It requires carefully spelling out differences and defining the relations (e.g., between an embedded description of some work practices and their formal specification, between what a particular person was doing to align conflicting demands and its general representation in a system function).

A related critical point in the COTERM project was the choice of the size and thematic focus of the unit to be studied. The team's social scientists opted for looking into complex, partly tacit coordination processes, involving multiple actors and their time-reckoning systems. Although they viewed the collected evidence as a sufficient basis for "trusting" that in hierarchical organizations with multiple professional cultures people may be faced with comparable temporal conflicts, the developers would have put more trust into a series of more narrowly defined and preferably standardized observations.

A bridge between those two perspectives was built by introducing the prototype (basically, a simulation of a series of user interfaces that allowed users to explore a variety of practices and tools without being able to perform the tasks) into meetings with staff and project teams from other hospitals (and countries). Feedback in these cases was not obtained by user testing but by using the prototype to trigger discussion about what a future system might look like. The fact that the initial prototype was designed on the basis of a site-specific ethnography, but could be used in other hospitals provided some additional confidence in its relevancy, because the truthfulness of the descriptions worked out in one particular study was implicitly corroborated.

"OPAQUENESS" VERSUS CONTROL

One approach to the design of computer support is to define time management as a pure scheduling problem. This is done by defining a goal function, that is, to optimize the utilization of surgery time. The task then consists in distributing limited temporal resources, given certain boundary conditions. An automatic scheduler would be a module that "knows" a series of restrictions and tests the compatibility of data. Experiences in the field showed the problems of an automatic scheduling approach, among them the existence of several competing "goal functions" (reflecting occupational diversity); the impossibility of representing the hospital hierarchy in the system, including the informal relations and arrangements it needs to be able to function (this would result in a far too complicated and in the end not flexible set of rules); the fact that the actor system is not well bounded; and the high level of temporal ambiguity. From the ethnographers' perspective, an adequate description was one that made these limits to automation explicit. On one hand, some clear-cut rules and conditions could be spelled out that lent themselves to what was called "collision management" (the automated checking of inconsistencies in a schedule). On the other hand, it was necessary to clearly demarcate what would have to be discussed and decided face-to-face and, consequently, had to be left implicit, open, and "unspecified."

Even though this view was explicated and shared on principle, it caused considerable confusion. Systems designers continued to request a *complete description* of time management practices on which to base the design of a prototype. Context, situatedness, and contingency (in particular sociologists' insistence on the subjective nature of time) were contrasted with an "automatic scheduling ideal." The project's focus had to be shifted from creating a formal representation of time-planning practices to more "modest" goals such as providing an overview, facilitating communication, and increasing the degree of inclusivity and participation in the scheduling process. Previous plans to ground design on graph-theoretic specifications seemed inadequate or at least premature.

This fundamental tension between the need for control (as expressed in a complete, often procedurally oriented description of activities) and "opaqueness" (leaving things implicit) has been repeatedly addressed in CSCW research. Different ways of "neutralizing" the automation agenda (which so often acts as the powerful standard image from which it is difficult to step back) are proposed and debated. These approaches stress the importance and richness of copresence in material environments and the inappropriateness of systems that try to substitute for, or restrict, dialogue and skill (e.g., Heath & Luff, 1992; Robinson, 1991; Suchman, 1987). Appropriate systems should give support for dialogue, not substitute for or restrict it; should provide new mediums of expression; and should help overcome limitations of distance, availability, and local knowledge (Clement, Robinson, & Wagner, 1994). Also, there is an extensive debate on the appropriateness of different types of representations (those created through systematic, highly formalized techniques and tools, prototypes, informal, incomplete sketches, scenarios, etc.) for design work. The direction of this debate is well reflected in Bødker (1995), who suggested "view[ing] representations in design as containers for ideas, not as mapping anything."

CONCLUSIONS

Exploring and understanding the conditions that shape research and design practices is an important part of the work needed to create a shared working culture in multidisciplinary design. This requires analyzing the "norms" of the participating disciplines—the role of theory building, empirical grounding, heuristics, aesthetics. The chapter has examined some practical ways of integrating such an analysis into ongoing project work:

- Exploring the "subject–process" distinction seems a fruitful route to some of the problems of multidisciplinary work. While sense making is indispensable for developing an understanding of what "provokes" actors to modify, re-initiate, justify, hide, and manipulate, a process-oriented perspective offers some common ground for learning what helps to ensure the ongoing flow of communication and cooperation within a field. Grounded scenarios should draw on both perspectives.

- Another meaningful approach is exploring the "workable versus true" distinction in its varied meanings for different participants and project outcomes. Layered folders defining the diversity of relevant "products" and their different status is one approach to making conflicting conceptions of what is relevant explicit. An additional possibility is creating rich descriptions of the accountability structures the various actors find themselves immersed in and analyzing how these commitments and dependencies influence the ethnographic and design work.

- A third focus is trust building. When disembedded and reembedded in an abstract system, a truthful description of some work practice may no longer be recognizable and distorted. Conversely, systems designers may have to cope with conflicting requirements—such as workability, formal correctness, tailorability, and "truthfulness" to the particularities of the work site—each of which requires different forms of confidence building. Although some of this confidence in interpretations and design decisions and in each other's work tacitly develops over time, trust building needs to become a project in itself. There is a small but growing recognition that the qualities of personal, lively interaction focused on concrete, rather than abstract, information-handling practices are often neglected in conventional systems development activities (Greenbaum & Kyng, 1991).

- Finally, multidisciplinary design requires finding and maintaining a delicate balance of what can be specified and controlled and what needs to remain implicit, opaque, and open to the discretion of users—of what can be captured by representations of a potential use situation and what is worked out in design practice. CSCW research addresses this particularly difficult point. It seeks to provide methods that allow working more closely to the realities of a work site, thereby making the act of connecting the worlds of work, ethnography, and design easier.

REFERENCES

Barley, S. R. (1988). On technology, time, and social order: Technically induced change in the temporal organization of radiological work. In F. A. Dubinskas (Ed.), *Making time. Ethnographies of high technology organizations* (pp. 123–169). Philadelphia: Temple University Press.

Beck, U., & Bonß, W. (1989). Verwissenschaftlichung ohne Aufklärung? Zum Strukturwandel von Sozialwissenschaft und Praxis [Scientification with no explanation? On the structural change of social science and praxis]. In U. Beck & W. Bonß (Eds.), *Weder Sozialtechnologie noch Aufklärung? Analysen zur Verwendung sozialwissenschaftlichen Wissens* (pp. 7–45). Frankfurt: Suhrkamp.

Bentley, R., Hughes, J. A., et al. (1992). Ethnographically-informed systems design for air traffic control. In *ACM 1992 Conference on Computer-Supported Cooperative Work* (pp. 123–129). Toronto:

Blomberg, J., Suchman, L., & Trigg, R. (1993). Reflections on the work-oriented design project in three voices. In *Workshop social science research, Technical systems and cooperative work* (pp. 75–90). Paris: CNRS.

Bødker, S. (1995). *Understanding representation in design*. Draft Paper, Aarhus University.

Clement, A. (1994). Ethical considerations in media space research. *IFIP WG9.1 Workshop on Ethics and Systems Design,* Havana, Cuba.

Clement, A., Robinson, M., & Wagner I. (1994). Supporting health care networks. *IFIP WG 9.4 Working Conference The Impact of Informatics on Society: Key Issues for Developing Countries.* Havana, Cuba.

Collins, H. M. (1987). Expert systems and the science of knowledge. In W. E. Bijker, T. P. Hughes, & T. J. Pinch (Eds.), *The social construction of technological systems* (pp. 329–348). Cambridge, MA: MIT Press.

Dupuy, J. P. (1980). Myths of the informational society. In K. Woodward (Ed.), *The myths of information: Technology and post-industrial culture* (pp. 3–17). London: Routledge & Kegan Paul.

Egger, E., & Wagner, I. (1993). Negotiating temporal orders. The case of collaborative time-management in a surgery clinic. *Computer Supported Cooperative Work. An International Journal, 1,* 255–275.

Egger, E., & Wagner, I. (1992). Time-management. A case for CSCW. In *ACM 1992 Conference on Computer Supported Cooperative Work* (pp. 249–256). Toronto:

Fetzer, J. H. (1988). Program verification: The very idea. *Communications of the ACM, 31*(9), 1048–1063.

Flores, F., Graves M., et al. (1988). Computer systems and the design of organizational interaction. *ACM Transcations on Office Information Systems, 6*(2), 504–513.

Geertz, C. (1987). *Dichte Beschreibung. Beiträge zum Verstehen kultureller Systeme* [Complete description. Contributions on understanding cultural systems]. Frankfurt: Suhrkamp.

Giddens, A. (1990). *The consequences of modernity.* Cambridge/Oxford, England: Polity Press.

Greenbaum, J., & Kyng, M. J. (Eds). (1991). *Design at work: Cooperative design of computer work.* Hillsdale, NJ: Lawrence Erlbaum Associates.

Grudin, J. (1991). Systematic sources of suboptimal interface design in large product development organizations. *Human–Computer Interaction, 6,* 147–196.

Habermas, J. (1968). *Erkenntnis und Interesse* [Recognition and interest]. Frankfurt: Suhrkamp.

Habermas, J. (1987). *Theorie des kommunikativen Handelns* [Theory of communicative behavior]. Frankfurt: Suhrkamp.

Heath, C., & Luff, P. (1992). Collaboration and control. Crisis management and multimedia technology in London underground control rooms. *Computer Supported Cooperative Work. An International Journal, 1*(2), 69–94.

Knorr, K. (1985). Zur Produktion und Reproduktion von Wissen. Ein deskriptiver oder ein konstruktiver Vorgang? [On the production and reproduction of knowledge. A descriptive or constructive process]. *Soziale Welt,* Sonderband 3, 151–178.

Luhmann, N. (1992). *Die Wissenschaft der Gesellschaft* [The science of society]. Frankfurt: Suhrkamp.

Robinson, M. (1991). Double-level languages and co-operative working. *AI & Society, 5,* 34–60.

Ropohl, G. (1979). *Eine Systemtheorie der Technik* [A system theory of technology]. München/Wien: Carl Hanser Verlag.

Shapiro, D. (1994). The limits of ethnography: Combining social sciences for CSCW. In *Proceedings of the CSCW '94 Conference on Computer-Supported Cooperative Work* (pp. 417–428). Chapel Hill.

Simone, C., & Schmidt, K. (Eds.). (1993). *Computational mechanisms of interaction for CSCW.* COMIC Deliverable 3.1, Lancaster University.

Suchman, L. (1987). *Plans and situated actions. The problem of human–machine communication.* Cambridge, England: Cambridge University Press.

Wagner, I. (1993). Neue Reflexivität—Zu einem kulturtheoretischen Verständnis der Realitätskonstruktion in Organisationen [New reflexivity—On a culture–theoretical understanding of the construction of reality in organizations]. In I. Wagner (Ed.),

Kooperative Medien. Informationstechnische Gestaltung moderner Organisationen (pp. 7–66). Frankfurt: Campus.

Whitley, R. (1988). The transformation of expertise by new knowledge. Contingencies and limits to skill scientification. *Social Science Information, 27*(3), 391–420.

18

Understanding of Work and Explanation of Systems

Kurt D. Keller
University of Copenhagen

The use of computer systems in organizations and in cooperative work has increased during the last three decades in a quantitative as well as qualitative sense. Nevertheless, until recently it has generally been possible to combine the development of computer systems and work organization on the basis of rather simplistic knowledge about the human performance of cooperative work (passing over the question of whether that has ever been prudent). Today, the conceivable utilization of advanced computer technology implies aspirations about influencing the organization of cooperative work rather thoroughly. As a result, the limits of both commonsense and ad hoc notions of human work performance have been surpassed as a frame for combined system and organization development. Now, some major problems in research and development (R&D) on computer-supported cooperative work (CSCW) are closely connnected to the understanding of social processes and social identity, both of which are essential concepts within social science.

Social processes include the micro- as well as macro-aspects of historical development, the interplay of all kinds of conflicting and converging customs and aims, which make up the dynamics of reproduction and change in social life. These processes are more concrete (and thus "more real") than the relatively permanent structures, relations, functions, and interactions found or built up in social life. Strictly speaking, these phenomena are abstractions of sociality in which only the reproduced (i.e., the relatively stable and thus most recognizable) aspects of social processes are focused, whereas the actual changes are disregarded. This also means the fundamental tension between future and past, the background for all our orientation in social life, is disregarded.

Difficulties concerning the understanding of social processes are clearly manifested throughout the attemts to integrate computer-based information and communication systems for work settings. The pertinent topics concern increasingly detailed ways of explicating the structures and dynamics of cooperative work, and attempting to ensure that these structures and dynamics are influenced in desirable directions through the application of new computer systems. The issue reflects a well-known theme in social science: To what extent and under what circumstances can social change be intentional?

Concepts of social identity (as opposed to purely physical or biological identity) have served to emphasize a view of social actors that cuts across distinctions between individual identity and collective identity. Furthermore, contrary to the usual notions of social agents and most notions of social roles, social identity points to the (sociocultural and socioeconomic) compound of a field of praxis with bodily social experience.

In the context of CSCW projects (cf. Baecker, 1993; CSCW, 1994; Greenbaum & Kyng, 1991; Marmolin, Sundblad, & Schmidt, 1995), the need to understand social identity has developed from two previous approaches to the design of computer systems for cooperative work settings: structured systems engineering (representing the predominance of technological expertise) and prototyping (representing the communication with the users-to-be). At best, combinations of these approaches may connect the creative dialogue between users-to-be and system developers with adequate concepts of computer technology. However, this does not at all guarantee a satisfactory conceptualization of the users' social identity.

This chapter suggests the application to social phenomena of the metascience distinction between understanding and explaining. Concepts of social processes make it easier to understand the way in which social structures are constituted, and similarly, concepts of social identity make it easier to understand the experience and praxis of social actors. But social structures and social actors may also be explained: namely, by being regarded as the components of social systems. Social processes and social identity, however, can only be modeled and represented in systems by disregarding the understanding (as opposed to an explanation) of their substantial characteristics.

In general, the superficiality of merely explaining sociocultural issues has become inadequate for CSCW projects. Now, the major challenge in these projects is to ensure that new computer-based information and communication systems can be succesfully embedded in the reality of human performance of cooperative work. Coping with this challenge requires a conceptual and theoretical "equipment" for R&D, which does not just deal with a simplistic "application" of computer technology to cooperative work, but with the possibilities of actually embedding the technological systems in the work settings. Accordingly, it seems inevitable that technological perspectives and knowledge have to be embedded in scientific perspectives and knowledge concerning human work. Furthermore, abstract comparison and unification of sociological and technological issues as the isomorphic components of sociotechnical systems can only be a subordinate part of the job. Clearly, first and foremost it is necessary to explicate the real differences between human work and computer technology in order to effectively bridge the various (conceptual, practical, and developmental) gaps between the two sides.

If social sciences are to be utilized seriously for this purpose, "the great divide" is not so much between computer science and social science: Rather, it is between combinations of human science and social science on the one hand (known for instance from organization development, adult education, and group therapy), and combinations of social science and computer science (e.g., in statistics, systems science, and game theory) on the other.

In the perspective inspired by human science, social life must be understood as processes of experience and praxis through which even the very identity of (conscious and responsible) social actors is marked by history, although objective traits of history (established institutions, etc.) are also manifestations of such experience and praxis. This "circular" view of social actors and social structures (which goes behind—but also leads back into communication with—the social actors' own perspectives) is in no way esoteric, though it is inconvenient for attempts to model social life as the structures and functions of systems. Rather, this view reflects the state of the art in social science: within the general theory of the social sciences it has been emphasized by Habermas (1972) and Apel (1976), as well as by Bourdieu (1977, 1981) and Giddens (1979)—albeit with different wordings and accentuations.

This chapter draws on a more basic approach—namely, the social philosophy in Merleau-Ponty's phenomenology—in which a coherent foundation for the various perspectives needed in an R&D methodology for computer-supported cooperative work can be found (cf. Keller, 1995). On this basis, computer technology (and also social systems) can be regarded as objectivations derived from our bodily-social experience and praxis. The phenomenological foundation also makes it obvious that, regardless how detached and "thinglike" a computer system might seem, it never functions (e.g., as a communication and information system) in human work performance without being reintegrated into this bodily social experience and praxis. It is equally important that, in Merleau-Ponty's writings (1963, 1964, 1968, 1974), there is a solid point of departure for distinguishing and connecting the various aspects of praxis, experience, and understanding in R&D: that is, as concurrent aspects of everyday life and theory (cf. also Keller, 1992; Waldenfels, 1987). The following discussion takes this point of departure, without suggesting that the involved considerations can all be directly deduced from Merleau-Ponty's writings.

UNDERSTANDING AND EXPLAINING IN SOCIAL SCIENCES

The distinction between knowing and doing has haunted the social sciences in a number of ways. In the shape of "explanation," knowing stands in a contrast to doing: There can easily be one of the two without the other. This section attempts to make it clear that the matter is different with understanding: This kind of knowing is more closely associated with bodily-social doing.

Obviously, people actively take part in social life in lots of important ways, without possessing any immediately objectified and communicable knowledge of this praxis (e.g., to be described as involving specific competences). Rather, if it is necessary at all, we objectify our praxis and communicate about it with the help of shallow indications and metaphors. Mostly, people perform, perceive, and understand everyday praxis in ways (by concrete example, intuition, etc.) that are quite immediate and intimate to their bodily social identity. Because we are not entirely transparent to ourselves, it is basically problematic to regard this perception and understanding as apt to be completely objectified and subject to verbal communication. Still, science must be based on knowledge that can be reported and discussed. Phenomenology offers a solution to this dilemma (or a way of living with it): Scientific descriptions and formalized notions are only conceivable because, strictly speaking, they never become completely abstract. Like a figure on its background or a theme in its context, they have to remain practically embedded in much wider networks (ultimately a whole lifeworld) of bodily social explications and implications. This is why the formal concepts and methods can be applied by turning the abstactions back into concrete examples and situations.

Of course, the problem of really respecting both sides, scientific knowing and social doing, is particularly significant as regards organization development and the various other development-oriented branches of applied social science. Clearly, R&D on computer-supported cooperative work is a case in point. R&D methods and methodology are there to help in these "direct encounters" between social action and scientific knowledge. The social dynamics of the R&D project can be influenced in diverse directions, depending on what trends and barriers it thematizes, and the ways in which these themes are treated. The reality of the R&D project is a social process in which many intentions and notions intermingle. It is possible to understand the phenomena of such dynamics through interpretation, and to stimulate learning processes that adhere to practical levels of engagement and knowledge.

For that purpose, it is fruitful (and seems necessary) to use the old distinction between explanation and understanding (cf. Apel, 1982; Ricoeur, 1991; von Wright, 1971), whereby knowing–doing problems have been transformed into another duality, which more specifically concerns conceptual reflection. The particular point to notice is that understanding differs from explanation by being integrated with our bodily social life to an extent that precludes objectifying the understanding in a number of distinct propositions.

If "knowledge" comes close to a sense of "explanation" typically to be found in the natural sciences, then people can only "know" about social life in very restricted ways: as it can be modeled on structures of reproduction or on constellations of functions (i.e., definite objectivations, which may only include some metaphorical—biological or physical—kind of "social dynamics"). Strictly speaking, we get pictures of a sociality that do not include social processes. Consequently, these models cannot really account for the trends in and tensions between a history and a future (i.e., realities which we experience all the time and are bound up with in our praxis).

The processes of social reality (be they intended development or unintended changes) have to be carried out in bodily social doing. In other words, there goes experience and praxis—which does not come down to consciousness and voluntary action, respectively—along with the unfolding of these processes. They can be understood, that is, known in a sense typically to be found in the human sciences, where "to know about doing" means to elucidate the composite of implicit intentionality and more explicit motives (again, not reducible to consciousness or will) in the doing. Although explanations belong to their differing functional frameworks, understanding is basically associated with the very identities of social actors (i.e., their common experience and praxis). In short, understanding is a basic principle of learning that elucidates a theme by integrating it more thoroughly into a sociocultural background. The microprocesses of understanding, for which the word "explication" is reserved in order to indicate the strict sense of "folding out" and "making explicit," are very different from, but may be combined with formalization and explanation (cf. Keller, 1995).

In accordance with Merleau-Ponty's concept of intentionality,[1] understanding is always (i.e., even as the simplest everyday understanding) more or less engaging (carries us into a different direction or a new perspective), and more or less creative. The understanding of social processes and social identity implies a generative structuring of meaning: A field of experience and praxis takes on a particular perspective and stands out with a corresponding figure-ground structure. In this way, thematizing and conceptual understanding is quite similar to immediate and spontaneous understanding: A field of experience and praxis is illuminated in a certain way through the coherence of a focus and a background. Within various fields, there are differing formalisms and ways of explaining that apply to the figures that we focus on. However, understanding requires in addition to this that the backgrounds of the fields (eventually associated with our entire lifeworld) are adequately structured as well. This has not simply to do with a regime of rules with its formalisms and informality, but is, rather, a question of the explicit and implicit order, themes, and rhythms in styles of social life.

The following sections attempt to outline some aspects of the way in which the duality of "understanding people and social processes" versus "explaining functions and systems" may be seen to mark (first) the application of R&D methods as well as (second) the conception of development in organizations and cooperative work. The practice of R&D with a predominance of understanding over explanation is found in various fields, such as organization development, informal education, and therapy. When social science is regarded as understanding, research comes closer to "interpretation," and "development" comes closer to "motivation." Consequently, *research* is used as a broad term for (interpretation-based) investigation and analysis, and *development* is used to indicate a broad sense of innovation through discussion and design (on the basis of motivation).

METHODOLOGY AND USAGE OF METHODS

Now, the focus is on highlighting why a methodology primarily based on understanding (without setting the utilization of explanations aside) can enhance the opportunities of intended and viable innovation in CSCW.

---

[1]The concepts of *intention* and *intentionality* traditionally associated with phenomenology have little in common with the meaning of the word "intention" in ordinary English. The phenomenological usage concerns the inevitable directedness of consciousness. Thus, points of departure in the purposes, goals, or motives of actions (Anscombe, 1957), or in states of mind (Searle, 1983), are quite different. For Merleau-Ponty, they are all superficial, and he rarely referred to intentions at all. However, he did elaborate on the notion of "operative intentionality," which Husserl came upon while realizing the philosophical importance of history and turning to the concept of lifeworld.

Such a methodology is not fully sketched here: This chapter takes for granted that there are adequate concepts about relatively static settings of CSCW, whereby it is possible to cogently distinguish suitable designs and applications from less suitable ones, and that there are (the descriptions of) relevant R&D methods, such as participating observations, semistructured interviews, and future workshops. In fact, there is adequate conceptualization (cf. Keller, 1994, 1995) of the very support with which a computer-based cooperation system might supply the human work performance (this support is associated with the usability of the system in the actual accomplishment of cooperative work).

Undoubtedly, qualitative methods have come to stay in the R&D on CSCW. This means not only participating observations, semistructured interviews, future workshops, and other methods, which have been "deliberately imported," but also prototyping, which is more like a kind of reinvention of action research from within the field of information systems designing (ISD) itself, including software engineering. Debates within the social sciences between defenders of qualitative methods and defenders of quantitative methods have only been meaningful because the topic of discussion was research solely. When development is on the agenda, there seems to be no possible alternative to qualitative methods.

ISD has managed for a long time without qualitative methods, or at least without discussing them explicitly. How can this be? Clearly, it results from differing terminologies. *Method* and *methodology* simply means something very different in applied computer science and in applied social science (cf. Keller, 1994). In relation to computer science, a method comes very close to an "algorithm," or even a single formalized "operation." And methodology either means "a collection of methods," or is simply used as a substitute for method (in the general sense of the word also known from social sciences): meaning something like "a structured procedure whereby to attain a wanted goal."

The qualitative methods for R&D on CSCW have to be understood in a different way. They cannot be implemented as computer programs, and they should be applied in accordance with a methodology (in the sense of the social and human sciences), or a "logos" (a coherent foundational reason) for the methods. A methodology informs researchers about the theory (principal assumptions) on a domain of reality, the aims with which researchers take up R&D within the domain, the main concepts about the domain, and the methods to be applied in the R&D (cf. Flick, Kardoff, Keupp, Rosenstiel, & Wolff, 1991; Heinze, 1987; Lamnek, 1988; Zedler & Moser, 1983). The necessity of methodology is due to the methods only being general descriptions of "what to do." The body of historical experience and praxis out of which a method has been developed is not explicitly preserved in the actual description of the method. It is the methodology that holds a well-informed perspective that can be applied to the various processes and situations of a R&D project by usage of the methods. The methods as such do not enable us to distinguish and interpret the most interesting phenomena in the research context, nor to explicate and motivate the most important aspects of the development context. It is a methodological requirement to bridge the R&D field and the available methods. This means that, from a methodological point of view, an R&D project encompasses a field of CSCW (that the project deals with) much more thoroughly than "simply to employ" methods on it (i.e., merely to "follow" prescribed procedures): The very application of qualitative methods is anything but a trivial matter.

Applied social science and human science can be very helpful in the quest for qualitative methods of research. But qualitative methods of development, such as the future workshop and group interviews, have not been studied as extensively. However, action research remains an important approach to integrated R&D (cf. Baskerville, 1991; Clausen, Lorentzen, & Rasmussen, 1992; Elden & Chisholm, 1993; Flick et al., 1991). Aspects of action research may also be found as independent research topics, such as experimental organization development or action-oriented research (e.g., qualitative evaluations of social initiatives or direct democracy). When system development is regarded on the basis of prototyping as a kind of action research, a theoretical bridging between the various perspectives, situations, and events of the R&D context is emphasized. Thus, the continuous processes of methodical understanding, interpretation, and intervention on social praxis and experience may be guided by concepts of social communication and human motivation (cf. Flick et al., 1991; Jensen, Keller, & Thorne, 1990).

Table 18.1 illustrates that methodological understanding absorbs the immediate conceiving in perspectives that Merleau-Ponty clarified (cf. Keller, 1995). Methodological understanding is itself a highly reflective

TABLE 18.1
The Relation of Methodological Understanding to Immediate Conceiving

Level of Thematizing	Aspect of Conceiving	
	Objectivated	Bodily–social
Perspective	figure	background
Concept	formalized	explicit
Method	description	application
Methodology	explanation	understanding

Note. More immediate levels are absorbed in the more reflective ones: Perspectives are embedded in all levels of thematizing; methodology encloses perspectives, concepts, and methods.

perspective that is mediated from everyday understanding through a thematizing usage of concepts and methods. As indicated, understanding differs from explaining by being coherent with bodily social experience and praxis. The hierarchical levels of thematizing may be noted by reading the table from its cells; for instance, explicit conceiving is a bodily social way of conceptualizing figure-background perspectives.

People always experience in perspectives. This is an insight of Husserl's, which Merleau-Ponty in turn radicalized beyond Husserl's philosophy of consciousness. The tight coherence between figure and background (which only permit retrospective distinction between the two) is more immediate than the routines and common sense of everyday life. This coherence does not imply any kind of basic consistency or constitutional foundation in human existence, but it does establish the rudimentary basis (below subject–object distinctions) for any more specific kind of intentionality and meaning.

At conceptual levels of thematizing, researchers attend to interpretations of perspectives in which the figures are generalized and abstracted. To formalized figures we attribute a high independence from background (historical and situational contexts), taking on language games (or praxis games) where form (e.g., syntax or roles) can be dealt with independently of contents (e.g., semantics or persons). On the contrary, explicit figures are characteristic signs (e.g., symptoms or icons) and significant expressions (e.g., gestures or statements) that inevitably structure our attention in accord with the context and horizon manifested through the figure (i.e., a concrete constellation of historical and situational experience and praxis).

The upper levels of thematizing indicated in Table 18.1, the levels of method and methodology, are directly related to the topics of knowing and doing. The distinction made by Ryle (1973) between "knowing that" and "knowing how" may be employed to outline this.[2] "Knowing that" designates propositional knowledge. "Knowing how" designates various dispositions to do something skillfully. Ryle made it clear that knowing how is a more basic kind of competence that is in play by the understanding of meaning and intentions, and cannot be reduced to knowing that.

---

[2]In fact, Ryle put forward several arguments that closely correspond to points raised by Merleau-Ponty (e.g., criticism of the body–soul dichotomy as "the legend of the ghost in the machine"). Thus, the interpretation of Ryle's concepts need not be restricted by his preoccupation with linguistic consistency and with the common sense that ordinary language permits. In particular, by rejecting the sharp distinction Ryle made between knowing how and habits, it may be emphasized that competences associate the efficient performance of any practice with some fluctuating awareness. Various levels of awareness are unfolded dynamically in any kind of skilled practice, be it a simple habit (once learned) or the understanding of complex issues. This awareness manifests the guiding experience of sociocultural custom, more as a rhythmic atmosphere, or "feel of the game," than as any clear consciousness.

This latter point has also been made as a result of regarding competences as "tacit knowledge" or "intuition." However, for the purpose of discussing methodology (as the theoretically reflected application of conceptually based methods), a concept of knowing how seems more appropriate than any of these alternatives. Concepts of intuition lead us into very general issues of competence and understanding (i.e., far beyond any focus on methodology). Tacit knowledge appears to me to be a confusing denotation. It comes very close to a mystifying contradiction in terms, because knowledge is usually defined as propositional (particularly in English and North American traditions of thought). Furthermore, it strongly aggravates the misguiding connotation, also found in "knowing how," that people are completely saturated with various kinds of knowledge, some of which are just too "deep" to be expressed. This "legend of the cognitive mind" entirely obscures the bodily-social foundation of our competences as emotional and motivational structures.

Now, it is possible to outline a notion of knowing how as the specialized kind of experience and praxis, which associates methodological understanding intimately with various kinds of competence: professional expertise as well as common sense and creativity. Potentially, this implies that the application of methods can be better integrated with the realities of social processes. In usual descriptions and models, social processes are regarded (or misconceived) as states and changes between them. It should be noticed, however, that this merely indicates a limit of descriptive knowledge, that is, "knowing that." Practical competences (knowing how) concerning social processes are much more potent.

The immediate understanding of social processes is comparable with the immediate understanding of ourselves, since our social identity is upheld and changed through these processes as an intertwining of praxis and experience. The dynamic flow of social events and situations is always a horizon (occasionally also a more direct theme) of experiences. People "know" the social processes as a mingling of structuring tendencies that are to some extent under their control, as well as emergent tendencies that are more or less out of their control. On the basis of this fundamental understanding, people know how to go about much more in social life than can be explained (knowing that). Applications of scientific methods are refined versions of (subsets of) general knowing how. In this light, methodology is required to bridge on the one hand various levels of knowing that, and on the other hand the knowing how whereby we find our way and make our way in the dynamics of social trends and constellations embedding an R&D project.

In the terminology of "a field" (from gestalt psychology and phenomenology) applied in Table 18.1, the knowing that is a subset of what can be experienced as figures, whereas the knowing how is more bound to the background of experiences (i.e., the contexts and horizons through which fields of praxis are embedded in the lifeworld). More specifically, the simple description of a method is a knowing that, and the actual application of a method in the perspective of a methodology is a knowing how.

This does not mean that knowing that is less valuable. It expresses, forms, and formalizes knowing how, and without it the contents of knowing how would be more futile and fragile and would vanish. Compared to knowing how, knowing that is simply objectified (or objectifiable), that is, more distinct in both of two different senses: It is (at least potentially) more clear and precise, but also necessarily apt to be separated from the very subjectivity of social praxis and experiences. Knowing that can be thematized in language, perhaps visually modeled, and so on, whereas knowing how always remains less clear (in theoretical, linguistic, and other possibly conscious representations), and closer to the reality of bodily-social praxis, which is experienced in immediate perceptions and routine actions, as well as in expressions and gestures that are well known to us.

By the knowledge acquisition from human experts for the purpose of implementing knowledge-based or expert computer systems, it has again been realized that the intuitive aspects of (expert) knowledge are more difficult to elucidate than the complex, but accurate, facts (which would often be regarded as most relevant for defining the knowledge domains). In this context, it has correctly been pointed out that the knowing how of experts has more resemblance to common sense than to the knowing that of the expert domain.

However, common sense is not itself an elementary kind of knowledge. It is a sociocultural sedimentation of everyday impressions, notions, and opinions, wherein the duality of knowing that and knowing how reappears. In the changing situations of everyday life, common sense helps to immediately recognize or take for granted the relevant aspects of huge resources of facts and preconceptions. But this competence is intertwined with and upheld by the creativity of bodily-social intentionality—the generative structuring of the praxis and experience fields into meaningful figures and backgrounds. It is through these rudimentary trends of knowing how that our experience and praxis always cohere with the order and disorder of social processes.

It is accurate to talk about the understanding of social identity and social processes as a structuring of experience and praxis. Understanding and structuring are the recursive aspects of social processes whereby individuals as well as groups share social identities and perspectives. In this sense, motives, imagination, initiatives, and learning are basically social processes. Although the here-and-now structuring of experience

and praxis can never be completely objectified and intended, this structuring is the very way in which social change is thoroughly marked by
sociocultural meaning and directedness (i.e., by intentionality). Of course,
this does not at all imply that social change is always "well structured"
in the sense of being in accord with a particular perspective. A field of
organization development can be explicated in creative and engaging
ways (i.e., "become more explicit") through a coherent association with
everyday life in this organization. This explication implies reintegration
of objectivations, because (contrary to explanations) the understanding of
a field of praxis must cohere with the lived experience of it. This means
that participants in development projects (users-to-be) become their own
"subject-objects" (Apel, 1982), thereby necessarily moving the borders
between their status as active sociocultural subjects and passive system
objects in the R&D project.

In summary, an R&D methodology can be based on principles of
understanding the social processes and the social identities in cooperative
work performance as a foundation for explaining the functioning of technical systems to be integrated in these processes. Table 18.1 indicated that
methodological understanding absorbs the principle of immediate conceiving of figures against their background. To only discern something
(an emergent 'gestalt' without any specified characteristics) in this prethematic way is the common origin of knowledge and doing. It is through
being rooted in this source of understanding that a methodology can
enable the establishment of the connection between the knowing that
(description) and the knowing how (application) of methods.

COOPERATIVE WORK:
FUNCTIONS AND PROCESSES

The following section discusses cooperative work as organization, because
topics concerning explanation and understanding have been touched on
quite extensively (though often not quite clearly) in organization theory.
The same explanation–understanding distinction is found in more direct
treatments of cooperation. Cooperation can be (and has been) looked on
as a system of labor division and coordination, regardless of who is going
to take on the roles of "agents" within this system. Or, it can be regarded
as an ensemble of cooperatively working people, performing the work
on the background of their social experience and praxis. In order to keep
this distinction clear, this discussion uses *cooperation systems* and *cooperative
work*, respectively.

A basic distinction is retained between social functions and social
processes. This section attempts to elucidate the way in which the domains

of CSCW can be explained with reference to systems (typically socioeconomic systems) and their functions, but must be understood by bringing sociocultural meaning and intentionality (which adhere to social identities and processes) into focus. The domains of CSCW are various areas of cooperative work regarded as (potentially or actually) integrating computer-based communication and information systems.

Common to formalization in a Weberian sense and formalization in a Taylorian sense is an exactness of abstract behavior patterns. This notion of formality is quite similar to the sets of uniform entities, relations, functions, and procedures in systems theory and information theory. The paradigm of organizational formality is nowadays being reinforced in a refined version. On the abstract level of exact systems, human action is treated as comparable with, interplaying with, and substitutable by computer processing. Furthermore, corresponding to the previous rise of the human relations and human resources schools of work organization, a growing number of CSCW researchers are now becoming interested in the investigation of informal structures of cooperative work.

However, in organization theories, the image of formality as an abstract exactness has frequently been confused with notions of normative, official, consciously planned, or collective activities (cf. Mintzberg, 1979; Scott, 1981). A major aspect of this problem is that the actual patterns of formal structure have not been clearly distinguished from the explicit aim or endeavor of formalization. Typically, what management has officially decided to be the stable structures in an organization are also taken to be the actual reality of such structures. The possible reasons for this lack of differentiation will not be analyzed in further detail here. Suffice to say that a fundamental distinction in social science is set aside: the distinction between the intentions that social actors consciously hold and the structures of social life that may persist or change regardless of the will of the particular social actors.

The problem of mixing divergent notions of organizational formality is hardly solved (but rather disseminated) by merely indicating informal structures as the deeper reality of organizational life. In this way, far too much is again mixed into one inconceivable category, now "the deep organizational matters." For instance, this has led to the unfortunate notion of informal structures as more or less merging with organizational culture (cf. French & Bell, 1990; Morgan, 1986). Worst of all, this view does not seem to make room for the concepts of social processes and social identity required for a methodological understanding of social development and social identity. Common sense is substituted for this substantial understanding.

Of course, the identification of these problems is connected with new challenges in the R&D on work organization. By now, for the purpose of CSCW, it is necessary to know much more about what the relatively permanent structures really are like and what they can be like. This is in order to conceptualize the integration of computer-based information and communication technology that (regardless of all attempts to design flexibility) remain highly formalized in comparison with the structures of human interaction and communication. Likewise, when the issue of R&D is a complicated organizational development, more than a commonsense notion of the social change and the social actors is needed. Finally, an understanding of work organization should include, but not be reduced to, explanations of social systems. Social systems make up our mediation between real social processes (such as cooperative work) and operating computer technology. It is therefore a crucial issue to acquire concepts and models of social systems that allow the consideration of the design of computer systems on the one hand, and the human experience of cooperative work on the other hand.

The indicated view of social and technical formality was elaborated in previous work on organization theory (Jensen et al., 1990; Keller, 1991, 1997) in which questions about formality were associated with the reproductive functions of social systems, and distinguished from questions about the sociocultural dynamics and change within an organization. Now, this view is going to be applied, as the difference for this:

This conception is outlined and the important difference between objectivated and bodily-social conceiving, which was emphasized in Table 18.1, is discussed: the difference between thematizing experiential perspectives through formalized conceptualization and through explicit conceptualization.

As previously discussed, conceptual interpretations may be regarded as perspectives with generalized and abstracted figures. Apart from this common aspect of concepts, formalized and explicit conceptualization are very different ways of making something clear. In *formalized perspectives,* there is a centripetal relation between figure and background; a convention of conceiving is used in which the figure has diluted the bearing of contextual meaning and the horizons of intentionality.

In contrast, the relation between figure and background is centrifugal in *explicit perspectives.* The appearance of the figure induces, as it were, a special structuration of the situational and historical context. Explicit figures need not be linguistic statements. They can be nonverbal gestures, or they may be symptoms and other signs that characterize some social trends, a general attitude, or a social atmosphere. A single explicit figure may be the significant expression of a huge (possibly very huge) constellation of experience and praxis. A few differing examples of this are the slogan of a political movement, the logo of an organization, the work organizational design metaphor for a computer system, the motivating impact of a recognition of social identity, and the exposure of a motive through a revealing action.

Conceptualizations are not solely intended constitutions and constructions. Rather, we may so to say stumble on or be caught by a conceptual perspective. It should also be emphasized that the notion of conceptual perspectives is an alternative to notions of conceptual categories: An explicit concept may also be formal, but in a different perspective.

Formality does not have to be designed, decided on, or objectified at all. To a large extent, formality is just given (as ordinary routines and habits), without being noticed by anybody, or it emerges by the actual accomplishment of tasks, independently of the planning of the tasks. Still, the exactness of such abstract entities and functions can, in principle, be identified by an observer.

The importance of informal patterns of action is connected with the flexibility of situated conduct and proceeding through ad hoc modifications. Formalizing can only lead to simplifying models of the fine details of informal complexity and concreteness. Between formal and informal patterns there is a borderland that is also a matter of functionality: A certain balance between formal and informal procedures is useful for the work organization, and variations of it may be disturbing.

In short, the informal organization comprises the aspects of organizational situations and conduct that are rather inexact, and therefore cannot conveniently be subject to strict regularization. Informality comprises the deep structures of organizational systems. However, there is more to organizational life than systems.

Talk about informality remains within the definite universe of an objectified social system. The appropriateness of informal conduct is a functional issue; it is a question of specific goals, states, rules, and resources, just like formality. Formal and informal structures are not sharply separated as to their functionality, but presuppose one another. The mechanisms and procedures at various levels of formality and informality have to match in order for the overall system to be efficient. Thus, the accelerating utilization of advanced computer technology is also completely dependent on some work organizational principles, which can guarantee the appropriate preconditions for informal cooperation and action.

All in all, an organizational system with its informal and formal patterns is a (definite) structure of socioeconomic functions. In principle, the complete system of informal and formal structures in an organization (or an organizational unit) can be observed within a socioeconomic perspective.

But an actor perspective can never be attained from this point of departure. The motivation to conform with formality and the intuition by which informality is accomplished are neglected in the socioeconomic perspective. Therefore, organization development, like any other social processes of structuration, cannot be conceptualized within this perspective either. These processes are inextricably bound up with generative

TABLE 18.2
Typology of the Developmental and Reproductive
Structuring of Cooperative Work Performance

Reproductive Functions	Development Processes	
	Explicit	*Implicit*
Formal	systematizing	adaptation
Informal	learning	habituation

Note. Predominant intentional structures in work organization (projects, styles, institutions, etc.) are regarded as bodily–social experience and praxis in the perspectives of sociocultural development and socioeconomic reproduction.

dispositions (such as creativity, intentions, intuition, and interpretations). The definitive patterns of socioeconomic functions are only a trivial basis for the generative processes of sociocultural experience whereby organizations develop. Therefore, organization development should be based on a sociocultural actor perspective (Table 18.2).

A culture approach to organization theory may point to a refinement of such actor-oriented perspectives.[3] This implies that the concept of culture must be understood as related to concepts of everyday life and lifeworld: It cannot be reduced to functional issues. Culture is predominantly a profound structure of experience: some implicit resources in people's everyday concerns. It makes us able to continuously reproduce, structurize, and "enliven" the social systems that we take part in (i.e., makes the systems work according to our intentions and interpretations).

Unintended social changes take place constantly, solely on the basis of implicit subjectivity. But, intended development of cultural resources goes through motivation and learning: A specific social identity becomes explicit about its own experience to an extent that allows adequate restructuring of its own praxis.

So, the sociocultural aspects of what organizations are indicate that, besides informality, there is another kind of "deep structure" in organi-

---

[3]According to the prevailing view of organizational culture, culture may appear to be an intractable organizational matter, but it is regarded as eventually subject to leadership. For instance, Schein (1986) stated that culture is created, embedded, and transformed in organizations through the actions of leaders. The life in an organization is regarded as a kind of social system, in which the cultural identity of the personnel can be managed in accordance with functional objectives. Here, the distinction between formality and informality has been disregarded. Furthermore, the difference between socioeconomic objectification and sociocultural experience is neglected. Consequently, the topic of formalization is reproduced in a way that is untenable, and substantial characteristics of sociocultural life are not exposed to view. Only in a highly metaphorical sense of "culture" can culture be subject to management (or leadership) and this metaphorical usage blurs the fact that social identity is rooted in culture.

zations, namely, implicitness. The implicit organizational spheres encompass all that takes place in the organizational being without much collective attention being paid to it. Implicit structures consist of matters that may be quite explicit to individuals or minor groups, but are not collectively accentuated because they are considered to be less important, too immature for articulation and discussion, or so embarrassing that they are actively repressed.

The explicit part of an organization is its *self-reflection*, or *collective consciousness* (i.e., the organization as a communicating public). Subjective resources of initiative, commitment, and enthusiasm are opened up by making room for social identity to express itself. Motivation, creativity, and thoughts are more likely to turn into articulation and dialogue when the common traits of sociocultural life are adequately explicit. In short, explicitness is to a social identity what formality is to a social system.

Thus, from a sociocultural point of view, an organization stands out as a substantially dynamic entity that is upheld by the common order of the lifeworld of its participants. The sociocultural perspective is the one in which the organization has experience, perceptions, and interests, out of which development processes can be actively initiated and influenced.

The dynamic relations between implicit and explicit experience determine the readiness and orientations of development within the organization. So, organization development may be stimulated and supported, but not precisely directed and controlled. Finally, consider two examples that illustrate the important difference between formality and explicitness.

First, the organizational life is wide open for the implicit prevalence of formality from the surrounding culture. Many roles, procedures, and functions are settled by unconscious delegations, attributions, and habits. Adaptation, or *mutual adjustment*, within working groups is an example of this, rather than being an example of informality as Mintzberg (1979) claimed. The participants of a semiautonomous working group, a project group or another group that only has a very general task definition do not have to informally invent their standards of work organization, or negotiate to find the standards that they can all adjust to. They immediately apply numerous norms and procedures that adhere to their common profile of social identity: being engaged in the same field, having some occupational background in common, and numerous other aspects of their life experience and everyday praxis. In this way, the work setting is immediately structured through its belonging to adjacent as well as remote parts of the surrounding culture (ultimately our global culture) in which the organization is embedded. Although problems of work organization do appear and may have to be dealt with more explicitly, the overall characteristics are that people can concentrate on the substance (instead of the form) of their cooperative work in such groups. Quite implicitly, they employ the vast resources of formalisms that never have to be officially pointed out in the organizational life because they are standard norms and default procedures of the surrounding culture.

Second, in contrast to formality, the essence of explicitness lies in decoding and expatiation. As indicated in Table 18.2, learning (as opposed to the systematizing and regulation of social behavior through models and schedules) elucidates this decoding and expatiation in a salient way. When an issue is made more explicit, it takes on a more significant figure. This figure serves to thematize and conceptualize an experiential perspective. The figure does not appear isolated from contextual background (as is the case with formalized objects), but is a symbol reflecting and structuring the background from which it stems. This centrifugal process clearly shows when an explicit figure rearranges portions of our experience and makes them stand in a new light. Quite informally (i.e., without being oriented to rules or submitted to schedules), the sparkling spontaneity and rudimentary initiative that are even linked with processes of habituation can become more explicit and crystalize into learning and innovative conduct. Most of what takes place by the collective acquisition and amplification of intuitive or dialectic knowledge—in project groups, in organizational politics, in any kind of discussion, or in the substantial steps of strategic development—is explicit and informal.

CONCLUSIONS

Referring to a useful distinction adopted from time to time during the last decade, it appears that system development *with* the users, proposed by Ehn and Kyng (1987), must be associated in some ways with the two approaches that Ehn and Kyng rejected: system development *for* the users and system development *by* the users. In other words, projects of applied research and development on CSCW have to take on a responsibility that goes beyond that which users-to-be can report on themselves (as to their knowledge as well as interests), but is assessible and attainable for the users-to-be, because it is based on understanding their situation, and not simply on explaining it.

Taking the preceding considerations one step further, it may be claimed that R&D on CSCW will soon have to address the topic of *late modernity* in our time. (Late modernity is used as a substitute for *postmodernity*.) In the theory of social sciences late modernity signifies a new historical situation, namely, the accelerating lability, change, and turbulence of socioeconomic systems together with sociocultural identities, including organizational systems and identities. Late modernity signifies the change of social life into a far more dynamic phenomenon than it used to be.

This situation can be illustrated more clearly by focusing on two opposing paradigms. First, the *system world* is expanding into the *lifeworld*. Of course, this paradigm is closely connected with the accelerating utilization of computer technology. Second, collectively, we still reproduce and develop our social systems by behaving as fallible and knowledgeable social actors. We actually manage to find coherence in and make sense of the fluctuating social life.

This scenario of opposing trends is associated with sociocultural identity: People incorporate late modern conditions, and consequently are socialized to uphold a late modern lifeworld. As a result, late modern organizations tend to be more anchored in the social identity and collective subjectivity of their participants. Therefore, the reproduction, structuration, and development of organizations now require more elucidation and interpretation of implicit organizational life. The explicit aspects of an organization are likely to be far behind the implicit evolution of the organization, particularly in rather dynamic organizations.

It is necessary to understand intuition and knowing how as a thoroughly bodily social topic. Researchers are able to take up the decentered (preindividual, precognitive, and preconscious) aspects of social life, and see it in connection with the responsible and deliberate actions of individuals. However, a phenomenological perspective of cooperative work cannot be reduced to a system model, so we have to respect some distinctions: between understanding and explaining in research and between stimulated emergence and controlled design in development. Therefore, in a phenomenological methodology on CSCW, one of the principal assumptions must evidently be the distinction between actor-oriented and system-oriented approaches to the differing topics and themes in ISD; and a central aim must be to combine these two kinds of approaches in practical R&D projects.

To some extent, the points accentuated here could also have been made on the basis of other approaches to the theory of social sciences (e.g., ethnomethodology; cf. Heritage, 1988; Suchman, 1987), which share some roots with Merleau-Ponty's phenomenology. So, what is the difference? Why should Merleau-Ponty's considerations be particularly interesting?

It is a radical sense of process-orientedness that characterizes Merleau-Ponty's approach to the understanding of social life. One of the most outstanding aspects of his works is an elucidation of bodily social intentionality. According to Merleau-Ponty, intentionality is first and foremost a structuration of meaning that emerges from below individuality, cognition, and consciousness. It is a bodily social origin of motives, attributions, and interpretations in our own experience and praxis.

The philosophy of Merleau-Ponty transcends the traditional oppositions between an active subject and a passive object (including the body–

soul dichotomy and the internal–external dichotomy). He made it clear that the most immediate conceiving is at bodily levels of existence without any opposition between individual and environment or between "I" and "You." On bodily levels of experience, the intentionality is a social interplay of established games in our praxis together with the initiative, creativity, and engagement, which is "always-already" about to carry the immediate conceiving into a new direction.

As responsible and rational social beings, people are "decentered" in relation to this bodily-social source. On the other hand, they are able to be responsible and rational in social situations (which strictly speaking never stand still, never appear twice, and always are equivocally delineated). It is by way of intentionality that we know of being centered as well as decentered in relation to the sociocultural processes that we take part in. That is because sociocultural processes cohere with our experience and praxis through the bodily-social intentionality. Consequently, our individuality, cognition, and consciousness can be regarded as important structures of sociocultural meaning and order, which are upheld and changed through bodily-social intentionality.

ACKNOWLEDGMENTS

I am grateful to Susan Leigh Star and to Graham Button, Rank Xerox EuroPARC, for their comments at the Paris workshop in March 1993 on the first version of this chapter. I am also grateful to Keld Bødker, Roskilde University Center, and Les Gasser for their critique of a subsequent version of the manuscript.

REFERENCES

Anscombe, G. E. M. (1957). *Intention*. Oxford, England: Basil Blackwell.
Apel, K. O. (1976). *Transformation der Philosophie* [The transformation of philosophy] (Vol. 2.). Frankfurt: Suhrkamp.
Apel, K. O. (1982). The Erklären–Verstehen controversy in the philosophy of the natural and human sciences. In G. Fløistad (Ed.), *Contemporary philosophy: Vol. 2. Philosophy of science* (pp. 19–49). The Hague: Martinus Nijhoff.
Baskerville, R. (1991). *Three perils for action research in information systems consulting*. Working Paper 91-201, SUNY—Binghamton School of Management.
Baecker, R. M. (Ed.). (1993). *Readings in groupware and computer-supported cooperative work*. San Mateo, CA: Kaufmann.
Bourdieu, P. (1977). *Outline of a theory of practice*. Cambridge, England: Cambridge University Press.
Bourdieu, P. (1981). Men and machines. In K. Knorr-Cetina & A. V. Cicourel (Eds.), *Advances in social theory and methodology* (pp. 304–317). Boston: Routledge & Kegan Paul.

Bourdieu, P. (1996). Understanding. *Theory, Culture & Society, 13,* 17–37.

Clausen, C., Lorentzen, B., & Rasmussen, L. B. (Eds.). (1992): *Deltagelse i teknologisk udvikling* [Participation in technological development]. Copenhagen: Fremad.

Computers in Context: Joining Forces in Design. (1995, August). Proceedings of the third decennial conference on Computers in Context, Department of Computer Science, Aarhus University.

CSCW '94. (1994). Proceedings of the ACM 1994 Conference on Computer Supported Cooperative Work. New York: ACM Press.

Ehn, P., & Kyng, M. (1987). The collective resource approach to systems design. In G. Bjerknes, P. Ehn, & M. Kyng (Eds.), *Computers and democracy: A Scandinavian challenge* (pp. 17–58). Aldershot: Avebury.

Elden, M., & Chisholm, R. F. (1993). Emerging varieties to action research. *Human relations, 46,* 121–142.

Flick, U., von Kardorff, E., Keupp, H., von Rosenstiel, L., & Wolff, S. (1991). *Handbuch Qualitative Soziaforschung* [Handbook of qualitative social research]. Munich: Psychologie Verlags Union.

French, W. L., & Bell, C. H. (1990). *Organization development.* Englewood Cliffs, NJ: Prentice-Hall.

Giddens, A. (1979). *Central problems in social theory.* London: Macmillan.

Greenbaum, J., & Kyng, M. (Eds.). (1991). *Design at work.* Hillsdale, NJ: Lawrence Erlbaum Associates.

Habermas, J. (1972). *Knowledge and human interests.* London: Heinemann.

Heinze, T. (1987). *Qualitative Sozialforschung* [Qualitative social research]. Opladen: Westdeutscher Verlag.

Heritage, J. C. (1988). Ethnomethodology. In A. Giddens & J. Turner (Eds.), *Social theory today* (pp. 224–272). Cambridge, England: Polity Press.

Jensen, H. S., Keller, K., & Thorne, M. (1990). *Knowledge engineering with personal computers.* Institute of Computer and Systems Sciences, Copenhagen Business School.

Keller, K. (1991, June). *Implicit and informal organization.* Paper presented at the Valhalla Conference on "Reconstructing Organizational Culture," Copenhagen.

Keller, K. (1992, September). *Sociality and intentionality.* Paper presented at the 17th Annual International Conference of the Merleau-Ponty Circle, Hartford, CT.

Keller, K. (1994). Conditions for computer-supported cooperative work: The significance of the psychosocial work environment. *Technology Studies, 1,* 242–269.

Keller, K. (1995). *Datamatstøttet samarbejde på fænomenologisk grundlag* [Computer-supported cooperative work on a phenomenological foundation]. Copenhagen: Samfundslitteratur.

Keller, K. D. (1997). Sociotechnics and the structuring of meaning: Beyond the idea of autopoietic social systems. In P. Mambrey, M. Paetau, W. Prinz, & V. Wulf (Eds.), *Self-organization: A challenge for CSCW.* London: Springer.

Lamnek, S. (1988). *Qualitative Sozialforschung. Band 1: Methodologie* [Qualitative social research: Vol. 1. Methodology]. Munich: Psychologie Verlags Union.

Marmolin, H., Sundblad, Y., & Schmidt, K. (Eds.). *Proceedings of the Fourth European Conference on Computer-Supported Cooperative Work.* Dordrecht: Kluwer Academic.

Merleau-Ponty, M. (1963). *The structure of behavior.* Boston: Beacon Press.

Merleau-Ponty, M. (1964). *Signs.* Evanston, IL: Northwestern University Press.

Merleau-Ponty, M. (1968). *The visible and the invisible.* Evanston, IL: Northwestern University Press.

Merleau-Ponty, M. (1974). *Phenomenology of perception.* London: Routledge & Kegan Paul.

Mintzberg, H. (1979). *The structuring of organizations.* Englewood Cliffs, NJ: Prentice-Hall.

Morgan, G. (1986). *Images of organization.* London: Sage.

Ricoeur, P. (1991). Explanation and Understanding. In *From text to Action: Essays in hermeneutics* (Vol. 2). Evanston, IL: Northwestern University Press.

Ryle, G. (1973). *The concept of mind*. Harmondsworth: Penguin.

Schein, E. H. (1986). *Organisationskultur og ledelse, -et dynamisk perspektiv* [Organizational culture and leadership—a dynamic view]. Copenhagen: Valmuen.

Scott, W. R. (1981). *Organizations: Rational, natural and open systems*. Englewood Cliffs, NJ: Prentice-Hall.

Searle, J. R. (1983). *Intentionality*. Cambridge, England: Cambridge University Press.

Suchman, L. A. (1987). *Plans and situated actions*. Cambridge, England: Cambridge University Press.

Waldenfels, B. (1987). *Ordnung im Zwielicht* [Order in twilight]. Frankfurt: Suhrkamp.

von Wright, G. H. (1971). *Explanation and Understanding*. New York: Cornell University Press.

Zedler, P., & Moser, H. (Eds.). (1983). *Aspekte qualitative Sozialforschung* [Aspects of qualitative social research]. Opladen: Leske Verlag & Budrich GmbH.

Author Index

Subject Index